ISSUES IN ENTREPRENEURSHIP & SMALL BUSINESS MANAGEMENT

Sara Miller McCune founded SAGE Publishing in 1965 to support the dissemination of usable knowledge and educate a global community. SAGE publishes more than 1000 journals and over 800 new books each year, spanning a wide range of subject areas. Our growing selection of library products includes archives, data, case studies and video. SAGE remains majority owned by our founder and after her lifetime will become owned by a charitable trust that secures the company's continued independence.

Los Angeles | London | New Delhi | Singapore | Washington DC | Melbourne

ISSUES IN ENTREPRENEURSHIP & SMALL BUSINESS MANAGEMENT

ARTICLES FROM
SAGE BUSINESS RESEARCHER

Los Angeles | London | New Delhi
Singapore | Washington DC | Melbourne

FOR INFORMATION:

SAGE Publications, Inc.
2455 Teller Road
Thousand Oaks, California 91320
E-mail: order@sagepub.com

SAGE Publications Ltd.
1 Oliver's Yard
55 City Road
London EC1Y 1SP
United Kingdom

SAGE Publications India Pvt. Ltd.
B 1/I 1 Mohan Cooperative Industrial Area
Mathura Road, New Delhi 110 044
India

SAGE Publications Asia-Pacific Pte. Ltd.
3 Church Street
#10-04 Samsung Hub
Singapore 049483

Acquisitions Editor: Maggie Stanley
Editorial Assistant: Ashley Mixson
Production Editor: Kimaya Khashnobish
Typesetter: C&M Digitals (P) Ltd.
Proofreader: Alison Syring
Cover Designer: Michael Dubowe
Marketing Manager: Ashlee Blunk

Printed in the United States of America

Library of Congress Cataloging-in-Publication Data

Title: Issues in entrepreneurship & small business management: articles from SAGE Business researcher / SAGE Business Researcher.

Description: First Edition. | Thousand Oaks: SAGE Publications, [2017] | Includes bibliographical references.

Identifiers: LCCN 2016059719 | ISBN 9781506381381 (pbk. : alk. paper)

Subjects: LCSH: Entrepreneurship. | Small business—Management.

Classification: LCC HB615 .I7545 2017 | DDC 658/.022—dc23
LC record available at https://lccn.loc.gov/2016059719

This book is printed on acid-free paper.

SFI Certified Sourcing
www.sfiprogram.org
SFI-00453

17 18 19 20 21 10 9 8 7 6 5 4 3 2 1

BRIEF CONTENTS

DETAILED CONTENTS

ACKNOWLEDGMENTS

SAGE wishes to acknowledge the valuable contributions of the following reviewers:

Lawrence S. Audler, University of Holy Cross

Diane Denslow, University of North Florida

Sara Kiser, Alabama State University

Michele K. Masterfano, Drexel University

Wallace W. Meyer Jr., University of Kansas

Charlie Nagelschmidt, Champlain College

Colette L. Rominger, Independence University

SOCIAL ENTREPRENEURSHIP
Can start-ups change the world?

Robin D. Schatz

EXECUTIVE SUMMARY

Global interest in social entrepreneurship is growing, as investors, corporations, academic institutions and foundations support individuals trying to solve intractable global problems, from abject poverty in the developing world to the ravages of climate change. Whether working in for-profit, nonprofit or hybrid organizations, these entrepreneurs are applying sound business principles and attempting to scale their solutions to reach the greatest number of people. The popularity and even trendiness of social entrepreneurship is attributed to the rise of the Millennial Generation, many of whom want businesses to prioritize social innovation and a concern for people over profit. But social entrepreneurs face a strong chance of failure, and serious challenges remain, from getting adequate funding to sustain growth to maintaining focus on social mission and impact as a venture grows. Among the questions under debate: Does a social enterprise need to be self-sustaining? Should investors and social entrepreneurs be allowed to profit from a social enterprise? Can social enterprises stay true to their mission if they become large and successful?

OVERVIEW

Brown University senior Gabi Lewis, an avid weightlifter, was trying to invent a healthier protein bar as a project for his 2013 social entrepreneurship class.

His roommate, Greg Sewitz, fresh from a climate change conference at the Massachusetts Institute of Technology, made a novel suggestion: Why not cook up something using insect protein?

Lewis was skeptical, until Sewitz told him about the nutritional and environmental benefits of eating insects, compared with, say, beef cattle, which take far more resources to raise and create far more greenhouse gases.

It wasn't long before the two friends had unloaded two boxes filled with 2,000 live, chirping crickets in their kitchen, Lewis recalls. They froze the bugs, roasted them in their oven and ground them up in their Vitamix blender to make cricket "flour," then blended it with fruits, nuts and other tasty ingredients. Their first protein bars were such a hit with their friends and professors at Brown that they took them to the local farmers market.

From *SAGE Business Researcher,*
December 7, 2015

By the time the roommates graduated from Brown, they were well on their way to creating a company called Exo, as in exoskeleton. They raised their first funds that summer on Kickstarter to finance their first production run, joined a food-focused accelerator program called AccelFoods and then raised another $1.2 million from investors in September 2014.[1]

Exo's protein bars contain 10 grams of protein and 40 crickets each. Their social and environmental mission is baked into each bar, too, Lewis says. "Our entire business is about shifting eating habits in a more sustainable direction."

Exo's founders aim for fast growth; they joined the food industry accelerator to help them through the process. Eventually, they hope to expand into other insect-based products—once they get people used to the idea of eating bugs. And they emphasize, they wouldn't be starting a business if they didn't think they could make a big social impact.

Lewis and Sewitz see themselves as social entrepreneurs, part of a growing movement of individuals who seek to transform and build institutions, including businesses, to tackle pressing and intractable social problems, from poverty and illiteracy to environmental destruction and climate change.[2] While the term social entrepreneurship has been used to describe these individuals since the 1980s, the field is gaining traction with the rise of the Millennial Generation, experts say. Millennials want businesses to prioritize social innovation and concern for people above profit, according to one international survey.[3]

A growing ecosystem—made up of impact investors, who generally accept lower rates of return and stay in their investments longer than typical venture capitalists in order to help solve social and environmental problems; foundations that support social entrepreneurs; academic programs around the globe; and a growing number of business plan competitions sponsored by brands that want to attract the Millennial market—is helping improve the prospects that social entrepreneurs will succeed. But serious challenges remain, from getting adequate funding to maintaining a focus on mission and impact as a venture grows.

Most impact investment occurs in post-venture stages

"Since social enterprises have a high probability of failure, the chances are pretty high that you will not be successful, and this means a lot of attention needs to be given to the unpleasant but probable downside," Ian C. MacMillan and James D. Thompson, both entrepreneurship professors at the Wharton School of the University of Pennsylvania, advised in *The Social Entrepreneur's Playbook*.[4]

Social entrepreneurs, by most definitions, seek to make an impact on a broad scale, which means they have to come up with a model that can be replicated and expanded to help as many people as possible—in business jargon, "scaled." They draw from the strengths of entrepreneurs: creativity, perseverance and an ability to muster scarce resources. They often apply sound business principles to expand their organizations. Their ventures come in many flavors, from nonprofit efforts that have little or no prospect of generating revenue to for-profit ventures with an environmental or social mission intrinsic to the business.

In between are so-called hybrid models, such as the benefit corporation, which is legal in 30 states, plus the District of Columbia, according to B Lab, a Wayne, Pa., group backed by a number of socially responsible organizations that lobbies for the corporate designation.

How impact investors distribute their capital, by stage of business

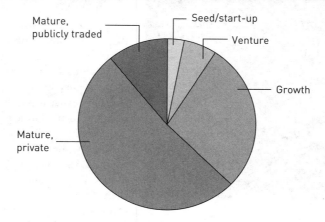

Impact investors have committed 91 percent of their managed capital during the growth and mature stages of the companies they invest in, rather than earlier stages, according to data from the Global Impact Investing Network. Only 9 percent of capital has been invested during seed and venture funding stages.

Note: Based on survey of 146 impact investors who manage at least $10 million and have invested in at least five transactions.

Source: "Eyes on the Horizon: The Impact Investor Survey," JPMorgan, Global Impact Investing Network, May 4, 2015, p. 7, http://tinyurl.com/orfvzdp

Hybrid organizations combine both worlds by linking profit to social mission and a concern for improving lives. They are proponents of the corporate philosophy of the "triple bottom line," or the 3 Ps, so-called because adherents account for performance in three areas: "people, profits and the planet." [5]

Catherine Clark, director of Duke University's CASE i3 Initiative on Impact Investing, says about 40 percent of the students who attend the Fuqua School of Business, which houses CASE, the Center for the Advancement of Social Entrepreneurship, say they chose the school because of its social emphasis.

"They're the first group in history to believe their primary purpose is to serve society, and they list making a profit as No. 2," says Clark, speaking of the Millennial Generation. "Our students are interested in education, development, energy and sustainability. They come in with all sort of interesting backgrounds and are trying to become more effective leaders doing the work they care about." (See Perspective "Q&A: Catherine Clark on Impact Investing.")

New York–based Echoing Green, a group that awards fellowships to early-stage social entrepreneurs, reported earlier this year that close to 50 percent of the 2015 applicants for its three fellowship programs want to start for-profit businesses.

In addition, contests sponsored by brands that market to Millennials increasingly honor young social entrepreneurs.

Actor Adrian Grenier helped judge an entrepreneurial business plan contest called *The Venture.*

In July 2015, actor Adrian Grenier, star of the HBO series and movie *Entourage*, and CBS Late Late Show host James Corden helped judge *The Venture*, a Chivas Regal–sponsored business plan contest that awarded a share of $1 million to five finalists pitching their social ventures. "Social entrepreneurship challenges society to reimagine what is possible and inspires us to create a better future and a better world," Grenier said.[6]

Meanwhile, *Forbes* Magazine's 2015 Change the World Competition, for social entrepreneurs under 30, drew more than 2,500 applicants from around the globe for $1 million in prizes. Prize winners were announced at the magazine's second annual Under 30 Summit in October 2015. The top prize—$250,000 in cash and a $250,000 media grant—went to SIRUM, a social enterprise started by Kiah Williams and her co-founders Adam Kircher and George Wang, all Stanford University alumni. They have created a tech platform to match unexpired surplus prescription drugs, which are often discarded, with hospitals that serve people in need.[7]

The magazine said that 42 percent of the applicants proposed for-profit businesses, 28 percent proposed hybrid business models with donated and earned revenue and 30 percent pitched nonprofit groups.[8]

Educators are responding to the interest in social entrepreneurship, too. In the United States and Canada alone, more than 200 colleges and universities offer programs and classes in social entrepreneurship.[9] Copenhagen Business School in Denmark offers a minor in social entrepreneurship and recently launched a MOOC (massive open online course) on social entrepreneurship to reach a broader audience.

A handful of fellowships support practicing social entrepreneurs, such as those sponsored by Echoing Green; Ashoka—Innovators for the Public, based in Arlington, VA.; the Skoll Foundation in Palo Alto, CA.; and the Schwab Foundation for Social Entrepreneurship, headquartered in Switzerland.

In addition, impact investment funds and angel investors who want to have a social impact are fueling the growth of social entrepreneurship. JPMorgan estimated that global impact investments could reach $400 billion to $1 trillion by 2020.[10]

However, Fuqua's Clark says a vast funding gap remains, with many early-stage social entrepreneurs still not considered established enough to attract investors.

Some early-stage impact funds and incubators are beginning to address that need, and groups such as Ashoka, a global organization that invests in social entrepreneurs with game-changing ideas, are expanding that "ecosystem" to help social entrepreneurs.

Social entrepreneur Björn Strüwer, who founded Roots of Impact, a Frankfurt, Germany–based consulting firm and accelerator for social entrepreneurs, is leading

Ashoka's efforts to foster an ecosystem for social innovators, focusing particularly on new ways to help entrepreneurs overcome the funding gap.

Starting any business is a risky proposition at best, and adding a layer of social accountability and mission is a tall order, notes Ted Ladd, who teaches social entrepreneurship at Hult International Business School in San Francisco.

"It's a harder row to hoe," he says. Such businesses have to take all the same steps as conventional ones, but the valuations and revenue tend to be lower, he adds.

Some social entrepreneurs struggle without mentorship and start-up funds. They may also lack the managerial expertise to build and lead a team. Social entrepreneurs sometimes fail to broadly execute change in a way that allows for maximum efficiency and impact, or scalability.

When social entrepreneurs start out, there are friends, family and other supporters to cheer them on, says Felipe Vergara, an Ashoka fellow from Colombia who started Lumni, a for-profit company that finances students who can't otherwise afford higher education. "As you want to scale, it's harder and harder to raise capital," he says. "The main challenge is not to lose faith, and also to understand your weaknesses and strengths."

Often, social entrepreneurs fail to think about the impact they hope to achieve when they start, says Cheryl Kiser, executive director of the Lewis Institute for Social Innovation and the Babson Social Innovation Lab at Babson College in Babson Park, Mass. She works with students to outline their goals and metrics from the start.

Erica Lock, director of fellowship programs at Echoing Green, says that her team tries to ensure success for those they support by seeking people who demonstrate leadership, passion and purpose, resilience to handle the inevitable ups and downs ahead and "resource magnetism"—the ability to attract both human and financial capital.

Often, she says, social entrepreneurs have a big vision and plenty of optimism but may lack the ability to execute that vision and run an organization. Echoing Green provides extensive mentoring and a network of advisers to try to overcome that challenge. They help the entrepreneurs develop a fundraising and short-term plan, internalize their philosophy of how to bring about change and then work toward it. That involves not just saying "this is my goal," Lock says, but also "how do you measure it?"

Social entrepreneurs often have great ideas and the best of intentions, but they still aren't able to achieve scale, Olivier Kayser and Valeria Budinich wrote in *Scaling Up Business Solutions to Social Problems*. Sometimes, solutions fail to scale because corporate executives don't see the value of reaching the world's 4 billion poorest customers. In other cases, giveaway programs supported by well-meaning foundations and governments can distort markets that social entrepreneurs are trying to serve. "And social entrepreneurs themselves are often encumbered by ideology or limited by their own capabilities," wrote Kayser and Budinich, who both work with groups that back entrepreneurs.[11]

Ashoka's Strüwer says the funding gap remains a major hurdle for most social entrepreneurs. "Most social enterprise models are not as profitable as traditional ventures." He points to one encouraging financial development, the creation in 2010 of the first Social Impact Bond in the United Kingdom to finance a nonprofit program to reduce recidivism among former prisoners. More than 100 social projects globally now follow this funding model: They pay investors a premium over their original investment, but only if the desired effect is achieved. Otherwise, investors don't get anything back.

Strüwer's firm is working with the Swiss Agency for Development and Cooperation on a project in Latin America that is trying to adapt the most successful features of the impact bond approach. Because some social businesses are not profitable or attractive enough to scale their ideas, Roots of Impact and the Swiss agency have designed a Social Impact Incentive, which is a payment from either a public entity or a donor agency. Funds would be provided for a limited time, until the organization is either self-sufficient or another funder takes over, Strüwer says.

Ashoka, which has named more than 3,000 fellows around the world since its founding in 1980, selects its entrepreneurs based on how innovative their idea is and whether it can be put into action on a broad scale and replicated elsewhere, explains Anne Evans, a leadership group member at Ashoka. Fellows must also have a track record achieving their mission.

"It was completely transformative to what we did," Sascha Haselmayer, the founder of Barcelona-based Citymart, says of his selection as an Ashoka fellow in 2011.

Citymart, a for-profit global social enterprise that recently expanded to New York City, lets cities around the world put out broad requests for solutions to their urban problems; its online platform promotes a wider range of responses than a traditional bidding process.

Finding like-minded peers who are going through similar experiences has been encouraging, Haselmayer says. "You work like an entrepreneur but with no prospect of becoming filthy rich from it," he says. "We take the economically least rational decision, choosing principle over profit. Then you walk into a room where everyone is like that."

As educators, funders and would-be social entrepreneurs consider the status of the sector, below are some of the issues under debate.

WEIGHING THE ISSUES

Does a social enterprise need to be self-sustaining?

When fledgling social entrepreneurs write business plans for their ventures, professors and mentors often ask them to describe their "earned income strategy."

In other words, where is the money going to come from to fund continuing operations, once start-up funds are exhausted? Is the venture going to sell a product or service as part of its business model, or will it depend on grants from nongovernmental organizations, foundations and government agencies? Will it have a long-term endowment or go begging for funds each year?

Social entrepreneurs who choose a for-profit model expect their business to eventually generate enough revenue to pay back investors and finance continuing operations.

However, an earned income strategy also works for many nonprofit organizations. The Girl Scouts of the United States of America, for example, earn revenue from cookie sales, but the profits get plowed back into supporting the group's activities.[12]

Regardless of whether a social enterprise is nonprofit or for-profit, becoming self-sufficient can assure that organizations actually survive to accomplish their social mission, says Kiser at Babson College.

For example, Lucky Iron Fish, started in 2012 by Gavin Armstrong, aims to vanquish iron deficiency anemia in the developing world with a small, fish-shaped iron ingot that's dropped into cooking water. For every fish it sells to a customer in the West, the company pledges to donate a second fish to a poor family. The company is now selling more than 10,000 fish a month to Western consumers and donating an equal number.

"The growing interest and demand in Western countries is actually fueling our impact," Armstrong says. "I never dreamed the buy-one, donate-one model would be as successful as it is."

Being a nonprofit or a for-profit doesn't typically limit a venture's ability to sell products or accept donations, according to a 2014 *Harvard Business Review* article by Rich Leimsider, then vice president of fellowship programs at Echoing Green. In the 2013 class of fellows, five of the 12 nonprofits had earned revenue, and five of seven for-profit companies had received donations.[13]

Most fellowship applicants aspire to profits

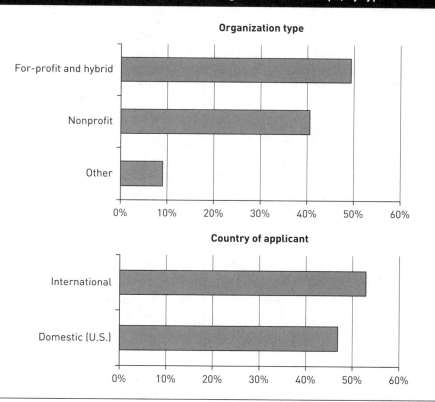

Percentage of applications for 2015 Echoing Green Fellowships, by type

Organization type

Country of applicant

Half the 2015 applicants for fellowships with Echoing Green, a New York–based social impact nonprofit, were for-profit organizations or hybrid organizations with both for-profit and nonprofit aspects, while 41 percent were nonprofit groups. More fellowship applications came from outside the United States than from within.

Note: From 3,165 submitted applications.

Source: Kayleigh Rogers, "The Data: Seven Trends We're Seeing in 2015," Echoing Green, March 10, 2015, http://tinyurl .com/o6f82t5

What's more, Leimsider argued, there's nothing inherently better about relying on revenue, rather than grants and donations. He says it's a common misconception that philanthropic revenue is somehow less reliable than earned income.

He noted that more than half of for-profit start-ups fail within the first five years and that earned revenue can also vary widely, depending on market conditions.

"In fact, according to the National Philanthropic Trust, when the S&P 500 fell by 45% after the 2007 recession, U.S. charitable giving dipped only 10%," he wrote.[14]

In many cases, though, it's not feasible for a nonprofit social enterprise to have an earned income model.

Echoing Green's Lock gives the example of fellows Robin Reineke and William Masson, co-founders of the Colibrí Center for Human Rights in Tucson, Ariz., which aims to end migrant suffering.

It's doing "super important work," helping to identify the dead along the borders of the United States and Mexico and establishing a database that will help provide grist for the policy debate on immigration, Lock says. In Colibrí's case, charging families for the identification service to raise revenue would be an "unethical model," she says.

An earned income strategy isn't always possible, agrees Lauren Booker Allen, senior manager for impact investing at the Omidyar Network, started by eBay founder Pierre Omidyar to invest in socially oriented nonprofit and for-profit ventures. However, she says, "For the vast majority, it's very important."

Omidyar Network helps its grant recipients determine how to eventually become self-sustaining. Sometimes it's through membership or subscription fees or by selling research. In other cases, it may involve securing an endowment for a fixed number of years.

"Similar to our for-profit companies, we don't like to create a dependency model," Allen says. Omidyar Network, on average, supports these nonprofit social enterprises for seven years, at an amount not exceeding 20 to 25 percent of their budgets, she says.

Should investors and social entrepreneurs be allowed to profit from a social enterprise?

For companies that need to raise a lot of capital to accomplish their social or environmental goals, a for-profit model allows them to seek funds from a growing community of impact investors, who want to make a difference while also making a profit.

"The biggest way to spread social good is in a for-profit model because then it's sustainable," says David Rosenberg, the CEO of AeroFarms, based in Newark, N.J., who has raised $35 million from impact investors to build an urban demonstration farm in Newark that grows plants "aeroponically" with a patented technique that requires very little water and no pesticides.

Social enterprises like AeroFarms, which haven't yet proven they will be profitable, can't easily attract investments from conventional venture capital firms. Impact investors offer "patient capital," because they're not looking for a quick exit, Rosenberg says.

However, making a profit isn't always desirable, or even possible when an organization's goal is to use the social enterprise to help support a mission.

REDF is a San Francisco–based venture philanthropy that provides funding and advice to social enterprises, mostly nonprofit, that help provide job opportunities to low-income and marginalized populations. Like a venture capital firm, they are looking for a return on their investment in these enterprises, but in this case, the return is social, not financial, explains President and CEO Carla Javits. They measure success by how many people gain meaningful employment as a result of their programs.

Most of the businesses in REDF's portfolio succeed at providing job opportunities while coming close to break-even. But they're not generating the level of returns that attract traditional investors. "They're basically covering all their costs with earned revenue," Javits says.

Still, that may be enough from a social perspective. In an analysis of programs it supports, REDF found that these organizations have helped 10,000 people go to work over an 18-year-period, with 3,000 of them in the last five years. Moreover, a cost-benefit analysis found that for every dollar spent, the programs generated $2.23 in value to the individuals they supported, Javits says.

Staying nonprofit can also help prevent what's known in the social enterprise world as "mission drift"—straying from the original social or environmental goals as a business grows, and in some cases, gets sold or changes leadership.

Nonprofit social enterprises are often more adept at monitoring their effectiveness and staying on course, Javits says. "I think many times the for-profits really fall short and really don't know how to measure social outcome, and so they don't."

Echoing Green's Lock says, however, that a for-profit structure can be perfectly compatible with achieving social or environmental goals. Echoing Green, as an organization, makes grants that must be paid back without interest when the entrepreneurs reach certain thresholds, either in valuation or revenue. About 20 percent of their entrepreneurs have reached those goals since the program took effect in 2011, according to Lock.

A changing business landscape is making it easier for these social entrepreneurs to succeed, as more investors look for companies that can help poor people or the environment, Lock says. "A lot more people are learning about social entrepreneurship and seeing the potential of capital markets and private investors to support this industry."

For social entrepreneurs who sell a useful product to poor populations around the globe—a strategy often referred to as base of the pyramid marketing, because there are so many more poor people than rich ones—charging customers a small fee, even if they are of limited means, may make them value a product more and take care of it better.

That's been the case for Essmart Global, a distribution business that sells solar lamps, water filters and other devices that improve the lives of the poor in southern India, Lock says. The company's founders, Diana Jue and Jackie Stenson, were 2013 Echoing Green fellows.

Omidyar Network's Allen says most businesses her firm invests in have integrated their social mission directly into their business model, so there's no conflict between profit and mission.

Many companies that consider themselves mission-driven yet adopt a more conventional corporate structure see no conflict between profit and purpose, says Babson's Kiser. Typically, they are seeking to reach a large scale quickly, and the best way to do that is by seeking venture capital or funds from impact investors.

Most impact investors want competitive returns

Kiser says she has no problem with social entrepreneurs making money for themselves and their investors. She cites the example of Brandon Arbiter, a social entrepreneur who created an app to control diabetes after he was diagnosed with the disease.

"If somebody is willing to come up with an amazing solution to better manage diabetes, I don't begrudge anyone making as much money as they want to," she says.

What does concern her, however, are entrepreneurs who don't clearly explain from the outset what impact they are seeking and how they will measure it. She says she wouldn't invest in any business that didn't provide this information to investors.

Ashoka's Evans notes the rise of many for-profit businesses with a social agenda.

Some, she says, are more about purpose with profit, where the entire business is geared to achieving a specific social or environmental goal. Others are more clearly about profit, with purpose taking a back seat. "Sometimes, the purpose part is more a marketing gimmick and other times it's very inherent to what the business is about. If it's really structured into what they do, then you can say at the very least, they're more about purpose."

Level of returns investors seek, by percent

Below market rate, closer to capital preservation

Market rate

Below market rate, but closer to market rate

Fifty-five percent of social impact investors said they seek market-rate returns on their investments. Another 27 percent target returns slightly lower than the market rate, while less than one-fifth aim for below-market-rate returns that simply prevent investment losses.

Note: Based on survey of 146 impact investors who manage at least $10 million and have invested in at least five transactions.

Source: "Eyes on the Horizon: The Impact Investor Survey," JPMorgan, Global Impact Investing Network, May 4, 2015, p. 15, http://tinyurl.com/orfvzdp

Can social enterprises stay true to their mission if they become large and successful?

All social enterprises face the challenge of preventing "mission drift."

"Everything out there can claim to be social entrepreneurship," warns Kai Hockerts, a social entrepreneurship professor at Copenhagen Business School who organized an online course for social entrepreneurs around the world. "The social motivation or mission needs to be first."

Social entrepreneurs and funders say this challenge of placing mission first can be addressed either by choosing a legal structure that protects against mission drift or by building the intended impact right into the business model.

For instance, in a much-publicized move, Kickstarter, one of the leading for-profit crowd-funding sites, officially relaunched on Sept. 21 as Kickstarter PBC, a public benefit corporation, which means that the company is obligated to consider the impact of its business decisions on society, as well as on shareholders.

In New Hampshire, Henry and Lisa Lovejoy founded EcoFish in 1999, expressly to assure consumers that they were buying seafood that came from fisheries that were behaving in an environmentally responsible way, careful not to deplete stocks of dwindling species or harm other animals, such as dolphins, in the fishing process. The company, which incorporated in 1999, projects $3 million in sales this year in canned and frozen, sustainably sourced tuna, cod, shrimp, sardines and salmon.

"One of the biggest challenges we had right out of the gate was that no one was doing this," Henry Lovejoy said. "You'd mention sustainable seafood and no one knew what it meant."[15]

To get around that problem, the Lovejoys created an advisory board, composed of conservation and environmental organizations, with veto power over every strategic decision the company makes. The structure remains in place and has enabled the company to stay on message and on target, Lovejoy says.

"We're highly regulated by design," he said. "We have eliminated a massive percentage of the average seafood a company could sell."[16]

But other organizations struggle with mission drift as they grow. That's particularly the case where a growing organization hires new employees from its industry, bringing in profit-minded people who might not necessarily share the social mission. The authors of a 2012 article in *Stanford Social Innovation Review* give the example of the Bolivian micro-finance group Banco Solidario, or BancoSol, which transitioned from a nonprofit to a hybrid in 1992 by spinning off its lending into "a regulated commercial organization."[17]

Under its new structure, BancoSol was able to meet the demand for loans from low-income entrepreneurs, because it generated income. However, staffing became an issue as the bank hired employees from both the social and business sectors and planned to train them to work together effectively, the authors wrote.

"According to Francisco Otero, BancoSol's first CEO, a balanced organizational culture would be created by 'converting social workers into bankers and bankers into social workers.' Despite BancoSol's training efforts, however, the single-purpose backgrounds of their employees made it hard for them to adjust to the hybrid model. Those with a social work background and those with a financial background ended up resenting each other and fighting constantly, so that the organization could hardly operate."[18]

Echoing Green screens heavily to make sure the entrepreneurs selected for its fellowships have a plan to keep the mission alive, whether via bylaws in their constitution or in their articles of incorporation.

Babson's Kiser, who co-authored the book *Creating Social Value: A Guide for Leaders and Change Makers*, emphasizes to her students the importance of defining what they hope to achieve with their social venture and figuring out how they will measure it. Such steps will ensure that as the enterprise grows larger and more successful, the mission won't get lost along the way, she says.

"If you wait until the end, it doesn't work," she says "Most people are remediating and backtracking. I say to them it's as rigorous as financing or anything else."

BACKGROUND

Ashoka and its aims

In his 2007 book, *How to Change the World*, author David Bornstein argued that many of history's most important social innovators—those who have worked to bring about major changes on a large scale—would fit today's definition of a social entrepreneur.[19]

These include religious leaders such as St. Francis of Assisi, who founded the Franciscan order and built multiple organizations that advanced systemic changes in his field, as well as Florence Nightingale, who completely transformed the system of nursing on the battlefield.

Social entrepreneurship pioneer Bill Drayton.

"What's different today is that social entrepreneurship is becoming established as a vocation and a mainstream area of inquiry, not only in the United States, but increasingly in Asia, Africa and Latin America," Bornstein wrote.[20] The emergence of what Bornstein called the "citizen sector"—a term he used to encompass nonprofit organizations and international nongovernmental aid organizations—has enabled change on a larger scale than was possible in the past, he said. These organizations are forging partnerships with government and business, approaching problems in a systemic rather than a stopgap fashion, he wrote.

To tell the story of social entrepreneurship's rise, Bornstein focused on the emergence and growth of Ashoka: Innovators for the Public, an organization founded in 1980 by Bill Drayton, then the assistant administrator of the U.S. Environmental Protection Agency.

Drayton had been mulling over his idea for about 15 years: to establish an organization that would support the world's leading visionaries, who combined entrepreneurial creativity and strong ethics to accomplish broad social change.

"To this end, Drayton set out like a modern-day explorer to map the world's social terrain in search of its most talented change makers," according to Bornstein.[21]

Ashoka, one of the best-known foundations in the field of social entrepreneurship, took an approach not unlike a venture capital firm, seeking a high return from very targeted investments.

The main difference: The returns Ashoka sought were not financial, but social.

Drayton's organization wanted to support individuals who were going to tackle some of the world's most intransigent problems: transforming education, protecting the environment, alleviating poverty, protecting human rights, caring for the disabled and aiding children at risk.[22]

"Like Bill Drayton, Ashoka is a lean organization that punches above its weight," Bornstein said. Its network includes tens of thousands of nominators and supporters who search out people who can cause major, positive system change.[23]

As Drayton is famously quoted: "Social entrepreneurs are not content just to give a fish or teach how to fish. They will not rest until they have revolutionized the fishing industry."[24]

Now 35 years old, Ashoka has elected nearly 3,000 social entrepreneurs from 70 countries to its fellowship program, providing them with start-up financing, professional support services and access to a global network.[25]

Ashoka funds fellowships in various sectors

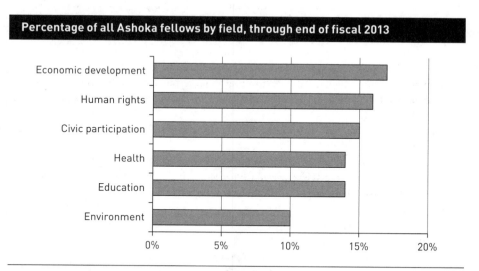

Percentage of all Ashoka fellows by field, through end of fiscal 2013

Seventeen percent of fellows funded by global social entrepreneurship nonprofit Ashoka through the end of fiscal 2013 worked in economic development. Human rights (16 percent) and civic participation (15 percent) were the second- and third-most common sectors, followed by education and health (each 14 percent).

Note: Total does not add to 100 because Ashoka did not classify all fellows by sector.

Source: Graphic courtesy of Ashoka: Innovators for the Public

Often, social entrepreneurs' personal experiences fuel their passion. Fellows include Vergara, the founder of Lumni, who saw firsthand in his native Colombia how the lack of access to financial resources was keeping poor students in developing countries from attending universities and bettering their lives. Not only was this a personal tragedy for these students and their families, but it also meant that local economies didn't reap the benefits of their increased education and earning power.

Lumni manages for-profit investment funds that lend money to students, mostly in developing countries. At the heart of Vergara's system is the "human capital contract," in which the investor partners with the student in a shared-income agreement. It requires the students to pay back a set percentage of their earnings to the investor over a predetermined period after graduation. The amounts students repay vary depending upon their chosen field of study, meaning that a graduate pursuing a career as a teacher would pay back less than someone who became an investment banker.

As of 2015, Lumni has found more than 150 investors and raised about $40 million for college students in Chile, Colombia, Mexico and the United States, as well as another $10 million to develop the business, according to Vergara. "My primary goal is to help people have a better education, pursue their goals and improve their quality of life," Vergara says.

As Ashoka views the world of social change, there are three levels of potential impact: direct service, where an individual or an organization is working to address a social problem in a repeatable, direct fashion, but not changing an existing system to eliminate the problem; system change, where a social entrepreneur comes up with a completely new solution that gets to the root of the problem; and the highest level, framework change—something that disrupts the pattern in a given industry and results in widespread policy change. Ashoka has sought out social entrepreneurs working at those two highest levels, Evans says.

Evans says Vergara's idea is changing the system of financing college education because he came up with "a completely new way of thinking about tertiary education." If he succeeds at a broad scale, resulting in a policy change within governments, he may completely change the framework, she says.

Over the past 10 years, Ashoka has evolved to promote the idea that everyone can be a "change maker."

"We've really done a deep dive into what is it these leading social entrepreneurs have learned at a young age that allows them to flourish and create these remarkable innovations," says Laxmi Parthasarathy, global media manager at Ashoka. "The idea is that social entrepreneurship is a mindset born of empathy, and that skill can be cultivated through the educational system, beginning at a young age."

To that end, Ashoka has begun recognizing outstanding "changemaker " schools and universities that are rethinking how to educate people to lead with empathy and find solutions to the world's problems. These include a diverse group of institutions of higher education, from Miami Dade College, a community college with more than 160,000 students and seven campuses in Florida, to the private Tulane University in New Orleans. At the primary- and secondary-school level, Ashoka has singled out schools like the Western Institute for Leadership Development in Tucson, Ariz., also known as "Changemaker High School," and Baltimore public charter school City Neighbors Hamilton. "We've been talking about how we can reimagine learning around the world to make everyone have this experience. This is where you get framework change: every child mastering empathy, and every child becoming a change maker," Parthasarathy says.

Changemaker schools and universities, like social entrepreneurship fellows, benefit from both the prestige of the designation and access to a network of peers with whom they share ideas and strategies.

Pioneering solutions in Bangladesh

Around the same time that Drayton was thinking about how to support social entrepreneurs, Bangladeshi economics professor Muhammad Yunus was developing a revolutionary way to eliminate poverty in destitute communities of his country, which became independent in 1971 in the aftermath of a disastrous cyclone and a bloody war for independence from Pakistan.[26]

No one had called Yunus a social entrepreneur yet, but he had become an example of how an individual could upset the status quo and bring about broad-scale change by getting to the root of a problem.

In 1974, Yunus took his Chittagong University students on a field trip to a poor village, where they spoke to a woman who earned her livelihood making and selling bamboo stools. They learned that to buy the raw bamboo, she had to borrow money from middlemen at sky-high interest rates, thus making only pennies per sale. Yunus reasoned that if she could borrow at better rates, she could move beyond a subsistence existence and build an economic cushion.

Later, Yunus defied the advice of both banks and his government by making tiny loans, known as microloans, out of his own pocket to poor female basket weavers in Bangladesh.

In 1983, Yunus founded Grameen Bank, which means "village bank" bank, on the foundation of trust and solidarity.

Since then, Grameen Bank has become a major economic force in Bangladesh, growing to more than 2,500 branches and serving 8.3 million borrowers from 81,379 villages, according to 2011 figures listed on its website. Almost all of the borrowers—97 percent—are women.[27]

Grameen Bank's methods have been adopted around the world, and microlending has become an established route to spur economic development in the world's poorest regions.

Yunus and Grameen jointly won the Nobel Peace Prize in 2006: "From Dr. Yunus' personal loan of small amounts of money to destitute basket weavers in Bangladesh in the mid-70s, the Grameen Bank has advanced to the forefront of a burgeoning world movement toward eradicating poverty through microlending. Replicas of the Grameen Bank model operate in more than 100 countries worldwide," according to the Nobel Foundation.[28]

In Yunus' 2009 book, *Creating a World Without Poverty*, he wrote that economic theory, by reducing human beings to "one-dimensional" profit seekers, has produced a "narrow" interpretation of capitalism that ignores the "essence of what it is to be human."[29]

In 2011, the Supreme Court of Bangladesh ruled that he was required to resign as managing director, citing a government provision that required retirement by age 60. (He was 70 at the time.) Observers said the move to oust Yunus was politically motivated.[30]

"Every time I wanted to go into retirement, you told me through your representatives that until you released me, I would have to continue with my responsibilities at Grameen Bank," Yunus wrote in an open letter to Grameen Bank members upon his resignation. "I accepted this and carried on. Recently, on the orders of Bangladesh Bank I have been forced to relinquish this responsibility. I am removing myself from the responsibilities of the Managing Director of Grameen Bank, but I am not distancing myself from you. My relationship with you will never be broken. Even after leaving Grameen Bank, I will remain close to you."[31]

Yunus has since formed Yunus Social Business, headquartered in Frankfurt, Germany. The accelerator program operates in the Balkans, Brazil, Colombia, Haiti, India, Tunisia and Uganda to encourage the formation of social businesses, which are dedicated to solving a social problem in "a financially self-sustainable way."[32]

The "double dip" at Ben & Jerry's

At the same time that pioneering social entrepreneurs such as Drayton and Yunus were working outside the system to spur social change, some businesses were questioning how as corporate entities they could behave in a more socially responsible manner.

Since then, the lines have blurred between so-called social entrepreneurs and larger companies that want to pursue a triple bottom line of people, profits and the planet.

In 1978, Ben Cohen and Jerry Greenfield opened their first ice cream store in a renovated gas station in South Burlington, Vt. As it grew, Ben & Jerry's became "a social enterprise icon" by stressing fair labor practices, environmental consciousness and humane treatment of the cows that supplied its milk.[33]

The founders called their pursuit of both profit and corporate social responsibility the "double dip."[34]

"In its heyday (circa 1990), the company was a kind of corporate hippie, wearing its convictions on its labels with funky-named flavors like Cherry Garcia, Whirled Peace, and Wavy Gravy. Peace, love, and ice cream," according to law professors Antony Page and Robert A. Katz.[35]

The company also sought to create business opportunities for disadvantaged groups. For instance, it bought the brownies for its chocolate fudge brownie ice cream from the

Ice cream company Ben & Jerry's is known as a social enterprise icon.

social enterprise Greyston Bakery in Yonkers, N.Y. Greyston was started in 1982 by Bernie Glassman to provide jobs and training to impoverished people who faced barriers such as previous incarceration, drug abuse and low education.[36]

Ben & Jerry's also committed to giving 7.5 percent of pretax profit to charity. However, the company's commitment to social responsibility failed to result in sufficient profit to buoy its stock price. The company's shares fell from almost $34 a share in 1993 to $17 in 1999.[37]

In 2000, the company's board accepted a $326 million acquisition offer from Unilever, then the world's third-largest consumer products company.

"While I would have preferred for Ben & Jerry's to remain independent, I'm excited about this next chapter," Cohen said in a prepared statement.[38]

Founders Cohen and Greenfield contended publicly that they had no choice but to accept the offer or they would have faced shareholder lawsuits. At the time, critics were outraged, calling the founders "sellouts" for putting profit above their ideals. By 2003, Unilever had discontinued one of their signature flavors, Wavy Gravy, because it wasn't profitable enough.[39]

Common wisdom has since held that Ben & Jerry's could have avoided being forced to sell if new corporate structures for social businesses had existed at the time, wrote Page and Katz. They contended that the company could have evoked its anti-takeover provisions for protection and would have been able to turn down the takeover offer without any change in its legal status.[40]

CURRENT SITUATION

Corporate structures for social enterprises

Social entrepreneurs must decide from the outset how they are going to structure their venture: Will it be a nonprofit organization, which is exempt from paying taxes, or a for-profit business, which pays taxes, but has more flexibility in raising capital from investors? Or will they seek some sort of hybrid option that combines the best of both worlds?

A small but growing number of social entrepreneurs are forming profit-making businesses, generally called hybrids, that value their social purpose at least as much as their profits. Many nonprofits also have revenue-generating businesses that support their social purpose because of the difficulty of obtaining philanthropic and government funding.

The two hybrid structures most used by for-profit U.S. social enterprises are the benefit corporation and the L3C. Both are taxable entities.

A benefit corporation must meet certain standards of accountability, transparency and purpose. While laws vary by state, in general benefit corporations must demonstrate a material impact on both society and the environment. Purpose is embedded in their DNA.[41]

At present, 30 states plus the District of Columbia allow benefit corporations, and legislation is pending in five more states. [42] There are about 1,200 benefit corporations in the United States, according to B Lab.

Kickstarter is one of the latest companies to join the club. On Sept. 21, 2015, it relaunched as a public benefit corporation. The co-founders explained their decision in a letter posted on the Kickstarter website: "Until recently, the idea of a for-profit company pursuing social good at the expense of shareholder value had no clear protection under U.S. corporate law, and certainly no mandate," they wrote.

"Companies that believe there are more important goals than maximizing shareholder value have been at odds with the expectation that for-profit companies must exist ultimately for profit above all. "[43]

San Francisco lawyers Doug Bend and Alex King wrote that start-ups should consider forming a benefit corporation when they have a strong social purpose. "Incorporating as a benefit corporation legally protects an entrepreneur's social goals by mandating considerations other than just profit," they said. Also, Bend and King said, with consumers increasingly making purchases at companies they feel are responsible corporate citizens, the benefit corporation status can help differentiate a business from the competition.[44]

While the benefit corporation path can align a company with its social and environmental goals, Bend and King acknowledged possible drawbacks: Benefit corporations have annual reporting requirements that benchmark performance against a third-party standard. Also, the very newness of the benefit corporation as a legal entity means that it's still unclear how courts will view such companies' mandates to consider societal benefits along with profit. It's also unclear, according to Bend and King, how the status will affect the ability of these companies to raise funds from angel investors and venture capitalists.[45]

The L3C, or Low-Profit Limited Liability Company, affords social entrepreneurs the legal and tax flexibility of a traditional LLC, the social benefits of a nonprofit organization and the branding benefits of being able to call one's business a social enterprise, says Marc J. Lane, a Chicago lawyer who drafted the L3C legislation for Illinois.

Under current tax law, foundations must distribute 5 percent of their assets annually to charitable causes related to their mission. Under Internal Revenue Service regulations, those distributions can include so-called Program-Related Investments (PRI) in organizations with a charitable or educational purpose, and L3Cs fall into this category.[46] There are 1,279 L3Cs in the United States, according to a quarterly tally by InterSector Partners, a consulting firm that advises social-purposes businesses and nonprofits.[47]

Just eight states allow companies to incorporate as L3Cs. (A ninth, North Carolina, rescinded its 2010 L3C law in 2014, deeming it unnecessary.[48])

In the United Kingdom, a social enterprise hybrid known as a Community Interest Company (CIC) gets tax benefits in exchange for limiting profit distributions to investors. Once the designation is approved, the government freezes the assets of the CIC and designates them for general community benefit. Investors can receive capped dividends on their investment, but the principal is never retrieved.[49]

A growing community

Allen, the senior manager of impact investing at Omidyar Network, says that even though she is seeing more social entrepreneurs who are exploring the benefit corporation concept, structure is less important than substance.

"We're certainly encouraged by this growing effort, as transparency, accountability, and commitment to impact are all great things," she says. "We don't think it matters, however, whether a company is structured in one way or the other: Benefit corps, certified B corps and companies not structured in this way can all have compelling profit and impact profiles, and vice versa."

However, Allen says, deciding to clearly brand a business as mission-oriented will appeal to some investors more than others. "Entrepreneurs have to be ready for potential market resistance if going this route."

Entrepreneurs who don't live in a state that allows L3Cs or benefit corporations can register their business in one that does, says Lane, who frequently helps social entrepreneurs set up L3Cs or benefit corporations.

For instance, Kickstarter, which has its headquarters in New York City, is incorporated in Delaware, legal home to thousands of corporations.[50]

Seal of approval: B Corp certification

In addition to choosing a hybrid for-profit business form, a growing number of companies are submitting to a voluntary review process called B Corp certification.

B Lab established the B Corp certification, which is different from the benefit corporation designation, in 2006. Currently, there are 1,498 certified B Corps, from 130 industries in 42 countries.[51] B Lab issues a report card assessing a company's commitment to social and environmental responsibility, accountability and transparency, benchmarking it against industry norms. Companies that pass can brand their business as a Certified B Corp, which can attract both consumers and impact investors, Lane says.

"B Corp is to business what Fair Trade certification is to coffee or USDA Organic certification is to milk," declares the B Corp website.[52] Such companies aren't necessarily small ventures run by new social entrepreneurs; they include large businesses, such as outdoor clothing maker Patagonia and two publicly traded companies, Etsy, the online sales platform for craftspeople, and Natura, a Brazilian cosmetics giant with 7,000 employees.[53] B Corps that are registered in states with a benefit corporation law are required to reincorporate as benefit corporations within four years to maintain B Corp certification.

Among B Lab's top-ranked B Corps is Better World Books in Alpharetta, Ga., near Atlanta. Better World is a triple bottom line business that is creating a nursing library in Somaliland, providing profit sharing and equity ownership opportunities to its employees and making carbon-balanced shipments. "They're not a company with an add-on 'cause' component. They create social good and protect the environment through their regular business transactions," according to a profile on the B Lab website.[54]

LOOKING AHEAD

Expanding the definition

Increasingly, players in the social innovation and impact investing community are looking to a broader definition of social entrepreneurship as the field evolves. In some cases, they have stopped using the term social entrepreneur altogether, preferring more inclusive terms that encompass efforts to solve social and environmental problems within larger organizations as well as entrepreneurial ventures.

In the future, Chicago lawyer Lane expects more charities will embrace earned revenue strategies. "We're seeing an enormous pickup in charities starting businesses to drive mission. It's healthy because it introduces sound business principles into the social sector, where they're desperately needed," he says.

As the lines continue to blur between the for-profit and the nonprofit worlds, more conversations will focus on how people can work together, across sectors to create social change, observers say.

Babson College, which requires all its business students to take an entrepreneurship class, was named a "Changemaker Campus" by Ashoka because of its strong socially oriented curriculum. Babson's Kiser stresses that entrepreneurs alone can't tackle the world's big social problems.

Nor is everyone cut out to run a venture. But individuals can work within larger organizations to foster social responsibility or join the nonprofit sector and steer investment funds to fledgling social innovators, she says.

"I love the notion of change-making. I think social entrepreneurship is very narrow," Kiser says.

Kiser sees a bright outlook for anybody interested in social and environmental change. While Millennials have been famously active in seeking social meaning in their lives, Baby Boomer entrepreneurs over 50, who are loathe to retire, will also play a big role in bringing about social change, she says.

Clark of Duke University's Fuqua School of Business sees social entrepreneurs acting as the catalyst for change, but says they can't succeed alone. "It's not just about creating the catalyst but about creating the helpers," she says. Clark maintains that social entrepreneurs can have the most impact when they work in tandem with major institutions, such as government agencies and private sector companies.

Vergara at Lumni, the higher education financing group, says he hopes companies generally will spend more time thinking about the social impact of their businesses on society and the environment.

Marina Kim, who is co-founder of Ashoka U, a program that identifies Changemaker Campuses, says she hopes as Ashoka's goal of promoting everyone as a change maker evolves, programs and fellowships won't be concentrated among socioeconomic classes perceived as having the luxury to think about making a difference instead of making a living.

"Social innovation has been a little bit elite. It's now spreading out of that, but it has a long way to go," she says.

To democratize social innovation, she says she would like to see more community colleges and historically black colleges starting social entrepreneurship programs, outside of the San Francisco Bay, New York and Boston areas.

"We will not get the type of innovation we need if it's only coming from a few places. For social innovation to have the impact it can have, and the democratization, there has to be some way for everyone to be a change maker," Kim says.

How to do that is the big question, she says. "Democratizing access is the No. 1 thing keeping us up at night."

Chronology

Pre–20th Century	Social entrepreneurship arises but lacks a name.
1209	St. Francis of Assisi establishes the Franciscan order.
1854	Florence Nightingale takes charge of British military hospitals in the Scutari district of Istanbul.

1970s–1990s	**Pioneers establish notable groups that blend business and social good.**
1971	Stanford University launches the public management program to educate socially conscious leaders.
1976	Muhammad Yunus starts a research project to lend to the poor in Bangladesh.
1978	Ben Cohen and Jerry Greenfield found ice-cream maker Ben & Jerry's as a "values led" company in South Burlington, Vt.
1980	Bill Drayton founds Ashoka Foundation to support social entrepreneurs. . . . Harvard University students launch the Nonprofit Management Club, now part of the Social Enterprise Club, one of the largest clubs on campus. . . . Yunus opens Grameen Bank to make microloans to poor borrowers.
1987	Global private equity firm General Atlanta starts Echoing Green, a foundation to support social entrepreneurs.
1989	Wendy Kopp founds Teach for America to recruit high-performing college graduates to teach in America's inner-city schools.
1999	Stanford University establishes the Center for Social Innovation to develop leaders to solve global social and environmental problems.
2000s	**New corporate structures evolve.**
2000	Unilever acquires Ben & Jerry's, promising to allow the company to keep its socially oriented policies.
2001	Harvard Business School adds a social enterprise track to its annual business plan competition.
2003	Oxford University's Saïd Business School establishes the Skoll Centre for Social Entrepreneurship.
2004	EBay founder Pierre Omidyar and his wife, Pam Omidyar, start Omidyar Network to fund entrepreneurs tackling social problems.
2006	Yunus and Grameen Bank are jointly awarded the Nobel Peace Prize for their microcredit innovation.
2007	Nonprofit B Lab certifies the first 19 B Corps, companies that agree to meet standards for environmental and social responsibility, transparency, workforce treatment and other criteria. . . . King Arthur Flour becomes first company to put Certified B-Corp logo on its packaging.
2008	Vermont creates a new corporate status, the Low-Profit Limited Liability Company (L3C), for social enterprises that put mission ahead of profit.

(Continued)

(Continued)

2009	President Obama establishes the Office of Social Innovation and Civic Participation to enlist nonprofits, foundations, social enterprises, businesses, faith-based and other community organizations to help solve problems facing communities.
2010–Present	**Social entrepreneurship reaches the mainstream.**
2010	The United Kingdom implements social impact bonds to help fund social enterprises. . . . Echoing Green establishes the first fellowship for social entrepreneurs working to improve the lives of black boys and men in the United States. . . . Maryland becomes the first state to enact a benefit corporation law, in which companies emphasize the importance of social and environmental missions to their business goals, along with profit.
2011	Yunus is forced to resign as managing director of Grameen Bank by the government of Bangladesh because he is 10 years beyond retirement age. . . . Yunus forms Yunus Social Business, an accelerator that's helping to finance and support social businesses in seven countries.
2012	Patagonia Inc., the outdoor outfitter, becomes California's first benefit corporation.
2014	Echoing Green launches its new Climate Fellowship for social entrepreneurs helping to mitigate or prevent climate change.
2015	Etsy, the Web platform for makers and crafters and a certified B Corp, goes public. . . . Crowdfunding giant Kickstarter, already certified as a B Corp, relaunches as a benefit corporation.

Q&A: Catherine Clark on Impact Investing

EXPECTATIONS OF CAPITAL SOURCES ARE "NOT REALLY ALIGNED WITH THE NEEDS OF EARLY-STAGE SOCIAL ENTREPRENEURS"
Catherine Clark
Founder and Director,
i3 Initiative

Impact investors are integral to the growth of social entrepreneurship, according to Catherine Clark, founder and director of the i3 Initiative on Impact Investing at Duke University's Center for the Advancement of Social Entrepreneurs (CASE) at the Fuqua School of Business.

Impact investors either put money directly into ventures that aim to alleviate major social and environmental problems or invest in impact funds that focus on such ventures. JPMorgan Chase estimated in its 2015 survey that impact investors had $60 billion in assets under management.[55]

Clark, a pioneer in impact investing and for-profit and nonprofit social entrepreneurship for 25 years, is an adjunct professor at Fuqua and coauthor of *The Impact Investors: Lessons in Leadership and Strategy for Collaborative Capitalism*. She spoke with SAGE Business Researcher reporter Robin D. Schatz about social entrepreneurship, the role of impact investors and CASE's philosophy on fostering innovation. This is an edited transcript of their conversation.

Does it matter how you define social entrepreneurship?

The field probably spent about 10 years arguing over the definition. I was at a series of research conferences over a decade where the first two sessions would always be people saying, "I think it should be this, and, no, I think it should be that." After a while, people just stopped arguing.

The definition that we use is based on a piece of writing by the founder of CASE, Greg Dees.[56] Greg is the one who basically founded the study of social entrepreneurship as an academic field. He was the first one to say this is not a hobby, this is not a variation on charity. It's a discipline, and it can be studied and written about as a research field, and it can be understood.

Dees said social enterprises are organizations that pursue social value as their primary goal. Then he

borrowed from a lot of the entrepreneurship literature: It's run by people who have a heightened sense of accountability to the impacts they're providing, that they are in an entrepreneurial sense not being limited by the amount of resources they currently have in hand.

There were a whole bunch of extremes of arguments in the field about whether a social enterprise needed to have earned income or whether a social enterprise needed to be in the nonprofit sector. Greg threw all of that away and said, "You'll know it when you see them."

And how do you know?

The two elements that I have pulled out from his six-point definition is the idea of intentionality and accountability. The accountability is that you're going beyond the norm, and that will change how you are articulating your ability over time to meet that mission, and that you're using business skills and tools to do it. It's an entrepreneurial style and attention to how you're getting your mission done. You're looking for resources and accounting for your work.

Is social impact investing critical to the growth of social entrepreneurship?

It's been really important, but there's still a large gap between the excitement of a new thing and the investable enterprise. And every book that's been written on impact investing in the last few years has emphasized this. I've been in rooms with investors on one side of the room saying, "There are no investable deals; we have all this capital, where are you?" and on the other side of the room are all these social entrepreneurs saying, "We're right here."

The problem is, the financial expectations of many of those sources of capital are not really aligned with the needs of early-stage social entrepreneurs. It takes a good five to

(Continued)

(Continued)

seven years for any social enterprise to be truly investable. What we're seeing is a bunch of people creating different kinds of funding structures. People call it patient capital, where instead of expecting a venture to grow and get big in five years, you have the capacity to wait for 10 years.

What have you learned from working with social entrepreneurs?

We've learned it isn't enough to fund a stellar social enterprise in the domain and think they're going to change that domain forever. They are not. They're catalysts; they're important catalysts and they're going to learn stuff, and they're going to communicate stuff and they're going to have a different way of looking at the problem that other people can pay attention to, but they need to work with major institutions in society for the change to actually happen.

Our theory of change as an academic institution is not to just create the catalyst but to create the helpers, whether that's someone in government who's going to change regulations around maternal health care in Kenya because of what they see that one incredible social enterprise has done, or whether it's a private company that is looking to social entrepreneurs to figure out what the innovations are that they can promulgate.

Social enterprise has become kind of this spark that is leading to a whole bunch of institutions changing the way they think about addressing social needs without many of them even using the word social enterprise anymore. . . . We are trying to put the carrot out in the marketplace to make it happen.

THE BUSINESS OF PHILANTHROPY

Can for-profit strategies work in the nonprofit world?

S.L. Mintz

EXECUTIVE SUMMARY

To support their philanthropic missions, U.S. nonprofit groups raise and spend trillions of dollars each year, and employ about 11 million people. They have access to unmatched wealth, dazzling technology and increasingly sophisticated and data-hungry donors. But challenges abound. They include an intense rivalry for dollars, whether fundraising is done face-to-face or by electronic means. In addition, nonprofits have learned that they cannot win or retain support based on the merit of their causes alone—they also must be able to show measurable, transparent results. To meet these challenges, managers increasingly emphasize the same bottom-line oriented techniques used by their for-profit counterparts. Among the questions under discussion: Can for-profit management principles and practices fit the philanthropic model? Can data measure good work? Can technology improve fundraising?

OVERVIEW

CARE, the iconic international human relief organization, got its start distributing packages of much-needed food and supplies to European survivors of World War II. Through cultural shifts, policy reversals, local political conflicts and volatile economic climates, CARE has not altered its ambitious philanthropic mission: to serve individuals and families in the poorest communities in the world.[1]

CEO Helene Gayle arrived at Atlanta-based CARE in 2006 with a mandate to multiply the impact of the sprawling global organization. "We determined that we needed to share information across countries more than we had done, be more rigorous about measuring our impact and make the best use of our voice as an advocate for policy change," Gayle told the *Harvard Business Review.*

To improve accountability, CARE not only tracks numbers such as the amount of food it delivers, but it also measures how it has improved access to clean water, sanitation, health care, agricultural expertise that targets malnutrition and skills that empower women, all in close cooperation with governments and the private sector. On Gayle's watch, the list of changes

From *SAGE Business Researcher,*
October 26, 2015

included a program to expand access to savings accounts, credit, insurance and other financial services to hundreds of millions of low-income Africans.[2]

Gayle left CARE in early 2015 to become the first CEO of the McKinsey Social Initiative. In her new role, she will advise other nonprofits under the aegis of New York–based McKinsey & Co., a corporate management consulting firm.[3] Her job switch signals a shift in the nonprofit sector, as many U.S. nonprofits assess how best to cope with a rapidly changing, crowded philanthropic landscape that increasingly requires business expertise to support do-good missions.

Tens of thousands of new public charities open in the United States each year, including those started for churches, schools and charitable aid groups.[4] (Donors to public charities can take tax deductions; the philanthropic sector also includes private foundations, which typically have just one source of funding, such as a wealthy family.[5] There are also nonprofit groups, such as fraternal societies, that are tax-exempt, even though contributions to them are not regarded as charitable and may not be deductible.[6]) Nonprofit groups today have access to unmatched wealth, dazzling social technology and increasingly sophisticated and data-hungry donors. But challenges abound. They include an intense rivalry for fundraising dollars, whether done face-to-face or by electronic means. In addition, nonprofits have learned that they cannot win or retain support based on the merit of their causes alone—they also must be able to show measurable, transparent results.

At a minimum, donors chastened by recent financial upheaval seek greater evidence that donations are making the world a better place. If a particular charity doesn't meet their expectations, alternatives are just a few clicks away on the Internet.

Philanthropic donations reach high

"The new philanthropists are challenging the whole setup," says Richard Feiner, the director of development at the Drugs for Neglected Diseases initiative, the U.S. arm of a nonprofit based in Geneva. "There is more of an expectation that the nonprofit sector will be run like a business," he says. It's not a new trend, he says, but it keeps accelerating: "There is more focus now, because so many philanthropists want to see [results] in their lifetimes."

Although many nonprofits operate on shoestring budgets—or fold for lack of funds—the nonprofit sector as a whole has impressive financial muscle.[7] In 2013, total assets surpassed $3 trillion across the 1 million U.S. public charities. Their revenue from government contracts, corporate largesse, charitable foundations and individual fundraising exceeded $1.7 trillion; they spent $1.6 trillion.[8]

Nonprofit organizations employed 11.4 million workers in 2012, almost 1 million more than in 2007.[9] That total jumped from 9.2 percent of the private-sector workforce to 10.3 percent, according to the Bureau of Labor Statistics.[10] Elite executive directors, meanwhile, take home high six-figure and even seven-figure salaries.[11]

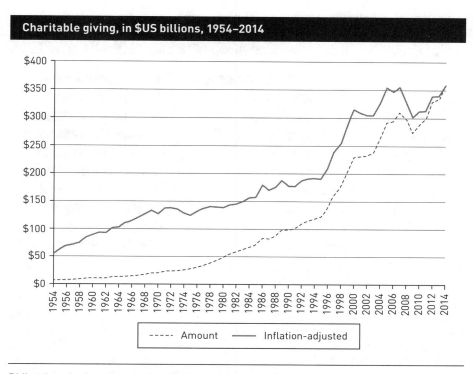

Charitable giving, in $US billions, 1954–2014

Philanthropic donations by foundations, corporations and individuals in the United States rose to a record $358 billion in 2014. Donations increased gradually from the mid-1970s through the mid-1990s before jumping 65 percent from 1995 to 2000, a period of strong stock market growth. While giving dipped during recessions in the early and late 2000s, donations have climbed the last five years.

Note: All figures are rounded.

Sources: Data from GivingUSA; original graphic from "Giving USA 2015: The Annual Report on Philanthropy for the Year 2014," GivingUSA and the Indiana University Lilly Family School of Philanthropy, June 2015; caption information from "Patterns of Charitable Giving," Congressional Budget Office, Oct. 18, 2011, http://tinyurl.com/n98ekzd

Giving varies among largest charities

Whether an organization builds widgets or advances a charitable cause, effective management can help it succeed. As Peter Drucker, a legendary management guru, wrote about nonprofits more than two decades ago, "They know that they need to learn how to use management as their tool lest they be overwhelmed by it. They know they need management so that they can concentrate on their mission."[12]

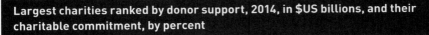

Largest charities ranked by donor support, 2014, in $US billions, and their charitable commitment, by percent

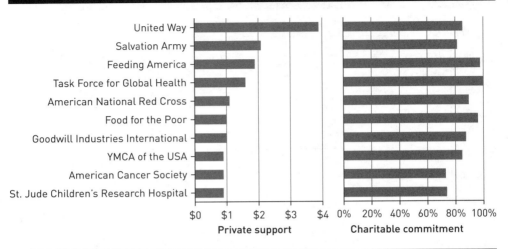

United Way received $3.9 billion in private donations in 2014, more than any other charity in the United States. Among the 10 largest charities, the Atlanta-based Task Force for Global Health was the only one to spend 100 percent of its expenditures for its charitable purpose; the American Cancer Society, by contrast, spent less than three-fourths of its expenditures on charitable services. Organizations that receive donations of goods, known as gifts in kind, tend to show a higher percentage of charitable commitment, according to Forbes, which performed the calculations.

Note: "Charitable commitment" measures how much of an organization's total expenses went directly to its charitable purpose, rather than to management, fundraising and certain overhead expenses.

Source: "The 50 Largest Charities," Forbes, December 2014, http://tinyurl.com/b4ujsqn

Like their for-profit counterparts, nonprofit professionals praise tools to gauge performance, as well as ever-more-sophisticated technology that streamlines operations and makes frequent use of social media. Strategic partnerships and mergers have ticked up in bids to cut costs and increase impact.

"By adopting a model that is increasingly common in the business world, nonprofit organizations can launch, test, and implement new programs and services more efficiently and more effectively," Peter Murray and Steve Ma of nonprofit incubator Accelerate Change wrote in summer 2015. They singled out "lean experimentation" that turns fresh ideas into a series of experiments. For example, they said, managers of the nonprofit Worldreader applied lean experimentation to support its mission of improving literacy in developing countries. They began by giving out e-readers to students in just one school in Ghana, rather than distributing them widely. That experiment showed them that the students kept breaking the e-readers; Worldreader learned that it should teach students to care for the e-readers and also that it should ask the manufacturer to make the devices sturdier.[13]

Fundraising strategies that resemble taxable investments or feature tax planning have become fixtures. Those include "impact investing," shorthand for "investment strategies that generate financial return while intentionally improving social and environmental conditions," according to Antony Bugg-Levine and Jed Emerson, nonprofit industry veterans at the Nonprofit Finance Fund and Gary Community Investment Co.[14]

Nonprofits and donors increasingly focus on return on philanthropic investment, or ROPI, a concept derived from return on investment (ROI) in the for-profit world. In taxable portfolios, total return measures investment results. For a stock or a bond, it equals the original price plus any subsequent increases in the price, plus dividends or interest, expressed as a percentage. A stock bought for $100 and sold for $110, with no other income, creates a 10 percent return.

Such thinking shapes the outlook at CARE. "What is the return on investment of the ways that we promote social change?" asks Nick Osborne, the group's vice president for program, partnerships, learning and advocacy. Donors used to settle for evidence that x dollars built x number of schools. "Today," Osborne says, "they are looking at underlying causes."

When organizations can demonstrate how they have accomplished their missions, it makes it easier for them to raise money—the most time-consuming activity for nonprofit professionals. "We have to be able to define success," says Amy Celep, CEO of Community Wealth Partners, a group that helps hundreds of charities promote leadership development, coaching, strategy and collaboration. "What does it look like and can we measure whether we get there or not? To me, it ties directly to return on philanthropic investment."

The financial crisis of 2008 and its aftermath increased the pressure to improve management. Steep stock losses depleted nonprofit coffers as donations declined for the first time in decades.[15] "Lightbulbs went on," says Beth Gazley, associate professor and teaching and learning faculty chair at Indiana University's School of Public and Environmental Affairs in Bloomington.

The scramble to attract new money and reassure existing donors propelled nonprofits toward the for-profit tool bench. Nonprofits "definitely spend more time on performance measurement," says Gazley, "not because there are more tools but because a greater range of tools has been adopted into the nonprofit sector."

Evaluation varies according to the organization. For instance, the New York–based Robin Hood Foundation, which provides charitable support to impoverished New Yorkers, has embraced a bottom-line approach and laid it out for donors.[16]

Another approach, the "pay for success" philanthropic model, attempts to appeal to socially conscious investors who are willing to risk losses in return for monetary rewards. If initiatives save money on government programs, donors and taxpayers both get a cut of the savings.[17]

"Pay for success" blends philanthropy with investment motives, "like nothing we have seen in previous generations," said Kippy Joseph, who heads the Rockefeller Foundation's social impact bond program.[18]

Legislation enacted or pending in 20 states, along with bipartisan bills in the House and Senate, would establish a $300 million federal pay-for-success incentive fund. More than 40 nonprofits and local and state governments have received White House grants to explore the feasibility of various programs. Blue-chip backers behind this form of impact investing include the Wall Street firm Goldman Sachs, the Rockefeller Foundation and the Federal Reserve.[19]

Not everyone's a fan, though. "For the most part, it's a heavily promoted idea but still half-baked," says Jon Pratt, executive director of the Minnesota Council of Nonprofits. He points to the New York City Adolescent Behavioral Learning Experience (ABLE) Project for Incarcerated Youth—also called the Rikers Island Pay for Success Social Impact Bond—which fell short of expectations. Investors received no payment after recidivism among juveniles did not decline, and the program ended in August 2015.[20]

Nonetheless, business principles and rigorous measurement increasingly shape nonprofit activity. "Everybody is doing it," says Barron "Buzz" Tenny, former general counsel at the Ford Foundation, now on the board of the New York Community Trust. To a point, Tenny applauds the trend. But he warns that rigid practices can overshadow charitable goals. At times, boards charged with oversight should step back from the numbers. He says, "Ultimately practical decisions are made on the threshold question: What is your primary purpose?"

As nonprofit executives, foundations, individual donors and other stakeholders consider how to get the most good from the charitable dollar, below are some of the issues under debate.

WEIGHING THE ISSUES

Can for-profit management principles and practices fit the philanthropic model?

Philanthropic institutions do not operate exactly like corporations, nor can they. Nonprofits can't sell shares or ramp up production to replenish coffers; their bottom lines don't boil down easily to profits and losses.

"Nonprofit financial management principles turn for-profit principles on their heads," according to The Bridgespan Group, a firm that advises nonprofits on goals and growth strategies. "In the nonprofit world, for example, increased demand for services often means an increase in costs (to provide those services) with no associated change in revenue. Such a scenario leaves an organization scrambling for funding to keep up with demand."[21]

Doug White, who directs the graduate program in fundraising in the business program at Columbia University, cautions against overreliance on for-profit approaches to solve nonprofit challenges, but adds that some management skills clearly overlap. For example, lofty aspirations without sound management imperil organizations regardless of their tax status. "Technical and managerial competencies help organizations exist as efficiently and productively as possible," White says.

In addition, experts in nonprofits say those organizations increasingly are becoming like corporations in seeking ways to increase accountability, though they say much still remains to be done.

Great ideas alone won't sustain philanthropic initiatives, warns Broc Rosser, executive director of the Florida Nonprofit Alliance, a statewide coalition. "A lot of people want to start a nonprofit but don't understand it's got to be run like a business in order to survive," Rosser says. Florida has more than 76,000 nonprofits, Rosser says, and at thousands of them, the annual budgets exceed $100,000—levels that can't be treated casually.

Companies find and keep investors by demonstrating a return on investment. Food banks, medical clinics, art museums, education programs and regional theaters find and keep donors by demonstrating satisfactory returns on philanthropic investment. They all contend with swings in economic cycles, husbanding resources at the top and parceling them out at the bottom. In both sectors, managers allocate assets, monitor performance and innovate to extend limited resources.

Religious groups are top charity recipients

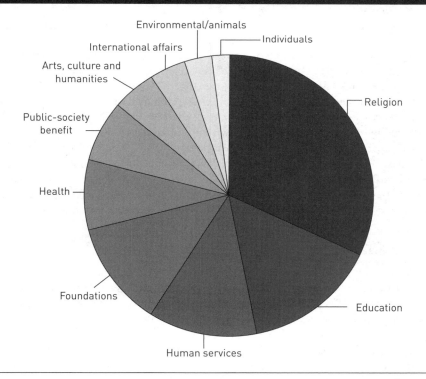

Percentage of charitable donations received, by type of organization, 2014

Environmental/animals

International affairs

Arts, culture and humanities

Public-society benefit

Health

Foundations

Human services

Individuals

Religion

Education

Religious organizations collected nearly one-third of all philanthropic donations in 2014. Education charities received the second-largest share (15 percent), followed by foundations and human services charities (12 percent). The remainder went to individuals and groups devoted to other causes, including health, the arts and humanities, international affairs and environmental concerns.

Source: Data from "Giving USA 2015: The Annual Report on Philanthropy for the Year 2014," GivingUSA and the Indiana University Lilly Family School of Philanthropy, June 2015

"There is opportunity cost if you are focusing on doing things that are not working," says Brian Quinn, assistant vice president for research-evaluation-learning at the Robert Wood Johnson Foundation in Princeton, N.J. "Money pumped into that intervention could have been used on interventions that work. Our goal at the end of the day is to help people or organizations make sure that support is going to interventions with the highest ROI."

Historically, while for-profit companies have shed underperforming divisions or embraced growth through sales, mergers, acquisitions and consolidation, nonprofits have resisted mergers because they are loath to surrender their independence. "Say the 'm' word and everybody runs in different directions," says Debra Jacobs, president of the Patterson Foundation in Sarasota, Fla., which underwrites learning, sharing and partnership initiatives in the nonprofit sector, including support for nonprofit mergers. Apart from hospital combinations in the tumultuous health care arena, nonprofits seldom merge, while thousands launch each year.

Yet combinations are on the rise, says Bob Harrington, a partner in La Piana Consulting in Emeryville, Calif. "Mergers get the headlines because they are the most dramatic," says Harrington, who advises nonprofits on strategic planning. He says he instead sees many more partnerships motivated by budgetary situations or expansion plans.

Nonprofit mergers do occur, though. In June 2015, the Lung Cancer Research Foundation (LCRF) and Uniting Against Lung Cancer (UALC) announced plans to merge. Between them, the two foundations have made grants exceeding $17 million, according to *The NonProfit Times*.[22] Both groups said they saw a sturdier business model by combining.

"This merger allows us to combine our expertise, resources and network of committed individuals to increase our impact and help close the funding gap for lung cancer research," Pippa Gerard, the LCRF board chair, said in a statement.[23] Just as with for-profit mergers, there may be other consequences, too. The new organization is housed in LCRF's Manhattan headquarters; UALC employees were reassigned and their headquarters was shuttered.

Can data measure good work?

No one needs to sell the chairman of the largest private foundation in the United States on the merits of performance data. Bill Gates, who with his wife started the Bill and Melinda Gates Foundation, gets it. While the couple has taken Melinda's lead in choosing to work to make birth control more available in developing regions, "they developed new metrics to satisfy Bill," according to *New York Times* columnist Nicholas Kristof.[24]

During a TED Talk last year, Bill Gates shared a slide showing "incredible progress" in fighting diseases that harm children. One comment hinted at his embrace of performance metrics. "My graph has numbers on it," said Gates, a founder of Microsoft. "I really like numbers."[25]

Numbers are big elsewhere, too. "There isn't a business now that doesn't have data specialists and measuring everything, capturing data and trying to discern all of it," says Eric Nee, managing editor of the *Stanford Social Innovation Review* (*SSIR*). "Why can't we do it in the social sector?"

SSIR has devoted many pages to weighing the value of data about nonprofit impact. "Ten years ago, critics dismissed impact measurement as too difficult, misleading, or simply not important," wrote Tris Lumley, director of development at New Philanthropy Capital, a London-based charity consulting group. "Today, 75 percent of charities measure some or all of their work, and nearly three-quarters have invested more in measuring results over the last five years."[26]

The move to measure nonprofit success arguably can be traced to a call to action in a 1999 *Harvard Business Review* article "Philanthropy's New Agenda: Creating Value." Authors Michael E. Porter and Mark R. Kramer, founders of the Center for Effective Philanthropy, proposed more rigorous management of charitable foundations.[27]

"Not enough foundations think strategically about how they can create the most value for society with the resources they have at their disposal. Little effort is devoted to measuring results," they wrote. "If foundations are to survive and thrive in the new century, those efforts and practices must change."

Other experts concur. "The rigour of corporate performance measurement should also be the standard in philanthropy," Jeri Eckhart-Queenan and Matthew Forti wrote in *Business Strategy Review*.[28] Eckhart-Queenan leads the Global Development Practice at The Bridgespan Group. Forti is managing director of One Acre Fund USA, which develops business solutions for farmers with tiny tracts of farmland. The One Acre website features multiple performance measures, including calculations by country of percentage gains in farm income stemming from its efforts.[29]

"A well-run performance measurement system can tangibly improve results for the people an organization is trying to help or the cause it supports," they said, urging corporate philanthropies to conduct timely, proactive measurement. "It can help leaders make better decisions about allocating scarce resources. It can support rapid innovation. It can also lower the cost of learning."

Educators have responded to the growing emphasis on performance measurement for nonprofits. In 2012, Indiana University–Purdue University opened the Lilly Family School of Philanthropy, the nation's first formal academic program concentrated solely on running nonprofits. Students can earn bachelor's degrees, master's degrees and doctorates in Philanthropic Studies.[30] More than 250 U.S. colleges and universities now offer nonprofit management programs, according to a census by Seton Hall University in South Orange, N.J.[31] Many also offer noncredit programs. Standard curricula span subjects from nonprofit leadership and financial management skills to digital fundraising via social media.

The Columbia University graduate program in fundraising added "The Wired Nonprofit: Social Media Strategy and Practice" to the curriculum in spring 2015. The course probes "new pressures on nonprofit organizations to be more responsive, accountable and transparent— and guided by newly available data and impact metrics to better target the expenditure of donor dollars."[32]

Experts who advocate cutting-edge accountability nevertheless warn nonprofits to use data with caution. "Measurement is essential for helping grant makers understand where their funding has the most impact," according to consulting firm McKinsey. "But using the right form of measurement is critical. Indeed, some types of measurement can have undesired effects: stifling innovation or missing what is truly meaningful for social impact because it cannot be measured easily."[33] Instead, McKinsey advises, prudent nonprofits listen to constituents, develop strategy and assessments in tandem, apply rigor tailored to strategic objectives, evaluate performance but don't impose an excessive burden on grantees or managers, and create "a learning culture" that invites honest review and feedback.

The Robin Hood Foundation, founded by wealthy hedge fund manager Paul Tudor Jones to raise money from the rich to ease burdens in New York City's poorest neighborhoods, has been especially active in using data.[34] In 2014, grants supported early-childhood education, job training, microlending, housing, emergency food and health programs.

"Metrics matter," the foundation declared in a 2009 document, "Measuring Success: How Robin Hood Estimates the Impact of Grants."[35] Explaining why, chief program officer Michael Weinstein wrote, "Every time that Robin Hood errs in allocating grant money—spending too much on one group and therefore, too little on another—it leaves behind more suffering among New York's poor than necessary."

In a detailed example, Robin Hood spelled out how it used benefit-to-cost calculations to estimate the bottom-line return on the grant it made to one program, Helpful Housing, which provided 672 studio or one-bedroom apartments to 887 homeless individuals or couples over 12 months.[36] Starting with an average fair-market price for similar units in New York City and the expectation that people served would otherwise remain homeless, the number of units times the fair-market value amounted to a $7.8 million benefit.

Additionally, Helpful Housing furnished pricier two-bedroom apartments to 75 low-income families who required fewer supportive services. Residents were expected to contribute 30 percent of their annual income toward rent. Assuming that one in 10 of these families would have found housing anyway, Robin Hood calculated an all-in benefit worth $760,000.

Step two used "quality adjusted life years," or QALY, to estimate the value of other benefits attributable to the housing program. Robin Hood judged that each QALY is worth $100,000. Medical referrals for 672 residents, valued at 0.07 QUALY per visit, adjusted by the number of residents who would have sought medical care without assistance, worked out to a value of $2.3 million per year for referrals. Similar calculations assigned dollar values to mental health care, employment training, case management and more.

Step three calculated lifetime impact subject to inflation that reduces the value of every dollar in the future, a process called discounting. Further steps calculated the value of all of the benefits arising from the housing program and assigned a share of the benefits to Robin Hood in the same proportion as the original donation. In the final analysis, benefits tripled the value of the donation—equivalent to a 300 percent return on investment.

Can technology improve fundraising?

Appeals via snail mail still snare the most donations, but the fundraising landscape nowadays looks different.[37] "Technology has redefined the art of the ask," says Marcia Stepanek, an instructor in the graduate program in fundraising at Columbia University.

The value of technology for fundraising became evident in early 2010, when an American Red Cross campaign using text messaging raised $43 million, $10 per text, after an earthquake devastated Haiti.[38]

"Philanthropy used to be a game for the 1 percent," Stepanek says. "Social media made it a game for the 99 percent."

Look no further than 2014's ice bucket challenge for clear evidence that technology has transformed fundraising. "Millions of people including celebrities, politicians and tech moguls [dumped] . . . buckets of ice water on their heads in an effort to raise money for amyotrophic lateral sclerosis (Lou Gehrig's disease)," according to *The Wall Street Journal*. Videos of dunkings went viral, spurring record donations to the ALS Association. The group raised $115 million in just over 45 days, versus $5 million in the same period a year earlier.[39]

Most nonprofits welcome digital fundraising assistance, if only to ease a major time drain. "The reality is when you cross the bridge to go to a nonprofit, fundraising has to be your favorite thing to do," especially if the group doesn't have an endowment, says Jacobs at the Patterson Foundation. "It doesn't matter how good a manager you are. You will spend at least half of your time raising money."

Shortcuts that cater to small donors free up time for big donors who still expect to be courted the old-fashioned way, in person. "From the very first time I meet someone," seasoned fundraiser Jennifer McCrea told the *Philanthropy News Digest*, "one of my goals is to sit down and say, 'Can I connect human being to human being?'"[40]

Taylor Hill/FilmMagic/Getty Images

Model Heidi Klum douses Tim Gunn, host of reality TV show *Project Runway*, with ice in September 2014 as part of the ice bucket challenge, a fundraising effort for the ALS Association.

Enlisting volunteers and staying connected via social media can be a powerful fundraising tool. "Volunteers give more," according to a study of wealthy givers by the Lilly Family School of Philanthropy and U.S. Trust. "Volunteerism has a strong connection to giving levels, and increasingly so," according to the sponsors. "Wealthy donors who volunteered in 2013 gave 73 percent more on average than those who did not volunteer ($76,572 compared to $44,137)." Donations from wealthy volunteers increased 23 percent from 2009 to 2013.[41]

At the loftiest levels of fundraising, where donor relationships hinge on human interactions, technology can help demonstrate accountability. "Super high net worth individuals with the capacity to have very significant impact are very interested in making wise investments and want to see the ways to measure impact," says Aggie Sweeney, vice chair of the Giving USA Foundation.

Online giving remains a slim slice of all donations but is growing rapidly. Growth exceeded 13 percent in 2013, nearly triple the inflation-adjusted growth rate for overall charitable giving, although that growth was from a small base. Online donations surpassed 6 percent of all charitable gifts, with small organizations seeing the biggest jump.[42]

In addition to speed, online fundraising extends reach in ways unimaginable before the Internet. Crowdsourcing mobilizes thousands or even millions of people around specific issues in real time. Team Rubicon, a California-based disaster relief group, arose in response to the 2010 earthquake in Haiti, when former Marines assembled supplies and delivered them where they were most needed.[43]

Cutting-edge fundraising technology is pricey. The market suits charities that can earmark tens of thousands of dollars a year in development and hosting costs. However, online vendors sell customizable off-the-shelf setups that can assist with fundraising and donor management in exchange for transaction fees. Razoo, Australian slang for a tiny bit of money, charges a 4.9 percent platform fee, plus a 2 percent payment fee and 30 cents per donation, to process donations worldwide.[44] FirstGiving, based in Boston, takes a 5 percent fee for product support plus a 2.5 percent credit card fee.[45] Units of Google Wallet and PayPal also support fundraising initiatives for similar fees.[46]

There's a catch to using technology: It can cut established nonprofits out of the process, Stepanek warns, a change known as disintermediation. It's similar to the way travel websites cut established travel agencies out of the business. "Now it's charities," Stepanek says. "People are saying we don't need you to take our money and decide how it gets done. We can go direct."

Groups born digital haven't just automated fundraising; they have changed the ground rules. Charity: Water, a New York–based group that focuses on ensuring safe water supplies in developing nations, invites individuals to donate cash or to launch their own fundraising campaigns—all with a smartphone. Charity: Water, founded in 2006, promises to send 100 percent of proceeds raised directly into the field and then track its use. "We'll report back to you with info about the actual people your money helps," the website promises.[47]

DonorsChoose.org, begun in 2000, has gained kudos from the likes of Stephen Colbert and Oprah Winfrey, who calls it "a revolutionary charity."[48] The mobile-friendly website posts requests from public-school teachers for funding for their classroom projects. Donors bankroll field trips or underwrite math projects; some large donors including foundations have backed matching-gift campaigns. The DonorsChoose.org website lets would-be donors see what happens with their money and to interact with the teachers who get the cash.

"My students need electric fans to battle hot weather," said art teacher Gil Ramirez at Waipahu Elementary School in Waipahu, Hawaii. Cost: $180. "My students need an easel, 23 subscriptions to *Scholastic News*, 15 subscriptions to *Time For Kids*," said Amanda Stilwell at Parkway Elementary in Fort Worth, Texas. Total cost: $870. Both appeals were designated "highest poverty," a measure of the percentage of students at a school who qualify for free and reduced-price lunch, which is considered a measure of economic need.

Fundraising technology appeals especially to a generation of Millennials who want more than the satisfaction of writing checks to good causes. "Millennial philanthropists are more data-driven than philanthropists in the past," says Angie Hyman-Robinson, associate director at the George H. Heyman Jr., Center for Philanthropy and Fundraising at New York University. "They want to make more of an impact, track that impact. If you want them to open their wallets, show it with data."

BACKGROUND

Roots of philanthropy

The United States has long been a generous nation. Voluntarism was so strong in a 19th-century evangelical America that French traveler Alexis de Tocqueville commented approvingly: "I have often admired the extreme skill with which the inhabitants of the

United States succeed in proposing a common object for the exertions of a great many men and in inducing them voluntarily to pursue it."[49]

After the Civil War, as the economy greatly expanded, the wealthy new captains of industry became captains of charity. Merchant banker George Peabody, dubbed "the father of modern philanthropy," reportedly gave away half of his fortune through a foundation. His and other names from the late 19th and early 20th century populate the Philanthropy Hall of Fame, maintained by the Philanthropy Roundtable: Andrew Carnegie, Leland Stanford, George Eastman, John D. Rockefeller and Henry Ford, among them.[50]

The government, however, was not always in the mood to be charitable. President Grover Cleveland in 1887 vetoed the distribution of seeds in drought-stricken Texas counties because he thought it was unconstitutional for the federal government to provide aid to individuals. Said Cleveland, "The lesson should be constantly enforced that, though the people support the Government, the Government should not support the people."[51]

Meanwhile, the wealthiest Americans financed libraries, universities, hospitals and primary schools across the United States. For instance, Sears Roebuck magnate Julius Rosenwald built schools across the South for African-American children who were ill served by their states.[52]

Sometimes, charitable initiatives raised doubts about the motives behind generosity. When Andrew Carnegie offered to build a public library in Homestead, Pa., union workers smelled an attempt to gloss over a four-month lockout at a Carnegie steel mill in 1892. Clashes killed several striking workers. The Pennsylvania National Guard arrived to protect strikebreakers. "For years after this, organized labor fiercely resisted the use of Carnegie's 'tainted money'—even for public benefit," wrote Tim Kelley in a history for the San Francisco Carnegie Branch Libraries.[53]

President Theodore Roosevelt also grew suspicious of the motives of some of the "representatives of predatory wealth." In 1908, he warned his attorney general they were "by gifts to colleges and universities . . . occasionally able to subsidize in their own interest some head of an educational body."[54]

Health and taxes

At the turn of the 20th century, the growth in passenger rail, the advent of telephones and a robust U.S. postal service fostered a larger sense of national community than ever before. New charitable initiatives tapped into this, especially initiatives that targeted public health.

Supporting sanatoriums around the United States strained the resources of the National Association for the Study and Prevention of Tuberculosis. Social activist Emily Bissell launched the U.S. version of Christmas Seals in 1907 in an attempt to keep the Brandywine Sanatorium near Wilmington, Del., open. By the end of the holiday season, she had raised $3,000. The next year, Christmas Seals raised $135,000.[55] Mass fundraising in the United States was born.

In 1913, the permanent imposition of an income tax changed philanthropy. Supporters of philanthropy mobilized, fearing that taxes would divert money that might have gone to charity. Some lawmakers pressed unsuccessfully to attach a tax deduction to the original legislation.

Congress changed course during World War I. The War Revenue Act of 1917 created deductions for "contributions or gifts made within the year to corporations or associations organized and operated exclusively for religious, charitable, scientific, or educational purposes, or to societies for the prevention of cruelty to children or animals." It set a limit at 15 percent of a taxpayer's net income.[56]

United Way historian Eleanor Brilliant has noted that before the Great War, fundraisers mainly tapped large donors. Afterward, fundraisers targeted middle- and lower-income Americans.[57] For instance, charitable "War Chests" became "Community Chests" and supported a wide range of humanitarian services funded by small donations.

The onset of the Great Depression in 1929 moved President Herbert Hoover to enlist private charity to ease misfortune. The Franklin D. Roosevelt administration that followed Hoover mobilized government instead. Through New Deal programs, government furnished a safety net, providing jobs, protecting savings and guaranteeing income in retirement through Social Security.

"The idea that social welfare assistance was a government responsibility rather than a private charitable function gained wider acceptance," according to the University of Michigan School of Social Work.[58]

Business titans still continued to give with dual aims. On Jan. 15, 1936, Edsel Ford, son of auto industry pioneer Henry Ford, started the Ford Foundation with $25,000 to support scientific, educational and charitable purposes.[59] The foundation's tax treatment also enabled the Ford family to skirt inheritance taxes and retain control of Ford Motor Co.

Conflict and relief

As World War II loomed, charity advanced national policy, according to historian Olivier Zunz. "President Roosevelt understood the potential benefit of this philanthropy for Americans' image in the world," Zunz wrote. "He saw the National War Fund [which coordinated local fund drives throughout the country] as evidence that 'Our men and our allies know they have made no covenant with our government alone. They know that they have the backing of all the resources and spirit of the American people themselves. In that conviction alone lies the winning morale which no slave of a dictator can ever know.'"[60]

Wartime charities aided refugees and victims of conflict. Such work earned the pacifist Quakers the 1947 Nobel Peace Prize. "The problem is not merely one of providing food and clothing," Nobel Committee Chairman Gunnar Jahn said in a presentation speech that cited three centuries of good works by members of the religion. "It is one of bringing people back to life and work, of restoring their self-respect and their faith and confidence in the future."[61]

In 1949, the Torch Drive campaign by the Detroit United Way mounted a torch atop a wooden structure in the heart of burgeoning postwar Motor City, launching the first orchestrated fund drive by a major city. Henry Ford II and labor organizer Walter Reuther made peace to promote its success.[62]

Community chests around the country eventually combined under the banner of the United Way, the largest U.S. public charity today.[63]

The anti-Communist fervor of the 1950s extended to charities. Rep. Eugene Cox, D-Ga., convened an investigation in 1952 to target foundations and organizations too liberal for his liking. Cox died before his inquisition ended. Rep. Brazilla Carroll Reese, R-Tenn., took his place in 1953. His aim was unmistakable, wrote Steven Alan Samson, a professor of government at Liberty University: "Once again, the purpose of the investigation was to uncover Communist subversion in relation to tax-exempt foundations."[64]

Congressional posturing led nowhere. Instead, wrote Zunz, "America now entered the golden age of mass fundraising." The 1950s brought "a dizzying array of overlapping charitable campaigns, involving both fundraising and volunteer work."[65]

The great society

In his 1965 State of the Union address, President Lyndon B. Johnson set forth goals that aligned government more tightly than ever with the nonprofit sector. "We do not intend to live in the midst of abundance, isolated from neighbors and nature, confined by blighted cities and bleak suburbs, stunted by a poverty of learning and an emptiness of leisure," Johnson said. "The Great Society asks not how much, but how good; not only how to create wealth but how to use it; not only how fast we are going, but where we are headed."[66]

Anti-poverty and other social programs multiplied as state and federal taxpayer funds flowed. "Right through 1968, a long series of major legislative changes followed in civil rights, health, education, housing and development, transit, Social Security, and cash and near-cash assistance programs like food stamps," according to Austin Nichols of the Urban Institute, a liberal-leaning Washington think tank.[67]

Public and private collaboration expanded in the 1970s. "Government found a partner in the nonprofit sector to deal with a lot of social issues," says Thomas McLaughlin, an adviser to nonprofits and an adjunct member of the Heller School for Social Policy and Management faculty at Brandeis University. "The government was able to get a good deal because a dollar in the nonprofit sector went a whole lot farther than in the government sector."

As foundations based on capitalist fortunes pursued new agendas, tempers sometimes flared. When he resigned from his post as Ford Foundation chairman in 1977, Henry Ford II spelled out a growing schism. "The foundation is a creature of capitalism, a statement that, I'm sure, would be shocking to many professional staff people in the field of philanthropy. It is hard to discern recognition of this fact in anything the foundation does," he wrote.[68]

Dubious motives

Philanthropic groups are not immune to controversy and criminality. Administrative bloat and arrogance reached epic proportions at some nonprofits in the 1990s. William Aramony ended his 22-year tenure as United Way president in shame when he was convicted of stealing more than $1 million from the organization.[69]

His transgressions paled beside those of John G. Bennett Jr. As president of the Foundation for New Era Philanthropy, Bennett raised more than $354 million from 1,400 donors and then generated $135 million in fraudulent losses to cover his tracks, according to the FBI.[70] The audacious scheme unraveled in 1995 and cost Bennett 12 years in prison.

In the wake of these scandals, nonprofits went through a period of self-examination, according to Robert O. Bothwell, an industry consultant who surveyed charity executives and regulators. "Many charitable leaders in the U.S. became concerned that the public, especially donors, would lose their confidence in the good of charitable organizations," he wrote. In response, he said, they moved to improve board oversight and to adopt codes of conduct. Both nonprofits and regulators emphasized increased transparency, in part by making all nonprofit tax filings public on IRS Form 990.[71]

Politics is at the base of one recent controversy. The Supreme Court's 2010 Citizens United decision allowed most people or entities to give unlimited amounts to advance political agendas. Afterward, the Internal Revenue Service stepped up efforts to review tax-exempt organizations to determine whether these groups were using funds for political ads, still a prohibited activity. Although IRS defenders pointed out that the agency had scrutinized organizations on the left and right, conservatives charged that the agency targeted their organizations, searching specifically for terms related to tea party groups. Lois Lerner, the IRS official who became the focus of conservative wrath, publicly apologized, then retired from the agency. The House voted in 2014 to hold Lerner in contempt of Congress in connection with her refusal to testify about the matter, and the House Oversight and Government Reform Committee continued its investigation into 2015.[72]

Meanwhile, criminal acts have also fueled public skepticism, as with this year's international arrests and guilty pleas over corruption at FIFA, the international soccer federation.[73] Amid speculation about a wider role for outside regulators, internal regulators promise change. "Its own ethics committee plans to request more freedom to reveal details of ongoing proceedings against FIFA officials," *The Wall Street Journal* reported in July 2015.[74]

CURRENT SITUATION

New vitality

Financial success elsewhere is paying off for charities. When American Pharoah crossed the finish line at the June 2015 Belmont Stakes and rode off with the first Triple Crown in horse racing since Affirmed in 1978, philanthropic initiatives won, too. Trainer Bob Baffert and his wife, Jill, announced their intention to give $50,000 to each of three horse racing-related charities that support disabled jockeys and retired racehorses. Victor Espinoza, the winning jockey, reportedly plans to donate his Belmont winnings to City of Hope, a cancer research facility and hospital in Southern California.[75]

Off the racetrack, a strengthening economy is bolstering the health of charities. Foundation endowments that looked shaky a few years ago are, for the most part, in excellent health because their investments have stabilized. Higher corporate profits have boosted corporate donations. For individuals, rising home prices in tandem with the bull stock market and falling unemployment have restored the so-called "wealth effect" that vanished in the recent recession. That gives rank-and-file donors confidence to contribute money to causes.

All told, charitable gifts from all four major sources—foundations, corporations, individuals and bequests—hit highs in 2014. The $358 billion peak marked the fifth successive annual increase and the first to surpass the prerecession top in 2007.[76]

Researchers at the Lilly Family School of Philanthropy at Indiana University, in collaboration with the international fundraising consultancy Marts & Lundy, expect continued growth—subject to economic health, which always affects giving. They predict that total giving by all sources will grow by nearly 5 percent in 2015 and 2016. In particular, the report said, giving by foundations and corporations is expected to be "quite strong." Giving by individuals and households will not increase as dramatically but is still expected to rise by more than 4 percent in each of those years. [77]

Some of the very richest Americans are contributing. Microsoft co-founder Gates actively heads the largest private foundation in the United States. The Bill and Melinda Gates Foundation, with $41 billion in assets at the end of 2013, earmarks billions of dollars each year to end abject poverty and hunger; harness science and medical technology to save lives; improve high school and postsecondary education in the United States; forge strategic relationships and promote policies that will advance philanthropic objectives.[78] In September, the Gateses joined with Facebook co-founder and Chairman Mark Zuckerberg, U2 singer Bono and other celebrities in calling for everyone in the world to have Internet access by 2020 as an important step toward eradicating poverty.[79]

Gates foundation leads in charity donations

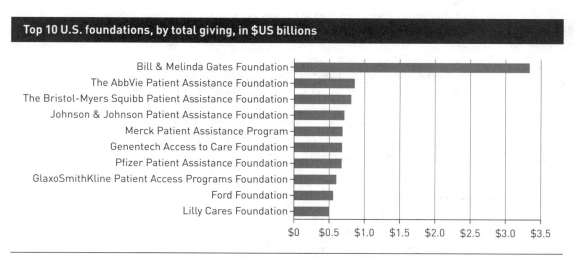

Top 10 U.S. foundations, by total giving, in $US billions

The Bill and Melinda Gates Foundation gave $3.3 billion to charities in 2013, more than four times as much as the second- and third-highest-giving foundations in 2013 or 2014. Among the top foundations by donations, eight were philanthropic arms of pharmaceutical companies.

Notes: Based on latest data reported by foundations, ranging from 2012 to 2014. Total-giving figures include grants, scholarships, employee matching gifts and giving reported as "grants and contributions paid during the year." Figures exclude all qualifying distributions under tax law, including loans, program-related investments and administrative expenses.

Source: "Top Funders," Foundation Center, updated Sept. 19, 2015, http://tinyurl.com/3nskw7h

Warren Buffett, the nation's second-richest man after Gates, set a very public standard with a pledge to bequeath the bulk of his wealth to charity. In July, he announced a gift of stock worth $2.8 billion to five foundations, including the Gates Foundation.[80] Buffett's act boosted "The Giving Pledge," a commitment by the world's wealthiest individuals and families to dedicate the majority of their wealth to philanthropy.[81] Dozens of billionaires have signed the pledge, a moral commitment that is not legally binding.

On Capitol Hill, nonprofits advocate permanently extending a few key tax incentives— for food donations, conservation easements and retirement account charitable rollovers—that have expired. Even though it has passed the House of Representatives twice in recent years, legislation aimed at preserving those incentives is in "an active state of limbo," pending Senate action, says David L. Thompson, vice president for public policy at the National Council of Nonprofits. In February 2015, Republicans and a few dozen Democrats in the House passed the America Gives More Act (H.R. 644), but hope for it becoming law this year soon faded, Thompson says.

Backers are determined to give "America Gives More" another try. If it gets a third nod in the House, says Thompson, indications of bipartisan support from influential senators "point in the right direction."

Nonprofits say another pending government change could put them in a bind. The U.S. Department of Labor has proposed rules that would make more low-paid white-collar workers eligible for overtime pay. As a result, nonprofits face higher costs, but unlike for-profit businesses, they can't raise prices to offset them.

The wider debate over the change has pitted employers against labor unions. "Both sides have tried to claim the allegiance of the non-profit sector, which is torn between a belief that the rule might help low-income people and the recognition that complying with it could strain their own budgets," *The Washington Post* reported.[82]

"We can't be dragged into it," Thompson told *The Post*. "The business community would love for us to be a shield. The labor community would love for us to be a champion."

But reporter and former nonprofit executive Rick Cohen observed that any nonprofits that fall below the $500,000 annual revenue threshold won't feel the pinch; the rest can seek exemptions. "The proposed regulations shouldn't make nonprofits think that the sky is falling," he wrote in *Nonprofit Quarterly*.[83]

The right stuff

With coffers healthy for now, leaders in the nonprofit sector are reexamining their priorities. Finding successors with suitable skills is one of their most pressing concerns.

A "CEO pinch" lurks for nonprofits, warns McLaughlin of Brandeis University. Visionary Baby Boomers and Gen X-ers who started or nurtured charities are handing over the reins in large numbers, creating more gaps in leadership than existing talent can fill. McLaughlin predicts that a shortage of CEO candidates will compel many nonprofits to merge in coming years.

Some leaders are shifting how they run their organizations. "There is a lot of talk in our sector about collective and shared leadership," says Celep of Community Wealth Partners, which aids nonprofits with leadership development. "You have to engage employees and change the way they work," she says. Engagement can occur through face-to-face conversation or, more commonly, across technology platforms and social media.

Millennials—donors and staff—bristle at rigid command-and-control environments, Celep says. "It's best to allow them to be part of decisions," she advises. Listening to ideas over coffee or across social media sends the right message, provided the best ideas make it into production. "At the end of the day it's my decision" as a top executive, Celep says, "but stakeholders want to be authentically engaged."

Nonprofits increasingly must accommodate tech-savvy donors who want to see measurable outcomes. "We are witnessing the 'democratization of philanthropy,'" says Feiner at the Drugs for Neglected Diseases initiative.

Wealthy young donors who made their fortunes in technology bring a "hacker" approach to giving, according to Sean Parker, the founding president of Facebook and chairman of the $600 million Parker Foundation. He used the term hacker in the good-guy sense, meaning successful entrepreneurs who make disruption a habit. They find conventional philanthropy "a strange and alien world made up of largely antiquated institutions," he said, whose principal mission appears to be self-preservation. "Instead, [donors] want to know that they are having an impact that can be measured and felt. . . . This new generation of philanthropists wants to believe there is a clever 'hack' for every problem, and they have launched a number of radical experiments."[84]

Sean Parker, founding president of Facebook and co-founder of Napster.

For instance, as an alternative to many failed conventional attempts to ease poverty in Nairobi slums, GiveDirectly lets donors send cash directly to cellphones of residents in need. Supporters include Facebook co-founder Dustin Moskovitz.[85] The group's website, which brags of "rigorous evidence," is dominated by data about results, rather than heartrending images of poor children.[86]

"A lot of changes in the nonprofit sector are direct results of people and money coming from tech and finance," says Nee at *Stanford Social Innovation Review*. "For better or worse, the focus on metrics and social entrepreneurs is directly attributable to that phenomenon."

Unlike horse racing, philanthropy seldom has a finish line. Each project informs the next, ideally improving outcomes and attracting new support, says Osborne at CARE. His group increasingly focuses on knowledge management and the power that knowledge can generate, Osborne says.

Meals served and lives improved or saved are paramount, of course. But it's not the whole story on nonprofit leadership. The key to sustainable success, Osborne says, lies in "understanding the value of the knowledge we gain from work that we do, and how we apply that knowledge."

LOOKING AHEAD

Future of fundraising

Against a hopeful backdrop for nonprofit fundraising, close observers see "business-minded tactics slowly gain[ing] ground," according to Rich Dietz, who handles digital fundraising at Abila in Austin, Texas.

Nonprofits increasingly are investigating customer relationship management tools that businesses use to convert prospects, including Web visitors, into sales, says Dietz, whose company stands to gain if that trend does take hold. Companies have poured gigantic sums into so-called CRM, and nonprofits can ride their coattails to build donor lists. In the process, engaging Millennials will gain in importance as income, assets and the reins of industry pass to a new generation.

Amid innumerable distractions, fundraising will depend on powerful storytelling to convey unique missions and robust returns. Always important, says Dietz, skilled storytelling is becoming an essential survival tool online and via social media. Consumers demonstrate a robust appetite for well-told stories. The WestJet Christmas Miracle, an advertisement in which the Canadian airline granted passengers' wishes in midflight, has drawn more than 40 million views on YouTube since its debut.[87]

Philanthrocapitalism, a term coined by authors Matthew Bishop and Michael Green in their book by that title, could produce a new golden age of philanthropy. Its avatars, notably Gates, Buffett and their billionaire peers, are on a mission to rescue the world from its ills. "Whether you call it 'venture philanthropy,' 'for-profit philanthropy' or 'philanthrocapitalism,' the motif is the same: in order to produce lasting change, philanthropic bodies need to be run less like charities and more like businesses," sociologist Linsey McGoey wrote in a review of the book.[88]

Fundraising consultant Gail Perry foresees the sector regaining trust from donors whose loss of faith in financial institutions after 2008 extended to nonprofits.[89] But in the words of former President Ronald Reagan, the message will be "trust but verify." Donors mulling support, says Perry, will want information on specific results, including the links between investment and impact.

Perry's list of 10 major fundraising trends features major donors and mega donors expressing their need to do good; financial performance tied directly to impact; the rise of passionate Baby Boomers who currently make up a third of all donors; the lure of big ideas and big data; and due recognition for women, who give 64 percent of all charitable gifts.[90] Perry also foresees a bigger role for donor-advised funds, which have caught on as tax-planning tools. Individuals set aside sums for charitable purposes to be selected later, but tax deductions are up front. Many billions of dollars now reside in donor-advised funds, where critics see idle wealth that largely rewards the banks and investment firms that collect management fees.

Big data, meaning vast troves of information captured electronically, can empower companies to identify prospective customers and tailor offers to them. Nonprofits are catching up. "Big data can watch thousands of donors, and based on their activities, create customized experiences for them," Perry wrote.

A developing trend looks promising to some observers but alarms others. Increasingly, for-profit companies support philanthropic initiatives not with donations, but by selling trendy products to consumers and using some of the proceeds for charity. Writing in *The Atlantic*, Amy Schiller tackled the subject in an article titled, "Is For-Profit the Future of Non-Profit? The troubling allure of turning philanthropy into consumer activity." To advocates, providing a product beats asking for donations if in both cases proceeds go to fight AIDS or breast cancer, she wrote.[91]

Critics foresee an insidious turn, she reported. "Democracy is reduced to a choice between competing charity brands, civil society is reduced to a subset of the market, stripped of its social and political content and significance. . . . Welcome to the path of least resistance, perfectly suited to our consumer society," said Michael Edwards, a former Ford Foundation executive who is now a distinguished senior fellow at Demos, a liberal think tank.[92]

The elephant in the room is age. As Baby Boomers and subsequent generations die, what's projected to be the largest transfer of wealth in history could change the philanthropic climate. An estimated $58 trillion will descend to heirs by 2061, according to a report from the Center on Wealth and Philanthropy at Boston College. If a slice of that goes to charity, "a golden age of philanthropy still beckons," as the report was titled. [93]

Chronology

1800s	**Philanthropy takes root in America.**
1835	In *Democracy in America*, Alexis de Tocqueville highlights the philanthropic spirit of Americans as one of the country's strengths.
1887	A Denver woman, a priest, two ministers and a rabbi plan the first united campaign for 10 health and welfare agencies, the birth of the United Way.
1889	Business tycoon Andrew Carnegie publishes an essay, "The Gospel of Wealth," arguing that the rich have an obligation to distribute their wealth in their lifetimes for the betterment of society.
1900s–1950s	**Congress pays increasing attention to philanthropy.**
1913	The Revenue Act of 1913, adopted after ratification of the 16th Amendment, exempts organizations "organized and operated exclusively for religious, charitable, scientific or educational purposes" from taxation. Subsequent acts add "prevention of cruelty to children or animals" (1918), "literary" (1921), "community chest, fund or foundation" (1921), and "testing for public safety" (1954) to the list of exempt organizations.
1917	To encourage charitable contributions as income tax rates rose, the War Revenue Act establishes an individual income tax deduction for contributions to tax-exempt charitable organizations.

(Continued)

(Continued)

1935	Congress passes another Revenue Act, which raises taxes on higher-income levels, corporations, and gifts and estates—a "wealth tax." Corporations are permitted to deduct charitable contributions up to 5 percent of taxable income.
1950	Under pressure from business executives, Congress passes a law to tax unrelated business activities of charities to prevent nonprofit groups from gaining a competitive edge.
1952	The congressional Cox Committee investigates whether communists have infiltrated foundations, as well as whether tax-exempt groups are "endangering our existing capitalistic structure." The committee's 1953 report endorses foundations, but recommends requiring them to do more public accounting.
1954	The GE Foundation, the philanthropic arm of General Electric, starts the first matching gifts program to encourage employee giving.
1960s–1990s	**American philanthropy jumps significantly.**
1964	The Civil Rights Act launches President Lyndon B. Johnson's Great Society initiatives. It's soon accompanied by wilderness protection, support for the arts and humanities and Medicare, which foster demand for a nonprofit sector to provide services.
1974	The United Way becomes the first nonprofit organization to raise more than $1 billion in an annual campaign.
1981	Congress refines payout requirements so that foundations have to give an amount equal to 5 percent of their asset value annually.
1983	American Express begins one of the first "cause-related marketing campaigns" when it gives a percentage of each card transaction to the restoration of the Statue of Liberty; donations totaled $1.7 million ($4.1 million in today's dollars).
1987	Despite the stock market crash in October, contributions to charities set a record fueled chiefly by individuals.
1992	Mutual fund company Fidelity creates the Fidelity Charitable Gift Fund using "donor-advised funds," a means to take immediate tax deductions on charitable gifts for distribution in subsequent years. The move sparks fresh interest in donor-advised funds and vaults financial services companies into the charitable giving marketplace.
1994	GuideStar launches, providing easy public access to tax returns and other information about charities and private foundations.
1996	David Packard, co-founder of Hewlett-Packard, dies. He bequeaths almost $4 billion to the David and Lucile Packard Foundation, the largest single U.S. bequest to date, establishing his foundation as the nation's largest.
1998	On his 43rd birthday in October, Bill Gates quietly contributes $1 billion to his foundation. In December, he and his wife, Melinda Gates, announce a $100 million gift for making vaccines for children more widely available.

2000s	**Technology transforms giving.**
2001	Americans donate $2.2 billion to various charities in the wake of the 9/11 terrorist attack, a spontaneous outpouring of unprecedented size.
2008	After a financial crisis and stock market collapse, charitable giving falls by the largest percentage in five decades.
2009	Twitter users help to generate more than $250,000 for charity in 24 hours as part of the "Twestival."
2010	Facebook chief executive Mark Zuckerberg pledges $100 million to transform education in Newark, N.J. Matching donations make the total $200 million. Warren Buffett joins Bill and Melinda Gates to launch "The Giving Pledge," through which billionaires promise to give away more than half their wealth.
2012	The 92d Street Y in New York City starts the annual "Giving Tuesday," harnessing social media to fundraising on the Tuesday following Thanksgiving in the United States, just after two of each year's biggest shopping days in stores and online.
2014	The ice bucket challenge goes viral, raising $115 million for the ALS Association.
2015	Citing Bill Gates as an inspiration, Saudi prince Alwaleed bin Talal pledges his entire $32 billion fortune to charity, with women's rights as a focus.

Q&A: Cheryl Dorsey on Business Approaches to Charity

"HEAD AND HEART"
Cheryl Dorsey
President
Echoing Green

New York City–based Echoing Green was begun in 1987 by founders of a private equity firm who wanted to nurture leadership and innovative ideas that advance global social change. It supports for-profit and nonprofit concepts. Its cornerstone program awards up to $90,000 in cash over two years, plus valuable guidance and networking support, to approximately 1 percent of fellowship applicants each year. Since its inception, the $40 million program has supported a roster that includes the founders of Teach For America, City Year, College Summit, Citizen Schools, One Acre Fund, SKS Microfinance and other flourishing for-profit and nonprofit initiatives.

Echoing Green President Cheryl Dorsey is a veteran of top posts in the U.S. Labor Department and a member of the Board of Overseers at Harvard University, where she earned her medical degree. She embraced the fledgling concept of social entrepreneurship, meaning innovation that unites capital markets, civil society and government to solve urgent social problems. In 1992, as an Echoing Green Fellow, she helped start The Family Van, a mobile unit in Boston that provides health care to residents of that city's most underserved communities

SAGE Business Researcher reporter S.L. Mintz talked with Dorsey about her perspective on financing good works. This is an edited transcript of the conversation.

How do you define social entrepreneurship?

It is definitely part of the landscape in the social sector today. The hallmark of the social entrepreneurship model is the blurring of sectoral boundaries between capital markets, civil society and government. The bleeding of the business sector into the social sector framework is the coin of the realm these days.

For-profit and nonprofit organizations both need capital. Do you see shared challenges?

In many ways, they are the same. The undergirding is relationship management with your investors or your donors. The best social entrepreneurs know that transactional relationships get you only so far. Relationships that will yield financial capital and social capital require mentoring and access to networks you would not penetrate otherwise. There is fluidity across boundaries that you didn't necessarily see 10 years ago.

How else has philanthropy changed?

Many of us in my generation came to nonprofit work without business training. We came mostly from a heart perspective, as opposed to a head perspective. Nonprofit social entrepreneurs today bring head and heart. They bring discipline and business acumen geared to revenue generation and earned income. They are clear about the need to build teams that can leverage all resources. Philanthropic capital is never going to be big enough to solve every problem.

What do you look for in fellowship candidates?

A Darwinian selection is pretty rigorous. The vetting process this year reviewed about 3,200 plans from more than 150 countries through a human capital development lens. We selected 38. We want to back the right entrepreneurs, because business plans become obsolete before the ink dries. Leaders are adept at critical thinking. They are resource magnets who can drive transformative social change. They attract financial capital, media attention and a volunteer workforce.

What does success look like?

Donnel Baird, for instance, pursued social entrepreneurship at Duke University and at Columbia University, where he earned his MBA. The fellowship supported his proposal for BlocPower, now an online marketplace where impact investors meet networks of energy efficiency projects in churches, synagogues, nonprofits and small businesses in low-income communities. Property owners and investors share savings from weatherproofing, use of solar panels and energy efficient projects.

How do you measure success?

We are very much like a business incubator or accelerator. What changes do we monitor? How many dollars did they raise after our investment seed capital? In the past couple of years, classes went on to raise 7.5 to 11 times our initial capital investment. We track the number of employees and the number of volunteers. Over time, we look at the hit rate, meaning how many enterprises made it in the short and long term, a really good indication that we support sustainable social transformation ideas. Two-thirds of the programs we have supported still improve lives.

How do you ensure the continuing success of Echoing Green?

Number one, I don't believe that any social enterprise needs to remain in existence in perpetuity. We compete in the open market where there are wonderful social enterprises that deserve support. We compete at a high level for oxygen in a crowded space. When you are passionate and believe very deeply in the product, at the end of the day, you are in the business of sales.

SUSTAINABILITY

Are businesses looking beyond profit?

Pamela J. Black

EXECUTIVE SUMMARY

Many companies, mostly large multinationals, are adopting sustainability programs and delivering annual reports on their progress toward creating a new kind of business. Within this burgeoning movement, sustainable companies give the environment and human rights the same priority as profits. Their goals include protecting the Earth to reduce the effects of climate change while innovating new products. Some of the biggest companies have succeeded in integrating sustainable principles into their corporate DNA and say that it gives them a competitive edge. Is sustainability really making a difference? Can a company go "green" and remain profitable? Will the movement spread or fade away? Many of these companies have been accused in the past of degrading the environment and depleting natural resources, and critics say they are only changing their ways because of pressure from regulations, investors, activists, communities and consumers. Others, often with the help of nonprofits, have voluntarily instituted change across their business model. But so far progress is slow.

OVERVIEW

In 2001, when Jack Welch stepped down as CEO of General Electric, the company was under attack for releasing some 1.3 million pounds of polychlorinated biphenyls (PCBs) from two plants into the Hudson River between the mid-1940s and 1977. PCBs, which are hazardous to all life forms, have invaded the food chain along miles of the Hudson and other waterways. Welch and GE denied for years that PCBs were harmful and said the river would clean itself.[1]

Welch's successor at GE, Jeff Immelt, has taken a different tack. In 2005, Immelt began "Ecomagination," which he describes as "GE's commitment to imagine and build innovative solutions to today's environmental challenges while driving economic growth."[2]

GE's $12 billion investment in Ecomagination generated $160 billion since 2005 in revenue. At the same time, GE reduced greenhouse gas emissions by 32 percent from 2004 levels and fresh water use by 45 percent from 2006 levels, according to GE's 2013 Global Impact Report, the latest available.[3]

In the impact report, Immelt offers a concise definition of a sustainable business: "To succeed as a global business, we need to help build the communities where we operate. We

From *SAGE Business Researcher,*
February 23, 2015

know this goes hand in hand with our ability to grow. At GE, we call this sustainability: aligning our business strategy to meet societal needs, while minimizing environmental impact and advancing social development."[4] Sustainability has become a buzzword in boardrooms around the world. In general, the movement strives to give the environment and human rights the same priority as profit. But sustainability remains amorphous and complex and is hard to measure. Libertarians and conservatives see it as a threat to individual freedom and private property. Advocates, including nonprofit groups and many academics, hail it as a revolution in corporate management—and even call it the "new capitalism." Statistics and anecdotal evidence vary on whether it's a growing movement or appropriate only for some giant multinational corporations. Becoming sustainable requires a significant investment of time and money. That might be why only 10 percent of companies, mostly big multinationals, have fully embraced it.[5]

Corporations such as Alcoa, GE, General Motors, 3M, Procter & Gamble, Hewlett-Packard, Intel, Nike and Unilever, to name a few, may be more motivated to become sustainable because their international reach makes them more vulnerable to the effects of climate change and social unrest in various parts of the world.[6] In addition, sustainable practices give them access to the fastest-growing markets in developing countries.[7]

Multinationals with long histories tend to plan 50 to 100 years in advance. That means anticipating possible risks from climate change. They are also vulnerable to reputational risk in developing countries. "In the Internet age, information travels much quicker," says Alexandra Cichon, senior vice president of business development at RepRisk, a global database of corporate sustainability risks.

Smaller companies may lack the means to make big investments, although a majority would like to reap the cost savings from sustainability, according to a survey by Cox Enterprises, the Atlanta-based cable television and Internet company.[8] "The reality is, they have a hard time justifying it without being able to see an impact right upfront," says Cox spokeswoman Elizabeth Olmstead. "Large business can make bigger investments with a longer time to make a return on their investment."

Nonetheless, more companies, big and small, are trying out sustainable practices, says John Weiss, a senior manager in the corporate program at the Coalition for Environmentally Responsible Economies in Boston, known as Ceres. "You would be hard-pressed to find some companies that aren't doing anything."

"The whole corporate responsibility movement has become irreversibly mainstream," says Bennett Freeman, senior vice president for sustainability research and policy at asset manager Calvert Investments, a sustainable and responsible investing (SRI) company based in Bethesda, Md. Although he says that the number of sustainable businesses he covers hasn't grown significantly, more and bigger asset managers are pursuing it.[9]

Whether it is growing or not, sustainability is gaining attention because of two worsening problems: climate change and population growth. Carbon dioxide emissions from fossil fuels and agriculture are raising global surface temperatures, leading to severe weather and more widespread and costly destruction of natural resources, according to scientists.[10]

Moreover, the planet's population of 7 billion is growing at the rate of 200,000 people a day. These newcomers will need food, water and shelter in a world where arable land and fresh water are disappearing. Already humans consume 50 percent more natural resources than the Earth is producing.[11]

The triple bottom line

To make sustainability more graspable, John Elkington, the founder of British consultancy SustainAbility, devised the triple bottom line (TBL) in 1994.[12]

TBL consists of three concentric circles representing the three P's: planet, people and profit. The confluence of these defines sustainability, although, as an *Economist* blog noted, these categories can't readily be measured. "One problem with the triple bottom line is that . . . It is difficult to measure the planet and people accounts in the same terms as profits—that is, in terms of cash. The full cost of an oil-tanker spillage, for example, is probably immeasurable in monetary terms, as is the cost of displacing whole communities to clear forests, or the cost of depriving children of their freedom to learn in order to make them work at a young age."[13]

PLANET

The environment includes energy, water, soil, air and biodiversity of plants and animals. Each of these could be assigned a cost as "natural capital," and all are threatened by climate change and consumption. Fossil fuels are woven through almost all aspects of modern life, and coal, oil and gas are the biggest producers of atmospheric carbon.[14] Sustainable companies try to reduce their carbon footprint by using renewable energy from solar cells and wind turbines. Renewable-energy markets have been growing with the help of government incentives. Apple, for one, gets 92 percent of its energy from renewable sources.[15]

However, it's becoming clear that multinationals can inadvertently encourage problems such as deforestation. Rainforests absorb carbon from the air and protect biodiversity. But producers in developing countries who supply multinationals with raw materials, such as coffee and palm oil, clear rain forests for farmland.

The amount of fresh water is limited and in some areas it's drying up because of overuse or climate change.[16] The supply is expected to shrink more within the next three years due to population growth and pollution. "No business can expand without water," says Lance Pierce, president of CDP North America (formerly the Carbon Disclosure Project, an international nonprofit headquartered in London). "Food and beverage companies are at the vanguard of that. It's central to their products. All over the world, watersheds are under pressure, so beverage companies are developing the capacity to understand community expectations around water."

PEOPLE

The social aspect of the triple bottom line refers to human capital. At the most basic level investing in people means providing a safe and healthy work environment, and many sustainable companies stop there. But the most valuable and loyal employees work for companies that are transparent about corporate operations and value employee contributions, according to China Gorman, CEO of Great Place to Work, a global human resources consulting and research company that provides the data for *Fortune* magazine's "100 Best Places To Work" issue.[17]

They need to trust their leaders to be fair and honest; they want to be proud of their work and to have strong bonds with colleagues, Gorman said. "They need the organization [that] believes in them, invests in their careers, in their skills."[18]

PROFIT

Sustainable initiatives need to be profitable so the company itself can be sustainable, experts say. Sustainability makes economic sense across the triple bottom line because companies require educated and motivated employees, electricity, water and air. "A lot of sustainability will make you more efficient, which will lower costs," says Jason Jay, director of the Sustainable Initiative at MIT's Sloan School of Management. "A more efficient refrigerator or solar panels entail some upfront costs, but you get a benefit over time."

Measuring sustainability

An ongoing challenge has been proving that sustainability goals contribute to the financial bottom line. As the business cliché goes, what gets measured gets managed. Many corporations still grapple with the best way to measure the value of water use, carbon emissions, and employee satisfaction. "It's critical that you have metrics. You have to measure to know how you're doing and set targets," says Weiss at Ceres. "It's one thing to quantify, but it's even more important to set a time-bound target to mark progress against—where we want to go versus the previous year. We push companies to set aggressive targets."

Most companies lack formal sustainability targets

The murkiness of gauging sustainability allows some companies to "greenwash," or mislead people, about their products and processes. For example, Walmart, which announced a big sustainability campaign in 2005, is still accused by employees, unions and environmental groups of increasing its carbon footprint and underpaying workers. Walmart officials reject the charges.[19] "Most fields don't have independent standards or boards regulating whether you're sustainable or not," says Janis Balda, associate professor of sustainable enterprise at Unity College's Center for Sustainability and Global Change in Maine. "So it's very hard to know where company values are across people—planet—profits. On the whole, some greenwashing is unintentional."

How do you know if a company is really sustainable or just saying it is? Balda says that corporate websites offer a clue. Numerous awards and certifications are another. "B corporation," a designation that applies mostly to smaller companies and start-ups that often begin sustainably and are certified as environmentally sound, is yet another.[20]

There is also a big difference between companies that have incorporated sustainability into their DNA, versus those that are making incremental changes, says Weiss.[21] Companies that are remaking their operations to be sustainable or have started out sustainably are focused on innovating whole new products, systems and strategies in which sustainability is a given.

Some proponents of sustainability go further than examining corporate strategies, calling for a new kind of capitalism. They see technology as the means to create a more equitable society. Unilever CEO Paul Polman has pushed for a sustainable and equitable capitalism that is based on long-term planning and inclusivity. "Capitalism has served us enormously well," he said. "Yet while it has helped to reduce global poverty and expand access to health care and education, it has come at an enormous cost: unsustainable levels of public and private debt, excessive consumerism, and, frankly, too many people who are left behind."[22]

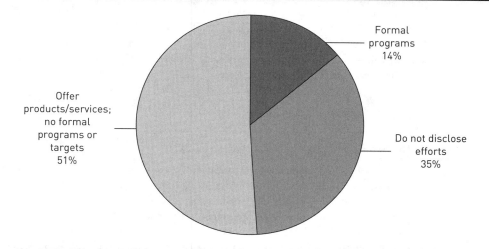

Companies with sustainable products/services, by offering

Formal programs 14%

Offer products/services; no formal programs or targets 51%

Do not disclose efforts 35%

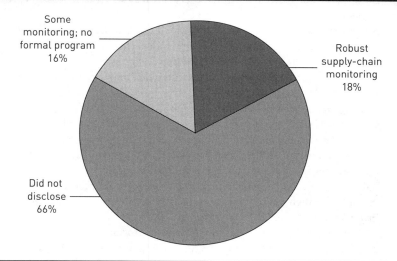

Companies with sustainable supply-chain management measures, by offering

Some monitoring; no formal program 16%

Robust supply-chain monitoring 18%

Did not disclose 66%

Sustainability remains elusive for most companies: Slightly more than half of the businesses surveyed by Ceres, a nonprofit that advocates for sustainability leadership, provide sustainable products or services without setting formal performance targets. The task is even tougher for those companies that try to monitor the sustainability of their supply chain: About two-thirds do not disclose how they measure their suppliers' sustainability performance. Among those who monitor their supply chains, 18 percent say they have robust monitoring systems to measure and respond to their suppliers' performance.

Source: "Digest of Education Statistics," Table 204.10, National Center for Education Statistics, September 2013, http://tinyurl.com/lwuxfpf

Although more companies seem interested in sustainability, actual change is glacial, Weiss says. Corporate sustainability efforts are falling way behind the pace of climate change. "It's disappointing. Companies have not gone as far as we hoped they would," he says. "We're looking out to 2020. But most companies aren't halfway toward meeting their goals."

Debate over corporate sustainability remains intense. Many of these issues will be resolved only in time—if at all. As companies struggle to define and adopt sustainable practices, they're wrestling with some of these key questions.

WEIGHING THE ISSUES

Is there a business case for sustainability?

The quest to find a link between sustainability and corporate value is ongoing. If such a link exists, stock prices don't always reflect it. Nevertheless, multinationals and other companies that have adopted sustainability believe their decision has led to higher profit because of savings from efficiency, innovative products and new markets.

A lot of the research on the financial value of sustainability is positive. In a study by asset manager Sustainable Insight Capital Management, fossil-fuel-free funds outperformed the S&P 500 in one-, three-, and five-year periods ending on Dec. 31, 2013.[23] A Harvard Business School study showed that every dollar invested in a portfolio of sustainable companies in 1993 would have grown to $22.60 by 2011, versus $15.40 for a portfolio of companies less focused on sustainability.[24] CDP's 2014 study, "Climate action and profitability," concludes that companies in its Leaders Index generated an 18 percent higher return on equity and 21 percent higher dividends than their less sustainable peers.[25] "The most recent look at the climate performance leadership index shows that it outperforms the Bloomberg world index by 9.6 percent," says CDP's Pierce.

However, other studies contradict this finding: A 2014 report by asset manager TIAA-CREF found no advantage over the long term, but no disadvantage either.[26]

The discrepancy between findings may have to do with varying definitions of sustainability among asset managers and corporations. A recent McKinsey study argued that the link between stock price and sustainability was weak because successful companies were failing to communicate their progress clearly. Instead, the companies were busy figuring out their own internal measures, which were often too voluminous and confusing for investors to evaluate.[27]

"Some people will tell you there's an outperformance and others will tell you SRI is a drag," says Freeman at Calvert Investments. "Like any other asset class, SRI funds go in and out of favor."

More companies say sustainability is good business

Anecdotal evidence is more emphatic. "We really do believe that good business and sustainability go hand in hand," says Todd Brady, global environmental manager at Intel, a leading semiconductor chip maker. "It doesn't cost money if you see where it aligns with business." Several years ago, Intel established a conservation fund, where engineers would contribute ideas for saving on energy costs—anything from replacing light bulbs to

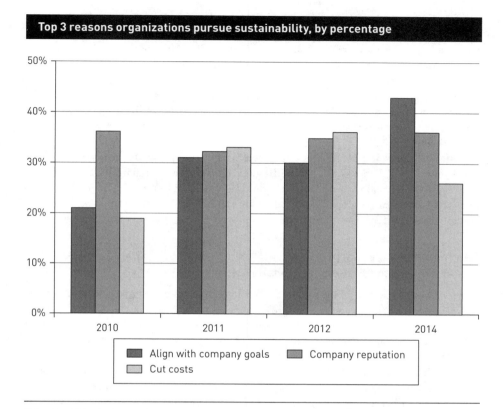

Top 3 reasons organizations pursue sustainability, by percentage

Legend:
- Align with company goals
- Cut costs
- Company reputation

Sustainability is becoming more popular because more businesses believe it helps the bottom line: 43 percent of executives in a 2014 survey said their companies adopted sustainable practices to align with their business goals in 2014, more than double the share citing that reason in 2010. Building company reputation (36 percent) and cutting costs (26 percent) were the second- and third-most commonly cited reasons.

Note: Number of survey respondents for each year: 1,749 in 2010, 2,956 in 2011, 3,847 in 2012; and 2,904 in 2014.

Source: "Sustainability's strategic worth: McKinsey Global Survey results," McKinsey & Company, July 2014, http://tinyurl.com/nsd52el

recapturing heat. "We thought we would get a return on investment in five years," Brady says. "But the first year we made $1 million to $2 million. Today, we have $30 million in the fund, and a savings to the company of over $65 million."

Focusing on sustainability takes significant risk out of portfolios, says Calvert's Freeman. Companies that are prepared for rising commodity prices or diminishing water supplies can prepare in advance to obtain commodities at reliable costs or to install water treatment and recycling systems.

Ideally, other stakeholders, including investors, benefit from sustainability, too. Customers buy a product that doesn't harm the environment, employees have a more satisfying experience and the community benefits from investments in its welfare and the environment. Sanya Carley, an associate professor of environmental affairs at Indiana University, surveyed leaders of 12 sustainable companies. Although the switch was difficult for many companies, she said, "not a single respondent claimed sustainability didn't contribute to the bottom line."[28]

Some nonprofits are trying to establish a link between corporate value and sustainability for investors. The Sustainability Accounting Standards Board (SASB) would do so by setting industry standards that would be combined with Securities and Exchange Commission (SEC) financial data.[29]

Establishing that missing link could help proponents persuade more companies to come on board. "There is a lot of willingness to support sustainability efforts, but a total lack of clarity on what business should do and why," said an unidentified CEO in a U.N.–Accenture report. "We need a plan that is progressive enough, and rigorous enough, to set real priorities for action."[30]

Can companies that adopt sustainable methods compete globally?

Competitiveness is the most significant economic concern of sustainable companies, followed by market pressure and revenue growth, according to "Sustainability's Next Frontier," a study by the Sloan Management School and the Boston Consulting Group. "There is little disagreement that sustainability is necessary to be competitive—86% of respondents say it is or will be."[31]

Even those CEOs who buy in to sustainability are having trouble scaling it up from individual projects to companywide strategy. They see improving the environment and people's lives as a cost rather than a strategy; they also view sustainability as a risk they can't afford to take. "People don't understand the positive gains from this type of enterprise, and some people are too scared to try," says Balda at Unity College. "Sometimes climate change is so huge, you need to break it down for companies, and they need to hear more stories of how [sustainable practices] can succeed for them."

CEOs increasingly see sustainability as a priority

Sustainability leaders, however, don't see improving the environment or society as a cost but as an opportunity to pursue innovative products, processes and markets. They have turned the double threat of dwindling resources and growing need into motivation for new business models with clearer values and purpose. This helps businesses differentiate themselves with consumers, attract top talent, protect their suppliers and compete globally. "We've set out to double the size of our business while reducing our environmental footprint and increasing positive social impact," says Jessica Sobel, manager of sustainable living and strategic initiatives at Unilever North America.

Electronics giant Siemens has sold offshore wind turbines that have saved 4 million metric tons of carbon dioxide a year, compared with traditional sources of power generation. Sales of turbines and smart electric grid meters have provided 42 percent of the company's business. The carbon savings was worldwide, and not just the company's own footprint.[32]

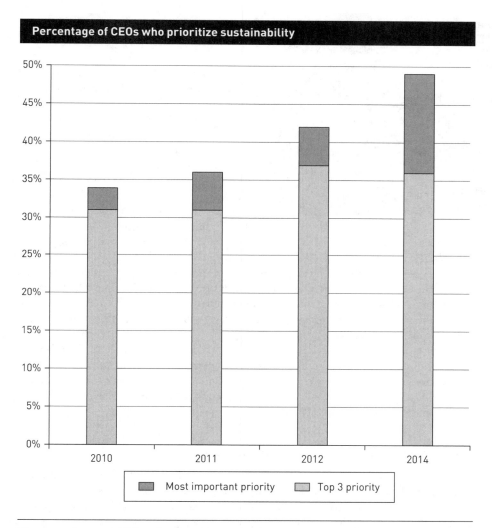

Percentage of CEOs who prioritize sustainability

Legend: Most important priority   Top 3 priority

The percentage of CEOs who viewed sustainability as either an "important" priority or a top three priority rose from 34 percent in 2010 to 49 percent in 2014. While 36 percent said it was a top three priority in 2014, down 1 point from 2012, the share who said it was important jumped from 5 percent to 13 percent.

Note: Number of survey respondents for each year: 175 in 2010, 265 in 2011, 364 in 2012; and 281 in 2014.

Source: "Sustainability's strategic worth: McKinsey Global Survey results," McKinsey & Company, July 2014, http://tinyurl.com/nsd52el

Vodaphone entered a joint venture to produce M-PESA, with Safaricom, the leading mobile communications company in Kenya. M-PESA allows people to bypass banks by storing and transferring money with their mobile phones.[33] A new Safaricom product, M-KOPA, is a solar lighting and charger system that people can buy with small payments over the course of year.[34]

Bloomberg/Bloomberg/Getty Images

Residents of Nairobi, Kenya, transfer money using the M-PESA banking by phone system, a success in places where people have access to mobile phones but not to banks.

In 10 years, 70 percent of global growth could occur in developing countries. To appeal to the new rising middle class, companies will have to build trust, listen to consumers and quickly innovate new solutions, according to McKinsey & Company.[35]

Companies, in other words, will need to create products that have resonance for local populations. They will need a "deep understanding" of local culture and customer segmentation, according to the Boston Consulting Group.[36]

"We source locally, market and produce locally, and hire and distribute locally, and that gives us a tremendous insight into the markets we serve and an edge in actually operating sustainably," said Coca-Cola CEO Muhtar Kent.[37]

Unilever's Sustainable Living Plan merges health and education with business: It teaches children in developing countries how to wash with soap and to brush their teeth. According to the company's website, these things improve oral health and raise self-esteem.[38] They also familiarize an up-and-coming market with Unilever's brand and products—and put the company in a favorable light.[39]

Some congressional Republicans and business leaders see a downside to sustainability: Efforts to go green can increase the cost of doing business and make American firms less competitive overseas, they say. They especially deride environmental regulations as anti-business; as the 2012 GOP platform put it, new greenhouse gas regulations "will harm the nation's economy and threaten millions of jobs over the next quarter century."[40]

Do sustainable business practices help society?

Unilever's Polman, who is seen as the leader of the sustainable business movement, says that the role of business is to serve society. In a commentary, he wrote: "In the next ten years, I think you are going to see many more initiatives undertaken by groups of businesses to protect their long-term interests and the long-term interests of society."[41]

Business and society cannot exist without each other, according to Michael Porter, a professor at the Harvard Business School and a leading authority on competitiveness. Business needs a healthy society to create evolving demand, and society needs businesses for jobs, wealth creation and innovation, he wrote in an article titled "Strategy and Society." He went on to say, "Any business that pursues its ends at the expense of the society in which it operates will find its success to be illusory and ultimately temporary."[42]

Porter cited how Nestle helped a dirt-poor town in northern India become prosperous. Farmers barely scratched out a living from their cow's milk. They were unable to travel to market without risking the milk going sour. Cows' yields were low and newborn calves kept dying. Nestle, which wanted to expand into India, aided the farmers by sending veterinarians and refrigerated trucks to transport their milk to a central processing center. The town flourished as a result.[43]

Ending poverty is one of the goals of sustainability, and helping people is one of the three bottom lines. Stories of creating better working conditions, sending kids to school instead of to a factory or farm and elevating the lot of women in villages are more and more common for companies. At the same time, the reverse outcome—stories about abusive working conditions at home and abroad—can badly harm a corporation's brand.

Big corporations have always had philanthropic arms. And this continues, but increasingly they have a sustainable bent. Some corporations contribute directly to communities through grants and gifts. Dow Chemical gives $25 million to science and technology education to "build the workforce of tomorrow."[44] Target awards grants to Feed America, UNICEF and school reading programs.[45] Ford Motor regularly buys supplies from minority- and female-owned businesses.[46] Hewlett-Packard works with Conservation International, using its technology to help scientists measure species' decline in 16 tropical rainforests in 14 countries, according to Nate Hurst, HP's global director of environmental progress.

Rather than making random donations to worthy charities, a recent *Harvard Business Review* article about Corporate Social Responsibility (CSR) suggested that the most productive social initiatives should be coordinated across the entire enterprise. The authors cited PNC, which consolidated its fragmented CSR budget behind a Grow Up Great program that helps under-served populations in its neighborhoods. This "correlates better with its employees' motivations and is likely to yield significant benefits to the communities the bank serves and relies on."[47]

Socially responsible programs can also generate value for the company. A cement company in India created a program to restore groundwater to arid areas around its mines. The land became farmable, and the company was able to bargain for more mining property.[48]

Sustainable companies in about 25 states in the United States have the option to become benefit corporations (similar to, but not the same as, B corporations like Ben and Jerry's), a status that commits them to meeting certain social and environmental goals of their choosing. This frees them to pursue social goals without being liable for suits claiming they're not putting shareholder value first. They could now, however, be sued by other constituents for not meeting their social and environmental goals.[49]

BACKGROUND

Silent Spring

Concern about sustainability originated with the modern environmental movement, which began in the years after World War II. The massive war effort spawned new technologies, materials and chemicals. As factories proliferated, U.S. manufacturers snapped up natural resources from around the world and freely spewed effluents, emissions and toxins from their operations into the environment.

Such pollutants, if noticed, were considered signs of prosperity until the marine biologist and nature writer Rachel Carson published her ground-breaking 1962 book *Silent Spring*, about the insecticide DDT. DDT was used during the war to delouse soldiers and clear South Pacific islands of mosquitos. After the war it was widely sprayed in the United States. In *Silent Spring*, Carson showed how DDT was killing insects, birds, fish and small animals, and was lodging in human tissue, where it causes genetic mutations and cancer.[50]

Biologist and author of *Silent Spring*, Rachel Carson.

Silent Spring raised public awareness of environmental problems. People started to worry about what other invisible chemicals might be affecting them.[51]

Paul Ehrlich's 1968 book, *The Population Bomb*, raised the specter of unchecked population growth and consequent consumption degrading the environment. This was apparent as postwar urban sprawl and the rise of the car reconfigured much of the country. The resulting smog in the biggest cities, Los Angeles and New York, caused stinging eyes, asthma, bronchitis and cardiac problems, much as it does in Beijing today.[52] Other causal links were established. Nitrogen oxides and sulfur dioxide from industrial smokestacks were combining with hydrogen and oxygen to form acid rain, which was killing plant and animal life in and around lakes and rivers.[53]

EPA versus business

Growing awareness of the destructive effects of oil spills, raw sewage, toxic dumps and overbuilding led to public pressure to clean up the environment.[54] A 1969 *New York Times* editorial called the environmental cause "more permanent, more far-reaching, than any issue of the era."[55] In 1970, President Richard M. Nixon established the Environmental Protection Agency (EPA) to direct the war on pollution. The new agency consolidated the duties of various governmental departments that had had jurisdiction over water, soil waste and air. A few months later, 20 million people turned out for the first Earth Day.

EPA's first administrator put business on notice when he announced that the agency had "no obligation to promote commerce or agriculture." [56] Congress then passed the Endangered Species, Clean Air and Safe Drinking Water acts.

EPA began slapping businesses with fines and lawsuits for pollution damage. As a result, manufacturers came to see the agency and the environment as the enemy, and pollution cleanup as an onerous cost and impediment to business. Where companies did comply with regulations, their solution, dubbed "end of pipe," was to spend money for costly cleanups of damage already done.[57]

In the 1980s, globalization, deregulation and growing friction between the developed and developing worlds fueled awareness of unrestrained corporate growth and degradation of natural and human resources. The United Nations responded by forming the U.N. World Commission on Environment and Development (WCED), which defined sustainability for the first time in its 1987 report, "Our Common Future." Sustainability was described as "development that meets the needs of the present without compromising the ability of future generations to meet their own needs."[58]

Also called the Brundtland report for its chair, Norwegian Prime Minister Gro Harlem Brundtland, the report reframed the world as a global system where universal issues were inextricably linked: "The environment is where we all live," development is how we get ahead and society is who we are.[59] These became the three pillars of sustainability: environmental protection, social advancement and economic development.

Besides environmental issues, competitive pressures were pushing businesses to look at sustainability. In the late 1970s and early 1980s, Japan outstripped the United States in the production and sale of all kinds of goods. By comparison, American conglomerates seemed bloated, unwieldy and unfocused.[60] Japan's secret was a highly systematic management method that originated in America in the 1920s and was taught to the Japanese in the 1950s by engineer W. Edwards Deming.[61]

The method, Total Quality Management (TQM), stressed continuously analyzing production processes to eliminate unnecessary steps, make operations more efficient, improve product quality and empower and educate employees. Above all, TQM demanded the elimination of waste. To compete, some U.S. executives also adopted these principles, trimming corporate fat.[62]

Moving toward metrics

In 1984, a toxic chemical leak at a Union Carbide pesticide plant in India killed and maimed thousands of people.[63] In the United States, EPA responded by requiring companies handling certain amounts of chemicals to fill out a Toxics Release Inventory (TRI) of some 650 chemicals. This information was made public so communities surrounding these companies could be prepared for potential leaks.[64]

"We could argue that the TRI was one of the most important and effective pieces of social legislation ever passed," wrote Stuart L. Hart in his seminal book on sustainability, *Capitalism at the Crossroads: Next Generation Business Strategies for a Post-Crisis World*.[65]

Although the inventory didn't require companies to do anything about these chemicals except report them, the TRI let companies, analysts and the public compare users, Hart said. As a result, many companies started reducing or eliminating their waste to improve their reputations. These published results were one of the first environmental metrics.[66]

Inspired by TQM and the push for greater efficiency, some companies began to reduce their toxic waste up front, in the design and production process rather than at the end of the pipe. By planning ahead, assessing and analyzing operations and products, corporations found they not only increased their brand value but also could save millions of dollars.[67] "If you're producing something in a really dirty way and have to invest to clean it up after the fact, it's not only expensive, but a pretty poor way to run your business," says Mark Milstein, director of the Center for Sustainable Global Enterprise at Cornell's Johnson Graduate School of Management.

One way to reduce waste up front was to substitute toxic ingredients with harmless agents that would do the same thing or to innovate new processes that recycle manufacturing materials.[68] Nike is a good example, according to MIT's Jay. Its original Nike Air shoe had a bladder under the heel that contained a potent greenhouse gas, sulfur hexafluoride. They replaced it with nitrogen, but being a smaller molecule, the nitrogen started leaking out. "So they stumbled on a new material that could hold nitrogen and allow them to extend the bladder under the whole shoe," says Jay. Still Nike's process left waste around cutouts of shoe tops. Its designers tried different ways to improve the process, ultimately inventing the Flyknit, in which the tops are all one thread interlocking with itself, says Jay.

In 1992, government and industry members attending the first worldwide economic development conference in Rio de Janeiro called for a standardized system of corporate practices to ensure the quality of products and to facilitate international trade. The International Standards Organization (ISO) had developed a series of standards for the Total Quality Management process called the ISO 9000 series. Now it developed a new series based on environmental improvements so companies could compare their processes. The ISO 14001 followed TQM principles of planning ahead, setting and implementing goals, measuring progress and starting over. This became the base line certification for sustainability.

Around the same time, Ceres began the Global Reporting Initiative (GRI), which became its own nongovernmental organization (NGO). This initiative expanded the reporting criteria beyond the environmental, social and financial goals to include governance, which required companies to report on involvement by corporate boards and behavior toward employees.[69]

The next step was eliminating waste altogether by reusing the components of a product through remanufacturing new or different products from waste in a closed cycle. The concept, called Cradle-to-Cradle (C2C), was introduced in 2002 by architect William McDonough and chemist Michael Braungart of McDonough Braungart Design Chemistry. The goal was to go beyond incremental improvements such as cutting a firm's carbon footprint by, say, 20 percent over the previous year. McDonough argued for creating a zero or positive footprint. Many companies now strive to achieve this.[70]

Shaw Floors, a leading carpet and tile maker based in Dalton, Ga., was an early C2C manufacturer. It built a machine that could chew up old carpet and spew out the basic nylon fiber it was made from. Shaw spins this fiber into fresh carpet, which it can do indefinitely without degrading the product. The company has collection centers around the country for its used carpet. By reclaiming and remanufacturing its basic raw material, it kept most of the finished product out of landfills.[71]

Supply chains

U.S. companies in the late 20th century began outsourcing their manufacturing to take advantage of cheap labor in developing countries. Starting in 1991, the press and activists denounced Nike for employing mostly women and children in Southeast Asian factories in abusive conditions where they were exposed to dangerous equipment and toxins, as well as subjected to emotional abuse. These laborers were paid little, and 70-hour workweeks were common.[72] The company at first blamed these problems on its subcontractors, but public protests and falling stock values forced Nike to take responsibility. "The Nike product has become synonymous with slave wages, forced overtime and arbitrary abuse," then-CEO Philip Knight said. "I truly believe the American consumer doesn't want to buy products made under abusive conditions." Nike started auditing the factories and publishing detailed reports on conditions there.[73]

The company went on to become a top sustainability leader, but the scandal became a warning to other executives about what attacks on their reputations could do.

U.N. guiding principles said businesses' corporate social responsibility extended to their "business relationships." Companies began looking into their supply chains and found plenty to worry about. They started urging their suppliers to abide by their sustainability goals and to follow environmentally sensitive practices. Yet only 54 percent of corporate leaders who thought they should be integrating sustainability throughout their supply chains believed this had been achieved within their company, according to management consultant Accenture.[74]

CURRENT SITUATION

Integrated reporting

Sustainability may be coming into sharper focus with the efforts to create a standard that would combine nonfinancial information with a company's hard numbers. This is called integrated reporting, which many in this business have been anticipating for a long time.

Three documents determine a company's health in the eyes of the financial market: a balance sheet, a profit and loss statement, and a cash flow statement. "But these are three documents which don't tell you very much about the overall impact of that business. So, we desperately need to develop a system to try and measure and quantify and communicate the wider stakeholder engagement," said Badr Jafar, managing director of the Crescent Group, an oil conglomerate in the United Arab Emirates.[75]

Sustainability reports have long served as adjuncts to corporate financial reports. Companies often disclose their numerical progress on carbon reduction or savings from a cleaner process, but this information is easy to dismiss as window dressing.[76] Integrated reporting would combine nonfinancial data with the hard financial data investors look at to assess the value of a company. An integrated report would link environmental stewardship, treatment of stakeholders and governance decisions with the financial value of the company now and in the future.[77]

"To many people, environment, society and governance sound like tree-hugging, or a good-versus-evil thing," says RepRisk's Chicon. "Not so; it's just common sense about how to do good business."

The oldest of the three nonprofits offering integrated reporting is the Global Reporting Initiative (GRI): Its format presents side-by-side reporting of financial and sustainability information. Many companies use it for organizing their sustainability information, so it's already familiar.[78]

In the past three years the International Integrated Reporting Council (IIRC) and the Sustainability Accounting Standards Board (SASB) have developed different frameworks for integrated reporting. IIRC calls for reporting six different capital flows: financial, manufactured, human, intellectual, social and natural. These are at once both broader and simpler than the GRI's latest iteration.[79]

SASB is modeled on the Financial Accounting Standards Board (FASB), a private-sector nonprofit group that works with the SEC and businesses to set and improve officially recognized corporate accounting standards.[80] SASB is creating detailed standards for 89 industries in 10 sectors across categories that include innovation, governance and human, social and environmental capital.[81] It is hoping the SEC will adopt its standards. "These are all mission-driven organizations trying to get sustainability taken as seriously as financial information," says Cichon.

But she adds that SASB, if adopted by the SEC, would make the most difference because companies could be held liable if they run afoul of the guidelines. "Volunteer reporting is not working as well," Cichon says. It's not clear what will happen with these three different plans. And some experts are getting frustrated by the choices. "Some of us would want to see them work together more," Cichon says.

Collaborations

More companies are teaming up to address challenges, such as air pollution, that are too big for any one entity to resolve alone. Supply chain sourcing has brought companies in the same industry together in roundtables on palm oil, cotton and beef, to ensure the sustainability of these ingredients from suppliers.

Once opposed to government, which regulated them, and "tree-hugging" nonprofits, which harassed them, sustainable corporations now regularly work with both of them. In fact, many companies are crying out for government policies that will define the terrain so they can know how to proceed. Until then, these companies are stuck in limbo, not sure how to plan for the future.[82]

In the meantime, they work with nonprofits, stakeholders and competitors. "The challenge is likely to encourage a much more collaborative form of capitalism," said Unilever's Polman. "Companies will have to work with each other, not just with governments, nongovernmental organizations (NGOs), and civil society. Issues like deforestation and species extinction cannot be tackled by just one company acting alone; they will require collaboration within, and across, industry sectors."[83]

GM and Honda have partnered to develop fuel cells for electric cars. Developing a battery to store significant amounts of electricity would be a huge breakthrough. Electric cars could drive much longer without recharging, and renewable energy could be stored for use when the sun isn't shining or the wind blowing. "For almost a century, we've been searching for batteries that are cheap enough to use in cars," says Julie Gorte, senior vice president for sustainable investing at Pax World Management, an investment company. "Now they cost $38,000 per kilowatt."

Honda and GM have filed the most patents in battery development, and Honda intends to introduce its offering in 2015. Fuel cell batteries enable electric cars to drive farther than existing electric vehicles before recharging (in minutes) and electric vehicles can accelerate quickly, according to the Greencar Congress, a website devoted to news about sustainable mobility.[84]

Ocean Spray and Tropicana teamed up to save on transportation costs. Tropicana was shipping its products to a distribution center in New Jersey in refrigerated trains, which returned empty. Ocean Spray was trucking its products to Florida because the train line didn't go close enough to its warehouses. But Tropicana trains did. Reluctant to share with a rival at first, Ocean Spray was able to save considerable money and emissions by shipping its products south on Tropicana's empty train.[85]

Regulations

EPA is set to go ahead with President Obama's clean-power plan announced in June 2014, which calls for a 30 percent reduction of carbon emissions from power plants over 2005 levels by 2030. These proposed rules are supposed to go into effect in June 2015.[86] More recently, the president announced a goal to cut methane gas emissions from oil and natural gas by 40 percent to 45 percent from 2012 levels by 2025. Methane is a more potent greenhouse gas than carbon.

EPA will work with industry and the states to achieve these goals while still allowing the fossil fuel industry to grow, the White House says. The plan would give money to the Department of Energy to develop ways to help natural gas companies seal leaks during transmission, for example.[87]

Congressional Republicans and fossil fuel industry leaders object to both plans. "The Obama administration's latest attack on American energy reaffirms that their agenda is not about the climate at all," said Thomas Pyle, president of the Institute for Energy Research. "It's about driving up the cost of producing and using natural gas, oil, and coal in America."[88] The National Association of Manufacturers has long lobbied for giving equal opportunity to all energy sources. The fossil fuel industry, led by logging, mining and oil conglomerate Koch Industries, has helped fill Congress and most state governorships with sympathetic Republicans via a PAC that allows unlimited giving.[89] Whether the clean power plan and other environmental regulations take effect may depend on who becomes the next president.[90]

LOOKING AHEAD

Optimistic predictions

Experts say the sustainable business movement is gaining momentum.[91] It may grow in fits and starts, but it will no doubt spread among more companies as it continues to be defined and to evolve, they argue. The growing threat of climate change, a new tech-savvy workforce, greater regulation and better understanding of how to profit from sustainability could mean that sustainability is here to stay. "Even if we ignore it, it doesn't cease to be real," says Christopher Cooke, manager of the measurement science working group at The Sustainability Consortium. "There is a groundswell of companies that realize if they want longevity and consumer respect and loyalty that sustainability really helps."

"We will see increased awareness of sustainability issues in business and investing, often prompted by some disaster or series of disasters," says Pax World's Gorte. "I think the perception of how to manage and measure corporate vulnerabilities to the physical risks of climate is a good bet to become more popular in investment and business over the next half-decade."

The need for skilled labor will be another incentive driving sustainable development. As more baby boomers retire, millennials will take over the workforce. These valuable "knowledge workers" are tech savvy and innovation minded. They want meaningful work and won't hesitate to leave if they don't get it, according to several experts.[92] Surveys show they are a good fit for sustainable values. They want corporate transparency and believe that success should be measured by more than profits.[93]

According to studies, millennials want training, career goals, feedback, competitive wages, work/life balance and other perks. They want to feel they are serving the greater good. Sustainable companies are more likely to attract and retain them, and millennials may reshape companies in sustainable ways.[94]

Some millennials, called "social entrepreneurs," are starting innovative programs to solve the pressing social needs of poor communities around the world. Others are founding companies based on new sustainable technology. For example, two college students worked for 10 years to find a cost-effective way to make plastic out of methane. Using a biological catalyst, AirCarbon, they developed a product that not only creates petroleum-free plastics but also removes a dangerous greenhouse gas from the atmosphere. The AirMaster carpet by Desso cleans the air in a room by attracting particulates and allergens. EcoATM by Outerwall is an ATM that takes recycled products in exchange for cash and sells them through a network of buyers. BioTrans collects and grinds up leftovers at restaurants into a biomass that it stores until it can be hauled to plants to be used as biogas.[95]

Technology, too, can further the cause of sustainability. Big data and the ability to analyze it will illuminate new sustainable business models and manufacturing operations. Most companies will need more and more powerful software to create smart products and run the Internet of Things. Accenture reports that "we may begin to achieve speed and scale in transformation only when business is able to capture the potential from digital infrastructure solutions and digitization." As Praveer Sinha, CEO of Tata Power Delhi Distribution, put it: "The technology transformation has to come; technology is the game-changer."[96] For example, GE, which manufacturers a variety of smart products, from toasters to jet planes, is increasingly run by smart technology.[97] The company uses a combination of sensors, software and nanotechnology to design planes and trains that can report in advance when the machinery needs maintenance, and jet planes with turbines that can adjust to save fuel.

"If you went to bed last night as an industrial company, you're going to wake up this morning as a software and analytics company," said GE's Immelt.[98]

Chronology

1960s–1970s	**Environmentalism takes hold, setting the stage for the rise of the sustainability movement.**
1962	Rachel Carson's *Silent Spring* describes the link between chemicals and human health. Her trail-blazing book leads to greater environmental awareness.
1968	Paul Ehrlich's *The Population Bomb* warns of environmental degradation from population growth and overconsumption.
1970	The U.S. Environmental Protection Agency (EPA) is established with independent powers to regulate the environment.... Millions turn out to attend the first Earth Day to celebrate the importance of the environment.

1971	The cause of acid rain—industrial pollutants—is discovered.
1973	OPEC cuts oil supplies to the United States, leading to gasoline shortages and long lines at the pump.
Mid–1970s	Leaks are found at a chemical dump at Love Canal in upstate New York; the government is forced to buy nearby poisoned homes.
1980s–1990s	**The sustainability movement emerges.**
1980s	Total Quality Management, a system for eliminating waste from the production process, is adopted by some leading companies.
1984	A leak at a Union Carbide chemical plant kills thousands of people in Bhopal, India.
1985	Chlorofluorocarbons (CFCs) used in refrigerants, cleaning fluids and aerosol cans are found to cause holes in the Earth's ozone layer.
1986	EPA establishes the Toxics Release Inventory, where companies list their toxic chemicals.
1987	The World Commission on Environment and Development, also known as the Brundtland Commission, defines "sustainability" in a report called "Our Common Future."
1989	Exxon Valdez spills some 11 million gallons of oil into Prince William Sound off Alaska. . . . Nonprofit Ceres is founded in the wake of the Exxon Valdez spill to bring together environmentalists and capitalists to form a sustainable business model.
1994	John Elkington introduces the triple bottom line as a way for companies to organize economic, social and environmental costs and achievements.
1996	The International Standards Organization publishes the first sustainability standards.
1997	The Global Reporting Initiative issues guidelines for reporting on sustainable issues. About 100 companies sign on.
2000s–Present	**Sustainability goes mainstream.**
2002	Architect William McDonough and chemist Michael Braungart publish *Cradle to Cradle: Remaking the Way We Make Things*, proposing a closed system for remanufacturing used products to eliminate waste.
2004	In *The Fortune at the Bottom of the Pyramid: Eradicating Poverty Through Profits*, management guru C.K. Prahalad writes about the huge potential market for companies able to sell to people making less than $1.25 a day.
2006	*An Inconvenient Truth*, the Academy Award-winning documentary by former Vice President Al Gore, publicizes the evidence for global climate change.

(Continued)

(Continued)

2010	BP's Deep Water Horizon rig explodes, spilling 210 million gallons of oil in the Gulf of Mexico. . . . International Integrated Reporting Council, an attempt to integrate sustainability and financial reporting, is founded.
2012	Sustainability Accounting Standards Board starts writing sustainability accounting standards that include environmental risks and social factors. These would be integrated with financial annual reports.
2013	Oil companies start putting a dollar value on carbon in anticipation of a possible carbon tax.
2014	President Obama announces a clean power plan, which would cut carbon pollution from existing power plants.

Pro/Con: Campher on Selling Green

YES

DO CONSUMERS BUY SUSTAINABLE PRODUCTS?
Henk Campher
Senior Vice President for Business and Social Purpose/Managing Director, Sustainability
Edelman

Written for SAGE Business Researcher, February 2015

We somehow cling to the belief that consumers don't care about sustainability and that price and quality are the main reasons why people buy things—that social and environmental issues just don't matter. But that's simply not true. The challenge is rather that the consumer world changes in an evolutionary—not revolutionary—way.

Imagine a world without Tom's of Maine or Ben & Jerry's, Tesla, Levi's, Starbucks, Stonyfield Farms, Timberland, Seventh Generation or Chipotle. Or organic food or fair trade products. All of these have become mainstream products. And they are growing fast. Who is growing rapidly at the moment—Chipotle or McDonalds? Where do you think the biggest growth in sales lie—hybrid cars or traditional? The list goes on. Imagine how few of those products were on that same shelf 20 years ago. Many of these products have become mainstream. They are so much a part of our lives today that we forget that they are still new when considering the life of a consumer product.

Sales continue to grow each year, some faster than others. That is simply the nature of evolution. Not every product is an iPhone—some take time to grow, and they grow by fits and starts. Companies aren't shrugging and turning their backs on consumers. They're using this evolution to transform their products and brands to drive new growth in sales and consumer support. We need to realize that sustainable products have grown up faster than we did—and so have consumers.

We are wrong when we think consumers aren't buying into sustainability and aren't buying products and brands they believe add to a more sustainable lifestyle and world. They are, but not the way we want it. That's our problem, not theirs. This is a business problem to solve, not a consumer's. We know they want to buy sustainable products (or products with sustainability as part of the brand value proposition), and we know they want to buy more. The problem is to find better ways to bring sustainability to life for consumers in ways that will resonate with them, and foster even faster growth. We know they will buy it—just don't try to sell them snake oil.

PERSPECTIVE

Pro/Con: Friedlander on Selling Green

NO

DO CONSUMERS BUY SUSTAINABLE PRODUCTS?

Jay Friedlander
Chair, Green and Socially Responsible Business
College of the Atlantic

Written for SAGE Business Researcher, February 2015

Reflecting on a decade of green consumerism, the executive editor of GreenBiz.com, Joel Makower, wrote, "Consumers, for all their good intentions, don't really want to change. They want what they want—and what they feel they need and deserve."

Survey after survey confirms that even if consumers say they want and care about sustainable products, they're not willing to pay extra for them. Faced with the realities of the register, most consumers would rather have the money for their own bills versus paying extra to "save the planet."

The payment barrier is exacerbated by an atmosphere of confusion created by proliferating claims about the eco-friendliness of products. U.S. consumers are overwhelmed by the amount of environmental messaging they receive. In addition, limited distribution and concerns about product efficacy further inhibit sales.

Given these findings, it is hardly surprising that the Greendex 2014 Report on Consumer Choice and the Environment by National Geographic and GlobeScan concluded: "It is clear that increased environmental concern is not manifesting in substantive behavior change" on the part of consumers.

Since consumers have not changed their buying habits because of sustainable claims alone, companies launching sustainable products need to put the desires of their customers at the forefront in order to succeed.

The story of Deja Shoe embodies these lessons. Begun in the 1990s as an environmental footwear company, groups as diverse as the American Marketing Association and the United Nations lauded Deja's recycled footwear. Given the high profile of climate change and the Rio Earth Summit in 1992, national retailers were eager to stock the shoes. Consumers, however, were another story. Sales were lackluster because shoes didn't meet customers' expectations on style, performance or price. Predictably, despite its environmental story and credentials, Deja went out of business a few years later.

Sustainably minded companies beat the competition by addressing a need that's less abstract than climate change. The sustainably focused car-sharing service Zipcar created a viable alternative to car ownership by providing the benefits of owning a car, such as convenience, along with access to multiple brands. Customers saved money and avoided hassles like parking, insurance and maintenance. In 14 years, Zipcar grew from a start-up with a few VW Beetles to being acquired by Avis for $500 million.

In a world where consumers are not motivated by sustainability alone, companies must merge their sustainability focus with customer expectations.

THE SHARING ECONOMY
Is it really different
from traditional business?

Patrick Marshall

EXECUTIVE SUMMARY

What's called the sharing economy—peer-to-peer transactions conducted via the Internet and smartphones—has changed how people arrange car rides, find vacation lodging and more. Revenue is projected to soar in the coming years, although profitability remains untested. But as businesses such as Uber, Lyft and Airbnb flourish, regulation and collection of taxes, primarily by state and local authorities, have become more difficult to enforce. Traditional businesses such as taxis and hotels complain that these newcomers are gaining an unfair advantage by ducking oversight that's meant to protect consumers. Additionally, debate has grown over whether service providers in the sharing economy are independent contractors or employees. Some of the key issues under debate: Is the sharing economy more efficient than traditional markets? Should regulators treat the sharing economy the same way as conventional competitors? Are sharing-economy companies platforms for independent contractors, or are they employers?

OVERVIEW

The "sharing economy"—in which consumers connect with service providers using Internet applications instead of relying on traditional providers—is booming. On a typical day, an estimated 247,000 items are sold on Etsy, 140,000 people rent accommodations through Airbnb and 1 million people ride with Uber.[1]

Because very few sharing-economy companies are publicly traded, it's unknown whether they are profitable. But many sharing-economy companies are attracting major investments and have quickly become players in the economy. Based on venture capital funds raised, *The Wall Street Journal* estimated Uber's value at more than $40 billion and Airbnb at $25 billion.[2]

In fact, according to the Federal Trade Commission, sharing-economy transactions totaled about $26 billion globally in 2013.[3] And PricewaterhouseCoopers (PwC), an auditing and consulting firm, estimates that in 10 years, the biggest sectors of the sharing economy could see $335 billion in global revenue. PwC projects that by 2025, sharing-economy companies will account for about half of the business in their market sectors, up from only 6.25 percent in 2013.[4]

From *SAGE Business Researcher,*
August 3, 2015

Sharing economy to match rental revenue by 2025

What's more, sharing-economy companies are emerging in numerous niche markets. It's not, in short, just about renting apartments and hailing cars. There is a platform that cities can use to share heavy equipment (MuniRent); a platform that skiers, bicycle and surfboard owners can use to rent their recreational equipment (Spinlister); and a platform that musicians can use to share their equipment (GearLode). There is also a robust group of platforms that connect investors to individuals and small businesses seeking funding (Funding Circle, LendingClub, Prosper, TransferWise).

"It's clear that consumers are embracing it," says John Breyault, vice president of public policy at the National Consumers League, a consumer advocacy group in Washington, D.C.

Of course, the sharing economy—which has also been described as a peer-to-peer economy—is not actually new.

"Peer-to-peer businesses were around long before the Internet," Philip Auerswald, associate professor of public policy at George Mason University, told a House hearing on the sharing economy last year. "Indeed, there was a time in this country and elsewhere in the world

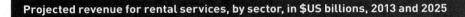

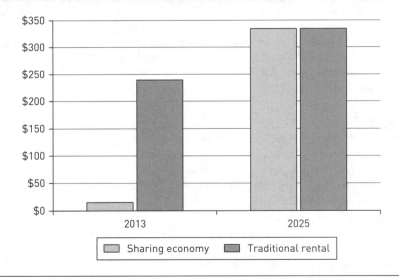

Internet-based sharing businesses will generate an estimated $335 billion in revenue by 2025, the same amount projected for five traditional rental sectors (equipment rental, B&B and hostels, car rental, book rental and DVD rental).

Note: 2025 estimates based on historical data and projected growth rates and economic outcomes for 10 industry sectors.

Source: "The sharing economy—sizing the revenue opportunity," PricewaterhouseCoopers, 2014, http://tinyurl.com/ophtwcf

(roughly until the end of the 19th century) when the peer-to-peer economy *was* the economy. Large corporations providing consumer services simply did not exist. Regulation governing consumer services was minimal. People provided services on a personal basis to other people who were very much like them."[5]

While peer-to-peer transactions may not be new, analysts say, how those transactions occur is. The Internet and smartphones have allowed transactions to take place around the block or around the globe, almost instantaneously. "It's these different technologies that are making things easier," says Dean Baker, an economist and the cofounder of the Center for Economic and Policy Research, a Washington, D.C., think tank. (See Perspective "Pro/Con: Dean Baker on Regulating the Sharing Economy.")

Indeed, the Internet has fundamentally changed the nature of peer-to-peer transactions. Where previously those dealings involved only the buyer and seller of goods or services, now they are mediated through a software platform, which is owned by a company or, in some cases, a nonprofit organization. That change has led to two developments. First, regulation and collection of taxes, primarily by state and local authorities, have become more difficult to enforce. Second, there is growing debate over whether service providers in the sharing economy are really independent contractors or employees.

The stakes involved are high. If regulators require sharing-economy companies to conform to laws governing employers' treatment of employees, the prices of their goods and services will likely rise and their competitive advantage against traditional companies will be reduced.

Corporate involvement in the sharing economy, some analysts say, means that much of this economy has little or nothing to do with sharing. "Make no mistake about it, today's sharing economy is big business, involving lots and lots of money and all kinds of players motivated powerfully by financial gain," said Nancy Koehn, a professor at Harvard Business School.[6]

Although the Internet has enabled the sharing economy to blossom, other factors also have contributed. "While some of these sharing models might have resulted from a need for frugal spending after the global economic recession of 2008," wrote entrepreneurship professors Boyd Cohen and Jan Kietzmann, "their success was also driven by a growing environmental consciousness combined with the ubiquity of Internet and associated information and communication technologies which make sharing possible at scale."[7]

Koehn speculated that deeper aspects of consumer psychology may explain the booming popularity of many sharing-economy companies. "There is a directness about calling a limo ride yourself on Uber or Lyft and then rating the driver and car after you get to your destination that is both empowering and seemingly more transparent than calling a car service or hailing a taxi," she said. "Individuals from all walks of life, particularly younger consumers, simply do not have much trust in established business, governmental, and other large-scale organizations. Against this backdrop, many consumers—and sellers—find peer-to-peer buying and selling to be more appealing because it is not so closely associated with a big business that may (or may not) have a mixed track record in their minds."[8]

The relatively new technologies that power the sharing economy have put many transactions outside the purview of regulators. While cities issue taxi medallions to a limited number of service providers, they have little control over the drivers who connect to passengers using

Portuguese taxi drivers join to protest against Uber, a popular ride-sharing service.

Uber, Lyft or Sidecar. And while cities license and tax hotels, they haven't yet developed a way to manage and monitor homeowners and companies renting through sharing-economy companies such as Airbnb.

As a result, although consumers generally seem happy with the savings and convenience delivered by sharing-economy companies, many of those companies are beginning to feel pressure from several directions. Those include their contractors (or employees) unsatisfied with wages and the lack of benefits; government agencies and competing businesses that claim sharing-economy companies are dodging needed regulation; municipalities that accuse service providers of failing to pay taxes; and consumer groups that say some companies are underserving certain groups of people.

Not surprisingly, the greatest amount of attention has focused on the most successful sharing-economy companies: Uber and Airbnb.

"The growth of illegal hotels is rapidly becoming one of the biggest obstacles in the struggle to protect and expand New York City's stock of affordable housing," Democratic New York state Sen. Liz Krueger told the Federal Trade Commission in May. "Online platforms like Airbnb lure individuals into breaking the law with promises of more income from operating illegal hotels, leaving residents with an increasingly scarce supply of affordable housing."[9]

Krueger also charged that the lack of effective regulation over Airbnb exposes consumers to drawbacks of which they may not be aware. "Most illegal hotels fail to meet federal, state and city accessibility requirements for people with disabilities," she said. "Far from being a harmless service that promotes 'sharing,' companies like Airbnb threaten public safety and make it more difficult for everyday New Yorkers to find an affordable place to live."

Airbnb did not to respond to repeated requests for comment. In a blog post in 2013, however, CEO Brian Chesky argued that the company actually helps New Yorkers stay in their homes. "In New York, our 15,000 hosts are regular people from all five boroughs. Eighty-seven percent of them rent the homes in which they live," wrote Chesky. "On average, they are at the median income level and more than half of them depend on Airbnb to help them stay in their home."[10]

Ride-sharing companies have drawn even greater criticism from competitors and regulators. "The thing with Uber and Lyft, what they're doing is they are cutting corners on safety and responsibility under the guise of the sharing economy," says Dave Sutton, a spokesman for the Taxicab, Limousine & Paratransit Association, which represents 1,100 taxicab companies. "Their insurance has gaps, which has come to light, and more and more will be revealed. Their background checks are not conducted by law enforcement and don't involve fingerprinting. And those are truly undercutting public safety."

Uber declined requests for interviews and responded to questions only by providing links to materials on the company's website. The materials do not indicate that Uber's background checks include fingerprints and reviews by law enforcement agencies.

The reaction to Uber by taxi drivers in some other countries has been even more dramatic. In early July, for example, Uber was forced to suspend its UberPop service in France after taxi drivers violently protested.[11]

Because sharing-economy companies are using new technologies that transform the way business is conducted, analysts say, a period of adjustment is inevitably needed to balance the competing interests of companies, regulators and consumers. "It is no surprise that Uber, Airbnb and other new companies find themselves operating in an area where the application of existing laws is potentially unclear," said Koehn. "It is also not surprising that these companies are fighting efforts by regulators to apply government rules and standards to their growing market."[12]

As the market presence of the biggest sharing-market companies has surged, friction with regulators—particularly at the state and local levels—has grown more pronounced in recent months.

For example, in the wake of an October 2015 report by the New York State Office of the Attorney General, which found that 72 percent of units booked via Airbnb in New York City appeared to violate state and local laws, city officials have begun filing suit and imposing fines on property owners.[13] The day after the report was released, the *New York Daily News* learned that New York City had filed suit against two property owners.[14]

In fact, many cities have long banned rentals of fewer than 30 days for properties that have not been inspected and licensed. And several cities have successfully pressed Airbnb to collect appropriate taxes from hosts for payment to the cities.

For its part, Uber has been banned by several communities and airports and has been sued by drivers who say that the company should be treating them as employees rather than independent contractors. In June 2015 in a ruling that could be portentous, the California Labor Commissioner's Office determined that an Uber driver should be classified as an employee, not an independent contractor. Uber was ordered to reimburse the driver, Barbara Ann Berwick, $4,152.20 in expenses and other costs for the eight weeks she worked as an Uber driver. While the ruling applies only to Berwick and Uber is appealing it, the case could significantly affect Uber's competitive pricing if other courts agree that drivers are employees.[15]

"The explosion of sharing or on-demand services like Uber and Airbnb is the beginning of an economic upheaval every bit as significant as the Industrial Revolution," warned Frank Shafroth, director of the Center for State and Local Government Leadership at George Mason University. "The on-demand economy promises to radically reshape the cost of services and change the face of the workforce. These upheavals, in turn, are altering state and local government policies—imposing unforeseen fiscal risks."[16]

Specifically, Shafroth wrote, in addition to the challenges of recovering lost tax revenue and ensuring public safety, policymakers will have to deal with an upsurge in the number of temporary or part-time workers in the economy. "These workers are providing on-demand services at rock bottom prices. They are not working in downtown or suburban office buildings or for traditional employers, nor are they eligible for traditional health-care or pension benefits," he said. "Leaders will need to be part of a discussion about changing rules for 'contract workers,' and of an even larger federalism and governance discussion about how pensions and health-care benefits are delivered in the future."

Number of part-time workers peaked during recession

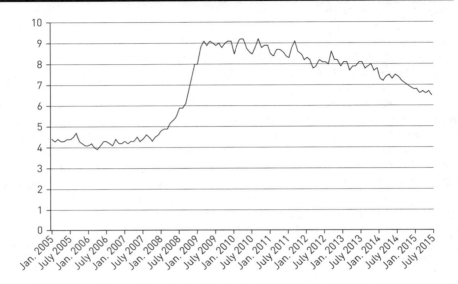

Number of Americans working part-time, ages 16 and older, in millions, 2005–15

About 6.5 million Americans work part-time for economic reasons, even though they say they would prefer to work full-time, a number that experts say could rise with a growing sharing economy. The number of these part-time workers jumped from 4.3 million in October 2007 to 9.1 million by March 2009 during the recession, hovering there for about two years before gradually declining.

Note: Part-time workers are those who indicated they would like to work full-time but were working 1 to 34 hours per week for economic reasons, such as being unable to find full-time jobs.

Source: "Labor Force Statistics from the Current Population Survey," U.S. Bureau of Labor Statistics, downloaded July 20, 2015, http://tinyurl.com/m6996nd

Additionally, the expansion of the sharing economy may have a lasting impact on other industries, such as automobile manufacturing. As consumers come to rely increasingly on sharing-economy transportation services, car ownership could decline. Indeed, a 2012 report by the U.S. Public Interest Research Group and the Frontier Group found that between 2001 and 2009, the average annual number of vehicle-miles of driving by young people (16- to 34-year-olds) decreased from 10,300 miles to 7,900 miles per capita—a drop of 23 percent. The report cites the rise of services such as Zipcar as a major factor in the trend.[17]

Shafroth said, "It's not for nothing that the on-demand economy is simultaneously dubbed the disruptive economy."[18]

As the controversy around the sharing economy grows, below are some of the questions being debated.

WEIGHING THE ISSUES

Is the sharing economy more efficient than traditional markets?

Sharing-economy supporters say that the companies and the platforms they offer are using technology not only to offer savings and convenience to consumers but also to make more efficient use of resources and to expand income opportunities for service providers.

The sharing economy, the staff of the House Committee on Small Business wrote in a January 2014 memo, more efficiently allocates "resources which in turn results in new consumption leading to new production."[19]

"Peer-to-peer marketplaces can have very different roles in an existing service industry," explains Chiara Farronato, an economist who is researching peer-to-peer Internet platforms. "They can actually take a thin local market and make it 'thick' and very global." She cites eBay's creation of global markets for goods that previously were difficult to sell locally. "And you can create new markets," she says. "For example, Instacart delivery options are creating a new [grocery] market that was not previously available."

Even Airbnb, which may divert some customers from traditional hotels, has expanded the market, especially in locations where the supply of hotel rooms is constrained by either regulations or geography, Farronato says. "In San Francisco, for example, there is a limit to expansion and demand is high," she continues. "So the entry of Airbnb has actually not led to people substituting away from hotels. It's possible for more people to come to San Francisco to visit the city." Farronato says her research has shown that hotels didn't experience a large reduction in mean price and occupancy.

Peer-to-peer markets growing more quickly than traditional sectors

Similarly, while Uber has no doubt diverted some riders—and drivers—from other transportation providers, at least one study has found that the company has expanded jobs and ridership overall. "The availability of modern technology, like the Uber app, provides many advantages and lower prices for consumers compared with the traditional taxi cab dispatch system, and this has boosted demand for ride services, which, in turn, has increased total demand for workers with the requisite skills to work as for-hire drivers, potentially raising earnings for all workers with such skills," write Princeton economist Alan B. Krueger and Jonathan V. Hall, head of policy research at Uber Technologies.[20]

The study has been questioned by some economists, who note that it is based on selected Uber data. "Krueger's study looks at gross income for Uber drivers and compares it with ostensibly net income for cab drivers in the same cities," Baker of the Center for Economic and Policy Research says. "The reason he doesn't have an estimate of the net for Uber drivers is that he doesn't know how many miles those Uber drivers drove. Uber has that data. They just chose not to give it to him."

Sarah Cannon, Google Capital manager, and Lawrence H. Summers, former U.S. Treasury secretary, defend the sharing economy. "These firms bring significant economic, environmental, and entrepreneurial benefits, including an increase in employment," they

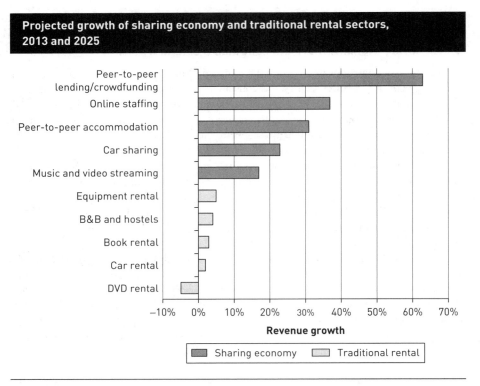

Projected growth of sharing economy and traditional rental sectors, 2013 and 2025

Sharing-economy sectors are expected to grow rapidly from 2013 to 2025, with the largest revenue growth in peer-to-peer lending/crowdfunding (up 63 percent) and online staffing services (up 37 percent). Forecasters project marginal or negative revenue growth for comparable traditional rental sectors.

Note: Growth estimates based on historical data and projected economic outcomes for industry sectors.

Source: "The sharing economy – sizing the revenue opportunity," PricewaterhouseCoopers, 2014, http://tinyurl .com/ophtwcf

argued in a *Harvard Business Review* article. They added that car-sharing services should reduce carbon dioxide emissions, benefiting the environment.[21]

Some analysts have estimated that for every shared vehicle, between nine and 13 private vehicles are removed from the roads, either by members selling a personal vehicle or postponing a planned purchase.[22] According to Susan Shaheen, an expert in innovative mobility research at the University of California, Berkeley, car sharers report reducing the vehicle miles traveled by 44 percent.[23]

While acknowledging that sharing-economy companies have had positive effects on markets, some analysts—as well as competitors—say that in some cases sharing-economy companies simply move jobs from existing industries to the new companies. They charge that these companies gain their competitive advantage by evading taxes, regulations and the cost of providing employee benefits.

"There are obviously some efficiencies there, using the technologies to connect buyers and sellers," Baker says. "And I'm sure there is some net job creation. But I suspect that for the most part it is displacement, that you have lost jobs in the traditional cab industry, and you're replacing them with Uber drivers."

Ride-sharing services, Baker says, are also evading regulations, and consumers may not even be aware of the hidden costs. "There are hidden costs in the sense that people are maybe getting a car that's not safe, or a driver who is not safe." Baker acknowledges that Uber has begun to take steps to ensure the safety of drivers and cars. "But they originally were trying to evade that," he says. "It remains an ongoing issue."

Some analysts say that while consumers may like the low prices that companies can offer by avoiding costly regulations, the overall impact on jobs is to drive wages down.

"There are a lot of articles coming out saying that these sharing-economy companies are turning people into mini-entrepreneurs, but in many cases, the way some people look at it, they are exploiting people," says Giana Eckhardt, professor in the School of Management, Royal Holloway, University of London.

Eckhardt notes that independent contractors not only often work for lower wages but also don't receive benefits, such as health insurance and sick leave. What's more, independent contractors must make their own payments for Social Security and Medicare, costs that are normally paid by a worker's employer.

Of the growing chorus of complaints by Uber drivers, Joseph De Wolf Sandoval, an Uber driver and the president of the California App-Based Drivers Association, told a reporter, "It's not just a small group of disgruntled or unprofessional drivers, as Uber would like to cast us. It's a nationwide feeling of general unhappiness and unease with policies and programs that are being promulgated by Uber without the drivers' input whatsoever."[24]

When Uber lowered fares in July, some drivers took exception. "Since Uber implemented the 20 percent off discount on all Uber rides, I've been losing $200 a week," Oris Fortuna, an Uber driver, said. "To make up for it, you have to work 20 percent more. That means more mileage and more gas. An $8 trip is not worth it."[25]

Should regulators treat the sharing economy the same way as conventional competitors?

Sharing-market companies, along with free market advocates, argue that the new platforms driving the sharing economy have features that make the old regulatory frameworks unnecessary.

"While some regulators are tempted to regulate sharing economy companies like their competitors, to do so would be a mistake that betrays a misunderstanding of how the sharing economy works," wrote Matthew Feeney, a policy analyst at the Cato Institute, a libertarian think tank.[26]

According to Feeney, the online customer ratings that sharing-economy companies such as Uber and Airbnb have made a central part of their business models are more effective than regulations at stopping misbehavior. "Badly behaved providers and consumers in the sharing economy do not last long, and the lack of anonymity means that anyone who does commit a crime is unlikely to escape justice," Feeney said.

As for dealing with bad actors, Arun Sundararajan, professor of information, operations and management sciences at New York University's Stern School of Business, says that the platforms can deal with them more efficiently than can regulators. "The interests of the platforms are well aligned with facilitating safe and profitable peer-to-peer trade (since their revenues are directly linked to the volume and continued growth of such trade)," Sundararajan told a House hearing in written testimony in January 2014. "The platforms are also better positioned to 'take action' against infringing entrepreneurs and consumers (for example, by simply disconnecting them from the platform)."[27]

Even in the absence of formal regulation, the review tools offered by sharing-economy platforms are not the only options for keeping bad actors in check.

"We have to remember there are always civil and criminal protections that will keep people safe," says Christopher Koopman, a research fellow at the Mercatus Center at George Mason University. "Just a few mistakes by these firms could sink one of these companies before they really have a chance to take off." (See Perspective "Pro/Con: Christopher Koopman, Matthew Mitchell and Adam Thierer on Regulating the Sharing Economy.")

Other analysts point out the review system poses several problems, starting with the possibility that sharing-economy companies can manipulate the process.

Asked what assurance consumers have about the integrity of companies' review systems, economist Farronato says simply, "It's their word." She notes that historically 15 percent of reviews on Yelp proved to be fake. "The peer-to-peer platforms are very different in how they handle fake reviews," she says. "Some are working much harder than others. My take is that large companies are probably doing a very good job of weeding out the fake reviews."

Koopman says, in fact, that companies have a vested interest in earning consumers' trust. "If people are not trusting the rating systems, they're no longer trusting the companies," he says. "If they are no longer trusting the companies, they're not going to want to do business with them anymore."

A second problem, some analysts say, is that a negative consumer review doesn't appear until after something bad has happened.

"Unfortunately it takes a tragedy and then people become aware," says Sutton of the Taxicab, Limousine & Paratransit Association.

Ideally, advocates of regulation argue, regulators require behaviors that prevent abuses from happening in the first place.

Uber has begun running background checks on drivers, which Baker calls "wonderful." But unless there's a regulatory framework that requires those checks, he adds, "there's no guarantee they will always be doing it."

Baker says the need for regulations is just as great for hostelry services like Airbnb. "With hotels we have a set of regulatory structures that ensure they're not fire traps, that they are not a nuisance to their neighbors," he says.

And regulations often go beyond simple safety issues to require companies to meet societal goals. "There are important services that we expect people to have access to, and that means all people," says Baker. He notes that because of the Americans with Disabilities Act, cab companies must have a certain number of handicapped-accessible cabs. "That is a totally legitimate public purpose," he says. "But Uber is not bound by that and as long as we have the two systems sidebyside, Uber is essentially dumping off the cost on the traditional cab companies."

Free market advocates say the problem is regulation itself—and that the solution is to remove the regulations that apply to traditional companies. "Rather than pursue legislation that seeks to regulate sharing economy companies like their traditional competitors," Feeney wrote, "lawmakers ought to deregulate these competitors in order to make the regulatory playing field as level as possible while allowing for innovative disruptors to enter markets."[28]

Are sharing-economy companies platforms for independent contractors, or are they employers?

Sharing-economy companies that connect service providers with customers say they are simply providing a convenient platform to help the two parties connect. An Uber spokesperson, talking on background, described Uber as a technology company that matches riders with drivers. The company classifies drivers as "partners," not employees.

As long as service providers are considered independent contractors, companies aren't bound by minimum wage and overtime laws, nor do they incur expenses for such things as unemployment insurance, workers' compensation and health insurance.

However, service providers have sued some sharing-economy companies—including Uber and Lyft—saying they are really employees and should receive benefits. Those lawsuits are pending, and neither company responded to requests to discuss them.

The initial indications are that the companies may face a tough sell of their argument that the companies are just platforms and not transportation companies with driver employees. Judge Edward Chen of the federal District Court in San Francisco called that argument "fatally flawed," noting, "It is clear that Uber is most certainly a transportation company, albeit a technologically sophisticated one."[29]

As for the argument that the drivers are independent contractors and not employees, Chen said that the issue will have to be decided at trial under California law.

The California Labor Commission's determination in early June that at least one Uber driver was, in fact, an employee, will likely be taken into consideration.

"Defendants hold themselves out as nothing more than a neutral technological platform, designed simply to enable drivers and passengers to transact the business of transportation," the Labor Commissioner's Office wrote in its decision. "The reality, however, is that defendants are involved in every aspect of the operation."[30]

While several other states—including Georgia and Texas—have ruled Uber drivers to be contractors, Florida authorities decided in May that a former Uber driver had been an employee for purposes of claiming unemployment benefits. Uber is appealing that decision.

There is no federal law defining the difference between independent contractors and employees, nor have states been consistent in defining the terms. But, according to Kai Falkenberg, senior legal counsel at the New York City Department of Consumer Affairs, there are a number factors the courts tend to consider in making such determinations, including the amount of control the company exerts over the service provider's activities.

For its part, the Internal Revenue Service applies "the usual common law rules" in determining employee status for tax purposes. This involves determining the extent to which the company exerts behavioral control and financial control over the service provider, as well as factors such as contract obligations, if any, and provision of benefits, such as health insurance.[31]

"One of the reasons that Uber drivers might be considered as employees is the degree of control that the companies are exerting," Falkenberg says. "And one of the manifestations of that is, interestingly, through the rating system. That seems to be a significant degree of control."

Falkenberg explains that Uber relies on its customer review system to cultivate trust in the service. If drivers get bad reviews from customers, they are likely to be let go.

"The companies really want to provide the best caliber service, and they want the people using the service to trust them," she says. "There's a tension between providing a high level of service but without changing your status from basically being a platform that provides a matchmaking service to a company that is actually employing people who are providing a service."

"For all practical purposes they are employees and if we're just going to play a semantic game here then there is no point in the regulations in the first place," Baker says of Uber drivers. "Obviously if you have the option to define someone as an independent contractor rather than an employee, and evade all of the regulations, then you've given companies enormous incentive to classify people as independent contractors."

Some analysts say the real problem is with the way important benefits are tied to employed positions versus independent contractors.

"The sharing economy in a lot of ways is putting a spotlight on weak spots in public policy," says Koopman. "One of those is why we continue to insist on tying health insurance to employment."

Sundararajan of the Stern School of Business agreed. "The dichotomy of employees and independent contractors is out of date," he wrote. Sundararajan called for labor laws to "be updated to provide a social safety net to people whose chosen form of work is something other than full-time employment. Health coverage, insurance against workplace injuries, paid vacations and maternity leave: these have long been universal entitlements in many economies. They should not become exclusive perks for a dwindling band of salaried employees."[32]

BACKGROUND

Out of the shadows

Before the development of effective monetary systems, nearly all economic activity took place within sharing economies that relied upon either barter or gifting to exchange goods and services. After the Industrial Revolution and the rapid spread of capitalism in the mid-1700s, the exchange modes of the sharing economy were relegated to an unofficial shadow economy in industrialized countries.

Some sources point to Harvard law professor Yochai Benkler as the first person to articulate the modern concept of the "sharing economy." Benkler coined the term "commons-based peer production" to describe activities in which numbers of people work together, primarily over the Internet, to create value. Benkler further developed the concept in his 2004 paper, "Sharing Nicely: On Shareable Goods and the Emergence of Sharing as a Modality of Economic Production."[33]

Benkler was describing a trend that had been developing for several years. Increasingly, individuals and companies were taking advantage of the emerging capabilities of the Internet to connect people to information, products and each other. As early as 1995, when a person had something to sell, she could simply post it on eBay or Craigslist and instantly reach thousands of people instead of having to take out a relatively expensive ad in the local newspaper that might reach a small number of people.

Not surprisingly, different sectors of the sharing economy developed independently and at different times as new technologies enabled more complex interactions.

The earliest companies in the modern sharing economy were those focused on connecting individual buyers of products and services with individual sellers.

Person-to-person (p2p) markets

"It's hard to believe now, but until 1991, commercial enterprise on the Internet was strictly prohibited. Even then, the rules favored public institutions and forbade 'extensive use for private or personal business,'" wrote *Wired* executive editor Keven Kelly.[34] In the eyes of the National Science Foundation (NSF), which at the time was the primary authority governing Internet activity, "the Internet was funded for research, not commerce," he said.

The NSF didn't officially lift its prohibition on commercial activity until 1995.[35] Even before then, however, e-commerce had begun. In 1992, Book Stacks Unlimited in Cleveland opened one of the first commercial sales websites that supported credit card processing. Only two years later, what would become a dominant e-commerce site—Amazon.com—was founded.[36]

Book Stacks Unlimited and Amazon were, of course, e-commerce sites rather than sharing-economy platforms. But they pioneered the technologies that would drive the emergence of online services that allowed consumers to share products through the Web.

And in 1995, two companies that would evolve into two of the largest drivers of the sharing economy appeared.

In early 1995, Craig Newmark began an email distribution list to inform his community of Internet developers in the San Francisco area about local events. The service proved popular—especially for its job listings and listings of items for sale—and as the mailing list grew others began to contribute items. By 1996, Newmark converted the mailing list to a website, craigslist.org.[37]

EBay, also founded in 1995, was intended from the start by its founder Pierre Omidyarto to be a commercial site for selling goods and services. Unlike Amazon, however, eBay aimed at connecting individual sellers with individual buyers through online auctions.[38]

Justin Sullivan/Staff/Getty Images News/Getty Images

Craig Newmark, founder of Craigslist, poses outside the company's San Francisco office.

In 2008, Shelby Clark, then a graduate student at Harvard Business School, realized that the P2P model didn't have to be limited to individuals buying and selling products. It could also be used for sharing things like personal cars. On Thanksgiving Day in Boston that year, Clark wanted to visit his cousins but he didn't have a car. "It was a frickin awful winter day in Boston," he recalled in an interview. "It was snowing and the freezing wind was coming from every direction and I'm biking through the snow and sleet to get this damned car. Meanwhile, I'm passing all these cars that are covered in snow. They clearly hadn't been driven in weeks."[39] That's when he got the idea to develop a platform on which car owners could offer their vehicles for rent.

Clark couldn't find any such service online, but he did discover the major hurdle he had to clear: insurance. Existing policies didn't cover car rentals between individuals. It took Clark 18 months to arrange appropriate coverage, after which he started RelayRides.

Also in 2008, Joe Gebbia and Brian Chesky were inspired to apply the model to another underused resource: living space.

"Joe Gebbia and Brian Chesky were two jobless friends living together when they received a terrifying letter from the landlord," wrote Alex Stephany, author and CEO of a European sharing company called JustPark.[40] The letter informed them that their rent was increasing by 25 percent. Chesky didn't have the money. "He had days to find a solution when the two noticed all the unused space in their living room," wrote Stephany. "What if someone would pay to sleep there? Gebbia had just been camping and had an airbed. They blew it up . . . and came up with the concept of 'airbed and breakfast': cheap accommodation on your beds with a no-frills breakfast of Pop-Tarts."

Two days later, www.airbedandbreakfast.com—later to be known as Airbnb—was born. The company grew so quickly that, in 2015, it has 1.2 million listings in 190 countries.[41]

But the power of the Internet-powered sharing economy isn't just about big markets. It also allows smaller communities to connect across great distances.

Poshmark, a platform founded in 2011 that runs on a mobile application, connects women who want to buy and sell used clothes with each other. Sellers take photos of their items to offer for sale. When an item is sold, the Poshmark app emails the seller a shipping label addressed to the buyer.[42]

Product sharing and renting

While P2P markets connect individual buyers to individual sellers, Robin Chase's idea in 1999 was to provide a platform and products that individuals could easily share.

She had met a friend at a café in Cambridge, Mass., Chase recalled. The friend had just returned from a vacation in Germany and mentioned that she had come across a car being rented to people by the hour or by the day. Chase, who would become a cofounder of Zipcar, wondered if that idea might work in Cambridge.

"My husband drove our car out to his suburban office every morning, where it would sit in the parking lot all day," Chase wrote. "And while I definitely needed a car sometimes, there was absolutely no way I wanted to buy another, park it on the street in our city neighborhood, maintain it, and shovel it out after snowstorms."[43]

Zipcar began with an initial investment of $50,000. "Four months later, Zipcar had $68 in its bank account and three days before going live," Chase said. "The plan was to place four cars in four reserved parking spaces, one near each of four consecutive subway stops in Cambridge and Boston."[44]

According to Chase, the company's goal was to make renting a car "as easy and convenient as getting cash from an ATM."[45] Chase and her team accomplished this by creating a website for making reservations, then placing devices in the cars that could read members' cards for unlocking, enabling the ignition and tracking distances.

At the same time as major sharing-economy companies were launching, so too were scores of nonprofit grassroots efforts that, collectively, have greatly affected the economy and communities' use of resources.

In May 2003, for example, Deron Beal started the Freecycle Network to connect his friends and a few nonprofits in Tucson, Ariz., so that they could exchange goods they no longer needed without charge. Freecycle Network now has 5,000-plus groups and more than 7 million members worldwide.[46] It's a grassroots and entirely nonprofit movement of people who are giving (and getting) stuff for free in their own towns and keeping good things out of landfills.

Peer-to-peer loans

As companies were helping people share goods and services, some companies turned to the Internet to allow people to loan each other money instead of going through banks and other financial institutions, which generally charge higher rates of interest.

The first such peer-to-peer lending service was Zopa, begun in Great Britain in 2005. Since then, Zopa has made more than $1.4 billion in loans with reserves pooled from more than 51,000 people.[47]

The next year, the first peer-to-peer lending company in the United States—Prosper Marketplace—launched in San Francisco.

According to a Federal Deposit Insurance Corp. report, however, early peer-to-peer lending platforms had few qualifications for borrowers, which led to defaults and high loss rates. The report noted that the major peer-to-peer services have tightened borrower requirements.[48]

Some platforms gave a twist to the peer-to-peer lending model by combining it with features of eBay-like auctions to create "crowdfunding." The best-known of these platforms—Kickstarter—was founded in 2009. Kickstarter provides a structured means for individuals or companies to pitch their products and services in order to enlist contributions. As of July 27, Kickstarter says it has funded 89,000 projects since 2009, with 9.1 million contributors pledging $1.8 billion.[49]

Fee-for-service markets

The preeminent example of fee-for-service firms are transportation network companies (TNCs), including Uber, Lyft and Sidecar. With TNCs—which offer rides to consumers, booked via websites or mobile apps—the vehicles aren't actually shared or rented. Instead, drivers with their own vehicles share the TNC platform to offer their services to consumers.

While car-renting companies such as Zipcar and car-sharing companies such as RelayRides had established themselves years earlier, TNCs, which deliver services on a moment's demand, had to await the development and ubiquity of smartphones and the apps that run on them.

Zipcar, founded by
Robin Chase

That technological hurdle was cleared by 2009 when Uber was founded as "UberCab"by Travis Kalanick and Garrett Camp.

The beginnings of regulation

Regulators have struggled to find ways not only to regulate the various types of sharing-economy companies but also to monitor their activities and collect appropriate taxes. For the most part, such efforts have taken place at the local level.

The TNCs have drawn the greatest attention, because they compete in an industry that has long been heavily regulated for public safety reasons and because governments want to control their effects on communities and public facilities, such as airports. This process of fitting TNCs into the existing regulatory frameworks has been a challenge that has resulted in a patchwork of requirements.

In June 2014, Colorado became the first state to pass legislation creating a statewide regulatory framework for TNCs.[50] The legislation specifies necessary levels of insurance and details requirements for regular background checks. The state Public Utilities Commission is empowered to revoke or suspend a company's permit, but penalties against drivers are prohibited. Other measures include yearly safety inspections of drivers' vehicles and exterior markings signifying them as vehicles for hire. In addition, the TNC cannot discriminate against riders based on their location or destination, nor can it charge additional fees for passengers with disabilities.

CURRENT SITUATION

Regulatory pressure grows

The sharing economy is filled with companies that have as many differences as similarities. In fact, the only thing they have in common is that customers access goods or services through the Internet.

Most of these businesses—such as Etsy, MuniRent and Zimride (a ride-sharing service for companies and universities)—pose few, if any, problems for consumers or regulators. That's because they simply connect providers to consumers and are not engaged in the types of activities that require safety regulations to protect the public. Most sharing-economy companies are also generally free of controversy because they are not directly competing with traditional companies. And most don't rely extensively, if at all, on service providers who might press claims for employee benefits.

Other companies—most notably, Uber, Lyft and Airbnb—are facing increasing pressure from regulators, employees and competitors.

In the last five months alone, legislatures, city councils, regulators and others have been active on numerous fronts:

In early March, the Vermont Department of Financial Regulation issued a consumer alert, "Be aware before you share." The alert warned residents wanting to drive that participation in sharing-economy businesses could expose them to major liabilities if they lack appropriate insurance. The state labor commissioner announced she was investigating Uber in Vermont to determine whether its drivers are employees or independent contractors.[51]

On April 21, the Portland, Ore., City Council voted 3–2 to end a prohibition on ride-sharing companies by allowing them to operate under a 120-day pilot program. The two dissenting council members indicated that they still have concerns about minimum insurance coverage and Uber's business practices.[52]

On May 4, California Democratic state Sen. Mike McGuire introduced legislation that would require companies such as Airbnb to adhere to local laws with regard to vacation rentals, including paying occupancy taxes. The legislation also calls for data reporting on room rates and the number of nights stayed by renters.[53]

On May 5, Uber announced that it was ceasing operations in Kansas after the state Legislature overrode the governor's veto to pass legislation with stricter insurance requirements and background checks for drivers.[54]

On May 12, the Santa Monica, Calif., City Council adopted a home-sharing ordinance that prohibits the rental of an entire unit for less than 30 days. The ordinance also requires hosts to obtain a business license and to pay a 14 percent hotel tax. Proceeds from the tax will help pay for enforcement officers and staff to search online for illegal rentals.[55]

On May 26, San Francisco International Airport and the San Francisco Municipal Transportation Agency petitioned the California Public Utilities Commission to impose tighter regulations on ride-sharing companies. Specifically, the agencies called for mandated vehicle inspections, a limit of 375,000 miles on vehicles, the use of permanent "trade dress" markers on vehicles and training for drivers.[56]

On May 29, Republican Nevada Gov. Brian Sandoval signed legislation providing a regulatory framework for ride-sharing services in the state. The framework includes a 3 percent tax on fares.[57]

On June 18, Lyft agreed to pay the state of New York $300,000 to settle claims that it was in violation of state and municipal laws. The agreement also placed tighter requirements on insurance for Lyft drivers, and required the company to comply with state and local laws covering for-hire car services.[58]

Companies responding

One of the major challenges facing sharing-economy companies is that to do business nationally, they must conform to not just one regulatory authority but potentially hundreds of state, municipal and port authorities.

"It's a problem for the companies," says John Browning, a Southern Methodist University adjunct law professor who also works with tech start-ups. "They have lobbyists going to 50 different state legislatures."

Browning says federal legislation could simplify things, although no bill has been introduced. "Are there companies, particularly in the tech sector, that have an interest in getting some sort of federal legislation? Absolutely," he says. "That would give companies some measure of predictability, reliability and, to a certain extent, protection."

Perhaps in anticipation of, or to fend off, regulation, many of the larger sharing-economy companies, in addition to stepping up lobbying efforts, have been introducing or increasing their own insurance coverage and taking other steps, such as performing background checks for relevant service providers.

"Generally, these companies want to at least have the appearance that they are in line with consumer expectations," says Breyault of the National Consumers League. "By and large, I think they are implementing these because they want to avoid more onerous regulations that could harm their business model."

Uber, for example, instituted background checks for drivers in 2014 that cover:

- County courthouse records going back seven years for every county of residence.
- Federal courthouse records going back seven years.
- The multistatecriminal database going back seven years.
- A National Sex Offender Registry screen.
- A Social Security trace, which ensures the number is valid and confirms names and addresses.
- Checks of existing motor vehicle records, as well as regular future checks.[59]

Critics, however, charge that the background checks aren't thorough enough because they do not include fingerprinting and processing through law enforcement agencies.

In July 2014, Uber also announced it had obtained a commercial insurance policy to provide $1 million of liability coverage per incident, as well as contingent comprehensive and collision insurance.[60] The new coverage applies to Uber's most widely used service, called UberX. (Commercial insurance already covered the company's other more specialized services such as black-car limo rides.)

In March 2015, Uber and the Property Casualty Insurers Association of America (PCI) announced model legislation for consideration by states that they jointly developed; 18 states have already passed laws that mirror the model, according to Robert Passmore, PCI's senior director for personal lines.

"Auto insurance is based on years and years of track records and loss history," says Passmore. "We don't have a lot of loss history behind these folks." Thus, says Passmore, it's especially important to have clear rules about what kinds of coverage are required.

Airbnb, too, has moved to provide insurance. As of January 2015, the company's Host Protection Insurance provides up to $1 million in coverage in the event a guest is injured on a host's property during a stay. The insurance applies only in the United States.[61]

Airbnb has also made agreements with some localities—including the District of Columbia, San Francisco, Phoenix, Portland, Ore., San Jose and Chicago—to collect taxes owed by hosts and pay them directly to the local government. While Airbnb did not respond to requests for comment, its website notes that these agreements make "the tax collection process easier for all parties involved."

"In many cases, these taxes were designed for hotels and folks with teams of lawyers and accountants, and the reality is that the person who's renting out his basement in Cleveland Park [in D.C.] once a month probably doesn't have tax experts on payroll," Nick Papas, an Airbnb spokesman, told a *Washington Post* reporter. "You shouldn't need a lawyer and a tax specialist if you want to rent out your house."[62]

According to Stephen Cordi, the deputy chief financial officer in the Office of Tax and Revenue in D.C., it was Airbnb that approached the city about making the arrangement to pay taxes.

"It's undoubtedly true that people particularly at the bottom end of this probably didn't know what to do," Cordi told *The Washington Post*. While individual Airbnb hosts should have been registering with the city and paying the taxes all along, he said, "this will eliminate the need for them to do that."

Still, according to Norton Francis, senior research associate at the Tax Policy Center, which provides research on taxes for the Urban Institute and the Brookings Institution, cities and states are "losing tax revenue because of these new forms" of services in the sharing economy. "The product isn't any different; it's the delivery," he said. "States are one step behind commerce in an effort to try to maintain their tax bases."[63]

LOOKING AHEAD

Rivals need to adapt

The technologies that define the sharing economy—the Internet-enabled applications that allow consumers to connect directly to service providers—are clearly not going to disappear.

"I think this is the beginning of the second-order issues of the sharing economy," says Koopman of the Mercatus Center. "The first-order issues were whether the sharing economy should exist at all. That debate is settled. The sharing economy is here to stay. Now comes the second wave of issues for sharing economy firms: How are the regulators going to treat them?"

Because the technologies driving the sharing economy are new, the old regulatory frameworks are no longer appropriate, most analysts agree. Even those who maintain the need for strong regulatory structures acknowledge that in some areas changes are warranted. "You can make plenty of arguments, and there some truth to them, that a lot of the regulations that we have in place are excessive," says Baker of the Center for Economic and Policy Research.

"Do you apply old regulations to new innovations or try to adapt and evolve the regulations to fit the market over time?" Koopman asks. "I think when you try to apply the old laws and the old rules to new innovation and new entrepreneurship, you end up hamstringing innovation. This should be an opportunity for everyone to critically reevaluate the regulations on the books."

In the meantime, say some analysts, it's time for traditional companies to adapt to the new technology environment. "The entry of these new platforms has put pressure on existing suppliers," economist Farronato says. "From the point of view of innovation, it is pressure for the better." She adds that as traditional companies adopt the new technologies—such as online review—old regulatory frameworks may no longer be needed. "It might be the case of the industry will actually evolve in a way that the regulatory environment will be more lax," she says.

While free market advocates worry about regulators stifling innovation, former Clinton administration Labor Secretary Robert Reich warns about the ramifications of an unfettered sharing economy.

"In effect, on-demand work is a reversion to the piece work of the nineteenth century—when workers had no power and no legal rights, took all the risks, and worked all hours for almost nothing," Reich wrote in an article on his website. "Uber drivers use their own cars, take out their own insurance, work as many hours as they want or can—and pay Uber a fat percent. Worker safety? Social Security? Uber says it's not the employer so it's not responsible."[64]

Of course, how consumers and investors will respond to higher costs caused by increased regulation of the sharing economy is unknown.

With respect to investors, they seem undeterred so far. "There have been very high investment levels within these areas where regulation hasn't been settled," says Eckhardt of the University of London.

Consumers' response, she says, may be more problematic. "When you start to see that competitive advantage eroding away, and prices rise, consumers may perceive [the companies] to be gouging," she says. "These so-called sharing-economy companies are, in a way, responsible for this because the way they tend to position themselves as, 'Oh, we're doing better for the world. We're somehow different than all of these regular companies.'"

Chronology

1990s	Technologies that will power the sharing economy appear, and pioneer e-commerce companies take advantage.
1991	The National Science Foundation (NSF), which controlled the Internet backbone, allows commercial access to the formerly government and academic network.
1992	E-commerce begins when Book Stacks Unlimited in Cleveland opens a website that supports credit card processing.

1994	Amazon is founded and would soon grow into a dominant e-commerce site.
1995	Craig Newmark launches an email distribution list that will be converted the next year into a website that allows people to buy and sell goods and to find jobs: craigslist.org. . . . eBay is founded as an online platform to connect individual sellers with individual buyers through online auctions. . . . NSF formally lifts its prohibition on commercial activity on the Web.
1999	Zipcar—an online car rental service—appears, with four cars stationed near subway stops in Cambridge and Boston, Mass.
2000–2007	**Early sharing-economy companies are founded.**
2003	The Freecycle Network goes online, allowing individuals and nonprofits to exchange goods they no longer need.
2004	Yochai Benkler, a Harvard law professor, publishes, "Sharing Nicely: On Shareable Goods and the Emergence of Sharing as a Modality of Economic Production," the first analysis of the modern sharing economy.
2005	Zopa, the world's first online peer-to-peer lending platform, debuts in London.
2007	Zimride, which became Lyft, begins offering on-demand rides; its drivers are independent contractors who own their own cars.
2008–Present	**Recession spurs growth of the sharing economy as regulators begin to take action.**
2008	Harvard Business School graduate student Shelby Clark launches RelayRides, a service that allows individuals to rent their personal cars to others. . . . Joe Gebbia and Brian Chesky, needing money to pay their rent, offer their living room online as a place for someone to sleep. A few days later, they launch www.airbedandbreakfast.com, which will soon become known as Airbnb.
2009	Kickstarter, a crowd-sourced platform for funding projects, opens. . . . UberCab, which will soon change its name to Uber, is founded in San Francisco.
2014	Colorado becomes the first state to pass legislation creating a statewide regulatory framework for "transportation network companies," such as Uber and Lyft. . . . In June, the California Labor Commissioner's Office rules that an Uber driver should be classified as an employee, not an independent contractor. . . . In October, the New York State Office of the Attorney General releases a report that finds that 72 percent of units booked over Airbnb in the state appeared to violate state and local laws. Within days, New York City files suit against two property owners.

(Continued)

(Continued)

| 2015 | On May 5, Uber announces it is ceasing operations in Kansas after that state passes legislation with stricter insurance requirements and background checks for drivers. . . . On May 12, the Santa Monica, Calif., City Council adopts a home-sharing ordinance that prohibits the rental of an entire unit for less than 30 days. The ordinance also requires hosts to obtain a business license and to pay a 14 percent hotel tax. . . . On May 26, San Francisco International Airport and the San Francisco Municipal Transportation Agency petition the California Public Utilities Commission to impose tighter regulations on ride-sharing companies. . . . On May 29, Nevada Gov. Brian Sandoval announces passage of a regulatory framework for ride-sharing services in the state; the framework includes a 3 percent tax on fares. . . . On June 18, Lyft agrees to pay the state of New York $300,000 to settle claims that it was in violation of state and municipal laws. The agreement also places tighter requirements on insurance for Lyft drivers, and requires the company to comply with state and local laws covering for-hire car services. |

PERSPECTIVE

Pro/Con: Dean Baker on Regulating the Sharing Economy

YES

SHOULD SHARING-ECONOMY COMPANIES BE BROUGHT INTO THE SAME REGULATORY FRAMEWORKS AS THEIR COMPETITORS?
Dean Baker
Economist, Co-founder of the Center for Economic and Policy Research

Written for SAGE Business Researcher, August 2015

Over many decades we have developed a long series of regulations that apply to taxi companies, hotels and other businesses that compete with upstart sharing-economy companies. These regulations cover a wide range of areas, including consumer protection, safety, worker protection and restrictions on discrimination based on race, gender and disability.

In some cases, these regulations are excessive, imposing unnecessary costs on business, which are in turn largely passed on to consumers. Some of the regulations were designed to protect the incumbents in the industry, most notably restrictions on the number of cabs that can be on the road. But most of these regulations do serve a public purpose. For this reason, it does not make sense to give the sharing-economy companies a pass, even if people order their service over the Internet. (For another perspective, see "Pro/Con: Christopher Koopman, Matthew Mitchell and Adam Thierer on Regulating the Sharing Economy.")

In the case of Uber, there should be guarantees that Uber's cars are safe, that passengers are covered by insurance in the event of an accident, that the drivers have good driving records, and that the drivers are not dangerous criminals who pose a threat to their passengers. This may not require the same sort of strict rules that are imposed on the traditional cab industry in most cities, but it does mean a mechanism should be in place to ensure that Uber meets basic standards.

Similarly, Uber drivers need the same sort of protections as other workers. This means they should be covered by minimum wage laws, overtime rules, workers' compensation and be insured not only when they have a rider in the car but also on their way to and from cab pick-ups. If this is too complicated for Uber to deal with, then they can be replaced by companies that are more computer-savvy.

Uber should be required to have a certain percentage of its cars handicap-accessible; the company also needs to either develop a mechanism for payment by customers without access to credit cards or to pay a fee to ensure that such people have access to taxi service.

Similarly, Airbnb facilities should not be fire traps and should comply with building and neighborhood rental codes. Airbnb must also take responsibility for ensuring that people have access to facilities it rents regardless of their race and ethnicity. We expect this of traditional hotels; Airbnb should be held to similar standards.

PERSPECTIVE

Pro/Con: Christopher Koopman, Matthew Mitchell and Adam Thierer on Regulating the Sharing Economy

NO

SHOULD SHARING-ECONOMY COMPANIES BE BROUGHT INTO THE SAME REGULATORY FRAMEWORKS AS THEIR COMPETITORS?

Christoper Koopman, Mathew Mitchell, and Adam Thierer
Research Fellows, Mercatus Center at George Mason University

Excerpted from testimony before the Federal Trade Commission, May 26, 2015

As the debate surrounding the sharing economy moves forward, policymakers must keep in mind that merely because regulations were once justified on the grounds of consumer protection does not mean they accomplished those goals or that they are still needed today. (For another perspective, see "Pro/Con: Dean Baker on Regulating the Sharing Economy.")

Markets, competition, reputational systems and ongoing innovation often solve problems better than regulation when they are given a chance to do so. There are two reasons for this. First, market imperfections create powerful profit opportunities for entrepreneurs who are able to find ways to correct them. Second, regulatory solutions too often undermine competition and lock in inefficient business models.

Exempting newcomers from traditional regulations could place incumbents at a disadvantage. Such regulatory asymmetries represent a legitimate policy problem. But the solution is not to discourage new innovations by simply rolling old regulatory regimes onto new technologies and sectors. The better alternative is to level the playing field by "deregulating down" to put everyone on equal footing, not by "regulating up" to achieve parity.

By trying to head off every hypothetical worst-case scenario, preemptive regulations actually discourage many best-case scenarios from ever coming about. For that reason, ex post remedies are often preferable to ex ante regulation. Private insurance, contracts, torts and product liability law, antitrust enforcement and other legal remedies can be utilized here when things go wrong, just as they are used in countless other segments of our economy.

The Internet and the information revolution have given rise to new online feedback mechanisms that have made it easier than ever for honesty to be enforced through strong reputational incentives. This has, in turn, alleviated many traditional concerns about informational deficiencies. With the recent growth of the sharing economy, even more robust reputational feedback mechanisms now exist that help consumers solve information problems and secure a greater voice in commercial interactions. These mechanisms have been integrated into the platforms connecting buyers and sellers and have become an essential feature of these sectors.

The Internet and real-time reputational feedback mechanisms should force a reevaluation of traditional regulations aimed at addressing perceived market failures based on asymmetric information. Such regulations have typically failed to improve consumer welfare and have undermined innovation and competition. This may explain why, when recently surveyed by PricewaterhouseCoopers, 64 percent of U.S. consumers said that in the sharing economy, peer regulation is more important than government regulation.

"FREE" AS A BUSINESS MODEL
Can companies thrive by giving away products and services?

Sharon O'Malley

EXECUTIVE SUMMARY

For a growing array of companies, giving their product away is now a business plan. Games, music, software—just about anything that can be digitally replicated and distributed via the Internet—all are available at no cost to consumers. Some businesses follow a cross-subsidy model, where one product or class of customer supports another. Some rely on free trials or on revenue from third parties such as advertisers. And other businesses are pursuing a "freemium" model, where the basic service is free of charge but upgrades cost. As the economy of free takes hold, companies and artists in some industries, such as music streaming, are pushing back against the pressure to offer their work for nothing. Among the questions now under debate: Is the freemium business model viable? Is free good for the economy? Can traditional businesses compete with free?

OVERVIEW

Since July 2015, anyone working on a PC just about anywhere has been reminded by constant pop-up ads that Microsoft's latest operating system, Windows 10, is ready for download—and that's it's free. Unlike prior Windows versions, which cost between $50 and $100, this one is gratis, just like the latest upgrades to Apple's operating systems and the Google Chrome Web browser, which has been free since its introduction in 2008.

Microsoft was a lonely holdout among the software giants when it came to converting its prize product from cash cow to complimentary. But the company finally—albeit reluctantly—embraced the inevitable: Comparable products from competitors who give them away for free have spoiled consumers. If every computer, smartphone and tablet user with an earlier Windows version upgrades to the latest edition, Microsoft will give away more than 1.5 billion free operating systems.[1]

"It will confirm people's expectations that you don't pay for operating systems," analyst Jan Dawson, of the Provo, Utah–based technology consulting firm Jackdaw Research, told *The New York Times*.[2]

Operating systems are not the only once-expensive product that people don't pay for any more. Like Microsoft, companies and whole industries involved in selling not only software

From *SAGE Business Researcher,*
November 23, 2015

but also music, video games, newspapers, cloud storage, apps and any other product that can be digitally replicated and distributed on the Internet are grappling with a major disruption: Their competitors are adopting business models at lightning speed that involve giving away some or all of a company's wares for free. Those that survive the disruption will find alternative ways to make money as they abandon the tried-and-true practice of selling what they create, because their customers can get the same products and services for free from a competitor. Those that resist are likely to fail in a free-product economy that has been growing stronger for a decade.

"The old saying that there's no such thing as a free lunch is not true anymore," says business consultant Peter Froberg, the founder of Copenhagen-based Freemium.org, which helps companies address the issue. "The company that's giving away that free lunch is paying for it."

"Free" isn't a single business model, and it's not new. Grocery stores have long offered complimentary bites of food to entice tasters, while shoe and clothing retailers for decades have advertised buy-one-get-one-free sales every holiday season. U.S. network television always has been free to watch. Nightspots have long let female patrons in for free on ladies' nights so men will flock to the bars and pay the cover charge. And over the last decade, technology products with household names such as Google, Dropbox, LinkedIn, Spotify, Skype and Facebook have cost consumers nothing as they have relied instead on advertisers or their other, paid product offerings to subsidize most of their users.

What's new is how prevalent—and how disruptive—giveaways have become as more businesses have embraced them and as consumers have come to expect them.

The disruption—to use the economists' term—is occurring mostly in industries whose products and services have become digital. That is, their makers no longer need to spend time and money manufacturing and shipping a physical product to their customers. Instead, they can digitally create the product once and share it online with an unlimited number of people while incurring little or no additional development, reproduction or distribution costs. In short, says Vineet Kumar, Yale School of Management professor of marketing, the recent explosion of free "is only for digital products, and there's a very good reason for that: It can work wherever the variable or marginal costs of serving the traditional customer are very low."

Still, says Fred Chen, an associate professor of economics at Wake Forest University, even a product with a very low production cost isn't free to produce or support for millions of users. "If you are a business," he says, "you are trying to make a profit. So you definitely can't give things away for free forever. If you don't generate revenue, you'll never make a profit."

And there's the irony of "free": Giveaways are helping businesses generate that profit. "The hope is: You offer something for free to people, they will try it, and maybe they will like it so much that they will be willing to pay money for it," Chen says. "Eventually, you expect people to pay."

Free games generate millions daily

Like any business model, "free" hasn't reaped profits for every company that has tried it. Google subsidiary YouTube, for example, attracted 1 billion users a month in 2014 and rang up $4 billion in revenue, yet it barely broke even.[3] Newspapers such as *The New York Times* gave away 100 percent of their content for free for years before erecting paywalls in response to dwindling revenues. Likewise, many digital start-ups that initially offered free access to their

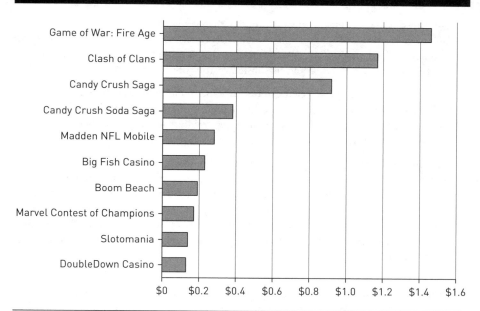

Top-grossing free iPhone games, by estimated daily revenue, in $US millions

"Game of War: Fire Age" generates more revenue than any other free iPhone app, bringing in $1.5 million daily as of the time of this snapshot. "Clash of Clans" ranked second with $1.17 million. Video game developer Activision Blizzard agreed to acquire King Digital, maker of both third-ranked Candy Crush Saga and fourth-ranked Candy Crush Soda Saga, for $5.9 billion in November 2015.

Note: Data as of Nov. 10, 2015.

Source: "Top Grossing iPhone Games," Think Gaming, updated Nov. 10, 2015, http://tinyurl.com/qjgnf9a

services switched to paid business models after failing to attract enough advertising or revenue through paid versions of their products to sustain their ventures.

And Joseph Farrell, CEO of BiTE Interactive, an app development company in Los Angeles, says "free" could have a downside for the broader economy: "It's having an unexpected negative consequence on our willingness to pay a fair price for fair work. As Millennials grow up, their concept is 'free' for everything."

Still, business strategists have identified four viable ways that companies are profiting, even as they offer free products:[4]

In the **cross-subsidy model**, a business gives away a product that won't work if the consumer doesn't buy a second product. For example, mobile phones used to be free to customers who paid for cell service. In a variation of this model, a company might charge higher prices to one group of customers, whose payment subsidizes another group.

Airlines, for example, use the proceeds from expensive first-class tickets to subsidize lower-priced coach seats.

The **three-party system** involves a product that is paid for by one group so another can use it for free. Network TV is the best example: Advertisers pay the networks for commercials that viewers, who pay nothing, watch as part of programming. Newspapers use this model, as do Google and its subsidiary YouTube.

Apple Music is the latest big business to experiment with the **free trial**, offering 90 days of free music streaming before cutting off customers who decide not to subscribe for $9.99 a month. The technology goliath reportedly had 11 million free users within five weeks of its June 29 launch.[5]

Freemium is boosting bottom lines in the digital industries of music, video games, social media, cloud storage and news, and has become one of the most common business models in use by Web-based industries. Companies offer a valuable, basic service for free—to as many users as possible—and reserve special upgrades for those who pay a fee. Dropbox, for example, allows users to store up to 2 gigabytes of data, which is more than enough for most people, for free. But those who need more space for photos and videos can get it for $9.99 a month.

Businesses that have attracted paying customers and advertisers by giving their products away have turned whole industries upside down. Craigslist, a mammoth classified ad website, tore the business model of American newspapers to shreds after it started offering free online ads in 1995. Classified ad revenue in the newspaper industry plummeted 70 percent between 2000 and 2009, from $19.6 billion to roughly $6 billion, revenue the news industry no longer had available to spend on reporting and printing the news.[6] The emergence of online booking sites that invite travelers to search for and reserve airline tickets and hotels led to the shuttering of almost 62 percent of travel agency locations in the United States between the mid-1990s and 2013, the same year job site CareerCast included "travel agent" on its list of "useless jobs."[7]

Those industries, Froberg says, "are dying because they have a production and distribution model for a different era. Now, that model doesn't necessarily make sense."

The pain involved with restructuring a bricks-and-mortar business for duplication and delivery online isn't dissimilar to what horse-and-buggy makers suffered when the Model T automobile debuted in 1908,

Photo by Harry Shipler

1910 Ford Model T

Froberg says.[8] Progress, he notes, is inevitable. So is the growing use of technology to produce and deliver goods and services at lower and lower costs—and then to give them away in an effort to hook enough paying customers to make a business profitable.

As economists, business owners and consultants consider the status of the free economy, below are some of the issues being debated.

WEIGHING THE ISSUES

Is the freemium business model viable?

LinkedIn, the 13-year-old business networking site that became a publicly traded corporation in 2011, is worth approximately $27 billion.[9] Dropbox, a private company, is an online file cabinet for documents and digital photos, and it was worth an estimated $10 billion in January 2014.[10]

The list of similarly situated companies is long: Music-streaming radio website Spotify, a privately owned company, is valued at $8.5 billion.[11] Spotify competitor Pandora, which is publicly traded: $2.5 billion.[12] Classified ad website Craigslist, private: nearly $3 billion.[13] Gaming giant Zynga, publicly traded: $2.2 billion.[14] Internet phone service Skype sold to Microsoft in 2011 for $8.5 billion.[15] The parent of dating site Match.com went public in November 2015, selling stock at a level that valued the company at $4.2 billion; the stock price jumped more than 20 percent in the first day of trading.[16]

Costs deter potential subscribers

Aside from their financial heft, these companies have something else in common: They subscribe to the freemium model of business and marketing, offering their basic services for free to millions of users and charging a subscription fee to those willing to pay for premium features.

While no organization keeps track of how many companies use the freemium model, economists estimate that freemium is quickly becoming the business model of choice for entrepreneurs in the digital marketplace.

Yale's Kumar calls the freemium strategy "cutting edge." "Companies should be paying attention to it," he says.

Its concept is simple, yet not intuitive: Businesses offer their high-quality digital products for free to anyone who wants them—and the successful ones draw tens of millions of takers. The companies make money by converting a small percentage of those customers—often just 1 percent to 5 percent—into paying subscribers, and to them, they offer extras, including ad-free music streaming (Spotify); computer-to-landline phone calls (Skype); or more gigabytes of cloud storage space (Dropbox). The more "freeloaders" who take advantage of the basic service, the bigger the pool of potential paying customers. And some convert larger proportions of that population into paying subscribers: One-quarter of Spotify's 60 million active customers, for example, pay for subscriptions.[17]

A freemium model, advocates say, can drive faster growth of revenue and profit than a system with a single, paid tier. And it can do it cheaply: John Tschohl, president of the Service

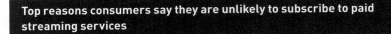

Top reasons consumers say they are unlikely to subscribe to paid streaming services

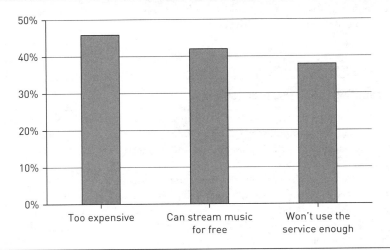

Forty-six percent of American consumers surveyed say they are unlikely to pay for any digital music streaming subscription because such services are too expensive. Slightly smaller shares say they won't subscribe because they can stream music for free (42 percent) or will not use the service often enough (38 percent).

Note: Based on survey of 3,305 American consumers from July 18 to Aug. 3, 2015; respondents could choose multiple reasons.

Source: "Nielsen Music 360 Report 2015 Highlights," Nielsen, September 2015, p. 6, http://tinyurl.com/ot3kzrw

Quality Institute, a Minneapolis-based customer service strategy and training organization, says a freemium strategy can whittle a company's marketing budget. "It brings a lot of eyeballs," he says, that otherwise might never have given a second look to a product if it hadn't been free. Companies, he says, "underestimate the power of price," while customers "value a price of 'free.'"

Self-titled "start-up guy" Dmitri Leonov, vice president of growth at SaneBox, a Boston-based $7-a-month online email organization service, on the other hand, said most business owners "are underestimating how difficult it is to make money when you offer your product for free."[18] He said the freemium model treats customers as a marketing cost, and that works for businesses such as LinkedIn and Skype, which he called "rare exceptions in a sea of start-ups. But because of a handful of wildly successful examples of freemium companies, most start-ups assume this model will work for them as well. . . . In most cases, this is simply not true."

A case in point: When DocuSign, an electronic-signature service, began in 2003, it offered a free product in an effort to attract as many "eyeballs" as possible in a short time. But its free, basic service proved to be all that nonpaying customers needed, so very few of them upgraded to the paid version.[19] After abandoning freemium and advertising a two-week free trial instead, the company attracted fewer customers, but those customers were more likely to be serious about the product and to upgrade at the end of the trial. Today, the company has millions of paid subscribers and is valued at $3 billion.[20]

Freemium, Leonov said, is a "take-it-home-and-keep-it" model that reaps few paying customers for a business. He advocates a free trial instead, noting that more than one-quarter of SaneBox customers who enroll in the free trial sign up for a paid subscription once it expires. "The remaining 75 percent leave," he said, "and we don't have to support them."[21]

According to Leonov, "If you're not charging money for your product, then your users are your product."[22] For some businesses—Facebook, for example—that strategy has translated into success, but Leonov said those successes do not come easily.

Kumar, on the other hand, says most freemium failures have a few things in common. First, like DocuSign, they give away too much. "If there is no incentive for the customers to upgrade to the paid version," he says, "they will use the free version."

The freemium dating app Tinder and the billing-management software provider Chargify found the same thing: The free version of their products gave users all they needed, and the upgrade did not add enough value to convince users to pay for it.[23] After nearly going bankrupt in 2010, the year-old Chargify switched to a paid-subscription service and became profitable within two years. Immediately after Tinder limited its free offering and enriched its premium features, the app's owner, IAC/InteractiveCorp., reported higher-than-expected subscription rates and profits.[24]

The free product has to be robust enough to attract users, but, Kumar says, businesses should not focus more on accumulating free users than they do on converting them to paid subscribers. He points to *The New York Times*, which, when it put up its paywall in 2011, allowed online readers to view 20 articles a month before the news site asked them to buy subscriptions. When few of them did, the publisher cut the number of free articles in half. In June, the newspaper enrolled its 1 millionth subscriber.

Is free good for the economy?

Giving away products for free—whether for 30 days or for an unlimited time with the option to pay for an upgrade—is forcing companies to focus more on quality and innovation, says BiTE Interactive's Farrell. Product innovation, he says, is good for the economy, as it both stimulates and satisfies consumer demand.

The introduction of software into areas that previously did not rely on it has provided much of the push toward a free business model in industries whose products are suited for digital duplication. That, in turn, "shifted the power dynamic from the suppliers to the consumers," Farrell says, because users who tire of one product—free or paid—can easily find a similar one they might like better.

In addition, the ease with which manufacturers and software developers can use the Internet to share mass quantities of their free, digital goods and services has cut out part of the distribution chain that manufacturers traditionally used to get their wares to market.

"The way we used to supply software for apps was, we built it, we talked to [consumer electronics retailer] Best Buy, we convinced them to sell it, and then they would sell it to their customers," Farrell explains. "So Best Buy was our customer. Best Buy said what we had to do or they wouldn't sell it. So the very few large megacorporations decided what was best for all of us."

Economists agree that freemium as a business model has started to disrupt the tried-and-true money-making operations of some large corporations because those established companies are not providing as much value to customers as firms that must constantly impress huge quantities of consumers. When just 1 percent to 5 percent of a product's players, readers or users are paying for it, they say, it has to be special enough to persuade millions—or billions—of people to try it out for free.

Free digital products, Farrell says, will force innovation on industries both online and physical that "haven't innovated in decades"—or force them out of business.

That innovation is already happening. Farrell points to dashboard navigation systems for which car dealers charge up to $5,000. "Your $700 phone is so much better and it updates every day," Farrell says. "Why would you pay $5,000 for a navigation system that does the same thing as a $700 phone" whose main purpose—as a phone—satisfies another, even more-important need and offers driving directions for free? Even with their larger, less-distracting big screens, sales of in-dash navigation systems—and other factory-installed auto electronics—have suffered a six-year-long decline in sales.[25]

Likewise, Amazon, which offers free shipping on most orders of at least $35, is pushing creative boundaries as it concocts ways to save money on deliveries so it can offer more of them for free. The company, which ships approximately 3.5 million packages a day, is pushing for Federal Aviation Administration approval to use unmanned drone aircraft for deliveries and is testing a plan to turn people into occasional couriers to drop off parcels in their own neighborhoods.[26]

A conveyor belt at Amazon, a company that offers free shipping on most orders over $35.

Plus, notes economist Peter Fishman, vice president of analytics for the online San Francisco human resources software firm Zenefits, what has become free online is putting upward pressure on some prices in the physical world.

For instance, streaming-music services such as Spotify, Pandora and Apple Music allow listeners to enjoy songs for little or no cost, a model that has, along with peer-to-peer file sharing and low-cost iTunes downloads, disrupted traditional sales of CDs. Musicians and producers are attempting to fill the financial gap.[27] Fishman points out that the price of attending a rock concert has skyrocketed—singer Bruno Mars was charging up to $250 for tickets to a December 2015 performance in Las Vegas.[28]

The concept is a variation of the kind of "price discrimination" airlines have practiced for years, Fishman notes: The very expensive first-class tickets that a dozen or so well-heeled fliers purchase on a 140-seat plane allow the airline to charge far less to travelers who fly in the more crowded, less-luxurious coach section. Applied to music, price discrimination allows those who can't afford the price of a concert ticket to enjoy Mars' music online because it's free.

Price discrimination, Fishman says, "is good. . . . It means two different people [of different means] can ride the plane. You've created more utility in the world."

Similarly, the technology behind the free economy lowers the barriers to entry for underfunded artists, programmers, writers and others. They can get what they create in front of millions of Internet users without having to raise large amounts of money up front to actually manufacture or market a product. "It's become much easier to start up a business with very little funding," says Yale's Kumar.

A lot of these companies would not start up otherwise, he says, which "increases the degree of entrepreneurship in the economy tremendously and enables a company to succeed without the backing of corporations like banks or venture capitalists."

That young programmer might not make any money for months or even years as she waits for unpaid users to convert to paid subscribers, Kumar acknowledges. "But if you were working in your parents' basement and wanted to create an app 20 years ago, you had to convince a software developer to bundle it or get in with Walmart," he says. "The distinction I see now is you can succeed without that."

Can traditional businesses compete with free?

"Never underestimate the power of somebody giving away a product for free," says online video technician Jonathan G. Mirow, former owner of a company called BroadbandVideo .com. The success of YouTube, he says, put his company out of business in 2008.

Just three years earlier, says Mirow, he and his colleagues "were looking at YouTube and laughing" as the newcomer to the online video space allowed its customers to upload videos for free. "We didn't even perceive of them as a threat to our business," says Mirow, now the director of video products for Denver-based technology company Epiphany Ai.

BroadbandVideo.com's business allowed its "hundreds and hundreds" of clients, including the Denver Broncos, Children's Hospital Colorado, several city and state governments, and many public speakers, to upload videos. It charged them $20 per upload, which repaid the company for leasing servers and bandwidth, encoding the videos, managing an office and delivering streaming video on the Web. "It looked an awful lot like YouTube does today," Mirow says.

The difference, of course, was that it wasn't free. And over the next couple of years, all of BroadbandVideo.com's customers closed their accounts and signed on with the newcomer. "They were simply giving it away," Mirow says. "There was no way for us to compete as a company with this vast-scale, cloud-based system." YouTube is owned by Google, which does not report its earnings separately.[29]

Venture capitalist David G. Cohen, founder of Boulder, Colo.–based Techstars, agrees with Mirow: "It's hard to compete with free," he says. "Customers still want the best product, but charging people for something is friction, and that rarely works against a free competitor."

But Wake Forest's Chen contends that companies that have been ruined by competitors with free products might have salvaged their organizations if they had figured out alternative money-making strategies—the same ones that made their competitors successful. For example, musicians and music producers have stepped up their sales of souvenirs such as T-shirts and have raised the price of their concert tickets to compensate for the death of CD sales, which was helped by free, online music-streaming services such as Pandora and Spotify. Newspapers that have so far managed to survive in an era of limitless free online information are slowly embracing a freemium model that allows readers a few free articles a month but then charges them a subscription fee.

"If you're a farmer and you're growing oranges," Chen says, "and everybody else has figured out how to grow oranges, you can't make money on growing oranges. You have to figure out what other products you can sell that are related to oranges: orange juice, marmalade, orange slicers. You can't sell the same thing you used to sell and make money. You've got to go forward."

Plus, says Chen, free products and services are a symptom of competition, not the cause of it. "If you go into the business blaming free, you're not on point," he says. "More competition is what's driving prices down—down to the free level. Something in the market condition has changed that's making it easier for competitors to come in and compete."

The driver behind free—aided by the low cost of digital distribution—is the abundance of products in crowded fields such as information, games, music and cloud storage, Chen says. "To get ahead, you have to have scarcity. You have to have something different. You have to come up with a new product or a new service."

In addition, the company trying to save itself will have to offer its original, abundant product for free.

In a five-year study of nondigital companies that tried to compete with rivals offering free products, three Brigham Young University professors found none that prevailed, even after giving their own goods away. The companies' failures weren't due as much to their competitors' strengths as to their own reluctance to embrace a free, digital business model and let go of their traditional models, the researchers said.

When facing off against a competitor with a successful free product, the professors wrote in *Harvard Business Review*, an established business's knee-jerk decision to introduce a free offering of its own could be wrong.

Instead, the authors recommended that "incumbents" step back and assess the strength of the threat when a competitor begins to offer a free service. That threat is immediate if the established business starts bleeding customers at a rate of 5 percent or more a year as they defect to a competitor with a comparable—but free—product. In that case, the researchers would advise the company's owners to quickly adopt a free business model of their own. If they don't do so, the academics said, "they will continue to deteriorate sharply without a fundamental rethinking of their business model."

But if fewer than 5 percent of customers defect, it is possible that the competitor is finding its nonpaying customers from a source other than the established business. In that case, the professors advised, the business owner can delay a wholesale change in business strategy and observe the impact over time. It could turn out that the competitor will not be able to convert its nonpaying clients into subscribers, and its business—not the established company's—is the one that will fail.[30]

Still, Mirow says he won't hedge his bets if he ever again faces a competitor who subscribes to the free model of doing business. His advice to business owners: "I would recommend that every company look at: Is there a way that another company could come along and put this free model to work and own this space?"

BACKGROUND

Free lunch

In the late 19th century, there was such a thing as a free lunch.

In 1875 New Orleans, saloons served complimentary lunches every day with the hope that their patrons would stick around and pay to drink alcohol at 15 cents per glass. Some diners drank and others did not, but one saloon owner, who acknowledged to *The New York Times* that it cost him $30 to $40 a day to serve the free meal, said "he would lose half his customers if he discontinued the practice."[31]

Free lunches were considered "a great leveler of social classes [because] when a man takes up a position before [a lunch buffet counter] he must give up all hope of appearing either dignified or consequential," *The Times* reported back then.[32] But as the practice faded into history, "free" became less "social leveler" and more "sales gimmick."[33] Still, many of today's effective marketing strategies involving "free" have roots in the19th and early 20th centuries.

Get this, buy that

As one of America's most popular desserts got its start in 1902, so did "one of the most powerful marketing tools of the 20th century: giving away one thing to create demand for another," said author and former *Wired* magazine editor Chris Anderson.[34]

The giveaway was an illustrated recipe book that suggested dozens of ways to use Jell-O in salads and as a dessert. The product that those books created demand for, of course, was Jell-O.

Jell-O was patented as a food in 1845, but sales never took off. Half a century and a couple of owners later, orator Francis Woodward of New York invested heavily in advertising the dried gelatin-in-a-box and sent "dapper-looking salesmen" from door to door to teach house-wives how to make the treat by adding boiling water. They distributed millions of free copies of the cookbook, and they handed out Jell-O desserts to immigrants arriving at Ellis Island.[35] Over the next 25 years, Woodward's company printed and distributed nearly 250 million free recipe books all over America.[36]

"From early on, Jell-O's marketers were masters at promotion," according to the nostalgia website Digital Deli.[37] Their decision to give away one thing whose use depended on another became the foundation of a marketing practice still widely used today: the loss leader.

Around the same time, inventor King Gillette of Boston was busy creating the world's first disposable razor blade and the razor handle to use with it. Like Jell-O, the product did not sell well at first. Eventually, Gillette persuaded the Army to buy millions of razors—at deeply discounted prices—to distribute to soldiers, and struck deals with banks, which gifted them to new depositors in "shave and save" campaigns. Likewise, the razors—useless without the disposable blades, which were not free—were packaged with products ranging from chewing gum to coffee.

"By selling cheaply to partners who would give away the razors . . . he was creating demand for disposable blades," Anderson wrote in his 2009 book, *Free: The Future of a Radical Price.*[38]

Although the banks and coffee distributors gave the razors away, Gillette did not. Yet his marketing strategy is widely touted as the grandfather of the "free" business model in which companies charge nothing—or next to it—for one product that depends on another to operate. For example, cellphone companies used to give away phones, which were useless unless their owners bought a calling plan. Coffee vendors sometimes install high-quality coffeemakers in offices, but charge their clients for the coffee pods.

Try one

As Woodward and Gillette learned during their struggles to introduce products to the public, giveaways are an effective way to capture the attention of a potential consumer base. But not all early businesses offered one free product to sell another.

Soap manufacturer Benjamin T. Babbitt is widely considered the first businessman to offer large quantities of free samples of his product with the hope that people who tried it would like it and buy some. His late-19th century ads for 1776 Powder contained the tagline: "A fair trial is all I ask for it."[39]

Nearly 40 years later, the owners of Wall Drug in South Dakota employed the "free sample" strategy in much the same way as those early saloon proprietors: The druggists offered free ice water to thirsty tourists traveling to Mount Rushmore. As word got around, Wall Drug became nationally known as a fixture on the road to the famous monument.[40]

Radio days

The fledgling radio industry, meanwhile, was struggling to come up with a way to pay for broadcasts, which had been free to listeners.[41] *Radio Broadcast* magazine held a contest asking listeners to come up with a solution. They proposed taxes, NPR-style listener donations and licensing fees.[42]

Radio advertising, which became the dominant solution, slowly took hold in the early to mid-1920s. The first paid commercials were one-offs at local stations in 1922 in New York, Seattle and Medford Hillside, Mass., a Boston suburb. The earliest radio station to sell purchased time, WEAF in New York, charged the Hawthorne Court Apartments in Jackson Heights $50 for a 10-minute ad.[43] By 1926, NBC had identified radio as a viable medium for advertising—joining newspapers, billboards and magazines. And after AT&T's telephone wires facilitated coast-to-coast transmission of radio broadcasts, a national market for radio advertising was born.[44] Free-to-watch television followed suit, and decades later, so did ad-supported websites across the world.

Not just a marketing gimmick

Over the next several decades, businesses used "free" in various forms to get products into the hands of new customers or to entice patrons to visit their stores.

By the 1990s, however, after a decade during which the public became used to working with personal computers and the Internet made its debut with the general public, "free" became less of a marketing gimmick and more of a survival strategy. By mid-decade, newspapers had begun publishing free articles on their websites in response to an abundance of free, online information. Web browsers such as Netscape became free, Google offered free email accounts, and software manufacturers started giving away some versions of their products for free. A few video game developers started offering free-to-play versions of their games in the late 1990s. Between 1993 and 2006, AOL distributed—via mail, in cereal boxes and even on seats at the Super Bowl—more than 1 billion CDs with free trial software and a way to access the Internet for a few hours.[45] Anderson, in his book, identified approximately 50 other ways in which businesses employed "free" in their marketing efforts, including selling paid advertisers access to an audience.[46]

Digital disruption

By the early- to mid-2000s, the widespread use of the Internet had substantially changed the business model for companies whose products could be digitized and distributed online. Instead of CDs containing software, for example, software became available for download from the Internet.

By the second half of the decade, hundreds of companies had started giving away those digital products. Although no organization keeps track of how many companies use some version of a "free" business model, those with digital products—or products that could be digitized, even if the industry resisted the change, such as newspapers—were forced to embrace "free" or forfeit their customers to competitors who did.

In a 2006 blog post, venture capitalist Fred Wilson defined the fast-growing business model that online companies such as Skype and Box increasingly had adopted: "Give your service away for free, possibly ad supported but maybe not, acquire a lot of customers very efficiently through word of mouth, referral networks, organic search marketing, etc., then offer premium-priced, value-added services or an enhanced version of your service to your customer base."[47]

At the end of that blog post, he invited readers to suggest names for the business model. The following week, he chose the winning label: freemium, coined by his associate Jarid Lukin of Alacra.

CURRENT SITUATION

Streaming wars

As testament that the concept of "free" as a business model is ever-evolving, two big names in music are challenging the notion that fans are not willing to pay to listen.

Apple Music and rapper Jay Z both introduced music-streaming services in 2015 that charge customers to listen to music online.

The effort, at least for Jay Z, is a rail against free music-streaming services such as Spotify, Pandora and Rdio, which allow users to listen to millions of tunes online for nothing and pay the musicians royalties that the rapper has said are too slim. His venture, Tidal, pays artists 75 percent of revenue, while Spotify shares 70 percent.[48] Tidal's competitors also offer ad-free listening to users who pay a monthly subscription fee that ranges from $3.99 for limited Rdio access to $9.99 for Spotify's premium tier. Tidal charges $9.99 to $19.99 with no ads and no free option.

"What Jay Z is doing is a backlash against free," says Wake Forest's Chen, who specializes in the business of music. "But that misses the point. If you don't like what's happening, you shouldn't be responding to free. You should be responding to the underlying market conditions"—which, Chen says, changed when the Internet made it possible to distribute digitized music for next to nothing.

Apple also competes with free music streamers, but its foray into that space is not a push against free, Chen says. "Apple is trying to capitalize on the large number of people who have bought music on iTunes," he says. "They're trying to bank on that and trying to outcompete the other people offering free services."

Apple Music, which came online on June 30, offers a free, three-month trial. By the time the free period ended for the first crop of samplers on Sept. 30, the streaming newcomer had attracted 15 million listeners, and 7.5 million of them had not deactivated its auto-pay function, indicating that they likely will agree to pay $9.99 a month for subscriptions.[49]

But a mid-August report by consumer research company Music Watch claimed that 48 percent of those who tried Apple abandoned it before their 90-day trials expired. Of the remaining listeners, however, 64 percent indicated they were "extremely or very likely" to pay for subscriptions once their trials ended.[50] Apple has not published its results.

Jay Z's Tidal, which is co-owned by 15 musicians, including the rapper's wife, Beyonce, and superstars Madonna and Rihanna, launched in March 2015 and has not fared as well.[51] In a series of tweets shortly after the service began, Jay Z claimed Tidal had 770,000 subscribers.[52] That compares with Spotify's 75 million users, including 20 million paid subscribers.[53] Still, Jay Z said in one tweet: "Tidal is doing just fine."

Yet many of his music-industry colleagues disagree. In a Billboard survey of top music executives, 71 percent said Tidal will be out of business within a year, and another 17 percent gave it two years.[54] Just 12 percent indicated the start-up is, as Jay Z said in another April 2015 tweet, "here for the long haul."[55]

Chen says he expects Apple Music will outperform Tidal, but he's not as sure it will displace free streaming services. "I'm not going to jump on the Apple bandwagon right now and say Apple is definitely going to dominate the market," he says, "because it's tough to compete with somebody who's offering the same thing for free."

In fact, the Billboard survey found that Apple Music so far has lured few of its competitors' customers: 11 percent of Apple Music listeners also listen to the free versions of Spotify, while 6 percent are also Pandora users, Billboard reported.[56]

Still, music executives seem to be in Apple's court. Bloomberg Business noted, "Many in the music industry believe that Apple is likely to become the dominant streaming player, setting the rules of the new format just as it did 12 years ago with digital downloads when it created the iTunes Music Store."[57]

Game on

In the world of free-to-play games, courts and regulators rather than market forces are setting the rules.

In response to parents' complaints that their children unwittingly spent thousands of dollars on upgrades and extras while playing freemium-style digital games, the Federal Trade Commission (FTC) and the European Commission have pressured Apple, Google and Amazon—whose online stores sell mobile apps and games—to become more transparent about what is not free in the so-called free-to-play games they stock.

Among the complaints: A Belgian teenager last fall reportedly used his grandfather's credit card to purchase $46,000 worth of what a digital game calls "gold" to spend on upgrades and extras over several months. The youth's mother told investigators he did not realize he was spending real money.[58]

His story is extreme but not unique: When 5-year-old Danny Kitchen of Bristol, U.K., asked his parents for permission to use their iPad so he could play a free online game, his father punched in his password and left him alone with the tablet. Within 10 minutes, the child had spent $2,500 on digital darts, bombs and other virtual weapons for sale in the app as part of the game.[59] Likewise, a 9-year-old Pennsylvania girl spent $200 on in-app purchases while playing free-to-play games. Her case triggered a class-action suit against Apple—she bought the virtual items through iTunes—in 2011.[60] The Cupertino, Calif., computer giant settled the complaint for $32.5 million in 2013 by making refunds to parents who proved that the purchases were unauthorized and by sending $5 iTunes gift cards to other users whose kids made in-app purchases. Likewise, as part of a settlement with the FTC, Google agreed last year to refund $19 million to Android owners whose children made in-app purchases.[61]

The European Commission, the executive body of the European Union, urged Google and Apple to alter the way they label games, as calling them "free" can mislead users who do not understand that players must pay for some of the games' components. The commission also said the apps should not entice children to buy items or persuade their parents to make those purchases for the young players.[62]

In response, Google agreed to remove the word "free" from games that offer in-app purchases and set defaults so every purchase requires authorization.[63] Apple, which in 2011 started requiring a password for every purchase, responded by saying its parental controls already "go far beyond the features of others in the industry."[64]

The European Commission did not name Amazon in its missive, but the FTC sued the online retailer in July 2014, saying that it failed to prevent children from making millions of dollars of unauthorized in-app purchases with their parents' credit cards.[65] Amazon sought to dismiss the lawsuit, contending the children had actual or apparent legal authority and that the FTC was trying to create a new legal standard. A U.S. District judge in December rejected that argument, enabling the lawsuit to continue.[66]

Some in the video game industry have argued that parents, and not game sellers or developers, are responsible for policing their children's purchases.

"I can't buy what Mom and Dad don't want me to buy because it's their phone" that is needed to make the purchase, BiTE Interactive's Farrell says. "If Mom and Dad give me a phone and a credit card, well, that's on Mom and Dad."

LOOKING AHEAD

Consumer expectations

Car buyers in the distant future might drive new sedans and sports cars off the lot without paying a dime—as long as they can tolerate an unending barrage of video and audio ads that would serve as the trade-off for a sticker price of zero. Airline executives might accept free jet engines equipped with software that will collect data that the manufacturer could sell elsewhere or use to build better, more expensive equipment.

"I could see that happening," Yale's Kumar says. "Free is going to be sustainable as long as you can monetize it some other way."

As more commerce moves online, the public's expectation will grow that more goods and services should be free. In response, manufacturers of physical goods will discover how to profit in creative ways that don't involve asking their customers—the bulk of them, at least—to pay.

Nevertheless, Kumar says, "Our economy is still made up of a lot of sectors that produce physical, tangible goods, where free is going to be difficult to implement." Industrial equipment, for instance, is unlikely to join the inventory of free products, he says. And, he adds, even five years from now, free won't be pervasive in the nondigital world.

However, Mirow, the onetime video company owner, says he expects what others see as the near-impossible. "Nobody could have predicted 10 years ago that video would be free, email would be free, browsers would be free," he says. "You would have said, 'That's not a sustainable business model.'"

Kumar says the digital economy will continue to grow quickly. "Every aspect of our life is becoming digitized," he says, "and everywhere you see digital, we know that digital has very low marginal costs. . . . To the degree that our economy is going to become digitized, we're going to see more free. Free and digital are increasingly intertwined."

He asks, "But will it dominate the entire economy? I don't think so."

Yet "free" is not finished disrupting the physical world, says Fishman at Zenefits. "How can the physical world compete? If I can go to the arcade and play pinball for a quarter vs. playing on my computer for free, I'll play on my computer," he says. "We will see a shift away from physical goods."

But the "free" of the future might look different, even in the digital world, Wake Forest's Chen says. "I don't think what we're seeing now is set in stone. The music market, for example, is still evolving; people are still figuring out what is the best way to make money off of music."

He says, "I don't think what we're seeing right now is anything like what we'll be seeing in the future."

Mirow agrees. "From a business perspective, I don't know what the next thing is that will be given away for free, but I know it will come out of left field," Mirow says. "Whatever industry it occurs in, it will probably blindside those involved in it."

Chronology

1800s	**"Free" emerges as a strategy to attract paying customers.**
1850s	Soap manufacturer Benjamin T. Babbitt becomes the first businessman to give away large quantities of free samples of a product as part of a marketing effort.
1875	Saloon keepers in New Orleans and elsewhere serve free lunches to patrons who they hope will buy alcoholic drinks.
1900–1920s	**Manufacturers give away products that depend on other, paid items to operate.**
1902	The owners of Jell-O distribute millions of free recipes to introduce homemakers to the dessert and how to make it. . . . King Gillette sells discounted razors to banks and other companies, which give them away. Gillette sells the blades separately. This becomes the foundation of the common business practice of giving away one product that relies on another, which is not free.
1922	First paid commercials air on radio stations in New York, Seattle and Medford Hillside, Mass., to support broadcasts offered free to listeners.
1960s–1980s	**Computers emerge as time- and money-savers.**
1969	The first host-to-host message, a precursor to email, was sent via the Internet.
1970	Intel co-founder Gordon Moore posits that processor power and speeds will double every two years as the price halves.
1980s	Software developers become the earliest adopters of the as-yet unnamed freemium business models, offering "lite" versions of their software on floppy disks that do not allow for printing or saving. Customers could use the software as is or buy a version with the premium features.
1984	Motorola sells the first cellphone to consumers. Cellular companies later provide some phones free to customers willing to sign via monthly service contracts.
1990s	**Digital disruption of mainstream businesses begins.**
1990	George Gilder writes the book *Microcosm* about the economics of bits, claiming that every iteration of a function diminishes in cost. . . . The first Web page appears on the open Internet.
1993	AOL begins giving away CDs containing a free trial of its software and limited online access.
1995	Craigslist launches free, online classified ads, leading to a financial disruption of the newspaper industry.

(Continued)

(Continued)

1996	Major newspapers such as *The New York Times* and *The Wall Street Journal* start websites, offering some content for free. . . . *The Village Voice* stops charging a cover price. . . . *Furcadia*, one of the earliest free-to-play digital video games, is introduced.
1998	Netscape becomes the first Web browser to be offered for free; others followed. The company also publicly releases its browser code, taking free, open-source software mainstream.
2000s	**Online products increasingly become free.**
2005	*The New York Times* begins charging readers $49.95 per year for online access to columns by its most popular writers through a subscription called TimesSelect; remaining content was free. The program ended in 2007, and all *Times* content was again free.
2006	Venture capitalist Fred Wilson brings early attention to the as-yet unnamed freemium business model in a widely read blog. . . . E-commerce specialist Jarid Lukin coins the word "freemium" to describe a business model that offers a basic product for free, but charges for a more premium version of it.
2009	Chris Anderson, then-editor of *Wired* magazine, popularizes the free business model with his book, *Free: The Future of a Radical Price*.
2010s	**Businesses settle in with the "freemium" business model and begin to profit.**
2011	*The New York Times* becomes the first major U.S. newspaper to restrict its website to paid subscribers after 20 free views per month. . . . LinkedIn, Pandora and Zynga—companies using the freemium business model—file initial public offerings (IPOs). . . . Parents file class-action lawsuit against Apple, alleging children do not understand that not all parts of its free-to-play video games are free. Apple settles the suit for $32.5 million in 2013.
2015	*The New York Times* sells its 1 millionth paid online subscription.

Q&A: Peter Froberg on "Freemium"

"COMPUTERS MAKE IT POSSIBLE TO DELIVER GREAT VALUE AT A VERY LOW MARGINAL COST"
Peter Froberg
Founder
Freemium.org

As popular brands like Google, Facebook, LinkedIn, Dropbox and Pandora flourish without charging their customers, more Internet start-ups will be testing "free" as a business model with the hope that it will work for them. Peter Froberg, a business consultant and the founder of Copenhagen-based Freemium.org, says the use of "free" also will increase as more businesses discover ways to make what they sell digital—so the cost of sharing their products is low enough to offer them for nothing. As the free economy evolves, Froberg says, "other kinds of free" could emerge that "will be more interesting."

Froberg spoke with SAGE Business Researcher reporter Sharon O'Malley about the strength of "free" as a business model. This is an edited transcript of that conversation.

Is free a viable business model?

Asking if free is a viable business model is a bit like asking if objects made from metal can float or fly. It seems counterintuitive. However, simply because of the vast amount of planes and ships most of us have seen, few would dispute that it is possible. This, however, does not mean that all objects made of metal can fly or float. Nor indeed does it mean that metal is always the best choice. Free has proven to be a viable business model through the sheer number of businesses that have used it with success. If you have doubts, just look at the revenue numbers from companies such as Google or Skype.

They say there's no such thing as a free lunch. Has that changed?

The conventional business wisdom is that there is no such thing as a free lunch. This term originates in the old West, where cowboys were drawn into a saloon to buy drinks with the promise of a "free lunch." However, this lunch was only available to those who were drinking. Thus, it was not really free. A narrow interpretation of this saying still holds true. No one has built a profitable business model around giving away a free lunch. The marginal costs of manufacturing and delivering such a lunch are simply too high for it to be possible. However, we can expand the interpretation of this saying to include things you can find today, such as free news, free music and free online services.

How can businesses give away their products and time for free and still make a profit?

The reason these things are free is that computers make it possible to deliver great value at a very low marginal cost, making it possible to build a profitable business around a free product. Most commercial uses of free are either monetized through advertising or through a freemium model, which offers a free product and an upgrade to a premium, paid product. Targeted advertising has made it possible for many companies to deliver great value to users for free. Just look at the example of Google or Facebook. In freemium models, the majority of users are able to enjoy a valuable free service, while a smaller percentage buy the premium service. So while the user will have to either look at advertising or offers to upgrade, the product or service is still 100 percent free to them.

Is "free" right for every business?

The scale and speed with which business models around free are spreading is causing many businesses to go into unchartered territory. Admittedly, there are examples of companies that work poorly with a business model based on free and of start-ups that provide a free product without any initial idea about how they will make money. This does not, however, disprove the viability of business models based around free, any more than a hunk of metal that sinks does not disprove the viability of boats built from metal. The challenge, rather, is for the broad business world to gain the understanding of how and when free is the right choice.

6

VENTURE CAPITAL
As money pours in for start-ups, can funds improve results?

Michael Fitzgerald

EXECUTIVE SUMMARY

Venture capital in the United States has matured as an industry, and with maturity comes fear of complacency. Many of its stars are reaching retirement age, and the sector faces questions about its inability to beat stock market returns, let alone match its storied performance of the 1990s, when the industry and high tech both rose to prominence. New types of investing approaches such as crowdfunding; increased vigor and coordination by "angel" investors; and greater interest in start-ups by private equity firms, hedge funds and mutual funds mean venture capitalists are facing growing competitive pressure. The industry's clubbiness has brought questions about its lack of diversity, and fears of a new tech bubble raise concerns that VCs are fueling conditions for another economic downturn. Even so, global interest in finding the next great start-up is soaring, opening up more opportunities for venture capital.

OVERVIEW

Venture capital

AS MONEY POURS IN FOR START-UPS, CAN FUNDS IMPROVE RESULTS?

As Etsy went public in April 2015, venture capitalists watched closely. The pioneering artisan e-commerce site's initial public offering (IPO) valued the company at well over $1 billion, affirming what its investors had already said: Etsy was a rare commodity, a start-up worth $1 billion. In the parlance of the venture capital (VC) industry, it was a "unicorn."[1]

According to venture capitalist Aileen Lee, who popularized the term, one of those rare unicorns can return the value of an entire fund all by itself.[2] Writing in 2013, she noted that only 39 $1 billion companies had emerged in the previous decade, or less than 1 percent of the enterprise and consumer software companies founded with venture money. Only one, Facebook, was worth more than $100 billion—what she called a super-unicorn. But in the ensuing two years, unicorns have multiplied: There were 13 privately held unicorns in 2013, and by mid-May 2015 there were 107, no longer including post-IPO Etsy.[3]

From *SAGE Business Researcher,*
May 25, 2015

This herd of unicorns seemingly signals that venture capital is thriving as the industry approaches levels it last achieved 15 years ago in terms of buzz and investment capital: VCs invested nearly $48 billion in 2014, the most since 2000, when a high-tech bubble collapsed and sent the U.S. economy into a brief recession.[4] Moreover, the average deal size ballooned to nearly $8 million. Overall, venture capitalists raised $32.2 billion in 2014, according to PitchBook, which tracks the VC industry.[5] In the first quarter of 2015, they raised another $7 billion, including a $1.6 billion fund raised by Bessemer Ventures.[6] That's a lower quarterly average than in 2014, but still solid.

But other signs are more troubling. Venture funds have not beaten the Dow Jones industrial average over the past decade, and they have only barely beaten the S&P 500, meaning that investors are not getting the "multiples" they expect to get from risky venture capital investments.[7] One study found that just a few VC firms were responsible for most of the industry's returns.[8]

The generally mediocre rates of return have caused people like Diane Mulcahy, the senior fellow at the Ewing Marion Kauffman Foundation responsible for its endowment investments, to question whether most VCs add any actual value to companies. "VCs have a great gig: They get paid well in fees, even if they lose money," she says.

Other problems are both deeper and murkier: Modern venture capital, which began taking shape in the 1970s, is hitting middle age, as is the high-tech industry that created venture's biggest successes. Critics say the days are gone when a venture capitalist could put $1.2 million into a fledgling computer company and see that investment worth more than $200 million a few years later, as happened with a 1975 investment in Tandem Computers.[9] Quite simply, VC is not generating the high returns that it experienced in the 1990s and earlier, when both it and the technology sector were thriving.

Meanwhile, some of the venture industry's biggest names are retiring or are close to retiring. Eugene Kleiner died in 2003, and Tom Perkins is no longer involved with Kleiner Perkins Caufield & Byers, long the Silicon Valley's signature firm; big-name partner John Doerr is 63. Donald Valentine of Sequoia Capital is in his 80s, and Michael Moritz, that firm's chairman, is 60, and has reduced his involvement with day-to-day investments because of illness. At New Enterprise Associates (NEA), founded in 1978 and the largest VC firm by assets under management ($15 billion), co-founder Dick Kramlich did not participate in its newest fund.[10]

Venture capital can be the jet fuel for starting companies, boosting the economy and creating jobs. But day to day, it is a more mundane business. Venture capitalists are partners in a kind of specialized mutual fund that invests money for large institutions, such as pension funds and university endowments, promising better returns than stocks. It's a form of private equity, a class of assets considered alternative investments to cash, stocks and bonds, the three most common asset classes.

Venture capitalists make their returns by providing money to entrepreneurs with great ideas but limited access to capital, and connecting those entrepreneurs with people in a position to make their business better—advisers, partners and customers for their product. In return, VCs earn what's called "2 and 20," 2 percent management fees drawn from the overall fund they raised, and 20 percent of the carried interest, or the profits generated over the life of the fund, which typically runs 10 years. Some limited partners say that VCs are paid too much and return too little.

Top 15 venture capital investors in start-ups

Some sovereign wealth funds—investment funds owned by governments—have tried to make their own investments out of dislike for the venture capital funding model and the inconsistent investing results VC firms generate. Were these to succeed, they could deprive VCs of a major source of institutional dollars. So far, though, the sovereign wealth funds have done far worse on their own.[11]

Steven Kaplan, a professor of entrepreneurship and finance at the University of Chicago's Booth School of Business, argues that venture capital is a cyclical industry emerging from a down cycle. He points out that funds raised between 2008 and 2012 have outperformed the S&P 500 by about 2 percent a year. Mulcahy is not impressed, arguing that these are paper profits based on valuations and that the real profits won't be known until companies in which the funds have invested actually go public or are purchased. This debate will play out over the next several years, and she believes VC will struggle to create better net returns than the public markets.

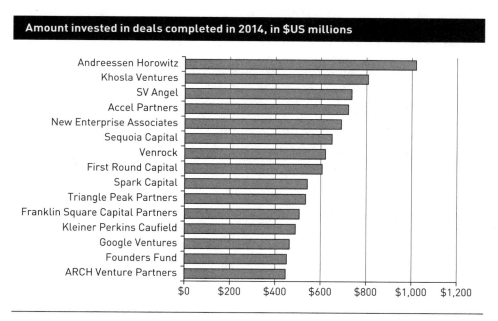

Amount invested in deals completed in 2014, in $US millions

Andreessen Horowitz of Menlo Park, Calif., topped the list of venture capital firms most active in early-stage investment in start-up firms in 2014, with more than $1 billion in deals completed that year. The company, founded by two former Netscape executives, has more than $4 billion under management.

Note: Firms are ranked on total capital amounts invested in early-stage deals. Data from PitchBook Platform, http://pitchbook.com/

Source: Tanya Benedicto Klich, "VC 100: The Top Investors in Early-Stage Startups," *Entrepreneur*, Feb. 19, 2015, http://tinyurl.com/opq8aop

One thing that's not debatable is the shift in the VC industry. VCs once routinely invested in companies as they were forming, but have ceded much of that traditional role in funding young companies to "angel investors," who often work alone and invest only their own money. While large VCs still maintain seed funds and will directly fund entrepreneurs they've worked with before, "that lower end of the market has been abandoned by VCs," says Josh Lerner, a professor of investment banking at Harvard Business School. He cites technology developments such as online platforms, which allow groups of angel investors to band together to invest, for the shift.

Other options for newly formed companies include "accelerators" and incubators that invest small amounts, $50,000 or $100,000, in entrepreneurs' firms, and introduce them to VCs after they have established their business model. Crowdfunding platforms, which allow much broader groups of people to invest in start-ups, are also on the rise.

VCs are drawing increased scrutiny on another front, too: At a time when income inequality is spawning protest movements and political pressure, the payments venture capitalists can receive, and the role they play in funding companies that sometimes destroy more jobs than they create, face criticism. The high-tech industry in 2014 publicly examined its lack of racial and gender diversity, with Google, Facebook and other companies posting reports on the small numbers of minorities and women they employed in technical and management roles. VCs have not been spared.[12]

In March, Kleiner Perkins, the venerable venture capital firm that has funded some of the biggest technology companies, from Genentech to Amazon to Google, found its inner workings exposed as part of a closely watched trial on gender discrimination, brought by Ellen Pao, a former junior partner.[13] She lost, but the bad press hurt Kleiner's image.[14]

Venture capitalists, though, are not ultimately judged on social issues. They're judged on performance, specifically returns for investors. Returns traditionally have come from about 10 percent of a venture fund's investments; the rest either break even or are a total loss. That's certainly true for the last decade, according to financing data from Correlation Ventures.[15] The glamour and wealth that comes from backing companies such as Facebook and Google mean that most countries and pretty much every U.S. state not named California would love to have its own Silicon Valley. Such an impact reflects how the venture industry has become a sophisticated manager of risk capital. Still, as modern venture capital approaches its 60th year, below are some of the questions the industry and others are asking.

WEIGHING THE ISSUES

Are we in another funding bubble?

Stock market indices are at or near all-time highs, breaking records set in 2000 during the Internet bubble. The Dow Jones industrial average topped 18,000 in December 2014 and since then closed as high as 18,288. Nasdaq exceeded 5,000 in March 2015. The S&P 500 broke 2,100 in February 2015. Along with record-setting stock markets, valuations for private companies reached record highs. In May 2015 there were as many as 91 venture-backed unicorns, led by China's Xiaomi, a privately owned electronics company valued at $46 billion. And a record number of venture-backed start-ups are valued at more than $1 billion. Leading the pack are household names such as Uber ($41.2 billion), Snapchat ($15 billion) and Airbnb ($10 billion).[16] For some analysts, these figures are worrisome. Even during the giddy heights of the dot-com boom in the late 1990s, when a frenzy over high technology and an expanding Internet sent stocks soaring, companies such as Amazon and Google were never worth $1 billion before they went public.[17]

"We are definitely in a bubble. This one is not as bad as 2000," when stock prices collapsed and many dot-coms went bust, Todd Dagres, founding partner at Spark Capital, told Bloomberg News.[18] "If you wake up in a room full of unicorns, you are dreaming, and you can't expect the dream to continue."

People are indeed dreaming big: Total venture investment in 2014 was $48 billion, more than any year since 2000.[19] But they aren't dreaming as big as they were in 2000, when nearly $100 billion in venture investment occurred.

In the late 1990s, investors abandoned metrics such as pricing stocks by a ratio of stock price to earnings (the P/E ratio) in the 10 to 17 range, in part because many Internet companies were not profitable. Instead, investors bought stocks based on perceived potential, starting in the wake of Netscape's explosive 1995 initial public offering, and the P/E ratio hit as high as 32 and was still at 26 before the market crash in 2000.[20] These investing trends were denounced in 1996 by then-Federal Reserve Chairman Alan Greenspan as "irrational exuberance."[21] Today, the stock markets do not seem to have bought into the hype surrounding private companies. "There's exuberance," says Anand Sanwal, CEO of CB Insights, which researches the VC market. "We haven't jumped on the bubble wagon because the public markets have not gone crazy," he says. "The performance of venture-backed companies when they go public has been pretty much rational."

Venture capital deals, 1995–2014

Longtime venture capitalist Bill Wiberg, of Advanced Technology Ventures and G20, agrees there is no bubble, despite the huge valuations of some companies. "Companies getting to that point [a $1 billion valuation] are for the most part really good, unique companies," he says. Most companies are not receiving huge valuations, he says, noting that 50 companies is not a big number considering the number of technology companies started every year. Instead, the high valuations reflect the longer period between founding a company and going public. "These would have been public companies in the past, and you would've said that's a sign of a healthy venture industry, to have 50 companies that have gone public and are really valuable," Wiberg says.

Others are not so sanguine. One skeptic is Dallas Mavericks owner Mark Cuban, who became a billionaire by selling broadcast.com to Yahoo during the Internet bubble. According

Dallas Mavericks owner Mark Cuban watching pre-game warm ups.

Bob Levey / Stringer/Getty Images Sport/Getty Images

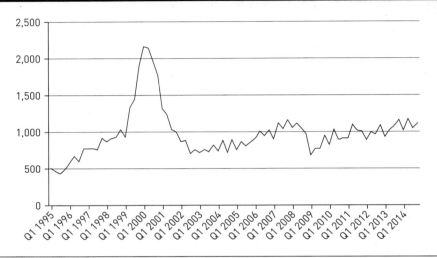

The number of venture capital deals spiked in the first quarter of 2000 with 2,160 deals at the height of the dot-com bubble. Venture capital rebounded modestly in the mid-2000s, then the number of deals fell again in 2008 during the recession. At 1,109, the number of deals in the final quarter of 2014 remained well below the 2000 peak.

Note: Based on data provided by Thomson Reuters and subject to change. For industry definitions, see https://www.pwcmoneytree.com/Definitions/Definitions

Source: "Historical trend data," PricewaterhouseCoopers MoneyTree, accessed May 12, 2015, http://tinyurl.com/omf3ryz

to him, today's companies are not going public because they cannot. Highly valued companies are still private because of a crisis in liquidity—the investors can't get cash for their assets, in this case shares in start-ups. "The only thing worse than a market with collapsing valuations is a market with no valuations and no liquidity," he wrote on his blog.[22]

Bubbles—when soaring investments create vastly inflated asset values, which eventually someone refuses to pay, bursting the bubble—tend to involve sheer speculation, and much of the value of a private company can be speculative until it goes public or is acquired. Steven Davidoff Solomon, a law professor at the University of California, Berkeley, wrote that start-ups such as Uber are being "priced to perfection," using values that assume they will reach their full business potential.[23] But there is also no question that venture-backed start-ups are taking longer to go public, eight years in 2014, versus five in 1994. That means investors have more time to see how a company performs.[24]

Larry Bohn of General Catalyst says companies such as Uber or Airbnb (a General Catalyst investment) might be overvalued, but still have business merit. While Uber may not prove to be worth $40 billion, it is on track to generate $10 billion in revenue in 2015.[25] That would put it at 283 in the Fortune 500, just below Avon Products.

Not all unicorns will do so well. E-commerce site Fab raised $310 million and was valued at more than $1 billion, but in 2015 it was in talks to sell for as little as $15 million.[26] Box, a cloud storage and content management company, successfully went public, but for less than its onetime $2 billion valuation.[27] Bohn says some unicorns should generate lots of cash and return money to their investors, but for at least some of them, the end will be unpleasant.

Sanwal says he has heard bubble predictions almost every year since CB Insights was founded in 2000. "Even a broken clock is right twice a day. Eventually, there will be that day of reckoning."

Is venture capital too big?

The law of diminishing returns holds that as a business or fund gets bigger, it gets harder for it to continue to generate high returns. VC firms invested nearly $50 billion in 2014, even though over the previous decade the industry produced smaller returns than the Dow Jones industrial average.

That meant investors could have done better by putting their money into an index fund, a fund consisting of stocks in market indices such as the Dow or the Russell 2000. Because venture funds are riskier than the stock market, VCs theoretically reward investors by beating the market, usually by 3 to 5 percent. Some observers, as a result, argue that too much capital is being deployed by an industry whose best years were from 1985 to 1995, when perhaps $5 billion to $10 billion a year was invested.[28] Because of the way venture funds are structured, with a 10-year investment cycle that can encompass numerous unpredictable "exits" (an exit is when companies cash out on an investment, usually through an IPO or an acquisition), it's difficult to say what impact the last two years have had on overall returns. But they should be positive for VCs; 2014 was the best year ever for private-company exits, with 845 for $78.4 billion. Even without counting Facebook's $22 billion buyout of messaging app WhatsApp, it was the best year in a decade, according to PitchBook.[29]

Another researcher, Jessica Duong of Preqin, which studies alternative assets, found that from March 2013 to March 2014, venture capital returned more than 27 percent on investments, beating every other type of private equity investment.[30] Duong concluded that venture capital was poised for a turnaround. PitchBook noted that 29 companies became unicorns in 2014. If stock markets remain strong in 2015, and these unicorns go public at high valuations, it could herald a new golden age for venture capital, PitchBook said.[31]

That would ease pressure on the industry, which has faced criticism that its performance was faltering because the high-tech industry itself was maturing. "While the Internet has provided many investment possibilities, including some resounding success for venture capitalists, like Google, the sector has changed," Paul Kedrosky, a senior fellow at the Ewing Marion Kauffman Foundation, which supports entrepreneurial activity, wrote in 2009. "The computer and enterprise software and networking markets are long past the peak of innovation in terms of being places for profitably investing significant early-stage money." The maturing of high tech means the venture industry should reduce its annual investing to about $12 billion a year to get consistently good returns, he added.[32]

Venture capital investment in Silicon Valley tech

Whatever the reason, some VCs are uncomfortable. Bill Draper, a longtime VC who founded Sutter Hill Ventures, said in 2013: "There's still too much money in Silicon Valley chasing too few deals," but added that while the excess capital created more risk for venture capitalists, it made it easier for entrepreneurs to raise money, which could lead to more good companies.[33]

The law of large numbers means big VC funds need to deploy more capital when investing. A $100 million fund that pulled off several $20 million exits has a good chance of breaking even. A billion-dollar fund needs much larger exits just to break even. But VCs can't really afford to spend much, if any, time on seed investments in new companies because of the time needed to help early-stage entrepreneurs build their businesses. Instead, VCs get involved with ideas only after they've taken shape—and some critics say that's a problem when VCs invest in unicorn companies in their late stages, when the chance of a large return is small.

Still, large funds of more than $700 million have their proponents. NEA created a $2.6 billion fund in 2010, then a $2.8 billion one in 2015, the two largest funds since the recession of 2007–09 (the latter was the second-biggest fund in VC history).[34] NEA's Kramlich said that VCs need large amounts of capital to fund companies that can solve tomorrow's problems.[35]

Large funds have outperformed smaller ones, although some very small, sub-$100 million funds have done well, creating a barbell effect, where the best returns come from small and large funds. Even NEA has maintained a small, $20 million seed fund to help it keep its ear

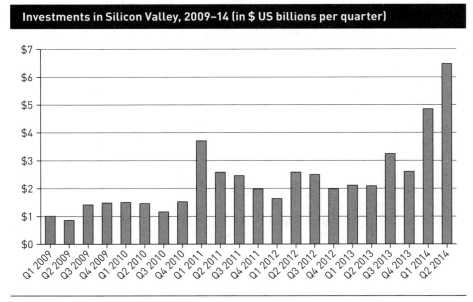

Investments in Silicon Valley, 2009–14 (in $ US billions per quarter)

The amount invested in Silicon Valley increased substantially between 2009 and 2014, peaking at $6.5 billion in the second quarter of 2014.

Source: "Silicon Valley Tech Investment and Exit Report," CB Insights, August 2014, http://tinyurl.com/otlxhuh

to the ground. One advantage of size: A big fund can invest from the seed stage to a Series E round or later. (A Series E represents a fifth investment of venture capital and would typically lead to an IPO.) And thus the big fund can share fully across the growth cycle of a start-up, unlike smaller funds that typically do not have enough capital to participate in B, C and later rounds of funding.

The Kauffman Foundation and others have criticized large funds for the lack of incentive: Partners can do very well for themselves even if the fund does poorly; they still get their 2 percent management fee to cover the costs of running the firm. For a billion-dollar fund, that's $20 million a year.

With a large fund "you lose alignment between investors, the venture firm and the entrepreneur," says Wiberg of ATV and G20. G20 was formed when ATV decided not to raise a ninth fund, and its partners split into two firms, one, G20, dedicated to enterprise software, the other, Lightspeed, to biotech.

Kate Mitchell, co-founder of Scale Ventures Partners, an early-stage Silicon Valley venture fund, acknowledges that big funds can generate huge management fees, but she notes that most funds have changed how they structure their fees so that they repay fees to investors before they take any profits from distributions. She says in some cases, funds have agreed to budgets, rather than a flat 2 percent management fee, and also have agreed to return all their investors' money before taking profits.

Some argue not only that more venture money is needed, but also that it should be distributed over a wider geographical area. "Way too much early-stage funding has been relegated to the coasts," says Jeff Fagnan, a technology partner at the Boston firm Atlas Venture, which in 2014 split into a biotech investing firm and a tech investing firm.[36] "I want to see funding much more broadly distributed across the country. Detroit needs it, Cleveland needs it. I'm looking for it to spread."

Harvard's Lerner disagrees. He points to Small Business Innovation Research funding grants from the federal government, which are spread throughout the United States. "The companies that succeed, from growth in employment or revenues, are almost overwhelmingly located in areas where there are already venture capitalists and a venture cluster," Lerner says.

Overall, the opportunities to spread technology to new business sectors in the developed and developing worlds leads Dave McClure, founder of the unusually structured venture fund 500 Startups, to say: "I'm not at all worried that there's too much capital. There is so much work to be done in innovating and disrupting companies which aren't technical."

Despite the criticisms, and the relatively poor returns, the last few years have seen a return to bigness; four funds accounted for $6 billion, or just under half of the new capital raised by VCs in the first six months of 2012, and seven mega funds closed in 2014, the best overall year for fundraising since the recession in 2008.[37]

Will venture capital become more diverse?

During the first few months of 2015, the venture industry found itself glued to its own version of Court TV, as Pao's lawsuit against her former employer, Kleiner Perkins, played out in a Silicon Valley courtroom. Pao accused Kleiner of not promoting her to senior partner because she was female, though at times that seemed almost incidental to the spectacle of the sometimes-sordid inner workings of a VC firm revealed in public. She lost her case, but between the trial, the recent filing of other lawsuits, a damning *Newsweek* article on Silicon Valley and women, and intense pressure from civil-rights advocate Jesse Jackson, the industry is on the defensive.[38]

Little wonder. Venture capital invests almost exclusively in companies run by men who are white or Asian. That reality reflects the industry itself. Few partners in venture capital firms are from other demographic backgrounds; a 2011 survey found 89 percent were male, and 87 percent Caucasian.[39] Most of the non-Caucasians are Asian, especially Indian; in the past, the proportion of non-Caucasians was even lower. But while VC was getting more diverse in this one area, it got less diverse in others: A 2013 survey found that the number of female partners at VC firms had dropped to 6 percent.[40] (The numbers were even smaller for African-Americans and Hispanics, at 1 percent and less than 1 percent, respectively.[41]) Critics see the VC industry's lack of diversity as a big reason why Silicon Valley firms themselves lack diversity, and why companies run by African-Americans and Hispanics receive less than 1 percent of all venture capital rounds.

Nobody in Silicon Valley is openly against diversity. The debate is over how to achieve it. The National Venture Capital Association, the industry's main trade group, in late 2014 formed a Diversity Task Force, co-chaired by Scale Venture's Mitchell and Ashton Newhall of Greenspring Associates, a Washington, D.C., area venture investor and fund manager.[42]

Mitchell says diversity would benefit the venture industry. She cites recent academic studies that show for mass manufacturing, a homogenous workforce improves performance, but for problem-solving, diverse workforces prove more effective. "One of our biggest challenges is knowledge and having the right mix of people. The more diverse group of people you've got, the more likely you are to have an overlaying network, [thus] improving your perspective on the world," Mitchell says. "We're about taking risks, helping to build great companies. Having different perspectives helps you to move forward."

The Diversity Task Force is new, but she says one idea under discussion is to adopt something similar to the "Rooney Rule" used by the National Football League, which requires teams with a coaching vacancy to consider minority candidates.

Silicon Valley's definition of a minority is a little different than the rest of America's. The data show that Asian entrepreneurs, especially Indians, on a per capita basis have a better chance of getting venture funding than any other ethnic group, and they represent about 10 percent of venture capitalists, far higher than their 5 percent share of the U.S. population.[43]

At the former Atlas Venture, the partners say their future partners will likely come from among the founders they back. "The percentage we're backing that are women are not high enough," Fagnan says. The company has begun reaching out more aggressively to female entrepreneurs by starting a women's entrepreneurial leadership seminar, where it brings in women who are in management roles at tech companies and encourages them to think about starting companies.

A new crop of female-run venture firms has also begun, including Scale, Aspect Ventures, Illuminate Ventures and Cowboy Ventures.[44]

Change will be slow, say Mitchell and other VCs, simply because of the way partnerships are structured. They tend to be limited to a handful of partners, and they last for 10 years. Partners aren't added to funds midway through, barring the death of a participant or some other catastrophe. "We lag the culture at large," says General Catalyst's Bohn.

But a decade from now, expect to see a more diverse venture capital world, says Mitchell. She thinks it will inevitably help create better returns for investors and will ease talent shortages at tech companies.

BACKGROUND

The gilded few

Although private equity investment has existed for as long as merchant banks have been around, venture capital as an asset class emerged over the 19th and 20th centuries and developed in three distinct stages—pre-Depression, the Depression and World War II years, and the post-war years.

Before the 1930s, very wealthy individuals and families (Andrew Mellon, J.P. Morgan, the Rockefellers) often put money into entrepreneurial ventures. Morgan funded Thomas Edison and put the capital syndicate together for what became General Electric, and he later backed Italian inventor Guglielmo Marconi's wireless efforts, which would become RCA. [45] Among other investments, Mellon supported what became Alcoa.[46] Other well-off people backed Alexander Graham Bell and the early aviation industry. These investors worked informally, using their own money. Today they would be known as angel investors.

The first known reference to the term "venture capital" was in 1920, when a report by the Investment Bankers Association of America referred to "speculative securities" and said they were "necessary for the development and growth of the country, as well as for the safety of all investment securities."[47]

The stock market crash in 1929 and sharply higher tax rates on the rich imposed during the Depression, plus difficult economic conditions, curtailed the desire for risk capital—money invested in new businesses that have a high chance of failure.

The drought

Between 1931 and 1946, the economy and changes in the tax code meant wealthy individuals had little incentive to invest in entrepreneurs. Still, some notable companies were born. John H. Whitney provided the capital to found Pioneer Pictures in 1933, and he also invested in Technicolor.[48] Laurance S. Rockefeller, grandson of John D. Sr., backed Eastern Airlines in 1938.[49] Companies such as Motorola and Hewlett-Packard were founded for less than $1,000 in capital. Meanwhile, regulations made it difficult for institutions to invest in risk capital. Institutions formed to invest were limited to publicly traded securities, bonds and Treasury instruments. Large corporations investing in research, and the U.S. government itself, were the most important risk investors.

During World War II, the government built networks with research universities and corporations and engaged in risk financing for firms seen as necessary to the war effort. For example, to create a synthetic rubber industry to replace supplies of natural rubber disrupted by the Japanese, the government backed 51 synthetic rubber plants, leading to the creation of a new industry.[50]

In 1942, capital gains rules were changed, allowing higher returns for risky investments. And federal and state governments began easing strict rules prohibiting speculative investments.

The post-war era

After World War II, systematic moves by the U.S. government to do things such as fund education for GIs brought a general increase in the flow of investment. The first private investment companies were formed around 1946, primarily on the East Coast: John Whitney set up J.H. Whitney and Co., and Georges Doriot established American Research and Development (AR&D) Corp. The Rockefellers founded Rockefeller Brothers Co., in effect a super-family fund engaging in risk capital.[51]

Some of these funds went on to make some famous investments. Rockefeller Brothers backed McDonnell Aircraft; Whitney invested in Florida Foods, creator of Minute Maid orange juice; and Doriot funded Digital Equipment Corp., which developed the minicomputer as a cheaper alternative to the mainframe.[52]

Rockefeller Brothers was the longest-lived of these funds, becoming VenRock in 1969, the year it invested in a promising start-up called Intel Corp. VenRock remains a successful VC (one recent success: Nest, the smart home device) and closed a $450 million fund in 2014.[53] Whitney and Co. would eventually become a buyout firm. American Research and Development was not the most successful of these funds or the longest lived, but it is widely considered the most influential.[54] It was the first venture capital firm to raise money from not just wealthy individuals but also institutions.

AR&D thus began the institutional structure of modern venture capital, leading some to call Doriot, its founder, the father of venture capital. AR&D's founding premise would fit into today's venture world: to find companies with a saleable product, significant intellectual property and the potential for substantial profit, and then invest in them. Doriot's attitude toward entrepreneurs also would fit with many of today's venture capitalists: He believed that good entrepreneurs were much more important than good ideas, writing once that "an average idea in the hands of an able man is worth much more than an outstanding idea in the possession of a person with only average ability."

Doriot was French but came to the United States and stayed, teaching an iconoclastic course on manufacturing at Harvard Business School. He was charismatic and brilliant and many of those who took his course were profoundly influenced by it, repeating maxims of his such as: "Somewhere, someone is working on a technology that is going to make your company's products obsolete."[55]

Many of his investments did not pan out, but one was brilliant: Doriot put $70,000 into Digital Equipment Corp., which commercialized minicomputers. They became workhorses and opened up a new market for technology. That $70,000 gave AR&D 70 percent of the company, a stake that eventually was worth $450 million.[56] It set the model for venture capitalists: take a number of calculated risks, and if one or two become big successes, a fund would create new businesses and valuable returns. Over its existence, AR&D recorded a 15 percent return on capital.

Doriot took one step that future venture capitalists would deviate from, however: AR&D raised its capital as a "closed-end" investment fund that was publicly traded. Being publicly traded with assets that were tied up in privately held start-ups that might not even have revenue, and whose values were unpredictable, caused the firm oversight problems with the Securities and Exchange Commission. It also vexed investors, who expected regular dividends, and this put a burden on AR&D, because most of its investments weren't in a position to give cash back. The final problem with its structure was that it could not properly reward its own personnel, who could make far more money by joining a successful portfolio company.[57] In 1973, Doriot sold AR&D to Textron.

In 1959, William H. Draper, father of Bill Draper, started what would become a family dynasty in venture capital, forming Draper, Gaither and Anderson with H. Rowan Gaither, who helped establish RAND Corp., and Frederick L. Anderson, a retired Air Force general. It was the first firm to blend Doriot's model with the family venture model, creating the limited-partner structure still used by today's venture capitalists.

While Draper, Gaither and Anderson did not make any famous investments, the firm did return profits to its investors. It closed in 1966. Draper died in 1974. But Draper's family legacy continues in the venture capital industry. His son Bill went on to form Sutter Hill Ventures, investing in a number of companies that were purchased for sizable returns, notably Apollo Computer, Integrated Genetics and Qume. Now in his 80s, Bill Draper stands as a kind of elder spokesman for the industry while still investing successfully, putting seed money into Skype. Bill's son Tim formed Draper Fisher Jurvetson in 1985; the firm has funded a diverse group of businesses, from Hotmail and Skype to *Parenting* magazine.

The industry's other seminal moment in the 1950s came when eight engineers working for Shockley Semiconductor Laboratory tired of the erratic, imperious nature of Shockley's founder, William Shockley, especially after he shared the 1956 Nobel Prize in physics for developing the transistor. The men, sometimes known as "the traitorous eight," quit in 1957.[58]

They "thought that they would like to quit Shockley and maybe get jobs together because there was no such thing in those days as forming a company and, what with the amount of capital that they needed to enter the semiconductor business," investment banker Arthur Rock recalled in an oral history.[59] Sherman Fairchild, an inventor, entrepreneur and the largest individual holder of stock in IBM, was one of his clients. Rock introduced the eight to Fairchild, who decided to hire them to start Fairchild Semiconductors, which aimed to develop and sell silicon transistors.

It was an accident of history that Fairchild was located in Palo Alto; Shockley's mother lived there, and he set up his lab in nearby Mountain View.[60] Fairchild is considered the original Silicon Valley start-up. The eight founders received stock options, a novel way to compensate founders, and worked without titles.[61] All would go on to found or run other companies. Two of them, Bob Noyce and Gordon Moore, in 1968 would launch Intel. Another, Eugene Kleiner, in 1972 formed Kleiner Perkins with Hewlett-Packard executive Tom Perkins, creating what became the most-storied Silicon Valley venture capital firm, and the first to be formed by entrepreneurs or people with industry experience, instead of finance backgrounds.[62] In all, some 400 companies trace their roots to Fairchild.[63]

Rock would move to San Francisco in 1971 and form a venture capital partnership. The Intel founders had already turned to him for financing. Noyce and Moore said they needed $2.5 million to start their company, and would each put in $250,000. Rock raised the other $2 million that day, without sending out a business plan he wrote. He would also provide money for Apple Computer, because of his friendship with a former Intel vice president named Mike Markkula, who had met the young Steve Jobs and Steve Wozniak, and had invested $300,000 for one-third control of the company.[64] Rock wound up as the first venture capitalist on the cover of *Time* magazine, in a 1984 article written by Michael Moritz, who would later leave journalism and become a highly successful venture capitalist in his own right at Sequoia Capital.

These early years of venture capital involved what today looks like tiny amounts of money. Indeed, the investments were so small that modern venture capitalists might not have made them, leaving them to angel investors. Kleiner Perkins put $1.2 million into Tandem Computers in 1975; it was worth $220 million seven years later. The firm's investment in Genentech grew 200 times in two years. The returns on companies such as Intel were astounding and drew interest to entrepreneurial start-ups developing new technologies. Sequoia put $600,000 into Atari and quadrupled its money in less than two years. Palo Alto Investments, formed in 1970 with $3.3 million in capital, returned $100 million to investors over the next decade.[65]

Despite these successes, the economic doldrums of the 1970s also affected venture capital, especially after the Employee Retirement Income Security Act (ERISA) of 1974 established criminal penalties for pension fund managers who lost money in high-risk investments.[66] In 1975, Venture Economics, a research firm, said that only $10 million in new investing capital was added to the field.[67] The industry was revived when the ERISA Improvements Act of 1979 allowed pension funds to put money into venture capital.[68]

The 1980s saw a run-up in the stock market, the rise of the personal computer and a boom in venture capital. The capital available to invest rose from $3 billion in 1980 to $31 billion in 1989.[69] But growth brought competition, transforming the business. On the industry side, Silicon Valley's semiconductor companies faltered against intense competition from the Japanese, driving many of them out of the business at the same time as venture capital went from a clubby group of financiers to 650 firms, all seeking to find good start-ups. The decade brought the first claims that the industry was overfunded and too risk-averse. A 1989 *New York Times* article noted that "rather than invest small chunks of money to start companies, many [VCs] put larger chunks in more mature companies, which are less risky and closer to going public, and in leveraged buyouts, which provide quicker and often better returns."[70]

But the stock market crash of October 1987 chilled the leveraged buyout market and the ability of many VC firms to raise money. Japanese companies, flush with cash, began swooping in to back promising American start-ups, offering better terms than American VCs. Among the start-ups they funded was Steve Jobs' NeXT Computer.

Overall, the 1970s and 1980s saw Silicon Valley grow in importance, surpassing Massachusetts' Route 128 as a center of technology development. As AnnaLee Saxenian wrote in her book *Regional Advantage*, some of this was happenstance. But it was also cultural: The older, East Coast tech firms, such as Digital Equipment, Prime and Wang, were vertically integrated, top-down companies, and so were the VCs that backed them. The firms that arose in Silicon Valley featured flat organizational structures, with project-driven teams that moved easily between companies. It created a culture that could respond quickly to change, and that proved a better model for the rapid shifts in technology that were coming.[71]

The rise of Silicon Valley

Today, the world's most valuable company by market capitalization (stock price times number of shares) is Apple Computer. Microsoft is second and Google is fourth, behind

Exxon Mobil.[72] Apple symbolizes the boom-and-bust cycles of venture investing and Silicon Valley; in the late 1990s, the company was all but given up for dead. The return of Jobs as CEO in 1997 and a cash infusion from Microsoft saved the company. Google is barely 17 years old. Facebook at 11 is one of the 10 most valuable technology companies.

Since personal computing emerged, followed by networked computing and the Internet, Silicon Valley's venture capitalists have played important roles and reaped rewards for doing so. Onetime upstarts such as Amgen, Cisco, Hewlett-Packard, Intel and Oracle are all now anchors of the valley and continue to provide talent for new generations of start-ups.

Tim Cook, current CEO of Apple Inc., often reveals new and innovative Apple products at Apple headquarters in Silicon Valley.

They also form part of its lore, several having survived near-death experiences, including Intel, which abandoned its original DRAM (dynamic random access memory) market and became a dominant supplier of microprocessors.

Boston, meanwhile, has seen only one large company, EMC, emerge since the early 1990s. Instead, Boston's VCs have largely become feeders, building companies to a point, then selling them to IBM or one of the big West Coast technology firms.[73]

Today's free-form, fail-fast-and-move-on culture in the valley was shaped in the wake of Marc Andreessen moving to California to start Netscape. Netscape's IPO sparked the five-year funding frenzy that became known as the Internet bubble.

Netscape's public offering saw its stock jump from $28 to $75, closing at $58 on its first trading day on Aug. 9, 1995. The company wasn't profitable. It had, in fact, little in the way of revenue.[74] That set the tone for the Internet bubble. Capital flowed to the valley's venture capitalists, and scores of new firms formed, the most prominent of which was Benchmark. Investor desire to reap the rewards of the Internet revolution led to mega-funds, with blue-chip VC firms able to pull together funds of $1 billion or larger. The valley is still dealing with the aftermath of this era, when there inarguably was too much capital chasing too few good ideas.

CURRENT SITUATION

Large numbers

Venture capital is not as big as it was in 2000, but it still invested nearly $50 billion in 2014. Billion-dollar valuations are becoming almost routine, in part because companies are taking longer to go public, as they build revenue and market share. In addition, says Scale Venture's Mitchell, venture capital funds are not funding many of these $100 million and larger rounds. "A lot of unicorn investing is happening in the later rounds, and not coming from traditional VCs," she notes. Instead, sovereign wealth funds, private equity firms and even some large mutual funds are participating in these rounds, along with very large VCs.

Bohn says this influx of capital makes sense. It's attractive for late-stage investors even if they pay high valuations. "If a company is within a year or two of going public, they can see a 2x return, and that's not bad in a year for a private equity group," Bohn says, particularly in a time of historically low interest rates.

Some VCs are now investing hundreds of millions of dollars in single deals. Overall, average deal size has ballooned to just under $8 million.[75] Bohn and others note that it's difficult to deploy large amounts of capital by making only small investments, which encourages VCs with large funds to take bigger bets.

The law of large numbers means if you have a big fund, it has to have big hits to create good returns on investment. That may help explain why over the last 10 years, fewer than 10 percent of venture funds have been able to beat the market indices.

The unicorn phenomenon, though, may lift returns. If the stock markets remain amenable to IPOs for the next two to three years, many of these companies should be able to go public and provide strong returns on their venture investments. The challenge, though, is that venture capitalists have put hundreds of millions of dollars, and occasionally more than $1 billion, into these companies. Creating great returns will require substantial IPOs. In VCs' favor were two outstanding 2014 IPOs: Alibaba, the Chinese Internet giant, which had the best-ever technology IPO, raising $25 billion and creating a company valued at $168 billion (it's now valued at more than $220 billion).[76] Late in the year, Juno Therapeutics set a record for biotech stocks by raising $265 million in its IPO, which valued the immunotherapy company at $2.2 billion, even though it had no revenue.[77]

Pulled from the edges

As Web technology has matured, and cloud services have made it possible for software and Internet start-ups to skip buying and managing servers, the costs of starting software and Internet companies have fallen. VC funds also place a premium on having at least one co-founder with a technical background who is capable of writing code or developing the core technology of a company, rather than paying others to do so. Technical co-founders aren't new—the Fairchild founders were mostly engineers; Bill Gates was an uber-programmer. But in the dot-com era, founders often outsourced their technology development, especially for companies that made semiconductors, computers and consumer electronics gear. Now, "you're battling up hill to get a venture capitalist to fund you without a technical co-founder," says Fagnan of the former Atlas Venture.

If it's cheaper to start companies, why are venture capitalists putting in so much capital? Part of the answer is that the venture capital comes into play not during the development stage but during growth phases. "The number of things that can be venture funded and grow fast and reach scale is much bigger than it was," Bohn says. Scale now means not just scale for the industry but also for acquiring the resources to compete globally. Also, he says, technology's spread is opening more economic sectors to new digital businesses, and they need to grow rapidly to stake out territory and to take market share from established competitors. Such tasks require substantial amounts of capital.

But part of the reason may also be "dumb money" that is drawn in by an up-cycle in the market, according to finance professor Kaplan. "The high valuations in later rounds are attracting a lot of nontraditional VC investors—the tourists," he says. "At some point, returns will be poor and the tourists will go home."

Number of venture capital funds continues to grow

Regardless, VCs often don't get involved in companies during the early stages. Instead, over the last decade, the industry has seen the rise of accelerators—programs that take applications from would-be entrepreneurs; pick the ones they like best; and give them a set amount of training and development time (often three months). The help includes mentoring and capital, ranging from $20,000 to about $120,000, in exchange for several percentage points of equity. These accelerators then host demo days or pitch days, where entrepreneurs pitch their start-ups, often to crowds of VCs. The best-known accelerator is Y Combinator, which began in 2004 in Boston and moved to Silicon Valley.

McClure's 500 Startups takes a similar approach. It is organized like a venture fund, with multiple investors, but it makes numerous small investments, usually about $100,000 per company. While some call this kind of investing "spray and pray," McClure says the point is

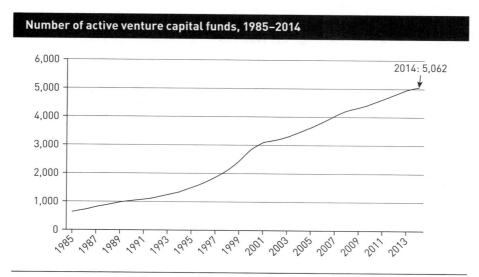

Number of active venture capital funds, 1985–2014

The number of venture capital funds increased from 631 in 1985 to 5,062 in 2014. The funds grew most rapidly from 1995 to 2000 as the technology industry boomed, nearly doubling before the Internet bubble burst in 2000. Funds typically remain in business for 10 years.

Source: "Yearbook 2015," National Venture Capital Association, March 2015, p. 20; downloaded from https://mthightech.org/wp-content/uploads/2015/11/NVCA-Yearbook-2015.pdf

to dilute risk by spreading it across far more investments than VCs typically make. "Almost nothing we do is conventional," he says. Unlike accelerators that invest similar amounts of early-stage capital, 500 Startups will make follow-up investments in its most promising companies, of up to $1 million.

Andreessen Horowitz represents another VC innovation. It was founded in 2009 by former Netscape colleagues Marc Andreessen and Ben Horowitz and quickly became an elite venture capital firm. Andreessen Horowitz decided that if it was going to compete with Silicon Valley stalwarts to get the best entrepreneurs, it needed to give entrepreneurs things they couldn't get from other firms. "They have a lot of skills in-house, experts in sales and human resources that they leverage for their portfolio companies. It's a completely different way to be organized for a VC firm," says Steven J. Kahl, associate professor at Dartmouth's Tuck School of Business, who is writing a history of venture capital.

The strategy is more expensive than the typical VC model, because it carries extra costs and affects the fund's investing strategy. Andreessen Horowitz was founded in the wake of the 2008 recession and has not yet experienced a serious market downturn. Its model is untested. If it continues to work, it could become more widespread.

LOOKING AHEAD

High winds or high returns?

The prominent VC and blogger Fred Wilson of Union Square Ventures said in 2013, "I believe that the venture capital business as we know it will not exist in 25 years."[78] VCs will still be around, he said, but they will be investing smaller amounts of capital and will have to reduce their management fees. Wilson also argued VCs invest in too many similar companies, rather than backing new ideas. He speculated they will have to use their brands to draw promising start-ups from accelerators and seed investors.[79] Capital increasingly will come via angel investors and more radical approaches such as crowdfunding, he said. Wilson added that there's too much money in venture capital to make consistent above-market returns possible.

Many disagree. Lerner of Harvard Business School says, "I don't think you can say that somehow venture returns have been some sort of a disaster, and as a result capital is going to dry up." In fact, since Wilson's statement, "there's been a real recovery in terms of returns and investor interest in terms of fundraising."

Mitchell of Scale Venture Partners also thinks venture capital is unlikely to disappear. "Fred Wilson is a great investor, but I don't think the venture industry is going to cease to exist," she says. "There's a ratio of failure in our industry. The failure rate is high and the wins finance the risk. That's the model."

Industry critic Mulcahy of the Kauffman Foundation concedes that some venture capital firms continue to create excellent returns, although she says "it's probably fewer than 10." And so far, big sovereign wealth funds and others that have tried to invest directly have not done well.[80] According to Robert Mah of the Alberta Investment Management Corp., the best deals gravitate toward Silicon Valley VCs, not sovereign wealth funds.[81]

So, many VC firms can probably continue to function much as they have in the past, but some changes seem inevitable. "Venture is different today than it was 10 years ago, or 10 years before that," says Wiberg of ATV and G20. He says, for instance, that 15 years ago many VCs thought they could scale up their model, and added staff and partners. But most venture capital firms did not improve results by adding people, with the possible exception of NEA. He argues venture capital does not scale well.

Accelerators and incubators are proving to be fertile, at least the very best of them, such as Y Combinator, which says its companies have gone on to net $3 billion in funding and more than $30 billion in market value.[82] Those numbers suggest excellent results, especially on investments that might be in the mere tens of thousands of dollars.

Harvard's Josh Lerner says it's becoming possible for entrepreneurs to entirely bypass the venture industry, thanks to crowdfunding and the rise of syndicates of angel investors. But Kaplan of the University of Chicago predicts trouble for both crowdfunding and syndicates of angels. "These two are the result of a hot market. When returns are poor, there will be a backlash," he says. Crowdfunding may open new geographic areas to investment funding, sparking ideas that VCs won't invest in simply because they're too far away. Also, at least one prominent platform, EquityNet, started in 2007 and has managed to survive the recession and its aftermath. Its CEO, Judd Hollas, distinguishes between it and platforms like Kickstarter, where the crowd by law can't actually buy ownership stakes. EquityNet investors, he says, "are not making a donation. It's a live investment. This is a different type of capital than Kickstarter and Indiegogo."

These next few years could be pivotal. If the companies founded by VCs are able to go public or be acquired for substantial premiums, more capital will likely flow into the industry. If the market drops sharply and kills the unicorns, the venture business will suffer. Veteran observers like Kaplan, though, expect the venture industry to continue operating in cycles, with booms and busts, a few notable successes and some spectacular failures.

Chronology

1880s to 1920s	The super-rich of an industrializing America spread the wealth by investing in new companies.
1878	J.P. Morgan backs Thomas Edison's research into electric lighting.
1887	Morgan and the Vanderbilts back Edison General Electric Light Co.; in 1892 it will merge with a rival to become General Electric.
1889	Andrew Mellon invests in the research that leads to the Pittsburgh Reduction Co., which will become Alcoa.
1903	Ten Detroit-area businessmen, including the Dodge brothers, put $100,000 into Ford Motor.
1920	An Investment Bankers Association of America report mentions venture capital—the first known reference to the term.
1929	Stock market crash leads to the Great Depression and a sharp drop in business activity.

(Continued)

(Continued)

1930–1946	**Business investment shrivels until World War II rekindles an interest in innovation.**
1938	Laurance Rockefeller funds Eastern Airlines. . . . Hewlett-Packard is founded in a Palo Alto, Calif., garage with $538 in capital.
1942	The federal government relaxes capital gains rules, making it more profitable to invest in risky ventures.
1946	First all-digital computer is unveiled at the University of Pennsylvania by J. Presper Eckert and John Mauchly, University of Pennsylvania researchers who built ENIAC (Electronic Numerical Integrator And Computer) for the U.S. government.
1946–1971	**Modern venture capital enters its formative years as business innovation shifts from large companies to entrepreneurial start-ups.**
1946	American Research and Development Corporation (AR&D) is formed and led by Georges Doriot; although publicly traded, it's the first venture fund with institutional money behind it.
1947	Bell Labs physicists John Bardeen, Walter Brattain and William Shockley invent the transistor, laying the groundwork for the emergence of digital computing and communications; many of the important innovations will come from venture-backed start-ups.
1957	AR&D funds computer-maker Digital Equipment Corp. . . . "The traitorous eight" form Fairchild Semiconductor, which features a novel flat organizational structure with stock options for all the founders.
1959	William H. Draper co-founds VC firm Draper, Gaither and Anderson, blending institutional money with the privately held family fund models.
1965	Moore's Law predicts that the number of transistors on a chip will double every 18 months.
1968	Semiconductor chipmaker Intel is founded.
1969	The Pentagon begins developing ARPAnet, the predecessor to the Internet.
1972–1995	**Silicon Valley emerges and venture capital is formalized.**
1972	Eugene Kleiner and Tom Perkins form Kleiner Perkins, the first VC started by entrepreneurs.
1975	Bill Gates and Paul Allen found Microsoft; the computer software maker does not take venture capital for most of its existence as a private company.
1976	Steve Jobs and Steve Wozniak found Apple.
1979	Restrictions in the Employment Retirement Income Security Act (ERISA) that hobbled investing are eased.

1984	The success of IBM's personal computer leads to a huge new industry.
1987	Stock market crash cools interest in new public offerings, chilling the high-tech field.
1989	Computer scientist Tim Berners-Lee, working for CERN, a physics research institute, creates the World Wide Web.
1995	Netscape, which developed a Web browser, goes public, igniting the Internet boom.
1996–Present	**Bubble and bust cycles plague venture capital; industry returns fall below those of market indices.**
1996	First billion-dollar venture capital fund is raised by New Enterprise Associates.
1998	Two Ph.D. students at Stanford University found Google; AltaVista was the dominant search engine of the day.
2000	Nineteen VC firms raise billion-dollar funds. . . . The Internet bubble bursts, after the tech-laden Nasdaq peaked at 5132.52 during trading on March 10 (it closed at 5048.62 that day).
2001	Apple releases the iPod, which will eventually save its business.
2004	Google goes public; Facebook is founded.
2007	Technology Crossover Ventures raises a $3 billion fund, the largest single fund ever raised.
2008	A deep recession leads to a drop in venture investing, and only 31 companies go public in the United States during the year. In 2009, VC funds raise only $13 billion, the lowest total since 2003.
2013	Nasdaq surpasses its 2000 high.
2014	Chinese e-commerce firm Alibaba goes public in the most valuable IPO ever. . . . Juno Therapeutics' IPO is the best ever for a biotech firm. . . . The industry as a whole invests nearly $50 billion.

Q&A: Lerner on Venture Capital

"THERE'S BEEN A REAL RECOVERY IN TERMS OF RETURNS AND INVESTOR INTEREST"

Josh Lerner
Jacob H. Schiff professor of investment banking
Harvard Business School

Josh Lerner is the Jacob H. Schiff professor of investment banking at Harvard Business School, where he teaches its popular venture capital and private equity course. He researches and writes extensively about the venture capital industry, and has written or co-authored three books on the topic, including *Boulevard of Broken Dreams*. He spoke with SAGE Business Researcher reporter Michael Fitzgerald about venture capital (VC). This is an edited transcript of the conversation.

VCs love to talk about "disruptive innovation." Are they ripe for disruption themselves?

I wouldn't say the word is "disruptive," but certainly there's a lot of change and evolution in the model going on. The big change is the bifurcation of the industry. Traditionally, it's been bell shaped: a few large firms, some small firms and a bunch in the middle. The largest firms have thrived, being able to raise billion-dollar funds or families of funds worth billions of dollars. On the low end, you've seen a whole flowering of micro VCs or super angel funds, typically under $100 million, doing much smaller deals and enjoying a lot of success. The ones in the middle have found themselves to be simultaneously without the global scale and reach of the big boys and lacking the specialization and laserlike focus of the more boutique-y firms.

The other thing is, we've also certainly seen interest on the part of angels and others to do venture-type investments in a more systematic way. Angels over the last decade have become much more systematized. Angel groups have created consortia for jointly investing, and in many cases these consortia have been Web-enabled through things like the Angel List syndicates. It's still unclear how much it will supplant the venture guys. But the possibility for entrepreneurs to bypass venture groups is great.

Is venture capital dead? Or at least does this asset class start to shrink?

It's true that a relatively small number of venture capitalists generate an attractive rate of return on a risk-adjusted basis. But that's been true since the earliest days of the industry. The idea that venture capital in aggregate hasn't generated attractive returns seems to be misplayed [in media reports]. I don't think you can say that somehow venture returns have been some sort of disaster and as a result capital is going to dry up. In fact, there's been a real recovery in terms of returns and investor interest in terms of fundraising.

What are the greatest pressures facing venture capital as an industry?

The fundraising situation has improved considerably, but it is very concentrated. There are only a certain number of groups that have the magic. It's an open question as to how much the venture model really carries over beyond the traditional ICT [information, communications, technology] kind of space into other areas. In the 1970s, VCs funded everything from new farming techniques to restaurants to advanced materials. Over the decades to follow, venture got extremely narrow in this band of ICT, largely because that was the only place where they were consistently successful.

In *Boulevard of Broken Dreams*, you detail government efforts to fund venture-style entrepreneurialism. Can we say governments are bad at venture capital?

It's been a mixed record. Certainly there've been spectacular successes like Israel, and you can point to New Zealand and Singapore, where government policy had a very positive impact in terms of promoting the development of a venture culture. But in many places a lot of money got spent with very little to show for it.

A great example in the United States would be the Small Business Innovation Research [SBIR] program. We have 435 congressional districts, and magically every year a company in each of those districts gets an SBIR grant. The companies that succeed, from growth in employment or revenues, are almost overwhelmingly located in areas where there are already venture capitalists and a venture cluster. So giving money to companies sitting in the center of Iowa, however fair a thing it is to do, if your goal is to boost economic activity you're unlikely to accomplish that goal.

What does government need to do to develop effective places for venture capital to operate?

The hard stuff of reforming labor laws and making sure that technology transfer is in place. Also, programs that condition public funding on the ability to raise funds from the private sector.

One of the big patterns worldwide is that labor mobility is extremely important. There's been a lot of controversy in Massachusetts around noncompete provisions [legal restrictions against leaving a company and joining or starting a competitor], where it would seem to have the effect of retarding labor mobility.[83] Having clear and understandable intellectual-property rights creates an attractive environment for start-ups. The U.S. has tremendous issues where successful start-ups are targeted by patent trolls [individuals or groups who buy up patents for the purpose of profiting by asserting intellectual-property rights, rather than develop new products and services] as well as large companies, which are no longer innovative but engage in programs to systematically litigate against anyone in their space.[84] Congress tried to reform it, but it's been a very contentious area, so reform is very slow.

There's almost universal hesitation on the part of governments on technology transfer policy. They want to encourage technology transfer but also want to make sure you don't make too much money on these transferred technologies. You can imagine that has a pretty chilling effect on private willingness to invest.

Many European countries until a few years ago had a system where they had registers of bankrupts.[85] So, even if you were a non-executive director [and not just a CEO] of a company that went bankrupt, you were put on this register to be banned for life from being able to serve as officer or director of another company. It curtails a willingness to engage in these kinds of risky experimental ventures.

CROWDFUNDING

Will Internet-based financing change how businesses raise capital?

Robin D. Schatz

EXECUTIVE SUMMARY

The explosive growth of social media and the Internet have paved the way for crowdfunding, a means of raising small amounts of money online from a large number of people without any financial intermediaries. Crowdfunding, say proponents, democratizes the fundraising process by helping start-ups, nonprofits, artists and others overcome barriers such as gender and geography to gain access to capital. Besides raising money, crowdfunding provides a way to test the popularity of a product or creative idea and solicit feedback from potential customers. In the United States, the JOBS Act of 2012 legalized investment crowdfunding, which allows for the issuance of debt or equity to both accredited and unaccredited investors. However, the rules implementing crowdfunding for the latter group have yet to be finalized. Some critics worry that ordinary investors will become victims of fraud or will simply make bad investment decisions, but the data remain too sparse to confirm those fears.

OVERVIEW

In 2005, three years after her father's death from brain cancer, Mikki Glass sought a way for her sister to include him on her wedding day. She crafted an ankle bracelet with a locket bearing their father's image, so he could, in spirit, accompany her sister down the aisle. A few years later, when Glass got married herself, she drew comfort from wearing that same locket.

Soon, friends were asking her to make them similar jewelry with pictures of their loved ones. That idea eventually grew into the small company With You, which produces a line of lockets, made of precious metals and stones and designed "with a modern vintage look and feel."[1]

Glass, a veteran entrepreneur who runs her own branding consultancy, Tilden Marketing, in New York City, had invested a substantial amount of her money to cover start-up costs, but she lacked the cash to actually produce the rings, bracelets, anklets and necklaces. "It is hard to get funding," Glass says. "I went to a bank first, and that's not the easiest road. They were willing to give us a loan, if I moved all my money into their bank, but I didn't." Glass says she also wasn't ready to seek outside investors, which would have required giving up equity.

Instead, Glass undertook a campaign on Kickstarter, one of the oldest and most popular crowdfunding platforms, with a goal of raising $40,000 to finance her inventory production.

From *SAGE Business Researcher,*
February 9, 2015

Crowdfunding has helped many entrepreneurs start and fund their businesses.

Crowdfunding allows individuals, artists, nonprofits, entrepreneurs and even big brands a way to raise money from a broad spectrum of people, using the Internet, without standard financial intermediaries.[2]

In less than a decade, Internet-based crowdfunding platforms, such as Kickstarter and Indiegogo, have helped filmmakers, video game producers and artists to finance their creative projects. They've also boosted numerous fledgling entrepreneurs like Glass, who want to raise start-up funds or test market demand, and they've helped the already-famous finance new projects. In some locales, crowdfunding has allowed small investors to take an ownership stake in businesses. U.S. regulators are working on rules that would permit wider use of this type of equity offering, which is limited now to wealthier investors. Boosters see crowdfunding as a way to open up access to capital to those who might not be able to get money through more traditional routes, and thus to help the wider economy by creating businesses and jobs. Others, however, worry about the possibilities for fraud and abuse.

For Glass, under Kickstarter's rules, the company would get nothing if she fell short of her fundraising goal; backers wouldn't pay a cent. But if she succeeded, everyone who pledged money would be charged for their contribution and Kickstarter would receive 5 percent of the take. With You would also pay credit card transaction fees.[3] Looking back on the process, Glass says the 30-day campaign was time consuming and stressful. But, ultimately, it paid off: When the campaign ended on Aug. 8, 2014, With You had raised $42,000 from 248 backers, with the help of a compelling video and various rewards—a selection of different lockets, based on the level of contribution.

Still in its infancy, crowdfunding campaigns of all types raised almost $2.7 billion world-wide in 2012, including $1.6 billion in North America.[4] The industry has its own trade associations, publications and research organizations. It boasts a growing roster of professionals, from accountants to lawyers to crowdfunding consultants.

Crowdfund Capital Advisors, a San Francisco–based research and consulting firm that has been a crowdfunding advocate, estimated in a report commissioned by the World Bank that that there were at least 672 crowdfunding platforms around the world in 2013.[5] Sherwood Neiss, a principal in the firm, says that number has almost doubled by now, with the greatest growth in Asia, Latin America and Europe.

Crowdfunding sites fall into four categories:

- Rewards or perk-based, where businesses solicit money in return for gifts or products, but not ownership interest.
- Donation-based, which are usually for nonprofit organizations or for individual causes.
- Peer-to-peer lenders, where groups of investors lend to individuals or companies for a fixed return.
- Equity, where investors get shares in the crowdfunded company.

Investment crowdfunding, which can be for debt or equity, is legal in many places, including the United Kingdom, France, Italy, the Netherlands and Australia.

Crowdfunding models vary by project, funding

Crowdfunding models, by project type and average funding sought		
Crowdfunding Model	**Most Suitable Project Type**	**Average Funding Sought ($US)**
Donation-based	Arts	Less than $10,000
Reward/presale	Project/product	Less than $100,000
Microfinance	Microdevelopment	Less than $1,000
Social lending	Microdevelopment	Less than $50,000
Investing/equity	Technology innovation	Less than $250,000

Some crowdfunding campaigns are better suited to specific projects, such as donation-based crowdfunding for community and arts projects or social lending for small enterprises. Models designed for smaller projects and short-term lending also set lower funding targets than models for entrepreneurial projects or larger business transactions.

Source: "Crowdfunding's Potential for the Developing World," World Bank, 2013, p. 34, http://tinyurl.com/o423cn8

Danae Ringelmann, co-founder of Indiegogo, which started in 2008, says rewards-based crowdfunding mitigates three common risks she learned about in entrepreneurship classes at the University of California, Berkeley, where she got her MBA: the risk you won't get sufficient financing; market risk, which means that demand for your product is insufficient; and the risk of poor execution—solving a need but doing it the wrong way or charging the wrong price.

Crowdfunding, at its best, addresses all these issues: "We help you find and grow your business idea before you launch, and we allow you to refine your product before you launch," Ringelmann says.

Even venture capitalists, hoping to discover the next Facebook or Google, are looking carefully at companies that successfully raise money from the public, particularly for new tech hardware.

"It's a really good validation of market demand, in my opinion," says Victoria Song, a principal at Flybridge Capital Partners, a venture capital (VC) firm in New York City and Boston that does early-stage investing. "In these cases, crowdfunding is actually very valuable and takes the risk away. It allows companies to raise money at higher valuations."

Since Kickstarter's founding in 2009, more than 74,000 projects have raised $1.2 billion via the site, according to the company. The potential for crowdfunding to transform access to capital is even greater in the developing world, said the World Bank study, which estimates that as many as 344 million households could invest in local businesses and deploy up to $96 billion a year by 2025, with some $50 billion coming from China alone.[6]

China leads developing world in crowdfunding potential

Rewards-based crowdfunding has fueled the popular imagination: Come up with a good idea, or even a harebrained one, then work furiously to build support on your social networks and you, too, can raise thousands or even millions of dollars. Highly successful campaigns are in the minority—just 40 percent of Kickstarter campaigns succeed.[7]

Even so, the success stories have been widely covered. The space video game *Star Citizen* from Roberts Space Industries had raised $63 million from fans as of late 2014, mostly from its own website, to fund new features in a game that hasn't even shipped yet.[8]

In 2012, the Pebble E-paper Watch turned to Kickstarter to raise $100,000 for a customizable smartwatch; instead, 69,000 backers gave $10.3 million. Equally noteworthy was the campaign for Oculus Rift, where 9,522 people contributed $2.4 million in September 2012 for the creation of 3-D virtual reality glasses.[9] That company went on to get millions in venture financing and was acquired by Facebook for $2 billion, stirring furor among some backers who, in retrospect, would have preferred a slice of the cash to a T-shirt.[10] And in August 2014, Ryan Grepper, the creator of the Coolest Cooler, a battery-powered picnic chest with a built-in blender and waterproof Bluetooth speakers, pulled in $13.3 million. His Kickstarter page lists 40 media outlets that covered the story.[11]

Until 2012, all U.S. Internet crowdfunding platforms by law were either reward-based or donation-based. People who contribute to a campaign aren't investors because they're not getting any ownership stake in the company in return for their money. Most rewards-based campaigns promise perks or gifts ranging from T-shirts to products not yet on the market, a practice known as "presale." Some rewards are intangible, such as a shout-out on a film's credits.

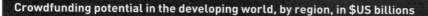

Crowdfunding potential in the developing world, by region, in $US billions

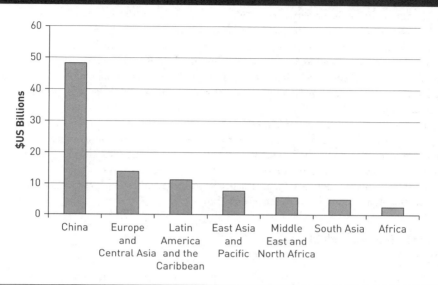

While crowdfunding now is concentrated in developed countries, analysts predict China will have the largest crowdfunding market potential of any developing region by 2025 at $48 billion. The next-largest potential regional markets will be Europe and Central Asia ($13.8 billion) and Latin America and the Caribbean ($11 billion).

Note: Estimates are averages of high and low projections for the potential crowdfunding market size in 2025. Analysts' projections are based on estimates of the number of households capable of making crowdfund investments; households' available funds to invest; and the amount of money investors will reallocate from savings and equity holdings.

Source: "Crowdfunding's Potential for the Developing World," The World Bank, 2013, p. 42, http://tinyurl.com/o423cn8

While rewards-based crowdfunding platforms continue to proliferate—there are niche crowdfunding sites for cannabis-related businesses and for athletes aspiring to compete in the Olympics—a whole new class of investment-oriented platforms has launched in the past two years to take advantage of the changing legal landscape. In April 2012, President Obama signed the JOBS (Jumpstart Our Business Startups) Act, which included provisions that for the first time allow companies to go directly to the public to solicit investments through crowdfunding.[12]

"Because of this bill, start-ups and small business will now have access to a big, new pool of potential investors—namely, the American people. For the first time, ordinary Americans will be able to go online and invest in entrepreneurs that they believe in," Obama said at the signing ceremony.[13]

However, until the Securities and Exchange Commission (SEC) releases final regulations for the law's Title III, which allows "unaccredited investors" to invest in private companies over the Internet, crowdfunding platforms may solicit funds only from "accredited investors" under what's known as Title II of the law. Accredited investors are those individuals with sufficient financial resources to risk investing in unregistered securities—earnings of at least $200,000 in each of the prior two years for individuals ($300,000 for a couple) or net worth of more than $1 million, not counting a primary residence.[14]

Academics have begun to study crowdfunding to understand what contributes to entrepreneurial success as well as how crowdfunding might affect the economy. "The research seems to suggest, if you have a slicker pitch, a better video, you're more likely to get support," says Jason Greenberg, an assistant professor of management at New York University's Stern School of Business.

It's one thing to throw in some money to be the first on your block to get your own cooler, but it might not make sense from an investment perspective to bet on its success as a going enterprise, given that a small number of players already dominate the industry. "This is where the equity-based model is going to be very intriguing," Greenberg says.

As this financing mechanism matures, below are some of the questions that entrepreneurs, investors, policy makers and researchers are asking.

Is crowdfunding a viable source of capital for start-ups and entrepreneurs?

Proponents say crowdfunding could democratize fundraising by providing access to capital for start-ups and creative projects. That is particularly true for those who can't attract investments from angel investors—the term for the very earliest investors in companies—or venture capitalists, often because of an entrepreneur's gender, ethnicity, location or industry.

"The beauty of crowdfunding, in general, is that it helps you [gain] access to larger pools of people that are motivated to help people like you," says Greenberg, who has studied rewards-based crowdfunding. He and his research colleague, Ethan Mollick, assistant professor of management in the Entrepreneurship Group at the University of Pennsylvania's Wharton School, found that female tech entrepreneurs on Kickstarter were 13 percent more successful than men in meeting their goals, and that they were primarily attracting investments from other women, who wanted to support female-led ventures.[15]

Minority and female entrepreneurs benefit from crowdfunding because it allows them to "raise capital for their businesses directly from investors in an open marketplace of ideas," Crowdfund Capital Advisors wrote in a July 2014 report. "While individual lenders may carry their own prejudices or may simply have a lower tolerance for the risk, the ability of crowdfunding to connect millions of potential investors with an entrepreneur's idea ensures that a greater cross section of society will be empowered to decide if the business plan has merit and if there is profit to be made."[16]

Neither venture capitalists nor banks have invested proportionally in women and minorities, according to that report. While women own about 41 percent of U.S. businesses, one study the researchers cited found that just 8 percent of women-owned firms got venture backing. Another study put that figure at 12 percent. "Crowdfunding can provide an alternative method of finding minorities and women, while providing investor protections and enabling risk sharing among a community," according to the report.[17]

Sutian Dong, a senior associate with FirstMark Capital, a New York–based venture fund that invests in early-stage companies, thinks crowdfunding may have the potential to help entrepreneurs in geographic areas that VCs ignore. "All the larger cities have a start-up culture," Dong says. "Outside of that, it's very hard to raise financing."

In addition, she says, some types of business don't make sense for angels or VCs, who generally look for high growth and scalable businesses, mostly in the tech sector, and who want to cash out their investment within seven years. "If you want to crowdfund a neighborhood bar, that might be an excellent way to get community support, but that's not a great investment for an angel, or for a VC," Dong says. Some entrepreneurs have no desire to give up equity or to eventually sell, she says. Depending on what the entrepreneur wants, crowdfunding could provide a better-fitting alternative. Says Dong: "A question is, do you want part of a watermelon, or a whole grape?"

Despite the hype about crowdfunding and its ability to help businesses gain visibility, develop vital marketing intelligence and raise capital, success is not guaranteed. To do it right, entrepreneurs need to invest in a good video, a strong marketing campaign and professional public relations, says consultant Sandeep Sood, CEO of both Monsoon, an app developer, and the RainFactory in Berkeley, Calif., which helps companies conduct crowdfunding campaigns. He says his clients spend an average of $200,000 on each fundraising effort.

Performing arts most successful on kickstarter

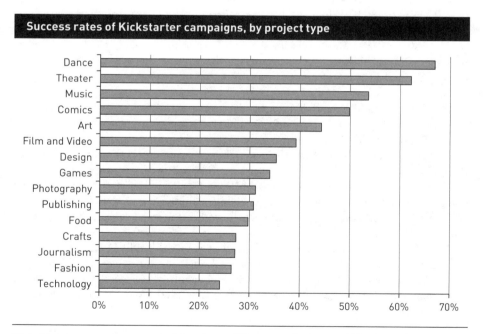

Kickstarter campaigns created for dance (67 percent), theater (62 percent) and music (54 percent) projects have the highest success rates for meeting funding goals. By contrast, fewer than 30 percent of campaigns created to fund craft, journalism, technology, fashion and technology projects have met their goals.

Source: "Stats," Kickstarter, updated Jan. 20, 2015, http://tinyurl.com/7bs6xbv

Preparing for and running a campaign can be expensive and time consuming. Although entrepreneurs on many rewards-based sites don't have to pay the crowdfunding site a commission if they don't raise enough money, the time they invested can't be recouped. The failure rate on crowdfunding campaigns is high—Kickstarter, which updates the statistics on its website daily, says 40 percent of some 197,000 campaigns have met their fundraising goals since the company's founding in 2009.[18] (With Kickstarter's all-or-nothing funding model, missing a goal means getting nothing.)

Entrepreneurs raising money online pay fees charged by the platforms, which run as high as 8 percent for a partially funded campaign on Indiegogo, plus 2 to 3 percentage points for credit card processing. There are other costs. For instance, money raised on rewards-based crowdfunding sites may be subject to taxation by the Internal Revenue Service and by states, which may levy a sales tax, although rulings are ambiguous.[19]

Accounting for the money can be tricky, and people should consult a tax accountant to make sure they get it right, says Neiss of Crowdfund Capital Advisors. Generally, equity investments go into Owners Equity on the balance sheet, while a loan goes under debt. For nonprofit organizations, donations are reported as donation income.

It behooves companies to follow through on their promises whether they have a legal and fiduciary responsibility to investors on debt and equity platforms, or a moral obligation to backers of rewards and donation campaigns. "Your reputation is on the line and will forever be scarred if you don't follow through," Neiss says. Best practices dictate that entrepreneurs are open and forthright with investors on how the funds are being used.

Successful crowdfunding, in theory, should help companies attracting follow-on financing because successful crowdfunders demonstrate themselves to be "accountable, reliable and transparent," he adds.

Boris Kogan, the CEO of start-up SwarmBuild, based in Tel Aviv, Israel, and Cedar Rapids, Iowa, is building a digital marketplace where hardware start-ups and designers connect with manufacturers. He sought $50,000 in October 2014 on Kickstarter, concurrent with efforts to raise a seed round from angels and venture investors. The campaign attracted little interest in its first 31 days, raising just $2,504, so the partners canceled their Kickstarter effort and moved to another platform where they perceived their chances would be stronger. The site, called Startup Rounds, allows 100 start-ups at a time to compete for presales and a pool of seed investment funds—significantly fewer than on Kickstarter. "We were competing for eyeballs with a thousand other tech projects on Kickstarter," Kogan says.

Even if they hit their crowdfunding goals, tech start-ups such as like SwarmBuild seldom raise all the money they need to sustain themselves through the early stages of building a business. "Had we raised a round on Kickstarter, it would not have been enough to get us past a couple of months," says Kogan, who developed his business at the Iowa Startup Accelerator in Cedar Rapids.

Is equity crowdfunding dangerous for investors?

Because equity crowdfunding for unaccredited investors won't take effect in the United States until the SEC releases the final rules implementing Title III of the JOBS

Act—regulations that are long overdue and not expected anytime soon—criticism to date revolves around hypotheticals. No one knows if people will make bad investments or become victims of fraud.

But the possibility that unsophisticated investors of limited means might lose their savings concerns even some fans of crowdfunding, such as NYU's Greenberg. "It's hard enough for professional investors with large and deep networks to do this properly," Greenberg says. "I do worry that it might become a casino of sorts. It's much more like gambling than investing because it's remarkably difficult to have a good sense of a very new idea succeeding."

Trying to determine how unaccredited investors might fare, Michael Dorff, a professor at Southwestern Law School in Los Angeles, reviewed studies tracking the performance of investments selected by angel investors. "What we see is that angel investing only makes sense on average because of a relatively few big winners," says Dorff.

"I just think it's fundamentally a bad idea," he says of unaccredited equity crowdfunding. "During the years that it will likely take for the middle class to see equity crowdfunding for the alluring trap that it is, investors are going to lose a lot of money. And these are not people who can afford the losses." In his article, Dorff said the only companies to go through the process of issuing equity on crowdfunding sites to unaccredited investors will be those with poor investment prospects and no other options.[20]

The U.S. Chamber of Commerce Foundation also raises flags about equity crowdfunding for unaccredited investors, even as it acknowledges its virtues. In a March 2013 blog, Rich Cooper, vice president of research and emerging issues, called crowdfunding a "legitimate and growing phenomenon."

He wrote, "While VC and other investments will always be a critical element in fostering new business, the explosion of digital capabilities has created a world-wide town hall that gives consumers an opportunity to directly support the products and services they want."[21]

However, Cooper said, crowdfunding carries risks: "In any new business, there is the potential that the company will fold, given changing consumer demand, business costs, competition and other factors that can depress the potential for success. Investors understand failure looms large in entrepreneurship, and it is a risk they are willing to take. Will the public accept this risk? Do they fully grasp that failure is a natural part of the entrepreneurial process?"

William Cunningham, a crowdfunding consultant, economist and author of *The JOBS Act: Crowdfunding for Small Businesses and Startups*, says that the SEC's proposed caps on investments in crowdfunded ventures won't shield all people from financial ruin. "You'll get somebody who lost the bulk of their savings through some fraudulent campaign the same way people lost their houses to an underwriting guy in subprime lending, but the downside is far lower and the potential for social and financial returns are so high that, in my opinion as an economist, it makes sense to pursue this."

Proponents also laud crowdfunding as an equalizing force in investing, a way to narrow the gap between the rich and everyone else by letting the masses participate in wealth creation before companies go public and their valuations soar.

"The JOBS Act lets ordinary investors invest easily for the first time," says Amy Cortese, author of a book about investing in one's local community to stimulate economic development and support area businesses.[22] She says crowdfunding is good not only for small companies and start-ups that can't raise money from VCs or get a bank loan, but also for the small, unaccredited investor who was previously shut out of investing in private companies. Crowdfunding rules will allow investors to lend money to companies, which means investors might be able to get a return much sooner through interest payments, Cortese adds.

David J. Paul, chief strategy officer of the real estate equity crowdfunding site Propellr and co-chair of Crowdfund Intermediary Regulatory Advocates, an advocacy group for equity crowdfunding platforms, has been active in negotiations over rules for Title III of the JOBS Act. He says that for years, regulations barred unaccredited investors from participating in the trillion-dollar market for private equity offerings. Right now, he says, it's an asset class that's available to only about 8 million wealthy families, and just about 1 million of them are participating. "If we get Title III close to right, it'll be available to everybody."

Paul says that the proposed caps on how much unaccredited investors can sink into any one deal could safeguard against losses. However, he adds: "No one should be putting more than 5 to 20 percent of their assets into alternative investments. At the end of the day, I think it's the government's job to protect people from fraudsters, but it's not necessarily the government's role to protect people from themselves, from the failure of a business. There's a difference between a company that genuinely tries and doesn't succeed and one that tries to rip you off."

Is crowdfunding good for the economy?

Besides democratizing the fundraising process, the White House and other proponents of crowdfunding say they hope it can foster viable enterprises that spur job creation and economic development in communities.

"The implication and opportunities for crowdfunding are much broader than just the piece of the world that VCs focus on," says Ellie Wheeler, a principal in New York City at Greycroft, a venture capital firm with $600 million under management.

Indications of crowdfunding's potential to transform businesses and to boost the economy come principally from anecdotes about reward-based and donation-based crowdfunding and in limited data from equity crowdfunding outside the United States.

The economic impact of a small business on its community can be powerful. The business can serve as a visible anchor on Main Street as well as a source of employment and tax revenue. Consider Lainie's Way in Port Jefferson, N.Y., a debt-strapped educational toy store that was on the verge of shutting down after suffering extensive damage from Superstorm Sandy in 2012.

Owner Lainie Litovsky took to the crowdfunding platform Tilt in March 2014, appealing to her community to save her store. With help from local media coverage and postings on social media, she raised $91,135 in donations, just slightly short of her $94,000 goal but past the "tilt" amount of $89,000, the bare minimum the store needed to stay open. On March 24 at 11:16 p.m., Litovsky posted a thank-you to the community: "Lainie's Way will be open tomorrow, and for many years to come. Good night."[23]

Survey: most kickstarter creators aim to launch businesses

Particularly for businesses in places not well served by venture capitalists, crowdfunding can spur economic growth. "The crowdfunding of securities under the Crowdfund Act has the potential to give rural entrepreneurs, farmers and small business owners a new source for venture capital and other business finance. What they choose to do with it, we can only wait and see," wrote University of Colorado law professor Andrew A. Schwartz.[24]

Kickstarter creators' reasons for seeking crowdfunding

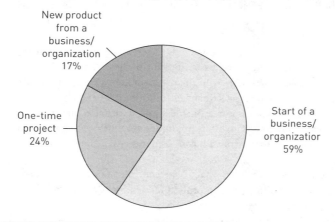

New product from a business/organization 17%

One-time project 24%

Start of a business/organization 59%

Fifty-nine percent of Kickstarter campaign creators using the platform between 2009 and July 2012 launched their campaigns to start new businesses. Twenty-four percent used Kickstarter to fund onetime projects, while 17 percent were business owners seeking funding to develop new products.

Source: Ethan R. Mollick and Venkat Kuppuswamy, "After the Campaign: Outcomes of Crowdfunding," UNC Kenan-Flagler Research Paper No. 2376997, January 2014, http://tinyurl.com/q3t9lk8

Crowdfunding lets people vote with their dollars to support their local economies and causes they believe in, says James Beshara, the CEO and founder of Tilt, which has raised funds for thousands of projects. "As people see the fruits of these platforms, they tend to think more through the lens of what can we do with our money," Beshara says.

Crowdfund Capital Advisors, which pushed for the JOBS Act, touted the economic benefits of successful crowdfunding in a 2013 study of 73 firms: crowdfunding campaigns by for-profit businesses on both rewards-based and equity-based platforms in North America, Asia and Africa.[25] The consultancy found:

- Crowdfunded companies overall saw a 24 percent quarter-to-quarter increase in revenue, not including sums raised through crowdfunding.
- For equity-crowdfunded companies, revenue increased 351 percent from quarter-to-quarter.

- 39 percent of companies hired an average of 2.2 employees after crowdfunding.
- 48 percent indicated they planned to use the proceeds of their campaign to hire more staff.
- Every hour invested in a successful crowdfunding campaign returned $813.
- 71 percent of companies that were successful with crowdfunding either had received or were in conversations to accept follow-on investment.[26]

Wharton's Mollick has also found that successful rewards-based crowdfunding on Kickstarter can benefit entrepreneurs and, by extension, the economy. In a survey of large design, technology and video game projects that had raised money on Kickstarter, 90 percent were still in business one to four years after their campaign. Moreover, Mollick and his survey co-author said that 32 percent reported revenue of more than $100,000 a year after their Kickstarter campaign.[27]

Circle Up, an equity crowdfunding site for accredited investors that specializes in consumer product companies, has been amassing data on the performance of its companies since 2012. Companies that raised money on the platform grew 80 percent on average in the year after their successful campaign, says Rory Eakin, co-founder and chief operating officer.

While crowdfunding can boost a business and its local economy, Southwestern Law's Dorff worries that middle-class investors might divert money from retirement, college savings or debt reduction into a crowdfunded business that is either fraudulent or just fails to deliver as promised.

Mollick found in a 2013 study that 75 percent of successful rewards-based campaigns experienced delays in producing the promised reward for backers, and that the more money received, the later they were likely to be.[28]

The blog Drop Kicker, which tracks crowdfunding flops and frauds, has devoted a lot of coverage to the Scribble Pen. Prospective funders raised doubts about the veracity of its creators' demo promising that the pen can write in any color by using a scanner that can replicate the hue of any surface. The company halted its campaign on Kickstarter in August 2014, after Kickstarter requested a new video within 24 hours.[29] Later, the campaign reopened on Tilt, but problems arose there too.[30]

Tilt's Beshara wrote in his blog that Tilt had learned about discrepancies in information given to Scribble Pen backers and potentially misleading representations in the demo video; Beshara requested additional information from the campaign organizers and gave them a deadline to provide either a new video of a working prototype or an in-person prototype. "Since these conditions were not satisfied, we decided that the best course of action to protect our community—both contributors and organizers—was to discontinue the campaign and refund 100% of all payments over the next three days."[31]

On Sept. 6, 2014, Scribble Pen noted on its website that a working prototype was never a condition of fundraising on Tilt. "Scribble is not a figment of our imagination or an attempt to defraud anyone in any way. We have been working tirelessly for the last two years to design and manufacture a product that we believe will change the world, and we are closer than ever to making that a reality." The company discontinued its crowdfunding efforts and is seeking to raise the money privately, according to the blog.[32]

Responding to a request from SAGE Business Researcher for comment, the "Scribble Team" said in an emailed statement in January 2015 that the company had "launched a little too early" on Kickstarter and Tilt. "As you know, we are creating an innovative product, never seen before, and we experienced some technical issues with the advanced color sensor that the pen uses. We shall be launching a finished consumer version of the Scribble Pen this year."

When it comes to equity crowdfunding, it's still not clear how much the economy might be helped, or hurt, once unaccredited U.S. investors are allowed to buy shares in private companies. To better understand how small investors make decisions, four academics from Canada and Germany studied offerings on the Australian equity crowdfunding platform ASSOB, in operation since 2006. Their conclusion: "Crowdfunding investors seem to pay a great deal of attention to the financial and governance material that firms provide. However, at this point, the industry is still in its infancy, and thus our data do not enable us to make a meaningful evaluation of firm outcomes yet.[33]

BACKGROUND

Before the Internet

In 1783, composer Wolfgang Amadeus Mozart needed some cash, fast. His goal: to stage the performance of his three new piano concertos in a Vienna concert hall. Appealing to his bewigged and perfumed fans in a newspaper advertisement, he offered an incentive that wouldn't seem at all strange to modern-day aficionados of Kickstarter. "These three concertos, which can be performed with full orchestra including wind instruments, or only a quattro, that is with 2 violins, 1 viola and violoncello, will be available at the beginning of April to those who have subscribed for them (beautifully copied, and supervised by the composer himself)."[34]

Mozart, like many a Kickstarter hopeful, didn't make his number. But a year later, in 1784, he tried again, and 176 patrons contributed enough for him to introduce his concertos in a three-part series known as the Lenten Concerts. He thanked his patrons by publishing a list of their names.[35]

Perhaps the best-known example of pre-Internet crowdfunding in the United States occurred in 1885, after the American Committee for the Statue of Liberty ran out of funds for the construction of the massive granite pedestal to hold the statue that was France's gift to America. Stepping forward to save the day, newspaper magnate Joseph Pulitzer appealed to everyday people to help. "Let us not wait for the millionaires to give this money," Pulitzer urged in his newspaper, the *New York World*. "It is not a gift from the millionaires of France to the millionaires of America, but a gift of the whole population of France to the whole people of America."[36]

Pulitzer printed in his newspaper the names of everyone who contributed. "One Hundred Thousand Dollars!" the *World* trumpeted on its front page. The final tally was $102,000, 80 percent of which came in donations smaller than $1, allowing for the completion of the pedestal.[37]

Internet revolution

Crowdfunding, by its nature, requires some way to get the word out efficiently to potential donors or investors. In the pre-digital age, successful efforts shared some common traits, according to author Dave Milliken. "Crowdfunding required the leadership of major influencers—a famous writer, newspaper publisher, a prominent businessman with federal backing—with access to mass media to generate awareness and interest from the general public. Otherwise, the cost of building awareness was generally far too great."[38] The Internet simplified getting the word out to large numbers of people in a community of like-minded individuals, regardless of their physical location. In 1997, the cash-strapped British rock band Marillion became the first to use the Internet to crowdfund, according to then-band member Mark Kelly. By appealing to fans via email, the band raised $60,000 to finance its U.S. tour.[39]

Crowdfunding took off after the global financial crisis in 2008. Entrepreneurs and artists alike were looking for alternative funding as bank loans and other traditional sources of capital dried up.[40]

Indiegogo, founded that year and now one of the world's leading crowdfunding sites, explains its genesis on its website: "Danae Ringelmann was an MBA student trying to open an Off-Broadway play. Eric Schell searched for funds for a Chicago theater company in his spare time. Slava Rubin started a charity event for myeloma cancer research after losing his father to the disease. Their struggles to find funding revealed a fundamental flaw in the system: For centuries, access to funds has been controlled by a select few. Danae, Eric, and Slava started Indiegogo in order to revolutionize the flow of funding, so it can reach and grow the ideas that matter."[41]

A year later, Kickstarter debuted, and other players have since piled into the reward-based crowdfunding sector, including RocketHub in 2010 and Crowdtilt (now called just Tilt) in 2012. Donation-based crowdfunding, including sites such as GoFundMe, are a close cousin of rewards- or perk-based models, helping people and nonprofit organizations raise money for personal needs and causes by reaching out through their social networks.

Investor protections

After the stock market crash of 1929, the federal government moved to protect investors with the Securities Act of 1933 and the Securities Exchange Act of 1934.[42] All securities sold to investors had to be registered with the newly created SEC, unless they fell into certain exempt categories, such as private offerings under Regulation D, which exempts small companies from SEC regulation for selling securities in a private placement. They must file an electronic form that includes the names and addresses of the company's promoters, executive officers and directors and some details about the offering.[43]

Those securities rules, which among other things, prohibited issuers from "general solicitation" and advertising of their offering, continued, without major changes, for decades. It took another disaster, the 2008 financial crisis, to open debate on new ways to encourage business innovation and job formation.

Entrepreneurs Sherwood Neiss, Jason W. Best and Zak Cassady-Dorian, now principals in Crowdfund Capital Advisors, helped form the Startup Exemption, a group that helped develop the framework for the crowdfunding portion of the JOBS Act.[44] Neiss recalls:

"The capital markets had seized up for people who create businesses, who innovate and create the majority of jobs. Our frustration led us to go to Washington."

Crowdfunding was just one of the measures of the JOBS Act, whose provisions aimed to help companies raise capital more easily by easing regulation. The act, signed into law by President Obama on April 5, 2012, drew support from the National Venture Capital Association, the Small Business and Entrepreneurship Council, the U.S. Chamber of Commerce and the International Franchise Association.[45]

Arguing that crowdfunding would endanger investors were groups such as AARP, which represents senior citizens, and the North American Securities Administrators Association, which represents state securities regulators.[46] The SEC also worried that equity crowdfunding might lead to more lackluster companies—what some refer to as "zombie companies." As a result of such objections, Congress revised the bill, including requiring a crowdfunding company to provide audited financials when raising more than $500,000.[47]

The JOBS Act enabled companies to publicly solicit and advertise private placements. The regulations for Title II took effect on Sept. 23, 2013, allowing companies to crowdfund from accredited investors.[48]

However, Title III, which legalizes equity crowdfunding for unaccredited investors, still hasn't taken effect. Congress mandated that the SEC issue these rules by the end of 2012, but the agency didn't issue its proposed regulations, which weighed in at 585 pages, until September 2013. To date, a final version has not been issued.[49]

The proposed rules would let small companies raise up to $1 million over the Internet from ordinary investors. These firms would no longer have to comply with certain reporting requirements that public companies must follow, such as disclosing executive compensation. Individual investors wouldn't be allowed to invest more than $2,000, or 5 percent of their net income, if their net worth is less than $100,000. Wealthier investors could spend 10 percent of their net income up to a "maximum aggregate amount sold of $100,000."[50]

"This could revolutionize everything because people who could not get access to capital will be able to do so on terms that are reasonable," says Cunningham, managing partner of the consultancy National Crowdfunding Services in Washington.

Industry growth

Since the release of Title II rules, numerous Internet portals have gone into operation to serve businesses seeking debt or equity from accredited investors. Niche sites specializing in real estate are among the fastest growing, according to Crowdfund Capital Advisors' Neiss. He says that may be because a tangible asset such as a building gives investors a sense of security.

Commercial real estate developers have long raised money from groups of private investors, either through limited partnerships or real estate investment trusts (REITs). Real estate crowdfunding lets lots of people invest smaller amounts of money, but unlike REITs, investors can choose a specific building or project. Many real estate crowdfunding sites structure the investments as debt notes or preferred stock.

Fundrise, a real estate crowdfunding platform based in Washington, was founded in August 2012 by brothers Daniel and Benjamin Miller, who work in their family's commercial real estate business. They aimed to spur economic development that reflected the desires of a local community—the potential equity investors, Daniel Miller says. "A lot of the real estate companies we work with now are existing developers with a real track record. We're now convincing them to go online to raise capital."

Neiss says that it's hard for many real estate projects to get bank loans and even when they do qualify, it can take months. Crowdfunding can deliver the funds in a matter of weeks.

In Fundrise's deals, the platform puts up the full amount of money each developer is seeking and then sells notes to investors.

Chad Gessin, a partner in Chatham Development in Manhasset, N.Y., decided to test crowdfunding by seeking $1 million on Fundrise in 2014 to build a house on Long Island. (Another $1 million came as cash provided by partners and family. No banks were involved, and Gessin says they didn't really need the money from Fundrise.) "We're a relatively small shop, and we were looking for a way to open up our development projects, large and small, to more investors, not just through crowdfunding but also through private offerings to accredited investors," he says.

Fundrise gave Chatham the $1 million upfront, then sold 10.5 percent preferred shares to investors. The investors will get their return on their investment before the developers, Gessin says. "It's a very safe deal for Fundrise, because $1 million is what we paid for the land." He says he liked that his company had to vet only one investor, Fundrise, instead of many.

Experts caution that such investing is by nature speculative and risky and investors must be willing to tie up their funds long-term.[51] Five financial consultants, interviewed by *The Washington Post*, don't recommend Fundrise to their clients because of concerns regarding risk, high fees and inadequate liquidity.[52]

Success in rewards-based crowdfunding has also led to follow-on investing by venture capital firms. CB Insights, which tracks venture capital, looked at 443 technology hardware companies that successfully raised more than $100,000 on Kickstarter or Indiegogo. The August 2014 report found that 9.5 percent of those companies raised venture capital funds, totaling $321 million.[53]

A case in point: After Oculus Rift's successful fundraising efforts on Kickstarter for its virtual reality headsets, venture capitalists came calling. The start-up secured two rounds of venture funding, $16 million and $75 million, respectively, on the strength of its crowdfunding success. Then in early 2014, Facebook acquired the firm. The Kickstarter backers didn't profit from the sale because they weren't shareholders; some complained about the deal and their inability to benefit. (Equity investing is still not legal for unaccredited investors, so the issue remains hypothetical.)

A man tries on an Oculus Rift virtual reality headset. The company was a major crowdfunding success.

ROBYN BECK/Staff/AFP/Getty Images

A disgruntled backer who identified himself on Kickstarter as Carlos Schulte groused: "I think I would have rather bought a few shares of Oculus rather than my now worthless $300 obsolete VR [virtual reality] headset. What's two billion dollars amongst 9,522 friends?

I'd be happy with my $300 back."[54] Greg Belote, the co-founder of equity crowdfunding site Wefunder, said that if Schulte's $300 donation had been an equity investment, he would have received about $43,500, or 145 times his investment.[55]

Still, some observers point out that even if equity crowdfunding had been a legal option, Oculus might not have chosen to sell equity so early, before it had a viable product.

David Marlett, executive director of the Dallas-based National Crowdfunding Association, says that the early backers of Oculus Rift got what they had signed on for, but adds the company could have behaved more sensitively. "The right thing would've been to take the $2 billion and give everybody their $300 back. What great PR that would've been."

Starting an Internet crowdfunding portal has become an attractive business venture in itself. Angel investors and venture capitalists have poured almost $1 billion into the industry since 2006, with activity intensifying in 2013, a "breakout year for crowdfunding," according to Neiss at Crowdfund Capital Advisors. Investments almost doubled, to more than $140 million, in the first three quarters of 2014, compared with the previous year, when investors put $71 million into seven major deals, mostly lending and rewards-based platforms.[56]

Most crowdfunding platforms are still privately held. However, Lending Club, a peer-to-peer-investing platform that lets individuals lend to other individuals profiled on the site, raised $870 million in an initial public offering (IPO) in December 2014.[57] Peer-to-peer lending involves issuing SEC-regulated securities, and is legal for investors in as many as 30 states to date. Unlike equity crowdfunding, it's not considered a private placement and is not covered by Title III of the JOBS Act, according to securities law firm Pepper Hamilton.[58]

It's also not clear when, or if, some of the biggest players in crowdfunding will go public. Speaking to interviewer Charlie Rose, Yancey Strickler, CEO of Kickstarter, said the co-founders have no intention of either selling or going public.[59] Indiegogo, which closed a $40 million round of funding in early 2014—the largest amount raised at one time by any single crowdfunding platform—maintains that it chose investors who take a long-term approach to building the business and aren't looking for a quick exit.[60]

Crowdfunding goes mainstream

As more of the famous and the well-heeled have turned to crowdfunding, some critics have complained that it is losing its populist spirit. An outcry ensued after director Spike Lee raised $1.4 million on Kickstarter in 2013 to make "*The Newest Hottest Spike Lee Joint.*"[61] A similar pushback accompanied the successful raising of $5.7 million for Rob Lee's *Veronica Mars* movie and the $3.1 million backers contributed for the Zach Braff movie project *Wish I Was Here.*[62]

Kickstarter's co-founders defended such celebrity campaigns, maintaining that high-profile figures help increase the pie for everyone. "Spike Lee brought three decades of fans to Kickstarter when he launched his project. He introduced many of them to this new way of funding creative works, and to the thousands of other projects that are funding on Kickstarter. Of Lee's backers, 47% had never backed a Kickstarter project before," they wrote in a 2013 blog post. "In the past 90 days alone, more than $21 million has been pledged to filmmakers on Kickstarter *not* named Rob Thomas, Zach Braff, or Spike Lee. Even without counting these projects, it's been the biggest three months for film ever on Kickstarter!"[63]

It's not just entrepreneurs and publicity-conscious celebrities trying crowdfunding. Major brands are also embracing the concept, not because they can't access capital, but because they want to market and promote new products, gauge consumer interest and foster a culture of innovation within the corporate environment. For example, in Japan, Sony Corp. is using crowdfunding to build employees' managerial and entrepreneurial skills with the development of new products. "Launching a business from scratch and seeing it through is a very valuable lesson to have regardless of whether you're becoming a Sony manager or going to other companies," according to Hiroki Totoki, who heads Sony's in-house entrepreneurship program.[64] Sony crowdfunded FES, a fashionable smartwatch with an e-ink paper display, without originally revealing its involvement.

Taking a different approach, consumer products giant Procter & Gamble in 2013 formed a partnership with the equity crowdfunding site CircleUp, which specializes in consumer products. P&G mentors some entrepreneurs vetted by the site and helps them bring ideas to market. The affiliation with CircleUp is also intended to help P&G keep abreast of consumer trends.[65]

CURRENT SITUATION

Regulatory challenges

The U.S. investment crowdfunding industry is in a holding pattern, as it awaits the SEC's final regulations for Title III of the JOBS Act. Since the act's passage in 2012, the commission's leadership has changed and it's now up to the new chair, Mary Jo White, who took over in April 2013, to act. She told the Senate Appropriations Committee that completing the regulations and studies mandated by the JOBS Act is among her top priorities.[66]

"No one knows when, or potentially if, the SEC is going to issue the equity crowdfunding regulations," says Marlett at the National Crowdfunding Association, which formed in 2012 to negotiate with the SEC. "It's such a political hot potato. If Obama puts it out there, and there is some fraud, he will get the blame, and there are not enough people with enough financial power pushing him to take that risk," he says.

Paul, co-chair of Crowdfund Intermediary Regulatory Advocates, told a House subcommittee in January 2014 that if the commission implements its regulations as proposed, the crowdfunding industry for unaccredited investors won't reach its potential. He said that the disclosure requirements for entrepreneurs raising $500,000 to $1 million are "actually more onerous and exhaustive than the current requirements for Regulation D offerings which does not mandate audited financial statements for issuers, nor ongoing annual audited disclosures."[67]

Ringelmann, co-founder of Indiegogo, doesn't want to see any more delays, either.

"I hope the regulators will be able to put a first pass out there and be ready to reassess and iterate, just like an entrepreneur would, based on what they learn from the marketplace. I don't know what needs to happen to make that happen," she says.

Ringelmann adds, "From what we've learned with a perks-based business, there is a need and desire for people to want to shape the world around them, whether it's to open a local restaurant or help a food truck get started, or get a school up and running or help a product launch."

Until Title III regulations are released, crowdfunding portals are focusing on either serving the accredited investor community or continuing to offer rewards- and donations-based models. Some new platforms that were poised to offer equity crowdfunding to unaccredited investors ran out of money and have disappeared, Marlett says. Impatient for the SEC to act, more than a dozen states, plus the District of Columbia, have legalized equity crowdfunding for unaccredited investors, using an SEC intrastate exemption. The catch: Businesses can raise funds from unaccredited investors only within that state's borders. Other states are drafting regulations or have bills wending through legislatures.[68] In Texas, where crowdfunding became legal in October 2014, lawyer Lee Polson, a partner at Strasburger & Price in Austin, is helping an investment crowdfunding portal launch. "We have been working through some of the operational issues and how to make this work in Texas," Polson says. "Texas is large enough, where somebody can raise some serious money operating these portals."

Industry growth

Even as regulatory inaction stalls the growth of U.S. interstate equity crowdfunding, rewards-based and donation-based campaigns grow in popularity.

"You can't put this cat back in the bag," says Marlett, the crowdfunding association executive, who is a senior research fellow in Arts & Emerging Media at the University of Texas, Dallas, and is leading the school's efforts to promote campus-based crowdfunding for professors' and students' projects. "Crowdfunding is a wonderful tool for vetting a project and developing a following."

Marlett, a filmmaker and script writer who incorporates crowdfunding into class assignments, often tells his aspiring filmmaker students that they should be grateful equity crowdfunding for unaccredited investors is not yet legal. Once that happens, he says, it may become next to impossible for projects such as indie films to get funding without offering backers a piece of the action.

Legal actions

In May 2014, Washington state Attorney General Bob Ferguson filed the nation's first consumer protection suit involving crowdfunding against Edward J. Polchlepek III, known as Ed Nash, and his company Altius Management. The suit, which is still pending, alleges that Nash's 2012 Kickstarter campaign failed to deliver the promised decks of Asylum playing cards with a retro-horror theme to backers by December 2012. Under Kickstarter's rules, companies that don't meet their promises to deliver rewards are supposed to refund the backers' money. Asylum raised $25,146 from 810 backers in a campaign that closed on Oct. 31, 2012. The company hadn't communicated with these people since July 2013, the suit alleges.[69]

"Consumers need to be aware that crowdfunding is not without risk," Ferguson said in a statement. "This lawsuit sends a clear message to people seeking the public's money: Washington state will not tolerate crowdfunding theft."[70]

Assistant Attorney General Jake Bernstein, who is handling the case on behalf of those Washington state residents who contributed to the Altius campaign, says his office brought the lawsuit to draw attention to the issue. "We tried to settle and didn't get anywhere. We're essentially working toward a court resolution, and we've had trouble serving him. He decided to hide and has been hiding effectively for a while."

Altius could not be reached for comment.

Meanwhile, backers, who contributed anywhere from $9 to $93, are outraged. "This project is dead and our money is long gone, we were all suckers and too many times now!" says a backer identified as Jericho in a Nov. 9, 2014, posting on the Kickstarter page.[71]

LOOKING AHEAD

Becoming the default

In a few years, crowdfunding as a term may become obsolete as the practice goes mainstream, some industry observers say.

Ringelmann, the Indiegogo co-founder, says crowdfunding "will become as common as buying" and that instead of crowdfunding, people will just be funding. Beshara, the CEO of Tilt, likens crowdfunding to blogging tools such as WordPress, which used to be considered novel but now are just the way people publish content on the Web. "The reason crowdfunding will seem archaic and dated is that it is just going to become the default of how people come together and make something happen," he says.

"I think 10 years from now a billion people will be crowdfunding around the world and from their phones," says Beshara, whose site recently released a mobile app. Most likely, he says, the majority of these global fundraising efforts won't be big, ambitious hardware projects but instead small "bite-sized" campaigns, such as raising money for a block party.

Beshara also sees a strong future for rewards-based crowdfunding for both small start-ups and major brands, based on Tilt's experience in selling an open-source crowdfunding tool to big brands to run major crowdfunding campaigns.

"I think we are going to see some massive crowdfunding campaigns, but it won't be dependent upon amateurs and early adopters," he predicts. "I think it's going to be Mountain Dew crowdfunding a new drink, Nike a new shoe and Lululemon a new apparel line."

Beshara says that as people grow more comfortable committing to buy items that haven't been produced yet, businesses will test demand before they spend a dime on production. "That is going to allow for what I call 'perfect demand,'" he says.

Beshara says he has no plans to expand Tilt's domain to include equity crowdfunding, once the SEC releases its rules for unaccredited investors. Increasingly, backers on crowdfunding platforms—such as the fans of the much anticipated video game *Star Citizen*, who have given more than $60 million to the company to build out new features—are showing their willingness to pay for cutting-edge products that they won't see for months. "If you can sell directly to these customers and build a community and not give away any equity, why would you look at an old-world alternative?" Beshara asks.

Proponents of equity crowdfunding see the future a bit differently. If and when equity crowdfunding becomes legal for ordinary investors, Paul of Crowdfund Intermediary Regulatory Advocates says he thinks the market could be worth "hundreds of millions of dollars" within five years—still small compared with the trillion-dollar accredited investor private-equities market.

Neiss at Crowdfund Capital Advisors says he expects the industry to grow in a slow and "rational" way. He expects asset-backed businesses such as real estate will keep growing, and that debt-based crowdfunding will experience the greatest growth. Women and minorities will benefit in particular from the growth of equity crowdfunding, he says, with new specialized platforms arising to serve them.

As an industry, crowdfunding will generate new businesses and job-creation, predicts Dong at venture capital firm FirstMark Capital. "You'll have services, platforms and tools that crop up around crowdfunding, and someone has to provide them."

Chronology	
1700s–1800s	**Poets, musicians and others appeal to patrons for money.**
1713	British poet Alexander Pope asks patrons to finance his six-volume English translation of Homer's *Illiad*.
1784	Mozart raises money from patrons to finance a concert to introduce his three new piano concertos.
1885	*New York World* publisher Joseph Pulitzer raises $102,000 from thousands of readers, in donations mostly under $1, to complete construction of the pedestal for the Statue of Liberty.
1930s	**Stock market crash of 1929 prompts securities regulation.**
1933	Securities Act provides for the registration of securities to protect investors and exempts small offerings from certain reporting requirements.
1934	Securities Exchange Act establishes the Securities and Exchange Commission (SEC) to regulate the securities industry.
1950s–1980s	**Invention of computers and the Internet pave the way for crowdfunding.**
1958	President Dwight Eisenhower creates ARPA, the Advanced Research Projects Agency, to develop technologies that eventually lead to the Internet.
1962	J.C.R. Licklider of MIT envisions a "Galactic Network" of globally interconnected computers.
1969	ARPANET, the precursor of the Internet, is founded to connect four university sites in California and Utah.
1972	First email travels over the network.
1977	Apple introduces its first personal computer.

(Continued)

(Continued)

1981	IBM unveils its first PC.
1986	The National Science Foundation connects regional networks to a backbone network, the NSFNET, or Internet.
1989	AOL users hear "Welcome, you've got mail!" for the first time.
1990	HTML protocol allows users to send text along with graphics to create hypertext pages.
1990s–2000s	**Internet Age crowdfunding appears.**
1997	English rock band Marillion raises $60,000 on the Internet from its fans to finance its U.S. tour.
2003	ArtistShare starts platform to help artists raise money online.
2004	Kiva.org, a crowdfunding and microfinance platform, makes small loans to business owners around the world.
2011–Present	**Crowdfunding grows in popularity.**
2011	Georgia allows companies to issue stock for up to $1 million without registration and to accept up to $10,000 from an unaccredited investor.
2012	President Obama signs Jumpstart Our Business Startups (JOBS) Act, allowing companies to go directly to the public to solicit investments through crowdfunding. . . . Pebble blows past its $100,000 goal and raises a record $10.3 million on Kickstarter. . . . Oculus Rift raises $2.4 million for its virtual reality headset from 9,522 backers on Kickstarter, on a goal of $250,000. . . . Philadelphia becomes the first city to crowdfund on Citizinvestor; it fails to raise $12,875 for Tree Philly to plant 15,000 trees.
2013	SEC issues draft proposals regulating equity crowdfunding for unaccredited investors. . . . Oculus Rift raises $75 million from venture capital firms. . . . Michigan passes intrastate crowdfunding legislation, called Michigan Invests Locally Exemption (MILE) law.
2014	Facebook acquires Oculus Rift for $2 billion, with some backers of the crowdfunding campaign complaining that they didn't get any of the money. . . . U.K. equity crowdfunder Seedrs acquires U.S. broker dealer/investment adviser Junction so it can move into American market. . . . Washington state Attorney General's Office sues the creator of the Asylum Playing Cards crowdfunding project on Kickstarter, for failing to deliver on its promises to deliver retro-horror themed playing cards. . . . Social media site Reddit launches beta version of Redditmade, a new crowdfunding platform. . . . Intrastate crowdfunding rule takes effect in Texas.
2015	In January, Tennessee and Oregon allow intrastate crowdfunding. . . . Kentucky Legislature discusses proposed crowdfunding legislation.

Q&A: Trends in Crowdfunding

"DEMOCRATIZING ENTREPRENEURSHIP IS VITALLY IMPORTANT"

Ethan Mollick
Assistan professor of business
Wharton School, University of Pennsylvania

Ethan Mollick, an assistant professor of business at the Wharton School, University of Pennsylvania, devotes much of his research to exploring the world of crowdfunding, where populist enthusiasm has bankrolled a $55,000 potato salad spree and funded a cooler with a built-in blender to the tune of $13 million. More important, he says, crowdfunding provides underrepresented groups with a chance to finance projects and products. Mollick spoke with SAGE Business Researcher reporter Robin D. Schatz about crowdfunding trends and his research. This is an edited transcript of the conversation.

What led you to study crowdfunding?

Online communities are interesting and user-driven innovation is interesting. I study and teach entrepreneurship—I'm a former entrepreneur—and I think democratizing entrepreneurship is vitally important. Somewhere between 2 and 6 percent of venture capital-backed companies have female cofounders, despite the fact that women make up 40 percent of business owners in the United States. We're clearly not drawing from a full pool when we're trying to make investments.

What's behind the field's rapid growth?

In some ways, there's a lot of pent-up demand for funding innovation. We have all these collaborative online communities that have developed ideas together, but there was never any way to get things funded. Also, there has been a rapid drop in price in everything associated with starting new businesses—recording an album, launching a software start-up. That puts things more into reach.

But some of your research also suggests people aren't turning to crowdfunding just to raise capital for their projects and businesses. What did you find?

If you look at one survey we did, money was the fourth most common reason why people sought funding. Far more important was finding out whether their idea was interesting to people, getting exposure, building a community of people who were interested.

What did you and New York University professor Jason Greenberg learn from your research into women and crowdfunding?

What we found is that you were 13 percent more likely to get crowdfunded if you're a woman than a man. But on top of that, it didn't come from the areas women traditionally do best in, where women are best represented, like fashion. Women were doing disproportionately well in technology and video games, areas in which they're underrepresented. So, we did experiments to find out why. Crowdfunding allows activist women, women who support other women, to help boost fellow females in underrepresented areas, and that's allowing them to do better than men.

Just how smart is the crowd?

Ramana Nanda, [an associate] professor at Harvard Business School, and I analyzed crowdfunding choices vs. the experts' choices in the theater, and we found that generally the crowd and experts agreed with each other. And when the crowd and the experts disagreed, the crowd liked things that the expert didn't. So the crowds are pretty wise.

In another study, I looked to see whether funders were rational: Were they looking for the kinds of things that professional investors look for before putting money into a company? Were they doing things like looking to see whether people had endorsements from the press; were they looking to see whether people had experience in an industry before they joined it; were they looking to see if people had prototypes? All of those things increased chances of succeeding. On the other hand, the thing that the Internet likes that aren't correlated with success—like do you have cat videos, or do you mention the word "bacon"—none of those things predicted success.

(Continued)

(Continued)

Then, how do you explain the success of the Kickstarter campaign that raised $55,000 to make potato salad?

First of all, the Internet is weird. It contains multitudes and sometimes those multitudes are really strange. Before potato salad, there was $40,000 raised to successfully build a statue of Robocop in Detroit. I mean, weird things will happen. Remember the potato salad guy ended up raising a huge amount for charity and started an endowment, so it's a pretty impressive outcome.

What role does social media play in all this?

To the extent that this is about making Internet things real, you need to have a presence for people to believe in you. I found the more Facebook friends you have, the more likely you are to succeed. This stuff moves through social networks.

How do crowdfunders fare after successful campaigns?

Out of the campaigns that are making products, 90 percent of them turned their campaigns into businesses and hired 2.1 employees in the next year or two, and a third of them had revenue of $100,000 or above. So it's a really impressive outcome.

Is there a danger if a crowdfunder raises too much money?

I think that's completely true. The more money you raise, the more delayed you are [in your project]. It's not uncommon to see that happen. Basically, expectations get larger and as you want to do something bigger, all the issues of producing get harder.

MEETINGS AND TEAM MANAGEMENT
Are traditional meetings still relevant in today's tech-driven world?

Joanne Cleaver

EXECUTIVE SUMMARY

Not for nothing are so many *Dilbert* comic strips set in meetings. Notorious for wasting time, dulling motivation and draining creativity, meetings are widely seen as a necessary evil—one poll found that 46 percent of Americans prefer almost any "unpleasant activity" over a meeting. Not surprisingly, managers are trying to reinvent meetings to make them more productive and to meet the changing needs of a 21st-century economy. Technology and start-up companies are experimenting with meeting formats and lengths, and some established organizations are following suit. And as staffs become more diverse, managers and researchers say meeting dynamics must include more points of view, communication styles and ways of arriving at decisions. Some experts agree that new technologies may help solve many problems associated with routine meetings. Yet others say that changing corporate culture is more important. Among the questions under debate: Is technology fundamentally changing the nature of meetings? Are planned meetings better than spontaneous meetings? Can women be heard in meetings?

OVERVIEW

Ask Jeanette Martin about the worst business meeting she ever endured and she will recount her stint at a German auto parts manufacturer. Everybody on the team spoke fluent English, but Martin was the only one who also wasn't a native speaker of German. Every week, the team held a meeting to review the status and progress of ongoing projects. And every week, the meeting opened in English and then quickly transitioned to German. She put up with it for a year, then snapped.

"I said, 'If you don't need all of us in this meeting, because you're speaking German then I've got other things to do.' And they apologized," says Martin, who teaches management at the University of Mississippi School of Business Administration and is co-author of *Global Business Etiquette: A Guide to International Communication and Customs*.[1]

Martin also has a happy meeting tale from her days as a staffer at a medical supply manufacturer. Managers were stymied by how to make the most of employees' often excellent suggestions for saving time or money. The suggestion program rewarded the person who came up with a good idea, even though the results often depended on how well others carried out the suggestion.

From *SAGE Business Researcher,*
March 14, 2016

Meetings are evolving as technology and corporate culture change.

"One person was getting rewarded while somebody else did all the work," Martin says. A cross-section of executives met to hash out the problem, well aware of the likely repercussions on employee morale and of the potential for blowback. "It was a good meeting because it took on a long-standing company practice—the suggestion box—and we saw people's minds change in the meeting" as participants came up with an innovative solution, Martin says.

Meetings: They're inevitable, inescapable and often intolerable aspects of any organization. Yet the meeting as a form of collaborative energy is so compelling that some meetings have achieved epic status: The Last Supper, the Constitutional Convention of 1787 and the post-World War II Bretton Woods conference on monetary policy, to name a few. In the best cases, the collective minds of meetings hash out agreements, breakthroughs and alliances impossible to engineer in individual conversation.

As the pace of business accelerates, managers are trying to reinvent meetings. Technology and start-up companies are experimenting with meeting formats and lengths, and some established organizations are adopting the resulting new practices. The emergence of the flat corporate structure (i.e., few bosses overseeing an army of self-directed, self-managing staff) appears to be diametrically opposed to traditional meeting culture. And as staffs become more diverse in terms of gender, generation and ethnicity, managers and researchers say meeting dynamics must adapt to include more points of view, more styles of communication and more ways of arriving at decisions.

This change is sending stress fractures through long-standing meeting culture and assumptions. From intern orientations to board of director assemblies, many meetings are happening in different ways, with different players, for different reasons.

Workers typically loathe meetings because they appear to wick away the one thing no one can make more of: time. For 18 percent of Americans, a trip to the Department of Motor Vehicles is a more appealing way to spend time than attending a "status" meeting—a prototypical form of meeting in which attendees update each other on the progress of various projects, according to a survey released in 2015 by software company Clarizen.[2]

The same poll found that 46 percent of Americans would rather do almost any "unpleasant activity" than sit through a meeting. For respondents, death by meeting was not hypothetical: The poll found that staff members spend an average of 4.6 hours weekly preparing for status meetings and 4.5 hours weekly attending such meetings—a full day of each workweek.[3]

A seminal study by University of Southern California (USC) researchers found that status and informational meetings (the latter is where announcements are made) accounted for 45 percent of all meetings.[4] Widespread dislike of these routine meetings has spawned an entire industry dedicated to eliminating them via "virtual collaboration platforms." Only 5 percent of the meetings identified in the USC study were creative or brainstorming meetings—the types, according to organizational psychologists, that are both the most fun and the most productive to attend.

But the USC study also had a cheerier side that validates Martin's best-meeting scenario. Purposeful, well-run meetings that achieve their goals generate high satisfaction among participants and goodwill for those who called and ran them. And a study found that 97 percent of workers consider the collaboration that meetings foster essential "to do their best work."[5]

Many consultants, psychologists and business anthropologists—those who study the underlying dynamics of meetings from a cultural point of view—agree that new technologies may solve or support many aspects of routine meetings, likely for the better. Technology innovators have introduced "collaborative project management systems" intended to eliminate the tedious status meeting. Such software creates online modes of continuously updating team members' progress on projects, eliminating the need to hold a meeting to accomplish that goal. In theory, tech company executives say, the remaining meetings would be productive, enjoyable and mission-driven brainstorming that can focus on idea development and strategy.[6]

Meetings don't just feel like they go on forever—meetings as a ritual actually have been going on forever, says Tomoko Hamada, a professor of anthropology at the College of William & Mary in Williamsburg, Va., who studies cross-cultural business customs.

Humans are hard-wired not just to communicate but to communicate in structured formats that reinforce who belongs to a group and that perpetuate the group's culture, she says. Contemporary business meetings are on the continuum that began with humans gathering to discuss how to stay alive by planning tasks. "We are social animals. From an anthropological point of view, meetings are corporate rituals," Hamada says. "Americans are always saying they're going to eliminate meetings, but they're not going to go away."

Routine meetings are platforms for power players to exercise their authority and for attendees to demonstrate that they are insiders who belong. Newcomers often must go through rituals of "rebirth" to affirm their status as learners, experts say, and to take their proper place (think of the notion that certain chairs are traditionally where certain attendees sit). Communication traditions, such as raising one's hand to signal the desire to speak, also affirm attendees' common culture. The corporate meeting even has a version of the tribal "talking stick": the PowerPoint projector remote.

Inherently, face-to-face meetings include the broadest spectrum of nuance, from side conversations to facial expressions to small gestures and tones of voice. Virtual platforms typically omit pre- and post-meeting rituals because technical requirements dictate the protocols of webinars, virtual meetings and similar formats. These formats are efficient, but the subtleties that reinforce the value of face-to-face meetings are lost, Hamada says. Often, participants make decisions in prior, private discussions so the actual meeting becomes a formality.

Layer on national culture, and it's a wonder that anything is accomplished in meetings that span companies, countries, time zones and generations. In some countries, anxious meeting-goers obsess over small points of protocol, such as when and how to present business cards to Asian colleagues, Hamada says. She once arranged a virtual group meeting between American and Japanese business school students. "The Americans were worried about how formal the Japanese usually are in how they dress, so they all put on neckties for the meeting. The Japanese were worried about how casual Americans are, so they all wore T-shirts and jeans. When they saw each other, they just laughed," she recalls.

Precisely because they are the stage for so much missed opportunity, meetings are ripe for reinvention. "The dilemma of meetings is that you have to invest time to make them more efficient, but then you have to have a meeting about it," says Alok Sawhney, a business psychologist and management consultant in South Florida. And there's no way to agree that a meeting is unnecessary except by having at least a brief virtual meeting to cancel the meeting, he says.

Ironies aside, Sawhney and other psychologists say meetings are prisms into an organization. Observant participants can read company culture, writ small, in a meeting.[7] Who leads, how they lead, how they shepherd the process, how they assign and measure results—all of this, says Sawhney, yields insights into the dynamics of power, influence and action.

Early in his career, Sawhney was excited to be invited to sit in on board and senior-level meetings at the hospital management company where he was a management intern. "It was fascinating," he says. "The most straightforward stuff took on a life of its own, with all the perspectives and conversations, the differences in personalities. That's the beauty of meetings."

"Meetings are a microcosm," says Bill Treasurer, CEO of Giant Leap Consulting, a team development consultancy in Asheville, N.C. He recalls a privately owned company whose leadership team would painstakingly plot meetings without consulting the owner. "They figured they'd show him the agenda for a three-day offsite meeting at the last minute, fearful that he'd change it. . . . And, of course, he changes it the very first time he sees it." That, Treasurer says, is the sign of a corporate culture driven by fear and obedience. "If there is a general dysfunction, you are likely to see it magnified."

As managers, consultants and researchers consider the role of meetings in a changing business world, below are some of the questions under debate.

WEIGHING THE ISSUES

Is technology fundamentally changing the nature of meetings?

The conundrum of meeting technology is that it makes good meetings better and bad meetings worse.

Now that webinars, conference calls and video conferences are standard formats, managers are realizing that these technologies are best used for transactional discussions: solving relatively routine problems and discussing concrete topics, says Jonathan Lane, managing partner of ProductWorks, a Massachusetts management consultancy that works with technology and start-up firms.

In fact, routine meetings seem to generate the most irritation. A 2013 study found that meeting-goers confessed to being late about one time in 20—with the cumulative effect of forcing 37 percent of all meetings to start late.[8] A quarter of meeting attendees reported through the USC study that "irrelevant issues" took up 11 percent to 25 percent of time in status meetings.[9]

Research indicates that new technology doesn't make attendees pay better attention to tedious topics. Standard conference calls have become notorious as gatherings for participants who are doing other things while listening: sending emails, eating and even going to the bathroom.[10] Video conferences command a bit more attention because participants can at least see each other, says Lane.

Conference calls persist for companies and teams that must communicate with workers across many locations because at least the call officially communicates the same information to everyone at the same time, Lane says. Information published via complementary technology, such as internal social media, intranets, email and digital company communications, might not be read.

But "if the purpose of the meeting is to do real work, the virtual platform degrades terribly," Lane says. A 2015 Boston College study found that telecommuting, while often popular with those working from home or other remote sites, left office-bound colleagues feeling lonely and disconnected. Nonverbal cues and the indefinable value of being together appear to reinforce team understanding and morale in ways not yet fully understood—and not replicated by virtual meeting platforms.[11]

But virtual meetings have their defenders. One is Edward Sturm, a self-employed video and digital marketing content creator in Brooklyn, N.Y., who specializes in collaborating with technology start-up companies.[12] He notes that virtual meetings address questions and decisions as they emerge, instead of batching them for resolution at a scheduled later time. In Sturm's experience, this timeliness prevents problems from snowballing.

"Virtual tools give the respondee time to think and time to continue in a flow state if they need it," Sturm says. "Face-to-face meetings are done more for the benefit of the person calling the meeting, so that person can advance in the company or get a connection that he or she needs."

At the same time, though, virtual platforms can undermine the value of face-to-face meetings, says Michael Randel, a Kensington, Md., consultant who specializes in facilitating meetings. "It's a counterintuitive attitude of 'let's *not* meet,'" he says. "People put all this information in shared folders and dashboards so they don't have to have a meeting."

Multitasking by participants during meetings via texting and sharing, often blamed on Millennials, is committed by all generations, says Paul Cooper, a professional facilitator based in Washington, D.C. He has seen many a meeting host struggle with "technology etiquette," with solutions ranging from forcing all attendees to park their devices in a basket that's put to the side, to actually asking attendees to do research during the meeting on their devices.

But don't blame technology for the easily distracted, Cooper says. The real issue is that the meeting topic and organization aren't interesting enough to hold people's attention. For meeting organizers, hosts and facilitators, "the task is to get people to focus on the here and now, and make it so compelling they don't want to do anything else," he says.

Even though technology itself does not appear to have transformed meetings, others note that management approaches pioneered by some technology companies have been adopted more widely.

For example, "agile project management," which has taken root in software development, is a "spiral process" in which projects are redefined as they progress, partially by ongoing collaboration and many short meetings.[13] (By comparison, traditional project management is linear: Define the project, break it into parts, get the parts done, assemble the parts and complete the project.)

Often, Lane says, agile project team leaders start each day with a short "getting on the same page" meeting. The meetings are intentionally so short—10 to 15 minutes—that everyone can stand, thus sidestepping the usual meeting protocol of sitting around a table. Typically, the team leader organizes the discussion around a board with notes, erasing project tasks just completed and adding tasks and problems to be solved that day. Stand-up meetings are often given nicknames borrowed from sports: "Scrum" and "huddle" are popular.

The concept of a short, stand-up meeting has spread to departments and companies beyond IT, Lane says.

He worked with one established technology services company that felt bogged down by meetings that took too long and accomplished too little. Adopting the agile team management approach, the CEO established a daily 15-minute, 11:45 a.m. standing meeting. "It was about getting visibility into what was happening that day," Lane says. "Everybody has a piece to bring in terms of service challenges, finance, new sales leads, whatever is happening in their departments. The time-boxing . . . moves it along, compared to other meetings where everyone leans back in their chairs with coffee."

The 11:45 meeting has "changed the company culture," Lane says. "It reduces anxiety and 'fire drills,' in which everyone scrambles to find out what's going on with a problem. Everybody knows a problem will be brought up at the 11:45. Over five years, this has become the basic organizing principle of the company."

Are planned meetings better than spontaneous meetings?

Traditional meetings follow a well-worn groove: set a time and agenda; prepare; attend; follow through. Thus, anticipating a meeting forces participants to prepare, clarify their thoughts and validate information, says Dana Ardi, founder of Corporate Anthropology Advisors, a New York City–based consulting firm that works with large corporations. Even short stand-up meetings require participants to bring items to present, she points out.

The collaboration needed to prepare for a meeting is so much a part of emailing, document-sharing and slide-designing that people don't realize how much actual work—analyzing, prioritizing, clarifying—gets done along the way, Ardi says. "It's a whole value chain that surrounds the meeting."

Preparation escalates along with a meeting's importance. When top executives are involved and the stakes are high, including significant decisions about people, money and corporate priorities, attendees prepare more. A "tribal council" meeting involving top leaders usually is preceded by bands of staff preparing research, presentations, charts and briefings. Young managers are often included as observers so they can see what's involved in staging such events.

Most office workers support meeting face-to-face

The structure of formal meetings, Ardi says, usually ensures that participants have an official chance to make their points.

Organizational psychologists and anthropologists agree that purely spontaneous meetings are valuable mainly for building relationships. By definition, spontaneous meetings don't involve preparation, agendas, research and goals, so the information exchanged is informal and may or may not achieve organizational goals.

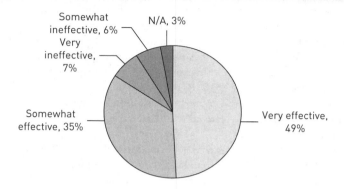

How effective or ineffective do you think face-to-face meetings are at your company?

Somewhat ineffective, 6%
N/A, 3%
Very ineffective, 7%
Somewhat effective, 35%
Very effective, 49%

About half of U.S. office workers at companies with 500 or more employees say their face-to-face meetings at work are "very effective," according to a survey conducted by Harris Poll for project-management software company Workfront. Thirty-five percent of workers said such meetings are "somewhat effective," while 13 percent said they are "somewhat" or "very" ineffective.

Note: Based on survey from July 6–24, 2015, of 617 full- or part-time U.S. office workers at companies with 500 or more employees.

Source: "The State of Enterprise Work," Workfront and Harris Poll, 2015, p. 19, downloaded from http://tinyurl.com/hyyo3y6

In fact, says Cooper, the professional facilitator, a frequent outcome of spontaneous meetings is the decision to call a formal meeting with all the attendant trappings.

Somewhere between spontaneous meetings and formal planned meetings sit periodic regular meetings, says Steven Hunt, vice president of customer research at SuccessFactors.

"There are certain people you should meet with on a regular basis, because there's something to talk about, but you don't know what it is until you get together," he says. Successful account representatives, for instance, will check in with key customers "whether or not there's something to discuss," Hunt says. The agenda for such regular meetings is implied: what's going right, what needs attention and what needs are emerging, he says.

Regular meetings also build relationships and trust, banking understanding for times when things might not be going so well. "Knowing the person in real life, you can 'hear' them in emails, read between the lines in emails and have context," Hunt says. "It builds a lot of tolerance into the relationship."

Focusing on *how* meetings are called overlooks the more important issue of *why* they are called, says Cooper. Format is less important than culture, he says. Northwestern University anthropology professor emerita Helen B. Schwartzman came to the same conclusion when she theorized that what the meeting is about is not what the meeting is. Meetings are not propelled by crises and decisions that must be made, Schwartzman says. For most organizations, it's really a case of the meeting "tail" wagging the issues "dog": Meetings are going to be held, thanks to human nature. The only real open question is, what issues are sufficiently important or pressing to justify the inevitable meetings?

Cooper saw this dynamic at a nonprofit where he frequently facilitated meetings. The group had been holding the same type of meeting in the same format, deciding the same types of things, for most of its 90-year existence. Its leaders realized one day during a sleepy meeting that they needed a wake-up call. Aimless meetings indicated a deeper drift of mission and culture. The organization was losing touch with its mission, just as its meetings were losing touch with attendees, he says.

"The meetings used to be easy. People didn't ask big questions," says Cooper. Now, with some new leaders and some reinvigorated old leaders, the meetings are the crucible for the converted culture.

"There used to not be any impatient people in the room. Now, they are more rambunctious," he says. "I have to be attentive to the fact that there are going to be people in the room who think that things are bull———. There's dissent, and energy."

Can women be heard in meetings?

As the only woman in an influential group of nine, a senior professional with several decades' experience, she often felt her views were overlooked in group debate. "When I will say something—and I don't think I'm a confused speaker—it isn't until somebody else says it that everyone will focus on the point," she told a reporter at a conference.[14]

Supreme Court Associate Justice Ruth Bader Ginsburg says women—including herself—have a hard time being heard in meetings.

The woman—Ruth Bader Ginsburg, inarguably at the top of her profession as an associate justice on the U.S. Supreme Court since 1993—added, "The same thing can happen in the public setting of oral arguments." She cited instances during which another justice would reiterate the question she had just asked during the oral argument and the lawyer presenting the case would direct his response to the male justice.[15]

If fellow justices don't hear the Notorious RBG, do other women have any hope of being heard in workplace meetings?

Women have a hard time being taken seriously in meetings, according to researchers. Academics at Northwestern and Cornell universities have found that in meetings, women's expertise is overshadowed by female identity and expectations of women in social settings. That makes it harder for the group to hear and use the skills that women offer. The group might not achieve its goals because it didn't make the most of the expertise represented by women—specifically because they were women.[16]

Researchers such as Deborah Tannen, professor of linguistics at Georgetown University and author of several best-selling books on gender communication, argue that it's up to both women and men to consciously negate dynamics drowning out women's voices in meetings.[17]

The stereotypical male style of being direct and straightforward isn't always better in corporate meetings, Tannen told one interviewer.[18] "And in some contexts, men tend to be more indirect than women," she said. "It's true that I have heard from women's groups who tell me that it's very hard sometimes to come to a decision, because people are so committed to consensus that they can never move on and say, 'OK, we're not all going to agree on this point, but we're going to have to do something, so let's do this.'

"At the same time, though, I would certainly say that there are things men could benefit from by adapting styles common among women. One is apologizing," Tannen said.

Women's communication style results in better corporate performance, according to a 2013 study of 624 board directors. Researchers, according to one summary, found that "women are more likely to consider the rights of others and to take a cooperative approach to decision-making." Male board members like to follow the rules and trust that their process will result in a valid and defensible decision. Women, though, are more willing to challenge the group, ask outside-the-box questions, request and respond to a broader array of perspectives and collaborate with colleagues more effectively. All of this adds up to impressive results, one study found: Boards with large female representation experience a 53 percent higher return on equity, a 66 percent higher return on invested capital and a 42 percent higher return on sales.[19]

Meetings involving sales and purchasing decisions are especially rife with gender communication problems, say gender communication researchers.

Women tend to examine the major attributes and details of a potential purchase, whether it's for their company or for themselves, according to Marti Barletta, a Winnetka, Ill., consultant who specializes in marketing to women.[20] They often use a time-consuming "discovery process" to get a 360-degree view of what they are considering, looking not just at the essential functions of the item or service but also, for instance, at how much training it might take to get staff to actually use it.[21] Thus, in a sales meeting, other women know they're taking a journey together, while the men grow impatient with the process and wonder when the women will make up their minds, Barletta said.

Perhaps because their views often are discounted and overlooked, even high-ranking women tend to believe they have less influence in their workplaces than men do.[22]

Because so much evidence is accumulating that women's voices are drowned out in meetings, many corporate executives are consciously trying to change the tenor of their meetings, to invite and include more perspectives of all types, says Bernardo M. Ferdman, an organizational psychology professor with Alliant International University in San Diego and a diversity consultant who specializes in working with Latinos and Latinas.

"Top leaders realize the meaning of diversity, but it's the middle who lose power, so they feel threatened," says Hamada of William & Mary. Women often are crowded out of important pre- and post-meeting informal discussions. Astute senior leaders detect these shunnings and step up to advocate for women and other diverse participants, she says.

In a key shift, Ferdman says, executives are starting to recognize that no one person speaks for all people with whom he or she primarily identifies. Market profiles and demographic data often assign common experiences to women—mothering, for example, and the attendant details of caring for small children. But that doesn't mean that any individual woman has that exact experience or represents the statistically average point of view, Ferdman says.

And company leaders are realizing that claiming to be "gender blind" or "race blind"' is misguided. Deliberately ignoring gender or race amounts to dismissing characteristics that have shaped people's life experiences.

The emerging practice, Ferdman says, is to focus on what each individual uniquely brings to discussions and collaboration. "We're all products not just of our own selves, but of our identities, cultures and histories," he says. "Our perspectives are valuable—when we use our perspectives."

BACKGROUND

In pursuit of the talking stick

From North American tribes to medieval guilds to New England town meetings, purposeful gatherings have shaped communication and culture for centuries. Native Americans often used their meetings to decide matters of state—whether to wage war or seek peace—and simply to socialize. In Europe, guild meetings also mixed business and pleasure, not only organizing commerce but formulating funeral and celebration traditions.[23] The famed New England town meeting of the 17th and 18th centuries brought residents together, at which every male citizen not only had the right but a responsibility to speak.[24] Painter and illustrator Norman Rockwell captured this democratic spirit in a painting that depicts a rough-hewn farmer taking the floor at a public forum.[25] The everybody-invited, everyone-can-participate meeting is so entrenched in American culture that even large political and corporate gatherings are often called "town hall" meetings.

One of the most consequential public meetings was the one that established the federal government: the Constitutional Convention, held in 1787.[26] Meeting behind closed doors for three and a half months, a group of male landowners, lawyers and merchants struggled to reach compromises on federalism, presidential powers and other difficult topics. Consensus was elusive, debate was fierce and leaks were common, but this meeting of federalists and anti-federalists, Northerners and Southerners, succeeded in producing a historic document that put the United States on a sound political footing. More prosaically, the convention showed what meetings could do when participants rallied around a common goal and evinced a willingness to compromise.

As the United States grew in the wake of the Constitutional Convention and a manufacturing economy blossomed during the Industrial Revolution, modern corporations emerged, complete with boards of directors, CEOs, marketing departments and products that were sold on international markets. Trailing close behind was the meeting, especially the "status meeting," where goals were assessed and progress was marked. Meetings became a part of corporate culture in the early 20th century and were emblematic of the button-down Eisenhower years in the 1950s, when corporations—and many workers—prospered.[27]

In the "Mad Men" era of the 1960s, committees, task forces, conferences and summits proliferated, each spinning off an orbiting constellation of meetings that were held in time-honored ways. The growing importance of meetings, however, began to produce murmurs of dissent: Midcentury sociologists noted the drain on time and drag on productivity that meetings often produced. And Melville Dalton, a University of California, Los Angeles, professor and author of *Men Who Manage*, was among the first to detect submerged purposes to supposedly task-oriented meetings.[28]

Bringing order to meetings

"Robert's Rules of Order" for meetings—a formal opening, asserting a quorum, asking that motions be made and seconded and then holding votes—set the basic expectations during much of the 20th century for how gatherings should be run, even though few modern companies strictly follow these guidelines in daily meetings. (Corporate annual meetings are a notable exception.)

There really was a Robert—Henry Martyn Robert, an Army engineering officer who was flummoxed when unexpectedly asked to run a public meeting. Determined to never again be caught by surprise, he created a formal template for how he thought meetings should proceed. Robert's Rules of Order was first published in 1876 and has been continually in print ever since.[29]

In effect, Robert's Rules created a default structure for Western meetings in the same way that tribal societies have default structures for their meetings. Many organizations incorporated Robert's Rules as their de facto legal structure. The Midwestern History Association was typical, referencing Robert's Rules in its constitution and bylaws.[30]

The underlying assumption of the traditional meeting was that everybody accepted the social relationships and structure of the meeting—who will come, the governing protocol and the supporting logistics, according to Schwartzman.[31]

While Robert's rules provided a common frame of reference for meeting structure, they also served as a handy weapon for those who either wanted to validate every decision "by the rulebook" or invalidate a decision by claiming that the meeting in question did not follow protocol and thus could not produce a valid result. Many a meeting broke down over the technical application of Robert's rules, to the degree that some public-speaking organizations actually provided cures for Robert's neurosis in the form of specialized training.[32]

Robert's Rules created a consistent way to structure meetings for companies and organizations, but it also created the expectation that simply following the rules would result in an orderly, respectful, productive meeting. In 1989, Schwartzman of Northwestern took this notion on, publishing a seminal work proposing that meetings should drive organizational culture, instead of serving the culture.

Schwartzman's breakthrough was to uncouple the Rules backdrop from what she said was the real purpose of meetings: to reaffirm power structures and relationships.

"The meeting is a specific type of focused interaction," wrote Schwartzman in *The Meeting: Gatherings in Organizations and Communities*. "More specifically, a meeting is defined as a communicative event involving three or more people who agree to assemble for a purpose ostensibly related to the functioning of an organization or group, for example, to exchange ideas or opinions, to solve a problem, to make a decision or negotiate an agreement, to develop policy and procedures, to formulate recommendations and so forth."[33]

The book is an anthropological field study of the meeting dynamics of one nonprofit organization and is considered pivotal to understanding the dynamics and value of Western organizational meetings.

"Meetings, however, may be most important in American society because they generate the *appearance* that reason and logical processes are guiding discussions and decisions, whereas . . . relationship negotiations, struggles and comments" are, she wrote. "It is this process that can make meetings such frustrating occasions because they appear to be doing one thing whereas, in many ways, they are accomplishing something entirely different."[34]

Reinventing meetings

While Schwartzman was peeling back the underlying layers of meeting culture, those going to business meetings in the early 1990s started to notice a change: Faster communication, propelled by email and the emerging Internet, was shifting how employees communicated and collaborated.

In their zeal to be No. 1, the initial wave of Internet companies reinvented meetings along with other aspects of corporate culture. They quickly realized the potential of virtual meeting platforms, such as Skype, to solve several problems at once: reducing costly, inefficient travel; minimizing the environmental effects of business transportation; and supporting collaboration among international teams across global time zones.[35] By 2009, consultants and business practitioners debated whether sophisticated meeting platforms could actually replace face-to-face meetings, or whether technology would essentially create a new type of meeting that would co-exist with traditional meeting formats.[36]

Yet, as meeting technology changed, meeting frustration grew, says Schwartzman, now a Northwestern University professor emerita.

Survey: "keeping focused" is most common challenge

She says there was a profound disconnect between the Robert's-steeped assumptions many people still held about how meetings should operate and what constituted a successful meeting.

Formalities such as Robert's Rules, along with defaults for meeting settings (coffee, pastries, a generic room) and courtesies (a bland greeting and bullet-pointed agenda), implied that meetings were a blank slate, an empty stage, that participants animated with personality, conflict, relationships and debate.

"People get frustrated because there's not a recognition that other things are actually happening in meetings," Schwartzman says. "These other things are speaking to issues that are relevant to what the group is doing, but that may not be recognized."

"Say people come together to make a hiring decision, but by talking in a meeting about that decision, they also are talking and enacting, and sometimes commenting on, their own set of relationships with each other," she says. "They may be jockeying, or negotiating, or renewing or underlining what their relationships are. The meeting becomes so important in so many different contexts because so many things are happening. There are a variety of things besides the agenda that are baked into the structure of the meeting."

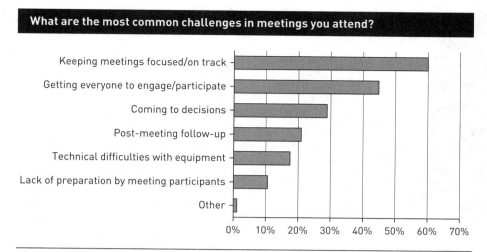

What are the most common challenges in meetings you attend?

Three in five employees say their most common meeting-related challenge is keeping them focused and on track, while 45 percent highlight participant engagement as the most common challenge, according to a survey by Mersive, a Denver-based collaboration software company.

Notes: Based on survey of 499 workers from Feb. 5–19, 2015. Respondents included workers from customer service, engineering, human resources, information technology, logistics, marketing and sales industries, among others.

Source: "The Truth about Meeting Culture," Mersive, April 2015, p. 4, http://tinyurl.com/pcqy6fs

CURRENT SITUATION

Meeting spaces evolve

Office-space planners currently allot about one meeting space for every four to six people, according to Gretchen Gscheidle, director of insight and exploration for Herman Miller, an office design and furnishings manufacturer. "And the spaces are smaller, both enclosed and open. That speaks to how business is done and how fluid collaboration can be," she says.

Smaller spaces, and more of them, indicate how meetings are evolving. They tend to involve fewer people, who are meeting more often. Designers at Herman Miller began seeing this change about 16 years ago. As the 20th century closed, the proportion of meeting rooms to employees started shifting rapidly. Before 2000, the standard was one meeting space for every 20 employees, says Gscheidle. Around 2003, clients started planning more meeting spaces—one for every 10 people—and arranging them throughout each floor of a building.

It's easier to track meeting activity and the space that meetings occupy than it is to monitor the effectiveness of meetings themselves. In fact, meetings are so much the wallpaper of corporate life that they are rarely studied in isolation. One study about meeting effectiveness, widely quoted in blogs, articles and infographics, is "Meetings in America," sponsored by Verizon and published in 1998.[37] A popular study with the same title was

AF archive / Alamy Stock Photo

The *Dilbert* comic strip portrays a satirized office environment, where work-related meetings are usually unsuccessful and unengaging.

published in 2003, a year after the company that sponsored it, WorldCom, filed for what was then the largest bankruptcy in America.[38]

Meeting metrics are slippery. Academics and consultants debate time lost, productivity eroded and morale dampened, yet they have not designed a metric for meeting effectiveness.[39] Meeting participants know a successful meeting when they experience it: a purposeful, inclusive process, focused on a meaningful topic, yielding breakthroughs that individuals could not have reached on their own, and, in many cases, applicable results.

Randel, the consultant who specializes in facilitating meetings, says there is no "overarching method" of measuring meeting effectiveness. "In a simple sense," he says, "a measure of success is, do the sponsors and participants feel that it achieved its objectives? But: Do they share those objectives? It comes back to whether there is an appropriate view of the mission of the meeting." Look no further than the *Dilbert* comic strip for the popular perception of unsuccessful meetings—dispirited, unengaged attendees manipulating what process there is for mutual sabotage, resulting in wasted time, eroded morale and undermined goals.

Part of the problem, says Lane at consulting firm ProductWorks, is that few companies bother to analyze why their meetings work, or don't work. Unlike the military and hospitals, businesses usually don't do postmortems of the underlying drivers of their meetings. Post-meeting discussions "tend to be about blaming, not learning," Lane says. Companies would do well instead to "take a deeper dive, structured as a learning meeting: 'How do we become smarter and better?'"

The chronic tension over the value of meetings is driving both a desire to move routine, repetitive communications to virtual platforms and to make more of the meetings that do need to occur, says Krystal D'Costa, an anthropologist who writes the "Anthropology in Practice" blog for *Scientific American*.[40]

Most workers, she says, want to be in on meetings, even if they claim otherwise. "You want to be an actor at some point. If you're not, you become ancillary, and they'll look to replace you," D'Costa says. This explains the persistence of status meetings, during which "a leader is rattling off milestones and deliverables. If you don't show up, there's no confirmation that you are fulfilling your role."

Having many meetings to complain about is in some ways a status symbol—especially at the C-level, where executives must meet with their teams and with each other. In 2009, an "Executive Time Use Project" tracked how executives of global companies spent and managed meeting time. It found that the most effective managers spent the most time in meetings with other executives and with clients.[41]

Still, employees and managers often struggle to control their time, especially when they feel they spend more time meeting than they do actually working at specific independent tasks D'Costa says. Power struggles erupt over planting meetings on others' schedules through online scheduling programs. Gscheidle, the Herman Miller executive, says that many meetings are doomed before they happen when the meeting request barnacles itself on participants' calendars. "People think, 'This is a block of time that has been added to my calendar, thanks to scheduling technology.' And we can't override the tools. So, the default is a tension that you can't control your own time."

Schwartzman says the fact that meetings are so loathed, and thus have become a rich target for satire, parody and platoons of consultants and technologies, only proves that they are not what they seem to be. Modern meetings are in a constant state of reinvention because "we believe that what meetings do or shouldn't do isn't what they actually do or should do," she says.

The more that consultants claim to quantify the ineffectiveness of meetings, the more attention and resources are devoted to transforming something that isn't what most people think it is, Schwartzman says. In fact, she says, those consultants and technology companies on a mission to reinvent meetings have a vested interest in perpetuating the notion that meetings are so bad that they deserve greater investment. Technology is not a solution, she says, if it simply adds layers of meetings in the absence of awareness about why an organization's staffers are chronically frustrated with its meetings.

Space for thought

Gscheidle says corporate clients still need large, technically equipped rooms for scheduled "show and tell" activity. But her clients also want informal spaces for spontaneous meetings, such as living room-like conversation pits and internal coffeehouses. Many clients specify multiple gathering places for stand-up meetings: a cluster of bar tables (but no bar stools) or slanted, waist-high counters perfect for resting a note-taking tablet.

Managers are paying more attention to how decisions pile up in anticipation of a decision-making meeting, while work coasts in the meanwhile, Gscheidle says. Some of this is inevitable: "Batching happens," she says. But tolerating bottlenecks and the resulting rush of work is, according to Herman Miller research, giving way to the expectation of ongoing collaboration. "Collaborative events," in Herman Miller parlance, take under 30 minutes, involve two or three people and occur at workstations or in casual settings.[42]

"Meetings are sort of the language of the company. Some companies say, 'We're only going to have 15 minute stand-ups,' or 'It's all open and collaborative.' It's an indication of what they want their culture to be," D'Costa says. "But at the end of the day, that need for face-to-face hasn't been removed. It's still a fundamental part of how we do business. You have to confirm that you belong to the company and to the team."

LOOKING AHEAD

Drilling down

"I meet. Therefore, I am." That's the existential essence of unnecessary meetings, says Sturm, the video and digital marketing content creator.

But, he says, the hidebound notion of meeting to meet is on a collision course with start-up culture. In fast-paced, resource-thin start-up organizations, meetings must be worth the time and attention they take away from productive work. Every minute spent in a meeting is a minute lost in getting a product to market.

Established organizations tend to view time as a commodity that they don't want to waste. Start-ups, in contrast, view time as a resource to be invested, he explains. Start-ups with such a philosophy find that they must struggle to retain it as they grow and as pressure mounts from within and without to default to the norm.

Sturm experienced this as he started his own company, and he deals with the dynamic daily as he works with clients that are start-ups. He thinks the start-up philosophy of meetings will prevail because other companies want to be like start-ups.

Paul Graham, a serial entrepreneur, programmer and co-founder of tech investment firm Y Combinator, crystallized the start-up philosophy of meetings in his seminal essay "Maker's Schedule, Manager's Schedule."[43] In it, he outlines the difference between "makers"—programmers, writers, designers and other creative or "making" jobs—and "managers," who translate daily operations into short-term and long-term results. Makers and managers have opposite requirements for time and meetings, Graham wrote. Makers need long stretches of uninterrupted "flow" time to stay in their creative grooves. Managers go from one conversation to another. When managers, who usually outrank makers, schedule meetings for their own convenience, it disrupts the creative flow of makers.

In traditional companies, that's just too bad for makers. Job titles such as "individual contributors" or "team members" barely disguise makers' lack of power to protect their most creative periods from meetings that not only take time but also make it difficult to be efficient with the time they do get.

Start-up culture, posited Graham, puts makers and managers on the same plane in terms of respect for their process and time. If the makers can't make, the managers don't have much to sell (and investors certainly won't reap returns).

"Each type of schedule works fine by itself. Problems arise when they meet. Since most powerful people operate on the manager's schedule, they're in a position to make everyone resonate at their frequency if they want to. But the smarter ones restrain themselves, if they know that some of the people working for them need long chunks of time to work in," Graham wrote.[44]

In his businesses, he reconciled the maker-versus-manager meeting culture by scheduling meetings in advance so that makers could plan accordingly. Graham also cross-pollinated his meeting approach through the start-ups that he backed and to other investors and start-ups through his voluminous network.

Key aspects of Graham's approach include: inviting only employees who must be in the meeting; setting and sticking to a clear, short agenda; and holding brainstorming sessions as separate meetings so free-flowing discussions do not hijack routine meetings.

Start-ups that grew into large companies, such as Google, have consciously tried to scale Graham-inspired scheduling even as they gain more makers and more managers. Mature organizations attempting to adopt aspects of start-up culture are exploring the approach, although it's not easy to retroactively integrate it into settled cultures. "Meetings are still the cockroaches that all companies think they are, but they're slowly dying," Sturm says.

Meanwhile, new technologies have put wheels onto Graham's concept. Sturm doesn't meet with clients face-to-face nearly as often as he used to. Instead, he's constantly in an endless meeting slowly scrolling across a window he keeps open on his computer screen. Virtual collaboration, project management and knowledge-sharing tools have created a new dimension. As with always-on social media, workers are physically in their own space, but virtually together (even if they physically are in adjacent offices).

Project management platforms—such as Slack, Asana, Igloo and Podio—enable workers to check off tasks as they are completed, find experts within their teams for troubleshooting and have quick online "huddles" to change plans or discuss a problem.[45] These are all functions that replace the standard status meeting, say the companies. And, popular virtual meeting platforms, such as Skype and Citrix GoToMeeting, let workers see each others' screens and support webinars and similar forms of virtual meetings.

"It's a constant stream of dialogue," Sturm says of the tools. It's quick and easy to review discussions and decisions, and such tools can be an introvert's best friend, enabling makers (especially) to develop relationships and trust before meeting face-to-face. "You feel smarter," he says. "If you're in a [face-to-face] meeting and you look something up on your phone, it looks like you're not paying attention. But through these tools, you have more resources . . . to look things up. It takes more time, but over the project, it takes less time," he says.

As they adopt technologies that redefine meetings, companies find that work and communication flow differently, forcing a sweeping revision of how work gets done, says Joe Staples, chief marketing officer of Workfront, in Lehi, Utah. Workfront designs, produces and supports cloud-based collaboration tools. And as it has used its own collaboration tool for its own projects, Workfront's own corporate meeting culture has changed, says Staples.

"Eliminating status meetings has allowed us to focus on other types of meetings," he says. For instance, "we'll bring a creative team together to work on a campaign. We'll do some things to structure the meeting, but it wouldn't be reliant on technology. We'd decide on goals and resources, kick around ideas, decide on an idea, and then we'd go into Workfront to assign resources to the campaign."

When everyone knows that the meeting's last phase is slotting work into a new project in the system, the meeting itself is organized around that goal, says Staples. "Now we're thinking about the deliverables that go into the Workfront," he says. "It helps us know what we need to identify, what's the timing, what creative resources do we need. Knowing that we have to define those things sets a structure for what the project looks like. Now, we ask the right questions in the meeting."

Chronology

1600s–1870s	Formal and informal meetings gain a foothold in American society.
1630s–1800s	New England towns hold public forums where residents gather to debate tax rates, land policy and other municipal matters—the beginning of so-called town hall meetings.
1787	Influential American landowners, lawyers and merchants convene for the Constitutional Convention in Philadelphia, where, in contentious meetings that last three-and-a-half months, they reach the compromises necessary to frame a constitution for the new nation.

(Continued)

(Continued)

1876	Army engineering officer Henry Martyn Robert writes and publishes "Robert's Rules of Order," a formal guide for meetings that becomes a generally accepted template in American culture.
1880s–1960s	**Industrialization gives rise to modern corporate structures.**
1880s–1920s	As a growing U.S. economy continues to industrialize, corporations featuring boards of directors, chief executives and other departments institutionalize a staple of modern life: the meeting.
1944	Delegates from 44 countries meet in Bretton Woods, N.H., to regulate international financial affairs in preparation for a post-World War II economy.
1950s	U.S. economy thrives and corporations prosper during the presidency of Dwight Eisenhower, further cementing the importance of meetings in American corporate culture.
1960s	A variety of new and more formal meeting types, including summits, conferences and task forces, emerge during an era typified by the male-dominated "Mad Men" of Madison Avenue.
1970s–Present	**New technologies transform American office culture, enabling workers and teams to meet virtually.**
1970s	Researchers invent word-processing software and laser printers and introduce new computer technologies to offices.
1983	Tandy and RadioShack introduce one of the first notebook-style portable laptop computers, the Tandy Radio Shack TRS-80 Model 100—a development that will soon enable employees to work from home or on the road.
1988	Microsoft releases first version of Microsoft Mail.
1989	Northwestern University anthropology professor Helen B. Schwartzman publishes a study of Western meeting culture, proposing that meetings should emphasize organizational communication and decision-making instead of following existing norms and traditional rules from Robert's Rules.
1989	Computer scientist Tim Berners-Lee invents the World Wide Web, which permits users to connect and meet virtually over the Internet. . . . Email becomes popular during the 1990s, led by America Online and other Internet pioneers; the explosive growth of email helps revolutionize the way workers communicate and meet.
1998	Verizon publishes "Meetings in America," a study that proposes ways for companies to reduce meeting costs and improve meeting efficiency.
2001	9/11 terrorist attacks halt international travel, requiring some multinational corporations to forgo face-to-face meetings with their foreign-based employees in favor of virtual ones.

2003	Swedish and Danish entrepreneurs create Skype, one of the first popularized videoconferencing software companies. . . . Meeting spaces begin to grow in number and become smaller, according to designers at Herman Miller, an office design and furnishings manufacturer; the average office goes from one meeting space for every 20 employees before 2000 to one for every 10 beginning around 2003.
2009	A study by Oxford Economics, a global research firm, concludes that face-to-face meetings are making a comeback despite the popularity of videoconferencing and says every dollar invested in business travel adds $12.50 in revenue. . . . Paul Graham, co-founder of tech investment firm Y Combinator, publishes "Maker's Schedule, Manager's Schedule," which calls for a start-up approach to meetings in which meetings are structured differently for creative "makers" and managers.
2014–15	A Harris Poll survey finds that more than half of U.S. office workers see "wasteful" meetings as the greatest obstacle to work productivity. . . . Globally, almost 3 billion people have Internet access, as electronic business communication continues to grow and evolve.

Q&A: Charles Steinfield on Virtual Meetings

"THESE TOOLS LET YOU DO THINGS YOU CAN'T DO IN A FACE-TO-FACE MEETING"

Charles Steinfield
Professor, Department of Media and Information
Michigan State University

Charles Steinfield is a professor in the Department of Media and Information at Michigan State University. He talked with SAGE Business Researcher contributor Joanne Cleaver about the respective merits of face-to-face and virtual meetings. This is an edited transcript of their conversation.

Technology companies and many consultants seem to believe that the reviled "status report" meeting can be eradicated through online meeting platforms. Would it be more effective to reinvent face-to-face status report meetings rather than seek to eliminate them?

The value of a meeting is that when there is information to be shared in a group and you bring all those people together, then everyone knows that everyone has been exposed to the same information. It's hard to reliably do that in other ways. You have other tools—posting it on the company intranet—but it's not the same quality of knowledge.

There's also symbolic value that when you bring people together, this is important enough to make everyone stop everything else that they're doing and come to this meeting.

Ensuring consistent pickup of information is a historic problem through virtual teams. Say you want to hold a meeting through Skype—it's not a perfect replica of a face-to-face meeting. You have four people in four locations, all on a Skype call; each person still misses some information about what's going on in the other person's context. You have a tiny window through the video camera. You don't know what's happening outside their office, and who else is part of their day. It's a situation that people underappreciate. You're literally not seeing the whole picture. You might not realize that there's someone sitting off camera who's hearing everything.

What are the inherent strengths of virtual platforms versus in-person meetings?

When you have a geographically distributed team, you have to rely on technology. These tools let you do things you can't do in a face-to-face meeting. You can quickly share things. You can engage in back-channel interactions. Say you're in a Skype meeting, but you're texting in a side conversation through your phone with one person. That's hard to do in a face-to-face meeting or even a traditional video conference. And collaborating virtually is a must for when teams involve self-employed professionals and for smaller companies with geographically dispersed teams.

And what are the inherent strengths of in-person meetings versus virtual platforms?

When people are connecting virtually in real time, the meetings tend to be shorter, and there's less socializing. There's a drive to be efficient. It feels artificial. But in person, there's pressure to do some chitchat and some socializing, and that has a benefit. It strengthens ties among people and has benefits for how teams function. To the extent that that doesn't happen through technology, then teams are a bit less cohesive and less trusting.

Can social media replicate the important informal communication of pre- and post-meetings, creating a more meaningful context for virtual meetings?

Social media can help a lot. With global teams, companies bring in people from different countries for face-to-face meetings, and they will periodically have team meetings virtually, but most companies have implemented their own internal social media platforms, and they provide rich capabilities, like microblogging and status updates. Other networks offer personal profiles that let people share personal information. It helps people build relationships. You can look people up and spark conversation in the meeting that wouldn't otherwise have occurred. Technology doesn't so much replace meetings as complement them. When groups do get together face-to-face, that meeting is very important, and in between, these other tools keep relationships alive.

FLAT MANAGEMENT
Can reducing hierarchy improve results?

Jane Fullerton Lemons

EXECUTIVE SUMMARY

Flat management techniques, spurred by the growth of technology companies, are becoming more popular, but it's an approach that can offer advantages to other types and sizes of businesses, too. Although it isn't applicable to all situations, flat management will likely keep gaining ground as the economy continues to evolve and businesses are forced to adapt. The increasing use of technology and social media, coupled with the need for businesses to make quick decisions to remain competitive, ensures flat structures will remain a viable option. Some companies take a dual approach by implementing a flat structure for certain elements of the business while maintaining a more traditional management hierarchy overall.

When Stephen Courtright teaches his business students at Texas A&M University about leadership styles, he cites the experience of a Fortune 500 health care company to illustrate flat management.

A former executive at Denver-based DaVita HealthCare Partners had been someone other employees expected to solve all their problems—and she did. "She was just kind of a do-it-all-er," Courtright says.

When a new executive took over and needed to revamp schedules for health care workers and for patient treatments, she could have done it herself, the way her predecessor would have.

But she chose a different path, opting to organize "a cross-functional team where they themselves came up with a proposal which they then proposed to the entire organization, got feedback on it, went and revised it, represented it to the other team, made final adjustments and then got the sign-off from the leader," says Courtright, assistant professor in the management department of Texas A&M's Mays Business School in College Station, Texas.

Even in the same "fairly hierarchical organization," he says, the executives took two very different approaches to handling a management issue. "Any leader in any organization can empower their workers to solve problems. I don't care what organization—you can empower people to solve their own problems," he says. "That's the principle I want my students taking away from flat management."

Since the mid-20th century, with a global marketplace and a changing economic environment, more companies are adopting leaner and flatter management structures to remain innovative, reduce costs and retain employees.[1]

From *SAGE Business Researcher,*
February 2, 2015

While the overall number of companies following flat management techniques remains relatively small, and they often are privately held, these firms are garnering attention for their nontraditional approaches. And data are beginning to indicate such methods can be effective, says Tim Kastelle, senior lecturer at the University of Queensland's business school in Brisbane, Australia.

"The level of success that these organizations are achieving is pretty high," he says, "so it adds up to a fairly suggestive set of cases."

Drawing on his own research, Kastelle says organizations that include front-line employees in decision-making are "way more innovative and their performance is better" than traditionally organized companies.

A traditional hierarchy is shaped like a pyramid, with one person, typically the CEO, perched at the top, followed by layers of managers, with front-line workers forming the base.

A flat structure can take various forms, but it essentially eliminates some, even all, those layers between the folks at the top and the folks at the bottom. The flattest companies, such as game maker Valve of Bellevue, Wash., are horizontal and essentially have no managers. But many companies regarded as flat, including Google and online shoe and clothing retailer Zappos, retain some kind of management structure, albeit pared down significantly from the traditional hierarchical pyramid.[2]

Even with such changes taking place, there are still plenty of business observers who contend that while modern managers might need to redefine their roles, the roles themselves are still necessary.[3] And the experiences of some flat companies underscore the point. Even the flattest of companies still have a leader or group of leaders who can make final decisions, and some have reinstated layers of management after running into operational problems.[4]

©iStockphoto.com/M_a_y_a

Some companies emphasize flat management as a way of encouraging employees to solve their own problems.

That balance of leadership—as well the differing approaches of publicly and privately held companies—is a key factor in determining whether a business can implement a flatter management technique.

"Flat organization structures require leaders to give up a lot of control, and they typically involve the company taking a long-term view on its development," says Julian Birkinshaw, professor of strategy and entrepreneurship at the London Business School. "So if you are on a quarterly earnings cycle, it is much harder to justify this model. And analysts are also skeptical of these nontraditional organizing models," so leaders of publicly traded companies "tend to opt for more traditional structures."

Jim Belosic, co-founder and CEO of Pancake Laboratories, a Reno, Nev.–based software company that makes ShortStack software, realized he was practicing flat management as his company grew from an initial trio to more than a dozen employees. He believed the company and its culture are better for having taken that approach and urges other small business to consider the same course.[5]

"When I hire these days, I bring on people who have a manager's mentality but a producer's work ethic," Belosic wrote. "In other words, they think like managers and figure out what needs to be done, and then they do the work."

The goal, according to Traci Fenton, founder and CEO of WorldBlu, a firm that advocates flattening management through workplace democracy, is to encourage businesses to shift away from a command-and-control, top-down management style to keep up with the changing demands of the marketplace.

"We've moved from the industrial age to the information age, and the information age has given birth to a democratic age, which is an age of unprecedented participation and collaboration unlike anything we've ever seen before," she says. For companies to remain relevant, Fenton says, they must redesign their operations and rethink their management technique. "What more and more companies are realizing is that in order to be competitive, in order to be nimble, in order to attract great talent, in order to be an environment where millennials will thrive," she says, "it needs to be a flatter, more democratic organization."

Similarly, Morning Star Self-Management Institute, a research and consulting firm affiliated with Morning Star Co., a California tomato processor that embraces flat management, contends that empowered workers are happy and creative workers. While WorldBlu calls its system organizational democracy, Morning Star uses the term self-management; each is a means to a flatter management end. "It doesn't make a lot of sense to give the decision-making authority to the person that [is] furthest (literally) away from the actual work being done," according to the institute's website.[6]

Employee engagement ticks up

Research demonstrates that groups of employees who manage themselves can be more productive. A study by Courtright and researchers from the University of Iowa and Texas A&M found that on the basis of data from 587 factory workers in 45 self-managing teams at three Iowa factories, "peer-based rational control corresponded with higher performance for both individuals and collective teams."[7]

Courtright explained how that translates into the workplace: "In high functioning teams, the group takes over most of the management function themselves. They work with each other, they encourage and support each other, and they coordinate with outside teams. They collectively perform the role of a good manager."[8]

At Pancake Laboratories, Belosic said a flat approach allowed his company to experience advantages other businesses have reported, such as:[9]

- Making faster decisions.
- Encouraging more collaboration among employees.
- Reducing spending on unnecessary or redundant jobs.
- Spending less time on human-resource issues and more on business development.
- Freeing up management-level people to spend more time doing what they're good at and were originally hired to do.

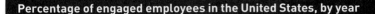

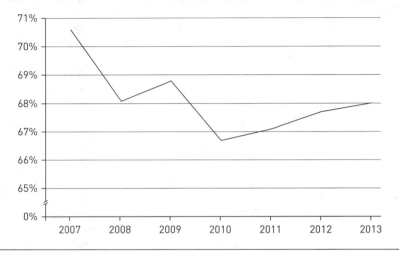

Percentage of engaged employees in the United States, by year

A common goal of companies with flattened management structures is to increase employee engagement by eliminating middle-management positions. According to an annual survey of nearly 5,000 organizations, the percentage of engaged employees fell to a four-year low in 2010 before rising to 68 percent in 2013.

Source: Natalie Hackbarth, David Weisser and Hilary Wright, "2014 Employee Engagement Trends Report," Quantum Workplace, July 2014, p. 11, http://tinyurl.com/klf8e2a

But flat management has its drawbacks. In terms of the impact on the business as a whole, companies always take risks when they empower people, Birkinshaw says.

"Some [employees] lack the competence or the will to do a good job, and this can result in mistakes being made or people doing things that take the company in the wrong direction," he says. "The ultimate case is Enron—supremely flat, but employees were given so much freedom that they ended up creating all sorts of poorly thought-out businesses that lost the company a lot of money and contributed to its eventual demise."[10]

And when things go wrong, Birkinshaw adds, "even the really flat companies tend to become more hierarchical when a crisis or external problem hits. It is human nature to 'circle the wagons' or to go 'back to basics' when faced with a threat."

In terms of the effect on employees, critics contend such an environment can stifle career advancement for those wanting to climb the corporate ladder or can mask hidden power structures and thus could shield employees from accountability. And as flat companies hire workers who will fit in with their culture, a procedure that frequently slows the hiring process, they also may be creating a homogenous workforce.[11]

Despite these criticisms, the use of flat management is growing.[12] Smaller companies and the technology sector have been the most enthusiastic converts to flat management because of the collaborative nature of the business, the creative nature of the products, the need to make rapid decisions and the influx of younger workers. But larger companies and other industries are also using it, albeit with different approaches and to different degrees. And the trend is not limited to the United States, either: Companies across the globe are implementing flat management practices. Even militaries in the United States and abroad are working on ways to reduce hierarchies and empower soldiers to make rapid decisions on the battlefield.[13]

As researchers and executives assess the results of flat management techniques, below are some of the questions under debate.

WEIGHING THE ISSUES

Can a flat management structure help the bottom line?

Flattening the management structure and thus empowering employees "certainly has made a big difference for companies like Google, like Southwest Airlines, 3M and many, many others," says Courtright of Texas A&M.[14]

Courtright has experienced some of the ramifications of worker empowerment during his own travels. "If you go to a Southwest baggage clerk for example, they can make a decision on the spot rather than consult with a manager above them, which is very different than say a lot of the rental car companies that you might go to," he says. "With rental car companies they have to ask their manager for anything and everything."

Clothing manufacturer W.L. Gore & Associates is "a perfect example" of nimble management, Courtright says. "They adopted this model back in the '50s, really structuring it to be more of an empowering environment, and they're one of the few privately held companies in their industry that has had as large a profit margin as they've had over the years." Gore, a Newark, Del., firm with about $3.2 billion in annual revenue and 10,000 workers—referred to as associates and sponsors, not employees and bosses—is run by the Gore family and its workers.[15] It doesn't report profit figures, but as the maker of Gore-Tex fabric, it is a leader in the outdoor gear industry.[16]

While many of the companies practicing flat management techniques began that way, some altered their structure. One example is the Brazilian conglomerate Semco Group, which grew from a family manufacturing operation. When Ricardo Semler took over the business, he restructured the company into a "radical workplace" operating with a participatory management structure.[17] The privately held firm has maintained about 20 percent growth annually for the past 30 years.[18]

Courtright and others point to research showing the correlation between employee engagement and enhanced productivity.[19]

Profits increase at companies with higher employee engagement

"We've found in our study that teams who felt more empowered through a psychological perspective achieved higher performance," says Courtright, adding that other studies he has conducted confirmed those results.

"So the fact is, this model does impact the bottom line, but it does all depend on the strategy, too," he says. The key is for a company to align its organizational design and its

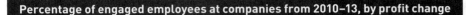

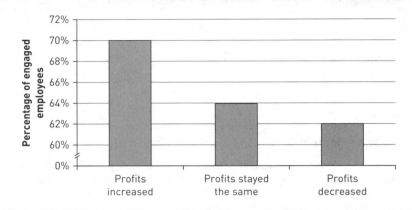

According to a survey of 5,000 organizations in 40 American cities, 70 percent of employees were "engaged"—given greater autonomy—at organizations where profits increased over the last three years, compared with 62 percent of employees who were engaged at organizations where profits decreased.

Source: Natalie Hackbarth, David Weisser and Hilary Wright, "2014 Employee Engagement Trends Report," Quantum Workplace, July 2014, p. 21, http://tinyurl.com/klf8e2a

business strategy. If the strategy requires constant innovation, such as a software company, then a flat approach could complement that. But if the strategy depends on product consistency, for instance, such as a fast-food company, then it might be more suited to a more traditional hierarchy.

Research by organizations such as Omaha, Neb.–based Quantum Workplace, which consults with companies about how to increase business by improving their employees' engagement, has found a correlation between productivity, profitability and employee engagement. An engaged workforce—meaning workers who are involved and enthusiastic about their jobs—can create a competitive advantage.

According to Quantum's studies, organizations with the highest level of engagement showed:[20]

- An 87 percent increase in revenue the following three years.
- An 86 percent increase in market share.
- A 57 percent lower employee turnover rate.

That link between employee engagement and company results illustrates the theory behind the service-profit chain, according to Greg Harris, Quantum's president and CEO. The service-profit chain, as first outlined in the *Harvard Business Review* in 1994, establishes relationships between profitability, customer loyalty, and employee satisfaction, loyalty and productivity. [21]

Links in the Service-Profit Chain

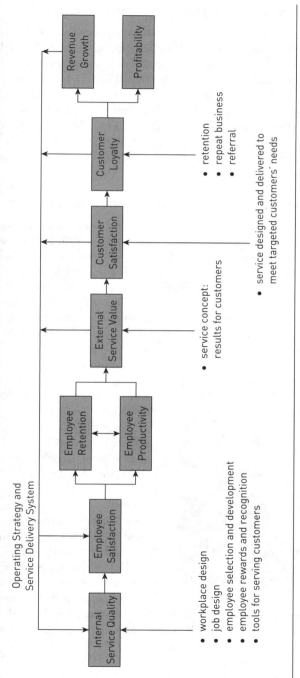

Companies with flatter structures aim to establish links between profitability, customer loyalty and employee productivity and satisfaction. The service-profit chain demonstrates the theory of how satisfied employees improve organizational results. "Internal service quality"—such as providing better workspaces—enables employees to better serve customers and leads to greater employee satisfaction. Companies with satisfied workers should have higher employee retention and productivity. Better services lead to higher levels of customer satisfaction. A satisfied customer base, in turn, leads to increased revenue and profits.

Source: James L. Heskett, Thomas O. Jones, Gary W. Loveman, W. Earl Sasser, Jr. and Leonard A. Schlesinger, "Putting the Service-Profit Chain to Work," *Harvard Business Review,* July 2008 (originally published March–April 1994), http://tinyurl.com/n9bc6vu

Profitability tied to employee satisfaction, customer loyalty

All of this relates to flat management because companies using flatter systems tend to possess more of the factors that lead to higher levels of employee engagement. So it follows that if flat management can increase employee engagement, it also can increase profitability.

"From a financial perspective that might make sense," Harris says, explaining that the flatter the organization, the more people there are who "actually touch customers and can impact the customer experience, [and] the more opportunity they have to drive client loyalty"—the elements of the service-profit chain. At the same time, he says, "the less hierarchical management you have, the fewer the layers of overhead expense."

Those factors together make the case that flat management structures can boost the bottom line, Harris says. "It's definitely a worthwhile hypothesis."

Can a flat management style work for any type of business?

Kastelle argued in "Hierarchy Is Overrated" that a flat organizational structure can work anywhere.[22] Flat management, he wrote, thrives under certain conditions, including a rapidly changing environment, the need for innovation and a shared purpose within an organization. Generally speaking, flat management works best in small and medium-sized businesses that are privately held, but Kastelle and others contend many of its principles can be applied in other scenarios.

The number and type of employees both affect a company's ability to flatten its management structure. Companies using flat structures range from small tech start-ups with a handful of employees, to the Brazilian company Semco with more than 3,000 workers, to manufacturer W.L. Gore with more than 10,000 employees.

Employees at a company that utilizes flat management can often participate in the hiring process as a way of building creativity and independence.

Size becomes a factor in establishing a management structure at some point between about 80 and 150 employees, says Birkinshaw.

"I don't believe it's possible to completely get rid of hierarchy," he says. "I think hierarchy has lots of negative connotations but, actually, some level of hierarchy is necessary to make an organization of more than about 100 people work."

So the question becomes how much structure to impose, how flat a company can go. Even the flattest of organizations ultimately have a leader or management team who can make final decisions. Google, for instance, attempted to rid itself of so many managers at one point that business was disrupted and some layers were added back into the structure.[23] With about 50,000 employees, Google still remains much less hierarchical than other companies of its size, Birkinshaw says.

"Flatter is easier in small and medium-sized companies," he says. "Big companies will always have some sort of hierarchy—it is just a necessary element of being big. So the question is, can a large company be relatively flat compared to its peers?"

©iStockphoto.com/kupicoo

Flat companies also need employees who thrive in such an environment—individuals who are independent and creative. That's one reason businesses with flat management can have a longer hiring process, or even a process where fellow employees do the hiring.

Courtright discusses these considerations with his students as they contemplate their own job options. For a flat organization to work well, he says, "you have to get people whose primary motivation for going into that organization is to work on creative and challenging projects. The corporate ladder isn't all that important to them. It's the notion of continually working on new and challenging tasks. If that's what their motivation is, they'll succeed in one of these organizations."

On the flip side, "if their motivation is to climb up the corporate ladder," Courtright says, "then they'd be much better suited for a hierarchical organization where that's more possible."

Another factor affecting a company's ability to flatten its management structure is its business strategy, for instance, whether it revolves around the need for constant innovation or a consistent product. "The design of your organization has to fit its strategy," Courtright says.

On the one hand, Courtright cites the Google example. "Their strategy is to continually come up with innovative apps or products, and they're all about innovation," he says. "That's ultimately their bread and butter." Because of that mission, he continues, "they have to structure the organization in a way that fosters innovation. So they configured a very flat structure. They give workers a lot of autonomy and freedom."

On the other hand, Courtright pointed to a company like McDonald's, whose business model centers on being consistent and familiar. Because they need to remain predictable to their customers, he says, "they structure their organization to be far more hierarchical."

Flat management vs. corporate hierarchy

Flat management means different things at different companies, some of which have followed the model for decades.

Morning Star, the tomato processor, has adhered to a self-management philosophy since its founding in 1970. According to the company's website, "We envision an organization of self-managing professionals who initiate communication and coordination of their activities with fellow colleagues, customers, suppliers and fellow industry participants, absent directives from others."[24]

At Morning Star, no one has a boss, employees negotiate their responsibilities with their peers, and workers have to get the tools they need to do their jobs—meaning if you need an $8,000 welding machine, you order it. The company's business units negotiate customer-supplier agreements, employees initiate the hiring process when they need help, and disagreements are resolved through a mediation process that can, but rarely does, end up on the president's desk for a final decision.[25]

Nick Kastle, a business development specialist, explained how his working for Morning Star differed from his previous employer: "I used to work in a company where I reported to a VP, who reported to a senior VP, who reported to an executive VP. Here, you have to drive the bus. You can't tell someone, 'Get this done.' You have to do whatever needs to be done."[26]

Valve, the software maker and game developer, has been bossless since it began in 1996.[27] The company's handbook—with the subtitle "A fearless adventure in knowing what to do when no one's there telling you what to do"—is available online.[28]

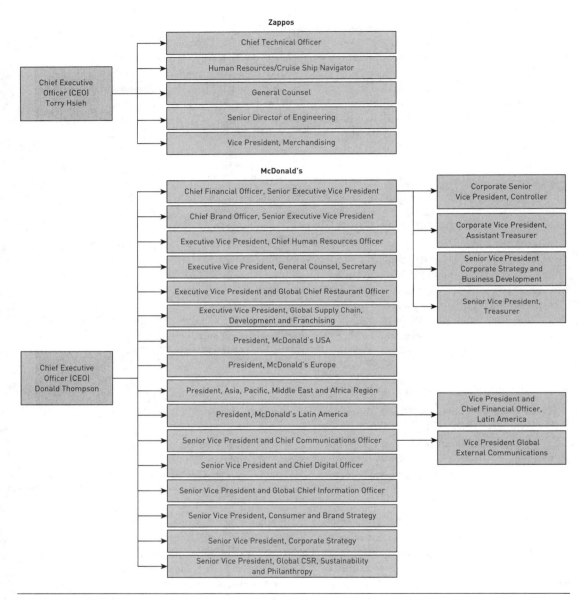

Online shoe retailer Zappos adopted a flattened approach to executive management in December 2013 and has six executives over two levels of its corporate hierarchy. McDonald's, by contrast, has a top-down hierarchical corporate structure with 16 different executive positions in just the second level of its hierarchy.

Source: Zappos organizational structure from "Zappos," The Official Board, updated June 20, 2014, http://tinyurl.com/okd8n4u; McDonald's organizational structure from "McDonald's," The Official Board, updated Sept. 9, 2014, http://tinyurl.com/d3er25l, and Our Company/Leadership, McDonald's, accessed Nov. 19, 2014, http://tinyurl.com/7r6nenm

"It's a classic example of one of the most extreme forms of flat management," says Cliff Oswick, professor of organization theory at City University London's Cass Business School. The company has no job titles, and the desks have wheels so employees can move around the office.[29]

"Your challenge is to add value where you can," he says. "So you decide which project you want to work on; you decide when you want to enter or leave a project, and the whole process of evaluating your performance is done by your peers, including the level for remuneration."

Since its founding in 1958, "Gore has been a team-based, flat lattice organization that fosters personal initiative," according to the company's website. "There are no traditional organizational charts, no chains of command, nor predetermined channels of communication."[30]

The company's president and CEO, Terri Kelly, said it's not realistic to expect a single leader to have all the answers. "It's far better to rely upon a broad base of individuals and leaders who share a common set of values and feel personal ownership for the overall success of the organization. These responsible and empowered individuals will serve as much better watchdogs than any single, dominant leader or bureaucratic structure."[31]

Zappos, the online retailer, recently adopted a management style known as holacracy, which seeks to integrate the advantages of top-down and bottom-up structures.[32] As the company's CEO Tony Hsieh told employees in announcing the plan, "Darwin said that it's not the fastest or strongest that survive. It's the ones most adaptive to change."[33]

"We're classically trained to think of 'work' in the traditional paradigm," John Bunch, a Zappos employee who is helping lead the transition to holacracy, told the online business news site Quartz.[34] "One of the core principles is people taking personal accountability for their work. It's not leaderless. There are certainly people who hold a bigger scope of purpose for the organization than others. What it does do is distribute leadership into each role. Everybody is expected to lead and be an entrepreneur in their own roles, and holacracy empowers them to do so."

For Zappos workers on a day-to-day basis, that translates to more clarity about who owns what, says Alexis Gonzales-Black, who also is helping lead the change to holacracy. "If you need to get something done, rather than emailing a bunch of people, you can look up exactly who is in charge of something," she says. "For many people, it's also meant expanding the scope of their work. In the old system, you might have been siloed into one kind of role, but now that it's more open, people are reaching across circles and taking on work outside of their main area."

Semco, the Brazilian portfolio manager that grew from a manufacturing company, has long practiced "what has variously been called participative management, corporate democracy, and 'the company as village.'"[35]

The military in the United States and elsewhere—long characterized by a hierarchical chain of command—also is working to adopt flatter management techniques to improve its ability to respond quickly to new forms of warfare.[36] That was underscored by comments about the military's future from retired U.S. Army Gen. Stanley A. McChrystal and Gen. Martin E. Dempsey, chairman of the Joint Chiefs of Staff, in which each acknowledged the need to streamline the management structure to allow for swifter decisions.[37]

Navy SEALs, for instance, must rely on distributed decision-making in the field.[38] The Israeli military also uses flatter management techniques to increase flexibility and efficiency.[39]

Military leaders "have been putting a huge amount of effort into figuring out how to make distributed decision-making more effective," says Oswick. "Because what they've discovered is that, in a battle, if you're relying on chain of command, you're not fast enough, and you will lose."

Can a company have a strong leader and a flat management structure?

The role of the CEO is changing along with the social and business climate that is fostering the move toward flatter management.

David Stein, the co-chief executive of software company Rypple, has a message fellow CEOs may find hard to hear: "They're just not that into you."[40]

"My job is important," Stein wrote in 2011, "but I don't flatter myself that I'm the most important person around in the eyes of my customers or most of our team. I certainly am not from my customers' perspective—or even from the perspectives of most employees."

But as many researchers have noted, flat structures still need managers.

"One of the things that is a little bit deceptive in all of this is that when people talk about flat, it's very rare that people are actually advocating we'll have a group of 2,000 people that are all exactly equal," says Kastelle of the University of Queensland. "What people are arguing for when they say flat is, 'Let's go from seven layers for 1,000 people down to three.' So if you do that you still end up with some leadership that is giving us some guidance and setting the course."

In a recent essay for MIT *Sloan Management Review*, professor of strategy and organization Nicolai J. Foss and economist Peter G. Klein made the case for why business managers still matter.[41]

"The new environment suggests the need for a redefinition of the traditional managerial role," Foss and Klein wrote. "Despite all the changes that have occurred, there is a strong need for someone to define the organizational framework within which a business operates. We argue that, in the knowledge economy, the main task for top management is to define and implement these organizational rules of the game."

That view is not so different from what proponents of flat management advocate. "They argue that you still need some source of entrepreneurial vision, strategy and guidance in your organization," says Kastelle, "which I think is, for the most part, true."

To reconcile the argument that managers still matter with the move toward flatter structures, the outsize roles that some CEOs have played may come under scrutiny, according to Oswick of City University London. "One of the things that's happened is the rock star CEO—the idea that in order to be successful you need a highly charismatic individual to lead—is becoming more difficult to sustain," he says.

Flat organizations don't buy into the concept that one individual knows best, Oswick says. Rather, it's a collective process.

"The successful, highly effective CEO of the future will be less concerned about what they think and more concerned with what the collective thinks and will involve a number of stakeholders in the decision making process," Oswick says. "It will be less about them as key individuals and will be more about them managing, coordinating, and engaging the efforts of others."

Courtright agrees. "In flat organizations, or these self-managing teams, it doesn't mean the leadership goes away." Rather, "it's just different. So instead of the top leader calling the shots, they provide information and resources so that the team can effectively self-manage."

BACKGROUND

Assembly lines and managers

Management principles have evolved significantly since Adam Smith put quill to paper in 1776 to write *The Wealth of Nations*, which outlined a new understanding of economics and the role of individuals in the economy.[42] As the manufacture of goods moved from the home and the guild to factories and mills, the Industrial Revolution in the 19th century changed thinking about how to manage business and labor.

Workers were brought together under one roof to manufacture products, increasingly using machines. As technology improved and markets expanded, entrepreneurs began experimenting with assembly lines and mass production. Elihu Root developed an assembly system for gunmaker Samuel Colt by dividing the manufacturing process to simplify it. Then, in 1913, Henry Ford perfected the assembly line so his motor company could churn out Model Ts cheaply and efficiently.[43]

The assembly line and other innovations required a new kind of business model, leading to modern management theories that developed around three broad concepts:[44]

Scientific management was developed by Frederick Winslow Taylor, an American engineer, in the late 19th and early 20th centuries. He was the first to apply scientific methods to workplace issues, with a specific focus on improving economic efficiency and worker productivity.[45]

Bureaucratic management was developed in the early 20th century by Max Weber, a German sociologist and political economist, who expanded on the principles of scientific management. He advocated dividing organizations into hierarchies and establishing strong lines of control and authority.[46]

The human relations movement in management, fostered by behavioral sciences, began in the mid-20th century, to counter the dehumanizing elements of earlier management theories and to emphasize that companies prospered when their workers prospered.[47]

Fast-forward another century: As society moved from the industrial era into one based on technology and information, many business observers argued management must change yet again to remain competitive.[48]

As Foss and Klein recapped in their essay for MIT *Sloan Management Review*, the Industrial Revolution brought the decline of small-scale, cottage production and the rise of large, integrated businesses. "Adam Smith's invisible hand was replaced with what business historian Alfred D. Chandler Jr. famously described as the 'visible hand' of management," they wrote. "But now that pendulum appears to be swinging in another direction."[49]

What Taylor saw as rigidly organized factories of docile and obedient workers, they continued, "has been eclipsed by loosely structured teams of highly trained and empowered knowledge workers. Indeed, the 'visible hand' of management has morphed into a system of loose networks, virtual businesses and peer-to-peer interactions."

"Seismic" changes

Hierarchical management styles trace their roots to the likes of Taylor, Weber and Ford, all of whom were born before the end of the American Civil War in 1865.[50] The change that's needed in an era of advancing technology, generational shifts and globalized workforces and marketplaces, says Oswick of the City University London, is of the same magnitude as the move away from scientific and bureaucratic theories that occurred in the mid-20th century. "On an organizational level, I think this is as significant as the shift from bureaucracy to flexible forms of organizing," he says.

In 2009, business consultant Gary Hamel published a landmark essay, "Moon Shots for Management," in which he argued that management styles dating to the late 19th century had "reached the limits of improvement."[51]

Business executives and experts "must face the fact that tomorrow's business imperatives lie outside the performance envelope of today's bureaucracy-infused management practices," Hamel wrote in the *Harvard Business Review.*

In 2008, Hamel convened a group of leading business scholars, executives and observers to outline a "roadmap for reinventing management." The consensus, Hamel said, was that "equipping organizations to tackle the future would require a management revolution no less momentous than the one that spawned modern industry."[52]

One of the scholars who attended that 2008 meeting with Hamel was Birkinshaw of the London Business School. The hierarchical management model, he says, "is coming under pressure because companies have to adapt more quickly to the rapid changes going on in the business markets." Hierarchy may be useful in stable times, he adds, but in a fast-paced, customer-oriented business environment, the old model has been found "wanting, it's been found to be deficient."

Others who study business trends share the view that management must change to succeed. "In this new world, 20th century management involving tight control of workers and measurement of outputs is no longer appropriate or effective," wrote business consultant Steve Denning. [53]

Japanese assembly lines

The roots of today's flat management structures date to the auto industry of the 1970s and 1980s, when American automakers realized they needed to learn from the Japanese approach.[54] Toyota gained notice when "they gave every employee on the assembly line the power to stop the entire line if there was something wrong," says Kastelle of the University of Queensland.

In the 1980s and 1990s, General Motors tried to emulate that approach with its Saturn line, following the Japanese automakers' flat management philosophy. And, for a while, Saturn proved to be a management success.

"The whole point of that was they had set up Saturn as an independent so that they could learn how to manufacture in a different way," Kastelle says. "The Saturn division did, in fact, do that incredibly successfully and then came back into the core business. The idea was, those ideas were going to flow through the rest of GM when, in fact, what happened was that the machine of General Motors just crushed all of that independent bit of Saturn so at that point the whole experiment fell over."

Honda and Toyota remain fairly hierarchical, Birkenshaw says, "but have figured out how to balance the need for top-down control with the opportunity for bottom-up input."

In contrast, General Motors seemed to tire of the Saturn effort after just a few years, according to John Paul MacDuffie, a Wharton management professor and co-director of what's now known as the Program on Vehicle and Mobility Innovation, a research consortium. "The story of Saturn is not so much the boldness of the ideas, but that GM was unable to follow through," he said. "It just never figured out how to take the lessons that could be learned at Saturn and apply them elsewhere."[55]

The management challenges in other industries were equally daunting. "Back when this was starting to come in the '80s, when the [flat] practice was starting to be talked about more and more, it really was the manufacturing organizations that were [experimenting], and it was a complete shift in *mindset* for them," Courtright of Texas A&M says. "In some cases they were successful, and in some they weren't."

"Engaged, not led"

In the 1990s and 2000s, technological change accelerated, and the Internet and social media became integral to business. This propelled the move toward flatter management techniques, in part because information no longer flowed down from the top of a management pyramid, but instead spread horizontally.

Oswick points to three social and technological changes that have allowed flat management to gain favor:

The ability to communicate and disseminate information in real time through technology and with social media. Informal channels can challenge information disseminated through formal channels. "If a message comes down formally from the top downwards," Oswick says, "already people who are stakeholders for the organizations are contacting people they know to come in to tweet on it in real time."

A shift in social attitudes that has occurred gradually over the last 20 to 30 years. Younger workers are more likely to "want to be engaged, not led," he says. "So that creates a very different dynamic."

The slow reaction time of traditional hierarchical organizations because they're very structured and rules-governed. "In an increasingly turbulent world," Oswick says, "organizations need to be flatter so they can be more responsive and dynamic in the way that they treat challenges within their environment, but also the way to drive innovation."

CURRENT SITUATION

Flat as philosophy

Companies increasingly are moving away from traditional hierarchies, incorporating techniques aimed at reducing bureaucracy and distributing decision-making.

Turning to a flatter structure requires a two-tiered approach, says Courtright, involving not only a company's organizational flow chart but also the mind-set of its employees. "When you think about flat management, what's really at the heart of it is to do away with layers of management and allow people to have more freedom and control of work," he says. "There's sort of this structural perspective to it, and then there's the psychological perspective to it."

Oswick agrees: "I think flat management has taken that one step further, insofar as it's not really about structure anymore. I think flat management is more about philosophy, a way of doing things that moves away from hierarchy more towards networks."

These networks encompass groups of employees, working together and managing themselves, and spread out horizontally; they sometimes represent the business form of societal phenomena, such as crowdsourcing, due to technology that allows for real-time communications. People want to be part of the process, Oswick says.

"We increasingly see the organizational equivalent of flash mobs and groups of employees self-organizing and instigating change," Oswick says, meaning "collective groups of employees coalescing around a common interest with mutual gain."

Generational changes appear to be a factor as well. When Courtright discusses flat management with his students at Texas A&M, "to them it's almost a given. They're not surprised that this is what should be done. I don't think that was the case 30 years ago when we were teaching business. It would've been a far more rogue practice than it is now. Now it just makes sense. And students of mine look for that when they go and get a job."

Although some researchers hesitate to put too much emphasis on the generational element, Harris of Quantum Workplace has seen similar indicators. Research by Quantum has found that flatter organizations draw younger job applicants because they offer more autonomy.[56]

"They want to have more impact quicker," Harris says. "They don't want to be a small cog in the wheel, and we're seeing that in recruitment. Today, talent is more likely to get excited about a role than they are a company name."

Different approaches to flatness

While the flat management concept covers many different approaches, there are companies that offer specific methods to help businesses streamline. Each aims to improve efficiency, speed communications and empower workers with more decision-making authority, but each takes a different approach. Among them:

"Holacracy" gained attention after Zappos announced it would implement this method, which is offered by its founding company, HolacracyOne.[57] The online retailer's move generated widespread interest and scrutiny about how holacracy works and whether it will be successful.[58] Another business using holacracy is Medium, a publishing website from the founders of Twitter.[59]

WorldBlu advocates a slightly different management approach based on what it calls "organizational democracy."[60] The underlying philosophy, according to founder Fenton, is that organizational design leads to organizational culture. "I believe in giving power to people; I believe in eliminating hierarchy as much as possible, but you still have to have some level of hierarchy," she says. "Hierarchy isn't necessarily bad. It's the bureaucracy and the mindless hierarchy that you want to get rid of."

The Morning Star Self-Management Institute espouses yet another model based on the principles developed at the Morning Star Co., "a fundamental mind-shift in the way we view human organizations, management and organizational strategy": Empowered workers, it has argued, are creative workers.[61] This approach has gained attention in business circles since the 2011 publication of the essay, "First, Let's Fire All the Managers."[62] In that article, business consultant Gary Hamel asserted that "with a bit of imagination, it's possible to transcend the seemingly intractable trade-offs, such as freedom versus control, that have long bedeviled organizations" and that "we don't have to be starry-eyed romantics to dream of organizations where managing is no longer the right of a vaunted few but the responsibility of all."[63]

Not without downsides

As companies grow, flat management structures can present problems, and some have dealt with issues concerning career development, employee grievances, office politics and even the lack of social diversity among employees with such similar workplace styles.[64] Two of the leading flat software companies—GitHub and Valve—have addressed problems, often in a public manner fueled by social media.

After leaving the company, former Valve employee Jeri Ellsworth characterized the experience as "a lot like high school."[65] "The one thing I found out the hard way is that there is actually a hidden layer of powerful management structure in the company and it felt a lot like high school. There are popular kids that have acquired power in the company, and then there's the troublemakers, and everyone in between," she said on the *Grey Area*, a podcast about game development.[66]

GitHub, another tech company with a flat management structure, also faced personnel issues, following public accusations of sexism and intimidation that played out on social media after a former employee left the company. That situation led the company to strengthen human-resource procedures and establish leadership-training programs as well as create distinct managerial positions.[67]

Jason Fried, founder and CEO of the Chicago-based software company Basecamp, formerly known as 37Signals, recounted his company's experience when a successful employee wanted to be rewarded with managerial duties and a new title. "The really strange thing was the reason this employee and I decided it was time to part ways," he wrote in a column for *Inc.* magazine. "The issue was ambition—not a lack of it, but more of it than we could use."[68]

None of this surprises researchers who study management techniques. They acknowledge that leaders—whether based on expertise, personality, initiative or other traits—will inevitably emerge. The question then becomes, according to Courtright, whether it is better to have formal leadership imposed on employees or informal leadership that arises naturally.

"That's how it's supposed to work," says Courtright, who explains, "With natural leadership emerging, that means there has to be consensus among the organization that this person is worthy of following, basically, versus in a hierarchical organization where you really have no choice."

These researchers also acknowledge what the companies on the leading edge have found: There's a risk in being among the first to make such changes. But, the other side of that coin is that if companies wait for such changes to become established knowledge, they will fall behind.

LOOKING AHEAD

"The trend is inescapable"

With societal factors propelling a move toward flatter management techniques, flat management observers say the approach will gain popularity.

"The trend is inescapable, just as the trend away from bureaucracy occurred from the 1920s to the 1950s," says Oswick of the City University London. Flat management "will be the dominant form of organization 15 to 20 years from now."

Karl Moore, an associate professor of strategy and organization at McGill University's Desautels Faculty of Management in Montreal, wrote about the situation from a generational perspective with business student co-author Kyle Hill.[69] "From business to the public service to the military, the conclusion is profound: hierarchy is not collapsing, but it is declining," they wrote. "All sectors need to rethink their organizational structure and work environment. The public service needs to shed its layers of hierarchy. The military needs to move from command-and-control practices to consultative leadership. And to remain competitive postmodern businesses need to reduce bureaucracy and facilitate engagement."

SABAH ARAR/Staff/AFP/Getty Images

The military is working to do that. In discussing his vision for 2020, Gen. Dempsey used the language of business to outline the need for military change: the impact of "viral effects," the "rapidity of change" and the "cascading and merging of technology" are compelling the move.[70]

"We have to be agile enough to see ourselves and to adapt on a far tighter cycle than ever before in our history, and I think we can do that," he said in a 2011 speech. Dempsey, chairman of the Joint Chiefs of Staff, was then Army chief of staff.

To accomplish that, Dempsey said, the Army plans to empower its forces from the

Gen. Martin E. Dempsey, then-chairman of the Joint Chiefs of Staff.

"bottom up." That was the theme of a 2012 "Mission Command" white paper that advocated allowing smaller groups to operate in a "decentralized" manner that would allow forces to adapt and respond more quickly.[71]

For Kastelle, that such changes are taking place in the military as well as the business community underscores the lasting nature of the transformation.

"I view that as a pretty important lead indicator in all of this," he says, "that the militaries of the world are trying to figure out, 'How do we give our lowest-ranking members more decision-making authority so that they can use it effectively.'"

Ultimately, Oswick says, "it's here to stay." The need for businesses to flatten organizations and move away from traditional hierarchies is more than a management fad. "This is something which is far more enduring, because it is a slow shift in social attitudes changing," he says, "and it's a slow but gradual shift in technological change."

He says, "This is enduring and significant, and I can't see how—short of us going back to not using technology, to using carrier pigeons rather than email—short of doing that, I can't really see how this trend would be reversed."

Chronology	
1770–1900	**Business complexity leads to development of new management techniques.**
1776	Adam Smith writes *The Wealth of Nations*, outlining a new understanding of economics.
1800s	Industrial Revolution brings the rise of mills and factories, where workers are under one roof to manufacture products, increasingly using machines.
1880s	Frederick Winslow Taylor introduces the concept of scientific management, designed to improve economic efficiency; he later publishes his *Principles of Scientific Management*.
1901–1960s	**Management techniques advance.**
1913	Henry Ford perfects the assembly line.
1920s	Max Weber introduces the concept of bureaucratic management, focusing on standardized procedures and a clear chain of command.
1940s	Drawing on behavioral sciences, human relations management begins to develop, emphasizing that companies prosper when their workers prosper.
1954	Abraham Maslow publishes his hierarchy-of-needs theory of what motives people, paving the way for his later work on what he called enlightened management.
1954	In his book *The Practice of Management*, Peter Drucker introduces the five basic roles of managers, which are to set objectives, organize tasks, motivate and communicate, measure performance, and develop people.
1958	Clothing manufacturer W.L. Gore & Associates is founded and becomes a pioneer of flat management techniques.

(Continued)

(Continued)

1970s–1990s	**Flat management gains a following.**
1970	Tomato processor Morning Star Co. is founded, employing self-management techniques.
1986	Six Sigma, a set of techniques and tools to improve business efficiency and production quality, is developed at Motorola. Although it began as a quality-control concept in the manufacturing sector, it has evolved into a widely used management philosophy focused on customer service and product improvement.
1988	General Motors prepares to open its first Saturn plant, where it attempts to emulate Japanese automakers' management and production techniques by giving its workers more authority. Production ends in 2009.
1990s–2010s	**Rise of the Internet and the spread of social media accelerate management changes.**
1996	Valve Software is founded with no formal management structure.
2001	A group of 17 software developers publishes the "Agile Manifesto," which proposes alternatives to traditional project management through collaboration among self-organizing, cross-functional teams.
2009	Management consultant Gary Hamel publishes a landmark essay in the *Harvard Business Review*, "Moon Shots for Management," in which he argues that management styles dating to the late 19th century have "reached the limits of improvement."
2010s	Business and military leaders implement flatter management strategies.
2012	Joint Chiefs of Staff Chairman Martin E. Dempsey issues white paper detailing the need for greater "mission command"—decentralized decision-making in the field—as a key element of military preparedness.
2013	Online shoe and clothing retailer Zappos becomes the largest company to adopt the holacracy management technique.

Q&A: Zappos and Holacracy

"WE'RE THE LARGEST COMPANY TO EVER DO THIS"
By Jane Fullerton Lemons

Alexis Gonzales-Black works at online shoe and clothing retailer Zappos, where she is leading the organizational change to holacracy, a management philosophy that seeks to replace the top-down approach with a managerial operating system that distributes power across all levels of an organization. She spoke with SAGE Business Researcher reporter Jane Fullerton Lemons about the shift. This is an edited transcript of the conversation.

Why did Zappos decide in 2013 to change its management structure?

The best way to describe the "why" behind holacracy is with an anecdote from a book called *Triumph of the City* by Ed Glaeser. [Zappos CEO] Tony [Hsieh] read the book and something really resonated with him, which is that as a city doubles in size, the productivity per resident typically increases. So as cities become more dense, they actually get smarter and more effective. The opposite tendency is true for organizations. As organizations get larger, they become less efficient, less productive. There is less flexibility and agility. The thinking behind [the change] was, "How can we make Zappos function more like a large city and less like a large business?" That's the "why" behind it, and when we looked around at different models of self-organization, holacracy emerged as the most comprehensive model.

How is the implementation going?

It's going well. One of the design challenges of holacracy is how complicated and nuanced it is. It's not easily implemented, particularly when you're challenging notions of rigid management hierarchy that have been around for as long as we all have been in the professional world. It is really difficult. We've begun to see some bright spots, and some case studies emerge, as to how people are using holacracy. There are no road maps for where we

are, because we're the largest company to ever do this. It's a lot of unknowns. The story is still unfolding.

What has been the most challenging aspect of implementing this new design?

What's challenging is that it is incredibly detailed, and it's not a bullet-pointed list. It's something that you really have to take the time to read and understand. Probably the most persistent challenge to change is the behavior and mind-set challenges that come with a new organizing system that really distributes authority and gives people the power and the responsibility to step up and own their roles in ways they haven't before.

What has been the most surprising element you've seen?

We really had our expectations set high, and we had a lot of ideas about what this could do for the company, so I wouldn't say surprising, but I would say inspiring. The most inspiring things that have happened is, it has really given a platform for folks in the company who are eager to find new ways to add value to the company and eager to maximize their value across functional areas to really address problems that haven't been addressed by the company for a while.

What advice do you have for other companies?

One of the lessons we've learned is the importance of addressing the behavior and mind-set shifts that are required early on. It's one thing to give people the technical tools, but it is quite another to begin the shift in thinking that's required. Another thing is that you learn through experience. So as much as you can teach people about self-organization, until they get really great models and stories for themselves—until they have that light-bulb

(Continued)

(Continued)

moment when they're like, "Wow, the way I do my work is truly different now"—then it doesn't really take hold.

Will Zappos stay with holacracy? Is there any chance you would switch to something different or return to the old ways of managing?

Tony always is the authority. As the person who signs and ratifies the holacracy constitution for the company, he retains the authority to take that back at any moment that he wants to. Eighty percent of the company's work is captured in holacracy, and we're beginning to see these stories emerge about how this is working for folks. But part of self-organizing is that you get real data about how things are operating, evolving the structure and working with that data. We really want that evolution. Tony always uses the Darwin quote: "It's not always the strongest or most intelligent of the species that survives; it's the most adaptable to change." Part of moving toward a self-organizing system is that evolution, and if at some point we get data that that's not actually serving the overall mission and purpose of our company—which is to deliver happiness to our shareholders, our customers, our employees—then we'll use that data to make whatever decision we need to. There are never any promises; changes are built into the DNA of what we do, but there's a lot of energy and excitement around this.

Looking down the road, how is this new management structure going to affect the company?

If we get this right, what you'll see over the next year, the next part of our story, is a lot more rapid evolution. You'll see more advancement and innovations, and at a pace that maybe you haven't seen before, which is exciting and also scary because as humans we naturally crave stability, we crave predictability. If we do this right, then our company will be smarter, more organized and more courageous—not just the company, but each person. The mission is that people leave Zappos better than when they got here, as both professionals and as humans. That's the larger vision that I would share.

10

BIG DATA
Marcia Clemmitt

EXECUTIVE SUMMARY

Big data—information that can be measured in millions of billions of bytes—increasingly allows businesses to understand their customers and gain advantage over their competitors. These data sets are huge and sometimes messy but, with ever-improving statistical tools, they can yield information that allows managers to act quickly and profitably. Manufacturers can produce what customers want, retailers can gauge when and where consumers will buy and shippers can offer same-day delivery. Even small businesses can benefit from previously inaccessible information. However, business analysts say few organizational cultures wholeheartedly embrace evidence-based decision-making, even if they are using smaller, easily accessible data sets. Moreover, managers generally lack the statistical and mathematical understanding needed to manage big-data projects or assess how big-data tools might help their companies. Thus, managers are challenged to glean insights from big data and measure the results. The growing importance of big data also may be increasing the value of employees with quantitative skills while reducing the need for middle managers.

OVERVIEW

For some businesses, at least, the big-data era is here. For evidence, look no further than companies that sell products essentially made from data, says Thomas Davenport, a professor of information technology and management at Babson College in Wellesley, Mass.

Agriculture giant Monsanto of St. Louis markets "precision planting," a service that tells farmers exactly when to plant, when to harvest and how much to irrigate. Monsanto bases its advice on computer analysis of massive amounts of weather and soil data.

"Big data" is defined as collections of facts too big and too various for traditional databases to accommodate. Over the past decade, though, computers' exponentially increasing data-storage capacity and speed have fostered big-data-based innovation at businesses worldwide, with the United States taking the lead in data investments and Europe close behind. Online retailer Amazon and shipping giant UPS have been especially adept in their use of big data, says Susan Athey, professor of the economics of technology at Stanford University's Graduate School of Business. The newfound ability to quickly and cheaply analyze masses of logistical data allowed them to "create products that wouldn't otherwise be feasible, like same-day shipping," she says.

From *SAGE Business Researcher,*
February 9, 2015

There's no question that big-data analysis has already provided significant competitive advantages to some companies, especially those for which massive amounts of data are an inescapable part of doing business, such as Internet companies. Such successes remain relatively rare, however. In part, that's because many tools and techniques for wrangling huge data collections into shape and then wresting meaning from them are in their infancy. A more significant barrier, business analysts say, is that few organizational cultures wholeheartedly embrace evidence-based decision-making, even if they are using smaller, easily accessible data sets. Moreover, say data experts, business-side managers generally lack the statistical and mathematical understanding needed to manage big-data projects or assess how big-data tools might help their companies. As a result, only about 10 percent of Fortune 100 companies now effectively use data to gain a competitive edge, according to Davenport.

While the term "big data" became common only in 2007, most observers agree that it has three key characteristics, which make it harder to handle but also give it the potential to produce greater insights than traditional data (the collection of facts, often numerical):

- Big data is huge.

A decade ago, a gigabyte of data storage—about 1 billion bytes—seemed hefty. Now, data analysts routinely talk of a petabyte—equal to 1 million gigabytes.

To produce its reports on weather, climate and marine conditions, a single federal agency, the National Oceanic and Atmospheric Administration (NOAA), collects more than 2 billion satellite observations and 1.5 billion observations from land- and water-based sensors daily, processing them with supercomputers that perform 2 million billion calculations per second.[1]

- Big data is diverse and often impossible to fit into traditional information storage such as tables or databases.

Besides longtime data such as measurements, street addresses and prices, today's data include many so-called unstructured items, such as "clickstreams" (generated when computer users click on different parts of their screens), Twitter posts, surveillance video and more.

- Big data includes information transmissible from the point of origin—for example, a retail checkout counter—to central computers for analysis in near-real time.

Big data allows managers to "measure, and hence know, radically more about their businesses, and directly translate that knowledge into improved decision-making and performance," wrote Andrew McAfee, associate director of the Center for Digital Business at the Massachusetts Institute of Technology (MIT), and center Director Erik Brynjolfsson, a professor of management at MIT's Sloan School of Management.[2]

In fact, "so many new, unexpected sources of data are available" that "often someone coming from outside an industry can spot a better way to use big data than an insider," McAfee and Brynjolfsson wrote. For example, Brynjolfsson and another researcher, neither with any "special knowledge of the housing market when they began," used "publicly available web search data to predict housing-price changes in metropolitan areas across the United States."

Their work produced more accurate predictions than the National Association of Realtors, "which had developed a far more complex model but relied on relatively slow-changing historical data."[3]

The term big data gained currency about eight years ago, when it began turning up in geek-oriented blog posts that discussed new software developed to bring big-data analysis out of the realm of science—fields such as astronomy and weather forecasting had relied on ultra-pricey supercomputer analysis of huge data sets for decades—and into the business world. Among the first of those tools, in 2005, was Hadoop—software developed at Yahoo to store and process big data, including unusual kinds of data such as video, by distributing the work among available computers. Many others followed.[4]

Soon the buzzword spread to the public. After a flurry of deletion battles beginning in November 2009, "big data" was enshrined in April 2010 in a so-far-permanent Wikipedia entry. By 2012, the phrase regularly appeared in job listings.[5]

Yet some began questioning how much big-data talk was substance and how much was hype. "Big-data rhetoric is at an all-time high" as technology vendors make claims "that seem incredible," wrote analysts from the Cambridge, Mass.–based consultancy Forrester Research in 2014.[6]

The Forrester analysts and other commentators note that many big-data experts at tech companies and in academia routinely describe its potential in the most expansive terms. Big data "has the potential to transform everything," declared Cornell University computer science professor Jon Kleinberg in a typical assessment.[7] Moreover, many software vendors market big-data technologies as one-stop plug-and-play solutions for gleaning answers to virtually any business problem, even though "big data is a perpetually changing process" that will require continued innovation and investment for companies to use it effectively, Forrester noted.[8]

As a result, many business analysts argue that, despite big data's potential to yield insight, much current rhetoric is overblown and potentially misleading for managers. It overemphasizes the power of data itself and of the software tools that manage it, while largely ignoring the business judgment and statistical skills managers need if they're going to use information productively, they say.

"I feel that the attention to big data is driven too much by vendors" selling products and services, says Claudia Perlich, chief scientist at the big data-oriented brand-marketing firm Dstillery in New York City and an expert in "machine learning"—the design of computer algorithms that allow computers to act based on information they glean from incoming data rather than on explicit programmed instructions.

"The underrepresented part of the conversation is that data is not the solution. It's just a tool, as many others are," Perlich says. "You can spend years on data and find interesting things," but to uncover useful insights for one's own enterprise "you need to know what you want to do." And "that's a human skill," she says.

Many early adopters of big-data technologies are becoming "disillusioned" as they discover that, contrary to some vendor promises, using big data productively is far from easy, according to Svetlana Sicular, a research director at the Stamford, Conn.–based information-technology consultancy Gartner. While "formulating a right question [to explore by analyzing data] is always hard . . . with big data, it is an order of magnitude harder," she wrote. For one thing, big-data analysis does not provide absolute answers but only "a proof of your hypothesis with a certain degree of confidence." That uncertainty leaves it "up to you to decide what level of confidence is satisfying."[9]

Big data brings new challenges

Many managers hoping to incorporate big data face a steep learning curve because they must oversee the formulation of questions to be answered by data analysis and decide whether to act on the answers that emerge, says Charles Davis, a professor of information technology management at the University of St. Thomas in Houston. "The key is not actually understanding computing technologies so much as it is understanding how to interpret and evaluate the results of the analyses," he says. "This is really a problem dealing with mathematical and statistical sophistication rather than a new form of computer literacy."

To become comfortable with big-data analyses, managers should start out small, says Stanford's Athey, who adds that she herself "went from a small-data statistician to a big-data statistician." It's not the use of big or small data that matters, but whether one is committed to basing decisions on evidence—data users must be "analytical and data driven," she says.

Becoming an evidence-driven decision maker is only the first step, however, said Rubina Ohanian, head of big data and analytics for Internet-connected products—such as cars, thermostats and smart watches that take blood-pressure and heart-rate readings—at telecom giant AT&T. Data-based insights won't get a fair shot unless confidence in evidence-based

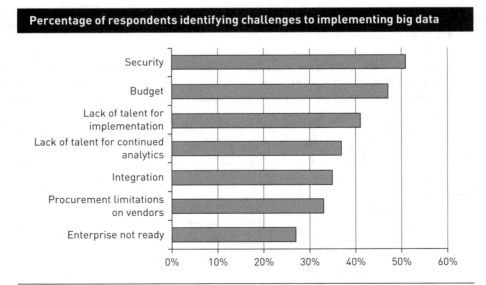

The major challenges for businesses using big data are security (51 percent), budget (47 percent) and lack of appropriate talent for implementation (41 percent), according to more than 1,000 professionals who responded to a survey.

Source: "Big Success With Big Data," Accenture, April 2014, p. 5, http://tinyurl.com/nornoxy

decision-making extends companywide, she said. "Big-data projects don't have to be expensive; start small, prove your point and then begin to grow by gaining credibility," said Ohanian. "Maintain visible executive sponsorship."[10]

"Be realistic about the value and limitations of big-data analytics," but also ensure that all staff members favor evidence-based decision-making over "touchy-feely" approaches, Ohanian added.[11]

Transforming an organization's culture so it can seek and use data for innovative purposes is hard work, and the secret is "continual coaching," wrote Jeanne Ross, director of the Center for Information Systems Research at the Sloan School of Management; Cynthia Beath, a professor emerita of information, risk and operations management at the University of Texas at Austin's McCombs School of Business; and Anne Quaadgras, a research project manager at MIT's Sociotechnical Systems Research Center.[12]

"It's not enough to tell people what the new rules or goals are," the authors said. "You have to help them shift from basing their decisions on instinct to basing them on data." For example, sales staff can develop a data mind-set if they are trained to spend less time delivering company-created product information to customers and more time asking customers about their product wants, needs and experiences – thus producing data that's useful for improving customer satisfaction, they said.[13]

Data experts point to certain problems that routinely arise when businesses try to incorporate big data into decision-making.

For one thing, as always with computers, garbage in means garbage out, says Jeffrey Stanton, a professor in the School of Information Studies at Syracuse University. Data sets, big or small, must be thoughtfully collected and checked for completeness and accuracy to be useful, and the more data they contain the tougher those tasks become.

For example, a large health plan tried to use its claims database to ferret out a subset of patients whose health would benefit from certain preventive care. Just one problem, wrote Sunil Soares, founder of a Harrington Park, N.J.–based data-governance consultancy, Information Asset: "Physicians were using inconsistent procedure codes to submit claims," which made predicting which patients would benefit nearly impossible. Moreover, fixing the problem meant cleaning up a data set that included "500 million claims per year, with each claims record consisting of 600 to 1,000 attributes."[14]

It's also common to find that "turning insights from data analytics into competitive advantage requires changes that businesses may be incapable of making," said Ross, Beath and Quaadgras, who based their analysis on interviews at 51 companies.[15]

In practical terms, the profit-enhancing moves suggested by data analysis "may be infeasible. They may require culture change that would cost more than the benefit," says Beath. For example, analyzing customer transactions might show that "getting all of your salesclerks to do one thing a little differently" every time they wait on a customer would increase sales. But in many cases, such behavioral changes involving multiple people are "not really small changes to make" but, in fact, prohibitively difficult, she says.

Many smaller businesses view their size as an insurmountable obstacle to adopting big-data analytics.

Big-data analysis requires "very separate areas of expertise" that aren't feasible to add to his 12-person staff, said Mat Peterson, founder of education-app developer Shiny Things

©iStockphoto.com/mediaphotos

Tracking data analytics can often be a factor in a company's decision-making process.

in Sydney, Australia. Furthermore, Peterson said, he hasn't seen other small or medium-sized businesses using big data effectively. "There are so many signals you can be distracted by. More often than not you're getting the right answer to the wrong question."[16]

Some data experts, however, say that small organizations should re-evaluate their stance.

Small organizations can do sophisticated statistical analysis with little investment, said Syracuse's Stanton. Data analysis that once required spending thousands of dollars on vendors' software packages can be done using free, open-source statistical software such as R and OpenOffice. Moreover, small organizations can draw on their own modest data collections, perhaps combined with big-data sets that are available free, from government agencies such as the Census Bureau and social media sites such as Twitter, where tweet analysis provides insights into consumers' opinions. "In the past, you had to be large enough and rich enough to buy the tools and have specialized people," Stanton says. "Now just regular folks can imagine ways of using data that would have been unthinkable before."[17]

As businesses debate the pros and cons of diving into the data pool, below are some questions that managers and researchers are asking.

WEIGHING THE ISSUES

Can companies glean insights more easily from big data than from traditional analysis?

The availability of larger and more diverse data sets allows today's analysts to bypass the complicated statistical methods once needed to pull general conclusions from limited information while revealing more meaningful patterns in data than ever before, some big-data enthusiasts say.

Other analysts, however, point out that the larger the data set, the more effort it takes to make the information usable. Moreover, they say, big data offers no escape from painstaking statistical work, because analysis of larger data sets also turns up more correlations that appear significant but actually result from pure chance.

Big-data analysis should be widely embraced by business managers and scientists alike because it makes it easier than ever to glean useful insights from information, wrote then-*Wired* Editor-in-Chief Chris Anderson in an influential 2008 essay. A case in point is Google's success at search-engine building and at translating foreign languages, Anderson said. Google Translate, for example, doesn't "know" any language or incorporate any language rules. The automated tool simply draws on hundreds of millions of online texts already translated by humans to generate best guesses for translating unfamiliar text. Sheer numbers make it work, said Anderson. The more translations available to scan, the more accurate new translations will be.[18]

Until now, data analysis has required devising hypotheses about how and why two variables might be connected and then testing whether the data support the hypothesized link, Anderson explained. But with massive data, he said, the need for humans to construct hypotheses and engage in complex statistical calculations before reaping insight is becoming obsolete. Having petabytes of data "allow us to say: 'Correlation is enough.' . . . We can analyze the data without hypotheses about what it might show. We can throw the numbers into the biggest computing clusters the world has ever seen and let statistical algorithms find patterns where science cannot," he wrote.[19]

Some businesses clearly have gained insights from large data troves in just this way.

Walmart is well-known for its longtime savvy use of its huge data troves to increase profit. In 2004, a week before Hurricane Frances was expected to hit Florida's Atlantic coast, Walmart Chief Information Officer Linda Dillman examined companywide sales data to find out what products besides bottled water and toilet paper were popular with shoppers in earlier hurricanes. For managers stocking up, two unexpected items jumped out: "Strawberry Pop-Tarts increase in sales, like seven times their normal sales rate, ahead of a hurricane," said Dillman. "And the pre-hurricane top-selling item was beer."[20]

But many information specialists warn that such revelations aren't necessarily easy to come by. For one thing, even a giant data set is not necessarily representative enough to ensure correct conclusions, because collection methods can easily introduce corrupting biases, they say.

For example, to locate street potholes, the city of Boston developed a downloadable Street Bump smartphone app using phones' GPS and accelerometer technology. Smartphone accelerometers—which rely on phone movements to orient screen views—detected cars' movements over bumpy streets and automatically sent reports to the city government. The city soon found, however, that Street Bump generated a flawed map that showed the streets most in need of fixing were in neighborhoods with young, affluent residents—those most likely to own smartphones—and it had to retool the program.[21]

Furthermore, in data sets with millions or billions of data points, patterns turn up and appear statistically significant when they are mere coincidence, says John Jordan, a clinical professor of supply chain and information systems at Penn State University's Smeal College of Business. "You'll find this beautiful thing where crime is up in correlation with the number of tons of cheese sold and the number of hairdressers opened. Once you get databases large enough, these things will be there. And they can mask actual insights."

That's for two reasons, said Nassim Taleb, a New York University professor of risk engineering. First off, mathematical tests for statistical significance reveal nothing about whether an observed pattern has any practical significance; other means are needed to determine whether statistically significant patterns have real-world lessons. Furthermore, in big-data analysis "the spurious rises to the surface. This is because in large data sets, large deviations are vastly more attributable to variance (or noise) than to information (or signal)."[22]

It's also vital to recognize the kinds of questions that big data simply can't answer, analysts say.

Bottom line: "Data by definition is a record of what was and maybe what is," says machine-learning expert Perlich, at Dstillery. This means data have predictive power only in future scenarios that are very similar to that in which they were collected, she explains.

The requirement that data be super-relevant to the question a user is exploring means that questions suitable for data-derived solutions are "primarily small and tactical, such as what particular offer should be made to each customer and how much inventory to keep in the warehouse," says Babson's Davenport. "Big decisions, and decisions that are made rarely, such as what company to acquire, whether my company should go public"—even what new products to introduce—"those are generally bad for analytics because we haven't got past data on which to base them."

Are businesses already getting good results from big-data projects?

In a 2014 survey by the management consultancy Accenture, 67 percent of the largest companies—those with more than $10 billion in annual revenue—rated big data as "extremely important" to their organizations.[23] Furthermore, business analysts note that companies in some sectors, such as finance and resource extraction, have long garnered insights from large data sets. However, many also say that the difficulty of establishing a company culture of data-based decision-making, along with practical challenges surrounding the use of large data sets, mean progress is slow.

In a 2013 survey, about half of large-company IT and other executives described their big-data projects as "somewhat successful" and only 23 percent deemed them a "success," at least in part because many big-data projects miss deadlines and run over budget, according to survey sponsor Kapow Software, a Palo Alto, Calif.–based software vendor. "It's really difficult to pinpoint and surgically extract critical insights without hiring expensive consultants or data scientists," and needed data are difficult to collect, the company noted.[24]

Although Internet companies pioneered big-data work, it's not clear how well even those firms are succeeding, according to Foster Provost, a professor of information systems at New York University's Stern School of Business, and data science researcher Tom Fawcett. Facebook's huge market valuation "has been credited to its vast and unique data assets," but it remains "an open question" whether Facebook effectively uses its data to improve procedures and create products that advertisers and other customers value, they wrote.[25]

C-Suite struggles with big data

Today, most data are not managed well enough to be of use in decision-making, said data analyst Juanita Walton Billings and Peter Aiken, founding director of the Glen Allen, Va.–based data-management consultancy Data Blueprint and an associate professor of information systems at Virginia Commonwealth University. Data management includes maintaining the proper infrastructure to store and share data; ensuring that data are complete and accurate; and integrating an organization's data to make it accessible to all potential users, and it is "a poorly understood concept" that isn't even taught in "the vast majority of information technology programs," they wrote.[26]

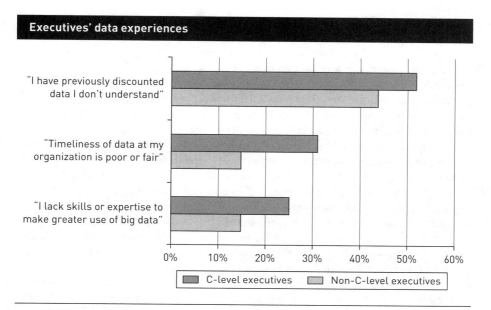

Executives' data experiences

"I have previously discounted data I don't understand"

"Timeliness of data at my organization is poor or fair"

"I lack skills or expertise to make greater use of big data"

0% 10% 20% 30% 40% 50% 60%

■ C-level executives ■ Non-C-level executives

A greater share of top executives said they lack the expertise to improve their organizations' usage of big data (25 percent), compared with their non-C-level counterparts (15 percent), according to a survey of 1,135 executives. C-level executives were also more likely to have discounted data they did not understand or to believe that their companies were not using data in a timely manner.

Note: C-level executives surveyed include board members, chief executive officers, chief operating officers and others with similar positions.

Source: "Gut & Gigabytes," PricewaterhouseCoopers, October 2014, p. 33, http://tinyurl.com/kjesgmf

Nevertheless, companies that have "a culture of evidence-based decision making . . . have seen improvements in their business performance—and they tend to be more profitable than companies that don't have that kind of culture," wrote MIT's Ross and colleagues.[27]

"Web-native companies" provide many of the best examples because they can capture so much data about customers, Ross and colleagues wrote. "One technique, which has become almost a governing ethos for Google, Amazon, Netflix and eBay, is A/B testing, in which some users are diverted to a slightly different version of a web page, which is presenting a new idea or product. The behavior of those users (B) is then compared with that of users on the existing page (A), and the results are often subjected to sophisticated statistical analysis. This technique transforms much product-development decision making from a subjective to an objective exercise."[28]

While big data is new to many businesses, a number of companies in sectors such as mining and drilling, insurance and finance for decades have harnessed huge data sets for competitive advantage, says Barbara Wixom, a principal research scientist in the Center for Information Systems Research.

One example is credit card giant Capital One, which began around 1990 as an audacious big-data project undertaken by what was then Richmond, Va.–based Signet Bank. Two young bankers, Richard Fairbank and Nigel Morris, convinced Signet that computerized data analysis had grown powerful enough to perform predictive modeling of the differing profitability of individual credit card customers. An information-savvy bank could therefore entice the most profitable customers with more favorable credit terms, they reasoned. At the time, though, banks used only a simple model of creditworthiness to qualify customers and offered a limited variety of credit terms, so no data existed on which to base predictive models.[29]

To acquire the copious data needed, Signet had to take the pricey risk of experimenting with different credit terms, offered to customers randomly. In the process, the bank went from an industry-leading 2.9 percent of credit card balances going unpaid to nearly 6 percent, raising shareholder alarms. Signet persisted, however, and, once completed, the new system proved its merit. In 1994, Signet spun off the profitable Capital One credit card unit, with Fairbank and Morris as chairman and president.[30]

Whether it involves big data or small, companies that use analytics—systematic data analysis for decision-making—"perform better. Every study done says that they do," says Babson's Davenport. Admittedly, it's not been possible to do "gold-standard" research that establishes a cause-and-effect relationship between a history of analytics use and better business results, he says, but research "consistently shows strong correlation" between a data-based culture and companies' productivity growth, returns on assets and equity and market value.[31]

Can small businesses take advantage of big data?

Affordability and a perceived lack of a "big" data trove to analyze stop some smaller businesses from adopting data-based decision-making. But analysts point out that today almost all businesses have access to customer information, such as from websites, and to affordable data-analysis software.

One Australian survey actually found that smaller companies used big data more for marketing than did larger businesses, with the firms reporting "higher levels of usage . . . and somewhat greater success."[32]

"In our experience, this is often driven by simpler data systems, nimbler administration and a strong drive to establish competitive advantage," according to the survey sponsors, Torque Data, a Sydney-based data-oriented marketing consultancy, and Sweeney Research, a Melbourne-based consultancy.[33]

Smaller companies should remember that the "big" in big data means more than just size and thus should seize overlooked opportunities to analyze data that may be hiding in plain sight, many experts note.

Between 14 percent and 18 percent of small businesses use so-called customer relationship management (CRM) software to track customer interactions, said Steve King, a partner at the Lafayette, Calif.–based small-business consultancy Emergent Research. At relatively low cost, CRM systems provide centrally stored data on sales, emails, calls and other communications with individual customers—all ready for a business to analyze, he said.[34]

Free public databases on topics from traffic patterns to weather, as well as companies' own websites, are overlooked data sources that even very small businesses can use, said Wilson Raj, global director of customer intelligence at analytics-software developer SAS Institute in Cary, N.C. Raj cited the example of a local yogurt shop that used forecasts of cold snaps to schedule promotions on days when sales would otherwise slump.[35]

While most data experts encourage managers to try some data-based decision-making, many also caution smaller businesses not to let hype push them into big-data investments without thoughtful consideration.

"I work with businesses that are being tempted by people promising big-data solutions," said Matt Young, founder of the Sydney, Australia–based consultancy Turning Leaf. For most small-to-medium-sized businesses, he said, "big data is a sham."[36]

"For most IT directors, if it's new and nifty, they want it," says Charlene Dykman, a professor of management information systems at the University of St. Thomas in Houston. "And because managers don't understand this stuff, the IT directors tell the managers what to do."

Dykman cautions business owners to remember the long history of big IT projects—they can cost smaller organizations more than they're worth. She cites ERP—enterprise resource planning software, intended to integrate all core business processes; it is sold customized for some sectors, such as higher education—that became a must-have in the 1990s. Her then-3,000-student university bought ERP for $8 million, Dykman says. But 16 years and significant additional dollars later, "they're still trying to get the automated registration system [included in their ERP software] working." The story is not unique, she says.

BACKGROUND

Data and insight

Scientists have long viewed data as a rich source of insight.

Based on hundreds of years of measurements, Polish astronomer Copernicus and others discovered by the mid-16th century that, despite appearances, Earth orbited the sun.[37] In 1854, English physician John Snow plotted onto a London map the addresses of residents stricken in a cholera outbreak. His visualization of mortality data traced the epidemic's source to drinking water from a single well.[38]

In business, too, the idea that data analysis could yield insight goes back centuries. Information collection contributed heavily to the success of Sir Henry Furnese, an English merchant and financier of the late 17th and early 18th centuries, according to Richard Millar Devens, a 19th-century American writer. By maintaining "a complete and perfect train of business intelligence" across Holland, Flanders, France and Germany, Furnese beat competitors to opportunities created by shifting military fortunes, Devens wrote.[39]

And there has never been a shortage of business questions that the right data could answer—if that data could be found and understood. A rueful adage attributed to 19th-century Philadelphia retailer John Wanamaker makes the point. "Half of the money I spend on advertising is wasted," the department store magnate purportedly said. "The trouble is, I don't know which half."[40]

As science's evidence-based worldview gained dominance, beginning in the 17th century and accelerating thereafter, many mathematicians sought techniques to unlock insights hidden in data. In new studies of statistics and probability, they tackled questions such as how to accurately describe and summarize sets of data and how to draw inferences—including predictions for the future—based on observational data.

"Many of the simplest and most practical methods" that statisticians use today were devised by 19th- and early 20th-century thinkers working in business, "solving real-world problems in manufacturing and agriculture by using data to describe and draw inferences," wrote Syracuse's Stanton.[41]

William Sealy Gosset, an English chemist born in 1876, worked on quality control at the Arthur Guinness Son & Company brewery in Dublin, Ireland. Charged with ensuring that batches of Guinness beer were of consistent quality, he devised some of the most widely used and powerful of statistical tools—small-sample statistical techniques, which provide "ways of generalizing from the results of a relatively few observations," according to Stanton.[42]

Gosset couldn't possibly test every batch of beer that might result when the same recipe underwent small circumstantial, procedural or ingredient variations, such as using hops stored at different temperatures, Stanton said. To draw meaningful inferences from limited samples, he "had to figure out the role of chance in determining how a batch of beer had turned out." To do it, he devised what's known as the t-test, a technique to determine how likely it is that two data samples differ by accident.[43]

Decision math

Guinness brewery managers were not the only turn-of-the-20th-century business leaders to embrace data.

Pennsylvania-born mechanical engineer Frederick Winslow Taylor extended the use of data into production-process planning and workforce management.

As a consultant for Pennsylvania-based Bethlehem Steel, Taylor concluded, based on observational data, that "a first-class pig-iron handler" should shift 47½ long tons (1 long ton equals 2,240 pounds) of iron per day into rail cars, rather than the 12½ long tons a worker typically moved. Taylor persuaded the company to hire workers that his data suggested were capable of loading 47½ tons; after overseeing their work for some time, he declared his conclusion upheld.

One early hire "worked when he was told to work, and rested when he was told to rest, and at half-past five in the afternoon had his 47½ tons loaded on the car," Taylor wrote. "He practically never failed to work at this pace during the three years the writer was at Bethlehem."[44]

Perhaps the most famous 20th-century management consultant was W. Edwards Deming, a professor of statistics at New York University's business school, who is often credited with the saying "In God we trust, all others bring data." (Unfortunately, the story is probably apocryphal, according to three Stanford University statistics professors who nevertheless made Deming's dictum the epigraph of their statistics textbook.)[45]

Whether or not he uttered the famous line, Deming's recommendations stressed data. For quality improvement, he prescribed systematic data collection on defects, analysis of their causes, correction of problems, then more data collection to ensure that improvements were made.[46]

One of the most significant 20th-century advances in statistics-based prediction dates back to an 18th-century discovery by an English clergyman and mathematician,

Thomas Bayes (1701–1761). Forgotten for nearly two centuries, Bayes' idea was resurrected in the mid-20th-century and forms the basis for much of today's work on big-data statistics.

Like many thinkers of his intellectually restless day, Bayes was preoccupied with how causes might be inferred from effects, how beliefs could be modified as new information emerged and how the probability of a future event might be calculated when one knew only how many times it had occurred in the past.[47]

Examining those questions mathematically, he hit upon a simple method that turned out to have enormous power: Start with an initial belief—even if it is a pure guess—then modify and improve it, gradually and repeatedly, with data derived from observation or experiment. The successive new estimates would gradually close in on accuracy, much as a poker player starts by assuming his opponent is playing with a straight deck, then modifies his assessment with each hand played until he forms a relatively accurate view of the other player's honesty.[48]

Bayes' theorem—which can be written as a fairly simple algebraic expression—was published by a friend after his death but mostly went unread. A few years after publication, though, the famous French mathematician and astronomer Pierre-Simon Laplace (1749–1827) hit independently on the same method. Trying out the process, Laplace used birth-record data from across Europe to establish the strong probability that male births slightly outnumbered female births worldwide. He also worked out numerous astronomical measurements to estimate the masses of Jupiter and Saturn. Both findings were later confirmed.[49]

Ironically, the continued rise of a data-focused worldview soon led to near-total abandonment of Bayes' theorem, although a few statisticians continued to use it for such practical problems as adjusting artillery fire to account for shifting enemy positions, wind direction and other variables. However, many dismissed a method that begins an inquiry with a guess, then nudges it closer to a probable correct answer as too subjective for a scientific age.

By the mid-20th century, though, evidence had piled up of the Bayesian method's success at solving practical problems, such as breaking wartime codes, setting insurance rates and locating the likely causes of some diseases. More statisticians came around to the view that most inquiries—even scientific ones—begin with what are essentially guesses, then move toward objectivity as data modify initial views.

In 1959, Harvard Business School professor Robert Schlaifer pioneered an influential theory of business decision-making using a Bayesian approach. Later, statistics rooted in Bayes' method were involved in the development of artificial intelligence and machine learning.[50]

Beginning in the mid-20th century, data collection, storage and analysis were automated. Researchers in the 1960s developed the first computerized systems to aid business decision-making. In some systems, mathematical representations—or models—of business processes are run with different sets of real or hypothetical data to find optimal modes of operation or to calculate the results of different choices by management. Some of these decision support systems (DSS) stored and manipulated large quantities of historical and current data. As far back as 1995, Walmart's DSS had more than 5 terabytes—5,000 gigabytes—of online storage capacity, which grew to more than 24 terabytes by 1997.[51]

Despite the proliferation of both data and tools to plumb it for meaning, only a handful of companies have long traditions of data-based decision-making, wrote MIT's Ross and

Tokyo-based
7-Eleven
convenience store.

Quaadgras and the University of Texas' Beath. "We've conducted seven case studies and interviewed executives at 51 companies" and "found that those that consistently use data to guide their decision making are few and far between," they wrote in 2013.[52]

The Tokyo-based 7-Eleven Japan convenience-store chain relies on data-based decision-making, Ross and coauthors noted. Since the early 1970s, local salesclerks have borne most of the responsibility for ordering their own stores' stock—much of it fresh and delivered three times daily. To guide clerks in their ordering, corporate headquarters forwards data on previous-day and previous-year/same-day sales for each clerk's store; weather forecasts; sales on days with similar weather and top-selling items at other stores. As a result, 7-Eleven has been Japan's most profitable retailer for more than 30 years, Ross, Beath and Quaadgras said.[53]

Big data

Meanwhile, one fact is clear: The amount and kinds of data collected, stored and—sometimes—analyzed never stop growing.

Decades ago, only a few fields, such as the astronomical sciences and the insurance business, wrested insights from huge data sets. As the capacity to store huge amounts of data spread society-wide, however, software developers created tools to allow any enterprise to do so, patterning their work on methods developed by the big-data veterans.

Weather forecasting—using models incorporating sensor data from weather stations on the ground and aloft—"has been a nasty big-data problem" for decades, wrote Jeffrey Needham, a San Francisco–based big-data expert. In the 1970s, weather models ran on expensive single supercomputers the size of high school gyms. But by the 1990s, computer scientists had figured out how to distribute the calculations "into a hundred smaller programs working at the same time on a hundred workstations," thus making the process faster and cheaper. In the 2000s, computer scientists at Internet businesses copied the 1990s approach to create software such as the Hadoop distributed-computing system, Needham noted.[54]

Over the past quarter century the digitization of media, the use of transmitting sensors on devices from phones to car engines and the rise of social media have all contributed to a 21st-century data deluge.

Declining costs of data-related technology played a big role in the proliferation, said Syracuse's Stanton. As barcode readers and other sensors dropped in price, every retailer—not just big chains—could use them. And, Stanton said, "the declining cost of storage has made it practical to keep lots of data hanging around, regardless of its quality or usefulness."[55]

What sets 21st-century "big data" apart from previous large data sets, however, is its variety and lack of structure: Big data includes media such as video that won't fit into a structured database or data table.

The data's immediacy—its speed of transmission and analysis—has brought even more significant changes, according to information experts. "Look at Twitter," says Penn State's Jordan. "Each tweet contains a massive amount of info." That includes words and their meaning as well as so-called metadata such as "when it was sent, who sent it, what their location was," he says. "We never had anything like that before."

Customer-transaction data, GPS locational data and much more is increasingly transmissible in real time. Moreover, the value of speed became clear years ago as financial companies speeded up analysis of fast-arriving credit card-transaction data to improve fraud detection, wrote Babson's Davenport.[56]

CURRENT SITUATION

Retooling for data

With some companies successfully using data—big and small—to improve decision-making, others now must step up their games, business analysts say. Most organizations face tough challenges before undertaking data analysis, however, and universities are only beginning to offer relevant training.

In a 2013 Gartner survey, 37.8 percent of U.S. businesses said they had made some investment in big data, the highest percentage in the world. Meanwhile, 26.8 percent of businesses in Europe, the Middle East and Africa had invested, 25.6 percent in Asia and the Pacific, and 17.8 percent in Latin America.[57]

More companies plan to invest in big data

Today, most managers likely think about creating data-oriented cultures in their organizations, says Babson's Davenport. Nevertheless, even among the largest companies—the Fortune 100—only about 10 percent now effectively use data to gain a competitive edge, says Davenport who, like many other analysts, generally gauges organizations' data savvy on how effectively they use small or large data sets for decision-making rather than on how much big data they employ.

A shrinking number of large companies are completely data-unaware, Davenport says, but the majority are "still in the second category from the bottom" on a five-level scale of data ability he has devised. At those companies, individual departments analyze data for insights, but data are locked into departmental silos, blocking development of an enterprise-wide analysis program, he says.[58]

"The most important thing is for people to realize what a primitive state we're in" when it comes to having data that are accessible companywide, clear, accurate and complete, says Syracuse's Stanton.

Furthermore, while much of the job will one day be automated, today "the amount of handwork required to get data in shape is amazing," even to move a single spreadsheet into an

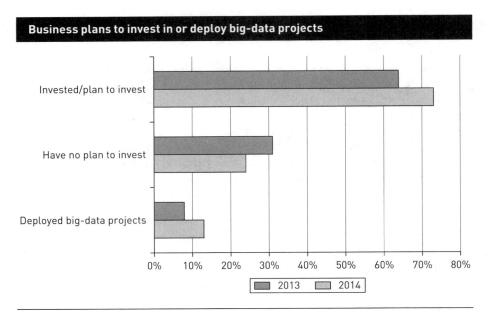

Business plans to invest in or deploy big-data projects

The share of businesses that had invested or planned to invest in big data rose from 64 percent in 2013 to 73 percent in 2014, according to a survey by information technology research firm Gartner Inc. A greater share of businesses also undertook big-data projects in 2014 (13 percent) than in 2013 (8 percent).

Source: Press release, "Gartner Survey Reveals That 73 Percent of Organizations Have Invested or Plan to Invest in Big Data in the Next Two Years," Gartner Research, Sept. 17, 2014, http://tinyurl.com/kfbxzdp

integrated company data system, says Stanton. "There's a huge, huge ramp-up time, just for that one 40-kilobyte file. Now multiply that by a thousand."

Because of the prep work needed, "data scientists will tell you they're only 20 percent productive" today, says Aiken of Virginia Commonwealth. Currently, "the average company has data about customers in 17 different databases," he says. "So if you have yours in 12 databases, you're way above average."

Moreover, while "every manager will tell you they make data-driven decisions" already, few really do, says Perlich of Dstillery. Without a basic understanding of both the statistics and the automated processes that underlie data-based decision-making, managers simply don't trust the results, and most lack such understanding today, she says. A common frustrated response data scientists hear is, "I don't understand the damned thing," says Perlich.

Qualms about potential legal implications and public backlash stemming from use of individuals' information for data analysis also are slowing companies' adoption of big-data tools, said Cheryl Metzger, director of creative strategy at the marketing agency OgilvyOne Worldwide, in Chicago. "Concerns about privacy are [rising] along with our collective blood pressure," she said.[59]

Academia's response

As more businesses look for technical staff with data-related skills and business managers face demands to learn the principles of data-based decision-making, new academic programs are emerging to fill these needs.

Many schools of information science—which teach information technology and specialties such as systems analysis—are introducing data science courses. A data science specialization is available in some degree programs at the Indiana University School of Informatics and Computing, in Bloomington, and the University of California, Berkeley, offers a data science master's degree.[60]

Technology giant IBM is working with 1,000 universities worldwide to expand programs in data analytics at schools of computer science and business management. For example, India's Mother Teresa Women's University will use an IBM grant to add training in predictive analysis and statistics to its management curriculum.[61]

The University of Southern California's Marshall School of Business and Arizona State University's W.P. Carey School of Business have recently opened stand-alone master's programs in business analytics, and applicants have been clamoring for spots.[62]

Some academics, however, argue that the business analysis degrees won't meet companies' needs. "We fear [graduates will be] neither as competent with data as real data scientists, nor have the leadership skills that you really need to drive change in analytics," said Florian Zettelmeyer, director of data analytics at Northwestern University's Kellogg School of Management, which requires MBA students to take some analytics courses but won't offer a stand-alone degree.[63]

Some business programs, such as at New York University's Stern School of Business and Stanford University's Graduate School of Business, are adding optional courses in statistical analysis and big-data-related coding. Such courses are important because MBAs hired as product managers at online retailer Amazon, for example, don't need advanced technical skills but must be able to "dive into data and be technically conversant," said Miriam Park, director of university programs there.[64]

Nevertheless, making such mathematically rigorous classes required rather than optional for business students would likely backfire, cautioned David Backus, a Stern School economics professor who has designed a business school course in data visualization and the programming language Python. "Students could get annoyed at you and think it's too hard."[65]

Backus' view encapsulates what some analysts call the biggest barrier to instituting evidence-based management. "The one thing that doesn't seem to change fast enough is mass education" that imparts comfort with mathematical ideas and statistics, says Beath of the University of Texas. "That shows up in people's lack of confidence and maybe a little shyness in using analytical results."

As a result, most managers "either accept [what data analysts] tell them on blind faith, without understanding the conclusion or its limits. Or they reject it for some bogus reason. Most data scientists will tell you that this is the response they get," Beath says. "In general, math skills are not what got people ahead in business."

LOOKING AHEAD

Goodbye, middle managers?

It won't happen this year or next, but, eventually, the power of decision-making based on automated big data will force radical shifts in at least some business sectors and potentially gut the managerial workforce to an unprecedented degree, many experts on data in business say. Although these scenarios may seem extreme, some predict that in the next few decades most top managers will have to grapple with their consequences.

The rise of big-data-based products will likely upend some large traditional markets, says Stanford economist Athey. The automobile industry is a key example, because a disruptive big-data game changer already exists—the self-driving car, Athey says.

At Google and other companies, big data has met machine learning and given birth to computers that can drive vehicles autonomously, with ever-increasing competence. The computers are trained to drive much as humans are. So-called supervised-learning algorithms "observe" many examples of humans driving correctly and gradually learn the principles well enough to apply them to new situations. So the machines can more easily navigate unfamiliar streets, Google is using its big-data capability to create precise digitized images of all roads its cars will use, including such details as the exact heights of curbs and traffic lights.[66]

Because self-driving cars likely represent the future and big-data-based companies are developing them far in advance of automobile makers, CEOs of traditional car companies are potentially looking at "a real existential moment," says Athey. "You'd ask, 'Do I invest in this? When only the very best would be accepted by consumers?' This is not something where you can put out a buggy product and fix it later. The first day your self-driving car drives you into a tree, you're kind of dead. Will you outsource this technology that's so crucial or try it yourself, even though you're far behind?"

Equally daunting for top managers throughout the business world—as well as for governments and society at large—will be workforce-related dilemmas, many business analysts predict.

San Jose Mercury News/Tribune News Service/Getty Images

Google unveiled a prototype of its self-driving car in May 2014. Big data allows the company to continuously improve the car's performance.

"The idea is to make some kinds of decision making completely automated," says Davis of the University of St. Thomas in Houston. "But with so much decision making done by machine [based on data gathered autonomously], will we need middle managers?

"In the '80s and '90s, companies had nine to 12 levels of management," Davis points out. "Then the computer replaced much of managers' main function—moving information up, down and across levels of the company," he says. "It took half the managerial jobs."

Managers who remained "were now coordinating maybe 13 to 20 people and making decisions. When machines start making decisions, that can change again. Machines are cheap."

The remaining human role will be the "intellectual oversight" of entire enterprises, including their big-data aspects, not the many detailed tactical decisions that managers spend their time on today, says Davis. "The technology is enabling this change," but businesses—or society—could reject it, he says.

Chronology

1940s–1950s	**Field of statistics advances.**
1940s	American management-consultant W. Edwards Deming helps war-torn Japan become an economic powerhouse by teaching managers to use statistical analysis of data to improve business processes. . . . A long-ignored statistical method discovered by 18th-century English clergyman Thomas Bayes is revived as the basis for a new era of predictive data analysis.
1944	Wesleyan University librarian Fremont Rider estimates that university libraries double in size every 16 years; by 2040 Yale's library will have more than 6,000 miles of shelves, he predicts.
1959	Harvard Business School professor of business administration Robert Schlaifer pioneers an influential theory of business decision-making that takes a Bayesian approach.
1960s–1980s	**Data storage and analysis are computerized.**
1982	The computer made the cover of *Time* magazine's annual "person of the year" issue, beating out politicians and scientists as the most influential force of 1982.
1985	Consumer-goods maker Procter & Gamble, a company with a long history of data-based decision-making, begins building a system to link sales information and point-of-sale scanner data.
1986	Despite the spread of computing, 99 percent of the world's data storage is analog.
1990s	**As computer speed and storage capacity rise, businesses begin mining data for insight.**
1994	Credit card giant Capital One of Richmond, Va., debuts, the product of a risky data-analysis experiment to learn how varying credit terms can attract the most profitable credit card customers.
1995	Walmart's decision support system tops 5 terabytes (5,000 gigabytes) of data.

(Continued)

(Continued)

1997	Storage capacity in Walmart's decision support system soars past 24 terabytes. . . . First recognized publication of the phrase "big data," by NASA researchers who dub the strain it puts on computer memory the "problem of big data."
1998	In "The Anatomy of a Large-Scale Hypertextual Web Search Engine," Google founders Larry Page and Sergey Brin lay out their method for sifting through the Web's vast data stores.
1999	The world produces 1.5 exabytes—1.5 billion gigabytes—of information.
2000s–Present	**Internet companies develop software to ease data handling; the phrase "big data" enters the public consciousness.**
2002	Amount of the world's information stored digitally surpasses the amount in non-digital storage for the first time.
2004	Walmart learns from data analysis that beer and Strawberry Pop-Tart sales soar during hurricane warnings.
2005	Computer scientists Doug Cutting, then of Yahoo, and Mike Cafarella introduce Hadoop software to facilitate storage and processing of big data by distributing the work among multiple computers
2006	The world generates 161 exabytes of data.
2007	Ninety-four percent of information storage is digital. . . . The term "big data" appears in computer-oriented blogs.
2009	In November a "big data" Wikipedia entry is created, then deleted.
2010	In April "big data" gets a permanent Wikipedia page. . . . World generates 1,227 exabytes of data. . . . Employers use phrase "big data" in job descriptions.
2012	World data production reaches 2,837 exabytes per year.
2014	Two White House advisory groups caution that personal-privacy protections that were adequate before big data won't adequately protect individual rights in a big-data age. . . . Among companies with annual revenue over $10 billion, 67 percent rate big data "extremely important."

Q&A: Davis on Using Big Data

"MOST MANAGERS AREN'T TRAINED IN THE RIGHT KIND OF STATISTICS"

Charles Davis
Professor of information technology management
University of St. Thomas, Houston

Charles Davis, a professor of information technology management at the University of St. Thomas in Houston who has worked for IBM, Occidental Petroleum and other companies, believes big data's potential is great—if businesses become smarter. He spoke with SAGE Business Researcher reporter Marcia Clemmitt about the challenges businesses face in using big data. This is an edited transcript of the conversation.

How new is the notion of big data?

At all the companies I worked for, I did a lot of big data. We've used statistics for a long time. We've been doing descriptive and predictive statistical analyses with increasingly larger data sets, in support of management decision-making, for generations. But the degree to which everyone is doing it is changing. It's becoming an imperative. Soon everything will be impacted—manufacturing, marketing, supply chain, human resources.

What do managers need to know about working in a big-data environment?

You have a smorgasbord of statistical tools, and depending on which you pick, you get different answers. Managers have to be able to question results and evaluate their credibility, and so they need to have some grasp of this.

But most managers aren't trained in the right kind of statistics. They learn descriptive statistics. That's what business schools teach. But you need predictive statistics. Many tend to think they know about that, or that they have people who know how to use it. In general, though, they don't.

There's a dearth of talent in the statistics area. Whether or not they know it or will admit it, most companies operate with only rudimentary capabilities in statistics, not only among managers but across the board. Schools tend to require one stats course of everybody, but statistics is not much fun. You don't get to the cool stuff until much later. I think I was in my sixth or seventh course before I got to the cool stuff.

An understanding of computing technology isn't needed nearly so much as greater mathematical and statistical sophistication—to have a basic understanding of the statistical methods that can be used to solve problems using big-data resources.

What's the best way to develop data scientists for business?

There aren't many data scientists yet. Data scientists have to be able to manage data well and employ statistics well—which is an art as much as a science—to use big data to solve problems.

Right now you're taking physicists and cross training them because they're good at working with very large amounts of data. But for the most part they don't really understand business. So you have a choice. You can try to train those physics people for business, or you can take business people and train them for analytics. More schools are putting in these programs, master's programs, now, to do that.

It doesn't just involve teaching people techniques, though. There's mathematical judgment involved, and how do you teach that? How do you identify people who have that talent? People who are attracted to these new master's programs [in data science] may have it, but it's not clear.

All in all, it's preferable to train business people in analytics rather than plugging in physicists and the like. The interpretation is as important as the analysis, and that requires deep knowledge of the [business] field.

What's the first step in a big-data project?

If people attempt to do big data without doing a profitability analysis, they'll end up equating big data with a big mistake. In profitability analysis you evaluate your entire business for profitability, as it's laid out in [the 2010 book] *Islands of Profit in a Sea of Red Ink*, by [Massachusetts Institute of Technology senior lecturer] Jonathan Byrnes.

(Continued)

(Continued)

Once you know exactly how much profit you get from each product line, then you can make your decisions about what data projects to do by understanding their impact on profitability. You want to look for the things you're making a profit on—to enhance that. Or you may want to invest in something low-earning because you believe it has potential. That's the kind of question you ask.

Once you've identified what particular thing you should focus on, only then do you do big data on that. But companies aren't doing it that way. They're working on marketing or on the supply chain, without thinking about the particular areas where improvement could really have an impact.

Has the average company made good use of data-based, evidence-based approaches up to now?

"Good" is a relative term and it evolves over time; all companies today have computers that accumulate and process operational data for operational, managerial and strategic decision-making. They all utilize data and evidence-based approaches for structured, routinized decision support. This is certainly good compared to earlier generations. But the issue now with big data is a shift in scope, the ability to assimilate data sources never contemplated before into the decision-making framework. And few companies have developed the necessary capacity to leverage big data—as it is understood in today's terms.

How much evidence is there of big-data projects producing tangible business improvements outside of oft-cited Silicon Valley examples such as the Google search engine?

There is a mountain of anecdotal evidence but nothing that can be substantiated. Every company is trying to get a handle on this within the context of its own business and technological situation. If you and I were competitors and I was using big data effectively to improve my position vis-a-vis you and the rest of our industry, would I tell you anything specific about the scope of these successes and how I am using big data to achieve them? Not likely. So you see the problem with getting specific examples. I know of many, but they are confidential, except for companies like Google where these kinds of efforts tend to enhance their mystique.

ACCOUNTING TRENDS
Should U.S. standards line up with the rest of the world?

David Milstead

EXECUTIVE SUMMARY

In matters of accounting and auditing, the United States increasingly is going it alone as the rest of the world settles on a different set of standards. U.S. companies must conform to the detailed rules known as Generally Accepted Accounting Principles (GAAP). Elsewhere, companies largely follow what are known as the International Financial Reporting Standards (IFRS), which rely on broad guidelines rather than the rules-oriented GAAP approach. In recent years, U.S. and international oversight bodies have discussed convergence of these different systems, but they remain far apart on almost all matters. Advocates for standards that will make financial statements as clear as possible for investors acknowledge that the United States may have the right answers in some areas, even as it resists investor-friendly rules elsewhere. But that raises questions about whether investors will best be served if the United States eventually has the only distinct set of accounting rules in the developed world, especially as business grows increasingly global. Among the questions under debate: Is U.S. GAAP, with its rules and regulations, better than IFRS? If the United States doesn't use IFRS, will its public companies have trouble attracting foreign investors? Will investors be better served if the United States adopts more rigorous auditors' reports used elsewhere?

OVERVIEW

When it comes to explaining to shareholders how its company's books are audited, the Rolls-Royce of the field is Rolls-Royce.

In 2014, the United Kingdom rolled out new rules that said the auditor's report in a company's annual financial statements, also known as an auditor's letter, needed to provide much more information about the choices the company made in preparing its numbers. For example: Were the company's assumptions cautious or optimistic?

Some auditors took it to heart: KPMG, which audited the books of Rolls-Royce Holdings PLC, produced a report so comprehensive, it's now held up as a model for how the auditor's letter to shareholders should be written.[1] The U.K.'s Investment Management Association has even instituted the Auditor Reporting Awards—with KPMG taking the inaugural "most insightful" prize.[2]

From *SAGE Business Researcher,*
November 9, 2015

The hood ornament and logo for luxury automaker Rolls-Royce are among the world's most recognizable; financial reports prepared for company stockholders under new U.K. accounting standards have been lauded as a model for how to present auditors' reports.

No auditor's letter in the United States will win an award anytime soon, however. That's because the country's auditing standards-setters have not joined an international movement toward beefing up auditors' reports. The global International Auditing and Assurance Standards Board has developed new standards that will take effect in 2017.[3] But the U.S. Public Company Accounting Oversight Board, a body that supervises the auditors of companies whose shares are publicly traded, has so far been unable to develop a set of rules palatable to its U.S. constituents.

In matters of accounting and auditing, the United States is increasingly going it alone as the rest of the world settles on its own set of standards. In 2002, the Financial Accounting Standards Board (FASB), the primary U.S. accounting rules-setter, agreed in principle to work with the newly formed International Accounting Standards Board (IASB) to develop a high-quality set of global accounting standards. But despite one significant success in the "convergence" project—new standards on how companies book revenue—efforts in areas such as insurance contracts and lease accounting have failed to produce converged rules because of differences of opinion among the constituencies of the two rules-setters. No more accounting topics are scheduled for convergence between the FASB and the IASB. The U.S. rulemakers are now "conceding that a one-size-fits-all global financial reporting model is a nice idea that doesn't work in practice," said the midsize U.S. accounting firm Baker Tilly.[4]

"I think on both sides of this issue . . . people have come to the realization of the difficulty of the transition," says William Ezzell, a former Deloitte executive who was chairman of the trade group American Institute of Certified Public Accountants (AICPA) when the convergence project picked up steam in 2002–03. "Some of these [converged standards] would cause significant change depending on which way you go . . . and people are uncomfortable with that. So I think that's caused everybody to slow down."

Without that one set of global standards, then, the United States is effectively wagering that its companies and their investors will be better off with its own Generally Accepted Accounting Principles (GAAP), developed over many decades, versus the IASB's relatively new International Financial Reporting Standards (IFRS). Russell G. Golden, chairman of the FASB, wrote in 2014 "when standards for convergence do not represent an improvement to U.S. GAAP, we must do what we believe is in the best interests of investors who use it."[5]

Advocates for stronger accounting standards that will make financial statements clearer for investors acknowledge that the United States may have the right answers in some areas, even as it resists investor-friendly rules elsewhere. But that raises questions about whether investors will best be served if the United States eventually has the only distinct set of accounting rules in the developed world. As business grows increasingly global, a U.S. multinational corporation will have multiple subsidiaries in countries that use IFRS. And separate rules also may create an obstacle for U.S. companies attempting to raise capital in an increasingly globalized marketplace for investments.

Company restatements peaked in 2006

"If we really believe in open international markets and the benefits of global finance, then it can't make sense to have different accounting rules and practices for companies and investors operating across national borders," said former Federal Reserve Chairman Paul Volcker in a 2012 interview.[6]

Part of the problem is the way the two sets of standards have evolved. Historically, IFRS relied more on principles of accounting, offering only broad guidelines on how companies should record their transactions. This gives company management more leeway. U.S. GAAP, by contrast, involve thousands and thousands of pages of precise rules that dictate proper accounting treatment.

The heavy U.S. reliance on rules is the product of a relatively strong enforcement regime—the Securities and Exchange Commission (SEC) and the Public Company Auditing

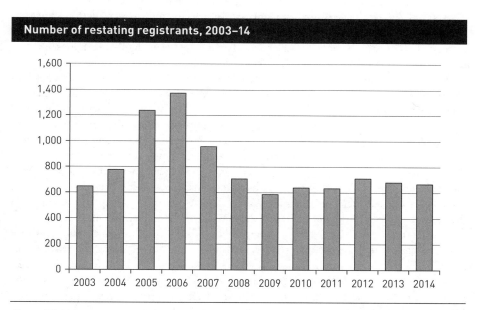

Number of restating registrants, 2003–14

About 670 U.S. public companies filed financial restatements in 2014, roughly half the number that did so in 2006, according to regulatory compliance research firm Audit Analytics. Companies file restatements when previous financial reports contain inaccuracies. The annual number of restating U.S. companies climbed to nearly 1,400 in 2006 before retreating to fewer than 600 in 2009. It has since fluctuated between 630 and 710.

Source: Mercedes Erickson,"2014 Financial Restatements Review," Audit Analytics, April 27, 2015, http://tinyurl .com/qexdye5

Oversight Board (PCAOB)—as well as a legal system that allows for plentiful securities lawsuits. But the rules have a downside, say experts: Companies can justify accounting decisions that may not reflect economic reality by saying they follow the letter, if not the spirit, of the accounting literature.

"It is so, so tough that I think what we find is accounting professionals like to hide behind a bright-line rule," says Jay Thibodeau, an accounting professor at Bentley University in Waltham, Mass., and co-author of a textbook on fraud and ethics in auditing and accounting. "Bright-line rules really allow the challenged to feel a whole lot better about what they're doing because they can point to a rule and say, 'Wait a minute, we can't get sued because we followed the rule.'"

Stephen A. Zeff, an accounting professor at Rice University and co-author of a book on the first 10 years of the IASB, says, "Historically, the SEC right back from the beginning in the 1930s has said that financial reporting must not be misleading. And to the SEC's accounting staff and the commissioners, misleading has meant, among other things, managements having excessive, unchecked, undisciplined discretion to put anything in the financial statements they like simply because they look better."

But outside the United States, Zeff says, "the IASB and other countries and their regulators and accountants and auditors have always been much more relaxed about that. . . . Their markets are different. The history of regulation is different and they say, within somewhat broader limits, 'As long as there is full disclosure we will allow companies to use their judgment to put figures in the financial statements that perhaps are not hard-core figures based on invoices, or prices established in writing somewhere.'"

Here's one example of how U.S. GAAP and IFRS differ in practice: When a company purchases equipment to be used in its business, it records the price it paid for that equipment as its value on its balance sheet, which lists assets and liabilities. This becomes known as its "historical cost," because as years go by, the equipment stays on the balance sheet at that price, minus depreciation each year to reflect its declining value. If a company finds that the asset can no longer produce profits that justify the amount on the balance sheet, it must reduce the value—a "write-down"—and reflect that reduction as an expense in its income statement, which tallies revenue and expenses. Under U.S. GAAP, the write-down is permanent because companies cannot mark up those hard assets if their prospects improve. Under IFRS, however, companies can reverse a previously recorded impairment and reflect the gains as income on their income statements.

A second example: Under IFRS, a company can choose whether the cash it spends for interest payments on its borrowings is recorded in the "operating" section of its statement of cash flows, or in the section for its "financing" cash flows. Under U.S. GAAP, interest expenses must be recorded in operating cash flows. This means that two companies in the same industry with similar cash interest expenses can report greatly different operating cash-flow numbers, both within IFRS, or in comparison to U.S. GAAP.

Some years after the FASB and the IASB decided in 2002 to work together to remove the differences between their two sets of standards, the boards settled on four major projects. One, "revenue recognition," would govern how companies recorded sales on their income statement, one of the most fundamentally important issues in accounting. The three others related to insurance contracts, financial instruments and leases.

The revenue recognition project succeeded, with the two boards issuing nearly identical standards in 2014.[7] They were set to go into effect for most companies in 2017, but both bodies said in July 2015 they would delay implementation until 2018 because companies and their auditors said they didn't have enough time to prepare for the changes.[8]

"I think that both boards had a big incentive to try to revise the current standards," says Robert Herz, who was chairman of the FASB when the two groups began the convergence project. "In our case, we had 200 pieces of disjointed literature that covered specific transactions in specific industries and . . . was outdated and contradictory. We had an incentive to try to put together a more overarching approach.

"On the other hand, the IASB had a very general standard that nobody knew how to use," Herz says. "So often people in other parts of the world would look to the U.S. GAAP to actually implement it, because you could almost do anything under IFRS, it was so broad. So you know, we worked on that one very hard, from probably the year 2003 onwards."

As accountants, regulators and investors continue to discuss the best ways to report corporate financial results, below are some of the questions under debate.

WEIGHING THE ISSUES

Is U.S. GAAP, with its rules and regulations, better than IFRS?

The failure to produce a global set of standards is not necessarily bad news to those who are skeptical about IFRS and its principles-based underpinnings.

"I am very much against it," says Michael C. "Chris" Knapp, an accounting professor at the University of Oklahoma and the author of a textbook on contemporary auditing issues. "The U.S. GAAP are much better than international standards. There are so many loopholes in those standards. They call them 'principle-based.' Well, it's just a transparent effort to allow these firms to report whatever number they want. Empirically, it's been proven repeatedly that U.S. earnings numbers have a much higher quality, are much more conservative than European numbers."

Dennis R. "Denny" Beresford, a former partner at the international accounting firm Ernst & Young who served as FASB chairman from 1987 to 1997, says, "The U.S. standards continue to be the best in the world, and while the IASB has made significant progress, they are not quite to the same level of the U.S and there's no reason for the U.S. to step down. . . . Relatively few of those countries use [IFRS] in the pure sense because they all have their carve-outs, or they don't really apply it in the same kind of rigorous, disciplined manner that we apply U.S. GAAP in our country."

The view that U.S. GAAP and its many rules make for better financial statements is not shared universally, even among U.S. accountants. Ezzell, a former AICPA chairman, says, "I don't buy the fact that any one set of standards is better than the other or that we're 'giving up something' if we switch."

He says, "I mean they are different, yes, but if you provide the readers with consistent application and sufficient information, they can make informed decisions. You can apply that to just about any area. If you say you're going to put leases on the balance sheet, or not put them on the balance sheet: OK, well, fine, just tell me what the rules are, and give me the disclosures. I'm an investor, I can make a decision."

Robert Mednick, a retired Arthur Andersen executive and chairman of the AICPA in 1996–97, says U.S. GAAP "has become far too rule-oriented. . . . [It's] an accounting standard that is written in such detail that it almost emulates the Internal Revenue Code or something like that that causes practitioners, whether in corporate America or in auditing firms, to have these huge checklists to make sure they follow every single detail. You lose sight of the forest for the trees. I like broad principles. . . . The more rules you make, the more people can find ways around and through the rules."

The SEC, which regulates U.S. stock markets, is the final arbiter of appropriate accounting in the United States. It often works directly with the FASB to offer guidance on rulemaking. At other times, it steps in and issues Staff Accounting Bulletins when it feels the FASB hasn't moved quickly enough in creating new rules.

That powerful presence is absent in the IASB/IFRS model, as there is no global securities regulator to take similar actions. Instead, each country that has adopted IFRS has its own regulator that enforces and interprets the standards as it sees fit. That void gives GAAP advocates pause—even though, despite arguments about the strength of GAAP, the United States has seen multibillion-dollar frauds and failures like Enron and WorldCom.

"We still have in our country the Securities and Exchange Commission that, by law set by Congress, has to determine what corporations must follow, and they are not going to give up the power to do that to some international body over which they have no direct authority," Beresford says. "That's how we feel in this country, and similar people in other countries feel the same way with their own situation."

Knapp asks, "Who's going to regulate this infrastructure now if we go to International Financial Reporting Standards? This idea that Europe, for instance, has adopted IFRS is a joke. If you study individual countries, you'll find out there's really loophole after loophole after loophole."

Zeff of Rice University says critics of the IASB's funding—it gets its money from contributions, many from the accounting and financial industries—conveniently forget that the FASB obtained its support in the same way until the 2002 Sarbanes-Oxley corporate reform law banned that practice and began to levy a charge on all public companies to fund it. Until then, "nobody in the U.S was complaining bitterly about how such a source of funding for the FASB in effect challenged its independence and objectivity. But, of course, as soon as the Americans changed, Americans think any program in the rest of the world which is unlike it is open to question."

Zeff says the IFRS Foundation's Monitoring Board was established in 2009 "to answer criticisms not just from the U.S. but elsewhere, especially from the European Parliament, that there was no oversight over the work and organization of the IASB by public interest authorities. . . . Well, that's the closest you can get to an SEC."

If the U.S. doesn't use IFRS, will its public companies have trouble attracting foreign investors?

In less than two decades, International Financial Reporting Standards have spread across the globe. The IASB estimates that 116 of 140 countries it has studied require use of IFRS for "all or most domestic publicly accountable entities."[9] (A publicly accountable entity is a company that has sold debt or stock to the public, or a financial company that has a large number of customers.)[10] "Capital market investors and lenders in jurisdictions with 58 percent of the world's GDP receive IFRS financial statements," the IASB says.[11]

According to accounting firm PricewaterhouseCoopers, the remaining major capital markets that do not mandate IFRS are Japan, where companies are allowed to use it if they choose; India, where regulators have said they intend to adopt the standards in 2016 or 2017; and China, which has said it intends to fully converge its standards but has not set a date.

And, of course, the United States, which, as PricewaterhouseCoopers notes, has "no current plans to change."[12]

In 2007, the SEC began allowing non-U.S. companies to list on U.S. exchanges using just IFRS, without also providing a reconciliation of numbers to match GAAP financials. But it has not said it will allow U.S. companies to adopt IFRS voluntarily, much less mandate all companies use IFRS rather than GAAP.

James Schnurr, the SEC's chief accountant, told the Baruch College Financial Reporting Conference in May 2015 that the agency had heard "reactions from a number of different constituents: preparers, investors, auditors, regulators and standard-setters." And while "there is continued support for the objective of a single set of high-quality, globally accepted accounting standards," he said, "there is virtually no support to have the SEC mandate IFRS for all registrants [and] there is little support for the SEC to provide an option allowing domestic companies to prepare their financial statements under IFRS."[13]

This will likely leave U.S. companies alone, among those in major capital markets, with their own set of national accounting standards. This may well be OK, for some time, given the dominance of U.S. markets: As of July 31, 2015, the market capitalization of U.S. stocks—the number of shares outstanding times the price—equaled nearly $20 trillion, or 52 percent of the total world market capitalization, according to Bank of America Merrill Lynch. The retreat of share prices in many emerging markets and the rising value of the U.S. dollar meant that the U.S. share of global capitalization was at its highest level since the 1980s, the bank said.[14]

U.S. stocks dominate world markets

"U.S. companies are not going to be penalized by the marketplace if there never is convergence," says Mednick, the former AICPA chairman. "We have not only the largest but [also] the most liquid capital market. The U.S. dollar is the reserve currency of the world. The U.S. is considered the safest place to invest. No one is going to penalize companies in the marketplace because they are not using the [international] standards."

Scott Taub, a former deputy chief accountant at the SEC who now is managing director for Financial Reporting Advisors in Chicago, says, "What I have heard is, No. 1, at this point U.S. companies can get all the capital they need from the U.S., so it doesn't matter. And No. 2, analysts and sophisticated investors are smart enough to deal with two sets of standards. They used to deal with 50 sets of standards, so two sounds pretty easy. So in that regard, I don't see that there is pressure that U.S. companies might bring to bear to say, 'You know, we've got to fix this because it's hurting us.'"

The SEC wields a weapon that may ensure that U.S. companies that want to list on foreign stock exchanges can do so even if they're not using IFRS. If any foreign exchange mandated IFRS, says Herz, the former FASB chairman, "then the SEC would have the counterthreat of saying, 'OK, you don't let our companies list with U.S. GAAP. We're [not] going to [let] your company use IFRS anymore.' You get a trade war by accounting standards."

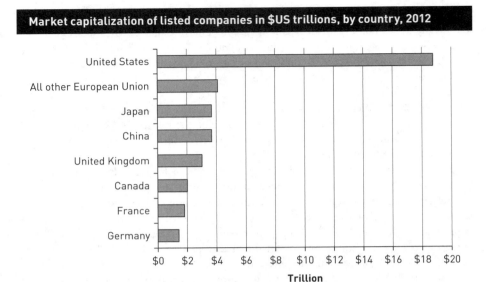

Market capitalization of listed companies in $US trillions, by country, 2012

The market capitalization of U.S. stocks totaled about $19 trillion in 2012, more than five times that of second-ranking China and third-ranking Japan. The United Kingdom led all European Union member countries with about $3 trillion in market capitalization, ahead of France ($1.8 trillion) and Germany ($1.4 trillion).

Notes: Market capitalization is the number of outstanding shares of companies listed on stock exchanges multiplied by their share prices. Does not include capitalization of investment companies, mutual funds or other collective investment vehicles. "All other European Union" excludes France, Germany and the United Kingdom.

Source: "Market capitalization of listed companies (current US$)," The World Bank, downloaded Oct. 27, 2015, http://tinyurl.com/qastjru

Those with a longer-term view express less certainty about the status quo. China will, by sheer virtue of its population, pass the United States in the coming years as the world's biggest economy. A recovery in global stock markets could push the United States back to less than half the world's market capitalization in the near term, with its share shrinking over time.

"I could foresee that," says Ezzell, a former AICPA chairman. "I don't have a crystal ball that says how long and how far out that could be. But if you look back far enough with what's happened in the last 20 or 30 years with a trend towards globalization and global companies, the U.S. stock market is not necessarily always going to be the always go-to first place. It's a natural evolution, not revolution."

Sir David Tweedie was the first chairman of the International Accounting Standards Board, serving from 2001 until 2011. "When I started in the IASB it was a case of, did you understand Latvian accounting? Did you understand French accounting? Did you understand German accounting? What were the differences? Have you got all the nuances? Are you sure you are right? . . . That's why the other countries adopted IFRS. . . . I think there is a risk premium if people don't fully understand [the accounting]."

He says, "I won't reveal the company, but it was an American company that was telling us how they were trying to raise capital in Asia and the markets demanded the IFRS numbers, and they couldn't provide them in time. Just couldn't do it in time. So they had to pay a higher price for countries who wouldn't accept U.S. GAAP."

Will investors be better served if the United States adopts more rigorous auditors' reports used elsewhere in the world?

Students know a pass/fail course may put less pressure on them than a graded one—but, ultimately, they'll get less detailed feedback about how they performed.

For decades, much of the world's auditors' reports have been constructed in the same way. These reports to investors, which take the form of brief letters included in a company's financial statements, simply signed off on the company's accounting—or, much less frequently, didn't do so. They were signed by the firm, not by any of the individual partners who performed the audit.

"Auditors' letters have been among the least interesting parts of annual reports," longtime *New York Times* financial reporter Floyd Norris wrote in 2014. "If the opinions said the accounting was proper—and virtually all did—and did not voice concern about whether a company could stay in business, the letters were basically the same. There was no reason for an investor to read them."[15]

That, however, began to change in 2014 when the United Kingdom revamped the requirements for the letters. "The Financial Crisis of 2008 brought into sharp focus the concerns of investors and others about the effectiveness of company stewardship generally and about the effectiveness of the audit in supporting this," the U.K.'s Financial Reporting Council, which sets the country's standards for accounting and auditing work, said in a March 2015 report reviewing the changes. "In particular, concerns were raised about whether the binary (i.e. pass/fail) auditor's report continued to be fit for purpose in providing adequate transparency about the audit and the auditor's insights about the company, based on its work."[16]

The new U.K. report identifies "key audit matters"—the things of greatest concern to the auditors when performing their duties—and how they responded. It addresses how the audited company defines "materiality," the concept of whether a piece of financial information is large enough to be of concern to the company's investors, and therefore disclosed. And it requires the disclosure of the name of the audit firm's partner who led the audit of the company's books.[17] The International Auditing and Assurance Standards Board (IAASB) is adopting similar rules that will go into effect in 2017 for countries that have agreed to use the group's International Standards on Auditing as part of their regulatory framework.

The U.S. Public Company Accounting Oversight Board, however, has no timetable to follow. It attempted in 2013 to introduce new standards for the auditor's report. The PCAOB's proposal kept the pass-fail approach but would have required auditors to discuss any "critical audit matters" in which the auditors "had to make their toughest or most complex judgments or which gave them the most difficulty in forming their opinion."[18]

Companies and accounting firms questioned whether the benefits to investors outweighed the costs. The accounting industry particularly opposes the idea of naming the audit partners in a company's annual financial statements, instead suggesting the disclosure occur in a separate document filed with the PCAOB.[19] (The AICPA and an affiliated group, the Center for Audit Quality, declined to be interviewed for this SAGE Business Researcher report.)

"I thought [the PCAOB] went too far, in particular, where they called for the auditors to be disclosing a lot of information that would be more management's responsibility, in terms of the information about the significant estimates and things of that nature that are included in the financial statements," says Beresford, a former chairman of the FASB. "In reality, . . . most investors still look to the auditor's report as more of what we would call a 'good housekeeping seal of approval.' They are more interested in just knowing that the auditors agree that the financial statements were fairly presented, and they are not looking to the auditors to give them a detailed analysis of those financial statements. They are looking to management for that responsibility."

Financial Executives International, a trade group for chief financial officers and other similar executives, expressed its opposition in a comment letter to the PCAOB. "It appears that one of the desired outcomes of the proposed rule would be to provide investors with additional insights into how an auditor has dealt with the complex and difficult issues that normally arise during the process and are highlighted by management in the financial statements. To the extent the information provided by management is not sufficient to enable investors to adequately understand the underlying financial statements; we believe any perceived shortcomings are better addressed by improved footnote or management discussion and analysis."[20]

Observers of the changes in the United Kingdom, however, say management's disclosures may improve as auditors highlight the key matters in an audit. "We think the new information may be helpful in prompting better dialogue between companies and their shareholders on accounting and audit issues," Citigroup Global Markets Inc. analysts Sarah Deans and Terence Fisher said in a March 2014 report. "We also suspect that companies may be prompted to provide better disclosure on matters highlighted in the auditor's report, provided auditors fulfill the spirit of the new requirements."[21]

Thibodeau of Bentley University says he believes the PCAOB will ultimately succeed in expanding auditors' reports, in part because auditing firms will eventually realize the reports could provide a competitive advantage.

"I've said to my colleagues in practice, 'I think the expanded reporting model allows you to differentiate yourself from your competitors on quality better than the pass/fail,'" he says. "The pass/fail does not really allow the market differentiation on the audit process that's been employed by that particular audit firm. It kind of treats the firms as basically the same. . . . I believe that the standard reporting model provides an opportunity to showcase your excellence to the marketplace and, most importantly, to audit committees that are making decisions."

BACKGROUND

Counting predates writing

Accounting is one of the world's oldest professions. While not all scholars agree on its origins, many have embraced the theories of Denise Schmandt-Besserat, an archaeologist who is professor emerita of art and Middle Eastern studies at the University of Texas;

she examined tiny tokens from archeological digs and concluded that the first systems of counting agricultural production dated to roughly 8000 B.C., several thousand years before the first written language.[22]

It makes sense: Commerce could not emerge and grow if participants could not keep track of what was traded or, ultimately, bought and sold. However, the idea that outsiders would examine a business venture's financial records is relatively new. England's English Companies Act of 1855–56 introduced a standard reporting method for balance sheets, "intended to prod companies to disclose financial information," author Mike Brewster said in *Unaccountable*, his 2003 survey of contemporary accounting.[23]

It was during this time—what Brewster, a former journalist and communications director for a large accounting firm, called "a golden age of accounting in England"—that many of the big accounting firms we know today were founded in London.[24] Samuel Lowell Price started Price Waterhouse in 1849. William Cooper launched Cooper Brothers in 1854; his firm would later be known as Coopers & Lybrand and would ultimately merge with Price Waterhouse in 1998 to form today's PricewaterhouseCoopers.[25] William Welch Deloitte rose to prominence in 1849 by auditing England's Great Western Railway; the firm would later combine with the operations of the first major U.S. firm, Haskins & Sells, to form Deloitte Haskins & Sells, now known simply as Deloitte.[26] Peat Marwick, the predecessor responsible for the middle two letters of today's KPMG, started in 1911 when Peat and Marwick merged.[27] (The only one of today's big firms with purely U.S. roots, Ernst & Young, was the product of a 1989 merger between Arthur Young & Co., formed in 1906 in Chicago, and Ernst & Ernst, started by two brothers in Cleveland in 1903.[28])

In the United States, where the accounting industry was not as mature, there were only sporadic, ineffective attempts in the latter half of the 19th century to get companies whose shares traded on the New York Stock Exchange to disclose financial results. "Nineteenth-century American industrial firms disclosed little to outsiders," wrote Thomas A. King in his *More Than a Numbers Game: A Brief History of Accounting*. In 1866, the Delaware, Lackawanna, and Western Rail Road treasurer responded to a NYSE request by saying the company would make "no reports and publish no statements and have done nothing of the sort for the last five years." Another railroad went two decades without a shareholder report. Said King: "Owner-managers saw little upside to sharing financial information, and they worried that disclosure could help competitors."[29]

The early 20th century saw a rise in accounting as a profession. Now, accounting and finance are staples of any business.

The public-accounting profession in the United States grew up in the early part of the 20th century. New York state introduced the first Certified Public Accountant designation in 1897, and it quickly spread. (To be a CPA, an individual must satisfy educational and professional requirements and pass a state licensing exam.) U.S. colleges began to develop accounting curriculums. The New York Stock Exchange, as well as British investors used to a more robust system of accounting, pushed U.S. companies to have outside firms audit their financial statements.[30] In 1903, United States Steel published financial statements that included all its subsidiary operations, allowing its auditor, Price Waterhouse, to assure the statements were "audited and found correct." This, said King, meant "the era of modern financial accounting had dawned."[31]

GAAP and greater disclosure

George May became head of Price Waterhouse in 1911 and quickly established himself as a leader in the profession. In 1927, he led a special committee of the American Institute of Accountants charged with cooperating with the stock exchanges.

"The committee's job, when it started out, was to develop ways that the NYSE could instill better accounting in the companies listed on its exchange," wrote Brewster. "For example, there were many reporting inconsistencies that plagued the NYSE: unreported sales figures, failure to account for asset depreciation, arbitrary asset revaluations, and failure to distinguish between expenses and capital expenditures."[32] The outcome was GAAP, which remain the standards to which U.S. companies must adhere for financial statements.

Greater financial information led to an expansion of the U.S. investor class, King said: He cites academic research that said the number of people investing in stocks increased from 500,000 in 1900 (out of a population of 76 million) to 2 million in 1920 (out of a population of 106 million); by the late 1920s, the number of individuals owning stocks might have been as high as 5.5 million, of a population of 120 million.[33]

While the Great Depression shattered investor confidence, the Securities Act of 1933 and Securities Exchange Act of 1934 cemented the ideas of disclosure and investor protection in American capital markets. Accounting firms, however, were often caught in the middle in subsequent decades. Hired by the companies, working with management to produce the audit, and often attempting to sell consulting services to the companies they audited, the accounting firms took a back seat to regulators and the exchanges in matters of compliance, Brewster said, citing a speech by Maurice Stans, a member of the Accounting Hall of Fame best known for his work as a Cabinet secretary and political fundraiser in the Nixon administration.[34]

The AICPA's Accounting Procedures Committee gave way in 1959 to a panel called the Accounting Pronouncements Board, which was to give the profession guidance on how to apply U.S. GAAP.[35] Within a decade, however, the accounting board was "hamstrung," Brewster wrote, as it was "strictly part-time, under the thumb of the AICPA, and clearly not interested in reform."[36] The successor, the Financial Accounting Standards Board (and its sibling organization, the Government Accounting Standards Board) were launched by the new Financial Accounting Foundation in 1973.[37] This structure took accounting standards-setting out from under AICPA control but left it in the hands of the private sector, rather than allowing government or regulators the primary rulemaking roles.

"Auditor prominence created a double-edged sword," wrote King. "While CPAs established brand positioning as members of a learned profession, their promotion efforts inadvertently influenced public opinion. Investors came to believe that CPAs' primary obligation was to the investing public, not to the firm actually paying audit fees, and their purpose was to root out management fraud, not opine on whether balances were prepared in accordance with [GAAP]. This expectations gap would haunt the profession for the balance of the century."[38]

Most of the time, the issues in accounting and auditing are discussed among accountants, regulators, lawyers and other sophisticated capital-market participants. At times, however, they explode into public view and capture the attention of politicians and ordinary investors.

Enron and WorldCom scandals

In the 1990s, as the American economy rode a wave of innovation from technology startup companies, the problem of how to account for stock options came to the fore. Options allow the holder to purchase a share of stock in a company for a pre-set price. If the shares grow in value, the right to buy the shares at the lower price grows in value, too. Cash-strapped tech companies made stock options their primary means of paying employees, more so than salaries or annual bonuses. At the same time, under the accounting rules of the day, they did not need to record this form of compensation as an expense, making their profits appear higher (or, in many cases, their losses appear smaller).

In 1993, the FASB attempted to draft rules that would force companies to expense employee stock options but was confronted with a public-relations campaign from the tech industry, which enlisted politicians to back its cause. Industry employees held anti-expensing rallies, and James Leisenring, vice chairman of the FASB, said he later learned that "one organization . . . spent $75 million to $90 million fighting the FASB on stock options. Obviously, the FASB did not have those kinds of resources."[39] Members of Congress began to suggest the FASB be put out of business and introduced bipartisan bills that directed the SEC to ignore the FASB if it published the new standard. The FASB abandoned the proposed standard in 1994. (Sen. Mike Enzi, R-Wyo., who is one of the few accountants in Congress, continued to oppose stock-option expensing for the next decade, but he ultimately lost that fight.[40])

James Nielsen/Stringer/Getty Images News/Getty Images

Employees of energy trading firm Enron walk past the company's Houston headquarters in 2001, just before the company went into bankruptcy amid accounting scandals.

Some of the most seismic changes to accounting and auditing came in the early years of the 21st century after the tech stock bubble burst in 2001. Houston-based Enron Corp. was seen as one of the most innovative companies in the United States, having moved beyond the pipeline business to trade in all types of energy-related products. But when investors realized the company had abused accounting rules to move billions of dollars of debt off its balance sheet, making the company seem healthier than it was, its shares plummeted, and Enron fell into bankruptcy in late 2001. Enron's auditor, Arthur Andersen, then one of the Big Five audit firms, admitted it had shredded Enron-related documents after the SEC began an investigation of the collapsed energy company. Clients began to leave, the U.S. Justice Department indicted Andersen on obstruction of justice charges, and the firm was convicted in June 2002. Although the U.S. Supreme Court overturned the conviction in 2005, citing overly broad jury instructions, the damage had been done: Andersen went out of business not long after the 2002 indictment.[41]

Despite the twin failures of Enron and Andersen that wiped out the wealth of tens of thousands of employees, corporate-fraud legislation had stalled in Congress in early 2002, in part because of opposition by accounting firms. Then came WorldCom—a huge telecommunications provider that admitted in June that it had overstated its profit by $3.85 billion. (Ultimately, it acknowledged $10.6 billion in errors, and recorded $73.7 billion in losses from 2000 to 2002.)[42] The next month, it filed for bankruptcy court protection, the largest Chapter 11 filing in history until that point.

Legislative reactions

The public's mood shifted, with Republicans the recipients of the ill will. "Until WorldCom announced their restatements, any major corporate fraud legislation was facing defeat in Congress," said Lynn Turner, the SEC's chief accountant in the late 1990s. "It was only after the Republicans thought they were going to be unemployed that they went against what the [accounting] firms wanted."[43]

Multibillion-dollar errors

The result was the Sarbanes-Oxley Act, a wide-ranging anti-fraud law. Among its provisions, it created the Public Company Accounting Oversight Board to regulate auditing firms and the audits they perform on companies whose shares trade on public exchanges. It required CEOs and chief financial officers to certify annual and quarterly company reports, subject to criminal charges for fraud. It established criteria for the independence of auditors from their clients.[44] And it required U.S. accounting standard-setters to consider whether their rules should converge with international ones.[45]

As the U.S. financial reporting system underwent this momentous change, the work on one global set of accounting standards began in earnest. The International Accounting Standards Board was formed in 2001 to replace a predecessor organization, the International Accounting Standards Committee, and to create a set of international rules called International Financial Reporting Standards. In 2002, the FASB and the IASB issued the Norwalk Agreement, named for the FASB's Connecticut headquarters city, which stated their commitment to develop compatible accounting standards. In 2006, the IASB and FASB identified several major areas—revenue recognition, leases, insurance contracts and "fair value" of assets—in which they would seek to converge U.S. GAAP with IFRS. In 2007, the SEC said it would begin allowing non-U.S. companies to be able to list on U.S. exchanges using just IFRS, without also providing GAAP financials.[46]

"The fact that we were working together and that we were making real progress prompted the SEC in late 2007 to lift the reconciliation requirement between U.S. GAAP and IFRS,"

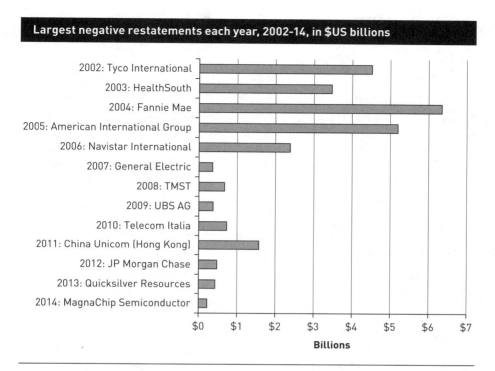

Largest negative restatements each year, 2002–14, in $US billions

2002: Tyco International
2003: HealthSouth
2004: Fannie Mae
2005: American International Group
2006: Navistar International
2007: General Electric
2008: TMST
2009: UBS AG
2010: Telecom Italia
2011: China Unicom (Hong Kong)
2012: JP Morgan Chase
2013: Quicksilver Resources
2014: MagnaChip Semiconductor

$0 $1 $2 $3 $4 $5 $6 $7

Billions

Corporations issue restatements when previous financial reports include errors. Electrical manufacturer MagnaChip Semiconductor's $203 million income adjustment was the largest negative restatement by any accelerated filer—businesses with tradable equity value ranging from $75 million and $700 million—in 2014. Mortgage market giant Fannie Mae's $6.3 billion adjustment in 2004 remains the largest negative restatement in recent years, but still trails WorldCom's 2000–01 adjustment of nearly $11 billion.

Source: Mercedes Erickson,"2014 Financial Restatements Review," Audit Analytics, April 27, 2015, http://tinyurl .com/qexdye5

says Herz, the chairman of FASB at the time. "But only for IFRS, not for other national standards. So all of a sudden, companies and countries around the world could use IFRS and register in our markets without having to redo their financials in GAAP or do their reconciliations to GAAP. The IFRS became kind of an international passport, from a financial statement point of view, to raising capital in any major market in the world including the largest market, ours. That move prompted a lot of countries to get off the fence. So you found that there was a whole wave of countries following that announcement that decided to either require or permit the use of IFRS for their companies."

"Bob [Herz] was a true internationalist," says Tweedie, chairman of the IASB during this time. "I think we both believed in the idea of one single set of global standards. So if the U.S. had the best standard, then the international standards should take the U.S. one, and vice versa. That's certainly the attitude that Bob and I developed, and was supported by the SEC."

But in contrast to the corporate scandals of the earlier part of the decade, the financial crisis of 2008–09 seemed to knock the convergence efforts off track, as the SEC and the FASB had a whole new set of fires to put out.

"Even though they may have intended them as short-term fixes and then 'We'll get back to working together on longer-term, more durable things,' by that time people [in leadership positions] had changed and business and the SEC said, 'This is a low priority.'" Herz says. "There was a lot of enthusiasm in this country for moving to convergence and moving to IFRS until the financial crisis."

"The crisis blew up and everybody was concerned more or less with staying alive, as opposed to converging standards," Tweedie says. "So you had a complete sort of hiatus."

CURRENT SITUATION

Convergence stalls

"I don't talk about convergence," says Linda Mezon, chair of Canada's Accounting Standards Board. Mezon has had a front-row seat over the last dozen years as the world's accountants have tried, in vain, to come to one set of global standards. "I talk about narrowing differences."

It's the best that can be hoped for now that the convergence project between the U.S. Financial Accounting Standards Board and the International Accounting Standards Board is ending. Of the four projects the two groups had identified for convergence, three (leases, insurance contracts and financial instruments) will be concluded without a uniform set of standards.[47] And for the one that succeeded—revenue recognition—both the FASB and the IASB have delayed implementation after complaints by companies and accounting firms that they haven't had enough time to prepare.

"People complain a lot right now about the fact that the IASB and the FASB are not ending up completely converged with the four standards," Mezon says. "But if you were to take a snapshot of what will happen after those standards are in place based on what we know today vs. where we were 10 years ago, what you would find is there are fewer differences between the IFRS and the USA today than there were 10 years ago."

Leases provide one example of a good result, short of convergence. Leases are financial arrangements in which companies use assets—think of an airline and its airplanes—but do not actually own them. In most of the world, for many years, companies were able to take on multibillion-dollar, multiyear leases for the equipment crucial to their businesses, yet never reflect that obligation as a liability on the balance sheet. By contrast, a company that issued debt to the public and used the proceeds to buy the equipment would record that debt obligation and seem, to the untrained eye, to be in a much weaker financial position.

While the FASB and the IASB have agreed to disagree on the final accounting for leases, that remaining dispute is over how lease payments will be reflected on the income statement, which records revenue and expenses. The bottom line, accountants say, is that the FASB and the IASB have agreed that leases, in nearly all cases, will now show up on the balance sheet, making balance sheets more comparable from company to company—and country to country. "In one important regard, they're going to converge," says Herz, who led the convergence effort for the FASB starting in 2002.

The SEC, which has the ultimate role in mandating IFRS in the United States or at least allowing U.S. companies to use it voluntarily, has done neither. A 2008 agency "roadmap" said a single set of global standards would benefit U.S. investors, and the SEC reiterated that position in 2010.[48] But a 2012 "final report" on a plan to incorporate IFRS into the U.S. system didn't make any recommendation to the commission on what should be done.[49] "I think the SEC has kind of come and gone, hot and cold, on this whole issue," says Ezzell, a former AICPA chairman.

FASB Chairman Golden wrote in his third-quarter 2015, "From the Chairman's Desk" blog: "In the past six months, it has become increasingly clear that the United States is unlikely to adopt International Financial Reporting Standards, or offer U.S. public companies the option to use IFRS when they file their financial statements with the Securities and Exchange Commission."[50]

The FASB's approach, going forward, is to participate in discussions at the Accounting Standards Advisory Forum (ASAF), a group created by the foundation that backs the IASB. It's one of 12 members. "The FASB's membership on the ASAF is an opportunity to represent U.S. interests in the IASB's standard-setting process and to continue the process of improving and converging U.S. GAAP and IFRS," the FASB said in a statement on its website.[51]

Sarbanes-Oxley hangs on

The 2002 Sarbanes-Oxley Act, referred to informally as "SOX," has survived court challenges and various legislative attempts to modify or weaken it. Opponents particularly have targeted as expensive and unnecessary Section 404 of the act, which requires management of companies with a market value of more than $75 million to certify the internal controls that produce the financial statements.

"Section 404(b) imposes very high costs and is of very limited utility with respect to small companies," David R. Burton, a senior fellow in economic policy at the Heritage Foundation, a conservative Washington think tank, testified before Congress in April 2014. "In these companies, a small executive team of a very few persons controls the company. If they want to abscond with company funds, a loose-leaf binder on the shelf is not going to stop them. Yet these internal control assessment loose-leaf binders can cost a quarter of [a] million dollars or more to produce."

The provision, he added, "is best thought of as the accountants' and management consultants' full-employment provision. As a practical matter, it does little to protect investors in small firms but imposes extremely high costs on law-abiding firms."[52]

The 2012 Jumpstart Our Business Startups Act loosened some disclosure requirements for companies that want to make an initial public offering (IPO) of their shares. For example, a company that qualifies as an "emerging growth company"—having less than $1 billion in revenue in its most recent fiscal year—may provide less financial and executive compensation information in its IPO documents than a larger company.[53]

Congressional Republicans continue to try to change or overturn Sarbanes-Oxley beyond the tweaks in that law—in 2013, the proposed Fostering Innovation Act aimed to raise the size thresholds for businesses covered by many of the SOX provisions.[54] That bill passed the House Financial Services Committee but was never taken up by the full House.[55]

Current business legislation activity focuses on Republican attempts, so far unsuccessful, to roll back or repeal the Wall Street Reform and Consumer Protection Act, better known as Dodd-Frank, that was passed after the 2008–09 financial crisis. The law created the Consumer Financial Protection Bureau (CFPB), which opponents say "has imposed fines at a rate never previously matched by a new regulatory agency."[56] While a handful of Dodd-Frank provisions could have accounting ramifications, the impact on financial reporting and auditing was minimal, compared with Sarbanes-Oxley.[57]

After years of criticism that regulators and law enforcement were forcing corporations into settlements but letting the individuals who ran them off the hook, the Department of Justice introduced new policies in September 2015 to make it easier to prosecute individuals. Under the rules, corporations that expect to receive leniency for cooperation must provide "all relevant facts relating to the individuals responsible for the misconduct."[58]

As 2015 came to a close, the primary showdown over accounting and auditing reform came at the Public Company Accounting Oversight Board, whose members are appointed by the SEC. The agency signaled frustration with the PCAOB's work, with some of its officials saying the board has prioritized disclosure over setting new rules that would dictate how accounting firms perform their audits.[59] In 2014, under industry pressure, the PCAOB had to back down from a rotation plan that would require companies to change auditors every 10 years; the idea was that requiring a fresh set of eyes each decade would improve audit quality and break up too-cozy relationships between auditors and the companies they audit.[60] PCAOB Chairman James Doty's term was set to expire in late 2015, and SEC Chair Mary Jo White said the SEC was considering "qualified" candidates to replace Doty, who is backed by a number of investor advocates.[61]

LOOKING AHEAD

Closer to global standards

With the big issues of convergence off the table, the agenda for the Financial Accounting Standards Board is filled with topics that only accountants can love.

Golden, the FASB chairman, outlined a number of issues for the FASB in coming years in a 2014 speech: Philosophy of measurement. Presentation of the income statement. Hedge accounting.[62]

Broadly, he said, "we at the FASB continue to believe that global accounting standards should be as comparable as possible—and we remain fully committed to the long-term, aspirational goal of developing global accounting standards that have the fewest possible differences."[63]

Although the FASB and the IASB "will continue to cooperate, communicate and liaise and all those kinds of the things," says Beresford, the former FASB chairman, "I don't see that there's going to be anything in the way of pure international accounting—at least adopted in the United States in the foreseeable future, put it that way."

Ezzell, a former AICPA chairman, says the United States would be better off simplifying the rules of disclosure. "We have to deal with an overload of information, and part of dealing with that is figuring out what truly is critical information. . . . [With] annual reports, the number of pages is growing constantly. So we're putting out more information, but too often that becomes boilerplate language or language that really doesn't get to the heart of the matter. . . . I think our liability system in the United States dictates a lot of that. . . . If the CEO could come out in just plain simple language and say why sales went down whatever without the fear of the company being sued out of existence, I think we would have a lot better understanding."

Herz and Tweedie, chairmen of the FASB and the IASB at the beginning of the convergence efforts, sound notes of optimism.

"If you asked me [my] expectations from 2001 whether most of the world would be using the same or very similar standards 14, 15 years later, I'd have said, 'Gee, that would have been a heck of an achievement.'" Herz says. "Most of the world does use IFRS, and we're pretty close to IFRS."

"I think eventually we will have one set of global standards," Tweedie says. "Slower than I would've liked to have seen, and I suspect slower than Bob would've liked to have seen. Some companies in the United States, if given the option, they'd go tomorrow to IFRS on the basis that they too believe it's easier for financing purposes and for their investors if everybody does the same thing."

Zeff of Rice University says, "We tend to forget how far we have come. Before 2005, it was a free-for-all among countries, and you couldn't compare at all unless you were an expert in the different GAAPs, and how many users were? So you've got to recognize how far IFRS has really brought us. It's not perfect, and never will be perfect, but it's a heck of a lot better than we were before 2005. I think everybody would concede that, but we take that for granted."

Chronology

1849–1890s	**Accounting moves from an internal means for managers to evaluate their companies to a method for outside investors to assess performance.**
1849–1870	Several of today's big accounting firms get their start in England in what's referred to as that nation's "golden era of accounting."
1855–56	England's English Companies Act introduces a standard reporting method for balance sheets.
1897	New York state introduces the first Certified Public Accountant designation in the United States.

(Continued)

(Continued)

1900s–1930s	**The modern idea of accounting takes hold in the United States, as stock exchanges and investors push companies to have their financial statements audited by outside firms.**
1927	The American Institute of Accountants forms a special committee to cooperate with the stock exchanges; the product is the first set of U.S. Generally Accepted Accounting Principles (GAAP).
1933–34	The Securities Act of 1933 and the Securities Exchange Act of 1934, passed during the Great Depression, cement the ideas of disclosure and investor protection in American capital markets.
1950s–1970s	**The accounting profession struggles to create a comprehensive set of standards.**
1959	The Accounting Principles Board (APB) forms to give the profession guidance on how to apply U.S. GAAP.
1973	The new Financial Accounting Foundation replaces the APB with the Financial Accounting Standards Board (FASB).
1990s–2000s	**Accounting scandals come to the fore as companies, investors and politicians debate the best ways to prepare financial statements.**
1994	The FASB abandons an attempt to make companies record the expense of stock options in their financial statements, one of a number of high-profile battles with the private sector over accounting rules.
2001–02	The failures of Enron and accounting firm Arthur Andersen, followed by the bankruptcy of WorldCom, spur Congress and regulators to reevaluate investor protections.
2002	Congress passes the Sarbanes-Oxley Act, a wide-ranging anti-fraud law, which requires CEOs and chief financial officers to certify annual and quarterly reports and establishes criteria for the independence of auditors from their clients.
2003	The Public Company Accounting Oversight Board (PCAOB), mandated by Sarbanes-Oxley, begins regulating auditing firms and the audits they perform on public companies.
2000s–Present	**U.S. and international accounting standards-setters start a convergence project with great fanfare—but ultimately see it crumble.**
2001	The International Accounting Standards Board is formed to replace a predecessor organization and to create a set of international rules called International Financial Reporting Standards (IFRS).
2002	The IASB and the FASB issue the Norwalk Agreement, which stated their commitment to develop compatible accounting standards.

2006	The IASB and the FASB identify several major areas—revenue recognition, leases, insurance contracts and "fair value" of assets—where they seek to align U.S. GAAP with IFRS.
2007	The SEC says it will begin allowing non-U.S. companies to list on U.S. exchanges using just IFRS, without also providing GAAP financials.
2008	A financial crisis wipes out trillions of dollars of investors' money, returning issues of accounting and disclosure to the spotlight.
2012	A "final report" from the U.S. Securities and Exchange Commission on a work plan to incorporate IFRS into the U.S. system makes no recommendations on what should be done.
2014	The IASB and the FASB issue a converged accounting standard on revenue recognition, but FASB Chairman Russell Golden says the two are likely to differ on the remaining issues where convergence was planned.
2015	The SEC and the Public Company Accounting Oversight Board squabble over the PCAOB's efforts to regulate audit firms.

Q&A: M. Darren Root on Accounting Careers

"HERE'S A BUSINESS WHERE YOU CAN GO GENERATE $1 MILLION PRETTY EASILY"
M. Darren Root
Co-founder and CEO
Rootworks

M. Darren Root is a longtime certified public accountant who has worked at Deloitte Haskins and Sells and owned his own firm. As a co-founder and CEO of Rootworks, a consulting firm for the accounting profession, he was named to *Accounting Today's* list of the Top 100 Most Influential People in Accounting. Root spoke with SAGE Business Researcher reporter David Milstead about the accounting profession. This is an edited transcript of the conversation.

The traditional career path at the big accounting firms was to join them after college, spend 30 or 40 years there and retire as a partner. Is that still a realistic path, going forward, for today's twentysomethings?

The path of "I want to graduate from college and go to a Big Four and make it to partner over the next 12 or 13 years" is still a realistic path. What's vastly different today than it was 30 years ago is today, those partners are expected to produce. In the old days those partners were expected to be rainmakers and take people to lunch and play golf. Today you might be asked to pick up and move away to Peoria, Illinois, so that you can be the partner on the Caterpillar job. I still think it's a realistic career path. The question I would have is whether it's a desirable career path.

A lot has been made of Millennials in the workplace and how they are different from previous generations. In what, if any, ways do accounting firms need to adapt to today's younger workers?

We help coach about 1,000 small CPA firms around the country. In my generation—I would be a very late Baby Boomer—our idea was that we would go into the accounting profession, and we would do it like it's always been done. That, to some degree, meant giving up your freedom, being willing to submit to the 60-to-80-hour weeks in the busy season and 60-hour weeks outside of the busy.

What I find with Millennials is that they are less willing to assume the status quo just because that's the way it's always been done, and they seem to have choices to do something different. It's not that they don't want to work hard. It's not that they don't have great skill sets. It's just that they are not quite as willing in the accounting profession to accept the status quo.

How has the accounting profession done on gender and ethnic and other forms of diversity and how can it do better?

Firms are trying really hard on diversity. I think there are probably more women entering the profession than men. You are not seeing them at the partner levels, still. It's because there are not that many who muddle all the way through the process to get to partner in a big firm. We're seeing a lot of women running small firms and owning small firms, because it allows them to have the balance between work and life that they are after. As far as ethnic diversity, I'm still not seeing much ethnic diversity in small firms at all. I occasionally teach at the Indiana University's Kelley School of Business. The classroom is very diverse there, but I am not seeing that equate itself into small accounting firm America.

There are plenty of small- to midsize businesses that have QuickBooks bookkeeping software and also have an accounting firm helping them. Do you see technology improving to the point where most businesses will just use software and CPA firms will only serve large, complex enterprises?

I see the exact opposite happening. I liken this to mowing my yard. I'm certainly capable of mowing my yard, I did it for years, but it's not a priority for me anymore. There are other ways for me to use my time. QuickBooks came out 30 years ago and Intuit said, "You no longer need your accountant, QuickBooks can handle it." What I didn't see was any falloff in the accounting profession; the profession grew. Ultimately business owners don't want, to use the analogy, to "mow their own yards." It's not their priority. So I see the small firms actually growing and helping small businesses.

How vulnerable is the U.S. accounting profession to the outsourcing of its professional jobs overseas?

The pendulum swung in that direction for a period of time. Then the IRS came out with Revenue Rule 7216, which said if you are going to outsource personal information outside of U.S. borders, you have to get written consent from your customer. At that point in time, eight years ago, there were a lot of tax returns being outsourced overseas, but that [rule change] really shut that spigot off. People are concerned with their personal data as it is, so signing an agreement that I can ship it offshore is a high hurdle. Most accounting firms that we see are not willing to go down that road.

What are some of the best opportunities for accounting students in the profession today?

The AICPA [American Institute of CPAs] has some statistics that say that about 75 percent of the leadership in the accounting space is set to retire in the next six years or so. Every city in America has multiple CPA practices. If I were a young undergrad or MBA student, I would look at finding an old guy, for lack of a better term, who's looking to retire. Here's a business where you can go generate $1 million pretty easily with a couple of hundred clients and you can put $500,000 to your bottom line and not have to deal with all the cycles of being on call, like being a doctor. That seems like a pretty good gig to me. And today with technology, you can actually do this from the beach. So to me that's the biggest thing that I want to see university students understanding. There's a whole business out here that you don't even know exists that is helping power small business in America, and you've got a great opportunity to be a part of that.

12

DIGITAL MARKETING
Has technology fundamentally changed how companies court customers?

Joan Oleck and Vickie Elmer

EXECUTIVE SUMMARY

Have you logged onto the Internet today? Used a mobile phone or tablet? Then you have seen digital marketing: ads that pop up on whatever website you are viewing. Not to mention placements on Google—and podcasts, electronic billboards and text messages, all vying for your attention (and business). You also likely have received invitations to play electronic games and become eligible for rewards, with—no surprise—tie-ins to products. All these channels are transforming today's advertising landscape. Since its arrival in the late 1990s, digital marketing has increasingly driven brand promotion. It's interactive and allows companies to collect user feedback immediately. These advantages mean that the growth in advertising is taking place in digital marketing. But its newness also means that businesses have to get creative to find the most effective campaigns.

OVERVIEW

"Sorry . . . sorry . . . sorry," rang out from YouTube videos and television screens around the world beginning in late 2013. Pantene's #ShineStrong "Not Sorry" ad gently chided women for their tendency to apologize, even when they have nothing to apologize for: An office staffer trying to make a point at a business meeting. A woman whose elbow has just been knocked off an armrest by a man sitting down next to her. A wife taking back her share of the bedcovers from her husband.

Viewers tweeted the ads, "liked" the ads, talked about the ads, endlessly. In short order, "Not Sorry" went viral—spreading from person to person, via blog, email and social media. YouTube recorded 2 million views within one week when one of the ads was released in mid-2014.[1] That viral popularity was exactly the response Pantene wanted. In fact, it's the response seemingly all brands seek.

Digital marketing—campaigns that use online tools, including social media and Web or mobile advertising—increasingly drives business and brand promotion, particularly plugs directed at millennial-generation consumers. Digital marketing differs from print and broadcast in two important respects. First, it's interactive. Users can respond and provide feedback to companies immediately. And, second, digital marketers can leverage user feedback to monitor and measure promotions in real time to determine what works—or

From *SAGE Business Researcher,*
March 2, 2015

doesn't. After they measure, marketers can concentrate on what they want most, which is converting clicks to customers.[2] The advantages inherent in instant consumer feedback, together with the savings from not wasting money on ineffective marketing, have fueled explosive growth in digital marketing since its emergence in the 1990s. However, its ever-changing options challenge business executives to create the most effective campaigns, and to determine whether trendy tools deliver the best return on investment.

By 2019, U.S. advertisers will spend $103 billion on search marketing, display advertising, social media marketing and email marketing—more than on broadcast and cable television advertising combined, Forrester Research forecasts. That's up from an estimated $67 billion in 2015. While interactive marketing will overtake television advertising by 2017, its growth rate is starting to slow slightly, according to Forrester.[3]

Global internet access rises

The Cambridge, Mass.–based research company in a report attributed this growth to three factors: the recovering economy; media proliferation, particularly the growth of interactive media; and a growing body of evidence that digital marketing works. "Marketers now have 15 years of experience from which to build the case for digital," Forrester said.

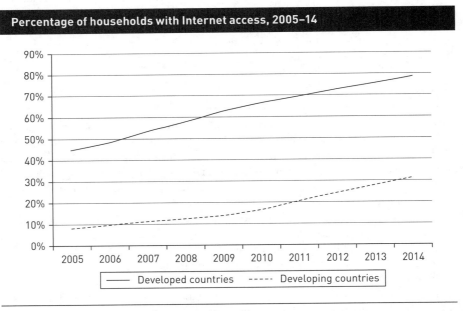

Percentage of households with Internet access, 2005–14

Legend: —— Developed countries - - - - Developing countries

Across the globe, more households are connected to the Internet, but developing countries still lag. In 2005, only 8.1 percent of households in developing countries had Internet access; in 2014, 31.2 percent did. The percentages are far higher in developed countries: 78.4 percent of households were connected in 2014, up from 44.7 percent in 2005.

Source: "Key ICT indicators for developed and developing countries and the world (totals and penetration rates)," International Telecommunication Union (ITU) /ICT Indicators database, undated, http://tinyurl.com/pyr44mv

Also from the report:

In a survey of 395 North American and U.K. enterprise marketers, 62 percent said they expected their digital marketing budgets to increase in 2014; only 8 percent expected a decrease. (Twenty-nine percent expected the budgets to stay the same, and 1 percent didn't know.)

Indications are that marketers are staffing up. The survey group said their interactive marketing teams consisted, on average, of 18 staffers. As a whole, more than 40 percent of companies surveyed devoted more than 25 workers to interactive marketing, and 12 percent devoted 16 to 25.

Consumers are spending more time on interactive media, but marketers' spending doesn't always track this trend. Surveys of U.S. adults online found they spent 32 percent of their media time watching TV in 2014, down from 34 percent in 2009, while TV ad spending increased to 43 percent from 31 percent of budgets. Media time spent on the Internet rose to 52 percent in 2014 from 45 percent in 2009; ad spending also increased, from 12 percent to 24 percent.

Digital marketing is "more than an incremental step in marketing," says Christine Barton, a partner at Boston Consulting Group (BCG). "I think it is shifting the way marketing and media are consumed."

She adds, "It's also changing the way that consumers interact with the retailer experience, as well as [with] retailer brands and branded-manufacturer brands."

By its nature, digital marketing is "two-way reciprocal marketing," Barton says, as opposed to traditional "push marketing" from companies to consumers. Reciprocal marketing involves "a more holistic and systemic engagement or conversation, where the company is listening and responding as much as talking and pushing its point," she says.

Digital marketing also takes advantage of millennials' obsessive use of mobile devices, especially smart phones, Barton says. Millennials are "just the lead indicators for the Gen X and baby-boomer generations" when it comes to new digital behavior such as using mobile devices as shopping aids, she says.

Global digital ad spending to top $200 billion by 2018

As with any marketing effort, a major question is whether digital marketing improves business results. "If you believe the capital being allocated towards it is any indicator that it works, the answer is overwhelmingly yes," says Scott Galloway, a marketing professor at New York University's Stern School of Business and the founder of business intelligence company L2 and of RedEnvelope, an online luxury gift company (now under other ownership). Digital marketing is "growing faster than any other marketing channel out there, so it either works well or we're all really stupid, because we keep spending more and more money on it," Galloway says.

Gartner Inc., the Stamford, Conn., information technology research consultancy, found in a survey of companies with $500 million or more in annual revenue that their marketing expense budget was 10.2 percent of revenue in 2014, with half the companies planning to increase

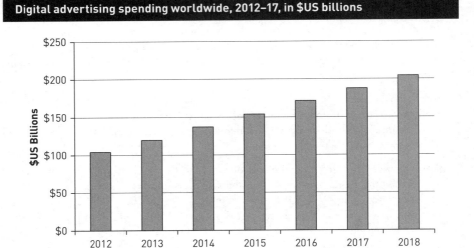

Market research analysts project worldwide spending on digital advertising will grow to more than $200 billion by 2018, nearly double the total spent in 2012. According to estimates, companies will spend $137.5 billion on digital advertising by the end of 2014.

Source: "Digital Ad Spending Worldwide to Hit $137.53 Billion in 2014," eMarketer, April 3, 2014, http://tinyurl.com/nwkn8qo

spending in 2015. Some 68 percent of these companies had a separate digital marketing budget, averaging a quarter of the total marketing budget, and this category showed a steady rise.[4]

"Progressive companies tend to place more priority and accountability on digital marketing," a Gartner analyst wrote.[5]

Yet marketers cannot count on digital taking over and other mediums disappearing, says the man credited with inventing the Web's banner ads. "A lot of people will predict banners will go away, or TVs will go away. They'll all be here. Nothing will replace something else," says Joe McCambley, co-founder and creative director of The Wonderfactory, which works in content marketing and app development, often for major publishing companies.

Of course, companies face pitfalls in back-and-forth online communication with customers. Even as companies are promoting a product, consumers may be slamming it via social media—think of online reviews and Twitter backlash. Just one blogger, Vani Hari, publicly shamed Subway into removing azodicarbonamide, a bleaching agent used in yoga mats, from its bread.[6]

Additionally, executives are not completely convinced that digital marketing works or that they know how to make a go of it. A 2014 Harris Interactive poll conducted for marketing agency Domus Inc. found that 64 percent of the advertising and marketing decision makers surveyed said their companies suffered from "digital dysfunction," meaning they were uncertain about how to integrate digital strategies into their marketing mix.[7]

The survey also found that 91 percent of respondents believed their companies needed better methods to measure results of digital marketing and social media. Eighty-two percent said their companies needed to achieve more with digital marketing, including increasing return on investment from social media.

One reason for confusion: Digital marketing requires a change in mind-set from mass media to niche and then to one-on-one connection and communication. "It's not about macro, it's about micro," says Nelson Freitas, marketing company Wunderman's chief strategy officer for New York. "It's the personal relationships you build with people."

Vani Hari, right, who blogs as the Food Babe, led an online campaign to shame Subway into removing a chemical from its bread. She has also criticized other companies for using ingredients she considers harmful.

Millennials have seemed particularly eager to embrace the brand "experience." They don't seem all that concerned—as their boomer parents might be—that they are being used to further the aims of marketers. In the 2014 PBS *Frontline* documentary, "Generation Like," for instance, young social media users were asked to define "selling out." The teens all looked puzzled, although one girl did hazard a guess: "I guess, I don't know, I think first about a concert that's, like, totally sold out, no tickets left," she said, innocently. [8]

Today's consumers use their smart phones, tablets, and game consoles to play, share and "like" the experiences brands offer them. Some examples:

Chipotle's "The Scarecrow": "The Scarecrow needs your help to foil the evil plans of Crow Foods," viewers are told. With animation from Moonbot Studios, the site offered an arcade-style adventure game (for the iPhone, iPod and iPad Touch) and a companion film (13.9 million YouTube views as of early 2015), aimed at promoting the fast-food company's use of organically farmed produce and meat from humanely treated animals. [9]

Nike's "Write the Future": The three-minute video ad tied to the 2010 soccer World Cup, which featured soccer superstars such as Didier Drogba, Fabio Cannavaro and Wayne Rooney, had garnered more than 5 million online views by early 2015. The ad, much copied for the 2014 World Cup, featured 236 visual effects made up of 106 soccer shots and a computer-generated stadium, plus in-jokes, like a nursery of babies all named Wayne (after Rooney), and appearances by celebrities Kobe Bryant and Homer Simpson, among others. During the soccer campaign period, Nike Football Facebook fan numbers quadrupled, from 1.1 million to 4.8 million fans; Nike became the most shared brand online in 2010. [10]

HBO's *Game of Thrones*: To promote the wildly popular series based on the fantasy novels of George R.R. Martin, HBO initiated several hashtag threads to build excitement in 2013 and 2014. #BeautifulDeath encouraged fans to create and post art inspired by the many noteworthy deaths of series characters; #RoastJoffrey called for insults about the evil boy king (resulting in 60,000 insults and 850 million impressions); #BringDowntheKing featured an online stunt in New Zealand whereby each click onto the Twitter account turned a "winch," which eventually felled a statue of King Joffrey.

"By giving people a channel to express their interest and enjoyment, HBO [has] created a devout fan base—in the same way clothing retailers often transform staff into brand ambassadors," Joe Marczynski of Label Media, a British Web design and marketing firm, wrote about the *Thrones* campaign. "The F.O.M.O. (fear of missing out) phenomenon comes also into play here, as people who have yet to watch the show are more likely to become more curious after seeing the bountiful social media buzz and the hundreds of thousands of comments, likes and shares of the many social media campaigns over the show's lifespan."[11]

"In the last five years, the industry has changed more than in the last 25. It's created chaos," Unilever Chief Marketing Officer Keith Weed said during the Cannes Lions Festival of Creativity. In recent years, said Miles Young, CEO of Ogilvy & Mather, the advertising festival feels more "like the Consumer Electronics Show" pitching digital technology, rather than a home for creative marketing types.[12]

The switch requires so much data, mobile optimizing and more that "many marketing organization aren't prepared to tackle," according to a Gartner report on "digital marketing technology integrators." With fast evolution and fragmented solutions and tools, marketers are looking for partners and new staff to bridge their limited knowledge or skills.[13]

As companies, marketers and industry observers wrestle with the best ways to take advantage of technology, below are some of the questions they are discussing.

WEIGHING THE ISSUES

Is digital marketing effective?

Companies have jumped into digital marketing, even as debate continues on how to choose effective techniques and to measure results.

Almost all of a sample of 160 top-level marketing executives at large firms reported that their companies are active on at least one major social network, according to a 2014 survey conducted on behalf of Spredfast, an Austin, Texas, social media marketing software and service firm. Among those same executives, 78 percent said they find it "challenging" to determine the return on investment (ROI) of social marketing techniques, and a similar percentage said they are "continually evolving" the way they measure business value created by social marketing.[14]

Yet many studies measure the returns on digital ads and show they are an effective part of the marketing mix. In a posting on a Rutgers University business school blog, Robert Petersen, a marketing executive who teaches an MBA course in digital marketing there, listed 11 studies showing the ROI of digital advertising. One of the studies, using information from Procter & Gamble, Kellogg, Nestle and others, found marketing-mix models underestimate the ROI of Facebook ads by as much as 48 percent and Google ads by as much as 39 percent.[15]

"I'm always baffled when I hear people say, 'It's really hard to prove the ROI,'" Stephen Quinn, Walmart's chief marketing officer, told industry publication *Adweek*. "We have ROI that's really strong. And, it's transforming our organization." Quinn's team claimed the giant retailer is getting a "marketing equivalent" 10X return-on-investment on Facebook and Twitter.[16]

He said, "This level of engagement we now have with customers is changing a whole bunch of other aspects of our marketing." Walmart has 31 million Facebook fans in the United States—more than any other brand—and 386,000 Twitter followers, according to *Adweek*, with a half-million pieces of user-generated content a month.[17]

Marketers expect quick returns on data investments

In addition to return on investment, marketers also measure the success of their campaigns by metrics such as the number of people who view a promotion and how long viewers spend engaging with it. Time and attention are increasingly the yardsticks used for digital campaigns, with various measures tracking the activity and engagement as well as time spent on the page.[18]

Measuring digital marketing is less about tracking a campaign and more about gauging how people react and use it, says Freitas at Wunderman. "Digital cares less about what you think— more about what are you doing with it, how are you incorporating it in your life?" he says.

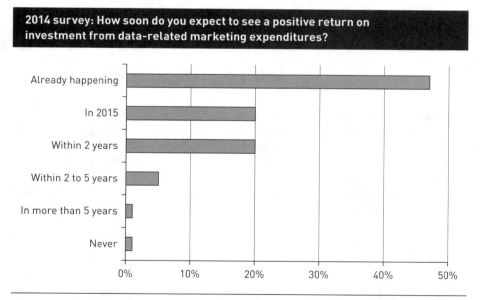

2014 survey: How soon do you expect to see a positive return on investment from data-related marketing expenditures?

Forty-seven percent of marketing companies that invested in big-data solutions had already received positive returns in 2014, according to a 2013 survey of about 600 marketers. Twenty percent of marketers expected positive returns in 2015, while another 20 percent expected returns by 2016.

Note: Numbers do not add to 100 due to rounding

Source: Digital Marketing Association Annual Conference 2014 Survey Results, Infogroup, January 2015.

Unlike a traditional advertisement that stands on its own, Freitas says digital goes through "the entire purchase journey: I saw it, acted on it, bought it and then made a comment on one of the social media sites."

As with other media, an industry has grown up to assist marketers in targeting and measuring their digital campaigns. For instance, Nielsen Digital Ad Ratings, a sister product of the well-known television ratings service, promises "transparent actionable audience measurement for digital advertising," via "the industry's only overnight measurements for campaigns, running across all digital screens."[19]

Microsoft Advertising collaborated with econometrics firm BrandScience to measure how digital advertising affected sales in the fast-moving consumer goods category, considering 455 campaigns in Western Europe over two years ending in May 2012. It found that digital campaigns were the second most effective at driving sales for items such as soft drinks and health and beauty items, after ads in movie theaters.[20] (Microsoft owns several brands, including MSN.com and search engine Bing that rely on digital advertising to stay in business.)

"Digital marketing is probably more measurable than traditional advertising," says Damian Ryan, who has written a half-dozen books about social marketing and is a partner in the London-based corporate financial boutique Mediaventura. (See "Q&A: Marketer Damian Ryan.") He says he has surveyed 1,700 digital marketing agencies worldwide about their campaigns and has compiled 700 case studies for a by-subscription database called the Global Academy of Digital Marketing.

In his 2014 book, *The Best Digital Marketing Campaigns in the World II*, Ryan outlined some of the promotions he considers effective and the results they achieved. Among them:

JetBlue's "Get Away with It": Online game show platform. **Market:** United States. **Aim:** Build awareness of the airline's JetBlue Getaways. **Budget:** Less than $300,000. **Strategy:** A game show with a real set was created in New York, with "contestants" Skyping in to participate. (Sample question: In what state are the Green Mountains located?) With a holiday vacation package as the reward, 13,000 people applied; custom apps managed and vetted the applications. Emails, "add to calendar" and promotional TV ads reminded participants of when to tune in. That day, the website synched to the live set, becoming one of the first to use live-streaming technology. **Results:** More than 42 million impressions followed, with more than 10 minutes each of average viewing time. The campaign won the airline the highest search volume seen for the term "JetBlue Getaways"; brand awareness spiked 117 percent.[21]

Harley-Davidson Open Road Festival: Film festival. **Market:** Australia. **Aim:** The motorcycle brand wanted to increase sales for its touring motorcycles and boost audience engagement. **Budget:** Less than $300,000. **Strategy:** The agency, 303Lowe, created an end sequence to a short film fantasy where a man wakes up with a Harley. Filmmakers were invited to view the film and create its beginning. The agency then hosted a live (and online) Open Road Film Festival event with the top eight films at Sydney's Bondi Beach. Winning filmmakers could score a motorcycle or cameras. Viewers could then join a waiting list for 24-hour test rides. **Results:** The site recorded more than 59,300 visits totaling 33,072 minutes. Ten thousand people watched the films; Harley sales in Australia rose 43 percent during the campaign.[22]

Fox Network's *Walking Dead* Kill Count: App. **Market:** United Kingdom. **Aim:** When Fox decided to export its hugely successful zombie television series to Great Britain, it needed to ensure that British fans would come back to the series despite a two-month break in the 12-episode season. **Budget:** About $83,500. **Strategy:** The agency created extra content to maximize engagement without compromising the plot; it created on-air teasers, website and social media content, and an app encouraging social chat before and after the show. Best received was the app, a game in which viewers competed to predict the number of zombie kills before the show. **Results:** More than 62,000 people downloaded the app in its first week. More than 300,000 game sessions took place. The game was named one of the 50 most innovative mobile apps by the British government group UK Trade & Investment.[23]

Of course there are epic fails in digital marketing, too. The Twitter hashtag #WhyIStayed was meant to collect stories about why women stayed with the men who abused them. But in September 2014, a DiGiorno pizza staffer, in a clueless attempt at humor, tweeted "#WhyIStayed You had pizza." The viral backlash was swift and merciless.[24]

In the United Kingdom in 2013, Kellogg got slammed for encouraging viewers to retweet "1RT=1 breakfast for a vulnerable child": "Please retweet to raise awareness about child hunger in the UK and Ireland," the first tweet urged viewers. Two little boys, presumably from low-income backgrounds, were pictured enjoying bowls of Fruit Loops. But viewers weren't impressed by the cereal maker's philanthropic effort. Typical was this response from @BotanyGeek: "Anyone else find this kinda creepy? Like sayin 'Help us advertise or kids go hungry.'" Kellogg promptly took down the tweet and apologized.[25]

Worst, Ryan says, are ads inadvertently linked to questionable content. In October 2013, Nissan, Sherwin-Williams, Wolverine shoes and vehicle manufacturer Polaris saw their pre-roll video ads—the 10- or 15-second commercials that appear before online videos—pop up on the tasteless website ForbezDVD. The website had posted a gruesome video seeming to show a woman in Mexico being decapitated, supposedly for unfaithfulness. Website Digiday, which covers news about digital media and marketing, only made things worse with an article headlined, "This beheading video is brought to you by Nissan."[26]

Ryan says technologies such as ADsafe and AdVerify, which track ads and where they appear, increasingly are preventing such terrible pairings of ads with tasteless or embarrassing content.

Should digital marketing targeting children and teens be more closely regulated?

For decades, companies have produced advertisements designed to reach children where they live. Considering that where they live these days is online and on their phones, flashy digital marketing tools have stepped up the appeal of sales pitches.

Take McDonald's Happymeal.com, with its array of videos, toys, games, bright colors and cartoon characters. Some pages are tied to upcoming children's movies or books; all of the pages sell, subtly or not, McDonald's food. What worries critics is that such enhanced marketing sites are attractive to kids who might not absorb so much advertising if they didn't click and download their way through their day.

Teens, meanwhile, are likely to be spending time on YouTube, Instagram and other platforms, watching young people demonstrate cosmetics while recommending specific products (supplied to them free by the manufacturers) or showing off skateboarding moves while pushing athletic gear.

Lawmakers and marketers have attempted regulation and self-regulation:

The Children's Online Privacy Protection Act (COPPA), effective in 2000, requires website operators to obtain parental consent for collection of personal information from children under 13.[27]

Blogger disclosure rules adopted in 2009 by the Federal Trade Commission (FTC) and updated in 2013 require bloggers, tweeters and other media creators who are compensated for endorsing brands to prominently disclose that fact, viewable on any device.[28]

The Children's Advertising Review Unit (CARU), a unit of the advertising industry's Advertising Self-Regulation Council created in 1974, reviews national advertising primarily directed to children under 12, for any medium. The reviews cover online data collection and other privacy-related practices.[29]

These moves, while well intentioned, are not very effective, argues Robert Weissman, president of the advocacy group Public Citizen, whose project Commercial Alert concentrates on children's advertising. "Confusion is the norm and the intent and purpose," Weissman says. Subtle brand promotion "is pervasive all over the Internet, especially in content targeting teens and children," he says, "and the direction is such as to get kids into a place where it's not just that they don't notice, but there's no conceptually meaningful difference" between neutral text and advertising.

"The games, the sharing, the 'liking,' the giveaways, that's all effectively hidden advertisements," Weissman says. "So [kids are] being exploited into being unwitting marketers for companies and purveyors of their marketing messages."

He finds "deeply troubling" what he describes as a societal shift toward "aggressive marketing to children and to invading kids' spaces that once were commercial free." That shift, Weissman says, began as far back as 1989, when Channel One, a television network, began providing schools with free youth-oriented newscasts that included ads. Today, commercialization is "the norm," he says, "especially because kids live so much of their real lives in virtual spaces."

Several companies have been found to violate COPPA and fined for collecting information from children without parental permission. Disney-owned Playdom operated virtual worlds, including Pony Stars and My Diva Doll. The FTC charged that the sites collected children's ages, email and locations, and also permitted children to publicly post personal information online.[30] The company in 2011 agreed to pay $3 million to settle, then a record amount.[31]

COPPA is a start, Weissman says, but he argues that its protections should be strengthened and expanded—especially to older children.

"Even highly wired adults don't know what's going on because they don't live in the children's world," Weissman says. "There's not a lot of adults who spend time in children's media, so a lot of this goes on under the radar."

Not everyone sees a problem. Mark Schaefer, an author, consultant and lecturer who advises companies on social media marketing, says the only effective influencer online is someone—a kid or a celebrity beloved by kids—"who really loves" a product. "It's not easy to nurture those people," Schaefer says, "but those are the real 'citizen influencers,'"—a term he takes credit for coining—"that you want to find because people believe them. People trust them." As for the teen girl with a home video camera promoting a line of teen-targeted makeup on YouTube in return for free products, or a skateboarder promoting athletic wear, those kids have little credibility among their peers, Schaefer maintains.

And even when they do, "what's the problem?" he asks. "You characterize these kids as hucksters. But who cares? If they want to be hucksters, if their parents say, 'Let's take the money; it's going to pay for your college education,' and they have their 15 minutes of fame, I'm not sure I know what the problem is. They're not being abused in any way."

In addition, Schaefer points to the FTC disclosure rule: "If these children are being paid to eat Snickers bars, then somewhere prominently in the context of that content, they have to say, 'I'm being paid to do this by the company,' and if they're not, they're breaking the law."

Danah Boyd goes even further to defend digital marketing to teenagers. Young people simply don't need all the protection adults want to provide them, Boyd, a Microsoft researcher and a fellow at Harvard's Berkman Center for Internet & Society, wrote in her book *It's Complicated: The Social Lives of Networked Teens*.[32] She argued that digital spaces should be seen as a kind of 21st-century update of the malt shop, where kids can meet other kids free of parental surveillance.

In an email interview, Boyd says, "Today's teens are growing up in a media-saturated world, in an advertising-saturated world. The key is to help them learn how to navigate what's in front of them rather than simply shielding them from it. We can have a different conversation about children, but with regard to teens, the worst thing that parents can do is send their kids off to college with no capacity to navigate American life, including the commercial world that we constructed."

She adds, "Are these [digital] spaces commercial? Absolutely. But they are also the only space that [kids] have. If adults don't like young people's deep engagement with commercial reality, we need to start allowing them to participate in public life. . . . But, given our culture of fear, their physical freedom has been massively eroded over the last 30 years. And thus, a collective action dilemma is born."

Will consumers resist digital marketing because of privacy concerns?

American consumers are only starting to understand that practically every click they make on a product website, every confidence they share with friends on Facebook, every tweet they send out about their latest activity, feeds information to marketers.

Facebook's "Check In" feature uses GPS to pin users' locations. The amount of geolocation data collected from features like this can be perceived by some as an invasion of privacy.

By feeding these tidbits of information into massive datasets, marketers compile information on what you look at, how you live and what you buy. Are you gay, straight? Italian? Muslim? Jewish? Do you suffer from cancer or diabetes? Or are you just really, really into Billy Joel? Marketers can use this information to target products and services just for you.

Some of that targeting may be desirable—people sell you items you actually want. But it also can be unwelcome—for instance, some say that geo-location data, collected via GPS, can unacceptably invade privacy.

"Geolocation information can divulge intimately personal details about an individual," Jessica Rich, director of the FTC's Bureau of Consumer Protection, testified at a June 2014 Senate subcommittee hearing on the proposed Location Privacy Protection Act (LPPA). "Did you visit an AIDS clinic last Tuesday? What place of worship do you attend? Were you at a psychiatrist's office last week? Did you meet with a prospective business customer?"[33]

The FTC, she pointed out, charged that Snapchat, maker of a mobile messaging app, deceived consumers by promising that photo and video messages sent through the service would disappear. Such assurances misrepresented the amount of personal data Snapchat collected as well as the security measures it took to protect that data, according to the FTC. Among other issues, "Snapchat transmitted geolocation information from users of its Android app, even though its privacy policy claimed that it did not track users or access such information," Rich said. A month before the hearing, Snapchat agreed to settle the charges and to establish a privacy program that will be monitored for 20 years.[34]

Sen. Al Franken, D-Minn., a sponsor of the LPPA legislation, railed at the hearing against "stalking apps" that help spouses, for instance, trail partners who they think are cheating. He also decried companies that collect user information and send it to third parties, called data brokers.[35]

"Some of the most popular apps in the country have been found disclosing their users' precise location to third parties without their permission. And it's not just apps," Franken said. "The Nissan Leaf's on-board computer was found sending drivers' locations to third party websites. OnStar threatened to track its users even after they cancelled their service; they only stopped when I and other senators called them out on this."[36] (Nissan said in 2011 that it had taken steps to halt unauthorized use of such data.[37] And while OnStar acknowledged making plans to collect data without consumer consent, it dropped those plans.[38])

LPPA would require companies to get permission before collecting and sharing location data off smart phones, tablets and in-car navigation devices. The bill also aims to stymie GPS stalking by preventing companies from secretly collecting location data. The legislation has been introduced in Congress twice as of early 2015, and has failed to pass both times.[39]

The industry prefers self-regulation rather than a new law. "Self-regulation is the appropriate approach for addressing the interplay of privacy and online and mobile advertising practices," Luigi Mastria, executive director of the Digital Advertising Alliance (DAA), a New York group that represents online marketers, testified at the hearing. "Laws and regulations can also serve as a disincentive to the marketplace to innovate in the area of privacy."[40]

LPPA is hardly the first effort to answer consumer fears surrounding mobile technology and privacy. Under COPPA, the 1998 law that deals with protecting children's privacy online, the FTC in September 2014 fined Yelp $450,000 for improperly collecting information on children via its mobile app.[41]

In Europe, the European Union has issued directives covering confidentiality of information, treatment of traffic data, spam and requirements for the use of cookies on websites.[42] However, there has been little enforcement, Mediaventura's Ryan says.

Aside from extreme abuses such as criminal stalking, consumers don't seem to care much about collection of their data, though. A 2014 Pew survey, for instance, found that even though consumers think companies have too much of their data, they are still willing to volunteer information.[43]

Schaefer, the social media consultant, explains this seeming inconsistency. "Whenever we go to Amazon and get interesting new products suggested to us, based on the vast amount of information Amazon is collecting on us, we like it," he says. "So, is that an invasion of privacy? You can't have it both ways."

Consumers are willing to give personal information if they receive something worthwhile in return, Freitas says. Privacy is important, however, and advertisers "are going to have to seduce people in different ways to share their information," he says.

Within 10 years, individuals will sell or lease their personal data and preferences to brands and companies, he predicts. But they'll do so selectively and only in exchange for something richer and relevant.

Pam Dixon, executive director of the World Privacy Forum, a San Diego–based nonprofit research group, says people are uncomfortable with some types of information collection and sale, such as data brokerage. "You could end up on a data broker list that you have diabetes," says Dixon. "Same thing with cancer. And then a marketer sends something [to you, the consumer] based on health data about you, maybe 'be part of a clinical trial,' or 'here's a book about cancer or diabetes.'"

She says, "People don't like it. They get creeped out, and it's a big issue. . . . Not everyone wants certain moments of their life to become a marketing opportunity."

Dixon has even heard of lists generating outreach to women who have suffered miscarriages. "The death of a child is another marketing opportunity," she says.

At least some companies experience a backlash for such activities, Dixon notes. "Companies are definitely starting to suffer brand reputational loss when they send out advertising that offends people," she says. "I know this because we get the phone calls."

BACKGROUND

ARPANET to dot-com

The Internet has its roots in a 1958 project of the U.S. Department of Defense's Advanced Research Projects Agency (ARPA, later known as DARPA). In 1965, researchers at the Massachusetts Institute of Technology hooked up their computer with one belonging to the Air Force in California; the subsequent ARPANET project in 1966 led to the first network to use packet switching, one of the data-transmission technologies underlying the Internet.[44]

A rudimentary form of email—what would later be called the Internet's "killer application"—was born in 1971. In 1989, Tim Berners-Lee, a British scientist working for the European physics research organization CERN, proposed a system of hypertext links to cross-reference and make documents available across the new Internet—what became the World Wide Web.[45] The Domain Name System had already debuted, in 1983, introducing .edu, .gov, .com, .mil, .org, .net and .int. These designations were easier to remember than the previous designation for websites: 123.456.789.10.[46]

In the 1990s, the development of the Web as a means of commerce made Silicon Valley a mecca for Internet entrepreneurs. Between 1991 and 1997, the number of websites grew 850 percent each year.[47] Dot-com stocks soared.

In March 2000, the dot-com bubble burst, sending stock prices and company values tumbling. But the Internet itself became increasingly important. By 2005, 1 billion people had Internet access. By the end of 2014, there were almost 3 billion Internet users worldwide, or 44 percent of the globe's households, two-thirds of them in the developing world, according to estimates from the International Telecommunications Union (ITU), a United Nations agency. Most people use their phones to reach the Internet, especially in poorer countries: The ITU estimated there were 2.3 billion mobile-broadband subscriptions globally in 2014, with 55 percent in the developing world.[48]

Three "revolutions"

Schaefer, the digital marketing consultant, refers to what he calls "the three revolutions of digital marketing": the founding of the Web, the growth of search engines and the rise of social media.

He dates the first stage to 1990–2000. As use of the Internet spread from campuses to homes, he says, marketers told themselves, "We need to get on the Web." At first, it was hard for the public to find them. The next revolution, discovery, unfolded from 2000–2010. Once search engines, especially Google, made it easier for users to find information, marketers tried to figure out how to profit from that. "If at the end of the second cycle you figured out search and got to the top of the search results, you had the advantage," Schaefer says.

It feels as if search has been with us forever, Ryan and Jones pointed out in their book, *Understanding Digital Marketing*.[49] But Google was founded only in 1998. Other search engines including Yahoo, Alta Vista, Ask and Bing all have roles, but Google dominates in the United States and many other countries.

For marketers, the importance of search means that techniques for rising to the top of results, known as search engine optimization (SEO), figure heavily in campaigns. So can paid search marketing and pay-per-click advertising, where advertisers pay for connections to keywords and for position on search pages.

What Schaefer calls the "third revolution," the rise of social media, with its emphasis on utility and mobility, is ongoing, he says. Marketers now aim to "help people where they are, in real time, using content," he says.

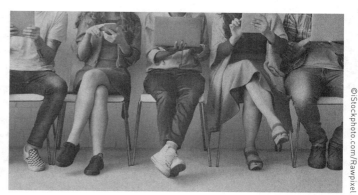

With the rise of social media, companies have increasingly begun to use online profiles to spread the word about their brands.

Today, marketers use Twitter, Facebook, email, Instagram and their own blogs to raise their profile, nurture brand loyalty and build customer databases. Nothing is sweeter to a marketer than to see a "social evangelist" spread the word through unsolicited Facebook postings or website reviews about a great product she tried.

"Once upon a time, consumers were quite happy to sit in front of passive broadcast media," Ryan and Jones wrote, but a more-interactive Web changed that, and broadband and rich media content allowed consumers control over what they wanted to see and when, as well as how to share it.[50]

"Digital natives"—young people who grew up using the Internet—have also changed marketing. Many treat their smart phones like extended limbs. "They are the mass market of tomorrow—and it's absolutely imperative that we, as marketers, learn to speak their language today," Ryan and Jones wrote.[51]

Banner ads

The fast-changing digital landscape raises the question of when individual advertising strategies lose their power. Consider the earliest digital marketing strategy, banner ads. Ad man McCambley is credited with helping create the first banner ad in 1994 for AT&T, to promote a tour of art museums. But in a February 2013 blog posting at the *Harvard Business Review*, McCambley argued that banners should have been scrapped after 1998. "We were back to delivering what TV spots, radio spots, and print ads had delivered for years: sales messages," he wrote. "The rest, as they say, is history."[52]

B2B marketers favor social media, videos

In an interview, McCambley estimates that more than 50 percent of mobile users click on banner ads by accident, which may trigger resentment or frustration, especially if their Internet connection is slow. Instead, he thinks advertisers should move to what's known as "native advertising," which places quality sponsored content within the headlines and articles produced by journalists at digital publishers and mainstream ones.

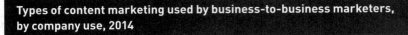

Types of content marketing used by business-to-business marketers, by company use, 2014

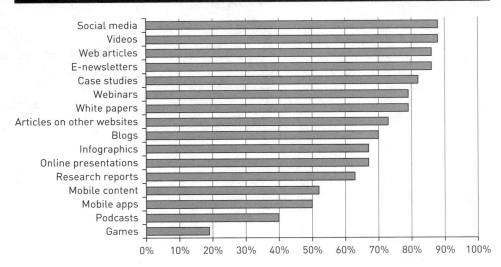

Nearly nine in 10 business-to-business (B2B) enterprise marketing companies use social media and videos to market content. Other popular tactics include posting Web articles, e-newsletters (both 86 percent) and case studies (82 percent); hosting webinars; and sending white papers (both 79 percent).

Note: Marketers surveyed served companies with more than 1,000 employees. Selected list of marketing tactics; see http://tinyurl.com/qaqkcza for full list.

Source: "B2B Enterprise Content Marketing: 2014 Benchmarks, Budgets, and Trends—North America," Marketo, 2014, p. 9, http://contentmarketinginstitute.com/wp-content/uploads/2013/10/B2B_Research_2014_CMI.pdf

Todd Wasserman, a columnist for Mashable, took exception to McCambley's *Harvard Business Review* piece. "Clearly, while McCambley thinks banners are a creative wasteland, there are lots of people still lining up to buy them," Wasserman wrote. He quoted figures from Nielsen estimating that the display business had grown 26.3 percent during the first quarter of 2013 and that eMarketer was predicting that display revenue would eclipse search advertising revenue in the United States in 2015.[53]

Web advertising—in banner or other formats—has been a boon to companies that want to take their message viral, with word of mouth, digitally amplified. Dove's 2013 "Real Beauty Sketches" video, where an FBI-trained sketch artist demonstrates to women that others see them as more beautiful than they see themselves, was dubbed the "most viral video ad of all time" (up to that time) by Business Insider because it attracted 114 million views its first month.[54]

Yet Google's own 2014 study indicates that 56 percent of all advertising impressions are not seen—and that vertical ads on the top half of Web pages are viewed more and longer.[55]

CURRENT SITUATION

Big data

Barton, the Boston Consulting Group partner, says that companies urgently need digital strategies in an era when print publications are rapidly becoming obsolete and electronic devices are in everyone's hands. "I do think the immediate opportunity in a lot of sectors is still about the land grab in terms of the ability to get their digital campaigns or their geolocation/ brand communications or promotions out to recipients first," Barton says. "So, right now the challenge in the U.S. or even globally is still about being first and getting distribution."

But increasingly, she says, "big data" is becoming important. Big data is defined as the compilation of massive and complex datasets, often containing a myriad of details about users of digital platforms. As businesses invest more in reaching consumers online as well as via mobile devices, their messages will be like other marketing messages, Barton says. "And then the game will be about relevance."

And relevance is where big data comes in. "Big data allows you, at least for a segment of people, and eventually for the individual, very relevant brand communications, very relevant promotions, very relevant pictures of the product, to try to get more impulse engagement by individuals with the product and the brand, depending on where they are," Barton says.

Small wonder, then, that *Harvard Business Review* dubbed "data scientist" the "sexiest job of the 21st century."[56]

Thomas H. Davenport, a distinguished professor at Babson College and senior adviser to Deloitte Analytics, wrote in a *Wall Street Journal* blog in May 2014 that among the lessons he has learned about big-data marketing were: (1) Marketing and big data are synonymous; (2) Marketing-spending optimization analyses are now happening every quarter or even every month, instead of every year, as in the past; and (3) Marketing analytics people are growing in influence. "It's obvious that these quantitative marketers no longer work unnoticed in the back office," Davenport wrote.[57]

Net neutrality

Net neutrality is the concept that all traffic and all information shared online get "a level playing field for Internet transport."[58] In this construct, nothing ought to get priority in speed or delivery, and nothing is discriminated against by service providers. Content providers tend to back net neutrality; Internet service providers (ISP) tend to say they should have the right to control their own networks.

In Washington, regulators and legislators are debating how net neutrality will evolve in practice. Neutrality has generally been the rule in the United States, but in early 2014, a federal court struck down the neutrality regulations then in effect.[59] Since then, the Federal Communications Commission (FCC) has been discussing how to rewrite the rules that cover how broadband providers such as Comcast or Verizon can treat content providers; the commission was scheduled to vote in late February. Republicans and Democrats on Capitol Hill are proposing their own versions, with varying degrees of regulation of the players.[60]

For marketers, how the neutrality debate works out could affect how quickly viewers see their content and whether access to the best spots for digital advertising is limited.[61]

According to Web marketing blogger Dan Shewan, without open access to the Internet for all, marketers will suffer. Say you're a business launching a marketing campaign with carefully thought out target words, he wrote. But when prospective customers click on your ads, they see their ISP "throttles bandwidth to your landing pages" because you did not buy the ISP's "preferential service agreement." He predicted, "Your landing pages take forever to load, and your conversion rates plummet."[62]

Content shock

Marketing expert Schaefer uses the term "content shock" to describe the glut of material on the Web competing for attention. Users have a finite amount of time to consume that ever-growing amount of material.

"The average user on Facebook can see 1,500 stories a day," he says. That's too much. "As companies put more and more content on the Web, that problem just gets worse. The amount of content is exploding, so I can see in some categories that the organic reach is zero"— meaning that marketers won't be able to post additional content because viewers will have reached full-consumption capability.

Schaefer says, "You've got to somehow spend more money on your content so somehow it gets through that algorithm," he says. It must be "so scintillating, . . . so remarkable, that people respond to it."

Chipotle, for example, has spent heavily on its animated "Scarecrow" marketing video, Schaefer says. There's little food in sight; instead, the video is a story designed to engage the audience due to its creativity (Wow! Cool video!) and its political sensitivities (the company's rejection of competitors' inhumane animal practices). Yet what people might want for dinner doesn't seem to matter, Schaefer points out. "That's an example where they bet the ranch on content," he says of the ad. "But let's be honest: They're spending millions on content to sell burritos."

A sponsored post or native ad can be another option for breaking through. These posts may look and feel journalistic, as demonstrated by a paid post on women in prison on *The New York Times* website that promoted the Netflix series *Orange Is the New Black*. Such attention-grabbing campaigns are not cheap, but they may be very effective, especially if the campaign matches both the advertiser's goals and the media company's brand, according to digital media consultant Dorian Benkoil.[63]

LOOKING AHEAD

Personal and mobile

Freitas at Wunderman in New York says a huge shift is under way, heading from mass media and marketing to more targeted, personal approaches. This requires marketers and advertisers to use big data and collected fragments of knowledge on a consumer and create messages that are relevant and engaging.

Marketing must be "relevant to us at that moment in time" and will become more benefit based, Freitas says.

The era of personalized pitches and products is coming, according to the Landor Trends Report, citing Coca-Cola's Share a Coke campaign, which featured bottles printed with 250 popular names. In Israel, Coke went further: It featured 2 million labels individually designed by consumers.[64]

Companies increasingly connect to consumers and customers with apps rather than Facebook or other social media, and brands will evaluate the app based not simply on frequency of use but on the utility and loyalty it creates with uses, wrote marketer Michael Della Penna.[65]

Gartner, the information technology research company, predicts that mobile advertising spending will grow from $13.1 billion in 2013 to $41.9 billion in 2017. The only thing holding mobile advertising back is tight ad space inventory, according to Gartner research director Stephanie Baghdassarian.[66]

Jeff Jones, chief marketing officer for department store chain Target, said shoppers increasingly will use mobile devices while shopping. "Mobile represents two-thirds of our digital traffic and will be 75 percent at the end of the year," he told a marketing conference in 2014.[67] So Target is focusing attention on mobile ads and on newer technologies that allow customers to click and buy on Instagram or to use an app to find the merchandise they want while in the store.

Marketers must strive to make their offerings useful, according to McCambley, the marketer who worked on the original banner ad. "To remain relevant to consumers who spend hours each day focused on smaller screens trying to get stuff done, marketers will have to think like publishers and technology companies," he wrote.[68]

In an interview, McCambley points to one very useful app, the Nike+: When used during a run, it creates a "beautiful map of the run, distance, pace, weather" and, over time, shares data on the individual's progress or lack of it. The app and related spinoffs had more than 18 million users in 2013 and were part of Nike's push into digital connections and gamifying fitness.[69]

"What's more popular to you than your [own] story?" McCambley asks. Nike teams up with *Runner's World* magazine and users give the two companies permission to share their information, so the magazine delivers more tailored and useful content. "That combination makes me more loyal to Nike and more loyal to *Runner's World*," McCambley says.

Marketers increasingly will use biometric data and insights to gauge emotional and physical reactions. "Imagine a world where entertainment choices are built around your emotional preference, where you would know before going into a movie or watching a TV show if it fit the pattern for your emotional preference," wrote Cavan Canavan, co-founder of a motion tracking tech firm, in TechCrunch.[70]

Brands from Domino's Pizza to Best Buy and MasterCard are using "new forms of interaction through voice, facial expression, body movement, temperature, eye movements and gestures," including voice-activated apps and mobile customer support.[71]

Before long, digital promotions may become trips into augmented reality—technologies that let a smartphone or tablet recognize real objects, then activate related video or graphics. Tech start-ups like Blippar, Layar and Daqri are testing new marketing features enabled by consumer mobile devices.[72]

With the Blippar app, for instance, a consumer can point a mobile device at a can of Pepsi and unlock interactive content from the National Football League—from recipes to Super Bowl ticket sweepstakes.

Then there is the growing trend of immersion, a term describing how social media sites are becoming more and more about users creating content themselves. Schaefer, the digital marketing expert, predicts that by 2020, the amount of data online will have grown by 600 percent and that 75 percent of it will be consumer-created. Immersion together with wearable technology will bring on the next digital revolution, he said, when "the Internet will surround us like the air that we breathe."[73]

Not everyone agrees, of course. Galloway, the NYU professor and founder of L2, says some developments such as wearables and 3D printing have been "overhyped."

Long form and backlash

Marketers that rely on tweets or six-second Vine messages may want to consider the return of the long-form story on a raft of websites and in podcasts. "Long form is involved, compelling and emotional, interesting" and is starting to show up in video, text and serial podcasts, McCambley says. He points to the success of the podcast Startup, in which the co-owner of a fledgling business shares his night terrors and his thoughts on how to bring in a partner. "His podcast became a native ad for his company" McCambley says, and within three episodes, that honest, unvarnished storytelling and "creative ways to engage" the audience drew in $1.5 million in venture funding.[74]

While digital marketing has become an almost unavoidable aspect of modern life, not all embrace it. Consider Ello, a new social platform that aims to compete with Facebook but with a big, big difference: Ello will have no ads. "We're growing very, very fast," CEO Paul Budnitz told CNBC.[75]

Currently in public beta format—meaning it's invitation-only—Ello says it will be forever ad-free and will never sell users' information to third parties. "Collecting and selling your personal data, reading your posts to your friends, and mapping your social connections for profit is both creepy and unethical," Ello proclaims, adding, "Under the guise of offering a 'free' service, users pay a high price in intrusive advertising and lack of privacy."[76]

Chronology

1950s–1960s	**The Internet begins.**
1958	In response to the Soviet Union's launch of Sputnik in 1957, the U.S. Department of Defense establishes the Advanced Research Projects Agency, or ARPA, later known as DARPA. Its mission: research and development that will expand technology beyond military needs.
1962–64	MIT researchers, including DARPA's first computer research head, J.C.R. Licklider, exchange memos about the notion of interconnected computers offering access to data and programs. They decide to use packet switching rather than circuits.

1965–66	MIT researchers get computers to "talk" to one another by connecting a TX-2 computer in Massachusetts to a Q-32 computer in California using a low-speed dial-up telephone line and the first computer network ever created. . . . MIT researcher Lawrence G. Roberts brings DARPA his plan for the packet-switching network known as ARPANET (Advanced Research Projects Agency Network).
1969	Four host computers are linked to form ARPANET, and the Internet is up and running.
1970s–1980s	**Email and the World Wide Web debut.**
1972	In response to ARPANET's need for a coordinating mechanism, researcher Ray Tomlinson writes the basic email message send-and-read software. An email utility program is then created to list, selectively read, file, forward and respond to messages.
1989	With scientists struggling to exchange data over the Internet, software engineer Tim Berners-Lee invents the World Wide Web. His proposals to make the Internet widely accessible include the technology for HTML, or hypertext markup language; URI, or uniform resource identifier, for a unique way to describe every resource on the Web; and HTTP, or hypertext transfer protocol.
1990s	**The Web undergoes explosive growth; marketers take note.**
1993	Software engineer Marc Andreessen releases a graphically rich browser called Mosaic with new features, such as support of in-line images that can be embedded with text.
1994	Berners-Lee founds the World Wide Web Consortium as a means for those on the Web to set guidelines to ensure that the Web works for everyone and evolves in a responsible manner. . . . Microsoft's Internet Explorer debuts.
1995	Dot-coms spring up everywhere. In June, there were an estimated 23,500 websites; by January 1996, 100,000—half of them dot-com.
1998	Google debuts.
2000s–Present	**The social media revolution takes off.**
2000	The dot-com bubble bursts; technology stocks dive.
2001	Apple opens first Apple retail stores.
2002	Friendster, a site that allows members to stay in contact and share content and media with another, is founded.
2003	WordPress is released, offering free and open source blogging. . . . LinkedIn starts professional job networking; Skype, the video chat service, begins. The first commercial mobile SMS appears.
2004	Facebook moves beyond the ivy walls of Harvard and quickly grows, reaching 802 million people worldwide by 2014.

(Continued)

(Continued)

2005	YouTube debuts; the Internet's billionth user is tallied.
2006	"You" becomes *Time* magazine's Person of the Year, celebrating user-generated content. . . . Twitter is started.
2007	Apple's iPhone debuts, bringing big things for mobile.
2008	Barack Obama, whose campaign makes innovative use of digital marketing, is elected president.
2010	Facebook hits 500 million active users; LinkedIn, 60 million; and Twitter, 15 million.
2013	Use of mobile apps and "couch commerce" explode, as does tablet shopping.
2014	Globally, almost 3 billion people have Internet access, two-thirds of them in the developing world.

Q&A: Marketer Damian Ryan

"IT'S EFFECTIVE IF YOU KNOW WHAT YOU'RE DOING"
Damian Ryan
Managing partner
Mediaventura

Damian Ryan, London-based author or co-author of six books about digital marketing, has compiled a database profiling about 700 successful campaigns and their results. The database is scheduled to be available this year on a subscription basis. Ryan, managing partner of corporate financing boutique Mediaventura, talked about this project and more with SAGE Business Researcher reporter Joan Oleck. This is an edited transcript of the conversation.

You've written several books about digital marketing and compiled this enviable database. What have you learned?

Two insights I've had over seven years of writing these books are, digital marketers are unlike their traditional counterparts. They are more global in nature; they think globally. They're more interested in what's happening in the markets around the world, be they Australia, Argentina, America, the U.K., whatever, because digital gives you the tools to be able to sell products and services globally.

Second, digital marketers require affordable access to case studies online, and they're struggling to get that. Each case study describes the challenge, the steps, the marketer went through; it displays how well they understood their audience, the tools deployed, whether search or affiliate or email or mobile or whatever. It outlines the results and, where possible, talks about budgets.

Here's the thing: We are, I believe, going through a transformation in the role of the marketer. Up till now, marketers have guarded their information quite jealously, and in my opinion it's a completely ineffective thing to do in terms of digital marketing. You have this dichotomy because marketers desire to be in the same arena as professional services. I think marketers are looking at other professions that have been out there for hundreds of years—architecture, engineering, medicine and science, and these guys haven't gotten to where they are today by being secretive. What we're finding is that more and more marketers, especially younger marketers, are more collaborative; they're thinking it's no big deal.

Is digital marketing effective?

It's a very subjective question; it's largely about whether the objectives you set for the digital marketing in the beginning have been met. So, you can have a task of digital marketing, but perhaps it doesn't meet its targets in terms of profitability, ROI [return on investment], customer engagement. That old adage about advertising, "I know that 50 percent of the money I've spent is wasted, but I don't know which half," applies. Digital marketing is probably more measurable than traditional advertising. But is it effective? It's effective if you know what you're doing. I've seen some brilliantly effective digital marketing without any budget—just pure common sense and understanding of the audience.

Is it ever ineffective?

I think if somebody doesn't want to repeat digital marketing exercises, [that's because] their audience isn't online, and I can't think of any brand in the world whose audience isn't online. Fifteen, 20 years ago, it would have been different.

Does anyone have "then" versus "now" data, pre- and post-digital marketing?

That stuff is hard to get because either they don't have comparable data to work from [or they're not sharing it]. But talking to people over the last couple of years—they've shared one piece of evidence with me, and that is that the percentage of money they've spent on digital has increased. That says to me that it's working.

Any trends you foresee for digital marketing in the near future?

The big question that is surfacing more and more is whether the Internet itself is just broken. Are we heading towards a new kind of Internet which is not going to tolerate privacy violations and tolerate hijacking and botnets

(Continued)

(Continued)

[an artificial way of inflating the effectiveness of an ad campaign by using robots instead of humans to click on advertisements]? If I was a brand, Mercedes or Coca-Cola, I would have serious thoughts about "Do I want to be associated with the medium?" I'm convinced that not tomorrow but at some stage we could look at an Internet I call the Good Internet—that's basically free from that kind of abuse.

The point is, if the advertising/marketing industry wants to clean up the Internet and [make it] part of something freer of these problems and privacy violations and abuse, then it needs to start to do something about it.

I am nailing my colors to the mast on the idea of a Good Internet because [the current Internet] is not sustainable, it's become so corrupt. I'm interested in collaborating with people on the notion.

13

FAILURE
What can businesses learn when things go wrong?

Vickie Elmer

EXECUTIVE SUMMARY

Failure has long carried costs and stigma, both personal and professional. In some business sectors, though, notably the technology industry, failure has become acceptable, even fashionable. It's inevitable that people who try new things will not always succeed. Fear of failure stifles creativity and innovation, advocates say. Bankruptcy has become a business decision, rather than a cause for personal shame, and it can allow firms to become stronger and more nimble. Nonetheless, critical oversights and bad financial moves still hurt entrepreneurs, shareholders, workers and communities. Among the questions under debate: Is failure good for the economy? Is failure necessary for long-term success? Are there cultural and regional differences in how people react to failure?

OVERVIEW

When three friends from Grand Rapids, Mich., started a storytelling event focused on failure, they met people over coffee to discuss such questions as, "What is an impactful failure that changed the trajectory of your life?"

Bloomberg/Bloomberg/Getty Images

Their project, Failure: Lab, debuted in early 2012, when the unemployment rate in Michigan still hovered around 9 percent and its largest city, Detroit, unsuccessfully debated budget cuts and alternatives to bankruptcy.[1] People shared stories of divorce and of bad career choices, of uprooting family to move to New York and of rock CDs that cost $1 million to produce and sold only 7,000 copies. For Brian Vander Ark and his The band Verve Pipe, that album resembled a "400 pound bowling ball covered in grease."[2]

"'In an age of constant change, the only real failure is the failure to try, improve and evolve,' says one futurist. But has the acceptance of failure in business gone too far?"

From *SAGE Business Researcher*,
January 4, 2016

Their stories, told in seven to 10 minutes, are shared on YouTube. Storytellers are asked to "dig deep for that intimate personal story of failure. It's . . . a public confession with no lessons," no uplifting comeback, said co-founder Jordan O'Neil.[3]

Humans have long feared failure. When people make mistakes, they can hurt themselves and others, their reputations and their futures. When managers and companies fail, customers, creditors, communities and employers can suffer. But public sharing of failure at venues such as Failure: Lab has become fashionable in some sectors, especially technology, where failure has lost much of its stigma. CEOs, experts and consultants share failure lessons at conferences, interviews for major media and in LinkedIn posts. The result: a business culture that increasingly celebrates what used to be shunned.

"In an age of constant change, the only real failure is the failure to try, improve and evolve. . . . These days, start-up flameouts are increasingly serving as badges of honor and—especially in Silicon Valley—failure has become a bragging right," Sheryl Connelly, Ford Motor Co.'s trend spotter and futurist, wrote in Ford's 2015 Trends report.[4]

For instance, LinkedIn co-founder Reid Hoffman has shared big lessons from his failed first venture—including the importance of finding customers from the start.[5] Start-up founders swap stories about "fail fast" and ideas that went south at F---up Nights, another global storytelling gathering, which sometimes goes by its acronym FUN. Writers and business leaders have poured out their perspective in a growing number of failure books, such as *The Up Side of Down* by Megan McArdle and *Rising Strong* by Brené Brown.

A handful of companies even give failure awards to encourage staff to dare something different and new. Among them is a "Heroic Failure" trophy that Grey, a large New York–based advertising agency, presents for most creative mistake. An early winner: One staffer used kitty poo buried in cat litter under a conference room table to pitch a possible cat litter client.[6] At Google X, the search company's laboratory working on shoot-for-the-moon projects, Astro Teller leads the teams of engineers and creators. He rewards failure, because it gives people courage to take risks.[7]

"The most successful people tend to be those with the most failures," Dean Keith Simonton, a University of California, Davis, psychology professor, told *The Wall Street Journal*.[8]

Australian futurist Wendy Elford sees value in failure and the trade-offs businesses make to manage risk while seeking innovation. "Preventing failure is enormously expensive. . . . We can't plan to succeed if everything we do is preventing losing," says Elford, who focuses on the changing nature of work.

Management guru Peter Drucker said he mistrusted any man who "never commits a blunder, never fails in what he tries to do. He is either a phony, or he stays with the safe, the tried and the trivial."[9]

Yet some companies or sectors fear losing or are so risk-averse that they cannot or will not join the "cheer failure" movement. When lives are at stake—in hospitals and nursing homes—or actuarial tables clearly spell out the risks, as they do for insurers, failure is viewed with trepidation.

What failure means and looks like may vary as widely as corporate strategies or worker ethics. At one extreme are catastrophic failures such as nuclear plant accidents; in the middle may be a missed opportunity to land a plum leadership role or a worker who ignores instructions and breaks the photocopier.

Harvard Business School professor Amy C. Edmondson suggested a "spectrum of reasons for failure," from deviance to "exploratory testing." She wrote, "In organizational life, it is sometimes bad, sometimes inevitable, and sometimes even good."[10]

The same holds true in personal life and careers; acceptance of a failure may depend on mind-set, financial and emotional health, self-confidence, support and other factors, researchers have found.

With such diversity, measuring failure requires many scales and data sets. Here are a few:

- Between 50 and 80 percent of all corporate mergers fail to add value, or may even cause serious damage.[11] Various researchers say that, historically, 50 to 75 percent to as high as 80 percent of all start-up businesses fail.[12]
- The recession of 2007–09—which some argue resulted from failed banking practices and lax regulatory oversight—cost the U.S. economy $14 trillion, or up to 90 percent of U.S. output in 2007.[13]
- In the United States, young adults are not landing full-time work. Of young men in their 20s, only 65 percent hold full-time jobs, down from 80 percent in 2000.[14] Forty percent of unemployed workers are Millennials, higher than their overall share of the population.[15]
- Approximately 1 million people and businesses in the United States file for bankruptcy every year, although the number fell 11 percent to 860,182 in fiscal 2015—the lowest tally since 2007.[16]

Bankruptcies on the decline

Such well-known companies as American Apparel, Conseco, Texaco, Pacific Gas & Electric and Washington Mutual have filed for bankruptcy court protection, and quite a few go through Chapter 11s two or more times.[17] In a Chapter 11, named for a section of the U.S. bankruptcy laws, a company or individual gets breathing space from creditors while restructuring debts. Sometimes the next step is failure, and sometimes it is a new and stronger enterprise freed from old obligations.

Billionaire Donald Trump trumpets himself as a great leader in his bid for the Republican presidential nomination, even though he has stumbled in and out of businesses selling vodka, mortgages and airline flights.[18]

Sometimes it's difficult to tell whether a company is failing or is just reinventing itself in the face of market changes. And sometimes the disruption may backfire: When banks and others started offering subprime mortgages, the loans were seen as an innovation that opened doors to low-income consumers.[19] Yet that lending sowed the seeds of the largest financial and economic meltdown since the Great Depression.

Researchers have found that bankruptcy's stigma has faded, starting in the 1970s. This occurred as media coverage suggested a bad economy, inflation or other external factors were to blame instead of an individual's mistakes or overconsumption, according to Rafael Efrat, a California State University, Northridge, accounting professor whose team

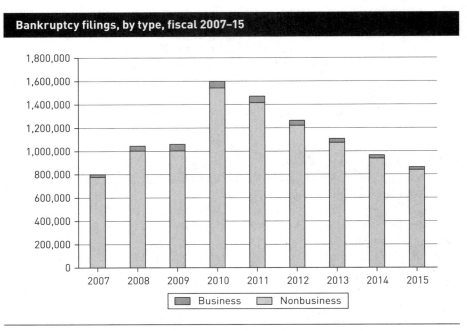

Bankruptcy filings, by type, fiscal 2007–15

U.S. bankruptcy filings have declined for five years since rising to nearly 1.6 million in the aftermath of the 2007–09 recession. Nonbusiness, or consumer, bankruptcies enable individuals to sell assets or restructure payments to creditors over time to repay debts for personal expenses. Business bankruptcies provide the same options to businesses and, while less common than consumer bankruptcies, generally involve more money.

Source: "Fiscal Year Bankruptcy Filings Continue Fall," United States Courts, Oct. 28, 2015, http://tinyurl.com/py2vsc6

analyzed 176 articles about personal bankruptcy published by *The New York Times* from 1864 to 2002.[20]

"Prior to the 1960s, newspaper articles depicted debtors largely as manipulators and fraud promoters," Efrat wrote. More recently, those who were bankrupt were portrayed as "simply rash and immature" and also victims of high inflation, stock market losses or increases in society's overall personal debt.

Even if they secretly feel embarrassed by their failure or foreclosure or a screwup at their university, Americans often share those moments on social media or in support groups.

"The shame factor has really declined," says Teresa Kohl, who has worked on corporate restructurings for almost 20 years.

Yet society's acceptance of failure and bankruptcy as more common does not remove the stigma from the individual—especially if she is a business owner whose identity is closely entwined with her enterprise.[21]

Failure may still trigger shame, grief, depression and loss, experts say. When the unemployment rate rises, so do drug and alcohol abuse, as well as spousal abuse. Crime may increase if some long-term unemployed individuals see that as the way to get money, says Carl Van Horn, professor of public policy at Rutgers University and an expert in employment issues.

Sometimes fear of failure creates incentives to excel, reinvigorate the business—or offer health insurance to workers. Starbucks CEO Howard Schultz could be Exhibit A. When he was growing up in Brooklyn, N.Y., his father held a series of jobs—truck driver, factory worker and cab driver—but then broke his ankle and couldn't work. The family had no health insurance and no income. His father's failure to provide is said to be the main driver of Starbucks offering workers, even part-time ones, health insurance coverage.[22]

Fear of failure also may have the opposite effect: It can stop women from starting businesses. It may reduce students' motivation to learn in school.[23] Executives may fear the wrath of Wall Street, which punishes stock prices if companies fail to meet profit numbers. So even those who want to experiment more or encourage risk taking must be mindful of the balancing act so they achieve profitability and other measures of success. "The pressure to perform to hit your numbers has never been greater," says Sydney Finkelstein, Dartmouth College professor of management.

People also may find it impossible to own up to an error without fear of reprisal—losing status or losing a job. "There are still plenty of cultures—which I hear discussed in executive education seminars—[where] the blaming culture exists," Finkelstein says. So managers never mention the mistakes or the misrepresented financials that could have been caught early.

Failure also may be embraced or accepted by executives "with a certain arrogance" about their decisions, Finkelstein says. They may be encouraged to experiment and undertake new products because of financial incentives that reward success with "unbelievable wealth" but carry no cost to salary if the initiative fails, he says.

Others suggest the start-up community, business professors and authors are merely branding and packaging failure. "Every age has a theory of rising and falling, of growth and decay, of bloom and wilt: a theory of nature," Jill Lepore, a professor of American history at Harvard, wrote in *The New Yorker*. She argued that instead of "progress" Americans now point to "innovation" to avoid questions about "whether a novelty is an improvement."[24]

As businesses and academics examine the mechanics and role of failure, below are some of the questions under debate.

WEIGHING THE ISSUES

Is failure good for the economy?

Kohl, the restructuring consultant, has experienced failure and bankruptcy from almost every angle, from childhood anxieties to a career as an adviser assisting troubled companies. While she acknowledges how tough such turmoil can be, she sees real value in failure and bankruptcy—both to the U.S. economy and to individual businesses.

Her first taste of failure came as a child in rural Illinois in the late 1970s, a time of record high gas prices and interest rates. Her parents filed personal bankruptcy after running a large farm for years. "It was a horrible, horrible experience," she says.

She skipped college and went straight to work, seeking a stable employer. She chose Laventhol & Horwath, a major accounting firm founded in 1915. She worked there for almost a year. One Sunday evening, her boss called her and told her to collect her personal belongings that evening. The next day, he warned, could be too late.

The 3,500-employee firm filed for Chapter 11 bankruptcy court protection in November 1990 after losing several malpractice suits.[25] Unlike numerous companies that restructure themselves and emerge from bankruptcy, Laventhol never recovered.[26]

Two of Kohl's subsequent employers folded or went through restructurings, so she investigated a career in business overhauls.

She landed a job with a small turnaround company and learned to negotiate with banks, to evaluate the underlying problems in a business and to "fix a company," she says.

"I see companies with no other choice but to shut down unless they go through a bankruptcy," says Kohl, who has worked on corporate turnarounds and restructurings for 15 years. She's now director of SSG Capital Advisors near Philadelphia and is active in the Turnaround Management Association's New York chapter. The restructuring process "creates a renewal that can spur growth and new jobs," Kohl says.

Some economists argue it is worthwhile to redeploy assets and pull the plug on "zombie companies"—firms that are unprofitable, relying on debt or state ownership in China and elsewhere to survive.[27]

For instance, all the bankruptcies and debt restructuring in 2008–09, coming out of the financial crisis and recession, helped revive the U.S. economy and improve corporate competitiveness, according to Stuart Gilson, a professor of business administration at Harvard.[28] Businesses used Chapter 11 to auction off valuable assets or to preserve value as they reduced their debt burdens.

Tight economic times also have produced some giants. "Some of the most successful tech investments of all time—among them Google and Facebook—came about in Silicon Valley's lean times," wrote Farhad Manjoo, a *New York Times* technology columnist. "This is a paradox of invention, as well as of investing: Bad times feed good ideas, which in turn lead to good times, which breed complacency, waste and lots of bad business plans."[29]

Those tech companies have created thousands of jobs. Successful corporate restructurings preserved many jobs, even when they involved layoffs. All the turnaround consultants, bankruptcy lawyers and distressed-debt investors contribute to the economy, although the numbers are difficult to quantify.

Making failure easier to manage may even support new business development, researchers found in a 29-nation study. Lenient, entrepreneur-friendly bankruptcy laws correlate significantly with levels of entrepreneurship development as measured by the rate of business start-ups. "The less the downside risk involved in filing bankruptcy, the more new firms are founded," according to the business school professors who conducted the research.[30]

Clarity about the rules of bankruptcy and failure encourages risk-taking, says Thomas B. Bennett, a retired U.S. bankruptcy court judge in Alabama who is now a lawyer in

Washington, D.C. "It encourages people to take risks so you're not going to be put in debtors' prison, like happened in early England [and America]. There's a way to rehabilitate yourself and move forward," he says.

Yet failure carries huge costs, to individuals and the economy. Millions of unemployed individuals and their families grapple with financial and health problems. Failed businesses and banks leave shareholders, suppliers and their communities unpaid, and in the extreme may even create ghost towns.

When businesses fail, stockholders lose—usually shares become worthless. In the case of banks, the U.S. government, which insures deposits, often arranges a marriage to a healthier bank—and gives the groom a nice check for the honeymoon. The 165 banks that failed in 2008 and 2009 during the financial crisis and recession cost the Federal Deposit Insurance Corp. (FDIC) $9 billion in incentives and loss-sharing agreements needed to entice other banks and investors to buy troubled institutions.[31]

At the individual and family level, long-term unemployment may be measured in lost confidence, repossessed cars, poor health and dunning creditor calls. In late 2015, 2.05 million workers were unemployed and looking for work for 27 weeks or longer, half the level of three years earlier but still about a quarter of all jobless individuals.[32]

When workers are unemployed or stuck in low-paying or part-time jobs, that hurts their community and the economy, says Rutgers' Van Horn. "They're not paying taxes. They're no longer consuming as much as they did before because they have no money," he says.

"It means a smaller economy, a less successful economy," Van Horn says, measured in declines to both consumer spending and GDP.

Failure can even lead to ghost towns where all the businesses have closed and all the residents departed—places such as Hashima Island, Japan, once an offshore coal-mining site where thousands lived (most recently famous as the fictional lair of a James Bond villain), or Bodie, Calif., a deserted gold rush boomtown that's now a state park.[33]

Corporate fraud, another type of failure by executives and the boards that oversee them, has been booming, with plenty of cases of accounting fraud, insider trading and kickbacks investigated by the FBI.[34] Half of senior executives worry about the effects of corruption and bribery on their business, and more than one-quarter of companies report bribery or procurement fraud.[35]

At its worst, fraud leads to a company disintegrating, as Enron did in 2001–02 after an accounting scandal by the formerly high-flying energy company led to thousands losing jobs, $2 billion in pensions disappearing and a few executives sent to prison.[36]

Even Gilson, the Harvard professor who is a big proponent of Chapter 11, acknowledged that not all firms come back strong. "Chapter 11 is likely to be prohibitively costly for a consulting firm, whose most valuable assets are intangible or capable of walking out the door; a steel manufacturer, in contrast, may suffer much less damage to its business if it files for bankruptcy," he wrote.[37]

Kohl says that while not every bankruptcy reorganization or failure ends in revitalization, turnarounds help the economy. One of her favorite cases involves Forum Health Care of Youngstown, Ohio, which owned several struggling hospitals that provided "a disproportionate amount of charity care." She represented Forum's bond insurance company, which would have to pay up if bonds defaulted; she says she still wanted to see "a win for everybody," including Forum's 4,000-plus employees. In 2010, Forum was sold out of bankruptcy to a Nashville firm that invested in new equipment but also laid off some employees.[38]

"You all have to share the pain to provide a platform for growth to the future," Kohl says. "We joke, 'Hold your nose and go forward.'"

Is failure necessary for long-term success?

Bill Gates was heading into his senior year of high school in the summer of 1972, working for a company that measured traffic patterns. The company used a machine that translated numbers into a custom paper punch tape, which then were manually repunched into computer cards.[39]

Gates' friend Paul Allen thought a machine powered by a then-novel microprocessor would work better. So they "scraped together $360" for the Intel 8008 chip and built what Gates dubbed Traf-O-Data.

"When the guy from the county that Seattle's in came to see it, it didn't work," Gates said in an interview.[40]

Traf-O-Data landed few clients, and Gates and Allen moved on. Yet their small company had served as a catalyst and a testing ground for something much bigger.

"It confirmed to me that every failure contains the seeds of your next success. It bolstered my conviction that microprocessors would soon run the same programs as larger computers, but at a much lower cost. . . . This was the essential step toward . . . the creation of Microsoft," Allen recalled.[41]

Gates and Allen, who co-founded Microsoft in 1975, are in good company in their faith that failure is a stepping stone to success, and a launching pad for innovation. Many start-up founders and business school professors—as well as super-successful author J.K. Rowling— say failure fosters better leaders and stronger companies.

For some, a stumble offers gifts: resilience, faith in the ability to come back, perhaps a new opportunity. For others, though, failure in career or business may lead to poverty and depression. How failure affects individuals and businesses has been widely researched, with myriad conclusions.

Lessons from failure last longer than those based on success, a University of Colorado, Denver, researcher found, based on his study of rockets and airlines. "Whenever you have a failure it causes a company to search for solutions, and when you search for solutions it puts you as an executive in a different mind-set, a more open mind-set," said Vinit Desai, an assistant professor of management who also has studied failure in other sectors.[42]

Not everyone learns from failure, though. Entrepreneurs need an "intuitive cognitive style" and mentoring to really extract valuable lessons from their huge mess-ups, entrepreneurship professors Brandon Mueller of Oklahoma State University and Dean A. Shepherd of Indiana University found.[43]

Many serial entrepreneurs continue to be overly optimistic and do not reflect on their missteps, so they fail a second time, according to others who have studied the process.[44] And even though the start-up community has embraced the "fail fast" mantra, it really applies to the little details of an enterprise, not the big things, wrote David Brown, co-founder of business accelerator Techstars.[45]

Yet failure leads some people to their big thing. Rowling was 28, jobless and poor, her marriage failing, when she returned to writing. The famous result: *Harry Potter*. She told part of her story in a 2008 Harvard commencement address: "Failure meant a stripping away of the inessential. I stopped pretending to myself that I was anything other than what I was, and began to direct all my energy into finishing the only work that mattered to me."[46]

That rebuilding grew into an empire, with seven *Harry Potter* books, eight movies, countless merchandising spin-offs and two Wizarding World sections at theme parks, collectively worth about $24 billion.[47] Rowling's personal net worth is estimated at $1 billion.

While the idea of failure as a necessary building block to success sounds enticing, there's plenty of contrary evidence—including people who string together success after success. Entrepreneurs with a track record of success are "much more likely to succeed than first-time entrepreneurs and those who have previously failed," a team of Harvard business professors found.[48]

J.K. Rowling: "Failure meant a stripping away of the inessential."

Despite many powerful comebacks, not every chief executive who goes down in flames returns stronger and better. Only about 35 percent of the 450 executives studied by two management professors ended up in another top job within two years of their departure.[49] The others either took consulting or teaching posts or disappeared into obscurity or retirement.

Trendy celebrations of failure are evolving into "failure porn" that "desensitizes one to the horrors of failure," wrote venture capitalist Geoff Lewis of Founders Fund. "I recoil when the merits of failure are so vastly overstated and its agonies are so trivialized."[50] People seem to ignore the costs: psychological trauma and a feeling of worthlessness for founders, huge losses for investors and jobs that evaporate, leaving families struggling.

"When you believe your vision is important, celebrating failure of any sort would be perverse. . . . (Yet) the failure pendulum has swung too far toward celebration. I'd like to see it swing back a bit toward fear," Lewis wrote.

Fear of failure certainly grips people who are stuck in low-paying jobs or out of work for months or years. About one-third of Americans worry they may not be able to pay their rent or mortgage, and 60 percent fear they will not have enough money saved for retirement, according to a 2015 Gallup Poll. Unmarried women, African-Americans, Latinos and anyone who earns less than $30,000 a year are the most likely to express worry about six or more financial areas of life.[51]

Americans worry about financial failure

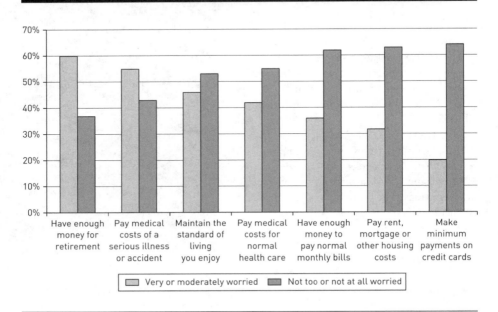

Poll: How worried are you about each of the following financial matters?

Legend: Very or moderately worried ■ Not too or not at all worried

A majority of Americans said they were very or moderately worried about being able to save enough money for retirement or being able to pay medical bills after a serious health problem, according to a Gallup Poll. About one-third of respondents said they were very or moderately worried about being able to pay for normal monthly bills or housing costs.

Note: Results based on surveys of 1,015 U.S. adults from April 9–12, 2015.

Source: Lydia Saad, "Americans' Money Worries Unchanged From 2014," Gallup, April 20, 2015, http://tinyurl.com/lhjp9jx

Are there cultural and regional differences in how people react to failure?

Bennett, who retired from the bankruptcy bench in June 2015, presided over thousands of cases a year during 20 years in Birmingham, Ala. They ranged from poor single parents to what in 2011 was the largest municipal bankruptcy in U.S. history, that of Jefferson County, Ala., which includes Birmingham. He was known for his rule-from-the-bench and work-through-the-holidays approaches.[52]

"There is no difference based on age, gender or race on how people react to bankruptcy," Bennett says, based on his experience.

At least in Alabama, the stigma of bankruptcy persists, even though it has declined, he says. "Nobody comes in and talks about failure in the way you're talking about," Bennett says. Celebration of failure seems rooted in Silicon Valley and a few other tech centers—although there's evidence it is spreading around the world.

Only 41 percent of those polled in Japan agree with the statement, "People today brag more about failure than they did in the past." But in Brazil, 73 percent see that happening. In the United States, 57 percent report more bragging about big setbacks.[53]

"In some Asian cultures, the ideas of speaking up when something's going wrong is unbelievably difficult," says Dartmouth's Finkelstein, whose book *Why Smart Executives Fail* was a best-seller in Japan.

Fear of failure may hold back people in some cultures from starting businesses more than others. For example, 50 percent of people in Vietnam said worry about failing could halt their plans compared with about 13 percent in Botswana and Uganda and 24 percent in Argentina. The highest levels were found in Greece, at almost 62 percent.[54]

Greeks fear business failure the most

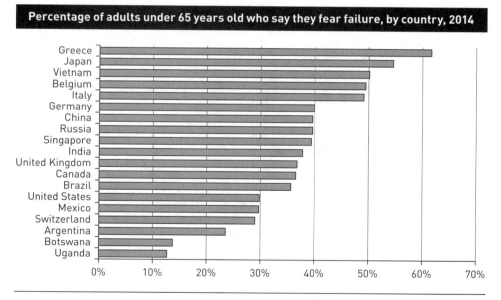

Percentage of adults under 65 years old who say they fear failure, by country, 2014

Sixty-two percent of adults under age 65 in Greece and 55 percent of those in Japan told researchers their fear of failure would prevent them from starting a business, well above the rate of 30 percent in the United States. Fear of entrepreneurial failure was even lower among adults in Argentina (24 percent) and African countries such as Botswana (14 percent) and Uganda (13 percent).

Note: Based on surveys of more than 206,000 people in 73 economies.

Source: "Global Entrepreneurship Monitor: 2014 Global Report," Global Entrepreneurship Research Association, 2015, pp. 32–33, http://tinyurl.com/j3fn7nb

Women are more risk-averse and have less experience with failure than men, researchers have found. They are more likely to take calculated risks and develop backup plans in case problems develop, while men are more likely to rely on their self-confidence.[55] Women also fear failure more than men, and their craving for success diminishes by their 40s.[56]

Young people ages 18 to 24 with a desire to start businesses are much more likely to say they fear failure than those who are over 35, and also are less likely to claim they hold the necessary skills and resources for entrepreneurship.[57]

Children may develop very different mind-sets about mistakes based on how they are reared. Those who are cocooned from their missteps can grow up stunted. "Out of love and a desire to protect our children's self-esteem, we have bulldozed every uncomfortable bump and obstacle out of their way, depriving our children of the most important lesson of childhood: that setbacks, mistakes and failures are the very experiences that will teach them how to be resourceful, persistent, innovative and resilient," wrote Jessica Lahey, a journalist and the author of *The Gift of Failure*.[58]

Geography, gender or parenting style do not explain all the nuances and variety of our feelings and behaviors around failure. Fons Trompenaars, a Dutch organizational theorist, and Peter Woolliams, a British international business culture expert, described five key dimensions that create differences around failure:[59]

- The degree over which an individual believes he controls his environment—or is controlled by it.
- Whether rules or relationships are more important.
- Whether failures are pinned to the individual or to the community or team.
- Whether the workers come from nonidentifying cultures (where failures are seen "as simply an idea that didn't work") or identifying cultures; two-thirds of American and Dutch survey respondents blame the idea, while only 12 percent of Japanese and 24 percent of Chinese respondents do.
- Whether status is granted based on performance or position.

Trompenaars and Woolliams cited an example of German and American engineers working for the same company, semiconductor maker AMD, in a joint brainstorming session in Dresden, Germany. American workers said the Germans were slow, risk-averse and lacked creativity in exploring new ideas. But the Germans felt the Americans offered undeveloped ideas without having done their homework. AMD found a middle ground for the two, but too often such encounters end in frustration or failure.

Companies may have a variety of micro-climates for failure, suggests Paul J.H. Schoemaker, a strategic management consultant who also teaches at the University of Pennsylvania's Wharton School. For example, for a pharmaceutical company, "failure is endemic" in research and development. "They start with 9,000 drugs to get to one that is interesting."

However, once a drug has been tested and is approved for sale, manufacturing "has to be a very tight process. Mistakes are frowned upon," he says. (See Perspective "Q&A: Paul Schoemaker on Mistakes.")

BACKGROUND

Debtors' prison

In imperial Rome, debtors could be arrested; if they did not repay, they were enslaved. In ancient Ireland and India, creditors would hold vigil outside the debtor's door until paid.[60]

In other places, failing to pay debts could lead to death, sometimes brought on by long imprisonments. "Not only freedom and honor but life itself was at the mercy of the creditor," wrote Louis Edward Levinthal, author of *The Early History of Bankruptcy Law*. Gradually though, creditor claims became directed at the borrower's property instead of his person, wrote Levinthal, a Philadelphia judge in the mid-20th century.[61]

An individual who went bankrupt in 16th-century England was a fraud and an "offender"; in France such people were labeled deceivers or squanderers.[62]

Debtors' prisons, imported along with bankruptcy codes from England, were common in the United States for almost 200 years, starting in the 1600s. Often overcrowded and disease-ridden, the prisons housed both criminals and debtors, who often received the only long-term sentences.[63]

The United States adopted its first bankruptcy laws in 1800, borrowed liberally from England's pro-creditor ordinances.[64] The bankruptcy codes applied only to merchants and cases initiated by creditors, and contained a five-year sunset provision. Congress repealed the laws after only three years, citing excess costs and corruption.[65]

Two more times in the 1800s, in 1841 and 1867, Congress passed federal bankruptcy legislation only to repeal it a few years later. Often the nation's leaders were pressed to act after economic crisis.

The new country's economy was turbulent, with panics and crashes interspersed with periods of growth and business development. The "Panic of 1819" was caused by loose credit, heavy debts by the U.S. government and farmers and plunging cotton prices. It was, according to one account, "America's first great economic crisis."[66]

Customers started runs on U.S. banks, withdrawing money because of fears the banks were unstable, while farmers and cotton farmers could not meet loan payments.[67] That panic was followed by the cotton market crash of 1825, which pushed the South into a depression.

Despite such setbacks, in the early 1800s, failure was mainly a business term—although preachers also would use it for "heathens" and others who fell from grace, historian Scott A. Sandage wrote in *Born Losers: A History of Failure in America*.[68]

That started to shift when success and ambition became more fashionable than piety. People began to abhor failure and blame it on a lack of initiative or talent, Sandage wrote. By the 1840s, the "go-ahead principles" took root and spread beyond New York as mining and railroads and more brought thoughts of success to many.

Failure and bankruptcy became accepted as part of American enterprise. "Business failure permeated the 19th century United States," wrote Duke history professor Edward J. Balleisen, who cited estimates that 95 percent of mercantile shops failed both before and after the Civil War. "Throughout the era, farmers from every part of the country lost their land because they could not make mortgage payments, while large numbers of artisans and manufacturers found themselves unable to meet their obligations. In the biggest cities and the smallest hamlets, a host of mercantile firms experienced bankruptcy."[69]

His analysis of 503 bankruptcies in New York City and vicinity from the 1830s and 1840s shows they were mostly filed by men (only nine women), usually in the "prime of their lives," and three-quarters were married.

During this time, many men were unable to pay their bills and landed in debtors' prisons. There were campaigns to abolish these unhealthy cells, including some penned from the prisons themselves.

Kentucky became the first state to outlaw those institutions, in 1821—just two years after nature painter John James Audubon was sent to a debtors' jail after his Kentucky business failed.[70] U.S. law forbade federal debtors' prisons in 1833.[71] By 1870, the "dismal cages" had been outlawed in almost all the states and territories.[72]

Bankruptcy laws in the United States gradually grew more liberal and helpful to individuals and business owners in trouble. By the 1850s, many states had extended help to families, exempting from seizure and sale not only clothing, furniture and household goods but also a home and 40 or 50 acres, plus the debtor's tools of trade.[73]

The Civil War and trying times caused Congress to adopt new bankruptcy codes in 1867, providing protection for corporations for the first time.[74] They were repealed in 1878.

The U.S. statutes were far more lenient than elsewhere; French historian and political writer Alexis de Tocqueville commented on the "strange indulgence that is shown to bankrupts" in the United States compared with Europe's still-stern laws.[75]

Evolution of bankruptcy

With rapid growth in commerce and movement into new territories after the Civil War, Americans embraced the "self-made man" approach. "The great American Assumption was that wealth is mainly the result of its owner's effort and that any average worker can by thrift become a capitalist," wrote W.E.B. Du Bois, co-founder of the NAACP, the nation's oldest civil rights organization.[76]

This sentiment led countless people to risk their life savings to buy farms or start businesses, only to fail. Ten years after Samuel Clemens wrote *Adventures of Huckleberry Finn* in 1884 to great acclaim, a company the man known as Mark Twain established filed for bankruptcy.[77]

A large-scale economic failure started in the South and Great Plains in the 1880s, punctuated by a deep agricultural crisis.[78] Wall Street took note in 1893, as one-fourth of U.S. railroads went bankrupt and a worldwide depression took hold.

Lawmakers debated the merits of various kinds of bankruptcy, voluntary as well as involuntary, in which creditors force a business or individual to liquidate. In 1898, Congress again passed federal bankruptcy laws that for the first time included a precursor to Chapter 13, which "really opened the doors for the modern understanding that businesses and individuals are vulnerable to shocks beyond their control," says Mary Hansen, an American University economics professor. "That thinking was the basis for the modern social safety net."

Chapter 13, then known as a "wage earners plan," enables individuals with regular income to create a repayment plan for part or all of their debts over three to five years. During this period, creditors are forbidden from continuing collection efforts.[79]

The 1898 law, though promoted by creditor interests, was "in many respects strikingly debtor-friendly," wrote David A. Skeel Jr., a professor of corporate law at the University of Pennsylvania.[80]

By 1900, as inventors were working on the first automobiles in Michigan and Indiana, bankruptcy had a solid foundation in the U.S. economy and legal code. Perfectionist Henry Ford's first company, Detroit Automobile, produced only 20 cars; the enterprise went bankrupt in 1901.[81]

Around that time, Michigan and Ohio were considered "cradles of innovation," Hansen says, with tinkerers working on horseless carriages of all sorts and the Wright brothers and others building airplanes. "Whenever you have high rates of business formation, you by definition have high rates of business failure," she says.

The Hindenburg airship that crashed in New Jersey in 1937 was not the first innovative transportation device to fail spectacularly—to "go up in flames" as some would dub a huge mistake. The Stanley Steamer, a transmission-less steam-powered car, debuted in 1897; its engines were smaller and more powerful than internal combustion gasoline engines.[82] The cars were fast, too: In 1906, steam-powered cars set a land speed record of 127 mph. Yet Ford Motor Co.'s assembly line-produced Model T cost much less, so by 1924, the last Stanleys were built.[83]

Fifty years later, Ford began a new car line called Edsel, named after the founder's only son. Because of low quality and an unusual front-end design that some said looked like a toilet seat, it never caught on. The Edsel was discontinued after three years, with only 2,846 cars sold in its final year, 1960.[84]

The panic of 1907 was a key turning point in U.S. failure history, Hansen says, because it led to the creation of the Federal Reserve system, which oversees the U.S. banking and money system. That panic was brought on by failed speculations and concerns about the safety of financial institutions and a weak U.S. economy.[85]

The other pivotal moment was the Great Depression of the 1930s, which sent families in search of new homes and lives in California and elsewhere. That 10 years of economic contraction resulted in some 7,000 bank failures and an unemployment rate of 25 percent.[86]

"The Great Depression really set the stage for the Great Society programs, which are our modern safety net," Hansen says. Social Security and many other government programs have their roots in President Franklin D. Roosevelt's Depression-fighting New Deal; other safety net programs, including Medicare and Medicaid, date to President Lyndon B. Johnson's Great Society of the 1960s.

Hansen is leading a project to digitize bankruptcy court records from the early 20th century, by taking samples from more than 2 million boxes of records in the National Archives. She has learned that many of the business bankruptcies of the Great Depression resulted not from bank failures but from trade credit evaporating. Small businesses just would not sell to other businesses on credit. Proprietors would say, "I can't extend you three months longer" on balances owed, and so the small grocer or milliner would go bankrupt, she says.

Access to credit for everyone

The 1940s and 1950s were prosperous times. After World War II, the Baby Boom, coupled with low unemployment and low inflation, meant Americans bought cars and stereos and invested in college educations.[87]

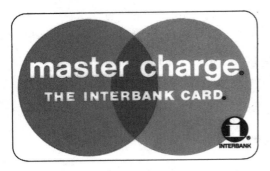

A credit card from MasterCard, which debuted in 1966 under the name Master Charge.

But credit cards and credit laws created a new avenue for failure. Introduced in 1958, Visa, then known as BankAmericard, and MasterCard, which debuted in 1966 as Master Charge, were held by 16 percent of U.S. families in 1970. By 1995, about two-thirds of all families had at least one card, and when single-store and other credit cards were added, that rose to three-quarters of all individuals and families.[88]

The seeds of overextension and rising consumer bankruptcies were sown in the 1970s, with the spread of bank credit cards and the 1974 passage of the Equal Credit Opportunity Act (ECOA), Hansen says. Before that law banned discrimination in lending based on gender, marital status, race and national origin, women found it difficult to land a mortgage or car loan.[89] Afterward, credit for women became more available, she says.

"The big story is access to credit. If you think of bankruptcy as being tied to access to credit, it no longer is a huge terrible thing. It's an obvious manifestation of risk in the modern economy," Hansen says. While consumers' debt grew from credit cards, businesses borrowed more money through private equity and junk bonds, used to create leveraged buyouts (LBOs) through the 1980s. But buyouts slowed markedly in 1989–90; by 1991, 26 of 83 big boom-time LBOs had defaulted on their debt, and 18 had filed for Chapter 11.[90]

Busts keep following booms

The 21st century brought another boom and bust cycle, fueled by new financial instruments. Lenders created an array of mortgages that made borrowing to buy a home seem easy, even for people with bad credit or shaky job histories. These subprime mortgages deteriorated in quality for six years, 2001 to '06, and the companies creating and reselling mortgage-backed securities were aware of the growing risks. Foreclosures mounted, and by late 2006, "an unusually large fraction of subprime mortgages" made just months before were delinquent or facing foreclosure.[91]

The problems that started in the mortgage market erupted in the financial crisis of 2008; financial companies including investment bank Lehman Brothers died or went bankrupt, while the government bailed out others. Millions of Americans lost their homes to foreclosure. The Federal Reserve Bank failed to halt the spread of "toxic mortgages," and it and other regulators were unprepared for the panic and fallout, according to numerous analyses.[92]

Lehman brothers tops largest bankruptcies list

From its peak in 2008 to 2010, the U.S. economy lost 8.8 million jobs in a wide variety of sectors, from construction to manufacturing and professional and business services.[93] From 2008 to 2011, almost 5 million Americans filed for personal bankruptcy.[94] Some 80 percent of Americans either lost their job or knew a family member or friend who were out of work in the recession, says Van Horn of Rutgers, author of *Working Scared (Or Not at All)*.

In the early 2000s, Richelle Shaw, who's now a motivational speaker and business coach, lost rental properties she owned in Las Vegas as well as her small telephone company. In her worst days, she "slept on the floor," she says. "I went without power for 18 days." She filed for

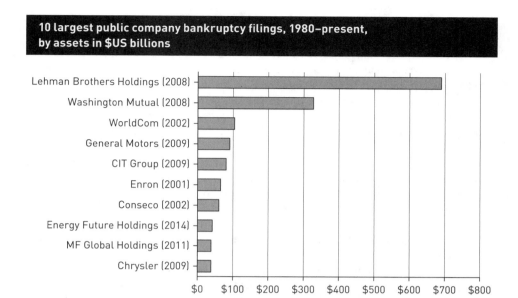

10 largest public company bankruptcy filings, 1980–present, by assets in $US billions

Investment bank Lehman Brothers filed for the largest-ever U.S. bankruptcy action in September 2008 with $691 billion in assets, more than twice that of second-ranked Washington Mutual, which filed that same month. Financial services firms filed for five of the 10 largest bankruptcies since 1980; the rest came from automotive, energy and communications companies.

Source: "20 Largest Public Company Bankruptcy Filings 1980 - Present," BankruptcyData.com, New Generation Research, undated, http://tinyurl.com/lphhuu

personal bankruptcy in 2006, after her business imploded from a heavy debt load. She laid off all her workers, including her mother.

A few years ago, Shaw started talking about her failure in her speeches and writing. "Failure happens throughout your life. If you're lucky, it will happen early so you can bounce back from it," she says.

"If you have never failed before, you haven't reached your fullest and best self," says Shaw, echoing the sentiments of more famous women such as Oprah Winfrey and J.K. Rowling.

CURRENT SITUATION

"A cultural moment"

Duke University adjunct professor Erin Parish is surrounded by failure, some of it intentional, in the first-year class she teaches and in her family and personal life.

She teaches students about failure and risk aversion, about social movements around failure and about tackling an "impossible task."

"It's definitely a cultural moment," Parish says, with failure praised, probed and feared in America today. She traces that partly to all the tech start-ups and to the growing number of standardized tests children take. "They talk about how there are no safety nets in high school to fail," she says.

She has experienced and studied stumbles for years, with a "failed job, failed marriage," she says. "I tried a graduate program and it didn't work for me." She ended up earning her doctorate in cultural anthropology from Duke.

"These students are more anxious at an early age than I was. They have more of a view of failure as this real thing to avoid," she says. Yet what they see as their big failures—receiving an 87 on a paper or not getting into Harvard—are shared easily in class and on social media.

Such is the dichotomy of failure today, where it's seen as a fashionable performer singing about "epic fails" and "superb smash-ups" as well as a tough headmaster doling out lessons and opportunities to innovate or reinvent. Yet not everyone embraces the performer or headmaster; a backlash against elevating failure is growing, too.

Failure has turned into a cliché, with not enough context and meaning, some say. "We don't want to set ourselves up to be a failure society where it's all wonderful and everyone will now get a trophy or kudos for failing," said Rebecca "Kiki" Weingarten, a career and education coach.[95]

For example, in Detroit, some people reject what's called "ruin porn"—photos of crumbling and abandoned buildings. One critic called it the "uncritical and exploitative celebration of Detroit's postindustrial landscapes."[96] Others dismissed the photos as intrusive and one-dimensional because they ignored Detroit buildings being rehabbed or those that remain well-tended.

Detroit, of course, has experienced years of decline and failure. One-third of the homes in the city have gone through foreclosure since 2005, a trend that has reduced property values and decimated neighborhoods.[97]

Yet the city's failings, which result in homes priced at $5,000 and commercial buildings at a fraction of what they would cost in Chicago or Los Angeles, are drawing investors and new residents. In the year before and after 2013, when the city filed for the largest U.S. municipal bankruptcy, Detroit and its backers have pushed a new message of Detroit as "a comeback city" with new investment, new art galleries and new restaurants.[98]

Corporate costs

Even though more companies see value in modest failure, big mistakes are costly to reputations and bottom lines. Some strong corporations have taken hits for major mistakes. Toyota paid a $1.2 billion settlement in 2014 to halt a criminal probe into its efforts to deceive regulators and the public about sudden acceleration problems and a sticky gas pedal that led to fatalities and accidents.[99] Volkswagen officials employed deceptive software so up to 11 million vehicles could pass emissions tests; the scandal exposed in 2015 is expected to cost the German automaker billions of dollars.[100] Also in 2015, Halliburton agreed to pay $18.3 million in back wages to more than 1,000 workers who were misclassified as salaried workers.[101]

Amid a mobile communications boom, some cellphone makers stumbled. "Motorola in the 1990s was more powerful than Apple today. It had 60 percent market share. . . . Just flying high," says Finkelstein at Dartmouth. Now Motorola's share is around 5 to 6 percent.[102]

"As powerful as the iPhone is today, it wouldn't surprise me that they would also be surpassed," Finkelstein says.

He sees the rate of failures increasing, and measures it partly by attrition of Fortune 100 firms. "The rate at which companies fall out of the top 100 has gone up by 50 percent since the ranking was first published in 1955. For example, the 10-year attrition rate from 1955 to 1965 was 20 percent; from 2005 to 2015 it was 30 percent—a 50 percent increase in attrition rate," he says.

Finkelstein's annual list of the worst CEOs shows three main storylines: CEOs who follow the wrong strategies and don't change things; corporate governance issues; and questionable, unethical or borderline illegal activity. Many of these executives lose their jobs within a year, he says.

Some of the CEOs work for companies that end up in Chapter 11, such as American Apparel's former CEO Dov Charney, who made the 2014 list.[103]

The American Bankruptcy Institute proposed changes to U.S. bankruptcy laws in December 2014, to shift power away from corporate creditors and make reorganization more affordable for small privately held companies with less than $10 million in assets. The proposal would also raise the amount an employee may collect as a priority creditor to $25,000 from the current $11,725.[104]

Bennett, the former bankruptcy judge, says Congress is unlikely to pass any significant changes to U.S. bankruptcy laws any time soon. One change that could take place could be to Chapter 9, the provision that covers municipalities such as Detroit and Jefferson County, Ala., Bennett's best-known case.

Selling failure and hating it

Sharing your failure has become so popular in the start-up world that the blog for venture capital database CB Insights gathered dozens of them in a 2014 post titled "51 Startup Failure Post-Mortems," updated by the end of 2015 to 146 failures.[105]

Michael Roberto, a management professor at Bryant University, said the embrace-failure movement has taken hold "because so many corporate cultures have become so intolerant of experimentation and people have become so afraid to fail that they have become reluctant to try new things." He added: "We still need to be careful about not labeling all failures as equally 'useful.'"[106]

Some experts say, though, that the "fail fast" and "fail forward" mantras are mostly just hype; leaders know a few social media posts will not erase the effects of a huge misstep. "The key, really, shouldn't be to embrace failure but to embrace resilience and the ability to bounce back," said Rob Asghar, a management consultant and the author of *Leadership Is Hell*.[107]

For some, resilience is a pipe dream. In a Rutgers report, seven in 10 workers 50 and older who hold part-time jobs because they cannot land better ones say they earn less than they need to live; 35 percent have sold possessions and 25 percent borrowed from family or friends.[108] More than a third are cutting costs—including food and upkeep on their homes—because most say their financial situations are "only fair" (about 50 percent) or "poor" (one-third).

Parish plans to talk to her undergraduates about creating a safety net for failure—financial, intellectual and emotional screwups. And she will highlight the "fictions of the self-made man" and the "shallow marketing of failure as the American Dream 2.0. It drives me crazy," she says.

"We talk about paradox a lot," Parish says. "Do you want stability or transformation? There's always paradox at play."

LOOKING AHEAD

Predicting and averting failure

Within a few years, a computer algorithm may scan the huge array of data collected by universities or employers for signs of flameouts—or to offer a prescription for avoiding catastrophe.

Already, at the Massachusetts Institute of Technology, by tracking how long students spend on a course website compared to their peers, a computer can anticipate when someone is about to drop out of an online course.[109] With the right intervention, perhaps that alert could avert a small failure for both the student and the teacher.

Increasingly, companies may use software to predict which workers are getting antsy. Candidates flagged are six times more likely to leave their job within 120 days than their peers.[110]

In hospitals and businesses, experts already use predictive analytics to anticipate such things as heart failure and which equipment components will stop working. Edward Altman, a New York University finance professor who focuses on bankruptcy, calculates a " Z-score" that provides a measure of corporate health or default by tracking liquidity, earnings, stock market valuation and solvency. "Many companies are repeating some of the mistakes of the past" by adding too much debt, according to Altman.[111]

In the future, predictive analytics may warn of larger failures, although tracking internal data on sales, repeat customers or employee turnover may not be enough to warn of a bankruptcy. "The information most likely to influence the future comes from looking out the window, not in the mirror," wrote Accenture's Jeanne Harris and Mark McDonald, referring to global economic and marketplace changes, vs. internal metrics.[112]

Managers must evolve and master new techniques for using predictive futures, instead of basing decisions on past experiences and data, whether they want to anticipate success or failure or something else, Harris and McDonald wrote.

And they must learn to get past the "blame game" and superficial lessons and head in "novel strategic directions," wrote Harvard's Edmondson. Even in companies with systems such as Total Quality Management to find problems, many staffers are loath to share bad news with bosses and colleagues. Edmondson suggested that management adopt strategies of openness and humility and of asking and answering questions.[113]

Elford, the Australian futurist, says acceptance of failure in business and life will continue to gain momentum. She expects a move toward finding "safe to fail" and recovery-from-failure strategies.

"We need to shift to being a master of failure and honoring failure and laughing at it. I don't think we are training people well enough," she says.

Yet Elford also notes that some trends may slow acceptance of failure. Helicopter parenting is one example, where parents coddle and protect their children. Another: Leaders fear ambiguity when they consider a huge array of future outcomes. Often, they seek to narrow the scope and focus of their future view to one point or set of questions. A manager thinks: "I will succeed or fail based on your answer to my question: 'Do you like your chair?'" she says. Yet for consumers, the important topic perhaps is not the chair, but a comfortable environment on the job or something else entirely. She says successful leaders must be open to such ambiguity.

"Everything you ignore is where failure begins," Elford says.

Chronology

1800s	**Bankruptcy laws take shape.**
1800	U.S. Congress adopts first federal bankruptcy laws, modeled after a 1732 English law.
1821	Kentucky becomes the first U.S. state to outlaw debtors' prisons.
1898	Congress approves changes to bankruptcy law that give businesses more financial options.
1920s–1930s	**Great Depression brings widespread failure.**
1929	After a speculative boom, the U.S. stock market experiences a devastating crash. In the years that follow, thousands of farms and small businesses close or are seized by banks for unpaid loans.
1930s	Throughout the 1930s, the Depression ripples globally, with unemployment rates at more than 30 percent in most European countries in some years, and even higher in Germany, still struggling to recover from its defeat in World War I.
1937	The Hindenburg, an airship that was considered a marvel of the skies, crashes in New Jersey, ending the dirigible era.
1950s–1970s	**Big companies suffer setbacks.**
1958	Toyota Motor Co. sells only 288 vehicles in the United States after its debut a year earlier. The company does not succeed until it introduces the Corona in 1965.
1970	Two years after a merger creates a huge railroad giant, Penn Central Transportation goes bankrupt in what at the time is the largest U.S. bankruptcy. The company's assets are sold off over the next several years, many of them to a new company, Conrail.
1978	The Bankruptcy Reform Act establishes Chapter 11 reorganization. Bankruptcy filings rapidly increase at an average annual rate of 7.6 percent between 1980 and 2004.
1980s–1990s	**Savings and loan crisis leads to widespread collapses.**
1982	The unemployment rate soars to a post–World War II record of 10.8 percent.
1988	The savings and loan crisis peaks, with 190 thrift failures.
1994	Euro Disney, open for two years, restructures its debt in an attempt to resolve financial problems.
1996	*Debt*, a game show in which winning contestants receive prize money to eliminate their debts, airs on Lifetime Television.

(Continued)

(Continued)

2000s–Present	The dot-com bubble bursts and financial markets buckle.
2000	The super-heated market in technology stocks plummets—what has become known as the bursting of the dot-com bubble.
2001	Energy giant Enron, which had been hailed for its innovation, files for Chapter 11 and lays off 4,000 employees.
2005	Congress passes the Bankruptcy Abuse Prevention and Consumer Protection Act, making it harder for individuals and families to file for Chapter 7 protection. . . . An early version of YouTube fails as a dating site, leading the founders to switch to video sharing.
2006	Bankruptcy filings plummet 70 percent to 618,000, down from more than 2 million the previous year.
2008	The growing subprime mortgage crisis erupts into a full-blown financial crisis, followed by the worst recession since the 1930s.
2009	FailCon, the first of a number of business conferences featuring executives who share their failure stories and lessons, launches in San Francisco.
2011	The European Commission Enterprise and Industry Group introduces "Second Chance" policy in the hopes of reducing stigmatization of failed entrepreneurs. . . . *Harvard Business Review* publishes a special "Failure" issue that discusses the many angles for identifying and learning from failure.
2013	With debts of $18 billion, the city of Detroit files for Chapter 9 bankruptcy, the largest municipal bankruptcy filing in U.S. history.
2014	The Science Gallery at Trinity College in Dublin, Ireland, debuts the "Fail Better" exhibition, a public display of failed ventures, to promote discussion of how failure sparks creativity.
2015	Business bankruptcies in Japan hit a 25-year low. . . . Because of low crude oil prices, dozens of U.S. oil and gas companies go bust. . . . Puerto Rico grapples with a debt crisis that could lead to default on its bond obligations.

—By Rivan Stinson and Vickie Elmer

PERSPECTIVE

Q&A: Paul Schoemaker on Mistakes

"EXPERIMENTATION AND MISTAKES WILL ADD UP TO SUCCESS AND BRILLIANCE, IF YOU ARE STRATEGIC"

Paul J.H. Schoemaker
Entrepreneur, consultant, educator
Wharton School, University of Pennsylvania

Paul J.H. Schoemaker knows a lot about mistakes, and believes in their power. An entrepreneur, consultant and educator who has taught at the University of Pennsylvania's Wharton School, he has researched such subjects as navigating the unknown future and how managers deal with emerging technologies. His numerous books include *Brilliant Mistakes: Finding Success on the Far Side of Failure*, which explores how businesses and business leaders can accelerate learning and innovation through mistakes.

"Success is really the sum total of many mistakes," Schoemaker says. Yet many people never "construct the silver lining" or see how they learn from their mistakes. "There is a tension in organization between learning and performing. Leaders have to balance that a bit."

Schoemaker discussed mistakes with SAGE Business Researcher reporter Vickie Elmer in an interview and follow-up emails. This is a consolidated and edited version of that discussion.

Give us a couple of examples of brilliant mistakes— not penicillin, but something any person could screw up.

To test their theories, David Ogilvy, the advertising genius, ran ads that he and his team did not believe would work. They knew they would waste half their budget—but they didn't know which half. So they experimented, including with a famous Hathaway shirt advertisement. Ogilvy added a man with an eye patch at the last minute. The ad was a brilliant success, ran for a long time and received several industry prizes.

This works well in training, too. If you want your team to get better, first, teach them to frame any mistake as a learning opportunity. Second, build on principles of positive psychology to deal with setbacks and failure as something temporary, isolated and valuable. Then emphasize that learning is the goal. A British girls' school declared a Failure Week because the headmistress wanted the girls

to understand it's acceptable and completely normal not to succeed at times.

Has anyone been able to measure the time it takes between a major failure and the context or resilience that turns it into something valuable?

This question is too general, for the range is wide: Penicillin took several decades to become a workable drug for humans, whereas other insights happen in a flash. One example: Physicist Michael Faraday discovered induction currents by accidentally moving some equipment sitting on his laboratory bench.

Companies in many sectors are expected to be risk averse and protect value and reputation. How could an individual or group encourage their bosses or company to open up to accepting or even embracing mistakes?

Clearly, it takes leadership to change an organizational culture to move away from only pursuing perfection, and leaving or creating some room for the kind of exploration that almost by necessity entails mistakes. To quote Einstein: If you have never made a mistake, you never tried anything new.

Tell us the story of your friend in the Netherlands whose father went bankrupt—and what ripples that caused.

In many Germanic cultures, perfection is prized and failure abhorred. I was born and raised in a small town in the Netherlands called Deventer. The father of one of my school friends had a company in the pharmaceutical business, which fell on hard times and was closed, with loss of jobs and much money. This failure was widely viewed as a very shameful event in the local community. He was no longer an accepted member of society and felt his only option to continue a seminormal family life was to

(Continued)

(Continued)

emigrate to North America. All this happened before it was cool to be an entrepreneur and take risks. If you failed big, you would essentially become a persona non grata in this traditional culture.

Many countries still suffer from such low tolerance for failure, and the price they collectively pay is low innovation. In more innovation-oriented economies, such as the USA or Israel, the market will sort out which failures were due to incompetence, negligence, fraud or bad luck—and people have a second chance if the latter. As [Microsoft co-founder] Bill Gates noted, he looks for people who took risks, have scars and want to try again. He reckons that they learned valuable lessons on someone else's dime and are the smarter for it.

If you could design a game that taught people to become comfortable with failure and mistakes in business and careers, what would it look like?

I think of business as "the game" that most of us play. And within the business world, we experience three distinct approaches to risk taking:

For the "innovation game," film makers, scientists and others use a strategy to "try a lot of things." Only a few of them will be winners, and that's all that success requires. So top economists or journalists may write 200 articles in a career, and only 10 of them are cited in the Nobel Prize, in the case of science.

In the "performance game," which airline or fast-food services play, you will mostly be judged by percentages or ratios—such as performance metrics about on-time arrivals. So you do not want to introduce too many variables here, and you emphasize consistency by keeping things simple and highly programmed, as McDonald's does so well.

Brain surgeons and nuclear power plants play the "loss avoidance game." They build in redundancies or strive for perfection in technique because the aim is to avoid a catastrophe.

These different environments require different leadership styles, and they each have very different capacities to tolerate and bounce back after a big mistake. In business, as well as in life, you need to know what game you are playing.

In the preface to *Brilliant Mistakes*, you observe, "For most people, the problem is not that they make too many mistakes but too few." Why is that a problem today, given that profit margins are often razor thin and change is a constant?

If that is your business environment, you should try to get out of it because it is mostly a red ocean; that is, a place where many competitors imitate each other and compete on the same basis. The promise of mistakes is that they get you out of this trap and create blue oceans, those new market spaces where there is unmet demand.

The caveat to that statement is you have to do it very strategically. Most people are risk averse, which means they don't explore as widely around their assumptions, or their mental models, as they should. Organizations exacerbate this because they reward people for results most of the time, and not so often on good intentions or good process. If your intention is to change a business model or if you're in a new environment, I think you should have more tolerance for mistakes than is typically the case in companies. Experimentation and mistakes will add up to success and brilliance, if you are strategic and willing to take some risks.

How can I start using my mistakes better to head toward success?

Think about which mistakes have taught you the most and least in your life. Assess the cost-benefit ratio of each and then try to make more of the favorable ones. These are the ones where the cost of experimentation is low and the rewards potentially enormous.

Once you start to test and challenge commonly held assumptions, take time to make midstream adjustments based on feedback, and try to turn early mistakes into stepping stones toward eventual success. In business, create an ecosystem of customers, employees, peers and friends who help manage the winding road of innovation through mistakes.

It is unfortunate that the terms "mistake" or "failure" have such negative connotations in common parlance. Better terms would include tests, experiments, or pilots. Or as a comedian once suggested, why don't we call failure "time released success"? They key is to make hay when things go haywire, while realizing that discovery can only occur when mistakes are allowed to happen. And to see setbacks and silver linings as an essential part of the journey.

NOTES

Chapter 1

1. "AccelFoods Alumnus, Exo, Secures $1.2 Million in Next Round of Financing," news release, AccelFoods, Sept. 25, 2014, http://tinyurl.com/oj6jnka.
2. David Bornstein and Susan Davis, *Social Entrepreneurship: What Everyone Needs to Know*, 2010, p. 1.
3. "The Deloitte Millennial Survey 2015: Mind the Gaps," Deloitte, 2015, http://tinyurl.com/myg2a6d.
4. Ian C. MacMillan and James D. Thompson, *The Social Entrepreneur's Playbook: Pressure Test, Plan, Launch and Scale Your Social Enterprise*, 2013, p. 157.
5. "Triple bottom line," The Economist, Nov. 17, 2009, http://tinyurl.com/3h7jbmx.
6. "Adrian Grenier and James Corden crown winners of The Venture receiving share of $1 million fund," news release, Chivas Regal, July 27, 2015, http://tinyurl.com/qzgx29z.
7. Samantha Sharf, "$1 Million Change The World Competition Goes to SIRUM For Recycling Unused Meds," Forbes, Oct. 6, 2015, http://tinyurl.com/pagztqd.
8. "Forbes Announces Finalists For $1 Million Under 30 Change The World Social Entrepreneurs Competition," news release, Forbes, Sept. 21, 2015, http://tinyurl.com/q29b9mq.
9. David Bornstein, *How to Change the World: Social Entrepreneurs and the Power of New Ideas*, 2007, preface, p. x.
10. Nick O'Donohoe, Christina Leijonhufvud and Yasemin Saltuk, "Impact Investments: An Emerging Asset Class," JPMorgan, Nov. 29, 2010, p. 6, http://tinyurl.com/mcn3eww.
11. Olivier Kayser and Valeria Budinich, *Scaling Up: Business Solutions to Social Problems*, 2015, pp. 1–2.
12. Issie Lapowsky, "The Social Entrepreneurship Spectrum: Non-profits With Earned Income," *Inc.*, May 2011, http://tinyurl.com/3jgjomv.
13. Rich Leimsider, "Five Bad Reasons to Start a For-Profit Social Enterprise," July 30, 2014, *Harvard Business Review*, http://tinyurl.com/oq39vbh.
14. Ibid.
15. Robin D. Schatz, "How Sustainable Seafood Pioneer EcoFish Avoids 'Mission Drift,' " Forbes.com, Nov. 8, 2015, http://tinyurl.com/pwzcxv3.
16. Ibid.
17. Julie Battilana et al., "In Search of the Hybrid Ideal," *Stanford Social Innovation Review*, Summer 2012, http://tinyurl.com/qeejqqs.
18. Ibid.
19. Bornstein, "How to Change the World," op. cit., p. 3.
20. Ibid.
21. Ibid.
22. Ibid.
23. Ibid, p. 12.
24. Ashoka website, undated, accessed Oct. 27, 2015, http://tinyurl.com/pmw3rue.
25. "About us," Ashoka website, undated, accessed Oct. 27, 2015, http://tinyurl.com/pz6k3gx.
26. Bornstein and Davis, op. cit., p. 13.
27. Grameen Bank website, updated Oct. 29, 2014, http://tinyurl.com/org7eq7.
28. "Muhammad Yunus—Biographical," The Nobel Prizes 2006, http://tinyurl.com/8x5obca.
29. Muhammad Yunus, *Creating a World Without Poverty: Social Business and the Future of Capitalism*, 2009, p. 18.
30. "Forced Out," Newsbook, *The Economist*, April 5, 2011, http://tinyurl.com/7lr2aav.
31. "A Letter Addressed to Grameen Bank Members from Nobel Laureate Professor Muhammad Yunus on the Occasion of his departure from Grameen Bank," May 15, 2011, http://tinyurl.com/4yv4cbq.
32. Yunus Social Business website, undated, accessed Nov. 13, 2015, http://tinyurl.com/qc4pptx.
33. Antony Page and Robert A. Katz, "The Truth About Ben & Jerry's," *Stanford Social Innovation Review*, Fall 2012, http://tinyurl.com/ncp7x4z.
34. Ibid.
35. Ibid.
36. Cheryl Kiser, Deborah Leipziger and J. Janelle Shubert, *Creating Social Value: A Guide for Leaders and Change Makers*, 2014, chp. 5.
37. Paula Caligiuri, "When Unilever bought Ben & Jerry's: A Story of CEO Adaptability," *Fast Company*, Aug. 14, 2012, http://tinyurl.com/8jwmv9g.
38. Constance L. Hays, "Ben & Jerry's to Unilever, With Attitude," *The New York Times*, April 13, 2000, http://tinyurl.com/2a75qwj.
39. Page and Katz, op. cit.
40. Ibid.
41. Marc J. Lane, "The Mission-Driven Venture," 2015, pp. 46–48.
42. "State by State Status of Legislation," Benefit Corporation, undated, accessed Nov. 13, 2015, http://tinyurl.com/qz8p5ng.
43. Yancey Strickler, Perry Chen and Charles Adler, "Kickstarter is now a Benefit Corporation," Kickstarter blog, Sept. 21, 2015, http://tinyurl.com/qd8gr69.

44. Doug Bend and Alex King, "Why Consider a Benefit Corporation?" Forbes.com blog, March 30, 2014, http://tinyurl.com/od22g4k.

45. Ibid.

46. Lane, op. cit., p. 56.

47. InterSector Partners website, updated Nov. 1, 2015, http://tinyurl.com/l8ml9wv.

48. Anne Field, "North Carolina Officially Abolishes The L3C," Forbes.com blog, Jan. 11, 2014, http://tinyurl.com/kfocvhb.

49. Battilana et al., op. cit.

50. Isaac and Gelles, op. cit.

51. B Corporation website, undated, accessed Oct. 27, 2015, http://tinyurl.com/ooukf8x.

52. Ibid.

53. "Natura," B Corporation, undated, accessed Nov. 13, 2015, http://tinyurl.com/q7vmh3f.

54. "Better World Books," B Corporation, undated, accessed Oct. 27, 2015, http://tinyurl.com/pmeg3gp.

55. Yasemin Saltuk et al., "The Impact Investor Survey," JPMorgan Chase, Global Impact Investing, 2015, p. 23, http://tinyurl.com/orfvzdp.

56. Greg Dees, "The Meaning of Social Entrepreneurship," Kauffman Foundation and Stanford University, revised May 30, 2001, http://tinyurl.com/pbtx6lt.

Chapter 2

1. "Mission and Vision," CARE, undated, accessed Sept. 26, 2015, http://tinyurl.com/ozb3ddn.

2. Rasika Welankiwar, "CARE CEO Helene Gayle on shaking up a venerable organization," *Harvard Business Review*, April 2009, http://tinyurl.com/nlcbu62.

3. "A new CEO for McKinsey Social Initiative," news release, McKinsey & Co., March 19, 2015, http://tinyurl.com/njgxs5e.

4. Paul Clolery, "Stats Show Huge Jump In Tax-Exempt Orgs, Applications," *The NonProfit Times*, March 24, 2015, http://tinyurl.com/qdhtclj.

5. "Public Charities," Internal Revenue Service, updated Jan. 8, 2015, http://tinyurl.com/ntvr8d6.

6. "Requirements for Exemption," Internal Revenue Service, updated April 23, 2015, http://tinyurl.com/ousc2bu.

7. "Frequently Asked Questions," National Center for Charitable Statistics, undated, accessed Oct.10, 2015, http://tinyurl.com/p72furv.

8. "Quick Facts about Nonprofits," National Center for Charitable Statistics, undated, accessed Sept. 25, 2015, http://tinyurl.com/2csfmhm.

9. "Nonprofits account for 11.4 million jobs, 10.3 percent of all private sector employment," Bureau of Labor Statistics, Oct. 21, 2014, http://tinyurl.com/kaupsoh.

10. Ibid.; "Announcing new research data on jobs and pay in the nonprofit sector," Bureau of Labor Statistics, Oct. 17, 2014, http://tinyurl.com/ogteh5w.

11. Kurumi Fukushima, "These 9 Nonprofit Executives Made Over $1-Million," The Street, Sept. 15, 2014, http://tinyurl.com/qjk8t8r.

12. Peter F. Drucker, *Managing the Non-Profit Organization: Principles and Practices*, 1990, Kindle edition, location 92.

13. Peter Murray and Steve Ma, "The Promise of Lean Experimentation," *Stanford Social Innovation Review*, Summer 2015, http://tinyurl.com/npchllz.

14. Antony Bugg-Levine and Jed Emerson, *Impact Investing*, 2011, p. x.

15. Abby Young-Powell, "Charity donations and donors decrease, says survey," *The Guardian*, Nov. 14, 2012, http://tinyurl.com/poqe3ve.

16. Michael M. Weinstein, "Measuring Success: How Robin Hood Estimates the Impact of Grants," Feb. 27, 2009, Robin Hood Foundation, http://tinyurl.com/nzdtupv.

17. "Pay for Success Learning Hub," Nonprofit Finance Fund, undated, accessed Oct. 13, 2015, http://tinyurl.com/pfmmtg8.

18. Michael J. Casey, "Profits Meet Philanthropy in 'Pay for Success' Investments—Horizons," Moneybeat, *The Wall Street Journal*, June 29, 2015, http://tinyurl.com/ozbbk7e.

19. Ibid.

20. "Results Released for Rikers Island Pay for Success Social Impact Bond," Nonprofit Finance Fund, undated, accessed Sept. 25, 2015, http://tinyurl.com/ofyjprq.

21. "How to Research a Nonprofit's Financial Strength—Deep Dive Approach," The Bridgespan Group, undated, accessed Sept. 14, 2015, http://tinyurl.com/pm7eevo.

22. "Cancer Charities Announce Merger Deal," *The NonProfit Times*, June 11, 2015, http://tinyurl.com/nvhqn5c.

23. Ibid.

24. Nicholas Kristof, "Bill and Melinda Gates's Pillow Talk," *The New York Times*, July 18, 2015, http://tinyurl.com/ozqqb4k.

25. Bill and Melinda Gates, "Why giving our wealth away has been the most satisfying thing we've done," TED Talk, posted April 2014, http://tinyurl.com/q9h8oh4.

26. Tris Lumley, "Raising the Bar on Nonprofit Impact Measurement," *Stanford Social Innovation Review*, July 10, 2013, http://tinyurl.com/pq6blb5.

27. Michael E. Porter and Mark R. Kramer, "Philanthropy's New Agenda: Creating Value," *Harvard Business Review*, November-December 1999, http://tinyurl.com/ncawvtw.

28. Jeri Eckhart-Queenan and Matthew Forti, "Case Study: Ten Thousand Strong," *Business Strategy Review*, June 1, 2011, http://tinyurl.com/nwrln29.

29. "Country Detail," One Acre Fund, undated, accessed Oct. 10, 2015, http://tinyurl.com/qdyovuc.

30. Lilly Family School of Philanthropy website, undated, accessed Oct. 10, 2015, http://tinyurl.com/qecdl3g.

31. Roseanne M. Mirabella, "Nonprofit Management Education; Current Offerings in University-Based Programs," Seton Hall University, undated, accessed Oct. 14, 2015, http://tinyurl.com/p7chuex.

32. "Fundraising Management Master of Science," Columbia University course catalog, undated, accessed Sept. 26, 2015, http://tinyurl.com/ogdlyhd.

33. "Learning for Social Impact: What Foundations Can Do," McKinsey & Co., April 2010, http://tinyurl.com/or65deg.

34. "Our Mission," Robin Hood Foundation, undated, accessed Sept. 26, 2015 http://tinyurl.com/plyzhbc.

35. Weinstein, op. cit., p. 6.

36. Ibid., pp. 84–90.

37. Jeff Brooks, "Questions I'm Most Often Asked about Direct Mail Fundraising," GuideStar, January 2014, http://tinyurl.com/qjbgr7v.

38. Amy Gahran, "Donating to charity by text message: Lessons from Haiti," CNN, Jan. 12, 2012, http://tinyurl.com/onplfwt.

39. Suzanne Vranica, "ALS Association Plots Return of Ice Bucket Challenge," *The Wall Street Journal*, July 1, 2015, http://tinyurl.com/osh5xn8.

40. "Exponential Fundraising," Foundation Center interview with Jennifer McCrea, 3:30 mark, April 4, 2012, http://tinyurl.com/omoytar.

41. "2014 U.S. Trust Study of High Net Worth Philanthropy Finds 28 Percent Increase in Charitable Contributions; Donors Forecast Positive Giving Trends for the Coming Years," news release, Bank of America, Oct. 21, 2014, http://tinyurl.com/njol8ph; "The 2014 U.S. Trust Study of High New Worth Philanthropy," U.S. Trust and the Lilly Family School of Philanthropy," October 2014, http://tinyurl.com/pgxuvkx.

42. "Charitable Giving Statistics," National Philanthropic Trust, undated, accessed Sept. 26, 2015, http://tinyurl.com/cszmc6b.

43. "The Story of Team Rubicon," Team Rubicon, undated, accessed Sept. 26, 2015, http://tinyurl.com/o7fyyo6.

44. "The Razoo Difference," Razoo, undated, accessed Oct. 10, 2015, http://tinyurl.com/of9sdoo.

45. "With FirstGiving Nonprofit Donation Software You Can Do More," FirstGiving, undated, accessed Oct. 10, 2015, http://tinyurl.com/py67xv3.

46. Marc Koenig, "5 Online Donation Tools to Delight Your Donors," Nonprofit Hub, undated, accessed Oct. 9, 2015, http://tinyurl.com/o8twdvx.

47. Charity: Water website, undated, accessed Sept. 26, 2015, http://tinyurl.com/5cqh3v.

48. "See what great teachers need for their students," Donors Choose.org, undated, accessed Sept. 26, 2015, http://tinyurl.com/j9mvk.

49. Alexis de Tocqueville, *Democracy in America*, via University of Virginia American Studies Program, 1835, Book II, Chapter V, http://tinyurl.com/m766cv.

50. "Philanthropy Hall of Fame," Philanthropy Roundtable, undated, accessed Sept. 11, 2015, http://tinyurl.com/o8hnzwf.

51. Lawrence W. Reed, "Government Should Not Support the People," Mackinac Center for Public Policy, April 8, 2005, http://tinyurl.com/np85k8g.

52. Karl Zinsmeister, "Julius Rosenwald," Philanthropy Round-table, undated, accessed Sept. 11, 2015, http://tinyurl.com/ps66yof.

53. Tim Kelley, "Landmark Nomination Carnegie Branch Libraries of San Francisco," Carnegie Branch Libraries of San Francisco, January 2001, http://tinyurl.com/ppzw5wx.

54. *Theodore Roosevelt: An Autobiography*, 1913, pp. 466–467, http://tinyurl.com/o9g5dug.

55. "Stamping Out Tuberculosis with Christmas Seals: Emily Bissell of the American Red Cross Begins Selling Christmas Seals," University of Virginia Historical Collections at the Claude Moore Health Sciences Library, undated, accessed Sept. 26, 2015, http://tinyurl.com/p7p3bao.

56. War Revenue Act, Public Law No. 65–50, Ch. 63, section 1201(2), 1917.

57. Martin Morse Wooster, "The Birth of Big Time Fundraising," Philanthropy Roundtable, undated, accessed Sept. 26, 2015, http://tinyurl.com/oqfavr4.

58. Nili Tannenbaum and Michael Reisch, "From Charitable Volunteers to Architects of Social Welfare: A Brief History of Social Work," University of Michigan School of Social Work, Fall 2001, http://tinyurl.com/qhhspae.

59. "Overview," Ford Foundation, undated, accessed Sept. 11, 2015, http://tinyurl.com/lzyk7mj.

60. Olivier Zunz, *Philanthropy in America: A History*, 2012, p. 139.

61. Gunnar Jahn, "The Nobel Peace Prize 1947: Award Ceremony Speech," Dec. 10, 1947, http://tinyurl.com/nkxfoqt.

62. Zunz, op. cit., p. 177; "United Way Celebrates the 50th Anniversary of the Torch Drive in Metropolitan Detroit," news release, United Way, Aug. 18, 1998, http://tinyurl.com/nwslwbm.

63. William P. Barrett, "The Largest U.S. Charities For 2014," *Forbes*, Dec. 10, 2014, http://tinyurl.com/qb66ruv.

64. Steven Alan Samson, "Charity for All: B. Carroll Reece and the Tax-Exempt Foundations," Liberty University, Dec. 14, 1980, http://tinyurl.com/oax2ngu.

65. Zunz, op. cit., p. 176.

66. Lyndon B. Johnson, "Annual Message to the Congress on the State of the Union," Jan. 4, 1965, http://tinyurl.com/qjmuymh.

67. Austin Nichols, "What happened to LBJ's Great Society?" Urban Institute, May 7, 2014, http://tinyurl.com/oxxv4ht.

68. Adam Meyerson, "When Philanthropy Goes Wrong," *The Wall Street Journal*, March 9, 2012, http://tinyurl.com/nbzndtk.

69. T. Rees Shapiro, "United Way leader's fraud scandal marred charitable legacy," *The Washington Post*, Nov. 14, 2011, http://tinyurl.com/pz2yefu.

70. "Foundation for New Era Philanthropy," FBI, undated, accessed Sept. 26, 2015, http://tinyurl.com/pesclbq.

71. Robert O. Bothwell, "Trends In Self-Regulation And Transparency Of Nonprofits In The U.S.," *The International Journal of Not-for-Profit Law*, March 2000, http://tinyurl.com/pe45thb.

72. Kelly Phillips Erb, "UPDATED: Timeline of IRS Tax Exempt Organization Scandal," *Forbes*, March 2, 2015, http://tinyurl.com/pkc6dgd.

73. "Ex-FIFA chief Chuck Blazer among 4 to plead guilty in $100m corruption case," The Associated Press, ESPN FC, May 27, 2015, http://tinyurl.com/n9zet39.

74. Joshua Robinson, "FIFA's Ethics Committee Seeks More Transparency," *The Wall Street Journal*, July 16, 2015, http://tinyurl.com/nssvbc4.

75. Mark Hrywna, "Triple Crown Winnings Will Fund Charities," *The NonProfit Times*, June 9, 2015, http://tinyurl.com/oromppm.

76. Danielle Curtis, "Good News for Giving: Record High Numbers in Giving USA's 2015 Report," *The Philanthropist*, June 16, 2015, http://tinyurl.com/oyo4pj8.

77. David Bivin et al., "The Philanthropy Outlook: 2015 & 2016," Marts & Lundy, February 2015, http://tinyurl.com/p9wc8f4.

78. "What We Do," Bill & Melinda Gates Foundation, undated, accessed Sept. 26, 2015, http://tinyurl.com/pdcejf7; Gates Foundation 2013 Form 990, via GuideStar, accessed Oct. 18, 2015, http://tinyurl.com/pjwafy3.

79. Jon Swartz, "Zuckerberg pushes Internet for everyone in U.N. speech," *USA Today*, Sept. 28, 2015, http://tinyurl.com/q8yql6h.

80. Alex Morell, "Warren Buffett Unleashes Another $2.8 Billion Donation," *Forbes*, July 6, 2015, http://tinyurl.com/q3ws4ue.

81. The Giving Pledge website, undated, accessed Sept. 26, 2015, http://tinyurl.com/28dhguu.

82. Lydia DePillis, "Inside the battle to overhaul overtime—and what it says about how lobbying has changed," *The Washington Post*, Sept. 4, 2015, http://tinyurl.com/pwv7jnw.

83. Rick Cohen, "The Debate over Reforming Overtime Regulations," *Nonprofit Quarterly*, July 29, 2015, http://tinyurl.com/qyyftq7.

84. Sean Parker, "Philanthropy for Hackers," *The Wall Street Journal*, June 26, 2015, http://tinyurl.com/o7q5psb.

85. Ibid.

86. GiveDirectly website, undated, accessed Sept. 14, 2015, http://tinyurl.com/plfx9ug.

87. "WestJet Christmas Miracle: real-time giving," Dec. 8, 2013, http://tinyurl.com/ngeh8qc.

88. Linsey McGoey, "Doing good and doing well," *The Spectator*, Nov. 12, 2008, http://tinyurl.com/ojfcp55.

89. Gail Perry, "Top10 Major Gift Fundraising Trends for 2014–2015," Fired Up Fundraising, undated, accessed Sept. 26, 2015, http://tinyurl.com/or4gav2.

90. Melissa McGlensey, "64% Of Donations Are Made By Women . . . And Other Facts About How We Give (INFOGRAPHIC)," *The Huffington Post*, April 29, 2014, http://tinyurl.com/l58jaq9.

91. Amy Schiller, "Is For-Profit the Future of Non-Profit?" *The Atlantic*, May 21, 2014, http://tinyurl.com/oj84luo.

92. Ibid.

93. John J. Havens and Paul G. Schervish, "A Golden Age of Philanthropy Still Beckons: National Wealth Transfer and Potential for Philanthropy Technical Report," Center on Wealth and Philanthropy, Boston College, May 28, 2014, p. 5, http://tinyurl.com/o7l5kbh.

Chapter 3

1. Brendan Lyons, "Dredging up the truth: The GE PCB files," [Albany, N.Y.] *Times-Union*, March 8, 2014, http://tinyurl.com/lxv3kha; "Hudson River PCBs Superfund Site," U.S. Environmental Protection Agency, Oct. 30, 2014, http://tinyurl.com/yttb3r.

2. "Fact Sheet," General Electric (GE), http://tinyurl.com/mm5fvat.

3. "Ecomagination," GE, http://tinyurl.com/l45l9lv; also see http://tinyurl.com/lfxhf2w.

4. Jeffrey R. Immelt, "A Letter from the CEO," GE, undated, accessed Jan. 22, 2015, http://tinyurl.com/knmmmaf.

5. David Kiron, et al., "Sustainability's Next Frontier," MIT *Sloan Management Review*, Dec. 16, 2013, http://tinyurl.com/lxxtfro.

6. Jo Confino, "Best practices in sustainability, Ford, Starbucks and more," *The Guardian* (U.K.), April 30, 2014, http://tinyurl.com/kjewham.

7. "Emerge, splurge, purge," *The Economist*, March 8, 2014, http://tinyurl.com/kzh8a6d.

8. "Cox Conserves Survey – A Study of Sustainable Solutions for SMB's [Infographic]," BLUE, Oct. 7, 2014, http://tinyurl.com/oozn5y7

9. "US Sustainable, Responsible and Impact: Investing Assets Grow 76 Percent In Two Years," U.S. Social Investment Forum, Nov. 20, 2014, http://tinyurl.com/mj9p7rp.

10. "Climate Change 2014, Fifth Assessment Report," Intergovernmental Panel on Climate Change, 2014, http://tinyurl.com/3e3zv.

11. "World Footprint: Do we fit the planet?" Global Footprint Network, accessed on Feb. 4, 2015, http://tinyurl.com/c8ga5p.

12. Stuart L. Hart, *Capitalism at the Crossroads: Next Generation Business Strategies for a Post-Crisis World*, 3rd ed., 2010; Timothy F. Slaper and Tanya Hall, "The Triple Bottom Line: What Is It and How Does It Work?" *Indiana Business Review*, 2011, http://tinyurl.com/7xt958c.

13. "The Triple Bottom Line," *The Economist*, Nov. 17, 2009, http://tinyurl.com/3h7jbmx.

14. "Climate Change, Overview of Greenhouse Gases," U.S. Environmental Protection Agency, updated July 2, 2014, http://tinyurl.com/cwneb4u.

15. "Fortune 500 Partners List," U.S. Environmental Protection Agency, Jan. 26, 2015, http://tinyurl.com/dbrmv2.

16. "Questions and answers about The WaterSense Program," U.S. Environmental Protection Agency, December 2014, http://tinyurl.com/m7ljak3.

17. "Fox Business Interviews China Gorman," Great Place to Work/Fox Business, undated, http://tinyurl.com/kk3wavz.

18. Ibid.

19. Steven Greenhouse, "On Black Friday, Walmart Is Pressed for Wage Increases," *The New York Times*, Nov. 28, 2014, http://tinyurl.com/mhl5gxl; Nilima Choudhury, "Walmart accused of 'greenwashing' over clean energy claims," RTCC, Nov. 18, 2013, http://tinyurl.com/ntjavhl.

20. "What are B Corps?" B Corps, undated, http://tinyurl.com/kfjdtc8.

21. Also see Robert Eccles, et al., "How to Become a Sustainable Company," MIT *Sloan Management Review*, Summer 2012, http://tinyurl.com/mknrw64; Jessica Cheam, "Sustainability needs to be in a company's DNA: interview with Martin Blake," Eco-Business, Aug. 28, 2013, http://tinyurl.com/qyrt7a2.

22. Paul Polman, "Business, society, and the future of capitalism," Insights & Publications, McKinsey Quarterly, May 2014, http://tinyurl.com/nwm8eye.

23. John Willis and Paul Spence, "The Risks and Returns of Fossil Fuel Free Investing," undated, Sustainable Insight Capital Management, http://tinyurl.com/jwtl3ge.

24. Tom Randall, "Saints Beat Sinners for Sustainable Investing: Stock Chart," Bloomberg, Feb. 17, 2012, http://tinyurl.com/7nmmxa8.

25. "Climate action and profitability," CDP, 2014, http://tinyurl.com/mqhkzul.

26. Lei Liao and Jim Campagna, "Socially Responsible Investing: Delivering Competitive Performance," TIAA-CREF, September 2014, http://tinyurl.com/oshb8b3.

27. Joel Makower, "Why sustainability leaders don't impress Wall Street," Greenbiz.com, Aug. 4, 2014, http://tinyurl.com/pvtsxpx; Sheila Bonini and Steven Schwartz, "Profits with Purpose: How organizing for sustainability can benefit the bottom line," McKinsey, 2014, http://tinyurl.com/lnkfl3v.

28. Sanya Carley, et al., "Success Paths to Sustainable Manufacturing," October 2014, School of Public and Environmental Affairs, Indiana University, http://tinyurl.com/oeotxet.

29. Doug Park, "Securities Law, Not Semantics," Sustainability Accounting Standards Board (blog), Nov. 17, 2014, http://tinyurl.com/mf8yczq.

30. "The UN Global Compact-Accenture CEO Study on Sustainability 2013," September 2013, Accenture, 2013, http://tinyurl.com/nvnte9p.

31. Kiron, et al., op. cit.

32. "The UN Global Compact-Accenture CEO Study on Sustainability 2013," op. cit.

33. David Herbling, "Safaricom opens talks with Vodafone on M-Pesa license fees," *Business Daily*, Aug. 18, 2014, http://tinyurl.com/qdpbdp5.

34. "The UN Global Compact-Accenture CEO Study on Sustainability 2013," op. cit

35. "Winning the $30 Trillion Decathalon: How to Succeed in Emerging Markets," McKinsey & Company, October 2012, http://tinyurl.com/oqhfr2n.

36. Arindam Bhattacharya, et al., "Competing for Advantage: How to Succeed in the New Global Reality," Boston Consulting Group, January 2010, http://tinyurl.com/msox9pq.

37. "Fit for the future: Capitalising on global trends," PricewaterhouseCoopers, 2014, http://tinyurl.com/mzg6mlj.

38. "Health & Hygiene," Unilever, undated, http://tinyurl.com/kjmd7nu.

39. John Maxwell, "Beyond the BRICS: How to succeed in emerging markets (by really trying)," PricewaterhouseCoopers, http://tinyurl.com/omx9x4b.

40. "Republican Platform," GOP.com, undated, http://tinyurl.com/lltq2l2.

41. Paul Polman, "Business, Society and the Future of Capitalism," McKinsey Quarterly, May 2014, http://tinyurl.com/nwm8eye.

42. Michael E. Porter, et al., "Strategy & Society: The Link between Competitive Advantage and Corporate Social Responsibility," *Harvard Business Review*, December 2006, http://tinyurl.com/pe5ha5q.

43. Ibid.

44. "Dow Chemical Company Foundation: Grants for Science Education," Inside Philanthropy, accessed Feb. 4, 2015, http://tinyurl.com/myem67e.

45. "Our Community Impact," Target Corporate Responsibility, accessed Feb. 4, 2015, http://tinyurl.com/mb36358 .

46. Dave Sorter, "Ford's supplier diversity development program celebrates 35th anniversary," Minority Business News, MBN USA, vol. 3, 2013, http://tinyurl.com/m8ujhmx.

47. Kasturi Rangan, Lisa Chase and Sohel Karim, "The Truth About CSR," *Harvard Business Review*, January 2015, http://tinyurl.com/nw4m9nl.

48. Ibid.

49. James Surowiecki, "Companies With Benefits," *The New Yorker*, Aug. 4, 2014, http://tinyurl.com/pst6txl; Melanie Colburn, "Making 'benefit corporations' more than just academic," Greenbiz.com, May 2, 2012, http://tinyurl.com/qx2leta.

50. Eliza Griswold, "How Silent Spring Ignited the Environmental Movement," *The New York Times*, Sept. 21, 2012, http://tinyurl.com/pay87b8.

51. Jack Lewis, "The Birth of the EPA," U.S. Environmental Protection Agency Journal, November 1985, http://tinyurl.com/p3lqqwy. Ibid.

52. Larry Cao, "The Price of Growth: Toxic Smog in China and Elsewhere," CFA Institute, April 7, 2014, http://tinyurl.com/pusuzy2.

53. "What Causes Acid Rain?" U.S. Environment Protection Agency, http://tinyurl.com/ybhh27l.

54. "The Birth of the EPA," op. cit.

55. Ibid.

56. Ibid.; Stuart L. Hart, *Capitalism at the Crossroads: The Unlimited Business Opportunities in Solving the World's Most Difficult Problems*, 2005.

57. Hart, "Capitalism at the Crossroads: Next Generation Business Strategies," op. cit.; Timothy F. Slaper and Tanya Hall, "The Triple Bottom Line: What Is It and How Does It Work?" *Indiana Business Review*, 2011, http://tinyurl.com/7xt958c.

58. "Report of the World Commission on Environment and Development: Our Common Future," United Nations, March 20, 1987, http://tinyurl.com/mtpt4pu.

59. Ibid.

60. Hart, "Capitalism at the Crossroads: Next Generation Business Strategies," op. cit., p. 27.

61. "History of Quality," Business Performance Improvement Resource, http://tinyurl.com/d8tdsxr; "Total Quality Management," *Inc.*, http://tinyurl.com/mmtoazp; and "History," Columbia Business School, The W. Edwards Deming Center for Quality, Productivity and Competitiveness, undated, http://tinyurl.com/oqlgv79.

62. Hart, "Capitalism at the Crossroads: Next Generation Business Strategies," op. cit., pp. 24–26; Shelly F. Fust and Lisa L. Walker, "Corporate Sustainability Initiatives: The Next TQM?" Korn Ferry Institute, 2007, http://tinyurl.com/mljle7u.

63. "1984: Hundreds Die in Bhopal Chemical Accident," BBC News, undated, http://tinyurl.com/6a499; Sanjoy Hazarika, "Gas Leak in India Kills at least 410 in City of Bhopal," *The New York Times*, Dec. 4, 1984, http://tinyurl.com/o62tnyh.

64. "Toxics Release Inventory (TRI) Program," U.S. Environmental Protection Agency, updated Jan. 28, 2015, http://tinyurl.com/pcfmenp.

65. Hart, "Capitalism at the Crossroads: Next Generation Business Strategies," op. cit., p. 27.

66. Ibid.

67. Magali A. Delmas, "Barriers and Incentive to the Adoption of ISO 14001 by Firms in the United States," *Duke Environmental Law & Policy Forum*, Fall 2000, http://tinyurl.com/mscq383.

68. Ibid.

69. "What Is GRI?" Global Reporting Initiative, http://tinyurl.com/7oeu2dg.

70. "William McDonough: Cradle to Cradle Design," TED Talks (YouTube), May 17, 2007, http://tinyurl.com/kfkv529; Oliver Balch, "C-suite interview: Rob Boogaard, Interface – Red carpet corporate sustainability," Ethical Corp., May 8, 2014, http://tinyurl.com/mrnfbhj; and Hanh Nguyen, et al., "Remaking the Industrial Economy," McKinsey Quarterly, February 2014, http://tinyurl.com/ly8kvwr.

71. "Our Story: Post-Consumer Carpet Recycling," Shaw Floors, http://tinyurl.com/lnnd9lo.

72. Jennifer Kesik, "Ethics of Sweatshops: Managing Global Labor Standards in the Sporting Goods Industry," Dec. 1. 2013, http://tinyurl.com/mkjnhwy; John Braddock, "Nike faces allegations of worker abuse in Indonesia," World Socialist Web Site, Sept. 8, 2011, http://tinyurl.com/m9vanpe; David Teather, "Nike lists abuses at Asian factories," *The Guardian*, April 14, 2005, http://tinyurl.com/kbjsrm7.

73. Max Nisen, "How Nike Solved Its Sweatshop Problem," Business Insider, May 9, 2013, http://tinyurl.com/cydqacl; James Epstein-Reeves, "The Parents of CSR: Nike and Kathie-Lee Gifford," *Forbes*, June 8, 2010, http://tinyurl.com/cpu97f4.

74. Peter Lacy, et al., "A New Era of Sustainability UN Global Compact-Accenture CEO Study 2010," Accenture, June 2010, http://tinyurl.com/pmyhgwl.

75. "The 17th Annual Global CEO Survey, Fit for the future Capitalising on global trends," PricwaterhouseCoopers, Jan. 20, 2015, p. 35 http://tinyurl.com/puwsxqp.

76. "Integrated reporting," Ernst & Young, June 30, 2013, http://tinyurl.com/kufm726.

77. Ibid.; David Kiron, "Get Ready: Mandated Integrated Reporting Is The Future of Corporate Reporting," MIT *Sloan Management Review*, March, 13, 2012, http://tinyurl.com/kclbmwx.

78. "GRI & SASB: An Understanding of Alignment," Brown-Flynn, May 21, 2014, http://tinyurl.com/kzj33fo.

79. "Integrated reporting," op. cit.; Dunstan Allison-Hope and Guy Morgan, "Navigating the Materiality Muddle," Business for Social Responsibility (BSR) Insight, Aug. 13, 2013, http://tinyurl.com/m88e8ga.

80. Rena Dietrich, "The Role of FASB to Business," *The Houston Chronicle*, undated, http://tinyurl.com/lkaekxh.

81. "The Hershey Company Joins Sustainability Accounting Standards Board (SASB) Advisory Council," Business Wire, Dec. 4, 2012, http://tinyurl.com/ks6gw97.

82. "2013 six growing trends in corporate sustainability," Ernst & Young and Greenbiz Survey, 2013, http://tinyurl.com/o6u87u3.

83. Paul Polman, "Paul Polman: The remedies for capitalism," op. cit.

84. "GM, Honda to collaborate on the next-generation fuel cell technologies; targeting commercial feasibility in 2020 time frame," Green Car Congress, July 2, 2013, http://tinyurl.com/mfctm75.

85. Justin Gerdes, "Shared shipping is slowly gaining ground between market rivals," *The Guardian*, Aug. 11, 2014, http://tinyurl.com/q5ubb2l.

86. Karel Beckman, "Perspectives on Obama's clean power plan: small step for US, big step for mankind?" Energy Post, June 11, 2014, http://tinyurl.com/lpz2l96.

87. "FACT SHEET: Administration Takes Steps Forward on Climate Action Plan by Announcing Actions to Cut Methane Emissions," White House, Jan. 14, 2015, http://tinyurl.com/kbpnwf8.

88. Ben Wolfgang, "Obama targets oil and gas industry, demands massive reduction in methane emissions," Jan. 14, 2015, *The Washington Times*, http://tinyurl.com/k8lnt8p.

89. Denise Robbins, "Myths And Facts About The Koch Brothers," Media Matters for America, Aug. 27, 2014, http://tinyurl.com/kxkwltg.

90. Michael B. Gerrard, "Obama's New Emission Rules: Will They Survive Challenges?" *Yale Environment* 360, June 16, 2014, http://tinyurl.com/p9jmewp.

91. Jennifer Kho, "Report: More Corporations Turn To Sustainability For Competitive Edge and Profits," *Forbes*, Jan. 24, 2012, http://tinyurl.com/7na4vkt.

92. Karen E. Klein, "How to Keep Millennials from Getting Bored and Leaving," Bloomberg, Aug. 22, 2014, http://tinyurl.com/pqbcrdo; Steve Cody, "Five Tricks for Working with Millennials," *Inc.*, updated April 18, 2013, http://tinyurl.com/al4x3w9; and Julie Honeywell and Brad Pease, "Attract and Retain Millennials with your Green Building," Paladino, undated, http://tinyurl.com/mvzwcro.

93. "What is Business For? The Millennial Survey 2011," Deloitte, January 2012, http://tinyurl.com/myg2a6d.

94. "Millennials Survey, Millennials at work: Reshaping the workplace," PricewaterhouseCoopers, 2015, http://tinyurl.com/yjdt4k8; for background, see Vickie Elmer, "Work-Life Balance," SAGE Business Researcher, Jan. 12, 2015.

95. "10 Leading Sustainability Innovations," *The Guardian*, June 16, 2014, http://tinyurl.com/mcuc2rt.

96. "The UN Global Compact-Accenture CEO Study on Sustainability 2013," op. cit., p. 49; "Computing sustainability," *The Economist*, June 19, 2008, http://tinyurl.com/lbszkoc.

97. Thom Patterson, "Amazing machines poised to fly travelers into a new era," CNN, Nov. 16, 2014, http://tinyurl.com/mp7cn6n.

98. Heather Clancy, "How GE generates $1 billion from data," *Fortune*, Oct. 10, 2014, http://tinyurl.com/kdf9qns.

Chapter 4

1. "Every day in the sharing economy, there are . . . ," Peers, undated, accessed July 15, 2015, http://tinyurl.com/q2czmqn; EllenHuet, "Uber Says It's Doing 1 Million Rides Per Day, 140 Million In Last Year," *Forbes*, Dec. 17, 2014, http://tinyurl.com/pjyhavq.

2. Scott Austin, Chris Canipe and Sarah Slobin, "The Billion Dollar Startup Club," *The Wall Street Journal*, updated July 2015, http://tinyurl.com/pbfqsfk.

3. "FTC ToExamine Competition, Consumer Protection, and Economic Issues Raised by the Sharing Economy at June Workshop," press release, Federal Trade Commission, April 17, 2015, http://tinyurl.com/ombw5u5.

4. "The sharing economy – sizing the revenue opportunity," PricewaterhouseCoopers, undated, accessed July 1, 2015, http://tinyurl.com/oxrhsbm.

5. "Written Testimony of Philip Auerswald," House Committee on Small Business, Jan. 15, 2014, http://tinyurl.com/nhu3o2u.

6. Colleen Walsh, "The big share: HBS historian examines a new kind of connectivity," *Harvard Gazette*, Aug. 5, 2014, http://tinyurl.com/pwon95b.

7. Boyd Cohen and Jan Kietzmann, "Ride On! Mobility Business Models for the Sharing Economy," Organization & Environment, Aug. 13, 2014, http://tinyurl.com/psqaqlp.

8. Walsh, op. cit.

9. Liz Krueger, "Letter to FTC Regarding the 'Sharing Economy,'" May 28, 2015, http://tinyurl.com/pzrn57o.

10. Brian Chesky, "Who We Are, What We Stand For," Airbnb blog, Oct. 3, 2013, http://tinyurl.com/o8sdzx6.

11. Mark John, "UberPOP halts service in France after clampdown, protests," Reuters, July 3, 2015, http://tinyurl.com/p6j4aje.

12. Walsh, op. cit.

13. Eric T. Schneiderman, "Airbnb in the City," New York State Office of the Attorney General,Oct. 14, 2014, http://tinyurl.com/m8pqffb.

14. Annie Karni, "De Blasio administration files first lawsuit against apartments operating as illegal hotels through sites like Airbnb," *New York Daily News*, Oct. 17, 2014,http://tinyurl.com/qguha7n.

15. Mike Isaac and Natasha Singer, "California Says Uber Driver Is Employee, Not a Contractor," *The New York Times*, June 17, 2015, http://tinyurl.com/qzmxqgl.

16. Frank Shafroth, "The Unforeseen Fiscal Challenges of Uber-Like Services," *Government Technology*, March 20, 2015, http://tinyurl.com/pmh3mlj.

17. Benjamin Davis, Tony Dutzik and Phineas Baxandall, "Transportation and the New Generation," U.S. PIRG Education Fund and the Frontier Group, April 2012, http://tinyurl.com/764qecl.

18. Shafroth, op. cit.

19. "Staff memo to the House Committee on Small Business," House of Representatives Committee on Small Business, Jan. 10, 2014, http://tinyurl.com/ovysxfu.

20. Jonathan V. Hall and Alan B. Krueger, "An Analysis of the Labor Market for Uber's Driver-Partners in the United States," Working Paper #587, Princeton University, Jan. 22, 2015, http://tinyurl.com/n5norw8.

21. Sarah Cannon and Lawrence H. Summers, "How Uber and the Sharing Economy CanWin Over Regulators," *Harvard Business Review*, Oct. 13, 2014, http://tinyurl.com/ntpcweq.

22. Cohen, op. cit.

23. Rachel Botsman and Roo Rogers, "What's Mine is Yours: The Rise of Collaborative Consumption," 2010, p. 114.

24. Maya Kosoff, "Uber Drivers Across The Country Are Protesting Today—Here's Why," Business Insider, Oct. 22, 2014, http://tinyurl.com/ojcwaxx.

25. Ibid.

26. Matthew Feeney, "Level the Playing Field—by Deregulating," Cato Unbound, Feb. 10, 2015, http://tinyurl.com/onphurf.

27. Arun Sundararajan, "Peer-to-Peer Businesses and the Sharing (Collaborative) Economy: Overview, Economic Effects and

Regulatory Issues," House Committee on Small Business, Jan. 14, 2014, http://tinyurl.com/pm3r3c5.

28. Feeney, op. cit.

29. James Niccolai, "Uber and Lyft fail to convince judges their drivers are merely 'contractors,'" *Computerworld*, March 12, 2015,http://tinyurl.com/ocwr69j.

30. Isaac and Singer, op. cit.

31. "Topic 762—Independent Contractor vs. Employee," Internal Revenue Service, updated May 27, 2015, http://tinyurl.com/yonzjs.

32. ArunSundararajan, "A Safety Net Fit for the Sharing Economy," *Financial Times*, June 22, 2015, http://tinyurl.com/q8w6ude.

33. Yochai Benkler, "Sharing Nicely: On Shareable Goods and the Emergence of Sharing as a Modality of Economic Production," *The Yale Law Journal*, 2004, Vol. 114, pp. 273–358.

34. Kevin Kelly, "We Are the Web," *Wired*, August 2005, http://tinyurl.com/p2zdsbw.

35. Ibid.

36. Dustin S. Klein, "Visionary in obscurity," Smart Business, July 22, 2002, http://tinyurl.com/o42v34t.

37. Nicole Achs Freeling, "The Nerd's Revenge," California CEO, February 2001, http://tinyurl.com/ojfvam8.

38. Zigmund, "Step Back in Time with Pierre Omidyar and Jeff Skoll," *The Chatter Newsletter*, eBay, 2005, http://tinyurl.com/qaqx4la.

39. Alex Stephany, "The Business of Sharing," *New York*, 2015, p. 71.

40. Ibid., p. 87.

41. Mimi Whitefield, "Airbnb Cracking the Cuban Market," *The Miami Herald*, July 5, 2015, http://tinyurl.com/noq6f5u.

42. Stephany, op. cit., p. 73.

43. Chase, op. cit., p. 8.

44. Ibid., p. 9.

45. Ibid., p. 13.

46. "History & Background Information," Freecycle, undated, accessed July 17, 2015, http://tinyurl.com/qjzml3k.

47. "About Zopa," Zopa, undated, accessed July 17, 2015, http://tinyurl.com/25g8bo.

48. "Alternative Financial Services: A Primer," *FDIC Quarterly*, April 27, 2009, http://tinyurl.com/p643omd.

49. For background, see Robin D. Schatz, "Crowdfunding," SAGE Business Researcher, Feb. 9, 2015, http://tinyurl.com/pk4alyg.

50. Patrick Hoge, "Colorado becomes the first state to pass law embracing Uber, Lyft et al.," *San Francisco Business Times*, June 5, 2014, http://tinyurl.com/pee39hf.

51. Alicia Freese, "Fair Share? Officials Struggle to Regulate Vermont's 'Sharing Economy,'" *Seven Days*, April 8, 2015, http://tinyurl.com/padu6gt.

52. Joseph Rose, "Portland Makes Uber and Lyft Legal – For Now," *The Oregonian*/OregonLive, April 22, 2015, http://tinyurl.com/ofp2fgx.

53. Brian Heaton, "California Bill Takes Aim at Home-Sharing Websites," *Government Technology*, May 4, 2015, http://tinyurl.com/ozytgds.

54. John Ribeiro, "Uber stops operations in Kansas over new legislation," *PC World*, May 6, 2015,http://tinyurl.com/nbkqqup.

55. Sam Sanders, "Santa Monica Cracks Down On Airbnb, Bans 'Vacation Rentals' Under A Month," NPR, May 13, 2015, http://tinyurl.com/oqgozky.

56. Joe Fitzgerald Rodriguez, "SFO, SFMTA ask state for stricter regulations of Uber and Lyft," *The San Francisco Examiner*, May 27, 2015, http://tinyurl.com/od9rnu3.

57. "Governor signs bills giving green light to rideshare services Uber andLyft," The Associated Press, *The Las Vegas Sun*, May 29, 2015, http://tinyurl.com/nheq467.

58. Martyn Williams, "Lyft to pay $300K, make insurance changes in settlement with N.Y.," *Computerworld*, June 18, 2015,http://tinyurl.com/nlxcr68.

59. "The Road Ahead," Uber document submitted to the Portland, Ore., Bureau of Transportation, undated, accessed July 17, 2015, http://tinyurl.com/omrzatv.

60. Don Jergler, "Uber Announces New Policy to Cover Gap," *Insurance Journal*, March 14, 2014, http://tinyurl.com/pbq2w4t.

61. Brian R. Fitzgerald, "Airbnb: Accidents Can Happen, So Here's $1 Million in Liability Insurance," Digits, *The Wall Street Journal*, Nov. 20, 2014, http://tinyurl.com/np4t583.

62. Emily Badger, "Airbnb is about to start collecting hotel taxes in more major cities, including Washington," *The Washington Post*, Jan. 29, 2015, http://tinyurl.com/nac6kdd.

63. Elaine S. Povich, "How Governments Are Trying to Tax the Sharing Economy," *Governing*, June 18, 2014,http://tinyurl.com/o6kgtao.

64. Robert Reich, "The Share-the-Scraps Economy," Feb. 2, 2015, http://tinyurl.com/mjyjwyg.

Chapter 5

1. Nick Wingfield, "Windows 10 Signifies Microsoft's Shift in Strategy," *The New York Times*, July 19, 2015,http://tinyurl.com/o7c9gs9.

2. Ibid.

3. Rolfe Winkler, "YouTube: 1 Billion Viewers, No Profit," *The Wall Street Journal*, Feb. 25, 2015, http://tinyurl.com/oo9e7m5.

4. Chris Anderson, *"Free: The Future of a Radical Price,"* 2009, Kindle edition, location 3775.

5. Andrew Tonner, "What Apple Music's Blistering Start Means for Spotify," The Motley Fool, Aug. 13, 2015, http://tinyurl.com/pp2ns2x.

6. Rick Edmonds, "Classified Ad Revenue Down 70 Percent in 10 Years, With One Bright Spot," Poynter, Feb. 1, 2010, updated Nov. 25, 2014, http://tinyurl.com/owl65po.

7. Rebecca L. Weber, "The Travel Agent is Dying, But It's Not Yet Dead," CNN, Oct. 10, 2013, http://tinyurl.com/ph6wp4s; Kyle Kensing, "When All Else Fails, Consider a Useless Job," CareerCast, 2013, http://tinyurl.com/nozvauy.

8. "Transportation: Past, Present and Future," The Henry Ford Foundation, 2011, http://tinyurl.com/qccwoyu.

9. "LinkedIn Corp," Google Finance, undated, accessed Oct. 27, 2015, http://tinyurl.com/po2grte.

10. Scott Austin, Chris Canipe and Sarah Slobin, "The Billion Dollar Startup Club," The Wall Street Journal, Feb. 18, 2015, http://tinyurl.com/pbfqsfk.

11. Ibid.

12. "Pandora Media Inc.," Google Finance, undated, accessed Oct. 27, 2015, http://tinyurl.com/o8eztpj.

13. "Update: eBay (EBAY) Sells 28.4% of Craigslist Equity Stake Back to Craigslist," StreetInsider.com, June 19, 2015, http://tinyurl.com/q5u6wqc.

14. "Zynga Inc.," Google Finance, undated, accessed Oct. 21, 2015, http://tinyurl.com/o6dqvbq.

15. Bill Saporito, "Microsoft's Call on Skype: Profits, $0; Value, $8.5 Billion," Time, May 10, 2011, http://tinyurl.com/nu8jgy8.

16. Lauren Hirsch, "UPDATE 2—Online dating company Match Group raises $400 mln in IPO," Reuters, Nov. 18, 2015, http://tinyurl.com/nbezmxy; Telis Demos and Corrie Driebusch, "Square, Match Surge in Trading Debuts," The Wall Street Journal, Nov. 19, 2015, http://tinyurl.com/nd3kx8m.

17. Luke Dormehl, "A Whopping 25% of Spotify's 60 Million Active Users Are Paying Customers," Fast Company, Jan. 12, 2015, http://tinyurl.com/o8s6jju.

18. Gene Marks, "Drilling Down: Does the 'Freemium' Model Really Work?" You're the Boss blog, The New York Times, June 11, 2012, http://tinyurl.com/qhps3as.

19. Carli Learly, "Is Freemium the Right Business Model? 10 Questions to Answer," Zuora Academy, undated, accessed Oct. 21, 2015, http://tinyurl.com/pyspbey.

20. Austin, Canipe and Slobin, op. cit.

21. Marks, op. cit.

22. Dmitri Leonov, "Why the Freemium Model Doesn't Work," Mashable, June 5, 2012, http://tinyurl.com/od59eua.

23. Aaran Fronda, "Freemium: You'll Pay Later," World Finance, May 29, 2015, http://tinyurl.com/nb2lult; Sarah E. Needelman and Angus Loten, "When Freemium Fails," The Wall Street Journal, Aug. 22, 2012, http://tinyurl.com/nozs4jl.

24. Sai Sachin, "Tinder's paid version is a hit," Reuters, Business Insider, April 28, 2015, http://tinyurl.com/n9lmrmd.

25. Joseph Palenchar, "Sales Decline Slows Among Top 25 Car CE Retailers," Twice, June 1, 2015, http://tinyurl.com/qzr6v7m.

26. Jacob Pramuk, "Why Amazon's Drone Delivery Is Growing Trickier," CNBC, June 17, 2015, http://tinyurl.com/q4f24wm; Greg Bensinger, "Amazon's Next Delivery Drone—You," The Wall Street Journal, June 16, 2015, http://tinyurl.com/qx888cx.

27. Amanda Ota, "How Much Does a Taylor Swift Concert Cost?" KUTV.com, July 13, 2015, ttp://tinyurl.com/o4xjaa6.

28. "The Chelsea at the Cosmopolitan," Pollstar.com, undated, accessed Oct. 21, 2015, http://tinyurl.com/ob2bfcu.

29. "Alphabet Announces Third Quarter 2015 Results of Google," news release, Alphabet, Oct. 22, 2015, http://tinyurl.com/nro2nac.

30. David J. Brice, Jeffrey H. Dyer and Nile W. Hatch, "Competing Against Free," Harvard Business Review, June 2011, http://tinyurl.com/oarggrh.

31. "Free Lunch in the South," The New York Times, Feb. 20, 1875, http://tinyurl.com/pegtjw2.

32. Ibid.

33. Anderson, op. cit., location 640.

34. Ibid., location 205.

35. "Jell-O History," Digital Deli Online, undated, accessed Sept. 30, 2015, http://tinyurl.com/pyqzgwj; "The History of Jell-O," Jell-O Gallery Museum, undated, accessed Oct. 27, 2015, http://tinyurl.com/o7mtp3r; and Reinhard Schrieber and Herbert Gareis, Gelatine Handbook: Theory and Industrial Practice, 2007, p. 182, http://tinyurl.com/oh8b2et.

36. Anderson, op. cit., location 205.

37. "Jell-O History," op. cit.

38. Anderson, op. cit., location 226.

39. "The First Free Sample: Benjamin T. Babbitt," GC Marketing Services, July 5, 2012, http://tinyurl.com/nzehmud.

40. Ted Hustead, "Our History Began with Wall and Water!" Wall Drug, 1982, http://tinyurl.com/pm9547.

41. Anderson, op. cit., location 2023.

42. Anderson, op. cit., location 2034.

43. John McDonough, "First Radio Commercial Hit Airwaves 90 Years Ago," NPR, Aug. 29, 2012, http://tinyurl.com/pdbveah.

44. Anderson, op. cit., location 2034.

45. Phil Edwards, "In memoriam: AOL CDs, history's greatest junk mail," May 12, 2015, Vox, http://tinyurl.com/nk5jjor.

46. Anderson, op. cit., location 3775.

47. Fred Wilson, "The Freemium Business Model," AVC, March 23, 2006, http://tinyurl.com/oynzzf6.

48. Devin Leonard, "That's Business, Man: Why Jay Z's Tidal Is a Complete Disaster," Bloomberg Business, May 28, 2015, http://tinyurl.com/oeyp4wq.

49. Claire Atkinson, "Apple Music has been a surprising success," New York Post, Sept. 21, 2015, http://tinyurl.com/p34p3rz.

50. "One in Ten iOS Users Listens to Apple Music," news release, Music Watch, Aug. 18, 2015, http://tinyurl.com/ostxj4y.

51. "Who Owns Tidal?" Tidal website, undated, accessed Oct. 21, 2015, http://tinyurl.com/q6ql6d7.

52. Amelia Butterly, "Jay Z Says Tidal Is 'Doing Just Fine' With 770K Subscribers," BBC Newsbeat, April 26, 2015, http://tinyurl.com/qatyusz.

53. The Spotify Team, "20 Million Reasons to Say Thanks," Spotify, June 10, 2015, http://tinyurl.com/ose6rt9.

54. "Billboard Music Executive Survey: Top Brass Weigh In On the Artists They Covet Most, Taylor Swift and More," Billboard, Aug. 25, 2015, http://tinyurl.com/q7fhbm7.

55. Butterly, op. cit.
56. "One in Ten iOS Users Listens to Apple Music," op. cit.
57. Leonard, op. cit.
58. Evan Narcisse, "15-Year-Old Kid Spends 37,000 Euros on Gold in Free-to-Play Game," Kotaku blog, Gizmodo UK, Oct. 3, 2014, http://tinyurl.com/pw6uny5.
59. "Five-Year-Old Runs up £1,700 iPad bill in ten minutes," *The Telegraph*, March 1, 2013, http://tinyurl.com/appvlfs.
60. "Garen Meguerian vs. Apple Inc.," U.S. 5:11-CV-01758-EJD (2013), http://tinyurl.com/q4pdoev; "Apple Offers Compensation for kids' in-app purchases," BBC News, Feb, 26, 2013, http://tinyurl.com/oxwdgfl.
61. "Google To Refund Consumers At Least $19 Million to Settle FTC Complaint It Unlawfully Billed Parents for Children's Unauthorized In-App Charges," news release, Federal Trade Commission, Sept. 4, 2014, http://tinyurl.com/lpayfw2.
62. "In-app Purchases Joint Action by the European Commission and Member States is leading to better protection for consumers in online games," news release, European Commission, July 18, 2014, http://tinyurl.com/osdhyly.
63. Ibid.
64. Stuart Dredge, "Apple Lets Parents Down Over In-App Purchases, Says EU," *The Guardian*, July 18, 2014, http://tinyurl.com/nsvwjy3.
65. "FTC Alleges Amazon Unlawfully Billed Parents for Millions of Dollars in Children's Unauthorized In-App Charges," news release, Federal Trade Commission, July 10, 2014, http://tinyurl.com/mej4q6n.
66. Khadijah M. Britton, "Amazon Can't Escape FTC's In-App Purchase Lawsuit," Law360.com, Dec. 1, 2014, http://tinyurl.com/purdtfu.

Chapter 6

1. Sarah Buhr and Alex Wilhelm, "Etsy Closes Up 86 Percent On First Day Of Trading," TechCrunch, April 16, 2015, http://tinyurl.com/ndbw4wr.
2. Aileen Lee, "Welcome To The Unicorn Club," TechCrunch, Nov. 2, 2013, http://tinyurl.com/n7w88mx.
3. "The Unicorn List: Current Private Companies Valued at $1B and Above," CB Insights, undated, accessed May 19, 2015, http://tinyurl.com/lz9hdfh.
4. "Annual Venture Capital Investment Tops $48 Billion in 2014, Reaching Highest Level in Over a Decade, According to the MoneyTree Report," news release, National Venture Capital Association, Jan. 16, 2015, http://tinyurl.com/kda4enq.
5. "2015 Annual U.S. Venture Industry Report," PitchBook, p 19.
6. "Venture Funds Raised $7.0 Billion During First Quarter 2015," National Venture Capital Association, April 9, 2015, http://tinyurl.com/mqofmo9.
7. Russ Garland, "Venture Capital Returns Rebound, But Beating Public Markets Remains a Challenge," Venture Capital Dispatch, *The Wall Street Journal*, Oct. 31, 2013, http://tinyurl.com/olvdg56.
8. Diane Mulcahy, Bill Weeks and Harold S. Bradley, "We Have Met the Enemy . . . and He Is Us," Ewing Marion Kauffman Foundation, May 2012, http://tinyurl.com/lwcn7lx.
9. Michael S. Rodes and Malone Fishburne, "Founding Funders," Forbes ASAP, May 29, 2000, http://tinyurl.com/l6u2km9.
10. "History," New Enterprise Associates, undated, accessed May 19, 2015, http://tinyurl.com/mc6a3st; Russ Garland, "New Enterprise Associates Cracks $3 Billion for Latest Funds," Venture Capital Dispatch, *The Wall Street Journal*, April 15, 2015, http://tinyurl.com/kyczjfp.
11. Jess Delaney, "Do Sovereign Fund Direct Private Investments Deliver Value?" *Institutional Investor*, March 24, 2015, http://tinyurl.com/ny5m2oy.
12. "Silicon Valley's Diversity Problem," *The New York Times* Editorial Board, Oct. 4, 2014, http://tinyurl.com/lz3h3bh.
13. "Kleiner Perkins and Ellen Pao: A Fortune Guide," *Fortune*, March 27, 2015, http://tinyurl.com/nlwjbnd.
14. Sarah Lacy and Michael Carney, "John Doerr's last stand: Can a dramatic shakeup save Kleiner Perkins?" PandoDaily, Dec. 11, 2013, http://tinyurl.com/n8en7av.
15. Seth Levine, "Venture Outcomes are Even More Skewed Than You Think," VC Adventure, Aug. 12, 2014, http://tinyurl.com/mr9st2p.
16. Scott Austin, Chris Canipe and Sarah Slobin, "The Billion Dollar Startup Club," *The Wall Street Journal*/Dow Jones VentureSource, Feb. 18, 2015, http://tinyurl.com/pbfqsfk.
17. Erin Griffith and Dan Primack, "The Age of Unicorns," *Fortune*, Jan. 22, 2015, http://tinyurl.com/oef3swz.
18. Serena Saitto, "This Venture Capitalist Says We Have Entered a Tech Bubble," Bloomberg Business, March 5, 2015, http://tinyurl.com/lu6yk9n.
19. "Annual Venture Capital Investment Tops $48 Billion in 2014, Reaching Highest Level in Over a Decade, According to the MoneyTree Report," news release, National Venture Capital Association, Jan. 16, 2015, http://tinyurl.com/kda4enq.
20. Robert J. Shiller, "Irrational Exuberance," 2nd ed., 2005, p. 5, http://tinyurl.com/lrmryft.
21. Alan Greenspan, "The Challenge of Central Banking in a Democratic Society," Federal Reserve Board, Dec. 5, 1996, http://tinyurl.com/5sje8.
22. Mark Cuban, "Why This Tech Bubble is Worse Than the Tech Bubble of 2000," Blog Maverick, March 4, 2015, http://tinyurl.com/mdyoa79.
23. Steven Davidoff Solomon, "Throwing Money at Start-Ups in Frenzy to Find the Next Uber," DealBook, *The New York Times*, Dec. 16, 2014, http://tinyurl.com/metgcpo.
24. TrueBridge Capital, "Too Many Unicorns? Why Billion-Dollar Startups Still Charm Us Today," Forbes.com blog, March 9, 2015, http://tinyurl.com/l3h9awz.

25. Alyson Shontell, "Uber Is Generating A Staggering Amount of Revenue," Business Insider, Nov. 15, 2014, http://tinyurl.com/lpncscl.

26. Max Nisen, "How Fab.com went from a $1 billion valuation to a $15 million fire sale," Quartz, Nov. 24, 2014, http://tinyurl.com/keb5qjf; Sarah Buhr, "PCH International In Talks To Buy Fab For $15 Million," TechCrunch, Nov. 20, 2014, http://tinyurl.com/kmms5xp.

27. Matt Egan, "Box jumps 66% in first big IPO of 2015," CNNMoney, Jan. 23, 2015, http://tinyurl.com/lag8cwb; Alex Konrad, "Box Raises $100M Round At $2B Valuation With IPO Filing Planned Before March," Forbes, Dec. 5, 2013, http://tinyurl.com/mkjxtz2.

28. Mulcahy, op. cit.; Paul Kedrosky, "Right-Sizing the U.S. Capital Venture Industry," Ewing Marion Kauffman Foundation, June 10, 2009, http://tinyurl.com/k2eme8u.

29. "2015 Annual U.S. Venture Industry Report," op. cit.

30. "The Turning Point for Venture Capital?" Private Equity Spotlight, November 2014, http://tinyurl.com/m93jly3.

31. "2015 Annual U.S. Venture Industry Report," op. cit., p. 18.

32. Kedrosky, op. cit., p. 5.

33. Carmel Deamicis, "Bill Draper: Why venture returns have fallen dramatically and will likely stay that way," PandoDaily, June 24, 2013, http://tinyurl.com/mpzgy5n.

34. Ainslie Chandler, "Buzzfeed Backer NEA Raises $2.6 Billion Fund as VC Values," Bloomberg, March 24, 2015, http://tinyurl.com/mr2xxed; Russ Garland, "New Venture Fund Raises $2.6 Billion," The Wall Street Journal, July 25, 2012, http://tinyurl.com/mou8pyw; and Garland, "New Enterprise Associates Cracks $3 Billion for Latest Funds," op. cit.

35. Tim Mullaney, "Venture Capitalist Dick Kramlich's Last Stand," Bloomberg Business Week, January 21, 2010, http://tinyurl.com/l5gq8bn.

36. Dan Primack, "Exclusive: Atlas Venture is splitting up," Fortune, Oct. 2, 2014, http://tinyurl.com/laxb64q.

37. "2015 Venture Industry Report," op. cit.; Garland, "New Venture Fund Raises $2.6 Billion," op. cit.

38. Margaret Cronin Fisk, "Next Up for Silicon Valley After Pao Loss: More Bias Suits," Bloomberg Business, March 28, 2015, http://tinyurl.com/n3y6n4z; Nina Burleigh, "What Silicon Valley Thinks of Women," Newsweek, Jan. 28, 2015, http://tinyurl.com/qjqj9f4; and Jon Swartz, "Jesse Jackson gets Silicon Valley to talk diversity," USA Today, Dec. 11, 2014, http://tinyurl.com/k9w4gfe.

39. Russ Garland, "Venture Industry Leaders Launch Task Force to Promote Diversity," Venture Capital Dispatch, The Wall Street Journal, Dec. 8, 2014, http://tinyurl.com/lznn3yl.

40. Steven Syre, "Venture capital's problem with women," The Boston Globe, March 31, 2015, http://tinyurl.com/l69edsj.

41. David Teten, "Why Are Venture Capitalists (76% White Men) Ignoring The Future?" Forbes blog, April 29, 2014, http://tinyurl.com/on6gw89.

42. "NVCA Forms Diversity Task Force to Foster Greater Inclusion across the Innovation Ecosystem," press release, National Venture Capital Association, Dec. 8, 2014, http://tinyurl.com/l6cw4cn.

43. Scott Austin, "White Men Still Dominate the Venture Industry," Wall Street Journal, November 21, 2011, http://tinyurl.com/ly9hmqe; "Asian American Populations," Centers for Disease Control and Prevention, undated, accessed May 14, 2015, http://tinyurl.com/mnsb7a9.

44. Claire Cane Miller, "Female-Run Venture Capital Funds Alter the Status Quo," DealBook, The New York Times, April 1, 2015, http://tinyurl.com/lwly5yt.

45. "John Pierpont (J.P.) Morgan," Netstate.com, undated, accessed May 13, 2015, http://tinyurl.com/mb7x42w.

46. William S. Dietrich II, "Andrew Mellon: Son of a judge," Pittsburgh Quarterly, Fall 2007, http://tinyurl.com/n8htqu9.

47. "Proceedings of the Annual Convention of the Investment Bankers Association of America," 1920, p. 157; available at http://tinyurl.com/odyp8gn.

48. "The Early History of Venture Capital and Silicon Valley," Risk Over Reward blog, Feb. 2, 2011, http://tinyurl.com/ow6vlgc.

49. "Laurance Rockefeller, philanthropist, dead at 94," NBCNews.com, July 11, 2004, http://tinyurl.com/pymaye5.

50. "United States Synthetic Rubber Program, 1939–1945," American Chemical Society, 1998, http://tinyurl.com/okachtu.

51. "The Early History of Venture Capital and Silicon Valley," op. cit.

52. Spencer Ante, "VC's First Home Run: Digital Equipment Corp.," Creative Capital blog, Jan. 4, 2008, http://tinyurl.com/pvrtlw9.

53. Ryan Lawler, "Venrock Closes $450 Million Seventh Fund To Invest In Tech And Healthcare Startups," TechCrunch, July 31, 2014, http://tinyurl.com/oq6menr.

54. Udayan Gupta, ed., "Done Deals: Venture Capitalists Tell Their Stories," 2000, pp. 223–224.

55. Howard Anderson, "20 People Who Changed Tech: General Georges Doriot," Government blog, InformationWeek, May 1, 2013, http://tinyurl.com/q4aynnn.

56. Andrew Beattie, "Georges Doriot and the Birth of Venture Capital," Investopedia, undated, accessed May 19, 2015, http://tinyurl.com/mbpmjgr.

57. David H. Hsu and Martin Kenney, "Organizing Venture Capital: The Rise and Demise of American Research & Development Corporation, 1946–1973," December 2004, http://tinyurl.com/opw5e82.

58. Therese Poletti, "The 'Traitorous Eight' have become California icons," MarketWatch, May 11, 2011, http://tinyurl.com/nbjudug.

59. "Interview with Arthur Rock," Silicon Genesis; an oral history of semiconductor technology, Stanford University, Nov. 12, 2002, http://tinyurl.com/nnulcje.

60. Leslie Berlin, "William Shockley Drove His Team Nuts," *San Jose Mercury News*, Sept. 2, 2005, http://tinyurl.com/noxdzjd.

61. Leslie Goth, "1958: The Birth of Integrated Circuits," CNN.com, May 19, 1999, http://tinyurl.com/nnc69fm.

62. Hervé Lebret, "A History of Venture Capital," SlideShare, Jan. 4, 2007, http://tinyurl.com/ojvgf6v.

63. Poletti, op. cit.

64. "Interview With Arthur Rock," op. cit.

65. Lebret, op. cit.

66. "Employee Retirement Income Security Act," U.S. Department of Labor, undated, accessed May 13, 2015, http://tinyurl.com/ypfhao.

67. Gary Klott, "Venture Capitalists Wary of Tax Plan," *The New York Times*, Jan. 9, 1985, http://tinyurl.com/n7jm2pc.

68. "S.209—ERISA Improvement Acts of 1979," Congress.gov, undated, accessed May 13, 2015, http://tinyurl.com/pw2fgkw.

69. Andrew Pollack, "Venture Capital Loses Its Vigor," *The New York Times*, Oct. 8, 1989, http://tinyurl.com/olzz4wp.

70. Ibid.

71. AnnaLee Saxenian, "Explaining Silicon Valley's Success," *Harvard Business Review*, Dec. 4, 2014, http://tinyurl.com/p9oytvn.

72. Dan Moskowitz, "What Makes Apple (AAPL) the Most Valuable Company?" Investopedia, May 4, 2015, http://tinyurl.com/lhykx6d.

73. Michael Fitzgerald, "Boston's Next Tech Gold Mine," *Boston Magazine*, May 2014, http://tinyurl.com/nlcuzu8.

74. Eric Niiler, "Netscape's IPO Anniversary and the Internet Boom," Aug. 9, 2005, http://tinyurl.com/pu6jyys.

75. "Annual Venture Capital Investment Tops $48 Billion in 2014," op. cit.

76. Matt Egan, "Alibaba 101: Inside the record IPO," CNNMoney, Sept. 10, 2014, http://tinyurl.com/ok4mnc5.

77. "Juno Therapeutics Prices Upsized IPO at $24," Renaissance Capital, Dec. 19, 2014, http://tinyurl.com/otgnfr8.

78. Cale Guthrie Weissman, "Fred Wilson: Venture capital as we know it will cease to exist," PandoDaily, June 17, 2013, http://tinyurl.com/qbmfrho.

79. J.J. Colao, "Fred Wilson And the Death of Venture Capital," *Forbes* blog, May 8, 2012, http://tinyurl.com/7p9kbdh.

80. Shai Bernstein, Josh Lerner and Antoinette Schoar, "The Investment Strategies of Sovereign Wealth Funds," *Journal of Economic Perspectives*, Spring 2013, http://tinyurl.com/oyfs3lz.

81. Jess Delaney, "Do Sovereign Fund Direct Private Investments Deliver Value?" *Institutional Investor*, March 24, 2015, http://tinyurl.com/oz97t7z.

82. Sam Altman, "YC Portfolio Stats," Y Combinator, July 16, 2014, http://tinyurl.com/onltx72.

83. For background, see Curt Woodward, "MA Won't Change Noncompete Law, VCs Pledge to Continue Campaign," Xconomy, July 31, 2014, http://tinyurl.com/p6qh84k.

84. For background, see "Patent Trolls," Electronic Frontier Foundation, undated, accessed May 13, 2015, http://tinyurl.com/7mo85yf.

85. For background, see "Les misérables," *The Economist*, July 26, 2012, http://tinyurl.com/butbord; Deborah Ball, "Europe Builds Own Chapter 11," *The Wall Street Journal*, April 5, 2013, http://tinyurl.com/otokztu.

Chapter 7

1. "With You: Reinventing The Locket," Kickstarter campaign page, accessed Dec. 11, 2014, http://tinyurl.com/myu2bbp.

2. Ethan R. Mollick, "The dynamics of crowdfunding: An exploratory study," *Journal of Business Venturing*, January 2014, http://tinyurl.com/nn9s5gu.

3. "Fees for the United States," Kickstarter, undated, http://tinyurl.com/o2999gl.

4. Crowdfund Capital Advisors, "Crowdfunding's Potential for the Developing World," World Bank, 2013, p. 19, http://tinyurl.com/o423cn8.

5. Ibid., p. 18.

6. Ibid, p. 10.

7. "Stats," Kickstarter, accessed Dec. 12, 2014, http://tinyurl.com/msrvgnp.

8. Chris Roberts, "Letter from the Chairman," Roberts Space Industries, Nov. 27, 2014, http://tinyurl.com/po7ofkj.

9. "Oculus Rift: Step Into the Game," Kickstarter campaign page, accessed Dec. 13, 2014, http://tinyurl.com/m65874o.

10. "Facebook to Acquire Oculus," Facebook, March 25, 2014, http://tinyurl.com/mahhcpl.

11. "Coolest Cooler: 21st Century Cooler that's Actually Cooler," Kickstarter campaign page, accessed Dec. 13, 2014, http://tinyurl.com/ngbzhtw.

12. "Remarks by the President at JOBS Act Bill Signing," the White House, April 5, 2012, http://tinyurl.com/o642okm.

13. Ibid.

14. "Investor Bulletin: Accredited Investors," Securities and Exchange Commission, Sept. 13, 2013, http://tinyurl.com/k9a2nea.

15. Jason Greenberg and Ethan R. Mollick, "Leaning In or Leaning On? Gender, Homophily, and Activism in Crowdfunding," July 3, 2014; available at SSRN, http://tinyurl.com/opaaqy6.

16. Habib Jamal, "Crowdfunding's potential for minority and women-owned Enterprises," Crowdfund Capital Advisors, July 2014, http://tinyurl.com/pn9eow7.

17. Ibid.

18. "Stats," Kickstarter, accessed Dec. 12, 2014, http://tinyurl.com/msrvgnp.

19. Christelle Xu, "Crowdfunding: Income or Gift," Crowdfund Capital Advisors, Aug. 14, 2013, http://tinyurl.com/qzul7ck.

20. Michael B. Dorff, "The Siren Call of Equity Crowdfunding," Sept. 13, 2013; available at SSRN, http://tinyurl.com/mke6uph.

21. Rich Cooper, "The Crowdfunding Conundrum: Embracing Reward, but What About Risk?" U.S. Chamber of Commerce Foundation blog, March 22, 2013, http://tinyurl.com/lmpn3cs.

22. Amy Cortese, *Locavesting: The Revolution in Local Investing and How to Profit from It*, 2011.

23. "Save Lainie's Way," Tilt campaign page, accessed Dec. 13, 2014, http://tinyurl.com/kr5cqsg.

24. Andrew A. Schwartz, "Rural Crowdfunding," U.C. Davis *Business Law Journal*, Nov.18, 2013, http://tinyurl.com/n2dfhhf.

25. Crowdfund Capital Advisors, "How Does Crowdfunding Impact Job Creation, Company Revenue and Professional Investor Interest?" Jan. 15, 2014, http://tinyurl.com/l4agb8w.

26. Ibid.

27. Ethan R. Mollick and Venkat Kuppuswamy, "After the Campaign: Outcomes of Crowdfunding," UNC Kenan-Flagler Research Paper No. 2376997, Jan. 9, 2014, http://tinyurl.com/m2gmo88.

28. Mollick, "The Dynamics of Crowdfunding," op. cit.

29. Samantha Hurst, "Creators of Scribble Pen Cancel Kickstarter Campaign After Backers & Crowdfunding Platform Ask Questions," Crowdfund Insider, Aug. 15, 2014, http://tinyurl.com/q3zcnf5.

30. "Scribble Pen shut down . . . again," Drop Kicker, Sept. 6, 2014, http://tinyurl.com/kfnro7z.

31. James Beshara, "The Scribble Pen," Tilt Blog, Sept. 6, 2014, http://tinyurl.com/lro924f.

32. Scribble Blog, Sept. 6, 2014, http://tinyurl.com/kh7bng8.

33. Gerrit K.C. Ahlers, et al., "Signaling in Equity Crowdfunding," Oct. 14, 2012, http://tinyurl.com/myn5csb.

34. "Mozart and the Keyboard Culture of His Time," Cornell University Library, Division of Rare and Manuscript Collections, 2002, http://tinyurl.com/krkdrrx.

35. Ibid.

36. National Park Service, "Statue of Liberty," http://tinyurl.com/oe2f5nj.

37. Sharon Shahid, "Joseph Pulitzer, 19th Century Crowdfunder," Newseum, March 28, 2014, http://tinyurl.com/n85bhv7.

38. Dave Milliken, *Crowdfunding in a Nutshell: A Concise History of Crowdfunding and How to Raise Money Today*, 2014.

39. Mark Kelly, "The birth of crowdfunding," July 15, 2013, TEDx Bedford, http://tinyurl.com/kycj3sj.

40. "Crowdfunding's Potential for the Developing World," op. cit.

41. "About Us," Indiegogo, undated, accessed Dec. 13, 2014, http://tinyurl.com/kh687tf.

42. William Cunningham, *The JOBS Act: Crowdfunding for Small Businesses and Startups*, 2012, Introduction.

43. "Regulation D Offerings," Securities and Exchange Commission, undated, accessed Jan. 7, 2015, http://tinyurl.com/cedxvw; "The Laws That Govern the Securities Industry,"

Securities and Exchange Commission, undated, accessed Dec. 13, 2014, http://tinyurl.com/lbeqjb.

44. Sherwood Neiss, Jason W. Best and Zak Cassady-Dorion, *Crowdfund Investing for Dummies*, 2013.

45. "House Passes JOBS Act," Office of Rep. Patrick McHenry, March 8, 2012, http://tinyurl.com/mk9zolk; Cunningham, op. cit., chp. 1.

46. Ibid., Cunningham.

47. Steven Davidoff Solomon, "S.E.C.'s Delay on Crowdfunding May Just Save It," DealBook, *The New York Times*, Nov. 18, 2014, http://tinyurl.com/mz9tvkp.

48. "Investor Alert: Advertising for Unregistered Securities Offerings," Securities and Exchange Commission, Sept. 13, 2013, SEC Investor Alerts, http://tinyurl.com/ls9rvgk.

49. Solomon, op.cit.

50. Cunningham, op cit., chp. 1.

51. Andrew Blackman, "Real-estate Crowdfunding Finds its Footing," *The Wall Street Journal*, April 13, 2014, http://tinyurl.com/lrkhytj.

52. Jonathan O'Connell, "Fundrise faces off with skeptical financial services industry over crowd-funded real estate," *The Washington Post*, June 9, 2013, http://tinyurl.com/pgsstw2.

53. "How Much Capital are Kickstarter and Indiegogo Hardware Projects Raising?" CB Insights, Aug. 11, 2014, http://tinyurl.com/lf7j5y2.

54. Oculus Rift Kickstarter comments page, accessed Jan. 13, 2015, http://tinyurl.com/khq4oml.

55. Quoted in Adrianne Jeffries, "If you back a Kickstarter project that sells for $2 billion, do you deserve to get rich?" The Verge, March 28, 2014, http://tinyurl.com/l3o7pzq.

56. Sherwood Neiss, "Investments in Crowdfunding Have Already Doubled This Year," Venture Beat, Sept. 8, 2014, http://tinyurl.com/kvcnv5g.

57. Leslie Picker and Noah Buhayar, "Lending Club Raises $870 Million in IPO Poised to Change Finance," Bloomberg News, Dec. 11, 2014, http://tinyurl.com/qhzxn8a.

58. Gregory J. Nowak and Brian Korn, "Crowdfunding and Peer to Peer Lending: Legal Frameworks and Risks," Dec. 18, 2013, Pepper Hamilton, http://tinyurl.com/mpc4xbs; The Wharton School, "Peer-to-Peer Lending: Ready to Grow Despite a Few Red Flags," Jan. 8, 2014, http://tinyurl.com/lvak7sv.

59. Charlie Rose, "Charlie Rose Talks to Kickstarter's Yancey Strickler," Bloomberg Businessweek, March 20, 2014, http://tinyurl.com/nyk7twc.

60. Christine Lagorio-Chafkin, "Why You Won't Use the Term Crowdfunding for Long," *Inc.*, Feb. 5, 2014, http://tinyurl.com/qe853pb.

61. "The Newest Hottest Spike Lee Joint," Kickstarter campaign page, accessed Dec. 13, 2014, http://tinyurl.com/kxm4tz9.

62. "The Veronica Mars Movie Project," Kickstarter campaign page, accessed Dec. 13, 2014, http://tinyurl.com/lb2hhmc; "Wish I Was Here," Kickstarter campaign page, accessed Dec. 13, 2014, http://tinyurl.com/ma8a6aq.

63. Perry Chen, Yancey Strickler and Charles Adler, "The Truth About Spike Lee and Kickstarter," Kickstarter blog, Aug. 19, 2013, http://tinyurl.com/ks5an4c.

64. Takashi Mochizuki, "Sony Looks to Crowdfunding As Way to Test Ideas," JapanRealTime blog, *The Wall Street Journal*, Dec. 22, 2014, http://tinyurl.com/mvnm7sy.

65. John Tozzi, "P&G Taps Crowdfunding Sites to Scout for Startup Brands," Bloomberg Businessweek, Jan. 29, 2013, http://tinyurl.com/bzlcuql.

66. Mary Jo White, "Testimony before the Subcommittee on Financial Services and General Government Committee on Appropriations"; the text can be found at Securities and Exchange Commission, May 14, 2014, http://tinyurl.com/m9u94sx.

67. "Congressional Testimony of David J. Paul, Co-Chair and Co-Founder of CfIRA (Crowdfunding Intermediary Regulatory Advocates), Chief Strategy Officer of Gate Global Impact, before the United States House of Representatives, Committee on Small Business, Subcommittee on Investigations, Oversight and Regulations," Jan. 16, 2014, http://tinyurl.com/m5csy5t.

68. Timothy J. Capen, "Tired of Waiting for the SEC, States Adopt Their Own Crowdfunding Rules," Ice Miller, Sept. 19, 2014, http://tinyurl.com/kxxccl5.

69. "Attorney General files lawsuit against company behind Asylum Playing Cards crowdfunded project," Washington State Office of the Attorney General, May 1, 2014, http://tinyurl.com/kgmb6rx.

70. Ibid.

71. "Asylum Playing Cards," Kickstarter campaign page/Comments, accessed Dec. 13, 2014, http://tinyurl.com/m6wtnvn.

Chapter 8

1. Jeanette S. Martin and Lillian H. Chaney, *Global Business Etiquette: A Guide to International Communication*, 2012.

2. "Clarizen Survey: Workers Consider Status Meetings a Productivity-Killing Waste of Time," Clarizen, Jan. 22, 2015, http://tinyurl.com/nbgpbye.

3. "American Time Use Survey," Bureau of Labor Statistics, 2014, http://tinyurl.com/yku9t89.

4. Peter M. Monge, Charles McSween and JoAnne Wyer, "A Profile of Meetings in Corporate America: Results of the 3M Meeting Effectiveness Study," Center for Effective Organizations, November 1989, p. 12, http://tinyurl.com/zb3hhwj.

5. Been Kim and Cynthia Rudin, "Learning About Meetings," Massachusetts Institute of Technology, June 8, 2013, http://tinyurl.com/zfxkzex.

6. Julian Birkinshaw and Jordan Cohen, "Make Time for the Work That Matters," *Harvard Business Review*, September 2013, http://tinyurl.com/jq9v9vg.

7. Sigal Barsade and Olivia A. O'Neill, "Quantifying Your Company's Emotional Culture," *Harvard Business Review*, Jan. 6, 2016, http://tinyurl.com/zmb6pfc.

8. Steven G. Rogelberg et al., "Lateness to meetings: Examination of an unexplored temporal phenomenon," *European Journal of Work and Organizational Psychology*, January 2013, http://tinyurl.com/jth9f4o.

9. Monge, McSween and Wyer, op. cit.

10. Gretchen Gavett, "What People Are Really Doing When They're on a Conference Call," *Harvard Business Review*, Aug. 19, 2014, http://tinyurl.com/z2fcj9a.

11. Phyllis Korkki, "Telecommuting Can Make the Office a Lonely Place a Study Says," *The New York Times*, Jan. 2, 2016, http://tinyurl.com/zbrrv5u.

12. Website of Edward Sturm, http://tinyurl.com/hm7xsx3.

13. Margaret Rouse, "Agile project management," TechTarget, August 2011, http://tinyurl.com/gws2ge9.

14. Bill Mears, "Justice Ginsburg ready to welcome Sotomayor," CNN.com, June 16, 2009, http://tinyurl.com/zpr5llw.

15. Ibid.

16. "When What You Know Is Not Enough: Expertise and gender dynamics in task groups," Insight/Kellogg School of Business, May 2007, http://tinyurl.com/hgnm56s.

17. Deborah Tannen's website, http://tinyurl.com/jhxftmf.

18. Gina Stepp, "Deborah Tannen: Communicating with Style," Vision, Winter 2009, http://tinyurl.com/hsv6bea.

19. Chris Bart and Gregory McQueen, "Why Women Make Better Directors," *International Journal of Business Governance and Ethics*, 2013, http://tinyurl.com/ztdwfkm; "Women Make Better Decisions Than Men, Study Suggests," ScienceDaily, March 26, 2013, http://tinyurl.com/zhofq2f.

20. Marti Bartletta, "Men Are So Emotional! Why Women Are Better Buyers," MartiBartletta.com, Feb. 9, 2016, http://tinyurl.com/hq9tx22.

21. Erin White, "Deloitte Tries a Different Sales Pitch for Women," *The Wall Street Journal*, Oct. 8, 2007, http://tinyurl.com/zfdpj8j.

22. Scott Schieman, Markus Schafer and Mitchell McIvor, "When Leaning In Doesn't Pay Off," *The New York Times*, Aug. 10, 2013, http://tinyurl.com/mmuzpxj.

23. Gary Richardson, "Medieval Guilds," EH.net Encyclopedia, March 16, 2008, http://tinyurl.com/zrshm23.

24. "An interview with Frank M. Bryan," University of Chicago Press, 2003, http://tinyurl.com/nzxxb.

25. "Norman Rockwell [1894–1978], Freedom of Speech, The Saturday Evening Post, 1943," Picturing America, National Endowment for the Humanities, http://tinyurl.com/jo9qtdt.

26. For a good account of the convention, see Catherine Drinker Bowen, *Miracle at Philadelphia: The Story of the Constitutional Convention, May to September 1787*, 1986.

27. Helen B. Schwartzman, *The Meeting: Gatherings in Organizations and Communities*, 1989.

28. Schwartzman, ibid., pp. 57–58; "Melville Dalton papers, 1941–2003," Online Archive of California, undated, accessed Feb. 2, 2016, http://tinyurl.com/zhlerf5.

29. "Short History of Robert's Rules," The Official Robert's Rules of Order website, http://tinyurl.com/ztphvhc.

30. "Constitution and Bylaws," Midwestern History Association, http://tinyurl.com/gunobjq.

31. Schwartzman, op. cit., p. 41.

32. "Chapter 17 – Strategies for Individual Motions Illustrated," Westside Toastmasters, http://tinyurl.com/jlk64xf.

33. Schwartzman, op. cit., p. 7.

34. Ibid., p. 43.

35. Peter Abrahamsson Lindeblad, "Organisational effects of virtual meetings," IIIEE Theses, September 2012, http://tinyurl.com/jxw8998.

36. Joe Mullich, "The New Face of Face-to-Face Meetings," *The Wall Street Journal* and Sprint, undated, http://tinyurl.com/mw9cz2.

37. "Meetings in America," Verizon, 1998, http://tinyurl.com/6kldp5c.

38. "Meetings in America V: Meeting of the Minds," MCI, 2003, http://tinyurl.com/gr8qxfp.

39. Kim and Rudin, op. cit.

40. "Anthropology in Practice" exploring the human condition," *Scientific American*, http://tinyurl.com/3jsdx99.

41. Rachel Emma Silverman, "Where's the Boss? Trapped in a Meeting," *The Wall Street Journal*, Feb. 14, 2012, http://tinyurl.com/jtkrgv7.

42. "What It Takes to Collaborate," Herman Miller, 2012, http://tinyurl.com/z4x7m4u.

43. Paul Graham, "Maker's Schedule, Manager's Schedule," PaulGraham.com, July 2009, http://tinyurl.com/nl5h5z.

44. Ibid.

45. Jill Duffy, "The Best Online Collaboration Software for 2015," *PC magazine*, Aug. 6, 2015, http://tinyurl.com/jgtd9la.

Chapter 9

1. Tim Kastelle, "Hierarchy Is Overrated," *Harvard Business Review*, Nov. 20, 2013, http://tinyurl.com/ksaur6h.

2. David A. Garvin, "How Google Sold Its Engineers on Management," *Harvard Business Review*, December 2013, http://tinyurl.com/oggkvhu.

3. Nicolai J. Foss and Peter G. Klein, "Why Managers Still Matter," MIT *Sloan Management Review*, Fall 2014, http://tinyurl.com/pzm64b4.

4. Garvin, op. cit.

5. Jim Belosic, "5 Ways A Flat Management Structure Can Empower Your Business," American Express Open Forum, Aug. 29, 2013, http://tinyurl.com/mf93gh8.

6. "What Is Self-Management?" Morning Star Self-Management Institute, http://tinyurl.com/ozkccme.

7. Stephen Courtright, G.L. Stewart and M.R. Barrick, "Peer-Based Control in Self-Managing Teams: Linking Rational and Normative Influence With Individual and Group Performance," *Journal of Applied Psychology*, March 2012, http://tinyurl.com/p3u5e58.

8. "Is Peer Pressure Better Employee Motivator Than Money?" *Insurance Journal*, Aug. 7, 2012, http://tinyurl.com/nlo24c4.

9. Colette Meehan, "Flat Vs. Hierarchical Organizational Structure," *Houston Chronicle*/Demand Media, http://tinyurl.com/3gdycj3.

10. For more on Enron, see Susan Boswell, "The Smartest Guys in the Room: Management Lessons from Enron's Leaders," *Baltimore Post-Examiner*, Dec. 22, 2012, http://tinyurl.com/kmmr6h8.

11. Klint Finley, "Why Workers Can Suffer in Bossless Companies Like GitHub," *Wired*, March 20, 2014, http://tinyurl.com/obu4gv6.

12. Jacob Shriar, "Can A Flat Hierarchy Really Work?" Officevibe, Jan. 8, 2014, http://tinyurl.com/kwdzj4g.

13. "Mission Command Center of Excellence," U.S. Army Combined Arms Center, updated Aug. 28, 2014, http://tinyurl.com/l6wqx32.

14. Drake Baer, "Does Google Need Managers?" *Fast Company*, Nov. 25, 2013, http://tinyurl.com/l97kcz3; "Strategic Alignment Business Cases," Advance! Business Consulting, 2009, http://tinyurl.com/lhvsfaw; and Marc Gunther, "3M's innovation revival," *Fortune*, Sept. 24, 2010, http://tinyurl.com/l6vhwye.

15. "W.L. Gore & Associates," *Forbes*, updated October 2014, http://tinyurl.com/nr4w5yu; "A Team-Based, Flat Lattice Organization," W.L. Gore & Associates, undated, http://tinyurl.com/yq6aup.

16. Mike Kessler, "Insane in the Membrane," *Outside*, March 7, 2012, http://tinyurl.com/cgaycx8.

17. Polly LaBarre, "Forget Empowerment—Aim for Exhilaration," Management Innovation eXchange, April 25, 2012, http://tinyurl.com/bu2y3rn; Mehdi Kajbaf, "The most radical workplace in the world and 10 reasons why it's worked for 30 years," Organizational Effectiveness Solutions blog, Oct. 8, 2012, http://tinyurl.com/ledzqak.

18. Kastelle, op. cit.

19. Courtright, et al., op. cit.

20. "Employee Engagement," Quantum Workplace, undated, http://tinyurl.com/p4dnk23.

21. James L. Heskett, et al., "Putting the Service-Profit Chain to Work," *Harvard Business Review*, July 2008, http://tinyurl.com/n9bc6vu.

22. Kastelle, op. cit.

23. Garvin, op. cit.

24. "Self-Management," Morning Star Co. Self-Management, undated, http://tinyurl.com/mfv5qtq.

25. Gary Hamel, "First, Let's Fire All the Managers," *Harvard Business Review*, December 2011, http://tinyurl.com/ms4ufk3.

26. Ibid.

27. "Welcome to Valve," Valve Software, undated, http://tinyurl .com/k6qfkpa; Claire Suddath, "Why There Are No Bosses at Valve," Bloomberg Businessweek, April 27, 2012, http:// tinyurl.com/kjj7kcp.

28. "Handbook for New Employees," Valve Software, March 2012, http://tinyurl.com/7a3jjyb.

29. Leo Kelion, "Valve: How going boss-free empowered the games-maker," BBC, Sept. 23, 2013, http://tinyurl.com/ l3jff98.

30. "A Team-Based, Flat Lattice Organization," op. cit.

31. Terri Kelly, "No More Heroes: Distributed Leadership," Management Innovation eXchange, April 8, 2010, http:// tinyurl.com/m6xqjmr.

32. "How It Works," Holacracy, undated, http://tinyurl.com/ nx3rojk

33. Aimee Groth, "Zappos is going holacratic: no job titles, no managers, no hierarchy," Quartz, Dec. 30, 2013, http://tinyurl .com/ppxhwc5; Tim Kastelle, "Two Great Innovation Misquotes," the Discipline of Innovation blog, undated, http:// tinyurl.com/7peof8f.

34. Groth, "Zappos is going holocratic," op. cit.

35. Lawrence M. Fisher, "Ricardo Semler Won't Take Control," strategy+business, Nov. 29, 2005, http://tinyurl.com/nkfsk6a; also see Semco Partners homepage, http://tinyurl.com/ q2zdp6x.

36. "Maneuver Self Study Program," U.S. Army Maneuver Center of Excellence, updated Nov. 21, 2014, http://tinyurl.com/ k26ponm.

37. "Stanley McChrystal, Military leader," TED Talks, undated, http://tinyurl.com/orscj2q; "Mission Command Concept," National Defense University Libraries, updated Oct. 7, 2014, http://tinyurl.com/mec5phr.

38. Minda Zetlin, "The Power of Flat: How organizations without managers succeed in the real world," Oracle Profit Magazine, February 2014, http://tinyurl.com/ngh2zdy.

39. Staff report, "Soldiers of Fortune," Newsweek, Nov 13, 2009, http://tinyurl.com/lrrjt7o.

40. David Stein, "Dear CEO: They're Just Not That Into You," Forbes blog, Feb. 2, 2011, http://tinyurl.com/lqyqho7.

41. Foss and Klein, op. cit.

42. Andrew Beattie, "Adam Smith and 'The Wealth Of Nations,'" Investopedia, 2014,http://tinyurl.com/k4pezer.

43. Michael T. Hannan, "The Assembly Line," Encyclopaedia Britannica, undated, http://tinyurl.com/lf3gkxf.

44. Carter McNamara, "Historical and Contemporary Theories of Management," Free Management Library, undated, http:// tinyurl.com/peus5os.

45. "They Made America: Frederick Winslow Taylor," PBS, undated, http://tinyurl.com/lzd8h76.

46. Lea Terry, "The Management Theory of Max Weber," Business.com, May 20, 2011, http://tinyurl.com/oqoosp3.

47. Jeanne Dininni, "Human Relations Management Theory," Business.com, Aug. 2, 2011, http://tinyurl.com/p4wx7ly.

48. Steve Denning, "The Management Revolution That's Already Happening," Forbes blog, May 30, 2013, http://tinyurl.com/ laldc4f.

49. Foss and Klein, op. cit.

50. Gary Hamel, "Moon Shots for Management," Harvard Business Review, February 2009, http://tinyurl.com/kkx 6wue.

51. Ibid.

52. Ibid.

53. Steve Denning, "Leadership's #1 Challenge: Transforming Management," Forbes blog, Feb. 28, 2011, http://tinyurl.com/ qcfxesr.

54. David Hanna, "How GM Destroyed Its Saturn Success, March 8, 2010, Forbes, http://tinyurl.com/yjxf934; "How GM Crushed Saturn," April 3, 2009, Newsweek, http://tinyurl .com/nn6ukdj.

55. "Saturn: A Wealth of Lessons from Failure," the Wharton School, University of Pennsylvania, Oct. 28, 2009, http:// tinyurl.com/pd9zypv.

56. Natalie Hackbarth, David Weisser and Hilary Wright, "2014 Employee Engagement Trends Report," Quantum Workplace, http://tinyurl.com/molc88r.

57. "How It Works," op. cit.; Steve Denning, "Making Sense of Zappos and Holacracy," Forbes blog, Jan. 15, 2014, http:// tinyurl.com/nye4tcv.

58. Nellie Bowles, "Holacracy or Hella Crazy? The Fringe Ideas Driving the Las Vegas Downtown Project," Re/Code, http:// tinyurl.com/kcs53k2; "The holes in holacracy: The latest big idea in management deserves some skepticism," The Economist, July 5, 2014, http://tinyurl.com/np4vvpv.

59. "About Holacracy," Medium, http://tinyurl.com/lhjw53p.

60. "Freedom by Design," WorldBlu, undated, http://tinyurl .com/5vtupth; Glenn Llopis, "Corporations Must Bring Democracy into the Workplace: A Conversation with WorldBlu, HCL Technologies and Groupon," Forbes blog, May 16, 2011, http://tinyurl.com/lopnk54; and Laurence McCahill, "Would You Want to Work in a Fear- or Freedom-Led Workplace?" The Huffington Post, Oct. 13, 2014, http:// tinyurl.com/mwtyukk.

61. "What Is Self-Management?" op. cit.

62. Josh Allan Dykstra, "Why Self-Management Will Soon Replace Management," The Huffington Post, July 16, 2014, http://tinyurl.com/q57hal4.

63. Hamel, "First, Let's Fire All the Managers," op. cit.

64. Bunkhuon Chhun, "Better Decisions Through Diversity: Heterogeneity can boost group performance," Oct. 1, 2010, Kellogg School of Management at Northwestern University, http://tinyurl.com/lmf8m4g. See also Katherine W. Phillips, Katie A. Liljenquist and Margaret A. Neale, "Is the pain worth the gain? The advantages and liabilities of agreeing with socially distinct newcomers," Personality and Social Psychology Bulletin, Dec. 19, 2008, http://tinyurl.com/lj9qxtz; and Finley, op. cit.

65. Philippa Warr, "Former Valve Employee: 'It Felt a Lot Like High School,'" *Wired*, July 9, 2013, http://tinyurl.com/qamqxoe; see also Twitter of former employee at http://tinyurl.com/33tfmsm.

66. Jeri Ellsworth (video), "Former valve Engineer talk about CastAR 3D glasses," Twitch (podcast), June 28, 2013, http://tinyurl.com/o7fngod ; Michael French, "Valve's 'perfect hiring' hierarchy has 'hidden management' clique like high school," Develop, July 8, 2013, http://tinyurl.com/m9j3td5.

67. Evelyn Rusli, "Torment Claims Make GitHub Grow Up," *The Wall Street Journal*, July 17, 2014, http://tinyurl.com/p2hxfbk.

68. Jason Fried, "Why I Run a Flat Company," *Inc.* magazine, April 2011, http://tinyurl.com/3wmhehp.

69. Karl Moore and Kyle Hill, "The Decline but Not Fall of Hierarchy—What Young People Really Want," *Forbes* blog, June 14, 2011, http://tinyurl.com/6sn5qxa.

70. See Gen. Martin E. Dempsey's speech before the Royal United Services Institute for Defense and Security Studies, June 1, 2011, found in "Mission Command Concept," op. cit.

71. Gen. Martin E. Dempsey, "Mission Command White Paper," U.S. Army Chairman of the Joint Chiefs of Staff, April 3, 2012, http://tinyurl.com/n6f5wpg.

Chapter 10

1. Wyatt Kash, "Federal Agencies Advised to Brace for Big Data," *InformationWeek*, Oct. 29, 2013, http://tinyurl.com/kd7fvpn.

2. Andrew McAfee and Erik Brynjolfsson, "Big Data: The Management Revolution," *Harvard Business Review*, October 2012, http://tinyurl.com/mvy79gg.

3. Ibid.

4. Vincent McBurney, "The Origin and Growth of Big Data Buzz," Toolbox.com, May 31, 2012, http://tinyurl.com/lagrogw; "Big Data: A Brief History," Outliers Collective, undated. http://tinyurl.com/lwghj2r; and Christophe Bisciglia, "5 Common Questions About Apache Hadoop," Cloudera, May 14, 2009, http://tinyurl.com/kguv4kd.

5. Ibid., McBurney.

6. Quoted in Elizabeth Dwoskin, "Beware 'Big Data' Hype, Reports Warn," *The Wall Street Journal* (blog), May 27, 2014, http://tinyurl.com/n6zrhml.

7. Quoted in Steve Lohr, "How Big Data Became So Big," *The New York Times*, Aug. 11, 2012, http://tinyurl.com/9c2whlc.

8. "Forrester Debunks Big Data Hype," press statement, Forrester Research, May 28, 2014, http://tinyurl.com/l98ggvy.

9. Svetlana Sicular, "Big Data is Falling into the Trough of Disillusionment," Gartner (blog), Jan. 22, 2013, http://tinyurl.com/o92ck9q.

10. Quoted in Sarah Reedy, "AT&T: Big Data Hype Confuses Executives," LightReading, Nov. 11, 2014, http://tinyurl.com/l458tv4.

11. Ibid.

12. Jeanne W. Ross, Cynthia M. Beath and Anne Quaadgras, "You May Not Need Big Data After All," *Harvard Business Review*, December 2013, http://tinyurl.com/ngblayk.

13. Ibid.

14. Sunil Soares, *Big Data Governance: An Emerging Imperative* (2012), Kindle edition, location 654.

15. Ibid.

16. Quoted in Claire Porter, "Big data and retail: saviour or sham?" *The Guardian* (U.K.), June 6, 2014, http://tinyurl.com/lh2mebj.

17. For background, see "The R Project for Statistical Computing," http://tinyurl.com/8a7pk; "List of Calc Statistical Functions," Apache OpenOffice wiki, http://tinyurl.com/pkvfq2f; Jeffrey Stanton, Introduction to Data Science (2012), http://tinyurl.com/mf9go79.

18. Chris Anderson, "The End of Theory: The Data Deluge Makes the Scientific Method Obsolete," *Wired*, June 23, 2008, http://tinyurl.com/k5y294p.

19. Ibid.

20. Foster Provost and Tom Fawcett, *Data Science for Business: What you need to know about data mining and data-analytic thinking* (2013) Kindle edition, location 306ff.

21. Tim Harford, "Big data: are we making a big mistake?" *FT Magazine*, March 28, 2014, http://tinyurl.com/qalr9kl; Elizabeth Good Christopherson, "Confronting the Data Dilemma," Rita Allen Foundation (blog), July 25, 2013, http://tinyurl.com/o4jcx74.

22. Nassim N. Taleb, "Beware the Big Errors of 'Big Data,'" *Wired*, Feb. 8, 2013, http://tinyurl.com/pfdtgdn.

23. "Big Success With Big Data: Executive Summary," Accenture, April 2014, p. 3, http://tinyurl.com/nornoxy.

24. Jeff Bertolucci, "Big Data ROI Still Tough to Measure," *InformationWeek*, May 29, 2013, http://tinyurl.com/ngpbzmj; "Deliver Actionable Insights by Making Big Data Consumable," Kapow Software, February 2013, http://tinyurl.com/ol5m9ot.

25. Foster and Fawcett, op. cit., location 502.

26. Peter Aiken and Juanita Walton Billings, "Monetizing Data Management," Data Blueprint, Sept. 4, 2013, p. 11.

27. Ross, Beath and Quaadgras, op. cit.

28. Ibid.

29. Provost and Fawcett, op. cit., location 454.

30. Ibid.

31. For background, see ibid., locations 358 and 416.

32. Quoted in Leon Spencer, "Small companies have data edge over big business: Torque Data," ZDNet, April 14, 2014, http://tinyurl.com/o2jyl7s; for background, see "The Big and Small of Big Data," Torque Data/Sweeney Research, April 2014, http://tinyurl.com/nhqk79x.

33. Ibid., "The Big and Small of Big Data."

34. Donna Fuscaldo, "How Small Businesses Can Use Big Data," Fox Business, May 19, 2014, http://tinyurl.com/qd98f3s.

35. Quoted in ibid.

36. Quoted in Porter, op. cit.

37. "Nicolaus Copernicus," *Stanford Encyclopedia of Philosophy*, Aug. 16, 2010, http://tinyurl.com/o8royc6.

38. Simon Rogers, "John Snow's data journalism: the cholera map that changed the world," *The Guardian*, March 15, 2013, http://tinyurl.com/k549eqs.

39. Richard Miller Devens, "Cyclopedia of commercial and business anecdotes" (1865), p. 210, http://tinyurl.com/nenuo3h; "Furnese, Sir Henry," *The History of Parliament* (2002), http://tinyurl.com/nrtgqfu.

40. "John Wanamaker," Advertising Age, March 29, 1999, http://tinyurl.com/oj5j7gc.

41. Stanton, op. cit., p. 37.

42. Ibid., p. 38; for background, see "Gosset, William Sealy," Encyclopedia.com, originally published in *International Encyclopedia of the Social Sciences* (1968), http://tinyurl.com/m7qylts; and Joan Fisher Box, "Guinness, Gosset, Fisher, and Small Samples," *Statistical Science*, February 1987, pp. 45–52, http://tinyurl.com/lhagj9a.

43. Ibid., Stanton.

44. Frederick Winslow Taylor, "The Principles of Scientific Management," National Humanities Center, chp. 2, 1910, http://tinyurl.com/mlmcfuw; "Frederick Winslow Taylor," *Who Made America?* PBS, http://tinyurl.com/lzd8h76.

45. Trevor Hastie, Robert Tibshirani and Jerome Friedman, *The Elements of Statistical Learning: Data Mining, Inference, and Prediction* (2013), pp. vii, http://tinyurl.com/ls94f2n.

46. "Quality Gurus," Reference for Business, undated, http://tinyurl.com/pf94luu.

47. For background, see Sharon Bertsch McGrayne, *The Theory That Would Not Die* (2011); lukeprog (blogger), "A History of Bayes' Theorem," LessWrong (blog), Aug. 29, 2011, http://tinyurl.com/olbn2c9; and Kevin Boone, "Bayesian statistics for dummies," Kevin Boone (blog), May 13, 2010, http://tinyurl.com/opmuut6.

48. Ibid., McGrayne, p. 11.

49. Ibid.

50. "Robert O. Schlaifer, 79, Managerial Economist," *The New York Times*, July 28, 1994, http://tinyurl.com/q6576pr.

51. For background, see D.J. Power, "A Brief History of Decision Support Systems," DSSResources.com, March 10, 2007, http://tinyurl.com/px5klal.

52. Ross, Beath and Quaadgras, op. cit.

53. Ibid.

54. Jeffrey Needham, *Disruptive Possibilities: How Big Data Changes Everything* (2013), http://tinyurl.com/p5zqyj8, Kindle edition, location 25.

55. Stanton, op. cit., p. 61.

56. Thomas H. Davenport, Paul Barth and Randy Bean, "How 'Big Data' Is Different?" MIT *Sloan Management Review*, July 2012, http://tinyurl.com/bg9e3l5.

57. Angus Macaskill, "Big data: Big hype or big hope?" ZDNet, Oct. 1, 2013, http://tinyurl.com/nhrwqpg.

58. For background, see Thomas H. Davenport, Jeanne G. Harris and Robert Morison, *Analytics at Work: Smarter Decisions, Better Results* (2010), p. 39.

59. Cheryl Metzger, "IoT & Marketing in 2015: 3 Ways Marketers Will Rethink Big Data," LinkedIn, Dec. 24, 2014, http://tinyurl.com/ngk2nc6.

60. For background on schools of information science, see iSchools, http://tinyurl.com/pyfgpwk.

61. "IBM Narrows Big Data Skills Gap By Partnering With More Than 1,000 Global Universities," press release, IBM, Aug. 14, 2013, http://tinyurl.com/pen9qzj.

62. Lindsay Gellman, "Big Data Gets Master Treatment at B-Schools," *The Wall Street Journal*, Nov. 5, 2014, http://tinyurl.com/nv2prbf.

63. Quoted in ibid.

64. Quoted in Cory Weinberg, "B-Schools Finally Acknowledge: Companies Want MBAs Who Can Code," Bloomberg Businessweek, July 11, 2014, http://tinyurl.com/pkgk7lp.

65. Ibid.

66. For background, see Udacity, "Machine Learning and Self-Driving Cars," YouTube, Oct. 27, 2014, http://tinyurl.com/k87reh9; Alexis C. Madrigal, "The Trick That Makes Google's Self-Driving Cars Work," CityLab, May 16, 2014, http://tinyurl.com/o3zg3t9.

Chapter 11

1. "Rolls-Royce Holdings PLC Annual Report 2013," Rolls-Royce Holdings, Feb. 12, 2014, p. 130, http://tinyurl.com/ovwyol4.

2. "KPMG wins big at the Investment Management Association's inaugural Auditor Reporting Awards," news release, KPMG, Nov. 21, 2014, http://tinyurl.com/otah3z4.

3. "Reporting on Audited Financial Statements—New and Revised Auditor Reporting Standards and Related Conforming Amendments," International Federation of Accountants, Jan. 15, 2015, http://tinyurl.com/lry4m74.

4. "Progress report: International convergence of accounting standards," Baker Tilly Virchow Krause, Oct. 31, 2014, http://tinyurl.com/pbteucg.

5. Russell G. Golden, "From the Chairman's Desk," Financial Accounting Standards Board, second quarter 2014, http://tinyurl.com/omcrtpu.

6. Robert Bruce, "The Bruce Column—Interview with Paul Volcker," IASPlus, Oct. 2, 2012, http://tinyurl.com/pcf5mbf.

7. "Project Update: Revenue Recognition—Joint Project of the FASB and IASB," Financial Accounting Standards Board, June 3, 2014, http://tinyurl.com/ohkgzaw.

8. Ken Tysiac, "FASB delays revenue recognition effective date by one year," *Journal of Accountancy*, July 9, 2015, http://tinyurl.com/pp737p5.

9. "Analysis of the IFRS jurisdiction profiles," IFRS Foundation, May 1, 2015, http://tinyurl.com/p4t2p4g.

10. "Reporting by For-Profit Entities," External Reporting Board, undated, accessed Oct. 13, 2015, http://tinyurl.com/pbftm7s.

11. "Analysis of the IFRS jurisdiction profiles," op. cit.

12. "IFRS and US GAAP: similarities and differences," PricewaterhouseCoopers, October 2014, http://tinyurl.com/pfbttoc.

13. James Schnurr, "Remarks before the 2015 Baruch College Financial Reporting Conference," May 7, 2015, http://tinyurl.com/kv8hhpo.

14. Luke Kawa, "Bank of America: These Five Maps Show the Major Global Trends Investors Need to Know," Bloomberg Business, Aug. 12, 2015, http://tinyurl.com/qj52q8r.

15. Floyd Norris, "Holding Auditors Accountable on Reports," *The New York Times*, May 8, 2014, http://tinyurl.com/q8bwkrd.

16. "Extended auditor's reports: A review of experience in the first year," Financial Reporting Council, March 2015, http://tinyurl.com/pzd54v9.

17. David Milstead, "Audit changes are good news. But the U.S. is holding Canada back," *The Globe and Mail*, May 27, 2015, http://tinyurl.com/ne8pduo.

18. Michael Rapoport, "Improving Audit Reports Is Focus of Hearing," *The Wall Street Journal*, April 1, 2014, http://tinyurl.com/ned6aat.

19. Michael Rapoport, "Regulators, Accounting Firms Bicker Over Audit Rule," *The Wall Street Journal*, Sept. 21, 2014, http://tinyurl.com/oh87nce.

20. Stephen J. Cosgrove, comment letter to the Public Company Accounting Oversight Board, Dec. 11, 2013, http://tinyurl.com/pl6vwuo.

21. Sarah Deans and Terence Fisher, "New UK Auditor's Reports: A Review of the New Information," Citigroup Global Markets research report, March 27, 2014.

22. Mike Brewster, *Unaccountable: How the Accounting Profession Forfeited A Public Trust*, 2003, pp. 22–26.

23. Ibid, p. 47.

24. Ibid, p. 49.

25. "History and Milestones," PricewaterhouseCoopers, undated, accessed Oct. 13, 2015, http://tinyurl.com/ngvf8yb.

26. *A timeline of our history*, Deloitte, undated, accessed Oct. 13, 2015, http://tinyurl.com/pla9do3; Thomas A. King, *More Than a Numbers Game: A Brief History of Accounting*, 2006, p. 17.

27. Brewster, op. cit., p. 51; "History," KPMG, undated, accessed Oct. 13, 2015, http://tinyurl.com/odef3oc.

28. "Two people. One vision," Ernst & Young, undated, accessed Oct. 13, 2015, http://tinyurl.com/odbqj39.

29. King, op. cit., p. 15.

30. Brewster, op. cit., pp. 51–53.

31. King, op. cit., p. 21.

32. Brewster, op. cit., p. 73.

33. King, op. cit., p. 56.

34. Brewster, op. cit., p. 116; "The Accounting Hall of Fame: Maurice H. Stans," Ohio State University Fisher College of Business, undated, accessed Oct. 13, 2015, http://tinyurl.com/nmpt8ge.

35. Ibid., Brewster, p. 114.

36. Ibid., p. 148.

37. "FAF, FASB, and GASB Timeline," Financial Accounting Standards Board, undated, accessed Oct. 13, 2015, http://tinyurl.com/ouho8hh.

38. King, op. cit., p. 67.

39. "Securities and Exchange Commission Historical Society Oral History Project Interview with James Leisenring," April 12, 2011, p. 27, http://tinyurl.com/ngbp5ur.

40. "Enzi—FASB Stock Options Process is Flawed," news release, Sen. Mike Enzi website, March 7, 2003, http://tinyurl.com/opmuaxq.

41. Charles Lane, "Justices Overturn Andersen Conviction," *The Washington Post*, June 1, 2005, http://tinyurl.com/bybbm.

42. Dana Cimilluca and Don Stancavish, "WorldCom Restates Results, Has $73.7 Bln of Losses," Bloomberg News, March 12, 2004, http://tinyurl.com/pyec23w.

43. Brewster, op. cit., p. 261.

44. Paul F. Wessell, "Key Provisions of the Sarbanes-Oxley Act of 2002," Rhoads & Sinon, Aug. 2, 2002, http://tinyurl.com/nosvqfm.

45. Robert Herz, *Accounting Changes: Chronicles of Convergence, Crisis and Complexity in Financial Reporting*, 2013, p. 84.

46. Teresa Conover and Frederick Niswander, *U.S. & International Accounting: Understanding the Differences*, 2011, pp. vii–viii.

47. For the FASB's explanation of the differences between it and IASB, see Golden, op. cit.

48. "SEC Approves Statement on Global Accounting Standards," news release, Securities and Exchange Commission, Feb. 24, 2010, http://tinyurl.com/y8awxo2.

49. "Comparability in International Accounting Standards—A Brief History," Financial Accounting Standards Board, undated, accessed Oct. 12, 2015, http://tinyurl.com/ouek5ln.

50. Russell G. Golden, "From the Chairman's Desk," Financial Accounting Standards Board, third quarter 2015, http://tinyurl.com/pkzj896.

51. "Comparability in International Accounting Standards," op. cit.

52. David R. Burton, "Proposals to Enhance Capital Formation for Small and Emerging Growth Companies," Heritage Foundation, April 11, 2014, http://tinyurl.com/osdav7o.

53. "Jumpstart Our Business Startups Act Frequently Asked Questions," Securities and Exchange Commission, Sept. 28, 2012, http://tinyurl.com/pchcvw9.

54. "April 9, 2014, Subcommittee on Capital Markets and Government Sponsored Enterprises Hearing Entitled 'Legislative Proposals to Enhance Capital Formation for Small

and Emerging Growth Companies,'" memorandum, House Committee on Financial Services majority staff, April 4, 2014, http://tinyurl.com/qek5kb9.

55. "Fostering Innovation Act of 2013," govtrack.us, undated, accessed Oct. 13, 2015, http://tinyurl.com/nwhn6kg.

56. John Alan James, "High cost of Dodd-Frank is harming US banks and citizens," Congress Blog, *The Hill*, Aug. 13, 2015, http://tinyurl.com/pykw68l.

57. For background, see "The Dodd-Frank Act: Could there be Accounting Consequences?" KPMG, 2011, http://tinyurl.com/prc87wq.

58. Kelly Johnson, "New DOJ policies target corporate executives over companies," Federal Securities Law Source, Sept. 24, 2015, http://tinyurl.com/pk3dlsr.

59. Michael Rapoport, "SEC: Accounting Board Is Dragging Feet," *The Wall Street Journal*, Dec. 14, 2014, http://tinyurl.com/pk55vul; Michael Rapoport, "SEC Presses Audit Regulator PCAOB on Priorities," *The Wall Street Journal*, Feb. 4, 2015, http://tinyurl.com/oaqnsz8.

60. Emily Chasan, "PCAOB's Auditor Rotation Project is Essentially Dead," CFO Journal, *The Wall Street Journal*, Feb. 5, 2014, http://tinyurl.com/op4ljhr.

61. David Michaels, "The Jockeying Has Begun to Fill a High-Paid Job in Washington," Bloomberg Business, Sept. 9, 2015, http://tinyurl.com/pk3ha7n.

62. Ken Tysiac, "Five key issues FASB may change in financial reporting," *Journal of Accountancy*, May 1, 2014, http://tinyurl.com/nvjlafz.

63. Golden, "From the Chairman's Desk," third quarter 2015, op. cit.

Chapter 12

1. "Pantene's branding strategy behind its 'Not Sorry' commercial," *The Branding Journal*, June 27, 2014, http://tinyurl.com/mu5nd72.

2. Much of the digital marketing industry has discarded "clicks" as a metric because of the possibility of fraudulent robotic click activity. Now, sites attempt to filter out fraudulent interactions, and many marketers measure "impressions."

3. Shar VanBoskirk, "US Interactive Marketing Forecast, 2014–2019," Forrester Research, Nov. 4, 2014, http://tinyurl.com/pg4fcp5.

4. Laura McLellan, "Presentation for CMO Spend Survey 2015: Eye on the Buyer," Gartner Inc., Oct. 29, 2014, http://tinyurl.com/k49ren5.

5. Laura McLellan, "How Much Progressive Companies Invest In Digital Marketing," Gartner Inc., April 25, 2014, http://tinyurl.com/lvlxmqd.

6. Vani Hari, "Subway: Stop Using Dangerous Chemicals in Your Bread," Food Babe blog, 2014, http://tinyurl.com/m5yv2pm.

7. Harris Interactive and Domus Inc., "Domus Client Needs Poll," 2014, http://tinyurl.com/5jb2t4.

8. "Generation Like," PBS *Frontline*, Feb. 18, 2014, http://tinyurl.com/q3oy6gw.

9. "The Scarecrow" YouTube video, Chipotle Mexican Grill, accessed Dec. 12, 2014, http://tinyurl.com/odmffvx.

10. "Nike: Write The Future, Themill.com, website of the British digital effects company that collaborated on the ad with agency Wieden + Kennedy, undated, accessed Jan. 22, 2015, http://tinyurl.com/pl8qx7f; and "Nike: Write the Future," Wieden + Kennedy, 2014, http://tinyurl.com/qhks9cm.

11. Joe Marczynski, "Game of Thrones: Digital Marketing is Coming," LabelMedia, June 10, 2014, http://tinyurl.com/qdlwu66.

12. Jack Marshall and Ruth Bender, "Ad Creativity Takes Back Seat to Tech at Cannes," *The Wall Street Journal*, June 19, 2014, http://tinyurl.com/p3j7dkf.

13. Jake Sorofman, Laura McLellan and Patrick J. Sullivan, "Market Guide for Digital Marketing Technology Integrators," Gartner Inc., Aug. 22, 2014.

14. "The 2014 State of Enterprise Social Marketing Report," Spredfast, 2014, http://tinyurl.com/pzahdf4.

15. Robert Petersen, "11 Studies Prove Digital Marketing ROI," Rutgers Business School, Dec. 19, 2014, http://tinyurl.com/qjd7yem.

16. Christopher Heine, "Walmart's Social Is Getting 10X ROI and Tens of Thousands of Daily Interactions," *Adweek*, Oct. 4, 2013, http://tinyurl.com/pdzvc3e.

17. Ibid.

18. Dorian Benkoil, "How Publishers, Marketers Measure Attention in a Post-Page-View World," PBS *MediaShift*, June 17, 2014, http://tinyurl.com/nebyxlw.

19. "Measure Campaign Audience Across Every Screen," The Nielsen Co., 2014, http://tinyurl.com/p86no97.

20. "Exploring digital ROI for FMCG brands," Microsoft, 2013, http://tinyurl.com/ozekqyv.

21. Damian Ryan, *The Best Digital Marketing Campaigns in the World II*, 2nd ed., 2014, pp. 29–31.

22. Ibid, pp. 39–45; "Harley-Davidson," p. 303; and Lowe, undated, accessed Jan. 21, 2015, http://tinyurl.com/n32etfg.

23. Ibid, *The Best Digital Marketing Campaigns in the World II*, pp. 201–205.

24. Kevin Short, "DiGiorno Interrupts Serious Conversation About Domestic Violence to Sell Pizza," *The Huffington Post*, Sept. 10, 2014, http://tinyurl.com/ke8jzha.

25. Felicity Morse, "Kellogg's Twitter campaign 'RT this to give a vulnerable child breakfast' sparks online anger," *The Independent*, Sept. 11, 2013, http://tinyurl.com/llqojmy; and Jonathan Pollinger, "Kelloggs' Twitter breakfast blunder," Intranet Future, Nov. 11, 2013, http://tinyurl.com/n2orou4.

26. Jack Marshall, "This Beheading Is Brought to You by Nissan," Digiday.com, Oct. 23, 2013, http://tinyurl.com/lnaf59h.

27. "Children's Online Privacy Protection Rule," Federal Trade Commission, http://tinyurl.com/l4lbplj.

28. ".com Disclosures," Federal Trade Commission, March 2013, http://tinyurl.com/ppa9mf2.

29. "The Advertising Industry's Process of Voluntary Self-Regulation," Advertising Self-Regulatory Council, Jan. 1, 2014, http://tinyurl.com/m9ya3ru.

30. "Operators of Online 'Virtual Worlds' to Pay $3 Million to Settle FTC Charges That They Illegally Collected and Disclosed Children's Personal Information," Federal Trade Commission, May 12, 2011, http://tinyurl.com/laly9rd.

31. Amy Lee, "Playdom Gaming Company Fined $3 Million by FTC For Using Children's Information," *The Huffington Post*, May 12, 2011, http://tinyurl.com/kk9xunw.

32. Danah Boyd, *It's Complicated: The Social Lives of Networked Teens*, 2014.

33. Testimony of Jessica Rich, Senate Judiciary Subcommittee on Privacy, Technology and the Law, http://tinyurl.com/lfgvnuu.

34. "Snapchat Settles FTC Charges That Promises of Disappearing Messages Were False," Federal Trade Commission, May 8, 2014, http://tinyurl.com/m7um6wb.

35. Statement of Sen. Al Franken, Senate Judiciary Subcommittee on Privacy, Technology and the Law, June 14, 2014, http://tinyurl.com/mkxr5hb..

36. Ibid.

37. John R. Quain, "Nissan Leaf Telematics May Leak Driver Data to Third Parties," Wheels, *The New York Times*, June 16, 2011, http://tinyurl.com/mgczut7.

38. Chris Woodyard and Jane O'Donnell, "Your Car May Be Invading Your Privacy," *USA Today*, March 25, 2013, http://tinyurl.com/ccv9t8z.

39. S. 2171 (113th Congress): Location Privacy Protection Act of 2014, Govtrack.us, accessed Jan. 21, 2015, http://tinyurl.com/lmyn6ja; and Kate Kaye, "Location Privacy Bill Gets Another Push," Advertising Age, June 4, 2014, http://tinyurl.com/msjajjh.

40. Testimony of Luigi Mastria, Senate Judiciary Subcommittee on Privacy, Technology and the Law, June 14, 2014, http://tinyurl.com/mmraxnu.

41. Edward Wyatt, "FTC Fines Yelp and TinyCo for Violating Children's Privacy Rules," Bits, *The New York Times*, Sept. 17, 2014, http://tinyurl.com/m6nr6oq.

42. Cynthia O'Donoghue, "First European Cookie Fine Issued by Spanish Data Protection Authority," Global Regulatory Enforcement Law Blog, Feb. 27, 2014, http://tinyurl.com/lescjlj.

43. Mary Madden, "Public Perceptions of Privacy and Security in the Post-Snowden Era," Pew Research Internet Project, Nov. 12, 2014, http://tinyurl.com/p2536wh.

44. Damian Ryan and Calvin Jones, *Understanding Digital Marketing*, 2nd ed., 2012, p. 7.

45. "History of the Web," World Wide Web Foundation, undated, accessed Jan. 22, 2015, http://tinyurl.com/npmj85s.

46. Kim Ann Zimmermann, "Internet History Timeline: ARPANET to the World Wide Web," June 4, 2012, Live Science, http://tinyurl.com/7pewr9s.

47. Ryan and Jones, op. cit., p. 10.

48. "ITU releases 2014 ICT figures," International Telecommunications Union, May 5, 2014, http://tinyurl.com/mdhykxt; "Statistics, Aggregate Data," International Telecommunications Union, undated, accessed Jan. 26, 2015, http://tinyurl.com/poehsmu.

49. Ryan and Jones, op. cit.

50. Ibid., p. 14.

51. Ibid., p. 27.

52. Joe McCambley, "Stop Selling Ads and Do Something Useful," *Harvard Business Review* blog, HBR.org, Feb. 12, 2013, http://tinyurl.com/mxgbxg5.

53. Todd Wasserman, "This Is the World's First Banner Ad," Mashable.com, Aug. 9, 2013, http://tinyurl.com/l9jl2q4.

54. Laura Stampler, "How Dove's 'Real Beauty Sketches' Became the Most Viral Video Ad of All Time, Business Insider, May 22, 2013, http://tinyurl.com/l6eun2w.

55. Laurie Sullivan, "More Than 56% Of Ad Impressions Are Not Seen, Google Says," MediaPost / SearchMarketing Daily, Dec. 4, 2014, http://tinyurl.com/mxo9kde.

56. Thomas H. Davenport and D.J. Patil, "Data Scientist: The Sexiest Job of the 21st Century," *Harvard Business Review*, October 2012, http://tinyurl.com/kam2tg3.

57. Thomas H. Davenport, "Lessons on Big Data Marketing," CIO Journal blog, *The Wall Street Journal*, May 14, 2014, http://tinyurl.com/kcra4ef.

58. "Definition of: Net Neutrality," *PC Magazine* Encyclopedia, undated, accessed Jan. 22, 2015, http://tinyurl.com/ml6qogj.

59. Gautham Nagesh and Amol Sharma, "Court Tosses Rules of Road for Internet," *The Wall Street Journal*, Jan. 14, 2014, http://tinyurl.com/kxdnbdm.

60. Brian Fung, "Congressional Democrats are itching for a fight over net neutrality," The Switch, *The Washington Post*, Jan. 21, 2015, http://tinyurl.com/mfp396m.

61. Dwayne De Freitas, "Why marketers need to fight for net neutrality," VentureBeat, Nov. 10, 2014, http://tinyurl.com/mfzxs5e.

62. Dan Shewan, "What Is Net Neutrality and Why Should Marketers Care?" WordStream blog, April 18, 2014, http://tinyurl.com/mjwqe6f.

63. Dorian Benkoil, "Predictions for 2015: Content Shakeout, More Tracking, Measurement Muddle," *Mediashift*, PBS, Jan. 5, 2015, http://tinyurl.com/kfq7kc2.

64. "Landor's 2015 trends forecast," Landor, November 2014, http://tinyurl.com/mwcobyw.

65. Michael Della Penna, "10 Digital Marketing Predictions for 2015," ClickZ, Dec. 15, 2014, http://tinyurl.com/kpona5r.

66. "Gartner Says Mobile Advertising Spending Will Reach $18 Billion in 2014," Gartner, Jan. 21, 2014, http://tinyurl.com/pwkqxcp.

67. Suzanne Vranica, "Target's Target No Longer Just the 'White Suburban Mom,' CMO Says," CMO Today, *The Wall Street Journal*, Oct. 17, 2014, http://tinyurl.com/majtfsb.

68. McCambley, op. cit.

69. Anya Kamenetz, "18 Million People Are Using Nike+ To Track Their Fitness," *Fast Company*, Aug. 21, 2013, http://tinyurl.com/mnuomqf.

70. Cavan Canavan, "The Future of Biometric Marketing," TechCrunch, Dec. 21, 2014, http://tinyurl.com/nq5yat8.

71. Steve McClellan, "2015: Brace For The Collision Of Entertainment, Marketing And Communication," MediaPost Agency Daily, Dec. 29, 2014, http://tinyurl.com/ng2u96g.

72. Katherine Rosman, "Augmented Reality Finally Starts to Gain Traction," *The Wall Street Journal*, March 3, 2014, http://tinyurl.com/nkjf6wj.

73. Suzanne McDonald, "Future of Social Media: Mark Schaefer at SXSW," Designated Editor, undated, accessed Jan. 22, 2015, http://tinyurl.com/ps76rds.

74. Christopher Zinsli, "'This American Life' Producer Raises $1.5 Million for Podcast Startup Gimlet," Venture Capital Dispatch, *The Wall Street Journal*, Nov. 11, 2014, http://tinyurl.com/nt8uvxd.

75. See Kit Tang and Nur Atiqah M. Hatta, "Can social network Ello stay ad-free for long?" CNBC, Jan. 1, 2015, http://tinyurl.com/qa5j89p.

76. "What is Ello?" Ello, undated, accessed Jan. 22, 2015, http://tinyurl.com/q3jl2ns.

Chapter 13

1. Quinn Klinefelter, "The Story of Detroit's Bankruptcy: A 'Takeover' or an Inevitable Financial Crisis?" WDET, Nov. 9, 2015, http://tinyurl.com/q4trpqs.

2. Brian Vander Ark, "Failure: Lab Grand Rapids," via YouTube, June 4, 2013, http://tinyurl.com/z9hu28h.

3. Vickie Elmer, "Putting unvarnished failure on stage, in Michigan and beyond," *Fortune*, Jan. 5, 2015, http://tinyurl.com/gvz2gpp.

4. Sheryl Connelly, "Looking Further with Ford: 2015 Trends," Ford Motor Co., Dec. 29, 2014, http://tinyurl.com/glyflut.

5. Richard Feloni, "LinkedIn founder Reid Hoffman shares 3 lessons he learned from the failure of his first company," Business Insider, July 29, 2015, http://tinyurl.com/zcg5mxs.

6. Sue Shellenbarger, "Better Ideas Through Failure," *The Wall Street Journal*, Sept. 27, 2011, http://tinyurl.com/j9cugpm.

7. David Grossman, "Secret Google lab 'rewards staff for failure,'" BBC News, Jan. 24, 2014, http://tinyurl.com/hqvac8t.

8. Shellenbarger, op. cit.

9. Rick Wartzman, "Drucker's Take on Making Mistakes," Bloomberg Business, June 19, 2008, http://tinyurl.com/hwaqtc7.

10. Amy C. Edmondson, "Strategies for Learning from Failure," *Harvard Business Review*, April 2011, http://tinyurl.com/peme4pu.

11. "Why Do So Many Mergers Fail?" Knowledge@Wharton, March 30, 2005, http://tinyurl.com/znw8qn3.

12. Glenn Kessler, "Do nine out of 10 new businesses fail as Rand Paul claims?" *The Washington Post*, Jan. 27, 2014, http://tinyurl.com/jhfw963; Carmen Nobel, "Why Companies Fail—And How Their Founders Can Bounce Back," Harvard Business School Research & Ideas March 7, 2011, http://tinyurl.com/ogonbv4.

13. Tyler Atkinson, David Luttrell and Harvey Rosenblum, "How Bad Was It? The Costs and Consequences of the 2007–09 Financial Crisis," Federal Reserve Bank of Dallas, July 2013, http://tinyurl.com/zp55lde.

14. "Georgetown study finds the age at which young adults get traction in their careers has increased from age 26 to 30, and to age 33 for African Americans," news release, Georgetown University, Sept. 30, 2013, http://tinyurl.com/zhsm646.

15. Leah McGrath Goodman, "Millennial College Graduates: Young, Educated, Jobless," *Newsweek*, May 27, 2015, http://tinyurl.com/phexd3h.

16. "Fiscal Year Bankruptcy Filings Continue Fall," U.S. Courts, Oct. 28, 2015, http://tinyurl.com/py2vsc6.

17. "20 Largest Public Company Bankruptcy Filings 1980-Present," BankruptcyData.com, undated, accessed Dec. 10, 2015, http://tinyurl.com/lphhuu.

18. Benjamin Snyder, "Donald Trump's business fumbles," Fortune, July 6, 2015, http://tinyurl.com/npornjs.

19. Jill Lepore, "The Disruption Machine," *The New Yorker*, June 23, 2014, http://tinyurl.com/kxrnt34.

20. Rafael Efrat, "The Evolution of Bankruptcy Stigma," *Theoretical Inquiries in Law*, 2006, http://tinyurl.com/o4qausb.

21. Smita Singh, Patricia Corner and Kathryn Pavlovich, "Self-Stigmatisation of Entrepreneurial Failure," paper at the 25th Australian and New Zealand Academy of Management Conference, 2012, http://tinyurl.com/owwgca7 and http://tinyurl.com/pxdl7cn.

22. Shana Lebowitz, "From the projects to a $2.3 billion fortune—the inspiring rags-to-riches story of Starbucks CEO Howard Schultz," Business Insider, May 30, 2015, http://tinyurl.com/npx6tvc.

23. "Fear of failure affects lifelong learning," news release, the British Psychological Society, Sept. 9, 2014, http://tinyurl.com/nbotopt.

24. Lepore, op. cit.

25. Nancy Hass and Rose DeWolf, "Laventhol & Horwath Collapses: Suits Battered Accounting Giant," *The Philadelphia Inquirer*, Nov. 20, 1990, http://tinyurl.com/nedecst.

26. Gregory Richards, "1990: The other big accounting firm melt-down," *Philadelphia Business Journal*, Aug. 5, 2002, http://tinyurl.com/pbeyev5.

27. Luke Kawa, "China Has No Good Plan to Deal With Its Achilles Heel," Bloomberg Business, Oct. 7, 2015, http://tinyurl.com/o4b9ttr.

28. Stuart Gilson, "Coming Through in a Crisis: How Chapter 11 and the Debt Restructuring Industry Are Helping to Revive

the U.S. Economy," *Journal of Applied Corporate Finance*, Fall 2012, http://tinyurl.com/q3r8btt.

29. Farhad Manjoo, "The Upside of a Downturn in Silicon Valley," *The New York Times*, Aug. 26, 2015, http://tinyurl.com/pmfascl.

30. Seung-Hyun Lee et al., "How do bankruptcy laws affect entrepreneurship development around the world?" *Journal of Business Venturing*, September 2011, http://tinyurl.com/od62n6r.

31. Robin Sidel, "FDIC's Tab for Failed U.S. Banks Nears $9 Billion," *The Wall Street Journal*, March 17, 2011, http://tinyurl.com/pgdgjzq.

32. "Table A-12: Unemployed persons by duration of unemployment," Bureau of Labor Statistics, modified Dec. 4, 2015, http://tinyurl.com/3gna7.

33. Aaron Schachter and Clark Boyd, "Update: The history of Hashima, the island in Bond film 'Skyfall,'" PRI's The World, Nov. 23, 2012, http://tinyurl.com/ncex6pl; "Bodie State Historic Park," California Department of Parks and Recreation, undated, accessed Dec. 10, 2015, http://tinyurl.com/kj7bbh.

34. "Financial Crimes Report to the Public; Fiscal Years 2010–2011," FBI, undated, accessed Dec. 10, 2015, http://tinyurl.com/nebmy3r.

35. "Global Economic Crime Survey 2014," Pricewaterhouse Coopers, undated, accessed Dec. 10, 2015, http://tinyurl.com/pf8uh6x.

36. "Former Enron CEO Skilling gets 24 years," The Associated Press, NBC News, Oct. 23, 2006, http://tinyurl.com/qywmlla.

37. Gilson, op. cit.

38. William K. Alcorn, "Forum Health gets new name," The Vindicator, March 25, 2011, http://tinyurl.com/of8kxcm.

39. Paul Allen, "My Favorite Mistake," *Newsweek*, April 24, 2011, http://tinyurl.com/qf25jv3.

40. David Allison, "Bill Gates Interview," National Museum of American History, Smithsonian Institution, undated, accessed Dec. 10, 2015, http://tinyurl.com/nwgn83s.

41. Allen, op. cit.

42. "Business School researcher finds organizations learn more from failure than success," news release, University of Colorado, Denver, Aug. 23, 2010, http://tinyurl.com/37syaqr.

43. Brandon Mueller and Dean A. Shepherd, "Learning from Failure: How Entrepreneurial Failure Aids in the Development of Opportunity Recognition Expertise," Frontiers of Entrepreneurship Research, June 9, 2012, http://tinyurl.com/opsozom.

44. Deniz Ucbasaran, Paul Westhead and Mike Wright, "Why Serial Entrepreneurs Don't Learn from Failure," *Harvard Business Review*, April 2011, http://tinyurl.com/zxxbuqg.

45. David Brown, "Here's what 'fail fast' really means," VentureBeat, March 15, 2015, http://tinyurl.com/mvbejqr.

46. J.K. Rowling, "The Fringe Benefits of Failure, and the Importance of Imagination," *Harvard Magazine*, June 8, 2008, http://tinyurl.com/3lgw8ce.

47. Karissa Giuliano and Sarah Whitten, "The world's first billionaire author is cashing in," CNBC, July 31, 2015, http://tinyurl.com/jklgkw5.

48. Paul A. Gompers et al., "Performance Persistence in Entrepreneurship," Harvard Business School working paper, July 2008, http://tinyurl.com/zvqx84e.

49. Jeffrey A. Sonnenfeld and Andrew J. Ward, "Firing Back: How Great Leaders Rebound After Career Disasters," *Harvard Business Review*, January 2007, http://tinyurl.com/p5jctgf.

50. Geoff Lewis, "Failure porn: There's too much celebration of failure and too little fear," *The Washington Post*, Dec. 4, 2014, http://tinyurl.com/h2o7jo8.

51. Lydia Saad, "Americans' Money Worries Unchanged From 2014," Gallup, April 20, 2015, http://tinyurl.com/lhjp9jx.

52. Steven Church, "Jefferson County Judge Known for 'Rule-From-the-Bench' Style," Bloomberg Business, Nov. 15, 2011, http://tinyurl.com/hgf39mj.

53. Connelly, op. cit.

54. Slavica Singer, José Ernesto Amorós and Daniel Moska, "Global Entrepreneurship Monitor: 2014 Global Report," Table 2.3, Global Entrepreneurship Research Association, 2015, http://tinyurl.com/j3fn7nb.

55. Alicia Robb, Susan Coleman and Dane Stangler, "Sources of Economic Hope: Women's Entrepreneurship," Ewing Marion Kauffman Foundation, November 2014, http://tinyurl.com/zcnksam.

56. Belinda Luscombe, "Why Failure Is the Key to Success for Women," *Time*, Aug. 19, 2014, http://tinyurl.com/hmppb9o.

57. Slavica, Amorós and Moska, op. cit.

58. Jessica Lahey, "Why we should let our children fail," *The Guardian*, Sept. 5, 2015, http://tinyurl.com/ot5fp69.

59. Fons Trompenaars and Peter Woolliams, "Lost in Translation," *Harvard Business Review*, April 2011, http://tinyurl.com/zmh829p.

60. Louis Edward Levinthal, "The Early History of Bankruptcy Law," *University of Pennsylvania Law Review* and *American Law Register*, April 1918, http://tinyurl.com/hnc78ld.

61. Ibid.

62. Efrat, op. cit.

63. Jack Lynch, "Cruel and Unusual: Prisons and Prison Reform" *Colonial Williamsburg Journal*, Summer 2011, http://tinyurl.com/hrekbcx.

64. Charles Jordan Tabb, "The History of the Bankruptcy Laws in the United States," *American Bankruptcy Institute Law Review*, 1995, available at SSRN: http://tinyurl.com/jsomu64.

65. "The Evolution of U.S. Bankruptcy Law," Federal Judicial Center, undated, accessed Dec. 10, 2015, http://tinyurl.com/o89cgvy.

66. James Narron, David Skeie and Don Morgan, "Crisis Chronicles: The Panic of 1819—America's First Great Economic Crisis," Liberty Street Economics, Federal Reserve Bank of New York, Dec. 5, 2014, http://tinyurl.com/hakbetw.

67. Quentin R. Skrabec Jr., "100 Most Important American Financial Crises," Greenwood, 2015, pp. 53–58.

68. Scott A. Sandage, *Born Losers: A History of Failure in America*," Harvard University Press, 2005, p. 14.

69. Edward J. Balleisen, *Navigating Failure: Bankruptcy and Commercial Society in Antebellum America*, University of North Carolina Press, 2001, Introduction.

70. Scott Jennings, "Kentucky's tradition of reforming nation's prisons," *Louisville Courier Journal*, Aug. 6, 2014, http://tinyurl.com/jc74wde; "The Evolution of U.S. Bankruptcy Law," op. cit.

71. Eli Hager, "Debtors Prisons, Then and Now: FAQ," The Marshall Project, Feb. 24, 2015, http://tinyurl.com/q99mvab.

72. Christopher D. Hampson, "The New American Debtors' Prisons," Harvard Law School 2015 Stephen L. Werner Prize: Criminal Justice, Aug. 4, 2015, http://tinyurl.com/hvjlvnn.

73. Balleisen, op. cit.

74. "A Brief History of Bankruptcy," BanruptcyData.com, undated, accessed Dec. 11, 2015, http://tinyurl.com/hmcgm39.

75. Alexis de Tocqueville, *Democracy in America*, via University of Virginia American Studies Program, 1835, vol. 2, section 3, chp. 18, http://tinyurl.com/hpchkkm.

76. Sandage, op. cit.

77. "A Life Lived in a Rapidly Changing World: Samuel L. Clemens, 1835–1910," The Mark Twain House and Museum, http://tinyurl.com/ptqcbuh.

78. Rebecca Edwards and Sarah DeFeo, "The Depression of 1893," 1896: The Presidential Campaign, Cartoons & Commentary, Vassar College, 2000, http://tinyurl.com/yzogaa9.

79. "Chapter 13—Bankruptcy Basics," U.S. Courts, undated, accessed Dec. 10, 2015, http://tinyurl.com/kz53tfk.

80. David A. Skeel Jr., "The Genius of the 1898 Bankruptcy Act," University of Pennsylvania, Bankruptcy Developments Journal, January 1999, http://tinyurl.com/pwj93xd.

81. Quentin R. Skrabec Jr., "Rubber: An American Industrial History," 2013, p. 75.

82. Tony Borroz, "June 1, 1849: Stanley Twins Steam into History," *Wired*, June 1, 2009, http://tinyurl.com/o6s4hmw.

83. Ryan Bradley, "A Brief History of Failure," *The New York Times*, Nov. 12, 2014, http://tinyurl.com/pagn94e.

84. Anthony Young, "The Rise and Fall of the Edsel," Foundation for Economic Education, Sept. 1, 1989, http://tinyurl.com/nwbzlcg.

85. Ben S. Bernanke, "The Crisis as a Classic Financial Panic," Speech, Board of Governors of the Federal Reserve System, Nov. 8, 2013, http://tinyurl.com/ltx68lf.

86. David B. Ballard et al., "The Great Depression, 1929–1939: A Curriculum for High School Students," Federal Reserve Bank of St. Louis, 2007, http://tinyurl.com/nsvnk35.

87. Gene Smiley, "The American Economy in the 20th Century," 1993, p. 9–1.

88. Thomas A. Durkin, "Credit Cards: Use and Consumer Attitudes, 1970–2000," Federal Reserve Bulletin, September 2000, pp. 623–634, http://tinyurl.com/nzxvu5q.

89. "Equal Credit Opportunity Act (ECOA)," Consumer Financial Protection Bureau, June 2013, http://tinyurl.com/npm7pbg.

90. Viral V. Acharya, Julian Franks and Henri Servaes, "Private Equity: Boom and Bust?" *Journal of Applied Corporate Finance*, Fall 2007, http://tinyurl.com/pwv6wta.

91. Yuliya Demyanyk and Otto Van Hemert, "Understanding the Subprime Mortgage Crisis," Federal Deposit Insurance Corp., Feb. 4, 2008, http://tinyurl.com/pu58fd5.

92. "Financial Crisis Inquiry Commission Report," Financial Crisis Inquiry Commission, January 2011, pp. xv–xxvii, http://tinyurl.com/c79hfv2.

93. Christopher J. Goodman and Steven M. Mance, "Employment loss and the 2007–09 recession: an overview," Monthly Labor Review, Bureau of Labor Statistics, April 2011, http://tinyurl.com/ps5r99u.

94. "Fiscal Year Bankruptcy Filings Continue Fall," op. cit.

95. Rachel Gillett, "What the Hype Behind Embracing Failure Is Really All About," *Fast Company*, Sept. 8, 2014, http://tinyurl.com/pxzh5ho.

96. Barrett Watten, "Learning from Detroit: The Poetics of Ruined Space," *Detroit Research*, Spring/Fall 2014, http://tinyurl.com/och4not.

97. Joel Kurth and Christine MacDonald, "Volume of abandoned homes 'absolutely terrifying,'" *The Detroit News*, May 14, 2015, http://tinyurl.com/nheaete.

98. Barnini Chakraborty, "Fixing Detroit: America's comeback city?" Fox News, Dec. 18, 2013, http://tinyurl.com/nvmtpr8.

99. Danielle Douglas and Michael A. Fletcher, "Toyota reaches $1.2 billion settlement to end probe of accelerator problems," *The Washington Post*, March 19, 2014, http://tinyurl.com/qh4sclp.

100. David McHugh, "Volkswagen suffers loss due to scandal but sales hold up," The Associated Press, Oct. 28, 2015, http://tinyurl.com/ncd9gee.

101. L.M. Sixel, "Halliburton pays $18.3 million in back wages after federal inquiry," *Houston Chronicle*, Sept. 22, 2015, http://tinyurl.com/nz68wew; "Halliburton pays nearly $18.3 million in overtime owed to more than 1,000 employees nationwide after US Labor Department investigation," news release, U.S. Department of Labor, Sept. 22, 2015, http://tinyurl.com/odd68er.

102. "Lenovo: strong quarter hit by one-off costs," *Financial Times*, Nov. 12, 2015, http://tinyurl.com/q2put4h.

103. "Tuck Professor Sydney Finkelstein Announces Best and Worst CEOS of 2014," news release, Tuck / Dartmouth Newsroom, Dec. 17, 2014, http://tinyurl.com/qesn7t6.

104. Katy Stech, "Bankruptcy Law Overhaul Would Mean Big Changes," Bankruptcy Beat, *The Wall Street Journal*, Dec. 8, 2014, http://tinyurl.com/ojzmj3s.

105. "146 Startup Failure Post-Mortems," CB Insights, Dec. 3, 2015, http://tinyurl.com/ngcfum4.

106. Gillett, op. cit.

107. Rob Asghar, "Why Silicon Valley's 'Fail Fast' Mantra is Just Hype," Forbes.com blog, July 14, 2014, http://tinyurl.com/no6e67u.

108. "The Joys and Disappointments of Older Part-time Workers," news release, Rutgers, Sept. 3, 2015, http://tinyurl.com/nb2vpav.

109. Larry Hardesty, "Automating big-data analysis," MIT News Office, Oct. 16, 2015, http://tinyurl.com/pqbj5qp.

110. Vickie Elmer, "A new tool tells companies when they're about to lose their best people," Quartz, July 31, 2014, http://tinyurl.com/pytega6.

111. James Sterngold and Matt Wirz, "Financial Crisis Anniversary: For Corporations and Investors, Debt Makes a Comeback," *The Wall Street Journal*, Sept. 5, 2013, http://tinyurl.com/o35zhoa.

112. Jeanne Harris and Mark McDonald, "What the Companies That Predict the Future Do Differently," *Harvard Business Review*, Sept. 25, 2014, http://tinyurl.com/gmhurxl.

113. Edmondson, op. cit.

REFERENCES

Chapter 1

BOOKS

Bornstein, David, *How to Change the World: Social Entrepreneurs and the Power of New Ideas*, updated ed., Oxford University Press, 2007.

A journalist discusses the growth of social entrepreneurship through the story of Ashoka and its founder, Bill Drayton, and recounts case studies of successful social entrepreneurs.

Bornstein, David, and Susan Davis, *Social Entrepreneurship: What Everyone Needs to Know*, Oxford University Press, 2010.

Journalist Bornstein and social entrepreneur Davis offer a primer on the meaning of social entrepreneurship, its execution and its exemplary leaders.

Kayser, Olivier, and Maria Valeria Budinich, *Scaling Up Business Solutions to Social Problems: A Practical Guide for Social and Corporate Entrepreneurs*, Palgrave Macmillan, 2015.

Two activists in the social entrepreneurship movement address the problem of increasing the scale of an organization's work, and they present case studies on effective approaches around the world.

Kiser, Cheryl, Deborah Leipziger and J. Janelle Shubert, *Creating Social Value: A Guide for Leaders and Change Makers*, Greenleaf Publishing, 2014.

Focusing on the importance of leadership and creating social change, this book from Babson College faculty includes examples of social innovation from both social entrepreneurs and large corporations.

Lane, Marc J., *The Mission Driven Venture*, Wiley, 2015.

A prominent lawyer in the field of social enterprise gives a detailed account of corporate forms and legal issues; he writes primarily for a legal audience, but the information is useful for social entrepreneurs.

MacMillan, Ian C., and James D. Thompson, *The Social Entrepreneur's Playbook: Pressure Test, Plan, Launch, and Scale Your Social Enterprise*, expanded ed., Wharton Business Press, 2013.

A guide that grew out of an e-book on social entrepreneurship offers solid advice to help businesses move from uncertainty to manageable risk, without sugar-coating the challenges for social entrepreneurs.

ARTICLES

Battilana, Julie, et al., "In Search of the Hybrid Ideal," *Stanford Social Innovation Review*, Summer 2012, http://tinyurl.com/n9mctl5.

Researchers from Harvard Business School and Echoing Green, which runs fellowships for social entrepreneurs, examine the challenges facing those hybrid organizations that combine aspects of non-profits and for-profits.

Bornstein, David, "The Rise of the Social Entrepreneur," Opinionator, *The New York Times*, Nov. 13, 2012, http://tinyurl.com/nf3vqg7.

A journalist who has written extensively about the field discusses the role of social entrepreneurs in solving big societal problems.

Caligiuri, Paula, "When Unilever Bought Ben & Jerry's: A Story of CEO Adaptability," *Fast Company*, Aug. 14, 2012, http://tinyurl.com/8jwmv9g.

A magazine for entrepreneurs recounts Ben & Jerry's history as a socially responsible business and discusses the plans of the international corporation that bought it.

Chen, Jane, "Should Your Business Be Nonprofit or For-Profit?" *Harvard Business Review*, Feb. 1, 2013, http://tinyurl.com/q2q2tkg.

The co-founder of a social enterprise uses her personal experience to discuss the challenges of choosing a for-profit or nonprofit structure.

Cooke, T.J., "4 Benefits that B Corps Didn't See Coming," *The Huffington Post*, Aug. 17, 2015, http://tinyurl.com/p28dpa6.

Social entrepreneur discusses the unanticipated benefits that four social enterprises discovered in becoming certified B Corps.

Dees, Greg, "The Meaning of Social Entrepreneurship," Kauffman Foundation and Stanford University, revised May 30, 2001, http://tinyurl.com/pbtx6lt.

This classic article defining social entrepreneurship was written by the late Greg Dees, who is considered the founder of social entrepreneurship as an academic discipline.

Isaac, Mike, and David Gelles, "Kickstarter Focuses Its Mission on Altruism Over Profit," *The New York Times*, Sept. 20, 2015, http://tinyurl.com/ocmxml4.

Crowdfunding site Kickstarter reincorporated as a public benefit corporation.

Kell, John, "What does social entrepreneurship mean to actor Adrian Grenier?" *Fortune*, March 30, 2015, http://tinyurl.com/nl52bvs.

Social entrepreneur and actor Adrian Grenier talks about his decision to judge a social entrepreneurship competition.

Leimsider, Rich, "5 Bad Reasons to Start a For-Profit Social Enterprise," July 30, 2014, *Harvard Business Review*, http://tinyurl.com/oq39vbh.

The former vice president of fellowship programs at Echoing Green looks at misconceptions about the for-profit model.

Milway, Katie Smith, "How Social Entrepreneurs Can Have the Most Impact," *Harvard Business Review*, May 2, 2014, http://tinyurl.com/ojrrruv.

A partner in the Bridgespan Group, a consulting firm that specializes in advising mission-driven organizations, discusses three tips for maximizing social impact.

Schatz, Robin D., "Are You Cool Enough To Eat Bugs?" Forbes.com blog, Aug. 6, 2015, http://tinyurl.com/q8dhzjk.

Exo makes cricket-based protein bars to promote entomophagy—eating insects—as a way to address food security and environmental impact.

Schatz, Robin D., "How a Social Entrepreneur Overcame His 'Arrogant Failure' And Won Kudos From Oprah," Forbes.com blog, Oct. 18, 2015, http://tinyurl.com/q8dhzjk.

Gavin Armstrong, founder of social enterprise Lucky Iron Fish, reexamined his business plan after he realized that Cambodians were reluctant to buy his product from door-to-door salespeople.

REPORTS AND STUDIES

"Impact Investment: The Invisible Heart of Markets," Social Impact Investment Taskforce, Sept. 15, 2014, http://tinyurl.com/pdks3yv.

A task force that examined impact investing globally makes a number of recommendations for ways that governments and other participants can improve legal systems, remove barriers, measure impact and otherwise support such investment.

Saltuk, Yasemin, et al., "Eyes on the Horizon: The Impact Investor Survey," JPMorgan and Global Impact Investing Network, May 4, 2015, http://tinyurl.com/q4khgfn.

Annual survey from JPMorgan and the Global Impact Investing Network highlights the growing global market for impact investments across all sectors.

The Next Step

B CORPS

Gili, Enrique, "B-Corps challenge environment vs. profit paradigm," *Deutsche Welle*, June 30, 2015, http://tinyurl.com/pq4hmle.

The nonprofit B Lab's certification process for B Corps companies requires them to closely monitor their supply chains and employment practices.

Lawson, Sarah, "Is B Corps or Fair Trade Certification Right For Your Company?" *Fast Company*, Oct. 6, 2015, http://tinyurl.com/qcpv8b8.

Companies should consider membership fees, workplace culture, organizational structure and their overall mission when choosing whether to apply for B Corps- or fair trade-certification, according to the founder of the world's only fair-trade shoe company.

Tabuchi, Hiroko, "Etsy I.P.O. Tests Pledge to Balance Social Mission and Profit," *The New York Times*, April 16, 2015, http://tinyurl.com/o8vpzlf.

Online craft marketplace Etsy became the second publicly traded, B Lab-certified company, a move that will require it to balance maintaining its social mission with meeting shareholder demands.

FOR-PROFIT

MacArthur, Kate, "Pipeline Angels fuels women-owned, socially conscious startups," *Chicago Tribune*, Nov. 10, 2015, http://tinyurl.com/q44ml93.

A New York-based angel investment network has trained 180 female philanthropists, many of whom once donated mostly to nonprofits, to invest in successful for-profit social ventures.

McBride, Elizabeth, "How Honest Tea conquered the US beverage market," CNBC, Nov. 11, 2015, http://tinyurl.com/ngjgynn.

Maryland-based organic beverage company Honest Tea has preserved its socially responsible mission to produce healthy, low-sugar drinks despite being acquired by soda manufacturer Coca-Cola.

Pledger, Marcia, "Successful small businesses with social missions find products, service have to come first," *Cleveland Plain Dealer*, Nov. 12, 2015, http://tinyurl.com/q3annem.

Start-up social enterprises become more successful by attracting customers with successful products rather than by marketing their social mission, according to the director of a Cleveland-area social enterprise accelerator.

GLOBAL IMPACT

Baritugo, Kei, "Changing the world, one startup business at a time: Spring Activator's mission expands globally," *The Vancouver Observer*, Oct. 22, 2015, http://tinyurl.com/ppglk5p.

Two social investment support organizations in Vancouver and Seattle have joined together to mentor entrepreneurs and raise capital for for-profit social start-ups from outside countries.

Foley, Stephen, "Gates cautious on 'impact investing,'" *Financial Times*, Oct. 30, 2015, http://tiny url.com/nchqlz4.

Microsoft founder and philanthropist Bill Gates said that while impact investing is popular among billionaire charitable donors, he expects charity to remain the dominant way to address global social issues.

Jenkin, Matthew, "It's not charity: the rise of social enterprise in Vietnam," *The Guardian*, March 31, 2015, http://tinyurl.com/qalp7p7.

Many Vietnamese investors doubt whether social enterprises effectively contribute to social causes in their country, although some are learning about their benefits from Western nations, according to the director of a consultancy for deaf education in Vietnam.

UNIVERSITY PROGRAMS

Adeniji, Ade, "Millions to Foster Social Entrepreneurship on a California Campus. Will More Follow?" Inside Philanthropy, May 8, 2015, http://tinyurl.com/pdn8y8b.

A Silicon Valley venture capitalist and his wife donated $25 million to Santa Clara University's Center for Social Entrepreneurship, which focuses on creating social change through science and technology.

Bing, Chris, "Life and Social Entrepreneurship Inside Georgetown's Halcyon Incubator," DC Inno, July 27, 2015, http://tinyurl.com/q4fh2z7.

Georgetown University in Washington, D.C., created its own on-campus incubator that offers start-up founders housing, a collaborative workspace and adviser networks.

Ladika, Susan, "Socially Conscious," International Educator, March and April 2015, http://tinyurl.com/oaus5rt.

Florida State University is among a number of universities that have founded social entrepreneurship programs in which students learn skills required to run a social enterprise by working alongside nonprofits in other countries.

ORGANIZATIONS

Ashoka—Innovators for the Public

1700 N. Moore St., Suite 2000, Arlington, VA 22209
703-527-8300
www.ashoka.org/

Fellowship program that invests in social entrepreneurs; supports education to foster empathy and social change.

B Lab

155 Lancaster Ave., Wayne, PA 19087
610-293-0299
https://www.bcorporation.net/

Group established by socially oriented firms to certify B Corporations, provide analytics for benchmarking and lobby for benefit corporation legislation in United States.

Center for the Advancement of Social Entrepreneurship

Fuqua School of Business, Duke University, 100 Fuqua Drive, Durham, NC 27708
919-660-7734
https://centers.fuqua.duke.edu/case/

Research and education center that prepares leaders and organizations to achieve lasting social change.

Echoing Green

462 Seventh Ave., 13th Floor, New York, NY 10018
212-689-1165
http://www.echoinggreen.org

Group that supports social entrepreneurs with three fellowship programs; impact investing; and curriculum and training for young leaders.

Global Impact Investing Network (GIIN)

30 Broad St., New York, NY 10004
212-852-8349
www.thegiin.org/

International group that represents the impact investment industry.

Schwab Foundation for Social Entrepreneurship

91–93 Route de la Capite, CH-1223 Cologny/Geneva, Switzerland
+41 (0) 22 869 1212
www.schwabfound.org

Internationally oriented group that highlights and advances models of sustainable social innovation; identifies select social entrepreneurs; and engages in shaping global, regional and industry agendas that improve the state of the world.

Skoll Foundation

250 University Ave., Suite 200, Palo Alto, CA 94301
650-331-1031
www.skollfoundation.org

Foundation that supports social entrepreneurs through fellowship program, including through direct investments; runs Skoll Center for Social Entrepreneurship in London.

Social Enterprise Alliance

41 Peabody St., Nashville, TN 37210
615-727-8551
www.socialenterprise.us

National membership organization for social enterprises.

Chapter 2
BOOKS

Acs, Zoltan J., *Why Philanthropy Matters: How the Wealthy Give, and What It Means for our Economic Well-Being,* Princeton University Press, 2013.

An economist contends philanthropy must be incorporated into the economic principles of capitalism to create policies that promote society's better aspects.

Bugg-Levine, Antony, and Jed Emerson, *Impact Investing: Transforming How We Make Money While Making a Difference*, John Wiley & Sons, 2011.
Two nonprofit advisers discuss practices aimed at meeting social and environmental challenges with profitable investments.

Drucker, Peter F., *Managing the Non-Profit Organization: Practices and Principles*, HarperCollins, 1990.
In a book that had a major impact on the field, the business guru weighs in on managing nonprofits, with an eye to sustaining missions that improve how people function.

Gazley, Beth, and Katha Kissman, *Transformational Governance: How Boards Achieve Extraordinary Change*, Jossey Bass, 2015.
A college professor and a nonprofit consultant highlight ways that nonprofit boards can remedy underperformance.

McLaughlin, Thomas, *Streetsmart: Financial Basics for Nonprofit Managers*, 3rd ed., John Wiley & Sons, 2009.
A nonprofit consultant and professor explains concepts of nonprofit financial management.

Ott, J. Steven, and Lisa A. Dicke, eds., *Understanding Nonprofit Organizations: Governance, Leadership, and Management*, 2nd ed., Westview Press, 2011.
The authors focus on governing, leading and managing nonprofit organizations and how they differ from the public and private sectors.

Zunz, Olivier, *Philanthropy in America: A History*, Princeton University Press, 2012.
A historian provides an overview on philanthropy from Andrew Carnegie to Bill Gates.

ARTICLES

"Cancer Charities Announce Merger Deal," *The NonProfit Times*, June 11, 2015, http://tinyurl.com/nvhqn5c.
Two charities unite to increase their impact and close the funding gap for lung cancer research.

Casey, Michael, "Profits Meet Philanthropy in 'Pay-For-Success' Investments—Horizons," Money Beat, *The Wall Street Journal*, June 29, 2015, http://tinyurl.com/pexnha8.
"A radical form of civic-minded financial engineering" invites investors to underwrite financial risk in social programs in hopes that a share of savings will produce profit.

Hall, Peter Dobkin, "Philanthropy & the Nonprofit Sector," *Daedalus*, American Academy of Arts and Sciences, Spring 2013, http://tinyurl.com/n9bsvt6.
A historian explains how nonprofit institutions have faced centuries of public skepticism and distrust.

Kasper, Gabriel, and Jess Ausinheiler, "Challenging the Orthodoxies of Philanthropy," *Stanford Social Innovation Review*, June 17, 2015, http://tinyurl.com/pjml4mo.
The authors argue that prevailing wisdom must be tested to identify future paths in philanthropy.

Kramer, Mark R., "Catalytic Philanthropy," *Stanford Social Innovation Review*, Fall 2009, http://tinyurl.com/nozjebs.
A co-founder of the social impact consulting firm FSG and the Center for Effective Philanthropy highlights innovative solutions to philanthropic challenges.

Kristof, Nicholas, "Bill and Melinda Gates's Pillow Talk," *The New York Times*, July 18, 2015, http://tinyurl.com/p33woa8.
The columnist assesses the decade and a half and many initiatives since Bill and Melinda Gates formed the country's largest private foundation.

Parker, Sean, "Philanthropy for Hackers," *The Wall Street Journal*, June 26, 2015, http://tinyurl.com/o7q5psb.

An ex-Napster and Facebook executive says technologists, engineers and even geeks dominate in this new era.

Porter, Michael E., and Mark R. Kramer, "Philanthropy's New Agenda: Creating Value," *Harvard Business Review*, November–December 1999, http://tinyurl.com/ncawvtw.

A plea to foundations that challenged nonprofit orthodoxy when it was published formed the foundation for performance measurement and strategic planning that are in growing use today.

"The butterfly effect," *The Economist*, Nov. 2, 2013, http://tinyurl.com/okdlqna.

Charities and companies promote togetherness to advance their respective missions.

REPORTS AND STUDIES

"Spotlight on the New Wealth Builders," The Economist Intelligence Unit and Citibank, undated, accessed Oct. 8, 2015, http://tinyurl.com/qywfg5a.

A 2013 survey of global households with financial assets of $100,000 to $2 million found regional variations in generosity.

"World Giving Index 2014," Charities Aid Foundation, November 2014, http://tinyurl.com/o3wqnn6.

More than 1 million interviews conducted by Gallup since 2005 and 2006 as part of its World Poll survey provide a picture of global charity.

Havens, John J., and Paul G. Schervish, "A Golden Age of Philanthropy Still Beckons: National Wealth Transfer and Potential for Philanthropy," Boston College Center on Wealth and Philanthropy, May 2014, http://tinyurl.com/owhzxqt.

The authors use a computer model to produce estimates of wealth transfer and household charitable giving through 2061.

McKeever, Brice S., and Sarah L. Pettijohn, "The Nonprofit Sector in Brief 2014," Urban Institute Center on Nonprofits and Philanthropy, Oct. 27, 2014, http://tinyurl.com/q576sgh.

Report highlights trends in the number and finances of 501(c)(3) public charities and key findings on private charitable contributions and volunteering.

The Next Step

FUNDRAISING

Gharib, Malaka, "At What Point Does A Fundraising Ad Go Too Far?" National Public Radio, Sept. 30, 2015, http://tinyurl.com/noekcwc.

More organizations are using images of starving children in fundraising advertisements that exploit poor people to extract money from sympathetic donors, some charity executives say.

Pallotta, Dan, "The Economics of Charity Telemarketing," *Harvard Business Review*, April 15, 2015, http://tinyurl.com/mk8yfyb.

Many people wrongly accuse fundraising telemarketing services of hoarding donations rather than giving them to their assigned charities, according to an expert in nonprofit marketing and fundraising technology.

Sullivan, Paul, "Gritty Details Are Behind the Glitter at Fund-Raising Galas," *The New York Times*, April 17, 2015, http://tinyurl.com/qcj6urh.

The most successful charity gala fundraisers in New York City provide guests with detailed views of the charity's management and day-to-day operations, according to organizers.

LEADERSHIP

Callahan, David, "Rare But Valuable: The Foundation Chief as Thought Leader," Inside Philanthropy, Oct. 1, 2015, http://tinyurl.com/p2yaxdm.

While charity executives usually come to the job with strong philanthropic experience, executives with academic backgrounds can be more adept at rethinking organizational frameworks and coming up with fresh ideas about their causes.

Dagher, Veronica, "How Family Foundations Can Pass on the Philanthropy Flame to the Next Generation," *The Wall Street Journal*, April 12, 2015, http://tinyurl.com/otf7ftz.

Family foundation leaders can groom younger generations for leadership roles by sharing histories with heirs, involving them in events at early ages and allowing them to vote on decisions.

Hope, Christopher, "32 charity bosses paid over £200,000 last year," *The Telegraph*, Feb. 26, 2015, http://tinyurl.com/nqmghyd.

The number of U.K.-based charities that paid executives more than 200,000 pounds (about $300,000) increased in 2014, despite a government-led push to rein in executive compensation.

TECHNOLOGY

Lee, Jasen, "BBB warns against Syrian refugee scams," *Deseret News*, Sept. 16, 2015, http://tinyurl.com/q2qsmv2.

People who want to donate online to Syrian refugee humanitarian groups need to be on guard against scammers posing as legitimate groups on social media, the Better Business Bureau says.

Love, Julia, "Apple pledges more aid to help with Europe's migrant crisis," Reuters, Sept. 18, 2015, http://tinyurl.com/qe2cwvk.

Apple, Google and other technology companies have offered to match donations by customers and employees to European refugee humanitarian groups and have created faster ways to donate from mobile devices.

Reich, J.E., "Kickstarter Makes Philanthropy Its Policy By Reincorporating As A Benefit Corporation," *Tech Times*, Sept. 22, 2015, http://tinyurl.com/qdngf75.

Crowdfunding platform Kickstarter reincorporated as a public benefit corporation, with an emphasis on how its operations affect society.

WEALTHY DONORS

Cohen, Rick, "Travel Writer Finds Poverty in the American Deep South and Hypocrisy in Corporate Philanthropy," *The Nonprofit Quarterly*, Oct. 6, 2015, http://tinyurl.com/ogvagjl.

Well-known travel writer Paul Theroux denounces companies for moving jobs overseas, then "offering a sop to America's poor" through charity.

Foley, Stephen, "Warren Buffett urges young tech titans to give big and early," *Financial Times*, Oct. 2, 2015, http://tinyurl.com/o8q6znw.

Investor and philanthropist Warren Buffett counsels Silicon Valley entrepreneurs who have quickly amassed fortunes to begin donating early and actively so they can make the greatest impact, but many have not heeded him.

Wallace, Nicole, "Silicon Valley vs. Philanthropy," *The Chronicle of Philanthropy*, June 1, 2015, http://tinyurl.com/nv7h5g6.

Although wealthy technology company executives have struggled to produce results as philanthropists, some charities desperate for their donations are altering their organizations or moving to Silicon Valley.

ORGANIZATIONS

Committee Encouraging Corporate Philanthropy
5 Hanover Square, Suite 2102, New York, NY 10004
212-825-1000
http://cecp.co

Coalition of CEOs founded by actor Paul Newman that seeks to include societal improvement in assessing businesses.

Community Wealth Partners
1825 K St., N.W., Suite 1000, Washington, DC 20006
202-618-4778
http://communitywealth.com

Consulting firm that helps nonprofit organizations become more self-sustaining through social enterprise ventures.

Foundation Center
32 Old Slip, 24th Floor, New York, NY 10005-3500
212-620-4230
http://Foundationcenter.org

Information source about philanthropy worldwide, providing data, analysis and training.

FSG
1901 L St., N.W., Suite 850, Washington, DC 20036
202-469-7540
www.fsg.org

Consulting firm launched by Michael Porter and Mark Kramer, the authors of a 1999 Harvard Business Review article that called on nonprofit organizations to adopt rigorous strategies to create value beyond their grant dollars.

Global Philanthropy Forum
312 Sutter St., Suite 200, San Francisco, CA 94108
415-293-4657
http://philanthropyforum.org

An initiative of the World Affairs Council acting as a peer-learning network of philanthropists committed to advancing equity and opportunity in the developing world.

Guidestar
1250 H St., N.W., Suite 1150, Washington, DC 20005
www.guidestar.org

Gathers and disseminates information about nonprofit organizations, including financial reports and tax filings.

Monitor Institute
101 Market St., Suite 1000, San Francisco, CA 94105
415-932-5382
http://monitorinstitute.com

Consulting firm and think tank that is part of the professional services network Deloitte.

Skoll World Forum on Social Entrepreneurship
250 University Ave., Suite 200, Palo Alto, CA 94301
650-331-1031
https://skollworldforum.org

Hosts an annual conference aimed at finding solutions to social challenges.

Urban Institute
2100 M St., N.W., Washington, DC 20037
202-833-7200
www.urban.org

Maintains the National Center for Charitable Statistics; conducts research aimed at solving challenges in rapidly changing urban environments.

World Association of Non-Governmental Organizations
866 United Nations Plaza, Suite 529, New York, NY 10017
212-588-1802
www.wango.org

International organization working to strengthen the nongovernmental sector and increase public understanding of the nongovernmental community.

Chapter 3

BOOKS

Elkington, John, *The Zeronauts: Breaking the Sustainability Barrier*, Routledge, 2012.
The creator of the "triple bottom line" looks at a new five-prong paradigm that moves well beyond incremental change to transformation.

Hart, Stuart L., *Capitalism at the Crossroads: The Unlimited Business Opportunities in Solving the World's Most Difficult Problems*, Wharton School Publishing, 2005.
The creator of the Sustainable Entrepreneurship MBA at the University of Vermont explains the history of sustainability and its possibilities.

McDonough, William, and Michael Braungart, *Cradle to Cradle: Remaking the Way We Make Things*, North Point Press, 2002.

The originators of circular or closed-loop production describe a seminal process of eliminating waste altogether.

Winston, Andrew S., *The Big Pivot: Radically Practical Strategies for a Hotter, Scarcer, and More Open World*, Harvard Business Review Press, 2014.
A business strategist gives a blueprint for how to incorporate sustainability in a business context.

ARTICLES

Bardelline, Jonathan, "How UPS makes the business case for sustainability projects," Greenbiz.com, May 6, 2013, http://tinyurl.com/ofk9xmc.
UPS successfully argued for alternative fuel or advanced technology to power its fleet.

Davis, Grant, "The Triple Bottom Line Goal of Sustainable Business," *Entrepreneur*, March 2013, http://tinyurl.com/pe36caw.
Entrepreneurs have successfully used the principle of the triple bottom line—profit, planet and people.

Kaye, Leon, "The Business Case for Sustainability Is Becoming Easier to Make," TriplePundit, March 15, 2013, http://tinyurl.com/bb4yy29.
The editor of GreenGoPost, a website devoted to sustainability, describes how "green" efforts have helped the bottom line.

Kelly-Detwiler, Peter, "The Upside and Waging Peace Through Commerce: William McDonough Wants Us to Design Our Way to Abundance," *Forbes*, Nov. 20, 2013, http://tinyurl.com/mb qet6w.
Architect William McDonough discusses the concept of closed-loop manufacturing, where everything gets recycled.

Kiron, David, et al, "Sustainability's Next Frontier: Walking the Talk on the Sustainability Issues That Matter Most," MIT *Sloan Management Review*, Dec. 15, 2013, http://tinyurl.com/lxxtfro.
Boston Consulting Group and editors at MIT Sloan Management Review present research on how companies are faring with integrating sustainable values and practices.

Rajaram, Dhiraj, "Making the Business Case for Sustainability," *The Harvard Business Review*, May 2, 2011, http://tinyurl.com/krn33z8.
CEO of an analytics firm explains companies can measure the financial impact of sustainability strategies.

Scott, Ryan, "The Bottom Line of Corporate Good," *Forbes*.com, Sept. 14, 2012, http://tinyurl.com/8 uy49tk.
CEO of Causecast, a firm that markets a technology platform to social cause-oriented organizations, explains the people, planet, profits framework.

REPORTS AND STUDIES

"The Business Case for Sustainability," International Finance Corp., 2012, http://tinyurl.com/mhhodsd.
A report from a World Bank affiliate puts the business case for sustainability in an international context.

"Planning for a Sustainable Future," National Association for Environmental Management, 2012, http://tinyurl.com/n364e4g.
Twenty-five sustainability leaders and experts discuss their current thinking about sustainability.

Makower, Joel, et al., "The State of Green Business 2014," GreenBiz and Trucost, 2014, http://tinyurl.com/kqcpcep.
The editors of GreenBiz, a leading website about sustainable business, discuss trends in everything from chemical transparency to corporate leadership.

The Next Step
ACCOUNTABILITY

Conti, David, "Center for Sustainable Shale Development aims to raise standards," *Pittsburgh Tribune-Review*, Jan. 11, 2015, http://tinyurl.com/o32g39t.

The Pittsburgh-based Center for Sustainable Shale Development, created in 2013 to certify natural gas companies for sustainable standards, aims to broaden its regulation of Pennsylvania's energy industry in 2015.

Leinaweaver, Jeff, "Might new financial tools translate ESG data into real-world loss and profit?" *The Guardian* (U.K.), Nov. 25, 2013, http://tinyurl.com/o2osvoh.

Bloomberg and Thomson Reuters have created databases containing economic, social and governance data from thousands of businesses to enable reporters and organizations to hold companies accountable for sustainability initiatives.

Roston, Eric, "Sustainable Companies Want to Be Transparent — But Not Too Transparent," Bloomberg, Feb. 11, 2014, http://tinyurl.com/p6b95tn.

Corporate counsel are wary of sharing too much information, as companies make environmental impact, social issue and corporate governance data more publicly accessible, according to the director of a sustainability consulting firm.

ENVIRONMENTALISM

Doyle, Alister, "IKEA may tighten carbon rules to protect environment," Reuters, Oct. 13, 2014, http://tinyurl.com/l32rtbt.

Swedish furniture retailer Ikea will shift energy investments away from fossil fuels and toward solar and wind power in 2015, while also purchasing more wood and cotton from sustainable sources.

Elgin, Ben, "No More Faking It: Companies Ditch Green Credits, Clean Up Instead," Bloomberg Businessweek, Dec. 17, 2014, http://tinyurl.com/n9h2zu3.

More companies are dismissing the positive effects of purchasing renewable-energy credits, each equating to one hour of renewable-energy supply, in favor of pursuing their own renewable energy.

Strom, Stephanie, "Walmart Aims to Go Greener on Food," *The New York Times*, Oct. 6, 2014, http://tinyurl.com/mzb97jx.

Walmart plans to collaborate with food suppliers to reduce its environmental footprint resulting from food production, to improve access to healthy foods and to reward farmers for sustainable practices.

PHILANTHROPY

Kozlov, Klara, "New survey shows FTSE 100 companies have increased charitable giving," *The Guardian* (U.K.), Aug. 14, 2014, http://tinyurl.com/nfwqyvm.

Research by the U.K.-based Charities Aid Foundation shows charitable donations by companies in London's FTSE 100 stock exchange nearly doubled between 2007 and 2012.

Seervai, Shanoor, "Indian Companies and Charities Aren't Ready for New Giving Law," *The Wall Street Journal*, April 11, 2014, http://tinyurl.com/pq864ju.

India's nonprofits must learn to manage more philanthropic donations after a new law took effect requiring companies to give 2 percent of their profits to causes such as hunger, gender equality and environmental sustainability.

Shwab, Klaus, "Business in a Changing World," *Foreign Affairs*, Jan. 6, 2015, http://tinyurl.com/ol6l4dt.

Global business will benefit long-term if companies innovate in corporate governance, philanthropy, social entrepreneurship, citizenship and accountability, according to the executive chairman of the World Economic Forum.

PROFITABILITY

Grene, Sophia, The bottom line is a sustainability one," *Financial Times* (U.K), Sept. 21, 2014, http://tinyurl.com/ps4vq22.

A study by researchers from the University of Oxford's Smith School of Enterprise and the Environment indicates that practicing sustainability directly correlates to improved stock price performance for companies.

Kukil, Bora, "New Report On Global Corporate Sustainability Practices Shows Talkers Outnumber The Doers," *International Business Times*, Dec. 18, 2013, http://tinyurl.com/p3cw572.

According to research by the MIT Sloan Management Review and The Boston Consulting Group, there are more companies claiming to pursue sustainability for increased profits and reputational gains than companies that actually pursue those actions.

Miller, Joe, "War on waste makes sustainable business more profitable," BBC, May 19, 2014, http://tinyurl.com/pevv485.

International waste management companies and sustainability nonprofits working with major corporations advise their clients that sustainable disposal makes most businesses more competitive.

ORGANIZATIONS

American Sustainable Business Council

401 New York Ave., N.W.
Suite 1225
Washington, D.C. 20005
202-595-9302
http://asbcouncil.org

A national advocacy group that works for a sustainable economy.

CDP (formerly the Carbon Discovery Project)

132 Crosby St.
8th Floor
New York, NY 10012
212-378-2086
www.cdp.net

Major nonprofit that works with companies and other stakeholders to transform business to prevent climate change.

Ceres (the Coalition for Environmentally Responsible Economies)

99 Chauncy St.
6th Floor
Boston, MA 02111

617-247-0700
www.ceres.org

Nonprofit for investors and businesses in sustainability that has numerous studies about industries, company rankings, and sustainability advice.

GreenBiz Group

350 Frank H. Ogawa Plaza
Oakland, CA 94612
510-550-8285
www.greenbiz.com

A varied and thorough source of news, reports and events.

International Institute for Sustainable Development

61 Portage Ave. E.
6th Floor
Winnipeg, Manitoba, Canada R3BOY4
204-958-7700
www.iisd.org.

International public policy research and lobbying institute for sustainable development.

Sustainability Consortium

Arizona State University Global Institute of Sustainability
P.O. Box 873511
Tempe, AZ 85287-3511
480-965-1770
www.sustainabilityconsortium.org

Trade association seeking a scientific foundation for innovation to improve consumer product sustainability.

Sustainable Manufacturer Network

833 Featherstone Rd.
Rockford, IL 61107
815-399-8700
http://sustainablemfr.com

Industry association that promotes "cost-effective, environmentally and socially responsible manufacturing."

U.S. Forum for Sustainable and Responsible Investment
1660 L St., N.W.
Suite 306
Washington, DC 20036
202-872 5361
www.ussif.org

Association for professionals, firms, institutions and organizations engaged in sustainable, responsible and impact investing.

Chapter 4

BOOKS

Botsman, Rachel, and Roo Rogers, *What's Mine Is Yours: The Rise of Collaborative Consumption*, HarperCollins, New York, 2010.
Botsman, a business consultant, and Rogers, the founder of several sharing-economy companies, trace the roots of the sharing economy and the changes in how people consume goods and services.

Chase, Robin, *Peers Inc: How People and Platforms Are Inventing the Collaborative Economy and Reinventing Capitalism*, PublicAffairs, New York, 2015.
Chase, a co-founder of Zipcar, draws on the relatively short history of the sharing economy and explores how it is changing the broader economy.

Stephany, Alex, *The Business of Sharing: Making It in the Sharing Economy*, Palgrave Macmillan, New York, 2015.
Stephany, CEO of JustPark, a sharing-economy company in Great Britain, outlines best practices for succeeding in the sharing economy by examining the experiences of his own firm as well as others.

ARTICLES

Asher-Schapiro, Avi, "The Sharing Economy Is Propaganda," Cato Unbound, Feb. 13, 2015, http://tinyurl.com/o2275be.
As part of a multi-author debate on a libertarian website, a journalist who has written about how Uber drivers see their work argues that much of the "sharing economy" is old-fashioned capitalism in disguise.

Badger, Emily, "Airbnb is about to start collecting hotel taxes in more major cities, including Washington," *The Washington Post*, Jan. 29, 2015, http://tinyurl.com/nac6kdd.
Airbnb agrees to be the tax collector for some cities to ease regulators' concerns about lost revenue.

Benkler, Yochai, "Sharing Nicely: On Shareable Goods and the Emergence of Sharing as a Modality of Economic Production," *Yale Law Journal*, 2004, pp. 273–358, http://tinyurl.com/nv384q2.
Harvard law professor's thorough analysis was the first real articulation of the modern sharing economy.

Cannon, Sarah, and Lawrence H. Summers, "How Uber and the Sharing Economy CanWin Over Regulators," *Harvard Business Review*, Oct. 13, 2014, https://hbr.org/2014/10/how-uber-and-the-sharing-economy-can-win-over-regulators/.
A manager at Google Capital (Cannon) and a former Treasury secretary (Summers) offer detailed advice on how sharing-economy companies can get the best treatment from regulators.

Cohen, Boyd, and Jan Kietzmann, "Ride On! Mobility Business Models for the Sharing Economy," *Organization & Environment*, Aug. 31, 2014, http://oae.sagepub.com/content/27/3/279.
The authors examine shared transportation business models to find the optimal balance between companies and local governments.

Feeney, Matthew, "Level the Playing Field—by Deregulating," Cato Unbound, Feb. 10, 2015, http://tinyurl.com/onphurf.
A policy analyst at the libertarian Cato Institute argues that new technologies have made much regulation counterproductive.

Kelly, Kevin, "We Are the Web," *Wired*, August 2005, http://tinyurl.com/p4kjdtj.

Wired magazine's founding executive editor offers a fascinating recounting of the development of the technologies that power the sharing economy.

Shafroth, Frank, "The Unforeseen Fiscal Challenges of Uber-Like Services," *Governing*, March 20, 2015, http://tinyurl.com/pmh3mlj.

The director of the Center for State and Local Government Leadership at George Mason University illuminates the challenges the sharing economy poses for government.

Sundararajan, Arun, "A Safety Net Fit for the Sharing Economy," *Financial Times*, June 22, 2015, http://tinyurl.com/qclxwu8.

A professor of information, operations and management sciences at New York University's Stern School of Business argues that benefits such as health coverage, worker's compensation and paid vacations should be available to sharing-economy workers.

REPORTS AND STUDIES

"Alternative Financial Services: A Primer," *FDIC Quarterly*, April 27, 2009, http://tinyurl.com/p643omd.

Report from the Federal Deposit Insurance Corp. explains how alternative financial services work, including peer-to-peer lending, and how the services interact.

Krueger, Alan B., and Jonathan V. Hall, "An Analysis of the Labor Market for Uber's Driver-Partners in the United States," Working Paper #587, Princeton University, Jan. 22, 2015, http://tinyurl.com/n5norw8.

A Princeton economist (Krueger) and Uber's head of policy analysis (Hall) examine Uber data and find mostly positive effects for communities and employees.

Schneiderman, Eric T., "Airbnb in the City," New York State Office of the Attorney General, Oct. 14, 2014, http://tinyurl.com/m8pqffb.

Report lays out the New York government's case against Airbnb, finding the rental activities supported by the platform frequently violate state laws and harm communities.

The Next Step
NICHE MARKETS

Goel, Vindu, "Start-Ups Clamor to Be the Airbnb of Boats," *The New York Times*, June 10, 2015, http://tinyurl.com/ndy7hu3.

Boat owners find a niche market in peer-to-peer boat rentals, but face new challenges due to insurance and safety requirements.

Sharam, Andrea, and Lyndall Bryant, "An Uber for apartments could solve some common housing problems," The Conversation, July 20, 2015, http://tinyurl.com/p2wy2v4.

Two-sided matching markets, commonly used in the sharing economy, could create a housing market that encourages quality and affordability by pairing consumers with developers.

Zhuo, Tx, "5 Lessons Entrepreneurs Can Learn From Niche Marketplaces," *Entrepreneur*, May 14, 2015, http://tinyurl.com/nj9ltuu.

Successful niche markets employ multiple tools, including partnerships with potential competitors, specialized services and an interest in consumer needs.

REGULATION

Badger, Emily, "Who millennials trust, and don't trust, is driving the new economy," *The Washington Post*, April 16, 2015, http://tinyurl.com/p9hjp78.

While trust in individuals has declined over the past 40 years, trust in crowds has increased, allowing for the rise of an industry with fewer regulations, according to a survey by PricewaterhouseCoopers.

Peltz, Jennifer, "Cities keen on 'sharing economy' but concerned about safety," The Associated Press, June 3, 2015, http://tinyurl.com/pqsok5y.

Officials in U.S. cities support growth in the sharing sector, but question the safety of an unregulated industry, according to a National League of Cities survey.

Popper, Ben, "Uber can't be stopped. So what's next?" The Verge, July 27, 2015, http://tinyurl.com/ppvl35j.

New York City becomes the latest locale to try to regulate Uber, but fail.

TECHNOLOGY

Bahceli, Yoruk, "Netherlands to make room in rules to stimulate 'sharing economy,'" Reuters, July 20, 2015, http://tinyurl.com/ou9xobv.

Officials in the Netherlands are adapting rules to meet the demands of new services, promising "technology-neutral" regulations that will not discriminate against less-savvy companies.

Howard, Alex, "Open data, crowdsourcing, and sharing economy tech take on new roles in disasters," Tech Republic, Aug. 8, 2015, http://tinyurl.com/q56uomg.

Some peer-to-peer companies are attempting to expand services to crisis response, offering "disaster technology" to those seeking information, aid and even housing during emergencies.

Kerr, Dara, " 'Sharing economy' apps to boom with their lure of cheap and easy," CNET, April 14, 2015, http://tinyurl.com/p7alnxb.

User-friendly apps and simple digital transactions help to engage a growing number of customers and entrepreneurs in the sharing economy.

WORKER TREATMENT

Lapowsky, Issie, "A Sharing Economy Star Shuts Down As Labor Issues Simmer," Wired, July 17, 2015, http://tinyurl.com/ovqkeug.

One start-up specializing in home cleaning services closed after failing to supply workers with basic benefits.

Macmillan, Douglas, "Sharing Economy Workers Need 'Safety Net,' U.S. Senator Says," The Wall Street Journal, June 8, 2015, http://tinyurl.com/ngn4xcj.

Sen. Mark Warner, D-Va., is calling for new programs that would protect independent contractors in the United States, providing insurance and other basic employee benefits to freelance workers.

Manjoo, Farhad, "Start-Ups Finding the Best Employees Are Actually Employed," The New York Times, June 24, 2015, http://tinyurl.com/q46u73l.

One tech company classifies its workers as employees, not contractors, arguing that valued employees provide better service.

ORGANIZATIONS

Airbnb
888 Brannan St., San Francisco, CA 94103
415-800-5959
www.airbnb.com

Company that provides a platform for peer-to-peer rentals of living spaces.

Cato Institute
1000 Massachusetts Ave., N.W., Washington, DC 20001-5403
202-842 0200
www.cato.org

Libertarian think tank that explores the impact of government policies, including regulation.

Center for Economic and Policy Research
1611 Connecticut Ave., N.W., Suite 400, Washington, DC 20009
202-293-5380
www.cepr.net

Think tank that focuses on the effects of economic policies.

Federal Trade Commission
600 Pennsylvania Ave., N.W., Washington, DC 20580

202-326-2222
www.ftc.gov

The U.S. commission that is charged with preventing business practices considered anticompetitive, deceptive or unfair to consumers.

Lyft
2300 Harrison St., San Francisco, CA 94110-2013
866-292-2713
www.lyft.com

Company that offers on-demand transportation network services.

Mercatus Center, George Mason University
3434 Washington Blvd., 4th Floor, Arlington, VA 22201-4508
703-993-4930
www.mercatus.org

Describes itself as "the world's premier university source for market-oriented ideas—bridging the gap between academic ideas and real-world problems."

Property Casualty Insurers Association of America
8700 W. Bryn Mawr, Suite 1200S, Chicago, IL 60631-3512
847-297-7800
www.pciaa.net

Trade association for property casualty insurers.

Uber
1455 Market St., 4th Floor, San Francisco,CA 94103
877-223-8023
www.uber.com

Company that offers on-demand transportation network services.

Chapter 5
BOOKS

Anderson, Chris, *Free: The Future of a Radical Price*, Hyperion Books, 2009.

The then-editor of Wired magazine writes the definitive book about what he calls "freeconomics," explaining the practice of various business models involving product giveaways and advocating for the growth of the free economy.

Baxter, Robbie Kellman, *The Membership Economy: Find Your Super Users, Master the Forever Transaction, and Build Recurring Revenue*, McGraw-Hill Education, 2015.

A consultant who has advised Netflix, SurveyMonkey and other start-ups discusses the pros and cons of the "freemium" model.

Seufert, Eric Benjamin, *Freemium Economics: Leveraging Analytics and User Segmentation to Drive Revenue (The Savvy Manager's Guides)*, Morgan Kaufmann, 2014.

A marketer outlines how to analyze data generated by freemium products to boost retention and add revenue.

ARTICLES

Doctor, Ken, "Newsonomics: 10 numbers on The New York Times' 1 million digital-subscriber milestone," NiemanLab, Aug. 6, 2015, http://tinyurl.com/pywg39j.

A media analyst gives his approval to The New York Times' strategy that reaped the newspaper 1 million paying subscribers after years of giving its content away for free.

Gladwell, Malcolm, "Priced To Sell," *The New Yorker*, July 6, 2009, http://tinyurl.com/pzozyzy.

The author of best-sellers "The Tipping Point" and "The Outliers" objects to author Chris Anderson's contention that "free" is the future of business.

Jefferies, Duncan, "Responsibilities of the Gaming Industry In Protecting Children's Rights," T Partner zone UNICEF, *The Guardian*, July 21, 2015, http://tinyurl.com/oz5lq92.

A brief produced by UNICEF details the efforts by a number of U.K. organizations to establish principles for free-to-play games popular with children.

Keep, Elmo, "The Case Against Free," Junkee.com, Nov. 3, 2013,http://tinyurl.com/d3htrge.

A digital media producer argues that artistic products have value, and that giving them away diminishes their value.

Leonard, Devin, "That's Business, Man: Why Jay Z's Tidal Is a Complete Disaster," Bloomberg Business, May 28, 2015, http://tinyurl.com/oey-p4wq.

This piece is part Jay Z biography and part scathing review of the rapper's latest effort, the subscription-only music-streaming service Tidal.

Sehlhorst, Scott, "The Freemium Business Model and Viral Product Management," Pragmatic Marketing, 2009, http://tinyurl.com/owrw4ku.

A product management consultant explains the economics of the freemium business model.

Wilson, Fred, "My Favorite Business Model," AVC, March 23, 2006, http://tinyurl.com/oh2kpuj; Wilson, Fred, "The Freemium Business Model," March 23, 2006, AVC, http://tinyurl.com/nkdrz3y.

A venture capitalist brings early attention to the emerging practice of giving a basic product away for free and then charging for a similar premium version. In his first article, he challenges readers to come up with a name for the business model. In his second, he coins the "freemium" label.

REPORTS AND STUDIES

"Is Freemium the Right Business Model? 10 Questions to Answer," Zuora Academy, http://tinyurl.com/pyspbey.

A business management company offers advice about when "free" is a viable business strategy.

"Mobile App Advertising and Monetization Trends, 2012-2017: The Economics of Free," App Annie, March 2014, http://tinyurl.com/q3hadjh.

Business intelligence company App Annie makes the business case for "free."

Bryce, David J., Jeffrey H. Dyer and Nile W. Hatch, "Competing Against Free," *Harvard Business Review*, June 2011, http://tinyurl.com/oarggrh.

The authors, professors at Brigham Young University's Marriott School of Management, explore the conditions under which an established business should combat a competitor that is using a free business model by adopting the same strategy or by waiting to learn whether the newcomer will be successful.

Kumar, Vineet, et al., "The New York Times Paywall," Harvard Business School Case 512-077, *Harvard Business Review*, February 2012 (revised January 2013), http://tinyurl.com/p743ooz.

Harvard Business School professors trace the history of The New York Times' experience with free content and examine the potential impact of the newspaper's 2011 decision to put up a paywall to convert nonpaying readers into paying subscribers.

The Next Step

"FREEMIUM" MODEL

Statt, Nick, "Jimmy Iovine wants Apple to save the world from free music," The Verge, Oct. 7, 2015, http://tinyurl.com/qg8pqv5.

Music-streaming services could earn more revenue and thus better compensate artists if they stop offering free versions of their products, according to a record producer and executive at streaming service Apple Music.

Titlow, John Paul, "YouTube inches toward Netflix with its new paid subscription tier," *Fast Company*, Oct. 21, 2015, http://tinyurl.com/qxkbszz.

Free video-sharing website YouTube launched a paid version of its service that allows viewers who pay $10 per month to watch ad-free videos and exclusive content, among other features.

Waters, Richard, "Zenefits stretches 'freemium' business model," *Financial Times*, Nov. 3, 2015, http://tinyurl.com/pup5fps.

Silicon Valley-based software provider Zenefits offers businesses free human resources software without additional benefits plans; it earns commission from brokering other companies' benefit offerings, such as insurance policies, to its clients.

FREE TRIALS

Butterly, Amelia, "Amazon Prime 30-day trial advert 'misleading' says ASA," BBC News, March 4, 2015, http://tinyurl.com/ng38a6n.

The United Kingdom's advertising regulator said advertisements by Web retailer Amazon for a 30-day free trial of its Amazon Prime service misled customers by not clearly stating that a paid subscription would automatically begin after the trial.

Jurgensen, John, and Barbara Chai, "Apple to Pay Artists After Taylor Swift Protest," *The Wall Street Journal*, June 22, 2015, http://tinyurl.com/oposvmv.

Apple Music reversed its decision not to pay royalties to artists during its initial three-month free trial period after popular singer Taylor Swift publicly objected to the company's policy.

Manning, Brendan, "Free trials return low profit but high engagement," *The New Zealand Herald*, April 28, 2015, http://tinyurl.com/qacwnb7.

Consumers who sign up for free trials subscribe for one-third as long as paying subscribers but respond more to marketing campaigns, according to a study by researchers from the Netherlands and New Zealand.

ONLINE GAMES

Bogost, Ian, "The Logic Behind the Sky-High Candy Crush Deal," *The Atlantic*, Nov. 4, 2015, http://tinyurl.com/np4jbx7.

American gaming company Activision Blizzard paid $3.6 billion of its $5.9 billion purchase of Irish mobile phone gaming company King Digital, maker of the popular free game Candy Crush, with money from offshore accounts, avoiding an additional $1 billion in repatriation taxes.

Chang, Andrea, and David Pierson, "Nintendo unveils its first game for smartphones in long overdue move," *Los Angeles Times*, Oct. 28, 2015, http://tinyurl.com/o7on52k.

Japanese electronics company Nintendo will release its first free online mobile phone game in spring 2016, a long-awaited move by the former top-selling console video game company.

Takahashi, Dean, "Game Insight's Anatoly Ropotov explains how to build sustainable free-to-play mobile games," Venture Beat, Oct. 19, 2015, http://tinyurl.com/ovbbwp3.

Mobile gaming companies can generate customer loyalty by offering updated games, offline play and graphically advanced products, according to the CEO of mobile game developer Game Insight.

NEWS INDUSTRY

Alpert, Lukas I., "For New York Times, a Gamble on Giveaways," *The Wall Street Journal*, Aug. 3, 2015, http://tinyurl.com/pac45hg.

The New York Times has developed low-cost or free mobile products to attract more young readers as potential paid subscribers while also raising online and print subscription fees to offset declining print advertising revenue.

Borchers, Callum, "Undaunted by others' setbacks, Brockton startup targets hyperlocal news," *The Boston Globe*, Sept. 27, 2015, http://tinyurl.com/p24rvxx.

A recently launched subscription-based news website devoted exclusively to local news will sell advertising space to businesses in Brockton, Mass., where other free hyperlocal news publications have failed.

Mance, Henry, "Rebekah Brooks to pull down Sun's online paywall," *Financial Times*, Oct. 30, 2015, http://tinyurl.com/o2f4zpy.

The Sun, Britain's top-selling tabloid newspaper and the only one with a paywall, will make its online content free to increase the publication's relatively low online readership.

Chapter 6

BOOKS

Ante, Spencer E., *Creative Capital: Georges Doriot and the Birth of Venture Capital*, Harvard Business Review Press, 2008.

A journalist examines the life and business times of Georges Doriot, making the case for him as the father of modern venture capital.

Bussgang, Jeffrey, *Mastering the VC Game: A Venture Capital Insider Reveals How to Get From Start-Up to IPO on Your Terms*, Portfolio/Penguin, 2011.

An entrepreneur turned venture capitalist lays out how investing works for start-up founders.

Draper, William H., *The Startup Game: Inside the Partnership Between Venture Capitalists and Entrepreneurs*, Palgrave Macmillan, 2012.

A longtime VC reflects on his family, three generations of which have been venture capitalists, and how the venture capital industry has evolved.

Rao, Arun, and Piero Scaruffi, *A History of Silicon Valley*, Omniware, 2012.

An investor/entrepreneur and a researcher/writer examine the emergence of Silicon Valley from the formation of Stanford University to the present.

Saxenian, AnnaLee, *Regional Advantage: Culture and Competition in Silicon Valley and Route 128*, Harvard University Press, 1994.

A University of California, Berkeley, professor who specializes in regional economics develops a novel theory for why Silicon Valley became a powerhouse for technology start-ups, displacing its East Coast predecessors.

ARTICLES

"Kleiner Perkins and Ellen Pao: A Fortune Guide," *Fortune*, March 27, 2015, http://tinyurl.com/nlwjbnd.

A business magazine collects its major articles on a prominent Silicon Valley venture firm and on a gender discrimination lawsuit.

Burleigh, Nina, "What Silicon Valley Thinks of Women," *Newsweek*, Jan. 28, 2015, http://tinyurl.com/qjqj9f4.

News magazine takes an in-depth look at gender discrimination in Silicon Valley over the last 20 years, with extensive reporting on how VCs shy away from funding female-run companies and avoid adding women to their ranks as partners.

Griffith, Erin, and Dan Primack, "The Age of Unicorns," Jan. 22, 2015, *Fortune*, http://tinyurl.com/oef3swz.

The technology industry is witnessing an unprecedented rise of start-ups that are valued at more than $1 billion by their investors; some observers ask whether that means another technology-driven stock market bubble is underway. (In conjunction with this report, Fortune compiled "The Unicorn List," a quarterly tally of unicorns, http://tinyurl.com/pssc2vo.)

Lacy, Sarah, and Michael Carney, "John Doerr's last stand: Can a dramatic shakeup save Kleiner Perkins?" PandoDaily, Dec. 11, 2013, http://tinyurl.com/n8en7av.

John Doerr and fabled VC firm Kleiner Perkins are going through a rough period, with poor results from missed opportunities and an unrewarding shift toward clean-tech investing.

Lee, Aileen, "Welcome to the Unicorn Club," TechCrunch, Nov. 2, 2013, http://tinyurl.com/n7w88mx.

A venture capitalist crunches the numbers on start-up valuations and explodes several myths about the start-up industry, in the process defining the term "unicorns."

Moritz, Michael, "Arthur Rock, the Best Long-Ball Hitter Around," *Time*, January 1984, http://tinyurl.com/ocnszpc.

For the first time, a venture capitalist makes the cover of Time magazine, in an article penned by a journalist who will go on to become a successful venture capitalist himself.

REPORTS AND STUDIES

"MoneyTree Report for 2014," the National Venture Capital Association and PricewaterhouseCoopers, February 2015, http://tinyurl.com/pumqomp.

A trade association and a consulting firm compile the latest annual report on the state of the venture capital industry in the United States.

"2015 Tech IPO Pipeline Report," CB Insights, http://tinyurl.com/l46ye7y.

A market research firm reports on the 585 privately held companies that are most likely to go public or be acquired in 2015.

"Venture Capitalists Oral History Project," University of California at Berkeley Library, 2010, http://tinyurl.com/o2oqo28.

In a series of 17 interviews, members of the first generation of Silicon Valley venture capitalists, investment bankers and lawyers discuss how the industry was formed and what their business was like.

"We Have Met the Enemy . . . and He Is Us," Ewing Marion Kauffman Foundation, May 2012, http://tinyurl.com/lwcn7lx.

The investment officer at a prominent foundation dedicated to entrepreneurship uses its own investing record to detail how limited partners have let venture capitalists get away with poor performance.

The Next Step

DIVERSITY

Guynn, Jessica, "Venture capital is facing up to its diversity problem," *USA Today*, Dec. 8, 2014, http://tinyurl.com/pnenzfo.

The venture capital industry's national trade group is forming a task force to promote diversity in the industry and publicly encourage companies to hire more women and minorities.

Hiles, Heather, "Silicon Valley Venture Capital Has a Diversity Problem," Re/Code, March 18, 2015, http://tinyurl.com/ldua6pd.

Deeply rooted sexism and insulated investing among groups of white male investors mean Silicon Valley's venture capital community is less welcoming to women and minorities than it is to men, according to the black female CEO of an online personal portfolio start-up.

Woodward, Curt, "Venture capital's diversity problem isn't just bad PR—it's bad for business," Beta Boston, March 31, 2015, http://tinyurl.com/q8bbj3w.

Researchers from Harvard Business School say that investors are far more likely to back a male entrepreneur over a female one, and that female investors are less likely than men to receive guidance from senior mentors.

FUNDING BUBBLES

Garofoli, Joe, "This is no bubble, but get ready for a 'correction,' top investment banker warns," *San Francisco Chronicle*, May 6, 2015, http://tinyurl.com/la2ww2b.

An investment banker and former U.S. Treasury Department official says while he believes there is no bubble in venture capital funding, the tech market will likely correct "fairly sharply."

Koh, Yoree, and Rolfe Winkler, "Venture Capitalist Sounds Alarm on Startup Investing," *The Wall Street Journal*, Sept. 15, 2014, http://tinyurl.com/olyn6cn.

The Silicon Valley-based venture capital community is undertaking an "excessive amount of risk" by investing heavily in tech start-ups, according to Bill Gurley, a venture capitalist who backed successful start-ups such as Uber, Zillow and OpenTable.

Waters, Richard, "Dotcom history is not yet repeating itself, but it is starting to rhyme," *Financial Times*, March 12, 2015, http://tinyurl.com/ndlbgqx.

Although differences exist, industrywide venture capital investment strategies are beginning to mirror those from the Internet bubble that exploded in 2000.

INVESTMENT RETURNS

Chayka, Kyle, "The Hubris of Venture Capital," Pacific Standard, April 24, 2015, http://tinyurl.com/k5rwa97.

In pursuit of the next "unicorn," venture capital firms invest billions of dollars in hundreds of start-ups each year, with the expectation that only a few will bring full returns.

Mulcahy, Diane, "Venture Capitalists Get Paid Well to Lose Money," *Harvard Business Review*, Aug. 5, 2014, http://tinyurl.com/kz25zey.

Venture capital investors are paid well, regardless of investment performance, thanks to fee-structured business models, says the director of private equity for the Ewing Marion Kauffman Foundation.

Weisul, Kimberly, "Venture Capital Funds Start to Make Decent Money. This is News," *Inc.*, May 29, 2014, http://tinyurl.com/ksma3qy.

The average 10-year return for a venture capital fund rose from 6.9 percent in December 2012 to 9.7 percent in December 2013, according to data from the venture capital industry's national trade group.

SOCIAL CAPITAL

Doom, Justin, "Musk Solar Strategy Used as Model for Record Investments," Bloomberg Business, Sept. 15, 2014, http://tinyurl.com/lsfz6z4.

The success of SolarCity, a solar energy provider backed by social venture capital firm DBL Investors, has led other firms to shift their renewable-energy investment strategies from solar panel manufacturers to solar energy suppliers.

Max, Sarah, "Venture Capital Firm Invests in Start-Ups With a Social Mission," *The New York Times*, Oct. 27, 2014, http://tinyurl.com/nfhxunq.

The venture capital firm DBL Investors has developed a reputation for generating returns by funding companies with social agendas, including electric car manufacturer Tesla Motors and Internet radio company Pandora Media.

Wallace, Alicia, "Colorado equity fund testing waters of 'impact' investments," *The Denver Post*, April 24, 2015, http://tinyurl.com/lbbwus9.

The Colorado Impact Fund, formed in 2013 by five private investors, aims to invest between $2 and $6 million in up to 20 Colorado-based start-ups with positive social and environmental goals to help them grow and remain in Colorado.

ORGANIZATIONS

Angel Capital Association
10977 Granada Lane, Suite 103, Overland Park, KS 66211
913-894-4700
www.angelcapitalassociation.org

Association that represents angel investors in the United States and provides a clearinghouse of information for angel investors and entrepreneurs, including network resources, research and webinars.

European Venture Capital Association
Bastion Tower, Place du Champ de Mars 5, B-1050 Brussels, Belgium
32 2 715 00 20
www.evca.eu/

Represents European venture capitalists and private equity investors; also offers information on how European entrepreneurs can find funding.

Ewing Marion Kauffman Foundation
4801 Rockhill Road, Kansas City, MO 64110
816-932-1000
www.kauffman.org

Foundation that is dedicated to entrepreneurialism and economic development.

Global Impact Investing Network
30 Broad St., 38th Floor, New York, NY 10004
646-837-7430
www.thegiin.org/

Organization that represents social impact investors and develops standards for measuring social and environmental investments.

National Venture Capital Association
25 Massachusetts Ave., N.W., Suite 730, Washington, DC 20001
202-864-5920
www.nvca.org

Trade association for U.S. venture capital firms that also provides research on the industry.

Small Business Administration
409 3rd St., S.W., Washington, DC 20416
800-827-5722
www.sba.gov

U.S. agency that helps Americans start and build businesses; also provides information on entrepreneurship and offers financing and advice.

The Indus Entrepreneurs (TIE)
415 Oakmead Parkway, Sunnyvale, CA 94085
408-567-0700
http://tie.org

International association of entrepreneurs that organizes conferences to support entrepreneurial development in 18 countries.

Chapter 7
BOOKS

Cortese, Amy, *Locavesting: The Revolution in Local Investing and How to Profit From It*, Wiley, 2011.
A veteran business reporter examines the local investment movement and how it can benefit investors and businesses.

Cunningham, William Michael, *The JOBS Act: Crowdfunding for Small Businesses and Startups*, Apress, 2012.
A crowdfunding consultant and economist explains the JOBS Act and how it can help small businesses and start-ups raise capital.

Milliken, Dave, *Crowdfunding in a Nutshell: A Concise History of Crowdfunding and How to Raise Money Today*, Amazon e-book, 2014.
An entrepreneur and business consultant reviews the history of crowdfunding and the opportunities that will be available under the JOBS Act.

Neiss, Sherwood, Jason W. Best and Zak Cassady-Dorion, *Crowdfund Investing for Dummies*, John Wiley & Sons, 2013.
Two crowdfunding consultants lay out the basics of equity crowdfunding for entrepreneurs and investors.

ARTICLES

Blackman, Andrew, "Real-Estate Crowdfunding Finds Its Footing," *The Wall Street Journal*, April 13, 2014, http://tinyurl.com/lrkhytj.
Article discusses the growth of real estate crowdfunding platforms that are attracting the interest of small investors.

Casserly, Martyn, "The top 5 Kickstarter success stories: Oculus Rift, Pebble smart watch, Ouya and more," *PC Advisor*, Oct. 2, 2013, http://tinyurl.com/lgqdns7.
Journalist profiles five top Kickstarter campaigns to understand the growing trend of crowdfunding.

Picker, Leslie and Noah Buhayar, "LendingClub Raises $870 Million in IPO Poised to Change Finance," Bloomberg News, Dec. 11, 2014, http://tinyurl.com/qhzxn8a.
Two reporters explain the significance of the $870 million IPO of Lending Club, a peer-to-peer lender.

Rosman, Katherine, "Crowdfunding Isn't Just for the Little Guys," *The Wall Street Journal*, July 9, 2014, http://tinyurl.com/leb2aue.
Bigger companies are turning to crowdfunding to test market demand for new products.

Saksa, Jim, "Kickstarter, but With Stock," Slate, June 23, 2014, http://tinyurl.com/kn9sxv3.
Lawyer/writer discusses the potential dangers of equity crowdfunding.

Shchetko, Nick, "Should Crowdfunding Sites Do More to Vet Projects?" *The Wall Street Journal*, Nov. 25, 2014, http://tinyurl.com/myha2pp.

Journalist asks whether crowdfunding platforms should vet projects before they launch.

Solomon, Steven Davidoff, "SEC's Delay on Crowdfunding May Just Save It," *The New York Times*, Nov. 18, 2014, http://tinyurl.com/mz9tvkp.

Law professor says the growth of intrastate crowdfunding might prove the viability of equity crowdfunding.

Xu, Christelle, "Crowdfunding: Income or Gift?" Crowdfund Investment blog, Crowdfund Capital Advisors, Aug. 14, 2013, http://tinyurl.com/qzul7ck.

Crowdfunding consultancy reviews tax implications of crowdfunding revenue and gives tips from tax experts.

REPORTS AND STUDIES

"How Much Capital are Kickstarter and Indiegogo Hardware Projects Raising?" CB Insights, Aug. 11, 2014, http://tinyurl.com/lf7j5y2.

Report from firm that tracks venture capital examines successful crowdfunded technology hardware projects that have gone on to receive venture capital investments.

Crowdfund Capital Advisors, "Crowdfunding's Potential for the Developing World," World Bank, 2013, http://tinyurl.com/o423cn8.

Report for the World Bank takes a global look at the potential for crowdfunding to improve the economies of developing countries.

Dorff, Michael B., "The Siren Call of Equity Crowdfunding," Sept. 13, 2013; available at SSRN, http://tinyurl.com/mke6uph.

Law professor looks at the poor performance of most angel investments and concludes that equity crowdfunding investments may fare much worse.

Greenberg, Jason and Ethan Mollick, "Leaning In or Leaning On? Gender, Homophily, and Activism in Crowdfunding," July 3, 2014; available at SSRN, http://tinyurl.com/opaaqy6.

Study examines the difficulty female founders face in getting start-up capital and why they are so much more successful at crowdfunding.

Mollick, Ethan, "The dynamics of crowdfunding: An exploratory study," Journal of Business Venturing, January 2014, http://tinyurl.com/nn9s5gu.

Management professor examines a data set of more than 48,500 crowdfunded projects and concludes that success is related to personal networks, project quality and geographical location.

Mollick, Ethan R., "Swept Away by the Crowd? Crowdfunding, Venture Capital and the Selection of Entrepreneurs" The Wharton School at the University of Pennsylvania, March 25, 2013, http://tinyurl.com/kwpgwqf.

Author concludes that crowdfunders and venture capitalists assess entrepreneurial quality in similar ways, but that crowdfunding alleviates some geographical and gender biases.

Mollick, Ethan R., and Ramana Nanda, "Wisdom or Madness? Comparing Crowds with Expert Evaluation in Funding the Arts," Harvard Business School Entrepreneurial Management Working Paper No. 14-116, June 20, 2014; available at SSRN, http://tinyurl.com/l8zzqfs.

Researchers compare how the crowd and professionals evaluate artistic ventures and finds they use similar criteria.

The Next Step

ENTREPRENEURS

Clifford, Catherine, "Food-Tech Startup Dinner Lab Is Crowdfunding a Cool $2 Million—From Its Customers," *Entrepreneur*, Dec. 3, 2014, http://tinyurl.com/pwz4etc.

Crowdfunding has enabled the founder and CEO of a food-focused start-up to pursue his own vision without ceding any creative control of his company to venture capitalists.

Kirsner, Scott, "A tale of two crowdfunding ventures," *The Boston Globe*, Sept. 21, 2014, http://tinyurl.com/n9k6525.

Two Boston-area crowdfunding campaigns demonstrate how some, but not all, entrepreneurs have been able to raise money online.

Robb, Alicia, "Why Crowdfunding Closes the Gender Gap," *Inc.*, December 2014-January 2015, http://tinyurl.com/p6cskzp.

More female entrepreneurs are seeking backing through crowdfunding platforms, which have a relatively high proportion of female investors compared with venture capital and angel investor communities.

INVESTORS

Fikes, Bradley J., "Science gets help from the crowd," *San Diego Union-Tribune*, Nov. 5, 2014, http://tinyurl.com/mtbvzym.

Some researchers who work for biotechnology laboratories that use crowdfunding platforms to raise money say the experience has improved their engagement skills with traditional investors.

Parmar, Neil, "Crowdfunding is Opening Investment Doors," *The Wall Street Journal*, Nov. 9, 2014, http://tinyurl.com/mazb6pa.

More investors are using crowdfunding websites, such as CrowdStreet and CircleUp, to purchase equity in real estate and consumer product opportunities that once were open only to larger investment institutions.

Weinstein, Joanna, "Crowdfunding real estate," CNBC, Dec. 10, 2014, http://tinyurl.com/mr9vzj8.

A real estate crowdfunding platform called iFunding allows accredited investors to search through development projects and choose between lending money to developers, with interest, or purchasing equity in their projects.

MARKETING

Dave, Paresh, "Gamers' funding fuels meteoric rise of 'Star Citizen,'" *Los Angeles Times*, Oct. 19, 2014, http://tinyurl.com/mroancg.

A massive crowdfunding campaign for videogame company Cloud Imperium to develop its "Star Citizen" game has enabled the company to spend its marketing budget on engagement programming, such as live events and video updates, for its backers.

Gumz, Jondi, "Fast start needed to generate buzz in crowdfunding efforts," *Santa Cruz* (Calif.) *Sentinel*, Dec. 27, 2014, http://tinyurl.com/n6eushg.

Founders of Santa Cruz, Calif.-based companies with crowdfunding experience say the success of a campaign is tied to the size of a project's fan base, its social media marketing presence and its engagement with backers.

Schultz, E.J., "Newcastle 'Crowdsources' Local Super Bowl Ad," Advertising Age, Jan. 12, 2015, http://tinyurl.com/mnp7fhp.

Heineken is funding a Super Bowl advertisement for its Newcastle Brown Ale brand by offering to include other companies' logos in the ad in exchange for contributions.

SUCCESSFUL CAMPAIGNS

Bajarin, Tim, "Pebble and Glyph: How Crowdfunding Is Creating Disruptive New Products," *Time*, Jan. 27, 2014, http://tinyurl.com/kahqrhh.

Crowdfunding has enabled small companies to develop technologies, such as smartwatches and wearable video displays, that will lead to new consumer product categories, according to the president of a market intelligence firm.

Heber, Alex, "A Campaign To Teach Kids An Hour Of Code Has Just Smashed The Indiegogo Crowdfunding Record," Business Insider (Australia), Nov. 5, 2014, http://tinyurl.com/lvoh95r.

The "Hour of Code" campaign, launched on the crowdfunding platform Indiegogo in October 2014 to fund computer science education initiatives around the world, raised more than $2.8 million in about one month.

Tate, Ryan, "How You'll Fund—And Wildly Profit From—The Next Oculus Rift," *Wired*, April 4, 2014, http://tinyurl.com/ogxdabx.

Pending U.S. Securities and Exchange Commission rules will allow backers of crowdfunded projects to purchase equity shares in those companies, unlike investors in the Oculus Rift virtual reality headset, who put up $2.4 million but didn't benefit from the company's sale to Facebook.

ORGANIZATIONS

Council of Better Business Bureaus
3033 Wilson Blvd., Suite 600
Arlington, VA 22201
http://www.bbb.org/council

Self-regulatory group that provides information about businesses to consumers, including warnings about scams.

Crowdfund Capital Advisors
1688 West Ave., #802
Miami Beach, FL 33139
www.crowdfundcapitaladvisors.com

For-profit advisory, research and education organization dedicated to promoting access to capital through crowdfunding.

Crowdfund Intermediary Regulatory Advocates
1345 Avenue of the Americas
New York, NY 10105
www.cfira.org

Advocacy and trade group for the equity crowdfunding industry.

Ewing Marion Kauffman Foundation
4801 Rockhill Road
Kansas City, MO 64110

816-932-1000
www.kauffman.org

Nonprofit research and grant-making organization that supports entrepreneurship.

National Crowdfunding Association
213-208-2148
www.nlcfa.org

Trade association of crowdfunding professionals, portals, venture capital firms, angel investors, lawyers, accountants, software vendors, educators and students.

Securities and Exchange Commission
100 F St., N.E.
Washington, DC
202-942-8088
www.sec.gov

Federal agency that regulates the U.S. securities industry and is preparing regulations for investment crowdfunding for unaccredited investors.

National Federation of Independent Business
1201 F St., N.W., Suite 200
Washington, DC 20004
202-554-9000
www.nfib.com

National advocacy and lobbying organization for small businesses.

North American Securities Administrators Association
750 First St., N.E., Suite 1140
Washington, DC 20002
202-737-0900
www.nasaa.org

Organization that represents state-level securities regulators.

Small Business Administration
409 3rd St., S.W.
Washington, DC 20416

800-827-5722
www.sba.gov

Federal agency that supports entrepreneurship and makes loans; offers online course, "Introduction to Crowdfunding for Entrepreneurs."

U.S. Chamber of Commerce Foundation
615 H St., N.W.
Washington, DC 20062
202-463-5500
www.uschamberfoundation.org

Nonprofit affiliate of the Chamber of Commerce, a business lobbying group, disseminates information on the economy and employment issues, including crowdfunding.

Chapter 8

BOOKS

Axtell, Paul, *Meetings Matter: 8 Powerful Strategies for Remarkable Conversations*, Jackson Creek Press, 2015.
An executive coach focuses on the organizational purpose of collaboration and outlines the tactics for meeting success.

Baker, Heather, *Successful Minute Taking: Meeting the Challenge*, Universe of Learning, 2013.
An executive-secretary-turned-administrative-trainer spells out the minutia of meeting protocol and process.

Field, Bryan, and Peter Kidd, *Powerfully Simple Meetings: Your Guide to Fewer, Faster, More Focused Business Meetings*, MeetingResult, 2014.
Two meeting-efficiency consultants examine ways to make meetings more successful.

Heinecke, Stu, *How to Get a Meeting with Anyone: The Untapped Selling Power of Contact Marketing*, BenBella Books, 2016.
A sales consultant explains how to win time with top executives—strategies that are especially useful in flat organizations.

Martin, Jeanette S., and Lillian H. Chaney, *Global Business Etiquette: A Guide to International Communication*, Praeger, 2012.
Business school professors outline cultural and international differences and similarities in formal business meetings, communication and etiquette.

Schwartzman, Helen B., *The Meeting: Gatherings in Organizations and Communities*, Plenum Press, 1989.
A Northwestern University professor of anthropology explores how various cultures conduct and view meetings.

ARTICLES

"Conference Planning Checklists," National Council of Teachers of English, 2015, http://tinyurl.com/h4m6rv2.
The organization details the ingredients of successful meetings, from a timeline for the event to a day-before site inspection.

"Planning Accessible Meetings and Events: A Toolkit," American Bar Association, 2015, http://tinyurl.com/jcx7gnx.
The voluntary association of lawyers and law students outlines ways to include in meetings people who have limited abilities to see, hear, move or speak.

Axelrod, Dick, "How to Change Your Company Culture One Meeting at a Time," SwitchandShift.com, July 10, 2014, http://tinyurl.com/zdz6aue.
An organizational-change consultant illustrates step-by-step methods of how to shift corporate or departmental cultures through structure and communication at meetings.

Barsade, Sigal, and Olivia A. O'Neill, "Quantifying Your Company's Emotional Culture," *Harvard Business Review*, Jan. 7, 2016, http://tinyurl.com/zmb6pfc.
Professors of organizational behavior at the University of Pennsylvania's Wharton School of Business (Barsade) and George Mason University (O'Neill) discuss how to track the emotional culture of workplaces.

Gallo, Amy, "The Condensed Guide to Running Meetings," *Harvard Business Review*, July 6, 2015, http://tinyurl.com/ohcbwan.

A business writer summarizes current wisdom on calling and managing meetings.

Heffernan, Virginia, "Meet Is Murder," *The New York Times Magazine*, Feb. 25, 2016, http://tinyurl.com/hdeavpv.

An essayist wonders how meetings "can be made bearable" and surveys a variety of experts.

Silverman, Rachel Emma, "Where's the Boss? Trapped in a Meeting," The Wall Street Journal, Feb. 14, 2012, http://tinyurl.com/jtkrgv7.

A reporter describes a study by London School of Economics and Harvard Business School researchers who tracked the schedules of more than 500 CEOs to learn how they spend their time and how that affects their companies' performance and management.

Spiro, Josh, "How to Run an Effective Meeting," Inc., Aug. 4, 2010. http://tinyurl.com/28hr5js.

A reporter delves into best practices for various types of meetings.

Sutton, Robert, "Tips for Better Brainstorming," Bloomberg Businessweek, July 25, 2006, http://tinyurl.com/hx4b4re.

A reporter outlines common pitfalls and assumptions about brainstorming.

REPORTS AND STUDIES

"American Time Use Survey," U.S. Bureau of Labor Statistics, 2014, http://tinyurl.com/hm2g2a8.

The federal agency charged with compiling workplace statistics measures how much time Americans spend at work as well as on various tasks.

"Guide to Meeting Facilitation, Best Practices and Talking Tips," Strategic Training Solutions, 2010, http://tinyurl.com/gtzoerd.

A consulting firm provides an overview of how to fulfill the intended mission of a meeting.

"Guidelines on Meetings Planning and Coordination," United Nations Conference Services Division, March 2006, http://tinyurl.com/zwfsneb.

The U.N. agency overseeing conferences gives an overview of the aspects of holding an international meeting, including invitations and seating charts.

"Running Meetings with Robert's Rules of Order," Alpha Rho Chi, March 2014, http://tinyurl.com/zmddnlv.

A professional fraternity for architecture simplifies Robert's Rules of Order.

Kim, Been, and Cynthia Rudin, "Learning About Meetings," Massachusetts Institute of Technology, 2013, http://tinyurl.com/zfxkzex.

Two MIT researchers assess ways to understand what happens in meetings and uncover complications that they attribute to contradictions between explicit and hidden agendas.

Rogelberg, Steven, et al., "Lateness to meetings: Examination of an unexplored temporal phenomenon," *European Journal of Work and Organizational Psychology*, 2013, http://tinyurl.com/zfqtt8g.

Researchers study punctuality at work and say the topic warrants additional exploration.

The Next Step
EFFICIENCY

Feloni, Richard, "A Facebook cofounder's productivity startup recommends 5 ways to dramatically improve your meetings," Business Insider, Feb. 8, 2016, http://tinyurl.com/j83jc79.

To increase meeting productivity, companies should impose caps on recurring meetings, designate one "no-meeting" day each week and allow employees five minutes at the end of meetings to ensure everyone is aware of their expected responsibilities, according to a list of best practices by technology company Asana.

Gallo, Amy, "The Condensed Guide to Running Meetings," *Harvard Business Review*, July 6, 2015, http://tinyurl.com/ohcbwan.

Organizations can make meetings more effective by limiting attendance to seven people, banning mobile devices and setting clear agendas, among other strategies, say two experts on meetings and decision-making.

Ha, Anthony, "Meetings Are Usually Terrible, But YC-Backed WorkLife Aims To Change That," TechCrunch, March 11, 2015, http://tinyurl.com/mcztnwe.

Technology startup WorkLife developed computer and mobile-device software that allows users to update meeting agendas, assign tasks, track time and generate shareable summaries from notes.

LEADERSHIP

Joseph, Arthur, "Leadership: Can You Learn to Communicate and Embody It?" *Entrepreneur*, Oct. 19, 2015, http://tinyurl.com/ordrugw.

Business classes often fail to teach students communication skills required of effective leaders, including how to facilitate and present information at meetings, says a communication strategist and speech coach.

Norton, Steven, "University IT Staff Gets Help Translating 'Geek Speech' to English," *The Wall Street Journal*, Aug. 25, 2015, http://tinyurl.com/gsh84lf.

A public-speaking group teaches information technology employees at the University of Arizona to improve their leadership and communication skills and has helped many to become more vocal during business meetings, says the university's chief information officer.

Tabaka, Marla, "How a Real Leader Runs a Company Meeting," *Inc.*, Sept. 3, 2015, http://tinyurl.com/p4lto55.

The best leaders establish clear purposes for calling a meeting, respect company hierarchies, manage time and distribute information to staff before the gathering, according to a small-business strategy consultant.

SPATIAL DESIGN

Gallagher, John, "Office design today embraces flexible workspaces," *Detroit Free Press*, Aug. 1, 2015, http://tinyurl.com/ptkd2hn.

The increasingly collaborative nature of office work over the past several decades contributed to a shift toward open meeting spaces, say employees of Michigan-based office-furniture maker Herman Miller.

Swanson, Ana, "Fascinating photos show the best and worst office designs for employees," *The Washington Post*, July 7, 2015, http://tinyurl.com/zeo2kwv.

A principal at architecture and design firm Gensler predicts offices of the future will feature smaller, more numerous meeting rooms—a change from the 1990s, when office layouts began to be more open and collaborative.

Zipkin, Amy, "Conference Centers Offer Companies Meeting Space Without Strings," *The New York Times*, April 6, 2015, http://tinyurl.com/jc7tdaj.

More stand-alone urban conference centers have appeared since the 2007–09 global recession, offering more flexible and comfortable meeting spaces for companies at cheaper rates than hotel-connected conference centers.

TECHNOLOGY

Segan, Sascha, "At Samsung Unpacked, Zuckerberg Ushers in the Year of VR," *PC Mag*, Feb. 21, 2016, http://tinyurl.com/jfshtmb.

Virtual-reality headsets will allow business colleagues to hold meetings from around the world, predicted Facebook CEO Mark Zuckerberg at an annual mobile technology conference in Barcelona.

Shah, Agam, "Quick start to meetings saves money, improves efficiency for Intel," CIO, Feb. 1, 2016, http://tinyurl.com/jeeyngm.

Technology company Intel installed wireless tools in more than 500 conference rooms, boosting meetings' efficiency by enabling on- and off-site employees to share information via monitors without having to waste time connecting cables to computers and other devices.

Warner, Kelsey, "Could Microsoft's humongous touchscreen make meetings bearable?" *The Christian Science Monitor*, June 10, 2015, http://tinyurl.com/zodwcy9.

Microsoft developed the Surface Hub, a touchscreen device available in 55- or 84-inch formats, to serve as a tablet computer, blackboard and TV screen and is marketing it to companies hoping to streamline boardroom meetings.

ORGANIZATIONS

American Anthropological Association
2300 Clarendon Blvd., Suite 1301, Arlington, VA 22201
703-528-1902
www.americananthro.org

Professional association for academic and practicing anthropologists, including business anthropologists, who study group dynamics and cultural history and evolution.

American Society of Association Executives
1575 I St., N.W., Washington, DC 20005
202-626-2723
www.asaecenter.org

Professional association for paid managers of trade, nonprofit and professional associations; provides training and advice on meeting logistics.

International Facilitators Association
15050 Cedar Ave. South, #116-353, Apple Valley, MN 55124
952-891-3541
www.iaf-world.org

Professional association for meeting facilitators.

International Society of Protocol and Etiquette Professionals
13116 Hutchinson Way, Suite 200, Silver Spring, MD 20906-5947
301-946-5265
www.ispep.org

Professional association for experts, trainers and coaches in meeting etiquette, business etiquette, international and cross-cultural etiquette and customs, among other communication and interpersonal dynamics.

Meeting Professionals International
2711 Lyndon B. Johnson Freeway, Suite 600, Dallas, TX 75234-7349
972-702-3000
www.mpiweb.org

Professional association for those responsible for organizing, planning and managing meetings, including nonprofit, business and academic gatherings.

National Speakers Organization
1500 S. Priest Drive, Tempe, AZ 85281
480-968-2552
www.nsaspeaker.org/

Professional association for current and aspiring professional speakers.

Chapter 9
BOOKS

Murray, Alan, *The Wall Street Journal Essential Guide to Management: Lasting Lessons from the Best Leadership Minds of Our Time*, HarperBusiness, 2010.

Management guide by a Wall Street Journal managing editor provides business strategies for being a successful manager and historical context on current management techniques.

Pontefract, Dan, *Flat Army: Creating a Connected and Engaged Organization*, Wiley, 2013.

A Canadian telecommunications executive and business speaker offers a guide for creating a culture of collaboration, engagement and employee empowerment by replacing command-and-control management techniques with collaborative methods.

Tapscott, Don, *Wikinomics: How Mass Collaboration Changes Everything*, Portfolio Trade, 2010.

A business consultant explains that the use of collaborative processes by employees is spreading to traditional companies.

ARTICLES

Birkinshaw, Julian, "Beware the Next Big Thing," *Harvard Business Review*, May 2014, http://tinyurl.com/kexgvy8.

A business scholar advises companies on how to evaluate new management theories before implementing them.

Finley, Klint, "Why Workers Can Suffer in Bossless Companies Like GitHub," *Wired*, March 20, 2014, http://tinyurl.com/obu4gv6.

A technology journalist examines some of the problems experienced by workers in companies using flat management techniques.

Foss, Nicolai J., and Peter G. Klein, "Why Managers Still Matter," MIT *Sloan Management Review*, Fall 2014, http://tinyurl.com/pzm64b4.

Two business scholars make the case that managers continue to be essential components of business success.

Garvin, David A., "How Google Sold Its Engineers on Management," *Harvard Business Review*, December 2013, http://tinyurl.com/pe638nl.

A Harvard business professor describes how Google examined the role of its managers and their contributions to the business.

Hamel, Gary, "First, Let's Fire All the Managers," *Harvard Business Review*, December 2011, http://tinyurl.com/77swj3x.

Management hierarchies have become inefficient, says a management consultant who has written frequently about innovation.

Hamel, Gary, "Moon Shots for Management," *Harvard Business Review*, February 2009, http://tinyurl.com/o9r89pk.

A leading management consultant lays out a road map for developing new management techniques, saying current structures can no longer be improved.

Kastelle, Tim, "Hierarchy Is Overrated," *Harvard Business Review* Blog Network, Nov. 20, 2013, http://tinyurl.com/ksaur6h.

A business scholar makes the case that flat organizational structures can work for any business.

REPORTS AND STUDIES

Courtright, Stephen, G.L. Stewart and M.R. Barrick, "Peer-Based Control in Self-Managing Teams: Linking Rational and Normative Influence With Individual and Group Performance," *Journal of Applied Psychology*, March 2012, http://tinyurl.com/p3u5e58.

University researchers find that groups that manage themselves can be more productive.

Friesen, Justin P., Aaron C. Kay, Richard P. Eibach and Adam D. Galinsky, "Seeking structure in social organization: Compensatory control and the psychological advantages of hierarchy," *Journal of Personality and Social Psychology*, April 2014, http://tinyurl.com/px5cgxx.

Researchers argue hierarchies offer structure and satisfy core motivational needs for order and control.

Ronay, Richard, Katharine Greenaway, Eric M. Anicich and Adam D. Galinsky, "The Path to Glory Is Paved With Hierarchy: When Hierarchical Differentiation Increases Group Effectiveness," *Psychological Science*, June 2012, http://tinyurl.com/p46x6vz.

Hierarchy helps teams work effectively on collaborative tasks, university researchers say.

Seibert, S.E., G. Wang and S.H. Courtright, "Antecedents and consequences of psychological and team empowerment in organizations: a meta-analytic review," *Journal of Applied Psychology*, September 2011, http://tinyurl.com/pu7edyx.

University researchers find that workers who felt psychologically empowered performed better.

The Next Step

LEADERSHIP

Hu, Elise, "Inside The 'Bossless' Office, Where The Team Takes Charge," National Public Radio, Aug. 26, 2013, http://tinyurl.com/ocyeqah.

More companies, such as software company Menlo Innovations in Ann Arbor, Mich., are adopting "bossless" office environments to more quickly serve customers and compete for the best employees.

Vasagar, Jeevan, "Experiment with a bit of anarchy," *The Financial Times*, Jan. 28, 2014, http://tinyurl.com/pwkyzsu.

Berlin-based technology start-up 6Wunderkinder eliminated middle-management positions after beginning to grow; it then introduced "ground rules" for self-managed project teams to follow that align with the company's business goals.

MILITARY HIERARCHIES

Boss, Jeff, "Why Hierarchy Is Outdated: The (Long Overdue) Need For Organizational Adaptability," *Forbes*, June 6, 2014, http://tinyurl.com/ozvgloc.

A former U.S. Navy SEAL says businesses should apply combat mission lessons such as removing deference to "rank" and changing decision-making routines to become more adaptable.

McCauley, James, "Quality Over Quantity: A New PLA Modernization Methodology?" The Jamestown Foundation, July 17, 2014, http://tinyurl.com/pvsa8qq.

A Chinese People's Liberation Army's colonel argued in a paper published in November 2013 that one of the military branch's top priorities should be flattening command structures to better integrate joint operations.

Sanborn, James, "Cyber steps up its role on the battlefield," *Air Force Times*, Aug. 25, 2014, http://tinyurl.com/nks56hn.

The U.S. Marine Corps gave cyberspace advisers more authority over tactical operations, rather than requiring them to gain approval from commanders.

PROFITABILITY

Brown, Jonathan, "Workers' co-operatives: One for all, all for one," *The Independent* (U.K.), Jan. 9, 2014, http://tinyurl.com/q7gxl2z.

The co-op food distributor Suma Wholefoods in West Yorkshire, United Kingdom, generates millions in profit and provides employees bonuses thanks to its flat structure and employee-based decision-making process.

Long, Yun, "Reno's Saint Mary's hospital in the black one year after turning for-profit," *Reno* (Nev.) *Gazette-Journal*, June 30, 2013, http://tinyurl.com/q4wq28o.

St. Mary's Regional Medical Center in Reno, Nev., became profitable immediately after being acquired in July 2012 by hospital chain Prime Healthcare Services, which introduced a flat structure that requires approval only from the CEO to implement decisions.

Sangani, Priyanka, "Harvard legend John Kotter advocates 'dual operating system' for winning in a turbulent world," *The Economic Times* (India), May 16, 2014, http://tinyurl.com/qx239d5.

Harvard professor and management consultant John Kotter believes large companies need to introduce flatter, more parallel management structures within existing hierarchies to remain efficient and successful.

RESTRUCTURING

Groth, Aimee, "Zappos is going holacratic: no job titles, no managers, no hierarchy," Quartz, Dec. 30, 2013, http://tinyurl.com/ppxhwc5.

Zappos CEO Tony Hsieh restructured the online shoe and clothing retailer by replacing top-down hierarchy with "holacracy," which distributes power among circles of employees with changing roles.

Hutson, Matthew, "Espousing Equality, but Embracing a Hierarchy," *The New York Times*, June 21, 2014, http://tinyurl.com/pbqyqu3.

Companies such as Internet search firm Google and design firm IDEO have retained some degree of structural hierarchy while adopting flatter management structures.

Jargon, Julie, "McDonald's Plans to Change U.S. Structure," *The Wall Street Journal*, Oct. 30, 2014, http://tinyurl.com/q4f3gm4.

Fast-food giant McDonald's plans to eliminate layers of management and create more autonomous consumer "zones" to adapt to local tastes after reporting declining quarterly profits.

FOR MORE INFORMATION

HolacracyOne

1741 Hilltop Rd.
Suite 200
Spring City, PA 19475
484-359-8922
holacracy.org

The company that developed the management theory of holacracy.

Morning Star Self-Management Institute

500 Capitol Mall
Suite 2050
Sacramento, CA 95816
916-925-6500
self-managementinstitute.org

Research and education company that advocates a management model based on the principles developed at the Morning Star Co.

WorldBlu

316 E. Court St.
Iowa City, IA 52240
202-251-8099
worldblu.com

A company that advocates the management theory of organizational democracy.

Chapter 10
BOOKS

Provost, Foster, and Tom Fawcett, "Data Science for Business: What You Need to Know About Data Mining and Data-Analytic Thinking," O'Reilly Media, 2013.

A professor of information systems at New York University's Stern School of Business (Provost) and a data-science researcher (Fawcett) explain the principles that underlie big-data analysis, using historical and current examples of real-life business problems.

Stanton, Jeffrey, *An Introduction to Data Science*, 2012, http://tinyurl.com/kb6w75l.

In this text for a certificate program in data science, a Syracuse University professor of information science explains how to approach practical questions using statistics and how to perform statistical analysis using free software tools.

ARTICLES

Crawford, Kate, "The Hidden Biases in Big Data," *Harvard Business Review* blogs, April 1, 2013, http://tinyurl.com/mcrluz4.

It's easy to be misled into believing large data sets are accurate and unbiased, according to Crawford, a Microsoft Research principal researcher.

Dwoskin, Elizabeth, "Big Data's High-Priests of Algorithms," *The Wall Street Journal*, Aug. 8, 2014, http://tinyurl.com/mepaota.

Data scientists need a rare combination of statistics and math skills, computer savvy and problem-solving ability; those who possess those traits are highly sought after by big retailers, manufacturers, Internet giants and other companies.

Harford, Tim, "Big data: are we making a mistake?" *Financial Times Magazine*, March 28, 2014, http://tinyurl.com/k6l7b5w.

Using big-data analytics effectively requires paying attention to traditional principles of statistics.

Marcus, Gary, and Ernest Davis, "Eight (No, Nine!) Problems With Big Data," *The New York Times*, April 6, 2014, http://tinyurl.com/knqc3bt.

New York University professors of psychology (Marcus) and economics (Davis) list the pitfalls that can afflict those who work with big data. Two common ones: It can generate statistics that aren't necessarily meaningful, and it can encourage users to ask useless questions.

O'Toole, Kathleen, "Susan Athey: How Big Data Changes Business Management," Insights by Stanford Business, Sept. 20, 2013, http://tinyurl.com/pd5qxyw.

Athey, a Stanford University professor of the economics of technology, says that the rise of data-based decisions makes it imperative that all executives understand the basics of decision statistics and automated data analysis.

Walker, Joseph, "Meet the New Boss: Big Data," *The Wall Street Journal*, Sept. 20, 2012, http://tinyurl.com/nlzpumr.

Hiring managers increasingly use automated big-data analytics to turn up unexpected characteristics that predict who will be the best hire. For example, a software program advised a company seeking call-center workers that people with creative personalities were more likely than those with inquisitive natures to stick with the jobs for six months or more.

REPORTS AND STUDIES

"Big Data and Privacy: A Technological Perspective," President's Council of Advisors on Science and Technology, May 2014, http://tinyurl.com/nu2oy5d.

White House technology advisers argue that technologies to protect privacy can't keep up with the big-data-related advances and that new laws and regulations will be required to protect individuals' personal information.

"Big Data: The next frontier for innovation, competition, and productivity," McKinsey Global Institute, May 2011, http://tinyurl.com/cplxu6p.

Analysts at the McKinsey & Company consultancy assess big data's effects on the workforce and market competition and its potential for boosting earnings and improving efficiency in retail, health care, manufacturing and government.

"Big Data: Seizing Opportunities, Preserving Values," Executive Office of the President, May 2014, http://tinyurl.com/n9vda93.

A panel of presidential advisers explores the opportunities big data will present for U.S. businesses and government privacy and security agencies, but cautions that current practices for protecting individuals' rights online will not be equal to the new threats posed by big data.

"Gut & Gigabytes," The Economist Intelligence Unit/PricewaterhouseCoopers, 2014, http://tinyurl.com/kjesgmf.

In a survey conducted by a U.K.-based business-forecasting group, 1,135 public- and private-sector executives describe their experiences with data-based decision-making and their expectations for future big-data use in their organizations.

The Next Step

JOBS

Bertolucci, Jeff, "Does Big Data Need A 'LinkedIn For Analytics'?" *InformationWeek*, Nov. 20, 2014, http://tinyurl.com/nhf94uo.

Companies undertaking big-data projects or adopting new data management methods would benefit from a crowdsourcing network that connects them with data professionals, according to the vice president of an analytics company.

Clark, Jack, "Big Data Knows When You're Going to Quit Your Job Before You Do," Bloomberg, Dec. 30, 2014, http://tinyurl.com/lgf4xzs.

Several Silicon Valley companies have developed software that allows companies to track a wide range of employee activity data and to help retain those who are likely to quit.

Schulte, Brigid, "Women flocking to statistics, the newly hot, high-tech field of data science," *The Washington Post*, Dec. 19, 2014, http://tinyurl.com/l5xzuuu.

More women are studying statistics and earning university faculty positions as demand grows for big-data professionals, bucking the trend in male-dominated science, technology, engineering and mathematics (STEM) fields.

PRIVACY

Bedoya, Alvaro M., "Big Data and the Underground Railroad," Slate, Nov. 7, 2014, http://tinyurl.com/lro69ey.

A privacy law expert suggests that while big data will benefit public health, business efficiency and other areas, ubiquitous collection may also harm vulnerable groups such as minorities.

Herold, Benjamin, "'Big Data' Research Effort Faces Student-Privacy Questions," *Education Week*, Oct. 21, 2014, http://tinyurl.com/q6noujq.

Data privacy advocates worry that the federally funded "Learnsphere" initiative, which will store behavioral data from high school and college students in online courses, violates students' privacy by sharing their personal information.

Perera, David, "Smart grid powers up privacy worries," *Politico*, Jan. 1, 2015, http://tinyurl.com/oxlrwxu.

The U.S. Department of Energy will begin collecting household electricity consumption data for utility suppliers through "smart meters," but some legal experts say the program violates consumers' privacy.

RELIABILITY

Lippert, John, "Lender Charging 390% Uses Data to Screen Out Deadbeats," Bloomberg, Oct. 3, 2014, http://tinyurl.com/qgwyyew.

To choose the most reliable borrowers, Los Angeles-based lender uses large pools of data to screen low-income applicants for high-interest loans that average $600.

Shinal, John, "If 'clean,' big data can improve U.S. health care," *USA Today*, Aug. 28, 2014, http://tinyurl.com/k8sosou.

Data collection companies might be able to profit from the digitization of all U.S. patients' medical records by integrating social media user and consumer data to ensure the records' accuracy.

Todd, Deborah M., "Study finds obstacles with social media data," *Pittsburgh Post-Gazette*, Nov. 3, 2014, http://tinyurl.com/kgchaz9.

Researchers from Carnegie Mellon and McGill universities say that anyone analyzing large sets of social media user data should adjust for factors such as public health, spending, political outcomes and false information to ensure reliability.

SMALL BUSINESSES

Grossman, John, "Finding Ways to Use Big Data to Help Small Shops," *The New York Times*, July 9, 2014, http://tinyurl.com/lrczsog.

The growing simplicity and shrinking costs of data analysis have led to a significant rise in the percentage of small businesses using intelligence software.

Hassemer, Jeff, "Think Small: Why Big Data Isn't For Everyone," Advertising Age, Jan. 6, 2015, http://tinyurl.com/qctwfso.

Businesses with insufficient resources to undertake big-data projects may benefit more from using "small data," or very basic sets of customer data, according to an executive of a digital advertising company.

Kelleher, Kevin, "What 3 Small Businesses Learned From Big Data," *Inc.* Magazine, July-August 2014, http://tinyurl.com/p4rxszc.

A North Carolina-based vacation real estate company, a zoo in Tacoma, Wash., and a Phoenix-based online car marketplace were able to improve customer service and be more competitive after working with big-data analytics providers.

ORGANIZATIONS

American Statistical Association
732 N. Washington St.
Alexandria, VA 22314-1943
703-684-1221
www.amstat.org

Membership organization for statisticians that provides information on predictive and Bayesian statistics as well as statistics for business.

Association for Information Systems
P.O. Box 2712
Atlanta, GA 30301-2712
404-413-7445
www.aisnet.org

Membership organization for information-systems professionals, academics and researchers.

Data Science Association
7550 E. 53rd Place, Unit 172622
Denver, CO 80217-2622
www.datascienceassn.org

Membership group that provides information on predictive analytics, algorithms, data visualization, machine learning and other topics.

Decision Sciences Institute
C.T. Bauer College of Business
334 Melcher Hall, Suite 325
Houston, TX 77204-6021
713-743-4815
www.decisionsciences.org

Membership organization that has information on quantitative methods for decision-making in business and other fields.

Digital Analytics Association
401 Edgewater Place, Suite 600
Wakefield, MA 01880
781-876-8933
www.digitalanalyticsassociation.org

Membership group with information and research on data acquisition, analysis and use.

Gartner Inc.
56 Top Gallant Road
Stamford, CT 06902
203-964-0096
www.gartner.com/technology/home.jsp

Business consultancy that specializes in technology, including big data.

International Institute of Business Analysis
701 Rossland Road E., Suite 356
Whitby, ON L1N 9K3, Canada
647-426-3735
www.iiba.org

Professional organization that provides certification and information on all aspects of business analysis.

McKinsey & Company
55 E. 52nd St.
New York, NY 10022
212-446-7000
www.mckinsey.com/insights/big_data_and_advanced_analytics

Business consultancy with news and information on analytics and big data.

Chapter 11

BOOKS

Brewster, Mike, *Unaccountable: How the Accounting Profession Forfeited a Public Trust*, John Wiley & Sons, 2003.

A journalist and former communications director at international accounting firm KPMG traces the history of the accounting profession and how the scandals of 2001-02 "tarnished the reputation of a once-respected profession."

Conover, Teresa, and Frederick Niswander, *U.S. & International Accounting: Understanding the Differences*, American Institute of Certified Public Accountants, 2013.

The authors, both CPAs, provide a brief yet comprehensive history of U.S.-international convergence and illustrate how the United States' Generally Accepted Accounting Principles (GAAP) and the International Financial Reporting Standards (IFRS) differ in various areas of financial statements.

Herz, Robert H., *Accounting Changes: Chronicles of Convergence, Crisis, and Complexity in Financial Reporting*, American Institute of Certified Public Accountants, 2013.

The former head of the Financial Accounting Standards Board details his career in the profession, including his eight years as the chairman of the primary setter of U.S. accounting standards.

King, Thomas A., *More Than a Numbers Game: A Brief History of Accounting*, John Wiley & Sons, 2006.

The treasurer of Progressive Insurance provides a history of the profession interlaced with examples of how financial statements have evolved over time.

ARTICLES

"Comparability in International Accounting Standards—A Brief History," Financial Accounting Standards Board, undated, accessed Oct. 12, 2015, http://tinyurl.com/ouek5ln.

The U.S. accounting standards-setter provides a lengthy timeline of attempts to create a set of international accounting standards.

"Progress report: International convergence of accounting standards," Insights, Baker Tilly, Oct. 31, 2014, http://tinyurl.com/odplbfs.

An accounting firm website provides a brief yet comprehensive summary of convergence efforts and where they stalled.

Norris, Floyd, "Holding Auditors Accountable on Reports," *The New York Times*, May 8, 2014, http://tinyurl.com/plvdtsm.

A veteran chronicler of accounting and financial reporting describes the challenges of getting auditing firms to accept the idea of expanded auditors' reports.

Rapoport, Michael, "SEC: Accounting Board Is Dragging Feet," *The Wall Street Journal*, Dec. 14, 2014, http://tinyurl.com/pk55vul, and "SEC Presses Audit Regulator PCAOB on Priorities," *The Wall Street Journal*, Feb. 4, 2015, http://tinyurl.com/oaqnsz8.

The Securities and Exchange Commission and the Public Company Accounting Oversight Board it supervises squabble over where to focus the board's attention.

Smetanka, Rick, "GAAP or Non-GAAP?" Financial Executive, November 2012, http://tinyurl.com/nnbpe9w.

A partner at an accounting firm argues that non-GAAP financial measures are essential tools for dynamic companies to describe their businesses.

Stocker, James, "Securities and Exchange Commission Historical Society Oral History Project: Interview with James Leisenring," SEC Historical Society, April 12, 2011, http://tinyurl.com/ngbp5ur.

An interview with a retired member of the International Accounting Standards Board describes the mid-1990s discord over accounting rules.

REPORTS, STUDIES AND ORIGINAL DOCUMENTS

"Analysis of the IFRS jurisdiction profiles," IFRS Foundation, May 1, 2015, http://tinyurl.com/p4t2p4g.

The organization that created IFRS tracks the adoption of the standards across the globe.

"Extended auditor's reports: A review of experience in the first year," Financial Reporting Council, March 2015, http://tinyurl.com/pzd54v9.

The U.K. regulator reviews its experience of requiring expanded auditors' reports.

"Final Rule: Conditions for Use of Non-GAAP Financial Measures," Securities and Exchange Commission, Jan. 24, 2002, http://tinyurl.com/6ju7qm.

The regulator sets out the rules for how a company may use non-GAAP measures, as well as the background surrounding them.

"IFRS and US GAAP: similarities and differences," PricewaterhouseCoopers, October 2014, http://tinyurl.com/p8exzw8.

The Big Four accounting firm provides a guide for comparing U.S. and international accounting rules.

The Next Step

AUDITORS' REPORTS

Ciesielski, Jack T., "What auditors ought to let U.S. investors know," *Fortune*, April 14, 2015, http://tinyurl.com/pfo6fjy.

An international accounting standards board developed a report template in which auditors are to identify companies' most significant issues, a proposed change the United States has resisted.

Deener, Will, "Audits of little help to investors," *The Dallas Morning News*, Oct. 25, 2015, http://tinyurl.com/q3djl2l.

U.S. auditors do a poor job of informing investors about who is auditing their companies in annual reports and disparately charge clients for their services, according to an accounting standards expert.

Freifeld, Karen, "Ernst & Young settles with N.Y. for $10 million over Lehman auditing," Reuters, April 15, 2015, http://tinyurl.com/oztklur.

An accounting firm agreed to a settlement with the New York Attorney General's Office after it was accused of hiding information in annual reports from 2001 to 2008 that were compiled for Lehman Brothers, the investment bank that failed in the 2008 financial crisis.

INTERNATIONAL STANDARDS

Crump, Richard, "IASB moves to help management understand materiality," AccountancyAge, Oct. 29, 2015, http://tinyurl.com/n9gvgnj.

The International Accounting Standards Board, which creates accounting rules for companies in most nations, published new guidance that helps company managers better determine which information is "material," or necessary to disclose on financial statements.

Rapoport, Michael, "IASB Staff Recommends One-Year Delay in New Global Revenue-Booking Rule," *The Wall Street Journal*, April 21, 2015, http://tinyurl.com/nhe8vmm.

The IASB plans to delay implementation of new revenue reporting standards until 2018.

Thomas Jr., Landon, "Greek Debt Vastly Overstated, Investor Tells the World," *The New York Times*, Feb. 20, 2015, http://tinyurl.com/perd2h7.

A millionaire investor controlling a large share of Greek government bonds struggled to persuade investors and policymakers that Greece's highly publicized government debt crisis was less severe than depicted under IASB standards.

MISCONDUCT

Alpeyev, Pavel, and Takashi Amano, "Toshiba Executives Resign Over $1.2 Billion Accounting Scandal," Bloomberg Business, July 21, 2015, http://tinyurl.com/nvapawu.

The president of Toshiba and two other executives resigned shortly after a report revealed that management pressured employees to delay reporting losses so that the Japanese electronics company could meet profit targets.

Armstrong, Ashley, "Sainsbury's questioned by accounting watchdog over income disclosures," *The Telegraph*, Oct. 3, 2015, http://tinyurl.com/pgvynfq.

The United Kingdom's independent accounting regulator will review Sainsbury's accounting for income from suppliers after the U.K.-based supermarket chain failed to follow an advisory to disclose such information to investors in 2014.

Morgenson, Gretchen, "Earnings Misstatements Come in Bunches, Study Says," *The New York Times*, Oct. 23, 2015, http://tinyurl.com/q9yotks.

Companies are more likely to misstate or manipulate their reported earnings if larger companies in their industries do so, according to a study to be published in the journal The Accounting Review.

U.S. STANDARDS

Chasan, Emily, "FASB Proposes Changes to 'Materiality,'" *The Wall Street Journal*, Sept. 24, 2015, http://tinyurl.com/p9c9o6k.

The Financial Accounting Standards Board is considering altering its general definition of "materiality," or the importance of companies' information to investment decisions, to match the legal definition set by the U.S. Supreme Court in a 1976 decision.

Katz, David M., "FASB Rids Income Statements of 'Extraordinary Items,'" CFO, Jan. 13, 2015, http://tinyurl.com/prfgp8l.

The FASB eliminated the requirement that companies must report on their income statements how seldom-listed "extraordinary events," such as natural disasters or terrorist attacks, affected their finances.

McKenna, Francine, "Investor advocates protest proposals limiting disclosure," MarketWatch, Oct. 19, 2015, http://tinyurl.com/pfndc89.

Members of a Securities and Exchange Commission committee objected to two changes proposed by the FASB because they could reduce companies' disclosures in annual reports.

ORGANIZATIONS

American Accounting Association
5717 Bessie Drive, Sarasota, FL 34233-2399
941-921-7747
www.aaahq.org
Twitter: @aaahq

Largest community of accountants in academia.

American Institute of CPAs
1211 Avenue of the Americas, New York, NY 10036-8775
212-596-6200
www.aicpa.org
Twitter: @CPALetter_Daily

World's largest member association representing the accounting profession, with more than 412,000 members in 144 countries.

Financial Accounting Standards Board (FASB)
PO Box 5116, Norwalk, CT 06856-5116
203-847-0700
http://www.fasb.org
Twitter: @FAFNorwalk

Private-sector accounting standards-setter for U.S. for-profit companies.

Financial Executives International
1250 Headquarters Plaza, West Tower, 7th Floor, Morristown, NJ 07960
973-765-1000
www.financialexecutives.org
Twitter: @FEInews

Trade group for chief financial officers and other high-level financial executives.

International Accounting Standards Board (IASB)
30 Cannon St., London, EC4M 6XH, United Kingdom

+44 (0)20 7246 6410
www.ifrs.org
Twitter: @IFRSFoundation

Global group that develops International Financial Reporting Standards (IFRS) and is backed by the IFRS Foundation.

International Federation of Accountants
529 5th Ave., New York, NY 10017
212-286-9344
www.ifac.org
Twitter: @IFAC_Update

Global trade group for accounting firms and their partners.

Public Company Accounting Oversight Board (PCAOB)
1666 K St., N.W., Washington, DC 20006-2803
202-207-9100
www.pcaobus.org
Twitter: @PCAOB_News

Private nonprofit corporation established by Congress to oversee the audits of public companies and investment dealers.

U.S. Securities and Exchange Commission
100 F St., N.E., Washington, DC 20549
202-942-8088
www.sec.gov
Twitter: @SEC_News

Federal regulator of financial markets and the final arbiter on accounting rules.

Chapter 12

BOOKS

Boyd, Danah, *It's Complicated: The Social Lives of Networked Teens*, Yale University Press, 2014.
Boyd, a principal researcher at Microsoft and a fellow at Harvard's Berkman Center for Internet & Society, defends teen social media use.

Quart, Alissa, *Branded: The Buying and Selling of Teenagers*, Basic Books, 2003.
Media critic slams extreme consumerism and the way corporations pursue teens and preteens.

Ryan, Damian, *The Best Digital Marketing Campaigns in the World II*, Kogan Page, 2nd ed., 2014.
CEO of the Global Academy of Digital Marketing profiles 40 digital campaigns between September 2012 and September 2013, describing their approach and hard-to-obtain ROI "results" figures.

Ryan, Damian, and Calvin Jones, *Understanding Digital Marketing: Marketing Strategies for Engaging the Digital Generation*, Kogan Page, 2nd ed., 2012.
Two experienced online marketers discuss in detail strategies for search, social media, mobile and more.

ARTICLES

Davenport, Thomas H., "Lessons on Big Data Marketing," CIO Report blog, *The Wall Street Journal*, May 14, 2014, http://tinyurl.com/mnplgp2.
Babson College professor of information technology looks at the growing influence of data marketers.

Davenport, Thomas H., and D.J. Patil, "Data Scientist: The Sexiest Job of the 21st Century," *Harvard Business Review*, October 2012, http://tinyurl.com/kam2tg3.
Two academics examine the demand for big-data professionals.

Heine, Christopher, "Walmart's Social Is Getting 10X ROI and Tens of Thousands of Daily Interactions," *Adweek*, Oct. 4, 2014, http://tinyurl.com/pdzvc3e.
Walmart's CEO talks about return on investment and social media strategy.

Hoffmann, Melissa, "A Glimpse into Marketers' Social Media Strategies: Even the Big Guys

Struggle to Measure ROI," *Adweek*, Sept. 16, 2014, http://tinyurl.com/muw2lql.

Infographic compares results of two studies that examine how companies measure returns from digital campaigns.

Marczynski, Joe, "Game of Thrones: Digital Marketing is Coming," LabelMedia, June 10, 2014, http://tinyurl.com/qdlwu66.

British advertising agency writer examines the much-praised "Game of Thrones" digital marketing campaign.

McCambley, Joe, "Stop Selling Ads and Do Something Useful," *Harvard Business Review* blog, HBR.org, Feb. 12, 2013, http://tinyurl.com/mxgbxg5.

One of the creators of the banner ad takes a critical look at how Web advertising has evolved over two decades.

Petersen, Robert, "11 Studies Prove Digital Marketing ROI," Rutgers Business School, Dec. 19, 2014, http://tinyurl.com/lawqa2y.

Executive who teaches MBA class on digital marketing examines 11 studies about return on investment from online strategies.

Schaefer, Mark, "Content Shock: Why content marketing is not a sustainable strategy," Grow blog, Jan. 6, 2014, http://tinyurl.com/k5ylnb3.

Digital marketing expert describes how the exploding amount of content marketing is not sustainable.

Stampler, Laura, "How Dove's 'Real Beauty Sketches' Became the Most Viral Video Ad of All Time," Business Insider, May 22, 2013, http://tinyurl.com/l6eun2w.

Dove's much-shared "Real Beauty Sketches" ad succeeded by touching emotions.

Wasserman, Todd, "This is the World's First Banner Ad," Mashable.com, Aug. 9, 2013, http://tinyurl.com/l9jl2q4.

On Mashable, business and marketing editor defends banner ads.

Woodyard, Chris and Jane O'Donnell, "Your Car May Be Invading Your Privacy," *USA Today*, March 13, 2013, http://tinyurl.com/ccv9t8z.

Cars collect increasing amounts of data about their drivers, which worries some privacy advocates.

Wyatt, Edward, "FTC Fines Yelp and TinyCo for Violating Children's Privacy Rules," The New York Times Sept. 17, 2014, http://tinyurl.com/luwo5d9.

The Federal Trade Commission fines a company for violating a children's privacy rule.

REPORTS AND STUDIES

"The Advertising Industry's Process of Voluntary Self-Regulation," Advertising Self-Regulatory Council, Jan. 1, 2014, http://tinyurl.com/m9ya3ru.

The Children's Advertising Review Unit, a subgroup of the Advertising Self-Regulatory Council, lays out its rules on advertising products for children.

"Children's Online Privacy Protection Rule," Federal Trade Commission, accessed Jan. 23, 2015, http://tinyurl.com/l4lbplj.

FTC rule tells marketers what they can and can't do in regard to children's privacy.

".com Disclosures: How to Make Effective Disclosures in Digital Advertising," Federal Trade Commission, March 2013, http://tinyurl.com/ppa9mf2.

The FTC lays out its blogger disclosure rules for bloggers promoting products.

"ITU releases 2014 ICT figures," International Telecommunications Union, May 5, 2014, http://tinyurl.com/mdhykxt.

United Nations agency provides annual updates to an array of statistics related to telecommunications and Internet access globally.

Madden, Mary, "Public Perceptions of Privacy and Security in the Post-Snowden Era," Pew Research Internet Project, Nov. 12, 2014, http://tinyurl.com/p2536wh.

Surveys find that Americans are concerned about privacy, but are willing to share information with companies when they receive free services in return.

McLellan, Laura, "Presentation for CMO Spend Survey 2015: Eye on the Buyer," Gartner Inc., 2014, http://tinyurl.com/k49ren5.

White paper examines digital promotion budgets.

OTHER RESOURCES

"Generation Like," PBS Frontline, Feb. 18, 2014, http://tinyurl.com/q3oy6gw.

"Frontline" documentary examines how marketers are using teens' online activities to promote brands.

"History of the Web," World Wide Web Foundation, undated, accessed Jan. 23, 2015, http://tinyurl.com/npmj85s.

Foundation established by the inventor of the Web provides a detailed, hyperlinked history on a site full of information about the

The Next Step

MARKETING TO CHILDREN

Chaker, Anne Marie, "Traditional Toys Add Digital Apps for Children Who Learned to Play on Tablets," *The Wall Street Journal*, Sept. 2, 2014, http://tinyurl.com/kbvmdgp.

To sell to an increasingly digital generation of children, companies such as Mattel and Hasbro are adding mobile applications to their traditional lineup of physical toys.

Evich, Helena Bottemiller, and Chase Purdy, "FTC not surveying junk food marketing to kids," *Politico Pro*, Dec. 31, 2014, http://tinyurl.com/mkhnesa.

Federal Trade Commission officials say the agency will not follow up on its 2008 and 2012 reports monitoring food industry spending on digital marketing to children.

Flacy, Mike, "Study: U.S. teens abandon Facebook and cling to iPhones," Digital Trends, Oct. 7, 2014, http://tinyurl.com/mm8q95u.

The mobile picture-sharing app Instagram has become a more popular marketing channel for reaching teens than Facebook, according to a study of consumer trends by investment bank Piper Jaffray.

PRIVACY

Alton, Larry, "Will Consumers Revolt Against Pervasive Online Advertising?" *Entrepreneur*, Nov. 12, 2014, http://tinyurl.com/l3m7snu.

A former entrepreneur suggests growing consumer dissatisfaction with ads on websites and social media will drive more Internet users to adopt advertisement-blocking browser extensions and join anti-advertising social media platforms.

Henschen, Doug, "SAP Helps Marketers Use Facebook Customer Data," *InformationWeek*, Nov. 11, 2014, http://tinyurl.com/otl7qey.

The German software corporation SAP will begin collecting audience data from Facebook for marketers and retailers, allowing companies to target Facebook audience segments and individual users.

Mitchell, Rick, "Consumers of Online Digital Content Need New Legal, Privacy Protections, OECD Says," Bloomberg BNA, Oct. 27, 2014, http://tinyurl.com/mvezvtl.

The Paris-based Organisation for Economic Co-operation and Development (OECD) recommends governments do more to prevent Internet providers and marketing companies from collecting citizen data.

SEARCH MARKETING

Frommer, Dan, "Why Google's earnings "miss" wasn't actually that bad," Quartz, Jan. 31, 2015, http://tinyurl.com/pzf57d3.

Despite Google's missed earnings mark for the fourth quarter of 2014, investors say they are optimistic about the company's future because of year-over-year growth in its core businesses—search, ads and applications—and a refined network of partner companies.

Peterson, Tim, "Amazon Tops List of Google's 25 Biggest Search Advertisers," Ad Age, Sept. 15, 2014, http://tinyurl.com/m48u6g4.

The Internet retail giant Amazon, one of Google's biggest advertising competitors, spent almost $158 million for Google search advertisements in the United States in 2013.

Winkler, Rolfe, "Ads Tied to Web Searches Criticized as Deceptive," *The Wall Street Journal*, Oct. 13, 2014, http://tinyurl.com/nvq5gdk.

The major search engines Google, Yahoo and Bing have inadequately distinguished advertisements from regular websites in their search results, according to some consumer advocates.

TWITTER

Bond Jr., Vince, "Study: Twitter Marketing Drives $716 Million in Car Sales," Ad Age, Oct. 28, 2014, http://tinyurl.com/lud8eqa.

Research by a marketing analytics company shows advertisements, brand mentions, rebroadcasts of TV ads and automotive company activity on Twitter led to $716 million in sales of 20 car models in 2013.

Ha, Anthony, "Twitter Expands Its Ad Retargeting To Include Data From Mobile Apps," TechCrunch, Dec. 9, 2014, http://tinyurl.com/o4wdlkk.

A new product from Twitter will enable companies to target Web users with advertisements by using mobile Twitter user activity data.

Nusca, Andrew, "Why IBM and Twitter did a data analytics deal," *Fortune*, Nov. 3, 2014, http://tinyurl.com/mzo8aw8.

Executives from software provider IBM and social media network Twitter say a partnership between the companies will allow IBM clients to analyze user data for marketing research and will encourage more companies to reach customer audiences using Twitter.

ORGANIZATIONS

American Marketing Association
311 S. Wacker Drive
Chicago, IL 60606
312-542-9000
www.ama.org

Professional association for marketers and marketing academics; founded in 1937.

Commercial Alert
1600 20th St., N.W.
Washington, DC 20009
202-588-1000
www.commercialalert.org

Project of the public interest group Public Citizen that aims to "keep the commercial culture within its proper sphere."

Digital Advertising Alliance
1120 Avenue of the Americas
New York, NY 10036
212-0768-7255
www.digitaladvertisingalliance.org

Consortium of media and marketing associations that collaborates with businesses, public policy groups and public officials; advocates industry self-regulation.

Digital Analytics Association
401 Edgewater Place
Suite 600
Wakefield, MA
781-876-8933
www.digitalanalyticsassociation.org

Nonprofit association of individuals and organizations who work with data acquisition, exploration and application.

Direct Marketing Association

1100 Avenue of the Americas

New York, NY 10036

212-768-7255

http://thedma.org

Trade association and lobbyist for direct, database and interactive marketing fields.

eMarketing Association

40 Blue Ridge Drive

Charlestown, RI 02813

800-496-2950

www.emarketingassociation.com

International group of digital marketers that runs conferences and certification programs.

Internet Marketing Association

10 Mar Del Rey

San Clemente, CA 92673

949-443-9300

http://imanetwork.org

Professional organization that includes marketers, business owners, Web developers and others.

Worldwide Privacy Forum

3108 Fifth Ave.

Suite B

San Diego, CA 92103

760-712-4281

www.worldprivacyforum.org

Nonprofit research group that concentrates on digital privacy, including medical privacy and the data brokerage industry.

Chapter 13

BOOKS

Gilson, Stuart, *Creating Value Through Corporate Restructuring: Case Studies in Bankruptcies, Buyouts, and Breakups*, John Wiley & Sons, 2010.

A Harvard University professor of business administration examines the process of corporate restructuring using case studies of prominent companies, including Delphi, General Motors and Kmart, as well as the Eurotunnel debt restructuring.

Kindleberger, Charles, and Robert Z. Aliber, *Manias, Panics, and Crashes: A History of Financial Crises*, Palgrave Macmillan, 2011.

Two academics detail how poor money management historically has given rise to financial crises.

Sandage, Scott, *Born Losers: A History of Failure in America*, Harvard University Press, 2005.

A cultural historian at Carnegie Mellon University explains how the meaning of failure changed from a business term to an identity marker for failed businessmen in 19th-century America.

Schoemaker, Paul J.H., *Brilliant Mistakes: Finding Success on the Far Side of Failure*, Wharton Digital Press, 2011.

A researcher and business consultant illustrates how many products, from ATMs to smoke-free cigarettes to penicillin, were initially judged as mistakes yet turned out to be money makers.

Skeel, David Jr., *Debt's Dominion: A History of Bankruptcy Law in America*, Princeton University Press, 2001.

A professor of corporate law at the University of Pennsylvania shows the political and economic roles in the United States' unique approaches to bankruptcy, from its inception in 1800 to the 1994 bankruptcy reform.

Tugend, Alina, *Better by Mistake*, Riverhead Books, 2011.

Drawing on research and behavioral studies, a New York Times columnist shares lessons from aviation and medicine on how to respond to errors, and why it's important yet difficult to accept and learn from mistakes.

ARTICLES

"The Failure Issue—Failure: How to Understand It, Learn from It, and Recover from It," *Harvard*

Business Review, April 2011, http://tinyurl.com/oj235a6.

A collection of articles, many by well-known professors and experts, on aspects of failure in career and business.

Bradley, Ryan, "A Brief History of Failure," *The New York Times Magazine*, Nov. 12, 2014, http://tinyurl.com/p59yuyu.

A photo gallery of innovative products that never took off, including the pneumatic railroad and a simplified typewriter keyboard.

Bruder, Jessica, "The Psychological Price of Entrepreneurship," *Inc.* magazine, September 2013, http://tinyurl.com/kht6mzo.

A journalist explains how leading a company through dark times can bring on depression, anxiety, despair and even suicide, leaving founders to feel alone in their emotional and financial battles.

Elmer, Vickie, "A coming-out party for business failures," *Fortune*, Oct. 21, 2013, http://tinyurl.com/pgct6pk.

FailCon, which started as a storytelling conference for business start-up failures, has grown to 10 cities and now has imitators.

Gillett, Rachel, "What the Hype Behind Embracing Failure Is Really All About," *Fast Company*, Sept. 8, 2014, http://tinyurl.com/pxzh5ho.

How the movement to celebrate failure began and how those in business should not go overboard in sharing their mistakes.

Lewis, Geoff, "Failure porn: There's too much celebration of failure and too little fear," *The Washington Post*, Dec. 4, 2014, http://tinyurl.com/h2o7jo8.

A Silicon Valley venture capitalist suggests Americans have swung too far in embracing failure stories while underestimating the risks in new ventures.

Moules, Jonathan, "From failure can come success," *The Financial Times*, Jan. 24, 2013, http://tinyurl.com/pasvq94.

British start-ups say a fear of failure in that country still holds back entrepreneurs, especially compared with the United States.

REPORTS AND STUDIES

Altman, Edward I., "Revisiting the Recidivism: Chapter 22 Phenomenon in the U.S. Bankruptcy System." *Brooklyn Journal of Corporate, Financial & Commercial Law*, 2014, http://tinyurl.com/pkfzhw6.

A New York University professor shows that 15 percent to 18.25 percent of firms that exit Chapter 11 reorganization return to it.

Atkinson, Tyler, David Luttrell and Harvey Rosenblum, "How Bad Was It? The Costs and Consequences of the 2007-09 Financial Crisis," Federal Reserve Bank of Dallas, July 2013, http://tinyurl.com/zp55lde.

Economists review the cost of the financial crisis, and determine that up to $14 trillion was lost or forgone in output, wealth and more.

Gompers, Paul A., et al., "Performance Persistence in Entrepreneurship," Harvard Business School Working Paper, September 2008, http://tinyurl.com/zvqx84e.

Entrepreneurs with a track record of success are more likely to continue succeeding than others. Those with market timing skills also have an edge, researchers found.

Lee, Seung-Hyun, et al., "How do bankruptcy laws affect entrepreneurship development around the world?" *Journal of Business Venturing*, September 2011, http://tinyurl.com/od62n6r.

Based on analysis of statutes in 29 countries, lenient, business-friendly bankruptcy laws lead to more firms being established.

Sonnenfeld, Jeffrey A., and Andrew J. Ward, "Firing Back: How Great Leaders Rebound after Career Disasters," *Harvard Business Review*, January 2007, http://tinyurl.com/p5jctgf.

Two business school professors interviewed 300 executives and found that only one-third of ousted CEOs returned to an active executive job, having done so by recovering their "heroic status" and fighting back.

Tian, Xuan, and Yue Wang, Tracy, "Tolerance for Failure and Corporate Innovation," *The Review of Financial Studies*, Dec. 5, 2011, http://tinyurl.com/zwgdmjd.

Initial public offerings of stock backed by more failure-tolerant venture capitalists are significantly more innovative, and less-experienced VCs are more likely to face capital constraints or career concerns, which may reduce their tolerance of failure.

The Next Step

BANKRUPTCY

Gleason, Stephanie, and Ted Mann, "GE Says Quirky Has Hurt Its Reputation," *The Wall Street Journal*, Dec. 3, 2015, http://tinyurl.com/qcqjdlg.

General Electric's partnership with a bankrupt home-technology invention start-up that reportedly failed to provide adequate customer service harmed General Electric's reputation, according to bankruptcy court documents.

Martin, Peter, "Free to fail in Malcolm Turnbull's new $1.1 billion innovation plan," *The Sydney Morning Herald*, Dec. 7, 2015, http://tinyurl.com/j4upsha.

New Australian laws will permit directors of bankrupt firms that have restructured debts to continue operating the businesses and allow them to start others, part of a national effort to help Australian entrepreneurs.

Schram, Lauren Elkies, "To Declare, or Not to Declare Bankruptcy?" *Commercial Observer*, Nov. 11, 2015, http://tinyurl.com/hbbbkyu.

Chapter 11 reorganizations can help real estate developers in weak markets to refinance projects, continue operating businesses while repaying creditors and push lenders to modify their original repayment terms, according to real estate lawyers.

CULTURAL DIFFERENCES

Duarte, Daniel, "Journalist Andrés Oppenheimer Tells Latin America to 'Create or Die,'" *PanAm Post*, July 15, 2015, http://tinyurl.com/zmnzls3.

Latin America has discouraged innovation by stigmatizing business failure and ostracizing entrepreneurs who do not succeed on first attempts, according to a book by an Argentinean journalist.

Nguyen, Hoang, "The entrepreneur teaching Japan how to take more risks," BBC, Sept. 14, 2015, http://tinyurl.com/pyo3vzb.

A Japanese entrepreneur who sold his first software company to Microsoft at age 33 now invests in start-ups in Japan, where he says disapproving cultural attitudes toward failure have stifled entrepreneurship.

Sheftalovich, Zoya, "EU pushes for business without borders," *Politico Europe*, Oct. 28, 2015, http://tinyurl.com/jd63ofl.

The European Commission has proposed regulations that aim, among other objectives, to make it easier for entrepreneurs behind bankrupt businesses to start new firms, although a Lithuanian member of the European Union Parliament says the EU could do more to improve the entrepreneurial climate.

ECONOMIC EFFECTS

Guilford, Gwynn, "China's latest refusal to fix its state-owned companies is bad news for the global economy," Quartz, Sept. 16, 2015, http://tinyurl.com/poyjhxj.

The Chinese government props up bankrupt state-owned enterprises by continuing to lend to them, leading to overproduction and market inefficiencies.

Howitt, Peter, "Failures and job losses are integral to economic growth," *The Globe and Mail*, Sept. 2, 2015, http://tinyurl.com/jxn2nhh.

Company failures and job cuts lead former employees to innovate and start competitive firms that create new jobs, thereby contributing to economic growth, says a Canadian economist.

Shane, Scott, "Is Declining Business Failure Holding Back Entrepreneurship?" *Entrepreneur*, March 11, 2015, http://tinyurl.com/h8r7sc2.

Government aid to failing businesses may inadvertently hold back the creation of start-ups, according to a professor of entrepreneurial studies at Case Western Reserve University.

TECHNOLOGY SECTOR

Griswold, Alison, "Startups With Shorter Names Are More Likely to Succeed, Study Finds," Slate, Feb. 9, 2015, http://tinyurl.com/konkyuw.

New businesses named after their founders are 70 percent less likely to succeed than other firms, and those with names of three words or less are 50 percent more likely to succeed, according to a study by Massachusetts Institute of Technology researchers.

Maney, Kevin, "In Silicon Valley, Failing Is Succeeding," *Newsweek*, Aug. 31, 2015, http://tinyurl.com/jmbgmbx.

Silicon Valley's technology industry has embraced failure as acceptable for many companies, an uncommon trait that has made the region's success difficult to replicate.

Voorhis, Dan, "Can Wichita get its entrepreneurial mojo back?" *The Wichita Eagle*, Dec. 12, 2015, http://tinyurl.com/jpm4pdp.

A group of entrepreneurs in Wichita, Kan., is working to attract investors to fund the city's technology businesses, but the director of an entrepreneurship nonprofit says many cities are unprepared for the high failure rate of such businesses.

ORGANIZATIONS

American Bankruptcy Institute

66 Canal Central Plaza, Suite 600, Alexandria, VA 22314

703-739-0800
www.abi.org

Membership-based institute that connects bankruptcy professionals and provides educational and research resources.

Business Plan Archive

3318 Van Munching Hall, College Park, MD 20742
301-405-0559
www.businessplanarchive.org

Online archive at the University of Maryland's Robert H. Smith School of Business that contains business plans and other documents of failed dot-coms and technology companies from the 1990s, with access limited to research and educational purposes.

FailCon

www.thefailcon.com

Conferences for start-up founders and others to discuss and study their past business failures to prepare for later success.

Failure: Lab

Grand Rapids, MI 49504
616-292-7277
http://failure-lab.com/

Group that organizes storytelling events around personal or professional failures.

International Failure Institute

Durham, NC 27708
http://internationalfailureinstitute.org/

Group of scholars, students, activists and artists seeking to understand the productive role of failure in learning and creativity by sharing stories, conducting classes and more.

Historical Bankruptcy Cases Project

4400 Massachusetts Ave., N.W., Washington, DC 20016
202-885-1000
http://www.american.edu/cas/economics/bankrupt/

A research effort at American University that is working with the National Archives to digitize bankruptcy cases from 1898 to 1978 for scholars; also offers research projects such as the extent to which women and African-Americans were involved in early bankruptcies.

National Association of Consumer Bankruptcy Attorneys

2200 Pennsylvania Ave., N.W., 4th floor, Washington, DC 20037
800-499-9040
www.nacba.org

Membership organization of consumer bankruptcy lawyers providing education, advocacy and some consumer resources.

The Success-Failure Project

5 Linden St., Cambridge, MA 02138
617-495-7680
www.successfailureproject.bsc.harvard.edu

An effort of Harvard University's Bureau of Study Counsel to provide resources aimed at students to discuss success and failure in context and to explore their own definitions of them.

Turnaround Management Association

150 North Wacker Drive, Suite 1900, Chicago, IL 60606
312-578-6900
www.turnaround.org

Membership organization of corporate turnaround-industry professionals that provides educational resources and hosts events.

U.S. Bankruptcy Court

E. Barrett Prettyman U.S. Courthouse, 333 Constitution Ave., N.W., Washington, D.C. 20001
www.uscourts.gov

One of the 94 federal judicial districts handling approximately 1 million business, individual and other bankruptcy cases filed each year.

ABOUT THE AUTHORS

Pamela J. Black is a New York City–based freelance writer specializing in personal finance. She was a writer and editor for *Businessweek*. Her work has appeared in a variety of financial magazines and websites.

Since 1981, **Joanne Cleaver** has covered businesses and business leaders for numerous publications, including Crain's *Chicago Business*, Crain's *New York Business, Working Mother, Inc.*, the *Chicago Tribune* and the *Milwaukee Journal Sentinel*. She also has written for consumer and trade publications.

Marcia Clemmitt is a veteran social policy reporter who previously served as editor in chief of *Medicine & Health* and staff writer for *The Scientist*. She has also been a high school math and physics teacher. She holds a liberal arts and sciences degree from St. John's College in Annapolis, Md., and a master's degree in English from Georgetown University. She wrote a report on "Minimum Wage" for SAGE Business Researcher. Her recent reports for CQ Researcher, an imprint of SAGE, include "Humanities Education" and "Government Spending."

Freelance writer **Vickie Elmer** has covered the media, advertising and "Mad Men" for *Fortune* and the *Ann Arbor Observer*, and edited articles for *Newsday* and the *Detroit Free Press*. She writes about business, careers and consumer issues for *Kiplinger, The Washington Post* and Crain's *Detroit Business*. She wrote the SAGE Business Researcher report on work-life balance. She shares on social media via Twitter @WorkingKind and @AwesomeDetroit.

Michael Fitzgerald is an award-winning freelance writer from Boston whose work has appeared in *The Boston Globe, The Economist*, MIT Sloan Management and other publications. He has written on a variety of business topics, including innovation and the digital transformation. He also has made numerous appearances on CNN, Bloomberg TV and CNBC.

Jane Fullerton Lemons is a freelance writer from Northern Virginia with more than 25 years of journalism experience. A former Washington bureau chief for the *Arkansas Democrat-Gazette* and *Farm Journal* magazine, she has covered the White House, Congress, food policy and health care. She is currently seeking a master's degree in creative nonfiction from Goucher College in Towson, Md.

Patrick Marshall is a freelance writer in Seattle who writes about public policy and technology issues. He is a technology columnist for *The Seattle Times* and *Government Computer News*. He holds a B.A. in anthropology from the University of California, Santa Cruz, and a master's degree in international studies from the Fletcher School of Law and Diplomacy, a program of Harvard and Tufts universities.

A Denver-based freelance writer, **David Milstead** is a regular contributor to *The Globe and Mail*, the national newspaper of Canada. He has individually or jointly won nine national awards from SABEW, the Society of American Business Editors and Writers. He passed the Level I exam in the Chartered Financial Analyst program in 2007. In a previous report for SAGE Business Researcher, he wrote about pensions.

S.L. Mintz covers personal finance, corporate finance, banking and financial regulation, and public policy. His articles have been published in *Barron's, Institutional Investor, The Economist, Bloomberg Personal Finance, Knowledge@Wharton* and other print and online venues. In a previous report for SAGE Business Researcher, he examined ethics and the financial services industry. Book credits include *Five Eminent Contrarians* and *John Neff on Investing*. He co-wrote the eight-part PBS Television series

Beyond Wall Street: The Art of Investing and a companion book with the same title. He served as a staff writer on the best-selling Financial Crisis Inquiry Commission report that probed reasons for economic upheaval triggered by collapsing home prices and excess on Wall Street. He lives in Montclair, N.J.

Freelance writer **Joan Oleck** is based in Brooklyn, N.Y. She teaches writing as an adjunct professor at New York University. She has held editing and writing positions at *Businessweek, Newsday, The Detroit News, Restaurant Business* and *School Library Journal.*

Sharon O'Malley, an instructor at the Philip Merrill College of Journalism at the University of Maryland, is a freelance writer, editor, consultant and trainer who has published articles in dozens of newspapers and magazines, including *The Arizona Republic, USA Today, Ladies' Home Journal, Working Woman*

and *American Demographics.* For SAGE Business Researcher, she has written reports about internships and mortgage finance. She has ghost-written three books, including *Where Winners Live: Earn More, Sell More, Achieve More Through Personal Accountability.*

Robin D. Schatz is an adjunct associate professor of journalism at the Columbia University Graduate School of Journalism and a New York–based business writer, who writes frequently for *Inc.* magazine on entrepreneurs and start-ups and is a contributor to Forbes.com. She previously worked at Bloomberg News as an editor, writer and television producer, and as an editor and columnist at *Businessweek.* She was also a Knight-Bagehot Fellow in economics and business journalism at Columbia University. For SAGE Business Researcher, she wrote a report about Crowdfunding.